W9-BTI-686

The Invention of Printing.

Theodore Low

Theo. L. DeVinne

The Invention of PRINTING

A Collection of Facts and Opinions Descriptive of Early Prints and Playing Cards, the Block-Books of the Fifteenth Century, the Legend of Lourens Janszoon Coster, of Haarlem, and the work of John Gutenberg and his Associates.

Illustrated with Fac-similes of Early Types and Woodcuts.

New York: Francis Hart & Co., 1876.

Republished by Gale Research Company
Book Tower, Detroit, 1969.

Library of Congress Catalog Card Number 68–17971

TO

DAVID WOLFE BRUCE,

IN ACKNOWLEDGMENT

OF INSTRUCTION ABOUT TYPES, NOT TO BE HAD BY READING,
OF ASSISTANCE IN STUDIES, NOT TO BE FOUND IN PUBLIC LIBRARIES,
OF COMPANIONSHIP MORE PLEASANT THAN BOOKS,

THIS WORK IS DEDICATED

BY HIS FRIEND,

THEO. L. DE VINNE.

CONTENTS.

ILLUSTRATIONS.

ILLUSTRATIONS.

PREFACE.

THE Invention of Printing has always been recognized by educated men as a subject of importance: there is no mechanical art, nor are there any of the fine arts, about whose early history so many books have been written. The subject is as mysterious as it is inviting. There is an unusual degree of obscurity about the origin of the first printed books and the lives and works of the early printers. There are records and traditions which cannot be reconciled of at least three distinct inventions of printing. Its early history is entangled with a controversy about rival inventors which has lasted for more than three centuries, and is not yet fully determined.

In the management of this controversy, a subject intrinsically attractive has been made repulsive. The history of the invention of printing has been written to please national pride. German authors assert the claims of Gutenberg, and discredit traditions about Coster. Dutch authors insist on the priority of Coster, and charge Gutenberg with stealing the invention. Partisans on each side say that their opponents have perverted the records and suppressed the truth. The quarrel has spread. English and French authors, who had no national prejudices to gratify, and who should have considered the question without passion, have wrangled over the subject with all the bitterness of Germans or Hollanders. In this, as in other quarrels, there are amusing features, but to the general reader the controversy seems unfortunate and is certainly wearisome.

It is a greater misfortune that all the early chronicles of printing were written in a dead language. Wolf's collection of Typographic Monuments, *which includes nearly every paper of value written before 1740, is in Latin; the valuable books of Meerman, Maittaire, and Schoepflin are also in Latin. To the general reader these are sealed books: to the student, who seeks exact knowledge of the methods of the first printers, they are tiresome books. Written for the information of librarians rather than of printer's, it is but pro that these books should devote the largest space to a review of the controversy or to a description of early editions; but it is strange that they should so imperfectly describe the construction and appearance of early types and the usages of the early printers. The mechanical features of typography were, apparently, neglected as of little importance, and beneath the dignity of history.*

A failure to present accurate illustrations of early printing is not the fault of modern authorities. Many of them are full of fac-similes bearing the marks of minute and conscientious care; but they are in foreign languages, and are seldom found in our largest American libraries. There are, it is true, a few books in English on early printing which have accurate fac-similes; but high prices and limited editions put them out of the reach of the ordinary book-buyer. They were written by and for librarians only.

Valuable as all these books are, they disappoint the printer. Some of them, though presenting fac-similes in profusion, are not accompanied with proper explanations in the text: others are devoted to one branch only of early printing, such as block-books, or the printed work of one nation only. Two of them are untrustworthy as authorities. Neither from one book, nor from all the books, can a printer get a clear description of the mechanical development of typography. This incompleteness was frankly acknowledged by Dr. Dibdin, when he said that there was no work in the English language which deserved to be considered as a complete general history of printing. This was an old complaint. Nearly a hundred years before, Prosper Marchand had said that the history of printing, voluminous as it then seemed, was but history in fragments.

The first attempt to supply this great deficiency was made by August Bernard, in the disquisition published at Paris, in the year 1853, under the title, De l'origine et des debuts de l'imprimerie en Europe. *His was the first book in which the printed work attributed to Coster and Gutenberg was critically examined from a typographic point of view. To readers who were not content with the vague descriptions of popular books of typography, the explanations of Bernard were of peculiar value. I had reason to think that a translation of the history of this eminent printer would be received by American printers with some measure of the favor which the original had met with in Europe. Impressed with this belief, I began the work.*

I found it necessary to consult many of Bernard's authorities. My admiration of the superior method and forcible style of Bernard, an admiration still unabated, was increased by the reading of the new books; but the esteem in which I hold his valuable work does not prevent the regret that, in his entire neglect of the block-books, he should have overlooked the most significant feature of early printing. The fac-similes of early prints, subsequently shown in The Infancy of Book Printing *of Weigel and in* The Typographic Monuments *of Holtrop, convinced me that the earliest practice of typography had its beginning in a still earlier practice of printing from blocks, and that a description of block-books should precede a description of the invention of types.*

Since these books were written, all the old theories about the origin of typography have been examined with increased interest, and discussed with superior critical ability, by many eminent European scholars. Discoveries of great importance have been made; old facts have been set forth in new lights; traditions accepted as truthful history for three hundred years have been demolished. Of the many able men who have been engaged in this task of separating truth from fiction, no one has done more efficient service than Dr. A. Van der Linde of The Hague, whose papers on the traditions of typography are masterpieces of acute and scholarly criticism. His researches and reasoning convinced me that it would be unwise to offer a translation of any previously published book as a fair exponent of modern knowledge about early typography. The newly discovered facts were opposed to early teachings; there could be no sewing of the new cloth on the old garment. I was led away from my first purpose of translation, and, almost unconsciously, began to collect the materials for the present volume.

Until recently, the invention of printing has been regarded as a subject belonging almost entirely to bibliographers. The opinions of type-founders and printers who had examined old books have been set aside as of no value, whenever they were opposed to favorite theories or legends. This partial treatment of the subject is no longer approved: a new school of criticism invites experts to examine the books, and pays respect to their conclusions. It claims that the internal evidences of old books are of higher authority than legends, and that these evidences are conclusive, not to be ignored nor accommodated to the statements of the early chroniclers. European critics do not hesitate to say that the confusing and contradictory descriptions of the origin of printing are largely due to the improper deference heretofore paid to the statements of men who tried to describe processes which they did not understand. They say, also, that too little attention has been paid to the types and mechanics of early printing. Criticisms of this character led me to indulge the hope that I might find gleanings of value in the old field, and that it would be practicable to present them, with the newly discovered facts, in a form which would be acceptable to the printer and the general reader. In this belief, and for this purpose, this book was written.

I would not have begun this work, if I had not felt assured that a thorough revision of the subject was needed. The books and papers on typography which are most popular, and are still accepted as authoritative by the ordinary reader, repeat legends which have recently been proved untrue; they narrate, as established facts of history, methods of printing which are not only incorrect but impossible. It is time that the results of the more recent researches should be published in the English language. But I offer them only as the compiler of accredited facts: I have no original discoveries to announce, no speculative theories to uphold. Nor shall I invade the proper field of librarians and bibliographers. I propose to describe old types, prints and books as they are seen by a printer, and with reference to the needs of printers and the general reader, avoiding, as far as I can, all controversies about matters which are of interest to book-collectors only. The historical part of the record will be devoted chiefly to the printed work of the first half of the fifteenth century. It will begin with descriptions of the earliest forms of printing, as shown in image prints, playing cards and block-books; it will end with the establishment of typography in Germany.

Believing that a verbal description of old books and prints, without pictorial illustrations, would be unsatisfactory, I have provided many fac-similes of early printing. No part of this work will more fully repay examination than its illustrations, which have been carefully selected from approved authorities, or from originals. Reproduced by the new process of photo-engraving, they are accurate copies of the originals, even when of reduced size. As they are printed with the descriptive text by the same method of typographic presswork, it is believed that they will more clearly illustrate the subject than lithographed fac-similes on straggling leaves.

In trying to make plain whatever may be obscure about the mechanics of printing, I have thought proper to begin the explanation with a description of its different methods. An introduction of this nature is not an unwarrantable digression. It is important that the reader should have an understanding of the radical differences between typography and xylography on the one side, and lithographic and copper-plate printing on the other, as well as some knowledge of the construction and uses of the more common tools of type-founders.

I do not propose to give any extended quotations in foreign languages. Wherever an approved translation in English has been found, it has been substituted for the original text; where translations have not been approved, they have been made anew. Writing for the general reader, I have assumed that he would prefer, as I do, in every book to be read and not studied, a version in English rather than the original text. Believing that the frequent citation of authorities, especially in instances where the facts are undisputed, or where the books are inaccessible, is an annoyance, I have refrained from the presentation of foot-notes which refer to books only. I have, in a few cases, deviated from this course where the matters stated were of a character which seemed to require the specification of authority.

One of the greatest impediments I encountered when about to begin the compilation of this work was the difficulty of access to books of authority. I do not mention this in disparagement of the management of our public libraries, for I know that old books are liable to injury in the hands of the merely curious, and that librarians have little encouragement to collect scarce books on typography. To prove that there is small inquiry for treatises of this character, it is enough to say that I have had to cut open the leaves of valuable books after their rest for many years on the shelves of one of the largest libraries of this city. But if these books were ever so abundant, the proper restrictions placed on their use were a hindrance to one whose chief opportunity for consulting them is at night.

Here I am pleased to acknowledge my indebtedness to Mr. David Wolfe Bruce. He has not only accompanied and aided me in repeated examinations of his very valuable collection of fifteenth century books, but has lent me all the books I desired, and has freely given me unlimited time for their study. This collection—replete with all the books of authority I needed, with specimens of types, wood-cuts, and curiosities of type-founding, which illustrate the growth of printing from its infancy—was more admirably adapted to my needs than that of any library on this Continent. Deprived of Mr. Bruce's generous assistance, my work would have been greatly restricted in its scope, and shorn of its best features of illustration.

I began this work intending to describe only the mechanical development of early printing, but I could not keep the matter strictly within this limit. Hedged in this narrow space, the story would be but half told. The true origin of typography is not in types, nor in block-books nor image prints. These were consequences, not causes. The condition of society at the close of the middle ages; the growth of commerce and manufactures; the enlarged sense of personal liberty; the brawls of ecclesiastics in high station, and their unworthy behavior; the revolt of the people against the authority of church and state; the neglect of duty by the self-elected teachers of the people in their monopoly of books and knowledge; the barrenness of the education then given in the schools; the eagerness of all people for the mental diversion offered in the new game of playing cards; the unsatisfied religious appetite which hungered for image prints and devotional books; the facilities for self-education afforded by the introduction of paper,—these were among the influences which produced the invention of printing. They are causes which cannot be overlooked. My inability to describe them with the fullness which they deserve would not justify their total neglect. I have devoted more space to them than is customary in treatises on early printing, but I have to admit, with regret, that they have been too curtly treated. I have done but little more than record a few of the more noticeable facts—enough, perhaps, to show that the state of education and society, in its relation to the invention of printing, deserves a more extended description than it has hitherto received. If I can succeed in awakening the attention of printers, and those who look on a knowledge of printing as a proper accomplishment of the scholar, to the nature and extent of these influences, to the curiosities of literature hidden in apparently dry books of bibliography, and to the value of the lesson of patient industry and fixed purpose taught by the life of John Gutenberg, the object of this book will have been accomplished.

I

The Different Methods of Printing.

Impression is used in many Arts...Printing implies the use of Ink and Paper...Four Methods of Printing...Steel-plate or Copper-plate, the artistic method...Lithography, the scientific method. Typography, the useful method...Xylography, the primitive method...Illustrations of Copper-plate and Lithographic Printing Surfaces...Process of Copper-plate Printing...Its Merits and its Defects...Process of Lithographic Printing...Its Advantages and Limitations...Theory of Typography, with Illustrations of the Face and Body of Types...Superiority of Movable Types over Engraved Letters...Stereotype...Superiority of the Typographic Method in its Presses and its Process of Inking...Xylography...Period when each Method was Introduced...A Meaning in their almost Simultaneous Introduction.

Printing, the act, art, or practice of impressing letters, characters, or figures on paper, cloth, or other material; the business of a printer; typography.
Typography, the art of printing, or the operation of impressing letters and words on forms of types. *Webster.*
Printing, the business of a printer; the art or process of impressing letters or words; typography; the process of staining linen with figures.
Typography, the art of printing. *Worcester.*
Print, to press, mark, stamp or infix letters, characters, forms, or figures.
Richardson.

THESE definitions of printing are based on its derivation from the Latin, *premo*, to press, and on the supposition that its most characteristic feature is impression. From a technical point of view, the definitions are incomplete; for printing and typography are made synonymous, while many leading, but totally different, methods of impressing letters, characters and figures, are not even noticed. Impression is employed in the manufacture of calico, paper-hangings, oil-cloth, figured crockery, and in many other arts which have no connection with each other. Under right conditions, the action or the impress of light makes a photograph. Under different conditions, the pressure of the breath makes hollow glassware. Moulding, coining, stamping and embossing are other methods of impression; but the men who practise these methods are not known as printers. The word printing has acquired a conventional meaning not entirely warranted by its derivation. It means much more than impression. It is commonly understood as a process in which paper and ink are employed in conjunction with impression.

Printing and typography are not strictly synonymous, as may be inferred from the definitions. Typography, although the most useful, is not the only form of printing. Printing on paper with ink is done by four methods. Each method is, practically, a separate art, distinct from its rivals in its theory, its process, and its application. These methods are:

Steel-plate or Copper-plate printing, in which the subject is printed from an etching or engraving below the surface of a plate of steel or of copper.

Lithography, in which the subject is printed from a transferred engraving on the surface of a prepared stone.

Typography, in which the subject is printed from a combination of movable metal types cast in high relief.

Xylography, in which the subject is printed from a design engraved on a block of wood in high relief.

The distinct nature of the substances in use for printing surfaces by the four methods should be enough to teach us that the methods are entirely different. But the manner in which the letters, designs or figures of each method are put on the respective printing surfaces will show the differences more noticeably. In typographic and xylographic work, the matter to be printed is cast or cut in high relief, or *above* the surface; in lithographic work, it is put *on* the smooth surface of the stone, in relief so slight that it is almost level with the surface; in steel and copper-plate, it is cut *below* the surface which receives the impression. The illustration on the next page shows, but in an exaggerated form, the appearance of a single line, cut across, or in a vertical direction, when it has been prepared for printing by each of the different methods: It will be seen that the line prepared for printing by the typographic or xylographic method can be inked with facility, and that, when compared with a similar line in lithographic or copper-plate work, it presents but a small surface and a slighter resistance to impression.

A
B B

Typography or Xylography.

A. Elevated line; the only part of a typographic or of a xylographic surface which receives the ink and impression.

B. The shoulder of the type, or the field of the block; it receives neither ink nor impression.

Lithography.

C. Transferred surface line; the only part of the surface which receives ink and repels moisture.

D. The surface of the stone, that imbibes moisture and repels greasy ink; it receives the full force of impression in every part.

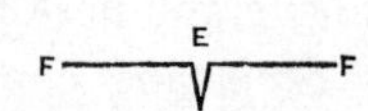

Copper-plate or Steel-plate.

E. The line printed, which is engraved below the surface of the plate, and is filled with ink.

F. The smooth face of the plate, which makes no mark on the paper, but which receives the full force of impression.

The process of copper-plate printing begins with heating the plate, and rolling it with ink, until the incised lines have been filled. The face of the plate is then wiped clean, care being taken that the ink in the incised lines is not removed. A moistened sheet of paper is then laid on the plate, and an impression is taken by forcing it under the cylinder of a rolling press. Under this pressure, the paper is forced in the sunken lines filled with ink, and the ink sticks to the paper.

Copper-plate printing is, in all points, the reverse of typographic printing. The engraved lines, cut below the surface, are filled with ink in a compact body, and not in a thin film, liable to spread under pressure, as it may on a type or on a wood-cut; the ink from a copper-plate is pressed in such a way that it re-appears on the paper in a low relief—it is not squeezed on and flatted out, but stands up with sharper line and shows a greater depth of color. The slenderness of the incised lines, the fineness and hardness of the metal, and the peculiar method by which the ink is laid on the plate and fixed to the paper, give to prints from engravings on steel or on copper a sharpness of line, a brilliancy of color, a delicacy of tone, and a receding in perspective, which have always won for this branch of printing the preference of artists. Yet it is a slow and expensive process. A steel-plate engraver may be engaged for many months upon a large plate, from which but forty perfect impressions can be taken in a day. On ordinary work on a large plate, three hundred impressions per day is the average performance of a copper-plate press.

Steel and copper-plate printing is largely used for bank-notes, portraits, fine book illustrations, revenue and postage stamps, and sometimes for commercial formularies, but it is in every way unfitted for the printing of books. It has not been much improved since its invention. Steel plates may be duplicated by means of electrotyping, or by the process of transfer to soft steel, but these duplicates cannot be made so cheaply as typographic stereotype plates, nor so promptly as transfers by lithography. The inking and cleansing of the plate, always dirty and disagreeable work, has hitherto been done only by hand. All the manipulations of copper-plate work are slow and difficult: they present many obstacles to the use of labor-saving machinery.

In lithography the design to be printed, which may be engraved on stone or copper, or written with pen on paper, is transferred by a greasy ink upon the smooth surface of a stone of peculiar fineness and firmness. This stone, which is found in its best state only in Bavaria, where the art was invented, is a variety of slate, which faithfully responds in printing to the slightest touch of a graver or a crayon, and permits the use of fine shades and tints which cannot be produced on wood or on copper. The transferred lines of the design cling to and dry upon the surface of the stone, which is then subjected to the action of a weak acid, which hardens the ink in the transferred lines, while it slightly etches and lowers the surface where it is unprotected. The process of printing begins by dampening the stone with a moist sponge, the water in which is absorbed by the unpro-

Surface Exposed to Impression by the Copper-plate Method.

The entire surface of the plate is covered with ink until the white lines are filled. The surface around the figures is wiped clean before the impression is taken.

1876

Surface Inked and Exposed to Impression by the Typographic Method.

Surface Exposed to Impression by the Lithographic Method.

This surface is rolled twice: once with water, which is absorbed only by the surface here shown in dull black tint; once with ink, which is retained only on the figures.

tected face of the stone, while it is repelled by the hard greasy matter in the transferred lines. The inking roller is then applied to the stone with a contrary result; the moistened surface repels the greasy ink, but the transferred lines attract and retain it. When an impression on paper is taken, the only part of the paper which receives ink is that part which touches the transferred lines. The theory of lithography is based upon the repulsion between grease and water. Lithographic printing is chemical printing.

Lithography is the most scientific and the most flexible of all methods of printing. It can imitate fairly, and it often reproduces with accuracy, a line engraving on steel, a drawing in crayon, the manuscript of a penman, or the painting in oil of an artist. By the aid of photography, it can repeat, in an enlarged or diminished size, any kind of printed work. It has many advantages over copper-plate and xylography. For some kinds of work, like autograph letters and rude diagrams, engraving is unnecessary; the design may be written with oily ink on paper, and can then be transferred direct from the written copy to a stone without the aid of a graver. The transferring process is another peculiarity of this art which allows the lithographer to duplicate small designs with greater facility and economy than a similar duplication could be effected by the stereotyper of types. These advantages are counterbalanced by one great defect: lithography is not a quick method of printing. The usual performance of the lithographic hand press when applied to ordinary work, is about four hundred impressions per day; on the steam press, the performance is about five thousand impressions per day.

The arts of lithography and copper-plate are useful and beautiful methods of printing, but they do not make books and newspapers.[1] The necessity which compels them to

[1] The *Daily Graphic* of New York, may be offered as an exception to this assertion, but this newspaper really confirms its correctness. It is the illustrated side only of this paper which is done by lithography. The side which gives it value as a newspaper is printed with ordinary printing types, and this result could be accomplished by no other method.

make a new engraving for every new subject restricts them almost exclusively to the field of art and ornament. If no other method of printing were known, encyclopedias and newspapers would be impossibilities. "The art preservative of all arts" is not the art of lithography nor of copper-plate.

This distinction rightfully belongs to Typography only. The theory upon which this method is based is that of the independence of each character, and of the mutual dependence of all its characters. Every character is a separate and movable type, so made that it can be arranged with others in an endless variety of combinations. The types used for this page are used for other pages in this book; they can be re-arranged for use in the printing of many other books or pamphlets; they cease to serve only when they are worn out. All other methods of printing require, at the outset, the engraving on one piece of wood or metal of all the letters or parts of a design, which, when once combined, cannot be separated; they can be applied only to the object for which they were first made.

Typography is most successful when it is applied to the letters of the alphabet. It fails totally when applied to maps, or to any kind of printed work requiring irregularly varying lines. It is only partially successful in the representation of combined ornaments and the characters of music. Its true field is in the representation of words and thoughts, and here it is supreme. There is no other method of printing which can do this work so perfectly.

Typography has a great advantage over other branches of printing in the cheapness of its materials. Type-metal is cheaper by weight than copper or steel, or the finer quality of lithographic stone: by measurement, it is cheaper than the box-wood used by engravers. Types are cheaper than engraved letters. A pound of the types by which this page is printed contains about 320 pieces of metal, the cost of which is but 48 cents. Types are made of many forms or faces, but they are always of uniform height, and are always truly square as to body, so that they can be fitted to each other with precision, and can be interchanged with facility.

The expense of combining types in words is trivial, as compared with the cost of engraving for lithographic or for copper-plate printing. An employing printer's price for the composition of a page like this would be, at the high rates of New-York city, $1.10. The engraving of such a page, by any method, would cost at least three times as much as the types and their composition. If never so carefully done, the engraved letters would not be so uniform, nor so satisfactory to the general reader, as the types. The engraved letters would cost more, but they could be used only for the work for which they were made. In typographic printing, there is no such restriction as to use, and no such loss of labor. It is only the labor of composition which need be lost; the types remain, but little more worn, or little less perfect, than when they were first put in use.

Letter H, from a type of Canon body.

Em, or full square of Canon body.

Face of the letter as it appears on the body.

The Face of a Large Type, showing the manner in which the Letter is placed on the Body.[1]

The labor of composition is not always lost. A page of movable types can be used for a mould, from which can be made a stereotype plate of immovable letters. Stereotyping is a cheap process. A plate of this page of type can be had for about one-half the cost of the composition. The stereotype plate has all the advantages pertaining to an engraving on a lithographic stone, and it is more durable and portable.

[1] This body of Canon type occupies about two-thirds of an American square inch. A square inch of the Small-pica type, in which this text is composed, contains about 44 ems to the square inch; a square inch of Agate, or of small advertising type, contains 177 ems to the square inch. There are types so small that 447 ems can be put in a square inch.

Typography has a marked advantage in the greater ease with which printing types are inked. In the copper-plate process, the plate must be first blackened over the entire surface, and then cleansed with even greater care, before an impression can be taken. This labor cannot be intrusted to machinery, but must be done by a practised workman. The inking of a lithographic stone is as difficult: the stone must be moistened before the inking roller can be applied. This double operation of inking and cleansing, or of inking and moistening, is required for every impression. The inking of types is done by a much simpler method; one passage, to and fro, of a gang of rollers over the surface is sufficient to coat them with ink. The types need no previous nor after application.

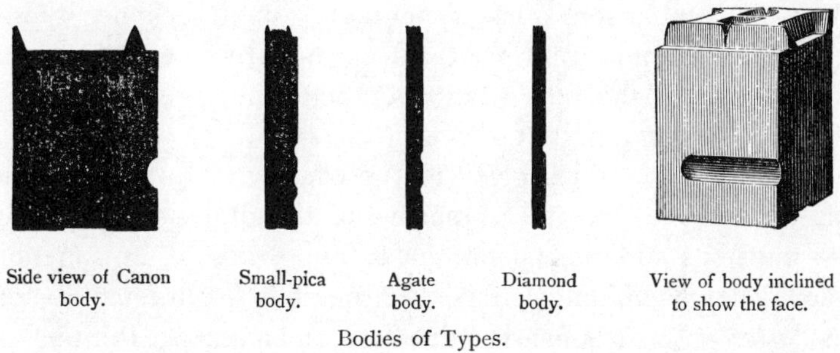

Side view of Canon body. Small-pica body. Agate body. Diamond body. View of body inclined to show the face.

Bodies of Types.

The impression by which typographic surfaces are printed is comparatively slight. The sunken lines of a copper plate or the transferred lines of a lithographic stone can be reproduced on paper only by means of violent impression, which is obtained by forcing the plate or the stone under an iron cylinder or scraper. Only a part of the surface is printed, but the entire surface must receive impression, which is, of necessity, gradually applied. A direct vertical pressure, at the same instant, over every part of the surface, would crush the stone or flatten the plate. In printing types of ordinary form, the area of impression surface is exactly the reverse of that of the lithographic stone or the copper plate. It is only the part which is printed that receives the ink and the impression. This printed part is the raised surface, which is rarely ever more than one-sixth of the area occupied by the types, and is often less than one-twelfth. The resistance to impression of types as compared with stones or plates is, at least, in the proportion of one to six.

As relief plates or types are more quickly coated with ink, and need less impression than lithographic stones or copper plates, the typographic process is, consequently, better fitted to receive the help of labor-saving machinery. The daily performance of the typographic hand press on plain work has been, almost from its earliest employment, about fifteen hundred impressions, which is about four times greater than that of the hand lithographic press. By the use of steam and of improved machinery, this inequality is put almost beyond comparison. The typographic single-cylinder type-printing machine can print fifteen hundred impressions in an hour, and the new newspaper perfecting press can print fifteen thousand perfect sheets in an hour.

The feature which gives to typography its precedence in usefulness over all other branches of the graphic arts is not so much its superior adaptation to impression as its superior facility for combining letters. Its merit is in the mobility of its types and their construction for combination. Printing is Typography. The printing which disseminates knowledge is not the art that makes prints or pictures; it is, as Bernard has defined it, "the art that makes books." The definition is not scientifically exact, but it gives a clear idea of the great breadth of the art. In its perfect adaptation to this great object, the broad generalization of the definition in the dictionaries may be justified. The method of printing which is most useful may rightfully claim the generic name.

Xylography is the scientific word for the art of making engravings on a single block of wood, in high relief, for use on the typographic printing press. A xylographic block may be an engraving of letters only, of pictures only, or of both letters and pictures, but in all cases the engraving is fixed on the block. The fixedness of the design on the block is the great feature which separates xylography[1] from typography. The printing surfaces of the two methods are alike. Types and xylographic engravings are printed together, by the same process, and on the same press.

Printing with ink, not as an experiment, but as a practical business, is comparatively a modern art. Lithography, the most recent method, was discovered by Alois Senefelder, an actor of Munich, in 1798. Unlike other methods of printing, it was, in every detail, an entirely original invention.

The introduction of copper-plate printing is attributed to Maso Finiguerra, a goldsmith of Florence, who is supposed to have made his first print about the year 1452. It cannot be proved that Finiguerra was the inventor, for prints by this method were made in Germany as early as 1446.

The period of the invention of typography may be placed between the years 1438 and 1450. There have been many claimants for the honor of the invention. Each of the following fifteen cities or towns—Augsburg, Basle, Bologna, Dordrecht, Feltre, Florence, Haarlem, Lubeck, Mentz, Nuremberg, Rome, Russemburg, Strasburg, Schelestadt and Venice—has been specified by as many different authors as the true birthplace of typography. The names of the alleged inventors are, Castaldi, Coster, Fust, Gensfleisch, Gresmund, Gutenberg, Hahn, Mentel, Jenson, Regiomontanus, Schœffer, Pannartz and Sweinheym, and Louis de Vaelbaeske. The evidences in favor of each claimant have been fully examined, and the more foolish pretensions have been so completely suppressed that it is unnecessary to review them. The limits of the controversy have been greatly contracted: but four of the alleged inventors of types, Castaldi, Coster, Gutenberg and Schœffer, have living defenders. The legend of an invention of types

[1] The word xylography is little used by printers or engravers, with whom the art of making engravings in relief is usually known as engraving on wood. It is most frequently used by bibliographers to distinguish early printed work: books printed from types are now defined as typographic, and those printed from engraved blocks as xylographic.

by Castaldi, of Feltre, has never been accepted beyond Italy, and barely deserves respectful consideration. The evidences in favor of Schœffer are more plausible, but they are not admitted by the writers who have carefully investigated the documents upon which this pretension is based. The real controversy is between Lourens Coster of Haarlem and John Gutenberg of Mentz.

There is no record, nor even any tradition, concerning an invention of xylography. It is admitted by all authorities, that xylographic prints were made during the first quarter of the fifteenth century, and that xylographic books were in use before typography was introduced.

Three of the four methods of printing here named were invented or developed within a period of fifty years. If the statements of some historians could be accepted, this period should be contracted to thirty years. There is no disagreement, however, as to the order of their introduction. Xylography, the rudest method, was the first in use; typography, a more useful method, soon followed; copper-plate printing, the artistic method, was the proper culmination. The order of invention was that of progressive development from an imperfect to a perfect method.

The introduction of three distinct methods of printing, by different persons and in different places, but during the same period, shows that a general need of books or of printed matter had given a strong impulse to the inventive spirit of the fifteenth century. It may also be inferred that the inventors of printing had been benefited, in some way, by recent improvements or developments in the mechanical processes of which printing is composed.

II

Antique Methods of Impression and their Failure.

Transfer of Form by Impression one of the Oldest Arts...The Stamped Bricks of Assyria and Egypt...Assyrian Cylinders of Clay...Greek Maps...Roman Theories about Combinations of Letters...Roman Stamps...The Brands and Stamps of the Middle Ages...English Brands. Stamping is not Printing...Ink then used was Unsuitable for Printing...Printing Waited for Discovery of Ink and Paper...Romans did not Need Printing...Printing Depends on a multitude of Readers...Readers were few in the Dark Ages...Invention of Printing was Not purely Mechanical...Printing needs many Supports...Telegraph...Schools...Libraries...Expresses. Post-Offices...A Premature Invention would have been Fruitless.

The stamps of the ancients, and the impressions from the seals of metal, found in deeds and conveyances of the lower ages, prove nothing more than that mankind walked for many centuries upon the borders of the two great inventions of typography and chalcography, without having the luck to discover either of them, and appear neither to have had any influence on the origin of these arts, nor to merit any place in their history. *Lanzi.*

SOME notice of the material and moral elements needed for the development of typography should precede a description of the work of the early printers. We shall form incorrect notions about the invention of printing unless we know something about the state of the arts of paper-making, ink-making and engraving at the beginning of the fifteenth century. We should also know something about the books and the book-makers of the middle ages. Nor will it be out of place to review the mechanical processes which have been used, almost from the beginning, for the preservation of written language. The review will show us what elements the inventor of typography found at his hand ready for use; what he combined from the inventions of others, and what he invented anew.

Engraving must be regarded as the first process in every method of printing. The impression of engraved forms on metal and wax, for the purpose of making coins and seals, is of great antiquity, having been practised more than three thousand years ago, and, by some people, with a skill which cannot now be surpassed. There are old Egyptian seals with faces of such minute delicacy that the fineness of the workmanship can be fully perceived only by the aid of a magnifying glass. There are coins of Macedonia which are stamped in a relief as bold as that of the best pieces of modern mints.

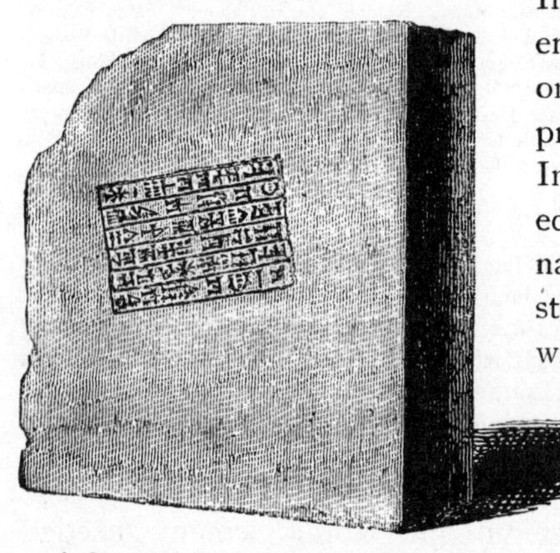

A Stamped Brick from the Ruins of Babylon.

[From Hansard.]

In Babylonia and Assyria, engraved forms were printed or stamped on clay specially prepared for this purpose. In the ruins of the ancient edifices of these primeval nations there is scarcely a stone or a kiln-burnt brick without an inscription or a stamp upon it. The inscriptions on stone appear to have been cut with a chisel, after the usual method of stone-cutters; but the stamps on the bricks were made from engravings on wood, or by the separate impressions of some pointed instrument. The preceding illustration is that of a stamped brick taken many years ago from the ruins of ancient Babylon. When in perfect condition, it was thirteen inches square and three inches thick. The inscription, which is in the cuneiform or arrow-headed character, is irregularly placed on the surface, but the letters or words are arranged in parallel rows, and are obviously made to be read from top to bottom. The characters of this inscription were not cut upon the brick, nor were they separately impressed. That they were made

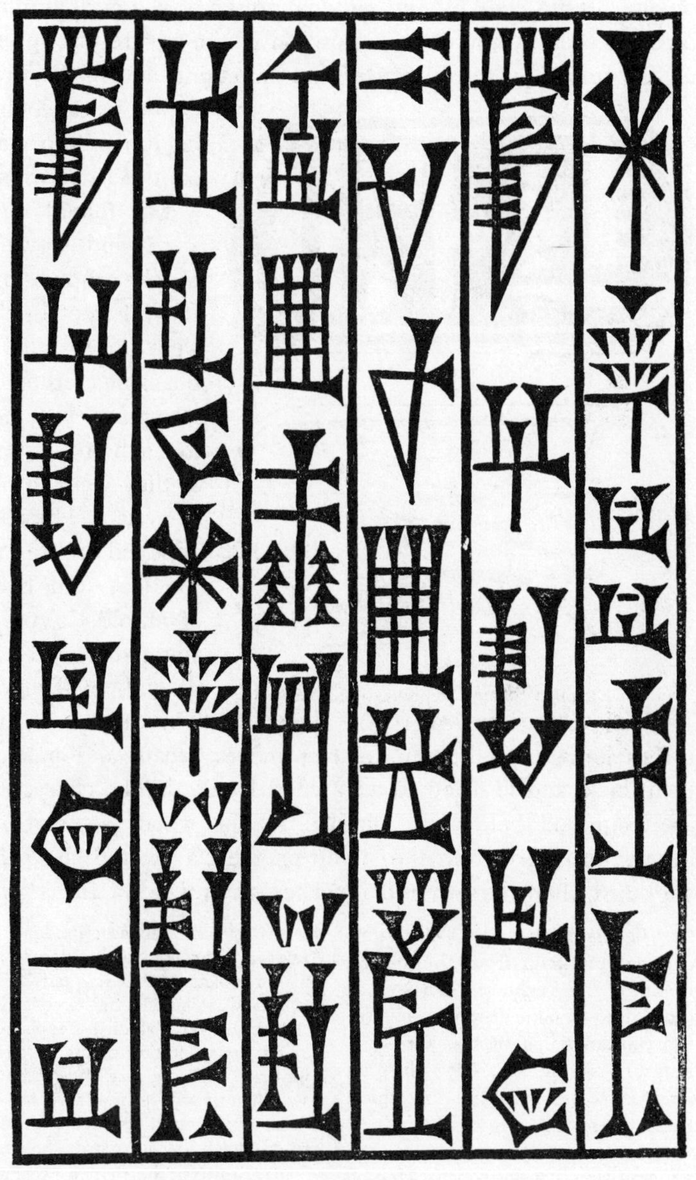

Fac-simile of the Impression on the Brick.

[From Hansard.]

on the plastic clay by the sudden pressure of a xylographic block, is seen by the oblique position of the square inscription on the brick,[1] in the nicety of the engraving and its uniform depth, in the bulging up of the clay on the side, where it was forced outward and upward by the impression. In old Egypt, bricks were impressed by the same method of stamping, but not to such an extent as they were in old Assyria. The cuts annexed represent the face and back of an old Egyptian stamp discovered in a tomb of Thebes. The stamp is five inches long, two and one-quarter inches broad, and half an inch thick, and is fitted to an arched handle. The characters are engraved below the surface of the wood, so that an impression taken from the stamp on the clay would show the engraved characters in relief. The inscription on the stamp

Face.

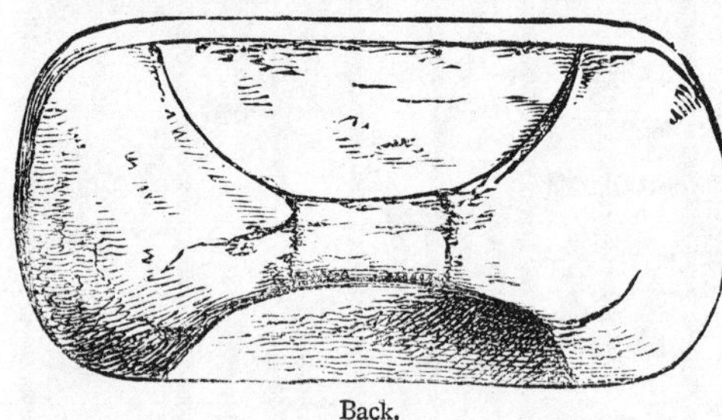

Back.

An Egyptian Stamp for Impressing Bricks.

[From Jackson.]

[1] The accompanying translation of a tablet taken from the record room of the second Assurbanipal (according to some original scholars, the Sardanapalus of the Greeks), king of Assyria, B. C. 667, will give an idea of one purpose for which the impressions were made:

Assurbanipal, the great king, the powerful king, king of nations, king of Assyria, son of Esarhaddon, king of Assyria, son of Sennacherib, king of Assyria; according to the documents and old tablets of Assyria, and Sumri and Akkadi, this tablet in the collection of tablets I wrote, I studied, I explained, and for the inspection of my kingdom within my palace I placed. Whoever my written records defaces, and his own records shall write, may Nabu all the written tablets of his records deface.

Mr. Smith of the British Museum is translating some of these tablets.

has been translated, *Amenoph, beloved of truth.* Amenoph is supposed, by some authorities, to have been the king of Egypt at the period of the exodus of the Israelites.

The characters on the Egyptian and Babylonian bricks are much more neatly executed than would seem necessary for inscriptions on so common a material as clay. But they are really coarse, when compared with the inscriptions upon the small cylinders of clay which were used by the Assyrians for the preservation of their public documents. Layard mentions a small six-sided Assyrian cylinder that contains sixty lines of minute characters which could be read only by the aid of a magnifying glass. Antiquaries are not yet perfectly agreed as to the method by which the cylinders were made. Layard, who says that the Babylonian bricks were stamped, thinks that the inscriptions on the cylinders were cut on the clay. But there are many cylinders which show the clearest indications of impression.

It is probable that they were made by both methods. The clay was prepared for writing as well as for stamping. Ezekiel, who prophesied by the river Chebar in Assyria, was commanded to take a tile, and portray upon it the city of Jerusalem. The Chaldean priests informed Callisthenes that they kept their astronomical observations on tiles that were subsequently baked in the furnace. Four large piles of tablets of unburned clay were found by Layard in the library or hall of records of Assurbanipal. Some of the tablets are the grammars and primers of the language; some are records of agreements to sell property or slaves; some are filled with astronomical or astrological predictions. On one of them was inscribed the Assyrian version of the deluge. The cylinders contained the memorials which were then considered as of most value, such as the proclamations of the king, or the laws of the empire. In the museum of the East India Company is the fragment of a clay cylinder which contains a portion of the decrees or annals of Nebuchadnezzar. For perpetuating records of this nature, the cylinders were admirably adapted.

They were convenient for reference, and their legibility, after so long an exposure, shows that they were perfectly durable.

We do not know by what considerations Assyrian rulers were governed when about to choose between engraving or writing on clay; but it is not unreasonable to assume that the inscription was written or cut on the clay, when one copy only of a record was wanted; if numerous copies were wanted, a die or an engraving on wood was manufactured, from which these copies were moulded. No surer method of securing exact copies of an original could have been devised among a people that did not use ink and paper. These cylinders are examples of printing in its most elementary form.

An Assyrian Cylinder.
[From Hansard.]

The accompanying illustration, copied from Hansard's *Typographia*, represents an Assyrian cylinder which presents the same indications of impression which have been noticed upon the bricks. This cylinder, which is seven inches high and three inches wide at each end, was baked in a furnace until it was partially vitrified. Around its largest circumference is a protruding line, about a quarter of an inch wide, which seems to have been made by the imperfect meeting of two moulding stamps. If the inscription had been cut on the clay, this defect would not appear; the vertical lines would have been connected, and the ragged white line would have been made smooth.

This method of printing in clay was rude and imperfect, but, to some extent, it did the work of modern typography. Writings were published at small expense, and records were preserved for ages without the aid of ink or paper. The modern printer may wonder that this skill in printing was not developed. The engraving that was used to impress clay could have been coated with ink and stamped on parchment. Simple as this application of the engraving may appear, it was never made. So far from receiving any improvement, the art of printing in clay gradually fell into disuse. It has been neglected for more than twenty-five centuries on the soil where it probably originated. For Layard tells us that an Assyrian six-sided cylinder was used as a candlestick by a reputable Turcoman family living in the village where it was found. A hole in the centre of one of the ends received the tallow candle. There is a practical irony in this base application of what may have been a praise of "the great king," which has never been surpassed by Solomon or Shakspeare in their reflections on the vanity of human greatness.

Engraving was used by the ancient Greeks in a manner which should have suggested the feasibility of printing with ink. Some of the maps of the Athenians were engraved on smooth metal plates, with lines cut below the surface, after the method of copper-plate printers, from which impressions on vellum, or even on papyrus, could have been taken. But, so far as we know, the impressions were not taken: for every new map there was a new engraving.

The Assyrian method of engraving stamps for impressing clay was practised by the old Roman potters, who marked their manufactures with the names of the owners or with the contents of the vessel. The potters clearly understood the value of movable types. On some of their lamps of clay, the inscriptions were made by impressing, consecutively, the type of each letter. These types must have been movable, and, in appearance, somewhat like the punches or the model letters of type-founders.

There were some men in ancient Rome who had a clear perception of the ease with which engraved letters could be combined. Cicero, in an argument against the hypothesis of logical results from illogical causes, has intimated that it would be absurd to look for an intelligible sentence from a careless mixing up of the engraved letters of the alphabet.[1] The phrase by which he describes the assembled letters, *formæ literarum*, was used by the early printers to describe types. His argument implies, conversely, that if proper care were exercised, it would be easy to arrange the letters in readable sentences. But the speculation of Cicero did not go beyond the idea of combination. It does not appear that he thought that the letters could be used for printing.

Quintilian had speculations about engraved letters. He recommended to teachers the use of a thin stencil plate of wood, on which should be cut the letters that a boy might be required to copy when learning to write. The boy who traced the characters with his writing implement would have his hand guided and formed by the outlines of the perforated letters. The curt manner in which stencil plates are noticed should lead us to think that they were then in common use. We can see that stencils of this nature could have been used, at least as an aid, in the mechanical manufacture of books; but it is not probable that they were so used.

[1] Balbus, the stoic, in replying to Vellejus, the epicurean, opposes his atheistical argument that the world was made by chance, and says:

He who fancies that a number of solid and invisible bodies could be kept together by weight [gravitation?], and that a world full of order and beauty could be formed by their accidental juxtaposition—from such a man I cannot understand why he should not also believe that if he threw together, pell-mell, a great number of the twenty-one letters, either of gold or of some other material, the *Annals of Ennius* could be legibly put together from the forms scattered on the ground. *De Natura Deorum*, book II, chap. 20.

We have some evidences that the old Romans practised, at least experimentally, the art of printing with ink. The British Museum has a stamp with letters engraved in relief, that was found near Rome, and which seems to have been made for the purpose of printing the signature of its owner. The stamp is a brass plate, about two inches long and not quite one inch wide. A brass ring is attached to the back of the plate which may have been used as a socket for the finger, or as a support when it was suspended from a chain or girdle. On the face of the stamp are engraved two lines of capital letters, huddled together in the usual style of all old Roman inscriptions, cut the reverse way, as it would now be done for printing, and enclosed by a border line. An impression taken from this stamp would produce the letters in the accompanying illustration, which may be translated, *the signature of Cecilius Hermias*. Of Cecilius Hermias we know nothing. He may have been a civic official who used this stamp to exempt himself from the trouble of writing, or a citizen who tried to hide his inability to write.

CICAECILI
HERMIAE. SN.

If this stamp should be impressed in wax, the impression would produce letters sunk below the surface of the wax in a manner that is unlike the impressions of seals. The raised surface on the wax would be rough where it should be flat and smooth. This peculiarity is significant. As this rough field unfitted it for a neat impression on any plastic surface, the stamp should have been used for printing with ink.

An Old Roman Stamp.
[From Jackson.]

The accompanying illustration is that of a brass printing stamp in the British Museum, which is preserved as a specimen of old Roman workmanship.[1] The letters were cut in relief, in reverse order, and with a rough counter or field. This roughness proves that it could not have been used to impress wax.

[1] Jackson and Chatto, *Treatise on Wood Engraving*, p. 8

Brass stamps of similar construction and of undetermined age have been frequently found in France and Italy. All of them are of small size, and contain names of persons only.

Roman Stamps.
[From Jackson.]

The illustrations annexed, of two engraved brass stamps of eccentric shapes, were also copied from the originals in the British Museum. As the letters are roughly sunk in the metal, and are not fitted for stamping in wax, it is supposed that the stamps were made for impression with ink. They are regarded as Roman antiquities, of undoubted authenticity, but the meaning of the inscriptions, the special purposes for which they were made, and the period in which they were employed, are unknown. The difficulty connected with the proper fixing of ink upon these stamps of brass, of which a subsequent notice will be made, is one of many causes which prevented the development of this experimental form of printing.

A favorite method of making impressions was that of branding. Virgil, in the third book of the Georgics, tells us of its application to cattle. The old laws of many European states tell us of its application to human beings. The cruel practice was kept up long after the invention of typography. During the reign of Edward VI, of England (1547–1553), it was enacted that, "whosoever, man or woman, not being lame or impotent, nor so aged or diseased that he or she could not work, should be convicted of loitering or idle wandering by the highwayside, or in the streets, like a servant wanting a master, or a beggar, he or she was to be marked with a hot iron upon the breast with the letter V [for vagabond], and adjudged to the person bringing him or her before a justice, to be his slave for two years; and if such adjudged slave should run away, he or she, upon being taken and convicted, was to be marked upon the forehead, or upon the ball of the cheek, with the letter S [for slave], and adjudged to be the said master's slave forever."

With these evidences before us of long continued practice in various methods of engraving and stamping, and of a fair knowledge of some of the advantages of movable letters, the question may be asked, Why did the world have to wait so long for the invention of typography? This question is based on the assumption, that the civilization of antiquity was capable of making and preserving the invention which was missed through accident or neglect. Here is a grave error. The elements of an invention are like those of a chemical mixture. All the constituents but one may be there, exact in quantity and quality, but, for the lack of that one, the mixing of the whole in a new form cannot be accomplished. Failure in one point is entire failure.

The ancients failed in many points. They were destitute of several materials which we regard as indispensable in the practice of printing. They had no ink suitable for the work. Pliny and Dioscorides have given the formulas for the writing ink that was used by Greek and Roman scribes during the first century. Pliny says that the ink of book-writers was made of soot, charcoal and gum. He does not say what fluid was used to mix these materials, but he does allude to an occasional use of acid, to give the ink encaustic property and to make it bite in the papyrus. Dioscorides is more specific as to the quantities. He says that one ounce of gum should be mixed with three ounces of soot. Another formula is, one-half pound of smoke-black made from burned resin, one-half ounce each of copperas and ox-glue. Dioscorides further says that the latter mixture "is a good application in cases of gangrene, and is useful in scalds, if a little thickened, and employed as a salve." From this crude recipe one may form a correct opinion of the quality of the scientific knowledge then applied to medicine and the mechanical arts.

These mixtures, which are more like liquid shoe blacking than writing fluid, were used, with immaterial modifications, by the scribes of the dark ages. Useful as they may have been for their methods of writing, they could not have been applied to the inking of a metal surface engraved in relief. If the brass stamps described on a previous page had been brushed over never so carefully with these watery inks, the metal surface would not be covered with a smooth film of color. The ink would collect in spots and blotches. When stamped on paper or vellum, the ink thereupon impressed would be of irregular blackness, illegible in spots, and easily effaced. Writing ink, thickened with gum, has but a feeble encaustic property. It will not be absorbed, unless it is laid on in little pools, and unless the writing surface is scratched by a pen to aid the desired absorption. The flat impression of a smooth metal stamp could not make a fluid or a gummy ink penetrate below the writing surface. It was, no doubt, by reason of the inferior appearance of impressions of this nature that the brass stamps described on a previous page found so limited a use.

An unsuitable ink may seem but a trifling impediment to the development of printing, but if there had been no other, this would have been an insurmountable obstacle. The modern printer, who sees that the chief ingredients of printing ink are the well-known materials smoke-black and oil, may think that an ignorance of this mixture, or an inability to discover it, is ridiculous and inexcusable. Modern printing ink is but one of many inventions which could be named as illustrating the real simplicity of a long delayed improvement. Simple as it may seem, the mixing of color with oil was a great invention which wrought a revolution in the art of painting.

This invention, attributed by some authors to unknown Italian painters of the fourteenth century, and by others to

Hubert Van Eyck of Holland, at or about the beginning of the fifteenth century, immediately preceded the invention of types. The early typographic printers, who could not use the ink of the copyists, succeeded only when they mixed their black with oil. After four centuries of experience in the use of printing ink made with oil, and after repeated experimentation with impracticable substitutes, it may be confidently asserted that an invention of typography would have failed, if this use of oil had not been understood. The invention of types had to wait for the invention of ink.

Typography had to wait for the invention of paper, the only material that is mechanically adapted for printing, the only material that supplies the wants of the reader in his requirements for strength, cheapness, compactness and durability. Paper was known in civilized Europe for at least two centuries before typography was invented, but it was not produced in sufficient quantity nor of a proper quality until the beginning of the fifteenth century.

The old Romans had no substitute for paper that could have been devoted to printing or book-making. The papyrus which they used was so brittle that it could not be folded, creased and sewed like modern rag paper. It could not be bound up in books; it could not be rolled up, unsupported, like a sheet of parchment. It was secure only when it had been carefully wound around a wooden roller. The scribes of Rome and the book copyists of the middle ages preferred vellum. It was preferred by illuminators after printing had been invented. But vellum was never a favorite material among printers. In its dry state, it is harsh, and wears types; it is greasy, and resists ink; in its moistened state, it is flabby, treacherous and unmanageable. The early books on vellum are not so neatly printed as those on paper. But these faults were trivial as compared with the graver fault of inordinate price. When we consider that the skins of more than three hundred sheep were used in every copy of the first printed Bible, it is clear that typography would have been a failure if it had depended on a liberal supply of vellum. Even if the restricted size of vellum could have been conformed to, there were not enough sheep at the end of the fifteenth century to supply the demands of printing presses for a week.

If the idea of printing books from movable types had been entertained by an ancient Roman bookseller, or by a copyist, during the earlier part of the dark ages, it may be doubted whether he could have devised the mechanism that is needed in the making of types. For types that are accurate as to body, and economical as to cost, can be made by one method only. It is, in the highest degree, improbable, that the scientific method of making types by mechanism could have been invented at an earlier date than the fifteenth century. There was mechanical skill enough for the production of any kind of ingenious hand work, but the spirit that prompted men to construct machines and labor-saving apparatus was deficient or but feebly exercised. There was no more of true science in mechanics than there was in chemistry. The construction of a suitable type-mould, with its appurtenances, during the dark ages, would have been as premature as an invention of the steam engine in the same period.

The civilization of ancient Rome did not require printing. If all the processes of typography had been revealed to its scholars the art would not have been used. The wants of readers and writers were abundantly supplied by the pen. Papyrus paper was cheap, and scribes were numerous; Rome had more booksellers than it needed, and books were made faster than they could be sold. The professional scribes were educated slaves, who, fed and clothed at nominal expense, and organized under the direction of wealthy publishers, were made so efficient in the production of books, that typography, in an open competition, could have offered few advantages.

Our knowledge of the Roman organization of labor in the field of book-making is not as precise as could be wished; but the frequent notices of books, copyists and publishers, made by many authors during the first century, teach us that books were plentiful. Horace, the elegant and fastidious man of letters, complained that his books were too common, and that they were sometimes found in the hands of vulgar snobs for whose entertainment they were not written. Martial, the jovial man of the world, boasted that his books of stinging epigrams were to be found in everybody's hands or pockets. Books were read not only in the libraries, but at the baths, in the porticoes of houses, at private dinners and in mixed assemblies. The business of book-making was practised by too many people, and some were incompetent. Lucian, who had a keen perception of pretense in every form, ridicules the publishers as ignoramuses. Strabo, who probably wrote illegibly, says that the books of booksellers were incorrect.

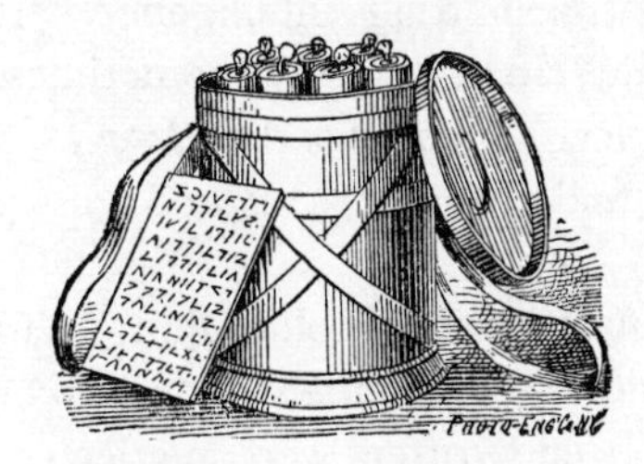

Tablet with Waxed Surface.
Scrinium or Case for Manuscripts.

Manuscript Roll, with Title on the Ticket.
Papyrus Manuscript partially Unrolled.

Roman Scrinium, with Rolls of Papyrus.

The prices of books made by slave labor were necessarily low. Martial says that his first book of epigrams was sold in plain binding for six sesterces, about twenty-four cents of American money; the same book in sumptuous binding was valued at five denarii, about eighty cents. He subsequently complained that his thirteenth book was sold for only four sesterces, about sixteen cents. He frankly admits that half of this sum was profit, but intimates, somewhat ungraciously, that the publisher Tryphon gave him too small a share. Of the merits of this old disagreement between the author and publisher, we have not enough of facts to justify an opinion. We learn that some publishers, like Tryphon and the brothers

Sosii, acquired wealth, but there are many indications that publishing was then, as it is now, one of the most speculative kinds of business. One writer chuckles over the unkind fate that sent so many of the unsold books of rival authors from the warehouses of the publisher, to the shops of grocers and bakers, where they were used to wrap up pastry and spices; another writer says that the unsold stock of a bookseller was sometimes bought by butchers and trunk-makers.

The Romans not only had plenty of books but they had a manuscript daily newspaper, the *Acta Diurna*, which seems to have been a record of the proceedings of the senate. We do not know how it was written, nor how it was published, but it was frequently mentioned by contemporary writers as the regular official medium for transmitting intelligence. It was sent to subscribers in distant cities, and was, sometimes, read to an assembled army. Cicero mentions the *Acta* as a sheet in which he expected to find the city news and gossip about marriages and divorces.

In the sixth century the business of book-making had fallen into hopeless decay. Ignorance pervaded all ranks of society.[1] The books that had been written were neglected, and the number of readers and scholars diminished with every succeeding generation.[2] The treasures of literature at Rome, Constantinople and Alexandria which were destroyed by fire or by barbaric invasion were not replaced. Books were so scarce at the close of the seventh century, that Pope Martin requested one of his bishops to supply them, if possible, from Germany. The ignorance of ecclesiastics in high station was

[1] The emperor Justin (518–527) could not write, and was obliged to sign state papers with a stencil.

[2] When Latin ceased to be a living language, the whole treasury of knowledge was locked up from the eyes of the people. The few who might have imbibed a taste for literature, if books had been accessible to them, were reduced to abandon pursuits that could only be cultivated through a kind of education not easily within their reach. Schools confined to cathedrals and monasteries, and exclusively designed for the purposes of religion, afforded no encouragement or opportunities to the laity. Hallam, *Middle Ages.*

alarming. During this century, and for centuries afterward, there were many bishops and archbishops of the church who could not sign their names. It was asserted at a council of the church held in the year 992, that scarcely a single person was to be found in Rome itself who knew the first element of letters. Hallam says, "To sum up the account of ignorance in a word, it was rare for a layman of any rank to know how to sign his name." Charlemagne could not write, and Frederic Barbarossa could not read; John, king of Bohemia, and Philip the Hardy, king of France, were ignorant of both accomplishments.[1] The graces of literature were tolerated only in the ranks of the clergy; the layman who preferred letters to arms was regarded as a man of mean spirit. When the crusaders took Constantinople, in 1204, they exposed to public ridicule the pens and inkstands that they found in the conquered city as the ignoble arms of a contemptible race of students.

During this period of intellectual darkness, which lasted from the fifth until the fifteenth century, a period sometimes described, and not improperly, as the dark ages, there was no need for any improvement in the old method of making books. The world was not then ready for typography. The invention waited for readers more than it did for types; the multitude of book-buyers upon which its success depended had to be created. Books were needed as well as readers. The treatises of the old Roman sophists and rhetoricians, the dialectics of Aristotle and the schoolmen, and the commentaries on ecclesiastical law of the fathers of the church, were the works which engrossed the attention of men of letters for many centuries before the invention of typography. Useful as these books may have been to the small class of readers for whose benefit they were written, they were of no benefit to a people who required the elements of knowledge.

We may imagine the probable fate of a premature and unappreciated invention of typography by thinking of results that might have been and have not been accomplished by printing among a people who were not prepared to use it as

[1] Hallam, *Middle Ages*, vol. III, pp. 286, 287.

it should be used. Printing has been practised in China for many centuries, but there can be no comparison between the fruits of printing in China and in Europe. The remarkable inefficiency of the Chinese method is the result not so much of clumsiness of the process, as of the perverseness of a people who are unable to improve it, and unwilling to accept the improvements of Europeans. The first printing press brought to the New World was set up in the City of Mexico about one hundred years before a printing office was established in Massachusetts. Books were printed in Constantinople, perhaps as early as 1490, certainly before types were thought of in Scotland. And now Scotland sends types and books to Turkey, and Boston sends printing paper and presses to Mexico. If the people of Turkey and Mexico are receiving benefits from printing, the benefits have been derived from the practice of the art abroad and not at home.

In making an estimate of the service that printing has done for the world, we frequently overlook the supports by which it has been upheld. It is a common belief that the diffusion of knowledge which was so clearly manifested in the fifteenth century was due to the invention of printing. This belief reverses the proper order, and substitutes the effect for the cause. It was the broader diffusion of knowledge that made smooth the way for the development of typography. In its infancy, the invention was indebted for its existence to improvements in liberal and mechanical arts; in its maturity, it is largely indebted for its success to discoveries in science, and to reforms in government.

The magnetic telegraph is the most recent discovery, and of the most importance, in its services to the daily newspaper press. The circulation of leading American daily newspapers has more than trebled since the invention of the telegraph.

The free public schools of America have done much to promote the growth of printing. If the State did not offer free books and free education, a large portion of the people would grow up in ignorance. Every scholar in a public school becomes for life a reader, and to some extent, a purchaser of books. The value of the school-books manufactured in the United States annually, has been estimated at fifteen million dollars. Of Webster's Spelling-Book alone, thirty-five million copies have been sold, and a million copies are printed every year. If printing were deprived of the support it receives from public schools, there would at once follow a noticeable decrease in the production of printed matter, and a corresponding decrease in the number of readers and book-buyers.

To foster the tastes which have been cultivated by public schools and newspapers, some States have established public libraries in every school district. There are, also, a great many valuable libraries which have been established by voluntary association or by individual bequest. These libraries create books as well as readers.

Railroads, steamboats and package expresses are aids of as great importance. The New-York daily newspaper, printed early in the morning, is sold within a radius of three hundred miles before sunset of the same day. Newspapers now find hundreds of eager purchasers in places where they would not have found one in the days of stage-coaches. The benefits of cheap and quick transportation are also favorable to the sale of books. A bookseller's package, weighing one hundred pounds, will be carried from New York to St. Louis, on the Mississippi, within sixty-five hours, at an average expense of three dollars. When there was no railroad from St. Louis to San Francisco, the overland charges on one hundred pounds of books were one hundred dollars. The long delays and great expenses of stage-coach transportation would operate almost as a prohibition to the sale of periodicals and new books.

The greatest legislative aid that printing has received is through the facilities which are furnished by post-offices and mails. They create readers. Weekly newspapers are now sent, for one year, for twenty cents, to subscribers in the most remote corner of the Union. Books are sent three thousand miles at the rate of one cent per ounce. The improvement of postal facilities has increased the number of readers and purchasers of newspapers to an amount unforeseen by the most sanguine projector.

All these aids are, comparatively, of recent introduction. The beginnings of the telegraph, the railroad and the express are within the memory of the men of the present generation. The systematic establishment of free schools and libraries is the work of the present century. Public mails and post-offices were introduced in 1530, but it is only within the past forty years that their management has been more liberal for the benefit of the people. It is by aids like these, and not by its intrinsic merits alone, that printing has received its recent development. It was for the want of these aids that printing languished for many years after its invention. One has but to consider the many supports printing has received to see that its premature invention would have been fruitless.

If, even now, when books and readers and literary tastes are as common as they were infrequent, it is necessary to the success of printing that there shall be schools and libraries, cheap and rapid methods of travel, generous postal facilities, a liberal government and a broad toleration of the greatest differences in opinion, what but failure could have been expected when the world was destitute of nearly all? Printing not only had to wait many centuries for improvements in mechanical appliances, without which it would have been worthless; it had to wait for a greater number of readers, for liberal governments, for instructive writers, for suitable books. It came at the proper time, not too soon, not too late. "Not the man, the age invents."

III

The Key to the Invention of Typography.

Conflicting Theories about the Invention of Typography...Was it an Invention or a Combination? Errors of Superficial Observers...Merit of the Invention is not in Impression...Not altogether in Types or Composition...Types of no value unless they are Accurate...Hand-made Types Impracticable...Merit of Invention is in the Method of Making Types...Is but One Method. Description ... Counter-Punch ... Punch... Matrix ... Mould...Illustrations ... Type-Making as Illustrated by Moxon in 1683...As Illustrated by Amman in 1564...Notices of Type-Making by Earlier Authors...Type-Mould the Symbol of Typography...Inventor of the Type-Mould the Inventor of Typography...A Great Invention, but Original only in the Type-Mould.

The character of typography is not pressing and printing but mobilization. The winged A is its symbol. The elements unchained, the letters freed from every bond in which the pen or chisel of calligrapher or xylographer held them entangled; the cut character risen from the tomb of the solitary tablet into the substantive life of the cast types — that is the invention of printing. *Van der Linde.*

THERE is a wide-spread belief that typography was, in all its details, a purely original invention. A popular version of its origin, hereafter to be related, says that it was the result of an accidental discovery; a conflicting version says that it was the result of more than thirteen years of secret experiment. Each version teaches us that there was no perceptible unfolding of the invention; that the alleged inventor created all that he needed, that he made his types, ink and presses, that he derived nothing of value from the labors of earlier printers. If typography was invented by Gutenberg, it was fitly introduced by the sudden appearance of the printed Bible in two folio volumes; if invented by Coster, by the unheralded publication of a thin folio of large wood-cuts with descriptive text of type. If either of these versions is accepted in the form in which it is usually told, we must also believe that printing, in the form of perfected typography, leaped, Minerva-like, fully equipped, from the brain of the inventor.

There is another belief, which is strongly maintained by a few scholars, that typography was not an original invention, that it was nothing more than a new application of the old theories and methods of impression which have already been described. According to this view, the practice of engraving is at least as old as the oldest Egyptian seal; the publication of written language can be traced to the Babylonish bricks; printing with ink, as indicated by old Roman hand stamps, was practised as early as the fifth century; the combinations of movable letters were suggested by Cicero and St. Jerome. All that was needed for the full development of typography was the invention of paper. Supplied with paper, the so-called inventor of typography did no more than combine the old theories and processes, and give them a new application. He really invented nothing.

In this conflict of opinion, the critical reader will note an inability to perceive the difference between impression and typography. Those who believe in the entire originality of typography ascribe its merit to the mind that first thought of the combinations of types; those who deny its originality find its vital element in pressure. With one class, the merit of the invention is in the idea of types; with the other, it is in the impression of types. Neither view is entirely correct.

A printer may see how these errors could be developed. The unreflecting observer, who, for the first time, surveys the operations of a printing office, finds in the fast presses the true vital principle of printing. With him, presswork is printing; type-setting and type-making are only adjuncts. He was the inventor of the modern art of printing who built the first press, and printed the first book. The conclusion is illogical, as will be shown on another page. If a radical improvement had not been made in the earliest method of printing books, the art would have been as unproductive in Europe as it has been in China. The fast press may do its work admirably, but its only functions are those of inking and impressing, and impression is not typography.

The thoughtful observer will perceive that the merit of modern printing is not in impression; that there would be neither fast presses, nor great books, nor daily newspapers, if there were no types. With him, whatever of greatness there is in printing is due to the mind that first imagined the utility of types. The grandness of the results that have been achieved by typography seem all the grander when he thinks that these results have been accomplished with such simple tools as little cubes of metal. The making of these tools he regards as a matter of minor importance. For in these types are visible no intricacy of mechanism as in the power loom, no indications of a mysterious agency as in the magnetic telegraph, no evidences of scientific skill as in photographic apparatus. There are in types, apparently, no more evidences of genius or science than there are in pins or needles. The grotesque types of the fifteenth century are rated by him, and even by many mechanics, as rude workmanship which could have been done by a carver in wood or a founder in metal. He who could imagine them could make them. To think was to do. The merit of the invention of typography is accordingly adjudged, not to the inventive spirit which constructed the mould by which the types were made, but to the genius which first thought of the utility of types. This is a grave error.

Speculations like these, which assign all the merit of the invention of typography to him who first conceived the idea of types, are opposed to many facts and probabilities. Cicero and Jerome could not have been the only men who thought of the combinations of engraved letters; nor were the old Roman lamp-makers and branders of cattle the only men who used types. The idea of stamping with detached letters could have been entertained, and practised, by hundreds of experimenters of whom there is no tradition. It is probable that there was such a practice, but the stamping of single types by hand pressure was not typography, nor did it lead to its subsequent invention. Experimental types like these, which had been cut by hand, were of no practical value, for they could not have been used on any extensive scale.

There is something more in types than is apparent at the first glance. Simple as they may seem, they are evidences of notable mechanical skill in the matter of accuracy. The page before the reader was composed with more than 2,000 pieces of metal; the large page of a daily paper may contain more than 150,000 of these little pieces. Whether the page is large or small, the types are always closely fitted to each other; they stand accurately in line, and the page is truly square. If the types of one character, as of the letter a, should be made the merest trifle larger or smaller than its fellows in the same font, all the types, when composed, will show the consequences of the defect. The irregularity of line that is scarcely perceptible in the first row will be offensively distinct in the second. It will increase with each succeeding row, until the types become a heap of confusion which cannot be handled by the printer. Advantages which might be secured from movable types are made of no effect by an irregularity so slight that it would be passed unnoticed in the workmanship of ordinary trades. The illustration proves that it is not enough for types to be movable; they must be accurate as to body; they must fit each other with geometrical precision.

The irregularity of this composition is caused by the types of the letters a and e, which are larger than the other letters, by accurate measurement, less than nine one-thousandths of an American inch. This minute difference is repeated and increased in every line, until the connection between words and lines is partially destroyed. If this use of the large a and e were continued through a dozen additional lines, the reader would be unable to understand what has been composed.

Illustration of Types of Irregular Body.

The accuracy of modern printing types is due more to the nice mechanisms employed by the type-founder than to his personal skill. He could cut types by hand, but the cost of hand-cut types would be enormous, and they would be vastly inferior to types made by the type-casting machine. He could make types by a variety of mechanical methods, but they would be imperfect and unsatisfactory. A careful survey of the impracticable inventions in type-founding, recorded in the patent offices of this country and Great Britain, proves that there is, virtually, but one method of making types. The requirements of accuracy and cheapness can be met only by making them of metal, and casting them in a mould of metal.[1]

Although it is clearly understood, by all persons who have a practical knowledge of the subject, that practical types can be made only by casting, many popular books repeat the old story that the first typographic books were printed with types which had been cut by hand out of wood or metal. Whether the mechanics of the middle ages could have done what modern mechanics cannot do,—cut types with bodies of satisfactory accuracy—need not now be considered. The stories about hand-made types—about types that were sawed out of wood blocks—about types that were cut out of wooden rods, and skewered together with iron wires—about types that were engraved on the ends of cubes of metal—will be examined at greater length on an advanced page. Even if these doubtful stories were verified, it would still remain to be proved that the cut types had advantages over letters engraved on wood. It would be difficult to give reasons for their introduction. Books composed with cut types could not be neatly printed; they would be inferior to good manuscripts in appearance, but not inferior in price. Cut types

[1] These observations apply only to the types used for the text letters of books and newspapers. The large types made for the display lines of posters are cut on wood, but these types of wood are used only for printing single lines; they are not combined with the compactness of book types, and do not require their precision of body. The wood types of Japan are, probably, the smallest wood types in practical use; but they are much larger than our book types; they are printed in smaller pages; they are not obliged to stand truly in line, nor to conform to the standards of European and American printers. The cheapness of types which have been cast, as compared with letters which have been engraved, has been explained on page 23 of this work.

were as impracticable in the infancy of the art as they are now. There is no trustworthy evidence that they were ever used for any other purpose than that of experiment.

Every method for making merchantable types, save that of casting, is a failure. Typography would be a great failure, if its types were not cast by scientific methods. This understood, we can see that the most meritorious feature in the invention does not belong to him who first thought of the advantages of types, nor even to him who first made them by impracticable methods. Its honors are really due to the man to whose sagacity and patience in experiment we are indebted for the type-mould, for he was the first to make types which could be used with advantage.

It will now be necessary to explain the scientific method of making types which is practised by every type-founder. The first process is the making of model letters. The work begins with the cutting on steel of a tool which is known as the Counter-punch. The illustration represents the face of a counter-punch for the letter H, of the size usually known among type-founders as Double-English. This counter-punch is an engraving, in high relief, of the hollow or the counter of that interior part of the letter H which does not show black in the printed impression. It has apparently, no resemblance to the letter for which it is made. When the proportions of the counter-punch have been duly approved, it is stamped or impressed to a proper depth on the end of a short bar of soft steel. Properly stamped, the counter-punch finishes by one quick stroke the interior part of the model letter, and does it more quickly and neatly than it could be done by cutting tools.

The short bar of soft steel is known as a Punch. When it has received the impress of the counter-punch, the punch cutter, for so the engraver of letters is called in type-foundries, cuts away the outer edges until the model letter is pronounced perfect. This is work of great exactness, for the millions of types that may be made by means of the punch will reproduce all its peculiarities, whether of merit or defect. The steel of the punch is then hardened until it has sufficient strength to penetrate prepared copper. It is then punched, by quick and strong pressure, on the flat side of a narrow bar of cold rolled copper. This operation makes a reversed or sunken imprint of the letter on the punch. In this condition, the punched copper bar is known among type-founders as a Drive, or a Strike, or an Unjustified Matrix. It becomes the Matrix proper, only after it has been carefully fitted-up to suit the mould. The exterior surface of the drive must be made truly flat, and this flatness must be parallel with the face of the stamped or sunken letter in the interior. The sides of the drive must be squared, so that the interior letter shall be at a fixed distance from the sides. The depth of the stamped letter, and its distance from the sides, must be made absolutely uniform in all the matrices required for a font or a complete assortment of letters. The object of this nicety is to secure a uniform height to all the types, and to facilitate the frequent changes of matrix on the mould. The justifying and fitting of matrices to moulds is one of the most exact operations in the art of type-founding.

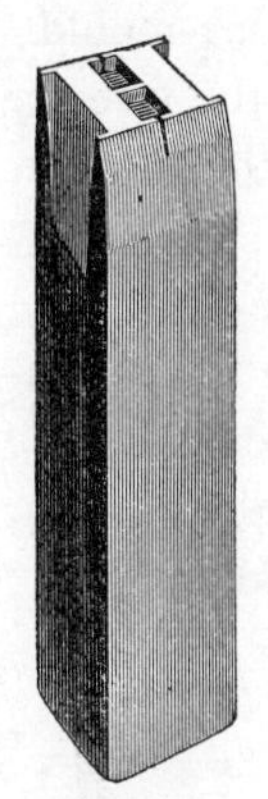

Punch.

For every character or letter really required in a full working assortment of types, the type-founder cuts a separate punch and fits up a separate matrix; but for all the characters or letters which are made to be used together, there is but one mould. Types are of no use, as has been shown, if they cannot be arranged and handled with facility, and printed in lines that are truly parallel. However unlike they may be in face, they must be exactly alike in body. This uniformity of body, which is as

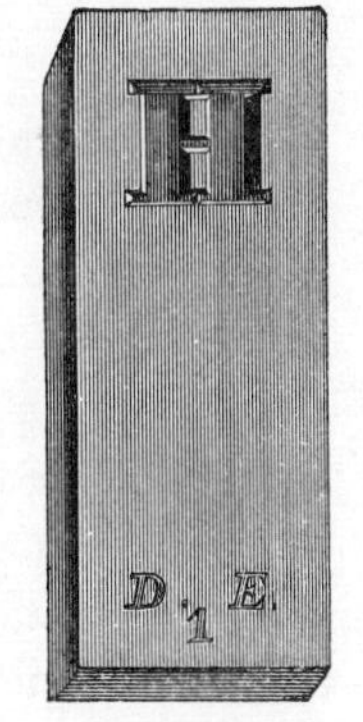

Matrix. [1]

[1] The characters D, E, 1 are the private reference marks of the type-founder. In this position they cannot be reproduced on the cast type.

essential as variety of face, can be most certainly secured by casting all the types in one mould. All the matrices are, consequently, made with a view to being fitted to one mould. The mould forms the body, and the matrix forms the face of the type. With nearly every change of matrix there must be a new adjustment of the mould.

The word Body, as used by printers and type-founders, means the measurement of a type in one direction only—in a direction at a right angle with the regular lines or rows of printed matter. The types of the accompanying illustration are of the same height, but they are of different bodies.

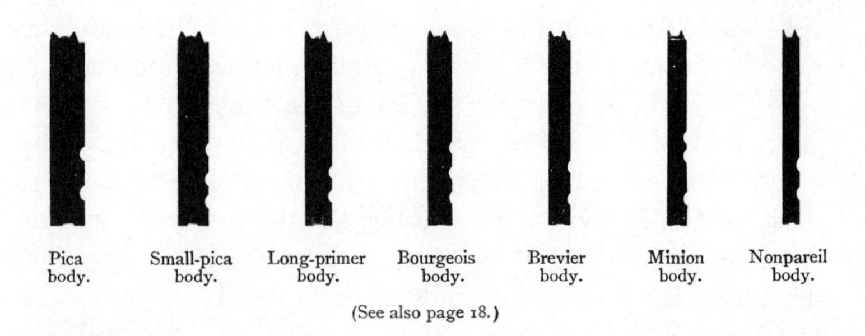

(See also page 18.)

Exactness of body could be secured with little difficulty if all the types belonging to the same font were of the same width, and could be cast in one fixed and unalterable mould. But types of the same font and same body are of all widths. They vary, in the letters from the l to the W; in the spaces or blanks used to separate the words, from the hair space to the three-em quadrat. The spaces in the following illustration are of the same body, but they are of different widths, to suit the peculiarities of different kinds of printed matter.

Six-in-em space. Five-in-em space. Four-in-em space. Three-in-em space. En quadrat. Em quadrat. Two-em quadrat. Three-em quadrat.

It is not practicable to make a mould for each character; the cost would be enormous, and the multiplicity of moulds would lead to fatal faults in inaccuracy of body. Exactness of body can be had only by casting all the characters in one mould, but this mould must be made to suit all the matrices. The matrices must be frequently changed, but with such nicety that the types of every letter shall be uniform in height, in line, and truly square. Any mechanic will see that the construction of an adjustable mould is work of difficulty, and that the fitting-up of a set of matrices for one mould is a very nice operation.

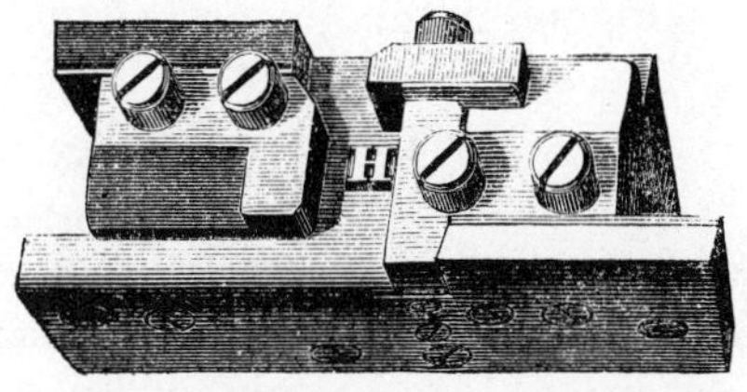

Figure 1. Type-Mould, without Matrix and with a Type in the Mould.

The Type-Mould of modern type-founders consists of two firmly screwed combinations of a number of pieces of steel, making right and left halves. In the first illustration of the mould, Figure 1, the halves are properly connected. In this form it is not practicable to represent the interior, but it may be understood that the interior faces fit each other snugly in every part but the centre, in which provision is made for a small opening which can be increased or diminished in a lateral direction only. One end of this opening is closed by the matrix; the other end is the jet, or the mouth-piece through which the melted metal is injected. In this opening, which is indicated by the letter H in the cut, the body of type is cast. The matrix which forms the face of the type is snugly fitted between the jaws on

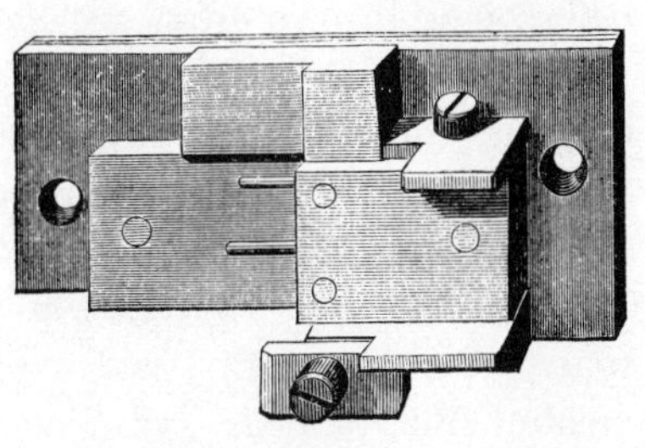

Figure 2. One Half of the Mould.

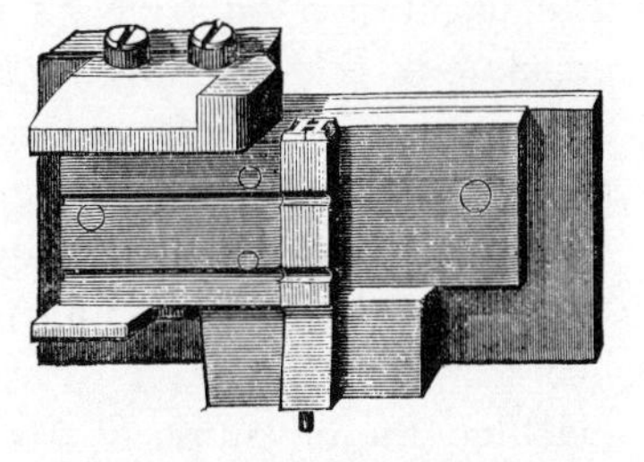

Figure 3. The Other Half of the Mould.

either side of this letter H. It does not appear in the cut; for the matrices, although indispensable parts, are always looked upon by founders as attachments to the mould.

Figures 2 and 3 represent the interior sides of the mould. For the purpose of clearer illustration, the half of the mould, Figure 2, is shown reversed, or upside down; but when this half is connected with its mate, the two halves appear as they do in Figure 1. These two halves differ from each other only in a few minor features. They are so constructed that, when joined, the sides which determine the body of the types are in exact parallel, and at a fixed and unalterable distance from each other. In Figure 2, the ridges which make the nicks are noticeable; in Figure 3 the cast type is shown as it appears before it is thrown from the mould, with jet attached.[1]

Although the two sides of the mould are fixed so as to be immovable in the direction which determines the body of the type, they have great freedom of motion and nicety of adjustment in the direction which determines its width. They can be brought close together, so as to make a hair space, or can be fixed wide apart, so as to cast a three-em quadrat, but they always slide on broad and solid bearings, between guides which keep them from getting out of square.

In the construction of the mould and adjustment of the matrices, every care is taken to insure exactness of body. The illustration on page 52 may be again referred to as an example of the necessity for minute accuracy. We there see that the feasibility of typography depends upon the geometrical exactness of its tools, and that types are of no practical use, if they cannot be readily combined and interchanged.

The casting or founding of types, in a mould constructed like that of the engraving, is now accomplished by a complex machine, the invention of Mr. David Bruce, Jr., of New-York city, and by him patented in the year 1838. Before this date

[1] The superfluous metal which adheres to the cast type, and is afterward broken off, is also called the Jet. The finishing of the types is comparatively simple work which does not require explanation.

all types were cast by hand, from a hand-mould, and by a process which received no noticeable improvement for two centuries. The following illustration, taken from an engraving

Type-Casting as Practised in 1683.

[From Moxon.]

published by an early English type-founder,[1] can be offered as a substantially correct representation of the method of casting which was practised by all type-founders in the first quarter of this century.

The type-caster took in his left hand the mould, which was imbedded in a wood frame, and shielded about the jet,

[1] *Mechanick Exercises, or the Doctrine of Handy-Works, applied to the Art of Printing.* By Joseph Moxon, Member of the Royal Society, and Hydrographer to the King, etc. London, 1683.

to protect him from accidental splashes of melted metal. Then, with his right hand, he took from the melting pot a spoonful of the hot metal, which he quickly poured into the jet or mouth of the mould. At the same instant, with a sudden jerk, he threw up his left hand, so as to aid the melted metal in making a forcible splash against the matrix at the bottom of the mould. This sudden jerk or throw was needed, in the casting of small letters, to make a good face to the type. If it was not done, the metal would cool too quickly, and would not penetrate the finer lines of the matrix. Long practice enabled the type-caster to do this work with apparent carelessness; but the trick of making this throw or cast with the left hand, at the right time and in the right manner, was slowly acquired—by some strong men, never acquired at all. In all cases, hand-casting was hard work. To face types, writes August Bernard, the type-caster must make the contortions of a maniac. It was slow work. Fournier the younger, writing in 1764, says that the performance of the type-caster of ordinary book types would vary from two thousand to three thousand types per day. When this throw was made, the type-caster removed the matrix with his right hand, and, giving the mould a toss, threw out the type. The matrix was then replaced on the mould, and the operations which have been described were repeated in the casting of every subsequent type.

It must be confessed that this method of making types is not simple. It is too circuitous in its processes, and too complex in its machinery, to be regarded as the fruit of the first lucky thought of the inventor. It is a scientific process, manifestly the result of thought and protracted experiment. In its series of impressions, it is an emblem of the art which it has created. The counter-punch impresses the punch, the punch impresses the matrix, the melted metal impresses the matrix and mould. One model letter on the punch is the instrument by which millions of types are made; one letter on a type may serve in the printing of millions of words.

The punch, matrix and mould are old inventions, but they are still in use in all type-foundries. They have not been changed in any important feature since they were explicitly described and illustrated for the first time, by Joseph Moxon. As Moxon did not claim these implements as his own invention—as we find in the writings of the authors who preceded him notices of the art of cutting letters, and mention of tools "which they called matrices," and of "making types in brass" [matrices or moulds], we have some reason for the belief that there has never been any radical change in the processes of type-making.

Unfortunately, we have no minute description of the art of type-making as it was practised before Moxon. Those who were competent to describe the work, refrained from description, either because they thought that the subject was trivial or technical, or because they intended to conceal the process. The authors who did undertake to describe the art were incompetent; they did not thoroughly understand the subject, and have treated it slightingly and incorrectly. But we are not entirely in the dark.

Our most authentic information is contained in a queer little book by Jost Amman, which is known to modern book-collectors as *The Book of Trades*,[1] and which was published at Frankfort-on-the-Main, in the year 1564. The title of the book, with text in German, describes it as *Hans Sachs' Correct Description of all Arts, Ranks and Trades*, with printed illus-

[1] *The Book of Trades* was popular. Two editions in Latin verse were published, one in 1568, and another in 1574, with descriptions by Hartmann Schopper. Chatto says:

> This is, perhaps, the most curious and interesting series of cuts, exhibiting the various ranks and employments of men, that ever was published. Among the higher orders...... are the Pope, Emperor, King, Princes, Nobles, Priests and Lawyers; while almost every branch of labor or trade then known in Germany, from agriculture to pin-making, has its representative. There are also not a few which it would be difficult to reduce to any distinct class, as they are neither trades nor honest professions. Of these heteroclytes is the *Meretricum procurator*, or, as Captain Dugald Dalgetty says, the captain of the queans. Jackson and Chatto, *A Treatise on Wood Engraving*, p. 409.

Jost Amman was one of the many famous German designers on wood. The publishers of Nuremberg and Frankfort esteemed his ability highly and gave him constant employment.

trations. The descriptions, so called, which were written in verse, by Hans Sachs, the cobbler poet, are of no value for this inquiry: they describe nothing. To men seeking trustworthy information about art or manufactures, all the merit of the book is in its numerous engravings on wood, which may be accepted as faithful illustrations of the methods and usages observed during the sixteenth century.

Among the illustrations is the *schriftgiesser*, or the type-founder, with the accessories of his art about him. We see the furnace for melting the metal, the bellows, the tongs and the basket of charcoal. That the man is founding types is apparent, not only from the bowl of cast types on the floor before the stool, but from his position with spoon in hand. Here we begin to note differences. The type-caster of 1683 stands up to his work; the *schriftgiesser* of Amman is sitting down. The mould of 1683, like the hand moulds that were in use forty years ago, is provided with a wire spring, to keep the matrix firmly in position; the mould of Amman has no spring of iron wire and it is nested in a pyramid-shaped box,

Type-Casting as Practised in 1564.
[From Jost Amman.]

which seems to be used as a protection to the hand. How the mould was nested in the box, how the matrix was attached to the mould, how the cast types were dislodged from the mould, is not shown in the engraving. We have to regret that the wood-cut is so small, and that Amman's engraving is so coarse. There are some indications that, in its more important features, the mould of Amman was like that of Moxon. The little opening in the side of the mould which rests on the shelf may have been an opening for the insertion of matrices. That metal matrices were used is dimly shown by the three little bars resting on the top of a small nest of drawers, which has the appearance of a chest for punches and matrices. The pyramidal box was not only the nest of the mould, but served also as a support for the matrix. The sitting position of the caster permitted him to give the box a throw or jerk; with his right hand at liberty, he could pull out the mould and dislodge the type in the usual manner.

There are other features in Amman's wood-cut requiring notice. Upon the lower shelf are two crucibles, which were put in use, probably, when making the alloy of type-metal. The use of the sieves is not apparent; they may have been needed to sift the sand for the sand moulds, in which bars of type-metal were made, and in which large initial types were cast. The crucibles, the furnace, the mould, the position of the type-caster, and the single types with jets attached, are enough to prove that types were cast, one by one, by the process subsequently described by Moxon. It is plain that the elementary principles of type-founding were as clearly understood in 1564 as they are at this day.

The most obscure feature in this wood-cut is the matrix. The three little bits resting on the chest of drawers are too rudely cut to enable us to decide positively that they are matrices. We infer that they are from their surroundings and from the apparent necessity for such implements; but it would be more satisfactory to know, and not infer, that the early type-founders used matrices of hard metal.

There are no engravings of type-founding of earlier date than this cut of Amman's, but we have some evidences which point to a very early use of moulds of hard metal. We find in many of the books of the sixteenth and fifteenth centuries occasional allusions to type-making. Considered separately, they are of little importance; considered together, they are ample proof that types were made of fluid metal in moulds and matrices of brass, not less than one hundred years before Amman made his wood-cuts.

In 1507, Ivo Wittig put up a stone to the memory of John Gutenberg, on which he had engraved that Gutenberg was the first to make printing letters *in brass*. We do not find in any record of authority that Gutenberg printed books by types cut out of brass. There are difficulties connected with the cutting and use of brass types which would make such an assertion incredible. If we accept the literal translation of the Latin epitaph, and supplement it with a little knowledge of type-founding, we shall then understand what Wittig meant—that Gutenberg, by using melted metal, made types in brass moulds.

Trithemius, writing in 1514, observes that Gutenberg and Fust "discovered a method of founding the forms of all the letters, which they called matrices, from which they cast metal types." The statement of the bishop is somewhat confused, and his specification of Fust as an inventor is, probably, incorrect, but every typographer who reads his description cannot fail to see that he has endeavored to describe the established method of making types—the method in use to this day.

Peter Schœffer, in a book printed by him in 1466, makes the book metaphorically say, "I am cast at Mentz." He says the types were cast, although he elsewhere praises himself as a more skillful cutter of letters than Fust or Gutenberg.

Bernard Cennini, writing at Florence in 1471, says that the letters of his book were first cut and then cast.

Nicholas Jenson, who calls himself a cutter of books, says in one of them, published in 1485, that the book, meaning the types of the book, was cut and cast by a divine art.

Husner of Strasburg, in the imprint of a book made by him in 1473, says (translating his language literally) that it was printed "with sculptured letters from brass," or, as it could be more clearly construed, with letters in high relief, made from brass matrices. That Husner did not mean to say that his printing types were cut out of brass, is more clearly shown in the imprint of another book printed by him in 1476, in which he says, literally, that it was printed, "without doubt, with sculptured letters, scientifically begun in brass."[1]

That the cutting, so frequently mentioned by the early printers, was the cutting of punches, is apparent to every modern typographer who knows that, in the manufacture of types, punch-cutting is not only the first process in order of time, but first in order of artistic importance. That the types said to be made of brass were made in brass moulds and matrices could, in the absence of other proof, be inferred from the appearance of the books of the fifteenth century. These types often show varieties of the same letter and have other peculiarities disagreeable to modern tastes, but there is strict uniformity in each variety, and an accuracy of body which could have been secured by no other method than

[1] The text of the *Speculum Durandi*, the book of 1473, is *exsculptis ære litteris;* the text of the *Præceptorum Nideri*, the book of 1476, is *litteris exsculptis artificiali certe conatu ex ære.* The language is plain and cannot be construed to mean cut types. When these books were printed, the arts of typography and copper-plate printing were new and had not yet received distinctive names. The reading public knew nothing of the theory or practice of either process, and confounded the productions of one art with those of the other. The early printers had to define the respective arts as they best could, with words made from Latin. A close examination of the words selected by Husner will show their propriety. The word *exsculptis*, sculptured, or cut out in high relief, is here used in contradistinction to *insculptis*, sculptured in, or cut in, as in engraving on a copper plate. It defines typographic work from copper-plate printing. The phrase *artificiali certe conatu ex ære*, means something more than skillful engraving; it suggests the use of mechanism, and of a beginning of the work in brass, which can be clearly understood only by construing *ex ære*, from or in a brass mould. The phrase here translated *in* brass has been rendered *of* brass, but the language will not bear this construction. The phrase *ex ære*, in, or out of, or from brass, was frequently used by many early printers. I have rarely met the form *æris*, of brass. To represent that early types were of brass is as much a violation of history as it is of grammar.

that of casting them in moulds and matrices of hard metal. There is other evidence which is even more direct. In the Magliabechi library at Florence is preserved the original Cost Book of the Directors of the Ripoli Press of that city, for the interval between the years 1474 and 1483.[1] In this book may be found, among other papers of value, a list of the prices which were then paid for the supplies or materials used in the type-foundry connected with the Ripoli Press. In this list we see the names of the metals that are used in all modern type-foundries. There can be no question of the statement that the types of this foundry were cast in metal moulds.

PRICES OF MATERIAL FOR THE TYPE-FOUNDRY.

Materials.	*Tuscan Currency per pound.*	*American Currency per pound.*
Steel, . . .	lir. 2 8 0	$2.18
Metal, (Antimony?)	11 0	.50
Brass, ...	12 0	.54
Copper, . . .	6 8	.30
Tin, ...	8 0	.36
Lead, ...	2 4	.10½
Iron Wire, . .	8 0	.36

It would not be difficult to present additional evidence tending to prove that the punch, the matrix and the mould of hard metal were used by the earliest typographers, but this evidence will be given with more propriety in another chapter. On this page, it is enough to record, as the result of the future inquiry, that printing types have always been made by one method. The significance of this fact should not be overlooked. It has been shown that printing, as we now use it, could not exist without types, and that there would be no types if we did not know how to make them in adjustable type-moulds. In this type-mould we find the key to the invention of typography. It is not the press, nor the types, but the type-mould that must be accepted as the origin and the symbol of the art. He was the inventor of

[1] This book was edited and republished in the form of an octavo pamphlet of fifty-six leaves, by Signor P. Vincenzio Fineschi, at Florence, in 1781. The equivalent in American currency of the Tuscan lira is calculated from a formula given with great minuteness by Blades in his *Life and Typography of William Caxton*, vol. II, p. xx.

typography, and the founder of modern printing, who made the first adjustable type-mould.

It is a curious circumstance, and not creditable to the sagacity of the historians of typography, that the importance of this implement, upon which the existence of typography depends, has never been fully appreciated. That the type-mould was first made by the inventor of typography need not be discussed. We have no knowledge that any method of founding different sizes and forms from an adjustable mould was attempted before the fifteenth century. There was no need for such a mould in any other art. But we have indirect evidences in abundance that the early printers considered their method of making types as a meritorious and original invention. Peter Schœffer described it as a new and unheard-of art; Bishop Trithemius said that it was found out only through the good providence of God; Jenson said it was a divine art; Husner said it was a scientific method; Wittig said that the inventor has deserved well of the wide world. It would be useless to attempt to add anything to these tributes—quite as useless to attempt to break their force. Typography, made practicable and perfect by means of the type-mould, was an original and a great invention. If the inventor had produced nothing more than the type-mould, this would be enough to entitle him to the highest honor.

It is tribute enough to acknowledge that the inventor of the type-mould was the inventor of typography. It is not logical nor truthful to attribute to him the introduction or the rediscovery of the simple elements of relief printing. It is not derogatory to his honor to confess that his labors were materially lightened by the services of men who had gone before him and had prepared materials for his use. The inventor of the type-mould did not invent paper, for that had been known for two centuries before; he did not originate engraving on wood, nor impressions from relief surfaces, for both processes were known before paper was made; he was not the first to print upon paper, for printed matter, in the forms of playing cards and prints of pictures, was a merchantable commodity before he was born. He was not the first to make printed books; it is not certain that he made the first printing press; it is not probable that he was the first to think of movable types. His merits rest on a securer basis. While others dreamed and thought, and, no doubt, made experiments, he was the first to do practical and useful work—the first to make types that could be used—the first to demonstrate the utility of typography. The first practical typographer, but not the first printer, he was really at the end of a long line of unknown workmen whose knowledge and experience in ruder forms of printing were important contributions toward the invention of the perfect method.

The contributions made by the men who practised ruder forms of printing demand a fuller description. The merit of printing with types cannot be fully appreciated until it has been contrasted with the printing that preceded types. It will be an instructive lesson to trace the origin of a great art to its sources.

IV

The Image Prints of the Fifteenth Century.

Were Engraved on Wood...Print of St. Christopher...Print of Annunciation...Print of St. Bridget. Other German Engravings on Wood...Flemish Indulgence Print...The Brussels Print...The Berlin Print...All Image Prints from Germany or the Netherlands...How were they Printed? Not by the Frotton...Methods of taking Proof now used by Engravers and Printers...Images copied from Illustrated Manuscripts...Not made by Monks...Images highly prized by the People...The Beginning of Dissent in the Church...Preceded by Ruder Prints.

Book printing and picture printing have both the same inner cause for their origin, namely, the impulse to make each mental gain a common blessing. Not merely princes and rich nobles were to have the privilege of adorning their private chapels and apartments with beautiful religious pictures; the poorest man was also to have his delight in that which the artist had devised and produced. It was not sufficient for him when it stood in the church as an altar shrine, visible to him and to the congregation from afar. He desired to have it as his own, to carry it about with him, to bring it into his own home. The grand importance of wood engraving and copper-plate is not sufficiently estimated in historical investigations. They were not alone of use in the advance of art; they form an epoch in the entire life of mind and culture. The idea embodied and multiplied in pictures became like that embodied in the printed word, the herald of every intellectual movement, and conquered the world.

Woltmann.

ONE of the purposes to which early printing was applied was the manufacture of engraved and colored pictures of sacred personages. These pictures, or image prints, as they are called by bibliographers, were made of many sizes; some of them are but little larger than the palm of the hand, others are of the size of a half sheet of foolscap. In a few prints there are peculiarities of texture which have provoked the thought that they may have been printed from plates of soft metal like lead or pewter; but this conjecture has never been verified. We find in many of the prints the clearest indications that they were taken from engravings on wood. With a few exceptions, these prints were colored; some were painted, but more were colored by means of stenciling, as is abundantly proved by the mechanical irregularities which are always produced by the occasional slipping of the stencil. The colors are gross, glaring, and so inartistically applied that the true outlines of the figures are frequently obscured. The quality of the engraving is unequal; some prints are neatly, and others are rudely cut, but in nearly all of them the engraving is in simple outline. We seldom see any shading tints, or any cross-hatchings, rarely ever any attempt to produce a perspective by the use of fine or faint lines. The absence of shading lines is not entirely due to the imperfect skill of the engravers. The engravings seem to have been cut for no other purpose than that of showing the colors of the stencil painter to advantage, by giving a definite edge to masses of color. The taste for prints in black and white had not then been developed. To the print-buyer of the fifteenth century, the attraction of the image print was not in its drawing, but in its vivid color, and its supposed resemblance to the paintings that adorned

The Print of St. Christopher.
Size of original, 8⅛ by 11¼ inches.

the walls of churches and monasteries. The image print of the fifteenth century was the prototype of the modern chromo.

The St. Christopher, a bold and rude engraving on wood, which represents the saint in the act of carrying the infant Saviour across a river, is one of the most remarkable of the image prints. This print was discovered in the cover of an old manuscript volume of 1417, among the books of one of the most ancient convents of Germany, the Chartreuse at Buxheim, near Memmingen, in Suabia.[1] The monks said that the volume was given to the convent by Anna, canoness of Buchau, who is known to have been living in 1427. The name of the engraver is unknown. This convent is about fifty miles from Augsburg, a city which seems to have been the abode of some of the early engravers on wood. The date is obscurely given in Roman numerals at the foot of the picture.

Christoferi faciem die quacunque tueris, Millesimo cccc.
Illa nempe die morte mala non morieris. xx° tertio.

In whatsoever day thou seest the likeness of St. Christopher,
In that same day thou wilt at least from death no evil blow incur. 1423.

The date 1423 is evidence only so far as it shows that the block was engraved in that year. The printing could have been done at a later date. As it is printed in an ink that is almost black (in which feature it differs from other early image prints, that are almost invariably in a dull or faded brown ink), there is reason to believe that this print was made some time after the engraving, when the method of making prints with permanent black ink was more common.

[1] Heineken, *Idée générale d'une collection complette d'estampes, avec une dissertation*, etc., p. 250.

According to the legend, it was the occupation of Saint Christopher to carry people across the stream on the banks of which he lived. He is accordingly represented as a man of gigantic stature and strength. One evening a child presented himself to be carried over the stream. At first his weight was what might be expected from his infant years; but presently it began to increase, and kept increasing, until the ferryman staggered under his burden. Then the child said, "Wonder not, my friend; I am Jesus, and you have the weight of the sins of the whole world on your back." St. Christopher was thus regarded as a symbol of the church.

This engraving has its merits as well as its absurdities. Chatto says that the design is better than any he has found in the earlier type-printed books; that the figure of the saint and that of the youthful Christ are, with the exception of the extremities, designed in such a style that they would scarcely discredit Albert Durer himself.

The accessories are grotesquely treated. One peasant is driving an ass with a loaded sack to a water-mill; another is toiling with a bag of grain up a steep hill to his house; another, to the right, holds a lantern. The relative proportions of these figures are but a little less absurd than those made famous in Hogarth's ironical study of false perspective.

These faults of drawing are counterbalanced by real merits of engraving. There is a noticeable thickening and tapering of lines in proper places, a bold and a free marking of the folds of drapery, and a general neatness and cleverness of cutting that indicate the hand of a practised and judicious engraver. This engraving of St. Christopher is obviously not the first experiment of an amateur or an untaught inventor.

The Annunciation.

In the book which contained this print of the St. Christopher was also found, pasted down within the cover, another engraving on wood, that is now known as the Annunciation. It is of about the same size as the print of St. Christopher. It is printed on the same kind of paper, with the same dull black ink. There is some warrant for the general belief that both engravings were executed at or about the same time, but they are so unlike that they cannot be considered as the work of the same designer nor of the same engraver. The lines of the Annunciation are more sharply cut; the drawing has more of detail; there are no glaring faults of perspective.

The Virgin is represented as receiving the salutation of the angel Gabriel; the Holy Spirit descends in the shape of a dove proceeding from a part of the print which has been destroyed, and in which was some symbol of the Almighty. The black field in the centre of the print was left unrouted by the engraver, apparently for no other purpose than that of lightening the work of the colorist, who would otherwise have been required to paint it black. This method of producing the full blacks of a colored print was practised by many of the early engravers. Full black shoes on the feet of human figures may be noticed in many of Caxton's woodcuts while other portions of the print are in outline. There are portions of this print in which the practical engraver will note an absence of shading where shades seem to be needed. The body of the Virgin appears as naked, except where it is covered by her mantle. It was intended that an inner garment should be indicated by the brush of the colorist. What the early engravers on wood could not do with the graver, they afterward did with the brush. They not only printed but colored their prints, and the colored work was usually done in a free and careless manner.

These prints do not contain internal evidences of their origin. They were found in Germany, but there is nothing in the designs, nor yet in their treatment, that is distinctively German. The faces and costumes reveal to us no national characteristics; the legends are in Latin; the architecture of the Annunciation is decidedly Italian.

But there is a print known as the St. Bridget, a print supposed to be of nearly the same age as the St. Christopher, which gives us at least an indication of the people by whom it was purchased and of the country in which it was printed.

St. Bridget.

Saint Bridget of Sweden, born 1302, died 1373, was one of the chosen saints of Germany. The print represents her as writing in a book while the Virgin and the infant Christ look down approvingly. The letters S. P. Q. R. on the shield, and the pilgrim's hat, staff and scrip are supposed to indicate her pilgrimages to Rome and Jerusalem. The armorial shield has the arms of Sweden. The legend, if it can be so called, at the top of the print is in German: *O Brigita bit got für uns*—O, Bridget, pray to God for us. The letters *M. I. Chrs* at the bottom of the print have been construed as, Mother of Jesus Christ.

The lines of this print are of a dull brown color. The face and hands are of flesh color, the gown, hat and scrip are dark grey; the desk, the staff, letters, lion and crown, as well as the glory or nimbus about the head, are yellow. The ground is green, and the whole cut is surrounded with a border of shining lake or mulberry color. This harsh arrangement of the colors is a proper illustration of the inferiority of the workmanship of the colorist to that of the designer.

Other prints in European libraries have been attributed to unknown engravers of Germany, who are supposed to have practised their art between the years 1400 and 1450. One of these prints, to which is attached a short prayer and the date of 1437, and which was discovered in a monastery in the Black Forest near the border of Suabia,[1] represents the martyrdom of St. Sebastian. These prints are rare: of the St. Christopher only three copies are known;[2] of the St. Bridget and Annunciation there is but one copy each. All of them were discovered in German religious houses, in which places it seems that they have been preserved ever since they were printed. They were found in a part of Germany that is famous as the abode of early engravers on wood, and as the birthplace of several great German artists. Prints of a similar nature were subsequently made in Germany in greater quantity than in any other part of Europe. The legend of St. Bridget is in German; the costumes of the archers in St. Sebastian are German. They are trustworthy evidences in favor of the hypothesis that engraving on wood was first practised in Germany.

This hypothesis has been disputed. It is opposed by several contradictory theories, which may be stated in the following words: (1) that engraving on wood was applied to the manufacture of playing cards in France at the end of the fourteenth century; (2) that it was derived from China; (3) that it was invented in Italy; (4) that it was practised in the Netherlands before it was known in Germany. As the theories of French, Chinese and Italian origin have no early

[1] The Suabia of the fifteenth century was separated by the Rhine from Switzerland and France on the south and west; its eastern boundary was Bavaria; its northern boundary, Franconia and the Palatinate of the Rhine.

[2] As these three copies have never been compared side by side, it has not been proven that they are impressions from the same block. The copy described on a preceding page has some peculiarities not found in the others.

image prints to offer, they need not now be considered. But the arguments in favor of an early practice of engraving in the Netherlands are based almost entirely upon these prints.

The Flemish Indulgence Print.

[From De la Borde.]

The illustration on the opposite page is the reduced fac-simile of an old print once known as the *Indulgence Print of 1410*, and then considered as of greater age than the print of Saint Christopher. The inscription at the foot of the indulgence, which is in old Dutch or Flemish, is to this effect:

Whoever, regarding the sufferings of our Lord, shall truly repent of his sins, and shall thrice repeat the *Pater Noster* and the *Ave Maria*, shall be entitled to fourteen thousand years of indulgence, which have been granted to him by Pope Gregory, as well as by two other popes and by forty bishops. [This has been done so that] the rich as well as the poor may try to secure this indulgence.

That this print was made in Flanders is apparent from the language, as well as from the peculiar shape of the letter t at the end of words. The perpendicular bar dropping from the top of this t was so seldom used in Germany that it may be regarded as the mannerism of a Flemish copyist. The Pope Gregory here mentioned is undoubtedly Pope Gregory XII, who reigned from 1406 to 1415. It was once believed that the two other popes mentioned in the indulgence were the Anti-pope Benedict XIII at Avignon and the lawful Pope John XXIII at Rome. It was supposed that this print was published during the life-time of Gregory,[1] and for this reason it has been usually described as the *Indulgence Print of 1410*.

[1]A book printed at Delft in 1480, says that when St. Gregory was pope, he celebrated mass in the church *Porta Crucis*. As he was consecrating the bread and wine, Christ appeared to him as represented in the engraving, with all the accessories to his passion. Robert of Cologne, who wrote a treatise on indulgences, published at Zutphen in 1518, adds, that Pope Gregory kindly granted 14,000 years of indulgences; that Pope Calixtus, after requiring the repetition five times of the prayers, again doubled the years of indulgence; that Pope Sixtus IV, adding two more prayers, again doubled them; and, finally, that Pope Innocent VIII, after adding seven more prayers, and two more of the *Pater Noster* and the *Ave Maria*, again doubled the length of the indulgence, so that the sum total amounted to at least 70,000 years—according to other computations, to 92,000 years, or 112,000 years. Holtrop, *Monuments typographiques*, p. 13. There is but one copy of this print, which recently belonged to the remarkable collection of Theodor O. Weigel of Leipsic, who published a fac-simile of it in colors, in his great work, *The Infancy of Printing*, plate 113, vol. I.

M. Wetter, a learned German critic, has pointed out the absurdity of the belief that three popes at enmity with each other should unite in the promulgation of this document.[1] It is now understood that the two other popes mentioned in the indulgence are Pope Nicholas V, who reigned from 1447 to 1455, and Pope Calixtus III, who reigned from 1455 to 1458. The publication of the indulgence is therefore placed between the years 1455 and 1471. Consequently, the print is of no value as an evidence of Flemish priority, for it was made more than thirty years after the St. Christopher.

A much more satisfactory evidence of the great age of Flemish engraving on wood is afforded by the *Brussels Print*, which was discovered in 1848 by an innkeeper, pasted down on the inside of an old chest. It was bought by an architect of the town of Mechlin, who sold it for five hundred francs to the Royal Library of Brussels, where it is now preserved. This print bears the date 1418, but the validity of the date has been challenged. It was alleged that the numerals that form the date had been repaired with a lead pencil in such a manner as to provoke doubts of its genuineness; that the true date is 1468, instead of 1418; that an alteration was made, by scratching out the L from the middle of the numerals [thus, MCCCC(L)XVIII] and by substituting a period—a fraud that puts the date backward fifty years. The charge of fraud has been denied with ability, and seemingly with justice. The print has passed the ordeal of hostile criticism, and is now accepted as a genuine print of 1418. It represents the Virgin and infant Saviour, when surrounded by St. Barbara, St. Catharine, St. Veronica and St. Margaret. The design is somewhat stiff and mechanical, but the composition is not devoid of merit. The lines of the engraving were purposely broken, for it was intended that the print should be more fully developed by the bright colors

[1] Wetter says that all letters of indulgence for thousands of years are spurious; that they were made by monks and ignorant traveling priests for no other purpose than to allure simple people to church.

of the stencil painter. The fac-simile is taken from Holtrop's *Monuments typographiques.* Holtrop says that the fac-simile is slightly reduced in height. The size of the block, as he represents it, is 9⅞ by 13¾ American inches.

The Brussels Print.

The Flemish origin of the *Brussels Print* is established by an image, in the Cabinet of Engravings at Berlin, now known as the *Berlin Print.* It is of the same size as the *Brussels Print*, and is, apparently, the work of the same designer, for in these prints a remarkable similarity of treatment in designing and engraving may be noticed in the wings of the angels, in the figure and position of the angel who crowns the Virgin, in the crowns of St. Catharine and the Virgin, in the flowing hair of the three saints, and that of the Virgin, and in the collars on the doves. This print represents the Virgin as carrying in her arms the infant Saviour. It is described in the catalogue as an early xylographic engraving, printed by friction about the middle of the fifteenth century. It is without date or name of artist. The language of the legend is Flemish. The Virgin holds in her right arm the infant Jesus, and in her left hand an apple. The child caresses the chin of his mother with one hand, while he drops a rose from the other. The Virgin, enshrined in an aureole of glory, encircled by four angels and four doves, placidly stands upon a crescent. The legend in the four corners is in metre, and is an exhortation to the reader to serve the Virgin, and imitate her example.

Who is this queen who is thus exalted?
  She is the consolation of the world.
What is her name? tell me, I pray!
  Mary, blessed Mother and Virgin.
How did she attain this exaltation?
  By love, humility and charity.
Who will be uplifted with her, on high?
  Whoever knows her best in life.

Connoisseurs in prints disagree as to the age and merit of this print. Passavant says that the *Berlin Print,* which he describes as of fine execution, is undoubtedly of Dutch origin, but he thinks it is the design of a German artist. He places its date in the same period as that of the *Brussels Print,* which, according to him, is 1468. Renouvier says that the outlines of the *Berlin Print* are in the style of well-known Dutch or Flemish prints. He hazards no conjecture as to the exact date of its publication, but intimates that it may properly be classified with the older prints of the Netherlands.

The Berlin Print.

Holtrop says that the language of the legend in the Berlin print decides its origin; the design is of the Netherlandish school; the language is Flemish, and not Dutch. He further says: "These two prints (of Berlin and Brussels) complement each other; the print of Berlin shows their common origin; the print of Brussels indicates their date. It may be said that they were engraved in the Netherlands, probably in Flanders, and perhaps in Bruges, at the beginning of the fifteenth century."

The prints herein described are the earliest prints with dates, but they are not, necessarily, the earliest of all. There are prints known to collectors as the *Crucifixion*, the *Last Judgment* and the *St. Jerome*, which are regarded by many bibliographers as the work of unknown engravers at or about 1400. There is a print of *St. George* which competent judges say was done in the thirteenth century. None of the prints contain the name or the place of the engravers, but it is plain that they were made in the Southern Netherlands, as well as in Southern Germany. It would be premature to assume that they were made nowhere else; but it must be acknowledged that there are no image prints on paper which can be ascribed to any engraver in France, Italy, Spain, Holland or England, during the first fifty years of the fifteenth century. There is a plausible statement on record, which will be reviewed on another page, that artistic engravings on wood were made in Italy before this period. We find, also, a more questionable statement, that engraving on wood was practised in France before the year 1400—a statement based entirely on a print in the public library of the city of Lyons, with a printed date which has been represented as that of the year 1384. The age of this print has been denied. It is alleged, with every appearance of probability, that there is mistake or fraud in the numerals, for the costumes of the figures prove that the print should have been made in the sixteenth century.

The question whether image prints were first made in the Netherlands or in Suabia need not now be considered. It is enough to say that, although the Brussels print bears the earliest date, the manufacture of these image prints was more common in Germany, not only in the first but in the latter half of the fifteenth century. That these few accidentally discovered prints represent the half, or even one-tenth, of the images then published, is not at all probable. We have good reason for the belief that they were as abundant in Southern Germany during the year 1450 as cheap lithographs were in the United States during the year 1830. That the greater part of these image prints have been destroyed and forgotten may be explained by the improved taste of the succeeding generation. The artistic copper-plate prints which came in fashion soon after swept away as rubbish the once admired image prints, just as the chromos of this period have supplanted the painted lithographic prints of 1830.

How were these images printed? Almost every author who has written on printing has said that they were printed by friction, with a tool known as the frotton, which has been described as a small cushion of cloth stuffed with wool. It is said that when the block had been inked, and the sheet of paper had been laid on the block, the frotton was rubbed over the back of the sheet until the ink was transferred to the paper. We are also told that the paper was not dampened, but was used in its dry state. The shining appearance on the back of the paper is offered as evidence of friction. This explanation of the method used by the printers of engraved blocks has been accepted, not as a conjecture, but as the description of a known fact. I know of no good authority for it. I know no author who professes to have seen the process. I know no engraver who has taken impressions with a cloth frotton. I doubt the feasibility of the method. The reasons for this doubt will be apparent when this conjectural method is contrasted with the methods used by modern printers and engravers for taking proofs off of press.

The modern engraver on wood takes his proofs on thin India paper. He uses a stuffed cushion to apply the ink to the cut. The ink, which is sticky, serves to make thin paper adhere to the block. He gets an impression by rubbing the back of the paper after it is laid on the block, with an ivory burnisher. If he is careful, he can take with a burnisher a neater proof than he could get from a press. But the only point of similarity between the imaginary old process and the present process is in the method of rubbing or friction. The materials are different: the modern paper is thin and soft, the old was coarse and harsh; modern ink is glutinous, medieval ink was watery; the burnisher is hard, the frotton was very elastic; the burnisher will give a shining appearance to the back, the soft frotton will not. If the modern engraver should attempt to use coarse, thick, dry paper, fluid ink, and a cloth frotton, he could not keep the sheet in place on the block during the slow process of rubbing. No care could prevent it from slipping when rubbed with an elastic cushion. The least slip would produce a distorted impression.

The modern printer takes his proof on dampened paper with a tool known as the proof-planer. This proof-planer is a small thick block of wood, one side of which is perfectly flat and covered with thick cloth. When the paper, which must be dampened, has been laid on the inked type or engraving, the printer places the planer carefully on the paper, holding it firmly with his left hand; with a mallet, held in his right hand, he strikes a strong hard blow on the planer. He then lifts his planer carefully and places it over the nearest unprinted surface and repeats the blow. In like manner he repeats the blow until every part of the type surface has been printed. Rude as this method may seem, a skillful workman can obtain a fair print with the planer. Although the wet paper clings to the type, and the ink is sticky, great care is needed to prevent the slipping of the sheet, and the doubling of the impression. The back of a thick sheet printed in this manner often shows a shining appearance in the places where the blow was resisted by the face of the type or by the engraved lines.

It will be seen that the printer's method of taking proof differs in all its details from the supposititious method of the early engravers. We have soft, damp paper, sticky ink, and a sudden flat pressure against a hard surface shielded with cloth, in opposition to fluid ink, dry paper, rubbing pressure and an elastic printing tool.

As we can find no positive knowledge of the method of printing which was adopted by the early printers of engravings on wood, it is somewhat hazardous to offer conjectures in place of facts. It is begging the question to assume that they were not printed by a press. The presswork of early prints is coarse and harsh, and could have been done with simple mechanism, with rude applications of the screw or of the lever, that could have been devised by any intelligent workman. It is more reasonable to assume that the early prints were made by a press, or with some practicable tool like a proof-planer, rather than with the impracticable frotton. One cannot resist the suspicion that the chronicler of early block printing who first described the frotton attempted to describe what he did not thoroughly understand—that he mistook the engraver's inking cushion for the tool by which he got the impression.

It should be noticed that all these old prints are of a religious character. Portraits of remarkable men or women, landscapes, representations of cities or buildings, caricatures, illustrations of history or mythology—none of these are to be found in any collection of the earliest prints. The early engravers were completely under the domination of religious ideas. Their prints seem to have been made with the permission, and possibly under the direction, of proper clerical authority. The designs are of much greater merit than any that could have been created by amateurs in the art of engraving on wood. They were, undoubtedly, copied from the illuminated books of piety which were then to be found in all large monasteries. Ecclesiastics of this period were careful of their books and jealous of their privileges, and not disposed to allow either to become cheap or common, but they must have favored an art that multiplied the images of patron saints. It was an age of great disbelief, and the image prints were of service as reminders of religious duty.

There is no evidence that these prints were made by the monks themselves. There is a statement current in German books of bibliography that one Luger, a Franciscan monk in Nordlingen, engraved on wood at the end of the fourteenth century. But this statement needs verification. It is not at all certain that the word which is here translated engraver on wood was written with clear intention to convey this meaning. The earliest typographers were not monks, nor were they favored with the patronage of the church.[1] It is not probable that any monk who had been educated for the work of a copyist or an illuminator, would forsake his profession for the practice of engraving on wood or printing. Prints, as then made, were coarse, mechanical copies of meritorious originals. The artistic scribe rightfully felt that engraving was beneath him. He must have looked on the people who bought image prints with the same pitying scorn that a true artist feels for the uneducated taste of those who now buy glaring lithographs of sacred personages, and he must have felt as little inducement to engage in their manufacture.

And yet the multitude received them gladly. Wealthy laymen who could afford to buy gorgeous missals, and priests who daily saw and handled manuscript works of art, might put the prints aside as rubbish; but poor men and women, whose work-day lives were unceasing rounds of poverty and drudgery, unrelieved by art, ideality or sentiment, must have hailed with gladness the images in their own houses which shadowed ever so dimly the glories of the church and the rewards of the righteous. The putting-up of the image print on the wall of the hut or the cabin was the first step toward

[1] Sweinheym and Pannartz, who were invited, in 1464, to establish a printing office in the monastery of Subiaco near Rome, were the first printers connected with any ecclesiastical institution. It may be remarked, that they did not thrive under clerical favor, for they soon found it expedient to remove to the city of Rome, where they were equally unfortunate in their efforts to find purchasers for their books.

bringing one of the attractions of the Catholic church within the domestic circle. It was the erection of a private shrine, an act of rivalry, pitiable enough in its beginning, but of great importance in its consequences. For it was the initiation of the right of private judgment, and of the independence of thought which, in the next century, made itself felt in the formidable dissent known in all Protestant countries as the Great Reformation.

Our knowledge of the origin of engraving on wood has not been materially increased by the recent discovery of the *Berlin* and *Brussels Prints.* We see that wood-cuts of merit were made during the first quarter of the fifteenth century, but we see also that they could not have been the first productions of a recently discovered or newly revived art. They present indications of a skill in engraving which could have been acquired only through experience. One has but to compare them with wood-cuts made by amateurs in typographic printing in Italy, Germany and Holland between the years 1460 and 1500, to perceive that the manufacturers of the image prints were much more skillful as engravers. If there were no other evidences, we could confidently assume that this skill could have been acquired only by practice on ruder and earlier engravings. Of this preliminary practice-work we find clear traces in the stenciled and printed playing cards which were popular in many parts of Europe before the introduction of images.

V

Printed and Stenciled Playing Cards.

Playing Cards not made by the Frotton...Their Manufacture an Industry of Importance...Decree of the Senate of Venice prohibiting the Importation of Cards...Early Notices of Card-Making in Germany...Probable Method of Manufacture...Illustrations of a Playing Card of the Fifteenth Century...Jost Amman's Illustrations of a Print Colorer and an Engraver on Wood...Playing Cards made from Engraved Blocks...Early Notices of Card Playing in France...Cards Prohibited to the People in France and Spain...Introduced in Italy in 1379...Not Invented in Germany. An Oriental Game...Illustrations of Chinese Cards...Originated in Hindostan...Transmitted to Europe through the Saracens...Popularity of Cards in Europe...Cards Denounced by the Clergy...New Forms and New Games of Cards, with Illustrations...Unsuccessful Attempts to make Cards a Means of Instruction...Cards not an Unmixed Evil...Induced Respect for Letters and Education...Cards probably made before Images...Made by Block-Printing...Most largely made by this process in Germany.

After innumerable experiments and disappointments, the art so eagerly sought and so sorely needed was at last discovered. And what is strange, although in accordance with the capriciousness of invention, this art that had eluded all the efforts and aspirations of intelligence, was discovered by makers of cards. It was by them, and for the peculiar requirements of their work, that xylography was invented.

Bibliophile Jacob.

THE hypothesis, for it is nothing more, that all the early prints were produced by the frotton does not satisfactorily explain the large production of merchantable printed matter during the first half of the fifteenth century. Friction would have served then, as it does now, for trial proofs or experiments, but it was a method altogether too slow and uncertain to meet the requirements of an extended business. The playing cards and prints so common during this period must have been made by a quicker method. That there was an established international trade in playing cards and in other kinds of printed work, as early as the year 1441, may be inferred from the following decree of the senate of Venice:

1441, Oct. 11. Whereas, the art and mystery of making cards and printed figures, which is in use at Venice, has fallen to decay, and this in consequence of the great quantity of printed playing cards and colored figures which are made out of Venice, to which evil it is necessary to apply some remedy, in order that the said artists, who are a great many in family, may find encouragement rather than foreigners: Let it be ordained and established, according to the petition that the said masters have supplicated, that from this time in future, no work of the said art that is printed or painted on cloth or paper—that is to say, altar-pieces, or images, or playing cards, or any other thing that may be made by the said art, either by painting or by printing—shall be allowed to be brought or imported into this city, under pain of forfeiting the work so imported, and thirty livres and twelve soldi, of which fine one-third shall go to the state, one-third to Giustizieri Vecchi, to whom this affair is committed, and one-third to the accuser. With this condition, however, that the artists who make the said works in this city shall not expose the said works for sale in any other place but their own shops, under the penalty aforesaid, except on the day of Wednesday at S. Paolo, and on Saturday at S. Marco.[1]

The engraved images here noticed were probably prints of saints or sacred personages like those of which engraved illustrations have been given on previous pages. The altar-pieces were prints upon cotton or linen cloth, of a similar character, but of much larger size.[2]

Playing cards, which are twice mentioned in the decree, seem to have been considered as of equal importance with images and altar-pieces. The specification of three distinct kinds of printed work, coupled as it is with the allusion to "any other thing that may be made by the said art," is an intimation that the manufacturers, "who were a great many

[1] I have used the translation as I find it in Ottley's *Inquiry into the Origin and Early History of Engraving*, vol. I, p. 47. The original is given by Temanza, *Lettere Pittoriche*, vol. V, p. 321. Temanza found this decree in an old book of regulations which belonged to a fraternity of Venetian printers.

[2] Weigel, in his *Infancy of Printing*, plate 10, presents the fac-simile of an old printed altar-piece, about eight inches wide and twenty inches long, which contains a representation of the Virgin and the infant Christ. The engraving is in outline only. The interior was colored by stencils. like the image prints.

in family," were even then applying the art of printing and colored stenciling to many other purposes.

The decree says that the art had fallen to decay. When it was in its most prosperous condition in Venice cannot be ascertained from the record, nor from any other source. The author[1] who found this document says that he had fragments of coarse engravings on wood which represented some parts of the city of Venice as they appeared before the year 1400. He thinks these rude engravings must have been cut in the latter part of the fourteenth century. That they could have been made at this time is not improbable, but the direct evidence is wanting. There are, however, abundant reasons for the belief that engravings on wood were made in Venice, not experimentally, but in the way of business, many years before the decree of 1441. And they must have been made elsewhere. The printers of playing cards and colored figures must have been many in family beyond as well as in Venice. If the foreign printers had not been formidable competitors, there would have been no request for the prohibitory decree.

Nothing is said in the decree about the nationality of the foreign competitors, but we may get this knowledge from another source. An authentic record of the town of Ulm in Germany contains a brief entry which tells us that playing cards in barrels were sent from that city to Sicily and Italy, to be bartered for delicacies and general merchandise.[2]

[1] Temanza had some old Venetian playing cards of unknown date, which he believed were made at or about the time of the publication of this decree. They were of large size, on thick paper, and elaborately decorated with gold and colors. The early Venetian playing cards were, probably, more expensively made, and were offered at higher prices than the German cards. In the field of art and ornament, and even in the trades which called for a higher degree of skill, the Venetians surpassed all their competitors. This pre-eminence was maintained many years after the invention of typography. The earlier books of Venice are famous for the whiteness of their paper and the beauty of their types, as well as for admirable presswork and solid bindings.

[2] Heineken, *Idée générale*, page 245. He does not give the date. The record from which he quotes, the Red Book of Ulm, so called because the initials were in that color, ends with the year 1474.

The same book contains a defense of the game of playing cards under the date of 1397. Another old German record, the Burgher Book of Augsburg for the year 1418, specifically notices card-makers. The Tax Book of Nuremberg, for the years 1433 and 1435, names Eliza, a card-maker. The same book, for the year 1438, mentions Margaret, the card-painter. The words *kartenmacherin*, card-maker, and *kartenmalerin*, card-painter, which are found in these books, do not clearly specify the process. It has been suggested that these cards could have been drawn and painted by means of stencil plates.

The word *formschneider*, form-cutter, the word now used in Germany as the equivalent of engraver on wood, appears for the first time in the year 1449, in the books of the city of Nuremberg. The same records mention one Wilhelm Kegler, *briftrucker*, or card-printer, under the date of 1420. They also mention one *Hans Formansneider*, in the year 1397, but Formansneider should not be construed as engraver on wood. It should be read Hans Forman, *schneider* or tailor. In this, as in some other cases, it will be seen that the facility of the German language for making new words by the compounding of old ones, is attended with peculiar disadvantages. The manufactured words are susceptible of different meanings.

These notices of card-making are not enough to prove that the process employed was that of xylography. They prove only that card-making was an industry of note in the towns of Ulm, Augsburg and Nuremberg. But when these notices of early card-making are considered in connection with early German prints, like the St. Christopher of 1423, which were discovered in the vicinity of these towns, there is no room for doubt. If prints of saints were made by engraving on wood, cards should have been made by the same art. The connection of cards and image prints in the decree of the Senate of Venice is evidence that they were made by the same persons and by the same process.

It may seem strange that the little town of Ulm, in the heart of Germany, should establish by a long sea route a trade in playing cards with cities on the Mediterranean and the Adriatic. It is but one of many evidences of the growing spirit of commercial enterprise which pervaded all the cities of Germany. It is not more strange than the fact that, in 1505, merchants of Augsburg, a city at a great distance from navigable waters, joined with the Portuguese in an extensive traffic with the eastern coast of Africa.

Playing cards may have been made at as early dates in other countries besides Germany and Italy. We shall soon see that they were in common use in many parts of Europe at the beginning of the fifteenth century, but we have no certain knowledge that they were made from engraved blocks in other places. Our knowledge of the fact that they were printed in Italy and Germany is based entirely on occasional notices in old manuscript records. We have indications that they were printed, but we lack the proof. There are no cards in existence which can be offered, with any degree of confidence, as specimens of the block-printing of 1440. The xylographic cards of which fac-similes are most common in books which treat of pastimes, are of the sixteenth century; the copper-plate cards described and illustrated by Weigel and Breitkopf were made either during the latter half of the fifteenth or in the sixteenth century.

The engraving on the following page is a fac-simile of one of a set of forty-eight playing cards now preserved in the British Museum. The entire set, printed on six separate sheets of paper, eight cards to each sheet, was found in that great hiding-place of discarded sheets, the inner lining of a book cover, for which, to adopt the bookbinder's phrase, it served as a stiffener. The sheets may have been rejected for imperfections, and put in the book cover because they were unsalable. The book in which they were found was printed and bound by some unknown or undescribed printer before the year 1500.[1] If rudeness of engraving could be considered

[1] Singer's *Researches into the History of Playing Cards*. This book abounds in curious information and has many valuable fac-similes.

as sufficient proof of superior antiquity, this card should be rated as one of the oldest pieces of engraving on wood. The cutting of this block could have been done by any carver on wood, or even by a carpenter. But the quality of the engraving is not a proper criterion of the condition of the art of engraving on wood during the period in which it was made. It is obviously a cheap card, made for the uses of people who could pay but a small price. There may have been other reasons for the rudeness of the work. The stiff and conventional manner of drawing the figures may have been as popular then as a similar method of designing playing cards is at this day.

Dull red and dark green were the only colors used in illuminating this set of cards. They were laid on with brush and stencil. The stencil is one of the oldest forms of labor-saving contrivance for abridging the labor of writing or drawing. It was used, as has been stated, in the sixth century by a Roman emperor who could not write; it was used for the same purpose by Theodoric, king of the Ostrogoths, and by the emperor Charlemagne. It is used to this day by merchants who mark boxes, in preference to writing, printing, branding, or painting. It has advantages of cheapness and simplicity that commend it to all manufacturers. It is even used by publishers of books for tinting maps, fashion plates, and illuminated pamphlet covers.

A Playing Card of the Fifteenth Century.
[From Singer.]

Jost Amman, in his Book of Trades, has presented us a representation of the print stenciler, as he practised his work in 1564. The method here shown is, probably, the method in general use in 1440, for the coloring of playing cards and image prints. We see the bowls that contain different colors, with their proper brushes, on top of the chest. The colorer is sweeping the brush over the perforated metal plate, and filling up the outlines of the print. The neat pile of sheets before him and near his right hand shows that he is working with precision and with system. Stencil painting was work of care and neatness, but it was so simple that we can clearly understand that it could have been done by women in Nuremberg as effectively as it is done now.[1]

The Print Colorer.
[From Jost Amman.]

The illustration of the engraver on wood which appears in the same *Book of Trades* puts before us a man in a richer dress, plainly a workman of higher grade than the stencil painter. He seems to be tracing outlines on the block. The technical accessories about this engraver are the same as those in use at this day—the graver, the whetstone, and, possibly, a water globe lens in the corner near the window casement.[2]

[1] Breitkopf says that the stencil painting of prints was done with great rapidity by the medieval colorist. He alludes to an old German saying of "painting the twelve apostles with one stroke," which, no doubt, refers to the expeditious painting of a once popular image print, of which there is now no fragment in existence.

[2] Some antiquarians say that this print is a representation of Amman.

Playing cards and engraving on wood bear to each other a curious relation. The introduction of the cards in Europe was soon followed by the revival, or as Bibliophile Jacob of Paris characterizes it, by the invention, of engraving on wood. Whatever differences of opinion may exist as to whether the art was revived or invented, it is certain that playing cards were the means by which early printing was made popular. Cards were the only kind of printed work which promised to repay the labor of engraving. People who could neither read nor write, and who had no desire to be taught either accomplishment, derived great pleasure from them. There was no other kind of printed matter, not even the image prints, which found so many buyers in every condition of society. The fixing of the earliest practice as a regular business of engraving on wood in Europe depends, in some degree, on the fixing of the date of the first introduction of playing cards. The determination of this date has been made a national question, and the theme of books containing much curious information.

The Engraver on Wood.
[From Jost Amman.]

Ambrose Firmin Didot[1] quotes a scrap of poetry from a French romance of 1328, which alludes to the folly of games of dice, checkers and cards. Other French writers maintain that playing cards were in use in France as early as 1350.

[1] Didot, *Essai sur la typographie*, p. 564.

Bullet says that playing cards were used in France in the year 1376. But the testimony in confirmation of these dates is ambiguous and insufficient. The first unequivocal notice of playing cards in France is to be found in an account book for the year 1392, kept by one Charles Poupart, treasurer to Charles VI. In this book is an entry to this effect: "Paid to Jacquemin Gringonneur, painter, for three packs of cards, gilded, colored, and ornamented with various designs, for the amusement of our lord the king, 56 sols of Paris." The mind of Charles VI had been seriously affected by sunstroke, and these cards were provided for his lucid intervals during which he suffered from melancholy. We are not told how these cards were made—whether they were first drawn by hand, or whether they were printed from cut blocks before they were painted. The price paid was not small: fifty-six sols of Paris in 1393 would be equivalent to one hundred and fifty francs in 1874. In 1454, a pack of cards purchased for the Dauphin of France cost but five sous of Tours, the equivalent of twelve or thirteen francs of modern French money.[1] The difference in these prices is some indication of a cheapened manufacture.

The earliest and most convincing evidence of the popularity of playing cards in Paris is contained in an order of the provost of that city, under the date of 1397, in which order he forbids working people from indulging in games of tennis, bowls, dice, cards, or nine-pins on working days. That the game was then comparatively new is inferred from the omission of playing cards in an ordinance of the city of Paris, for the year 1369, in which other popular games were minutely specified.

The Cabinet of Prints attached to the National Library at Paris contains seventeen cards which are supposed to be the relics of the three packs made for Charles VI by Gringonneur; but these cards were, without doubt, drawn by hand. This cabinet has no printed cards which can be attributed to the

[1] Bibliophile Jacob, *Curiosités de l'histoire des arts*, etc., p. 48.

fourteenth century. Its oldest relics of this kind are eighteen printed cards which may have been made in France during the reign of Charles VII, or between the years 1442 and 1461.[1]

Playing cards seem to have been popular in Spain before they were known in France. They were supposed to be so demoralizing to the people, that John I, king of Castile, in the year 1387, thought it necessary to prohibit them entirely. To have acquired this popularity, the cards should have been made by some process as economical as that of printing. We have, however, no knowledge that the cards were printed. They could have been made by stencils. Chatto says that the relics of playing cards which he thought were the oldest were made exclusively with stencils.

Cards were known in Italy as early as 1379. An old manuscript history of the town of Viterbo, which states this fact, says that "In this year, a year of great distress [occasioned by the war between the anti-pope Clement VII and the pope Urban VI], was brought into Viterbo, the game of cards, which came from the land of the Saracens, and by them is called Naib."

[1] One of the cards bears the name of the maker, F. Clerc. The costumes of the figures are French, and of the fashion of the court of Charles VII. One of the queens is a rude copy of the well known portrait of the queen Marie of Anjou; another queen is from an authentic portrait of the king's mistress, Gérarde Cassinel. The robe of one of the kings is plentifully sprinkled with the *fleur-de-lis;* the figure of another king is that of a hairy savage with a torch in his hand. These singular cards illustrate a frightful accident which made a profound impression on the people of France. To divert the half-crazed king Charles VI, a masquerade was planned for a ball given by Queen Blanche, on the 29th of January, 1392, in which masquerade the king and five of the gentlemen of the court took the parts of savages. The costumes were made by encasing the actors in tight-fitting linen garments, covered with warm pitch and tow. In this uncouth attire, and linked together with clanking chains, they danced in the ball-room to the amusement of the men and the terror of the ladies. Wishing to discover one of the maskers, the Duke of Orleans snatched a torch from the hand of a servant, and thrust it too near an unhappy masker's face. In a moment he was covered with a blaze which quickly spread to his fellows. The king was rescued in time, but four of the masqueraders were burned to death.

Many German authors claim that playing cards were in common use throughout Germany at a much earlier period. Breitkopf quotes the following passage from a book called the *Golden Mirror*, said to have been written about the middle of the fifteenth century by a Dominican friar of the name of Ingold: "The game is right deceitful, and, as I have read, was first brought in Germany in the year 1300."[1] Another writer quotes an old chronicle, that describes the emperor Rudolph as amusing himself with cards in the old town of Augsburg at some undefined time before his death in 1291. It cannot be proved that the cards here mentioned were true playing cards. It is more probable that the amusement noticed was the game of king and queen, which was forbidden to the clergy by the synod of Worcester in 1240, and which has sometimes been erroneously understood as a game of cards. The notices of card-makers and card-printers in the town books of Nuremberg and Augsburg should be regarded as the earliest records of the use of playing cards in Germany.[2]

A review of the dates proves that playing cards were not popular in any part of Europe before the last quarter of the fourteenth century. The Italian record which attributes their derivation to the land of the Saracens is fully corroborated by other testimony of authority. Students of oriental literature assure us that the Saracens were taught the uses of playing cards by the inhabitants of Hindostan, in which country they were invented.[3] Playing cards were made in China from printed blocks long before the game was known in Europe.

[1] Breitkopf, *Versuch den Ursprung der Spielkarten*, p. 9, note g. The fac-similes of playing cards in this book are exceedingly grotesque.

[2] Cards are not mentioned in a specification of popular games in the Stadtholdt Book of Augsburg for the year 1274. The ordinances of the town of Nuremberg for the period between the years 1286 and 1299 prohibit gambling, but they do not mention cards. For the period between 1380 and 1384, they are both mentioned and permitted.

[3] In Singer's *Researches into the History of Playing Cards* may be found many fac-similes of early Hindostanee cards, some of which, we are told, were engraved on plates of ivory. These fac-similes show that the primitive game was a modification of the old Indian game of chess.

Chinese Playing Cards.
[From Breitkopf.]

The introduction of this oriental pastime in civilized Europe has been attributed to the Moors of Spain, to eastern Jews who traded on the shores of the Mediterranean, to Gypsies who made their appearance in Germany at the beginning of the fifteenth century. Whether they were introduced by Moor, Christian, Jew or Gypsy is of minor importance. It concerns us more to know how they were received. We have abundant evidence that the cards supplied a universal want, and that they soon became as popular with the poor and ignorant as they had been with the rich and noble. While the Duke of Milan found amusement, as he did in 1415, with a suite of cards elaborately painted by artists of renown on plates of ivory, at a cost of fifteen hundred crowns, and while Flemish nobles were playing at games of hazard with cards engraved on silver plates, the working people of France and Spain, soldiers in Italy, and traveling mechanics in Germany were diverting themselves in wine-shops and public gardens, in huts and by the road-side, with similar games, played with greasy cards which had been printed or stenciled on coarse paper. The cards were adapted to all tastes, and there was a fascination in them which made men neglectful of duty.

The evil results of this infatuation were soon perceived. Playing cards were denounced not only by kings and the provosts of cities, but by the more zealous and conscientious priests of the church. At the synod of Langres held in 1404, the fathers of the church forbid all games of playing cards to the clergy. On the fifth day of May, in the year 1423, St. Bernard of Sienna preached against playing cards from the steps of the Church of St. Peter, with such effect, that his hearers ran to their houses, and brought therefrom all the games of hazard that they owned—cards, dice and checkers—and burnt them in the public square. One card-maker, who felt that his business had been ruined by the sermon, went in tears to the saint, and said, "Father, I am a card maker, and know no other trade. You have forbidden me to make cards and have consequently condemned me to die from starvation." Whereupon the ready priest said, "If you know how to paint, paint this image"—showing him the figure of Christ, with the monogram I. H. S. in the centre of a halo of glory. The card-maker, we are told, followed the judicious advice. The proper sequel is not wanting: virtue had proper reward; the converted image-maker soon became rich. In 1452, the monk John Capistan preached for three hours in Nuremberg with a similar result. The conscience-stricken people brought into the market-place "76 jousting sledges, 3,640 backgammon boards, 40,000 dice, and cards innumerable," and burnt them in the market-place.

The attacks of the clergy had no permanent effect. At the end of the fifteenth century, playing cards were more popular than ever. Other games were invented, and new forms of cards of quainter or of more graceful patterns were produced. Sometimes they were engraved on copper plates, and were painted with all the delicacy of fine miniatures. Despairing of success in their attempts to entirely abolish the practice, moralists undertook to divert cards from their first purpose, and to make them a means of instruction as well as of amusement. Of this character is an old pack of fifty cards engraved on copper plates, and supposed to be the work of Finiguerra, which has been preserved in an Italian library. One of the cards bears the printed date, 1485. The pack is divided in five suites: the first suite contains cards that represent, by figures and words in the Venetian dialect, the various conditions of men from the pope to the beggar; the second suite contains the names and figures of the nine muses, with Apollo added to make the complement; the third illustrates branches of polite learning from grammar to theology; the fourth exhibits cardinal virtues, like justice and prudence; the fifth, displays the heavenly bodies, the Moon, Saturn, the stars, Chaos and the First Cause. This game, obviously made up for the benefit of young collegians, was, probably, no more popular with them than the scientific story books of 1820–30 were with the boys of that period. The combination of abstruse sciences with a frivolous amusement may rightfully be considered a problem of despair.

The illustration on the next leaf is the reduced fac-simile of a suite of twenty-two playing cards, intended, apparently, to convey solemn religious truths in the form of a game of life and death. We do not know how the game was played: we have to accept the figures upon the cards as their own explanation and commentary. In the figures of Jupiter and of the Devil, we see the powers which shape the destinies of men. The Wheel of Fortune is emblematic of the fate which assigns to one man the condition of a Hermit, and to another that of an Emperor. The virtues of Temperance, Justice and Strength which man opposes to Fate, the frivolity of the Fool, the happiness of the Lover (if he can be happy who is cajoled by two women), and the pride of the Empress, are all dominated by the central card bearing an image of the skeleton Death—Death which precedes the Last Judgment and opens to the righteous the House of God. In these cards we have a pictorial representation of scenes from one of the curious spectacle plays of the middle ages, which were often enacted in the open air to the accompaniments of dance and music. The union of fearful mysteries with ridiculous accessories, and the ghastly suggestion of the fate of all men, as shown in the card of Death the reaper—these were the features which gave point and character to the series of strange cartoons popular for many centuries in all parts of civilized Europe under the title of the *Dance of Death.*

This was but one of the many innovations proposed as substitutes for the older oriental games. In the latter part of the fifteenth century, playing cards were made in Italy with figures which represented the four great monarchies of the ancient world, with which a childish game was played in imitation of war and conquest. Suitable marks on the cards designated the four different classes of society; hearts were the symbol of the clergy; spades (from the Italian *spada*, a sword) were for the nobility; clubs stood for the peasantry; and diamonds represented the citizens or burghers.

Thomas Murner, a professor of philosophy at Cracow in 1507, undertook to make use of playing cards for teaching high scholastic science. He published a book which he called

1 The Juggler.
2 Juno.
3 The Empress.
4 The Emperor.
5 Jupiter.
6 The Lovers.
7 The Chariot.
8 Justice.
9 The Hermit.
10 The Wheel of Fortune.
11 Strength.
12 The Hanged.
13 Death.
14 Temperance.
15 The Devil.
16 The House of God.
17 The Stars.
18 The Moon.
19 The Sun.
20 The Last Judgment.
21 The World.
22 The Fool.

Reduced Fac-Simile of French Copper-plate Playing Cards of the Sixteenth Century.

[From Breitkopf.]

Logical Playing Cards, or Logic Realized and Made Comprehensible through Pleasant Exercises with Pictures. The cards were filled with mysterious symbols intended as keys to the entire art of reasoning. The difficult science was adapted to the meanest capacity, by puerile methods which subsequently provoked the contempt of Erasmus. Each card had some pedantic name like Proposition, Predicate or Syllogism. Could there be a more unattractive game?

Eminent German artists—among them Martin Schongauer and the Master of 1466—undertook to supplant the stiff and barbarous figures that had been used on playing cards, with designs of merit. They drew and engraved new face figures of most extraordinary character, in which satirical and poetic fancies were strangely blended. The amorousness of the monks and the coquetry of the ladies, the quarrels of termagants among the peasantry, the revenge of hares who are roasting their enemy man and his friend the dog, are the subjects of some cards. On other German cards of this period are represented, in startling contrast, the sweet and saintly faces of pure women, heroic men riding in triumph, and filthy sows with their litters.

Jost Amman[1] designed, and perhaps engraved, a full pack of cards which was published in book form with explanatory verses in Latin and German. Rejecting the established forms of hearts, clubs, spades and diamonds for the designation of the suites, he substituted books, printers' inking balls, wine pots and drinking cups. The moral that he endeavored to inculcate was the advantages of industry and learning over idleness and drunkenness. But the intended moral is not as clear as it should be. Some of the figures are exceedingly gross, although they are drawn with admirable skill and spirit.

These innovations had but a transient popularity. The people played cards, not for instruction in art, science or

[1] The industry of Jost Amman was as remarkable as his skill. The old historian of early painters, Sandraart, says, on the authority of his pupil George Keller, that during the four years in which Keller lived with him, Amman produced designs enough to load a wagon.

French Card of the Fifteenth Century.
[From Lacroix.]

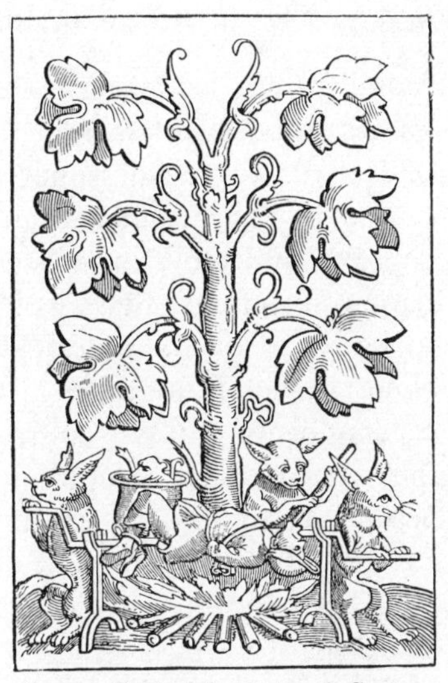

German Card of the Sixteenth Century.
[From Lacroix.]

German Card of the Sixteenth Century.
[From Lacroix.]

German Card of the Fifteenth Century.
[From Breitkopf.]

morality, but for amusement, and they would not suffer the games to be diverted from their first purpose of the pleasure of hazard. The old games and the old figures were deeply rooted in their memories and habits. They would have no changes, and there have been none of any importance. The hard conventional figures of king, queen and jack which are to be found on the oldest playing cards have been repeated almost without alteration in the popular cards of every succeeding century. We can readily understand the reasons why the scholastic and scientific games were rejected, but it would be difficult to account for the preference always manifested for coarse outlines and clumsy drawing in the figures.

Although playing cards led to gambling, and to forms of dissipation which required restraint,[1] their general use was not an unmixed evil. To the common people, they were a means of education; a circuitous and a dangerous means, no doubt, but not the less effectual. The medieval churl whose ignorance was so dense that he failed to see the advantages of education, and who would have refused to learn his letters by any persuasion, did perceive that there was amusement in playing cards, and did take the trouble to learn the games. With him, as with little children, the course of instruction began with bright-colored little pictures and the explanation of hidden meanings in absurd-looking little spots or symbols. In the playing of the game, his dull mind was trained to a new and a freer exercise of his reasoning faculties, and he must have been inspired with more of respect for the dimly seen utility of painted or printed symbols. To the multitude of early card players, cards were of no other and no greater benefit as a means of mental discipline. To men of thought and purpose, they taught a more impressive lesson of the value of paper and letters. They induced inquiries that led

[1] The ordinances of Nuremberg between the years 1380 and 1384 permitted gambling and betting, but in moderation: "Always excepting horse-racing, shooting with cross-bows, *cards*, shovel boards, tric-trac and bowls, at which a man may bet from two pence to a groat." Von Murr, as quoted by Chatto, *Treatise on Wood Engraving*, p. 42.

to important resolves. If a few arbitrarily arranged signs on bits of paper could greatly amuse a party of friends during a long evening, would not the letters of the alphabet as they were combined in books, furnish a still greater and an unfailing source of amusement?

The meagre notices of card-makers and card-painters in old town-books of Germany and in the decree of Venice do not tell us whether cards were made before or after image prints. Those who have written most learnedly on this subject,[1] tell us that the cards were made before the images; that at first they were drawn and painted by hand; that they were afterward colored by stencils; that when this method was found too slow, blocks were engraved and printed; and that the image prints were subsequently introduced for the purpose of counteracting the evil influences of cards. These propositions are ingenious, but it must be confessed that we have no certain knowledge that the improvement was made in this order. This theory of gradual development is based on conjecture, and its best support is derived from a consideration of the fact that cards were in common use before we have any indications of the existence of image prints. That the cards should have been made by engraving before the images seems reasonable when we consider that the workmanship of the cards was of a much ruder nature. The experimenting amateur who knew that he was unable to cut a block like that of the *St. Christopher*, would readily undertake to engrave the spots and face figures of the earlier cards.

Breitkopf, an expert type-founder and a writer of authority, stands almost alone in his opinion that playing cards were

[1] Having visited many convents in Franconia, Suabia, Bavaria, and the Austrian States, I everywhere discovered in their libraries many image prints engraved on wood and pasted either in the beginning or the end of old volumes of the fifteenth century. These facts taken together confirm me in the opinion that the next step of the engraver on wood, after playing cards, was the engraving of figures of saints, which, distributed and lost among the laity, were carefully preserved by the monks, who pasted them on the inner covers of the books with which they furnished their libraries. After the engravers had succeeded in making prints of saints, they found it very easy to engrave historical subjects, with explanations in words. Heineken, *Idée générale*, etc., p. 251.

made after the image prints. He says that the engravers who made cards also made images, and he adds the curious fact that in some places cards and images were called by the same name.[1]

The curt and careless manner in which the business of card-making is mentioned in the old records is an indication that the process used was not novel. We do not find in the writings of any author of the fifteenth or sixteenth centuries a statement that the earliest playing cards were made by a new art. That they were made by block-printing at the beginning of the fifteenth century in Italy and Germany seems clearly established. That they were made at a corresponding period in Spain and France, where cards were as common, cannot be proved. It is probable that the Germans derived their knowledge of cards from Italy, but the evidences of an early manufacture by printing are decidedly in favor of southern Germany, a district in which the most famous image prints have been found, and which, at a later period, was the birthplace of many eminent engravers on wood.

[1] Wood-cuts of sacred subjects were known to the common people of Suabia, and the adjacent districts, by the name of *Halgen* or *Halglein*, saints or little saints, a word which, in course of time, was also applied to prints of all kinds. In France also, the earliest prints were known as *dominos*, or lords, a word which was intended to convey the same meaning. The maker of prints was known as a *dominotier*, whether he made profane cards or pious images. In time the word so far declined from its first meaning that it was applied not only to printers of cards and images, but to the makers of fancifully colored wall-papers. *Versuch der Ursprung der Spielkarten*, etc., vol. II, p. 174.

VI

The Chinese Method of Printing.

Antiquity of Printing among the Chinese...Statement of Du Halde...Its Perversion...First Chinese Method, the Gouging of Letters...Didot's Hypothesis...Second Method, of Xylography...Third Method, a Combination of Xylography and Typography... A Peculiarly Chinese Invention. Method now used...Its Advantages over Types...Chinese Paper... Performance of Pressmen. Curious Method of Binding...Expense of Engraving no hindrance to Chinese Printing...The Xylographic Method necessary... Chinese Practice in Typography... Cheapness of Chinese Books...Similarity between the Chinese and the European Methods of Block-Printing...The Hypothesis of its Transmission to Europe through Marco Polo, or other Venetian Travelers.

In both arts, writing and printing alike, the Chinese have remained stiff, stolid, and immovable at the first step, with the characteristic unchangeability of the yellow races of Eastern Asia.

D. F. Bacon.

MANY eminent authors are of the opinion that we are indebted to China not only for playing cards, but for the means of making them. They tell us that playing cards could not have been popular, as they were at the beginning of the fifteenth century, if they had not been made by a cheaper process than drawing by hand. The inference attempted is that block-printing and playing cards were brought to Europe together. The reasons presented in support of this opinion are far from conclusive, but they are based on many curious facts which deserve consideration.

The Chinese claims for priority in the practice of block printing have been disallowed by some critics, chiefly because they have been presented in the form of perverted translations. That oriental people practised printing before this art was applied to any useful purpose in Europe is admitted by all who have studied their history. Du Halde, a learned Jesuit father, who traveled in China during the earlier part of the eighteenth century, was the first author who furnished Europeans with a description of Chinese printing. He quotes the following extract from a Chinese book, supposed to have been written in the reign of the emperor Wu-Wong, who was living 1120 B. C. "As the stone *me* (Chinese for blacking), which is used to blacken the engraved characters, can never become white, so a heart blackened by vices will always retain its blackness."[1] This is an allusion to some primitive method of blackening incised characters, for the purpose of making them more legible. It is a method which is still observed in the inscriptions on memorial stones in churches and graveyards. But it is an allusion to engraving and blackening only. There is no mention of printing ink, and no suggestion of printing. Du Halde quoted it only to show the antiquity of engraving, yet it has been used by many authors as a warrant for the assertion that printing was practised in China eleven hundred years before the Christian era. If we could accept this statement, we should have to believe that printing was invented in China but a few years after the siege of Troy, before Rome was founded, before Homer wrote and Solomon reigned. Du Halde's words do not warrant this statement. He says, with due caution, "In printing, it seemeth that China ought to have the precedence of other nations, for, according to their books, the Chinese have made use of this art for sixteen hundred years," or since the first century.

The practice of blackening characters was not printing, but it may have led to its development. Du Halde says that the Chinese printed not only on wood blocks, but on tables of "stone of a proper and particular kind." The writing or design to be printed, while it was still wet with ink, was transferred by pressure from the paper upon which it was written to the smooth surface of a slab of stone. When the

[1] This method is still in use in many parts of the East Indies. A dried leaf is written on with a pointed steel which scratches the smooth surface. A bit of charcoal is then rubbed over the leaf; the places scratched are filled with atoms of charcoal, which make the writing as legible as it would have been if written with fluid ink.

black lines of the writing or design were firmly set on the stone, the paper was peeled off. The black transferred lines were then cut out, or cut below the surface, as they are now done in the copper-plate process. The surface was inked, paper was laid on the stone, and an impression was taken. The result was, the appearance on the paper of the writing or design in white on a field of solid black. This method of cutting out the lines, so that they should appear white in the printed impression, is the simplest form of engraving. It is like that of the boy who cuts his name in the bark of a tree. He finds it easier to gouge out the letters than it is to raise them in high relief. Reasoning from probability, we should say that it should have been the earliest of the methods. Didot believes that it was known to the old Romans.[1] Du Halde says that this method of printing on stone was used chiefly for "epitaphs, pictures, trees, mountains and such like things." He does not fix the date of its invention, but it was probably the earlier method. Didot says that he had in his

[1] In support of this opinion he quotes the following from Pliny:

It would be improper to omit the notice of a new invention. We have been accustomed to preserve in our libraries, in gold, silver, or bronze, the personages whose immortal spirits speak to us from distances of leagues and centuries. We create statues of those who are no longer living. Our regrets invest them with features which have not been given to us by tradition, as, for example, is shown in the bust of Homer. The idea of making a collection of these portraits is due to Asinius Pollio, who was the first to throw open his library, and to make these men of genius the property of the public. That the love for portraits has always existed is sufficiently proven by Atticus, the friend of Cicero, who published a book on the subject, and also by Marcus Varro, who had the enlarged idea of inserting in his numerous books not only the names, but, by the aid of a certain invention, the images of seven hundred illustrious persons. Varro wished to save their features from oblivion, so that the length of centuries would not prevail against them. As the inventor of a benefit which will fill even the gods with jealousy, he has clothed these persons with immortality. He has made them known over the wide world, so that everywhere one can see them as if they were present. Pliny, book XXXV, chap. I.

This invention has never been clearly explained. A new invention, which exhibited in books the features of seven hundred men, which multiplied them so that they were known over the wide world, and preserved them for posterity, should have been the invention of printing. Pliny speaks of it as a well-known fact, but no other writer of his age makes any mention of it. Why did not Pliny describe the new art instead of praising it?

library the portraits of four Chinese emperors of a dynasty which began A. D. 618, and ended during the ninth century, and also some fac-similes of the imperial writings, which were made by the same process.[1]

Sir John Francis Davis, for many years British Minister to China, and author of two valuable books on that country, places the invention of block-printing in China in the tenth century of the Christian era. He attributes the discovery of the art to Foong-Taou, the Chinese minister of state, who had been greatly hindered in the discharge of his duties by his inability to procure exact copies of his writings. After many trials and failures, he dampened a written sheet of paper, and pressed it on a smooth surface of wood until he had produced a fair transfer. He then cut away every part of the surface that did not show the transferred lines, and thus produced a block in relief. The lines in relief were next brushed with ink; a sheet of paper was laid on the block, and impression was applied. The result was, a true fac-simile of his writing, and the birth of block-printing.

There was another Chinese method, which, paradoxical as it may seem, was a combination of xylography and typography. It was invented A. D. 1041, by an ingenious Chinese blacksmith, named Pi-Ching, whose process is thus described by Davis. The inventor first made a thick paste of porcelain clay, and moulded or cut it in little oblong cubes of proper size. On these cubes he carved the Chinese characters that were most frequently used, thereby making movable types. The next process was to bake them in an oven until they were hardened. But the types so made were irregular as to height and as to body. In printers' phrase, they would not stand together: some would be larger than the standard, others would be too high to paper, and all would be crooked. This difficulty could be remedied only by fixing the types firmly on a surface or bed-plate of unequal elevation. This surface was formed by pouring a melted mixture of wax, lime and

[1] Didot, *Essai sur la typographie*, p. 563.

resin on a plate of iron. Pi-Ching then took a stout frame of the size of the page he proposed to print, filled with iron wires in narrow parallels, and placed it on the prepared bed-plate. The types of clay were next forced between the iron wires on the mixture, and pressed close together. Then the plate was put on a furnace and heated until the composition became soft. A planer was put upon the face of the types, to force them down in the composition until they were firmly secured at a uniform height. So treated, the composed types were made as solid as a xylographic block or a stereotype plate. The form was then ready for printing. The method of printing was like that subsequently used for printing blocks engraved on wood, a method that will be described hereafter. When the form had been printed, heat was again applied; the types were withdrawn from the composition, cleaned of ink and adhering composition by the aid of a brush, and put back into a case for future use. Signs and unusual characters not in constant use were wrapped up in paper.

There is nothing incredible in this curious story: on the contrary, it bears internal evidences of its probability. The selection, for printing purposes, of so unpromising a material as clay, the patient labor given to each character before it reached the condition of a type, the sagacity that foresaw and evaded the difficulty of irregular bodies and heights by the use of iron parallels, and a yielding bed-plate—all these are characteristic of the eccentricities of Chinese invention. The process was ingenious, but it was not entirely practical. It depended for its success more on the zeal and ability of Pi-Ching than it did on its own merits. When Pi-Ching died, his process died with him. His friends preserved his types as mementos of his ability, but none of them were able to use his method with success.

The present Chinese method is, practically, the method originally used by Foong-Taou. For the purpose of block-printing, Chinese printers select the wood of the pear-tree, which has close fibres that yield readily and sharply to the touch of the graver. Contrary to western usage, the blocks are cut from wood sawed in boards, or sawed parallel with the fibres. The thickness of the boards or blocks is about a half-inch, but, in the Chinese method, it is not important that the blocks be made of uniform thickness.[1] Each block is cut large enough to contain two pages, and is carefully planed and truly squared. The surface is then sized with a thick solution of boiled rice, which saturates the pores of the wood. When the sizing is hard, the block is ready for the engraver.

The writing or design to be engraved is neatly drawn or written on thin, strong, transparent paper, and is transferred, face downward, to the surface of the block. The rubbing of the back of the paper permanently transfers the writing in its inverted position to the block. The engraver then cuts away the field, leaving the transferred lines in high relief. If the graver slips and spoils a letter, the defective part is cut out; the vacant space is plugged with new wood, on which plug the letter is redrawn and cut. Labor is cheap, and skill is abundant: the cutting of a block of Chinese characters which conveys as many ideas as a page of large Roman book types costs no more, often less, than the composition of the types. The block has advantages over metal types or stereotypes. It is, practically, a stereotype: correct to copy, it needs no proof-reading; light, portable, and not so liable to damage as the stereotype, it can be used for printing copies as they are needed from time to time.

For printing the block, a press is not needed. The block is adjusted upon a level table, before which the printer stands, with a bowl of fluid ink on one side, and a pile of paper, cut to proper size, on the other. In his right hand the printer holds two flat-faced brushes, fixed on the opposite ends of the same handle. One brush is occasionally dipped into the ink,

[1] American engravers on wood use box which has been cut across the fibres in flat disks, ninety-two hundredths of an inch thick. Wood so cut, with its fibres like columns, perpendicular to the touch of the graver and to the line of impression, can be engraved with more delicacy, and, for printing, has more strength than wood cut in line with the fibres.

and afterward swept over the face of the block. This done, the printer places a sheet on the block; he then reverses the position of the wet brush, and sweeps the paper lightly, but firmly, with the dry brush at the other end of the handle. This light impression of the brush is all that is needed to fasten the ink on the paper. The success of this operation depends largely on the quality of the paper, which is soft, thin, pliable, and a quick absorbent of fluid ink.[1] If American book papers were substituted for Chinese paper, the process of printing by the brush and with fluid ink would be found impracticable: the sheet would not adhere to the block; the ink would smear on the paper; the brush would not give enough pressure to transfer the ink.

Chinese presswork is done with rapidity. Du Halde said that a printer could perfect, without exertion, ten thousand sheets within one day. As this performance, about thirteen impressions in a minute, for a working day of twelve hours, is really greater than that of ordinary book-printing machines in modern printing offices, this part of the description of Du Halde may be rejected as entirely untrustworthy. We must believe that the good father did not count the work, and that his credulity was imposed upon by some Chinese braggart. Davis, with more reason, says that the usual performance of the Chinese printer is two thousand sheets per day, which is about one-fourth more than the daily task of an American hand-pressman. The simple nature of the work favors speed. The sheets are printed on one side only, and the printer is not delayed by the setting-off, or smearing of the ink, on the back of the white paper.

Although the Chinese book is printed on paper of the size of two leaves, in pairs of two pages, it is not stitched through the back or centre of the double leaf. The paper is folded between the pages, and the fold is made the outer edge of the book; the cut edges are the back of the book,

[1] The buff-tinted wrappers around fire-crackers and Chinese silks will fairly represent the quality of the paper used for Chinese books.

through which the stitching is done. Clumsy as this method of binding may seem to our standards of propriety, it is done in China with a neatness and thoroughness which are almost beyond criticism.[1]

The labor of engraving separate blocks for every work, which would be regarded as an insuperable difficulty in the Western World, is esteemed but lightly by the patient and plodding Chinese, and is no hindrance to a very broad development of printing. A daily newspaper, known to European residents as the *Peking Gazette*, has been printed in Peking for centuries. This paper, which is made up chiefly of the orders of the emperor and the proceedings and papers of his general council, is printed from a composition of hard wax, which can be more quickly engraved or indented than wood. The presswork, as might be expected, is inferior to that done from engraved wooden blocks. The cost, in China, of engraving a full page, about twice the size of the fac-simile opposite, would be about forty-five cents; a careful imitation of the same page by a competent engraver on wood in New-York would cost about thirty-five dollars.

Adherence to old usages, in neglect of improved methods, is a true oriental trait, but the preference of the Chinese for block-printing is not altogether unreasonable. Their written language is an almost insurmountable obstacle to the employment of types. Chinese characters do not stand for letters or sounds; they represent complete words or ideas. As their vocabulary contains a great many of these words, estimated by some at 80,000, and by others at 240,000, it is impracticable, by reason of its expense, to cut punches for all these characters. European type-founders, at various times, have made up an assortment of Chinese characters for printing the New Testament, and for other books requiring a limited

[1] I have before me a thick Chinese pamphlet which is bound in this style. In the essential points of strength, flexibility and convenience, this binding is much superior to that of American or European sewed pamphlets. The most famous bookbinder would be justly proud of the combination of firmness and elasticity in the sewing.

黄三分射香二分珍珠
共爲細末 此散耑治
驗中風中痰中氣傷暑
見關鎖發冷發熱吐瀉
暈身熱霎時不醒人事
能下之所治各症屢驗
用藥擦眼吹鼻男左女
散一分至三分量人大
子死腹中用朴硝一錢
途中遇有急症不用茶

Fac-Simile of part of a Page from a Chinese Book.

number of words, but a complete collection has never been attempted beyond the Chinese Empire.

The type-foundry attached to the National Printing Office at Paris, which founded types for 43,000 distinct characters, has, probably, reached the highest practicable number; but this performance was accomplished only by repeated alterations of punches and matrices. The punches were cut on wood, and pressed in prepared plaster. The matrices so made were broken when a sufficient quantity of types had been cast from them. By shortening or cutting off a line or lines, the old punches were altered to form new characters. The matrices, also, after they had received the prints of these punches, were sometimes altered by the

於勇華盛頓異人也起按
勝廣割據雄於事疆鳴其亦
國駸呼畫迴乎崇法傳曹
不之開哉倫見功治駸舉號
劍傑矣絶嘗武其公推位尺
毅余尚意爲爲僭三人雄異
不遺下創不提謂貌國俗之
天而乃已不氣諸善代於孫
里既可像與讓三幾子萬劉

Chinese Types Made in London.

[Furnished by Mr. John F. Marthens of Pittsburgh.]

separate prints of dots, lines, or angles, which gave them a different meaning. The imperfection of the process is obvious, for it required the destruction of many matrices and punches.

The difficulties in the way of using types, if they could be made with advantage, are too great to be overlooked: they could not be classified nor handled with economy. The American compositor picks types from cases with boxes for 152 characters, and covering an area of 1088 square inches; but experts in type-setting say that the American case is too large, and that the speed of the compositor would be much increased by reducing the area of the case. The performance of the compositor decreases with an increase in the size of case and in the number of characters. To provide for 80,000 Chinese characters, cases covering an area of 550,000 square inches would be required. In other words, the Chinese compositor would need the room occupied by five hundred cases; he would unavoidably waste the largest portion of his time walking through alleys in search of types, and vainly trying to recollect the places where he had distributed them.

The Chinese are not entirely insensible to the advantages of European typography. There is a story current in books on printing, that Jesuit missionaries, during the latter part of the seventeenth century, cast 250,000 Chinese characters in the form of movable types.[1] Here is an obvious error: if we consider the work done afterward with these types, the quantity stated is altogether too small for the types and too large for the punches. It is further said that the Jesuit missionaries, with the permission of the reigning emperor,

[1] To this description of Chinese typography is usually added the untrue statement that the types were made of copper. Why the Jesuit missionaries, who were amateurs in type-founding, should add to their labors by the use of such a troublesome and slowly melted metal as copper, when European type-founders preferred lead, tin and antimony, cannot be explained. I cannot find a copy of the original statement, which was, no doubt, in Latin. The phrase, types of copper, is, probably, an incorrect translation, a repetition of the error explained in a note on page 65 of this book. The missionaries intended to say, and no doubt did say, that they made types *in* copper, or in copper matrices.

printed a collection of ancient and standard works in six thousand octavo volumes. Of this edition, there are now in Paris, the *History of Music* in sixty volumes, the *History of the Chinese Language* in eighty volumes, and the *History of Foreign Peoples* in seventy-five volumes.[1] A printing office, in which movable types of cast metal are used, has been in operation in Peking since the year 1776. The types of this office are of home manufacture, made from punches of hard wood and matrices of baked porcelain. There may be other instances of an occasional use of types for special purposes, but they are exceptions to the general practice.

Ever since their invention of the art, the largest part of Chinese printed work has been done, as it is now done, by xylography. So long as they continue to use these peculiar characters, this simple method of printing must be preferred for its great cheapness and simplicity. We may smile at the clumsiness of the method, but we should not overlook the fact that it is efficient. "Every one," Du Halde says, "hath the liberty to print what he pleaseth, without the supervising, censure or licence of any one, and with so small charge, that for every hundred letters perfectly engraved in the manner above said, they pay four pence half-penny, yet every letter consists of many strokes." In no country are books so cheap and so abundant as they are in China. The American book or pamphlet in paper cover, sometimes sold for seventy-five cents, more frequently for one dollar, seems of exorbitantly high price when contrasted with a Chinese book of similar size, which can be had in China for the equivalent of eight or ten cents. If the Chinese have not derived great benefits from printing, it is obvious that their failure has not been produced by the high price of printed work.

There are many points of similarity between the Chinese method of printing and the early European practice of the art. The preliminary writing or drawing in ink of a design on paper; the transfer of lines from the paper upon the wood,

[1] *American Encyclopædia of Printing*, p. 104.

and the cutting away of the field; the use of a fluid writing ink; the fashion of printing upon one side only of the sheet: these were features in use by both peoples. If we had a more thorough knowledge of the processes of the early European engravers on wood, other points of similarity might be found. These resemblances seem still more significant when they are considered with the fact that playing cards, supposed to be of oriental origin, were among the earliest productions of European engravers on wood. They have been regarded as a sufficient warrant for the hypothesis that our knowledge of engraving on wood must have been taken from China. It is the belief of many that block-printing was introduced in Europe by Venetian travelers of the thirteenth century, who had acquired a full knowledge of all the details of printing through long residence in China. This is a specious proposition, but it will not bear close examination.

Venice took the lead of all European cities in the establishment of commercial intercourse with China. Venetian merchants, in 1189, occupied an allotted street in Constantinople, from which port they sent vessels through the Black Sea, with bales of merchandise, which accompanying agents introduced into Thibet, Tartary and China. To promote this traffic, Venice sent to the courts of the Eastern potentates some of her most reputable citizens as diplomatic and commercial agents. Marco Polo, the most distinguished of these embassadors, resided more than twenty years in the great empire of Cathay, or China, in high favor with the emperor, and provided with every facility for acquiring a knowledge of the arts and industry of the country. Soon after his return to Venice, in 1295, he dictated a narrative of his travels, but his statements were received with general disbelief, and they have usually been considered as extravagant and improbable. Of late years, the travels of Marco Polo have been defended as substantially truthful, but his most zealous defenders have to confess that he was remarkably credulous. It is a noteworthy circumstance that he does not describe printing or printed books, although he does mention the paper money of China, formally stamped in red ink with the imperial seal. This paper money must have been printed, but he does not say anything about the printing.[1] The commercial relations between Venice and China were continued many years, and it is possible that other travelers may have acquired some knowledge of the peculiarities of Chinese printing, and may have communicated this knowledge; but it was a communication of details only, and not of the principle of printing. Printing could not have been a novelty, for we have many evidences that it was practised in Italy before Marco Polo was born. The mechanics of Europe had nothing to learn of the theory, and but little of the practice, of the art of xylography. All they needed was something to print, and something to print on. They were waiting for paper and for playing cards.

[1] Polo was more deeply interested in the simplicity of the financial method by which the Emperor filled his impoverished treasury.

He transferred the bark of the mulberry-tree into something resembling sheets of paper, and these into money, which cost him nothing at all: so that you might say he had the secret of alchemy to perfection. And these pieces of paper he made to pass current universally over all his kingdoms and provinces and territories, and whithersoever his power and sovereignty extended. And nobody, however important he thought himself, durst refuse them on pain of death. *The Book of Ser Marco Polo, the Venetian.* Translated and edited by Henry Vale, London, 1871.

With all his power, the Great Khan met the fate which comes to every financier who tries to fill up a depleted treasury by the issue of paper money. In a very short time the notes were worth but one-half of their original value. But the Emperor was equal to the emergency: when the notes fell to one-fifth of the nominal value, he called them in, and exchanged five old for one new note of the same denomination.

VII

The Early Printing of Italy.

Printing with Ink in Italy during the Twelfth Century...Printed Initials in Manuscripts...Printed Signatures and Monograms, with Illustrations...Medieval Trade-Marks, with Illustrations. Engraved Initials probably made by Copyists who could not draw...Texts of Books printed from Engraved Letters...The Codex Argenteus of Sweden...Weigel's Fac-Similes of Printing on Silk and Linen Cloth...Probable Method of Printing...Printed Fabrics made in Spain, Sicily and Italy...Art not derived from China...Antiquity of Stained Cloths...No Connecting Link between Hand-Stamping and Card-Printing...No Early Italian Image Prints...Story about the Two Cunios...Its Improbability...No Early Notices of Engraving on Wood...Not considered a New Art, nor a Great Art...Its Productions of Paltry Nature...Early Engravers had nothing to print on.

Nor is it any proof or strong argument against the antiquity of printing, that authentic specimens of wood engraving of those early times are not to be found. Their merits as works of art were not such as to render their preservation at all probable. *Ottley.*

At the beginning of the seventeenth century, a student of old Italian books called the attention of bibliographers to the strange uniformity of the initial letters in many old manuscripts,[1] some of which had been made as early as the ninth century. Each ornamental letter, wherever found or however often repeated in the same book, was of the same form. He reached the conclusion that this uniformity had been produced by engraved stamps. The announcement of this discovery induced other persons to make similar examinations, the result of which confirmed the original statement.

[1] Papillon, *Traité historique et pratique de la gravure en bois*, vol. I, pp. 76, 77. Papillon does not name this student. Lanzi describes him as the ecclesiastic Padre della Valla. Passavant (*Le peintre-graveur*, p. 18) says that the initials of like character which have been found in German manuscript books of the twelfth century, were printed.

It was proved that there was a uniformity in the shapes of the letters which could not have been made by drawing.

The statement that a rude method of printing had been practised three centuries before its supposed invention, was received by the bibliographers with incredulity. Authors who had advocated theories of a Chinese, a German or a Netherlandish discovery of printing would not admit that printing with ink could have been done at an earlier period. They said that the initials were made by stenciling, or by tracings

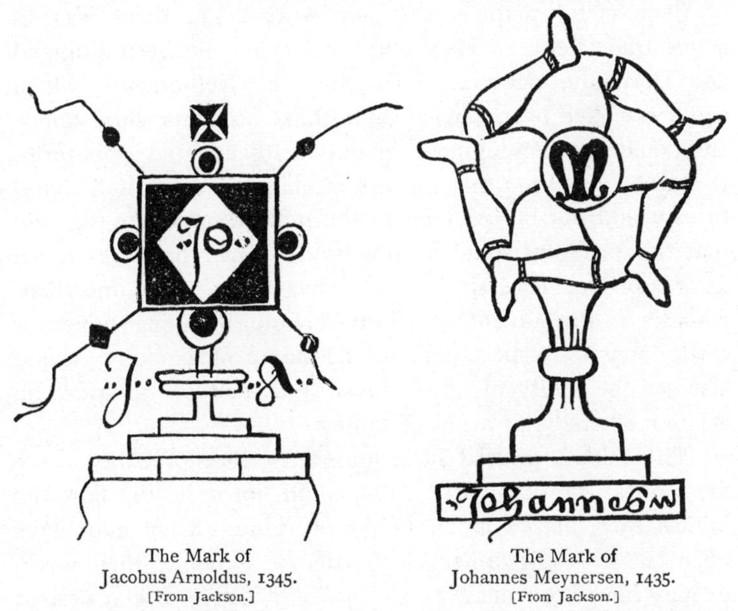

The Mark of
Jacobus Arnoldus, 1345.
[From Jackson.]

The Mark of
Johannes Meynersen, 1435.
[From Jackson.]

taken from a model letter. But they had a peculiarity which could not have been produced by stenciling, for they showed the marks of hard indentation in the parchment. Papillon, a practical engraver on wood, accepted the indented letters as the impressions of wood-cuts; Lanzi, the historian of Italian fine arts, said that the initials were certainly printed.

Signatures which show all the mechanical peculiarities of impressions from engravings on wood have also been found on Italian documents of the twelfth century. Printed signatures or monograms of notaries, which seem to have been made to serve the double purpose of signature and seal, in imitation of the kingly practice of affixing the signet, were frequently used in Italy, Spain and Germany from the ninth to the fourteenth century. It was customary, also, for the manufacturer or merchant[1] to stamp or brand merchandise with a sign or mark through which its origin could be traced. It does not appear that merchants made use of these trade-marks instead of signatures on paper or parchment, but many of them could neither read nor write. Yet there was an active trade between Italy and the Levant, between England and Germany, between Spain and the Netherlands, which could not have been carried on without accounts, correspondence, and the employment of duly authenticated signatures. It may be supposed that the use of stamped or printed signatures would not be confined to the notaries and copyists, and that this printing would be practised by merchants, as much for reasons of necessity as of convenience. The merchant who knew the advantages derived from branding boxes or cattle, and the respect paid to the stamp of a notary, would also see the utility of an engraved and stamped signature on a letter of credit or a bill of lading.

The initials printed in manuscripts were probably made for scribes who could write, but could not draw the floriated initials then placed in all books of value. They may have been cut by calligraphers, who tried to expedite their work, or may have been made to the order of copyists who desired to free themselves from their dependence on the calligrapher. In either case there would have been sufficient reason for the engraving. These initials are, for the most part, of unusually intricate design, but they were engraved in outline only, so

[1] . . . If he was a wool-stapler, he stamped it on his packs; or if a fish-curer, it was branded on the end of his casks. If he built himself a new house, his mark was frequently placed between his initials over the principal doorway, or over the fireplace of the hall; if he made a gift to a church or a chapel, his mark was emblazoned on the windows, beside the knight's or the nobleman's shield of arms; and when he died, his mark was cut upon his tomb. Jackson and Chatto, *Treatise on Wood Engraving*, pp. 17, 18.

that they could be filled in with bright color, by hand-painting or by stenciling. They were printed with a fluid writing ink, which may have been black, but is now of a dingy brown.

A recent Italian author, D. Vincenzo Requeno, who has published an essay on this subject, tells us that the employment of engraved letters by the Italian book-makers of the middle ages was not confined to floriated initials. He says that they were sometimes used for the texts of books, and that many so-called manuscripts were printed by stamping cut letters one after another upon the page. This method of printing a book, letter by letter, could have been made a quicker process that that of careful writing. Not more than sixty-six engraved characters would have been required for the copying of any ordinary manuscript. A skillful workman,

Mark of Adam de Walsokne, who died 1349.

Mark of Edmund Pepyr, who died 1483.

Mark of an unknown person from a tomb in Lynn.

[From Jackson.]

who had the characters before him, fitted up as hand-stamps, lettered so that he could select them at a glance, resting on a surface which kept them coated with ink, could take them up one after another, and produce on paper the impressions of letters faster than they could be produced by the penman who was obliged to carefully draw each letter and to paint or fill in its outlines with ink.[1]

In a library at Upsal, Sweden, is a volume known as the *Codex Argenteus*, or the Silvered Book, which seems to have been made exclusively by this method of stamping one letter

[1] The letters in the most meritorious manuscript books of the middle ages were not made with running hand, closely connected, like the letters of modern penmanship. The form of writing most in fashion was a spurred or pointed Gothic of remarkable blackness. Each letter was separate, carefully drawn, angled and painted, by many strokes of the reed.

after another. The book is so called because the letters are in silver, and present a brilliant appearance, like the glittering letters of bookbinders, on their leaves of purple vellum. The *Codex Argenteus* presents many indications of hand-printing: the letters are depressed on one side of the leaf, and raised on the other, as if made by indentation. Under the letters that have been too rudely pressed with the stamp, the vellum is thin; in some parts the leaf has been broken by pressure and patched with bits of vellum. Occasionally, letters are found turned upside down—an error possible to a hand-printer, but not to a penman. John Ihre, who described the book, in a pamphlet published at Upsal in 1755, says the silver leaf of the letters was affixed to the vellum by means of sizing, and that the letters were produced by stamping on the leaf with engraved punches of hard metal, which had been heated and used as bookbinders now use gilding tools. The use of heat has not been proved, but the blemishes of the work are most satisfactorily explained by the hypothesis that the book was printed letter by letter.[1]

This explanation of the method by which the book was made has not been generally accepted. It was said that silver letters are found in medieval books made entirely by writing. But this is negative evidence, for these books do not present the mechanical imperfections of the *Codex Argenteus*. There has, evidently, been a vague apprehension that the admission of an early use of single types for printing would invalidate all subsequent claims to the invention of typography. One can hardly imagine a grosser error, for the hand-printing of single types is not typography. It is even farther removed from it than the printing of letters on engraved blocks.

[1] The text of the *Codex* is a translation of the four Gospels, written in the Gothic character, by Ulphilas, bishop of the Goths, about the year 370. This book, which is supposed to have been made not later than the sixth century, was discovered in the year 1587, in an abbey in Westphalia, and was taken to Prague. When that city was captured by the Swedes in 1648, the book was sent as one of the trophies of war to Queen Christina. It has ever since been regarded as a great curiosity.

The doubts that once existed as to the genuineness of the printed initials in manuscript books have been dissipated by recent investigation in another direction. It has been conclusively proved that woven fabrics of silk and of linen, ornamented with designs printed in bright colors, not unlike those of modern chintzes and calicoes, were produced between the twelfth and fifteenth centuries. The designs or patterns were printed in ink from engraved blocks of wood, by the tedious process of hand-stamping. Of this curious primitive printed work, there are, in several European collections, fragments of images, priests' robes, altar cloths, and ecclesiastic apparel of like nature. The genuineness of these relics of early printing, and the process by which the printing was done, have been established in the most satisfactory manner Weigel, in his valuable work on the *Infancy of Printing*, has illustrated this part of his subject with fac-similes of these fragments which prove that Italian workmen not only knew how to print, but that they printed in colors with great precision.

The modern printer who fairly appreciates the difficulties of printing colors in register, and the force required to secure a good impression from a large, flat surface, may be puzzled by the neatness of this early printing. His experience tells him that these designs should have been printed upon strong and accurately adjusted presses, and from large surfaces, in sections or forms of two or more square feet. But the method of the Italian printers was quite different; the designs were engraved on many pieces of wood of small size, made to fit each other with accuracy, and each piece was separately inked and struck by hand, or by a mallet, on the fabric. A careful workman could readily connect the different impressions of different blocks, keeping the colors in true register, and could pursue the pattern in a neat manner over any surface, however large. The work was tedious, but not more so than that of finishing, or gilding by hand tools, in ornamental book-binding, which is now done by a similar method. Slow as it may seem when compared with the rapidity of modern calico-printing, it was an improvement on all methods then known, and much quicker and more exact than any form of stenciling or hand-painting.

The fragment adjudged by Weigel the oldest of the ten specimens illustrated in the book, is a bit of red silk, woven and printed during the last ten years of the twelfth century. He says that we must search for its origin where silk fabrics were most extensively manufactured; that it must have been made by Moorish artisans of Almeria, Grenada and Seville in Southern Spain, or by Saracens in Sicily in the rich manufacturing cities of Palermo[1] and Messina. Printed fabrics of silk, cotton, linen, and woolen stuffs were subsequently made in Lucca, in Genoa, and the free cities of Northern Italy.

The art of staining cloth with colors is older than history. Homer writes about the magnificent colored cloths of Sidon; Herodotus mentions the garments of the people of Caucasus, which he says were covered with figures of animals; Pliny describes the decorated linens of the old Egyptians.[2] The Spanish invaders of Mexico brought back statements that all the people of the New World were clothed in cotton cloths

[1] Moorish authors tell us that in the days of the last Norman kings of Sicily, ten thousand silk looms were in active operation in Palermo; but this statement is an oriental exaggeration of a fact that required no embellishment. Others say that Jewish and Italian traders carried these silks to Italy, Germany, and the North of Europe. The earliest silk-weavers of Palermo were the captured inhabitants of Greece who had been taken there in 1147.

[2] Pliny says that the colors were produced by dyeing, but the garments described by Herodotus could not have been made by this process. We have to infer that they used some form of impression. Breitkopf tells us that the colored cloths of the Egyptians were made by printing. His conclusions seem reasonable when we consider how largely engraved stamps were used by the Egyptians for printing upon clay, and how short was the step from printing on clay to printing on cloth. The art of staining, printing or stenciling cloth with bright colors by different processes, has been practised in Hindostan from a very early period. The antiquity of the Indian manufacture may be inferred from the European adoption of Indian names. The English word *chintz*, and its German synonym *zitz*, are derived from a Hindostanee word that means both a colored printed cloth and a flower. The word *calico* is from Calicut, the town on the Malabar coast from which calico was first exported to Europe.

of brilliant colors, which Stephens says were certainly printed. Cook, the discoverer of islands in the Pacific, says that the Polynesians beautified their garments by a method of stamping. It is not even necessary to attribute the early Italian practice of printing upon woven fabrics to the Saracens of Sicily; the Italian practice may have been the revival of a disused but unforgotten Roman art—a revival made possible through the growth of commerce and manufactures.

There is no connecting link between the Italian hand-stamps of the thirteenth and the Venetian playing cards of the fifteenth century. There are no Italian prints of images, and no Italian block-books, which can be attributed to this period. Papillon, the author of a treatise on engraving, is the only person who has attempted to supply this deficiency in the record. He gives a description of eight large prints, which he thinks were made at Ravenna, in the year 1286, by a twin brother and sister, known as the two Cunios:

When I was a young man, and employed by my father almost every week-day in different places, to paste or arrange our papers for the hanging of rooms, it happened that, in 1719 or 1720, I was sent to the village of Bagneux, near Mount Rouge, to a Mr. De Greder, a Swiss captain, who there possessed a very pretty house. After I had papered a closet for him, he employed me to paste certain papers in imitation of mosaic upon the shelves of his library. One day after dinner, he found me reading in one of his books, and was, in consequence, induced to show me two or three very ancient volumes which had been lent to him by a Swiss officer, one of his friends, that he might examine them at his leisure. We conversed together about the prints contained in them, and concerning the antiquity of engraving on wood. I will now give the description of these ancient volumes, such as I wrote in his presence, and as he had the goodness to dictate to me: "Upon a cartouche, or frontispiece, decorated with fanciful ornaments, which, although Gothic, are far from disagreeable, and measuring about nine inches in width by six inches in height, with the arms, no doubt, of the family of Cunio at the top of it, are rudely engraved the following words, in bad Latin, or ancient Gothic Italian, with many abbreviations:

"The Heroic Actions, represented in Figures, of the great and magnanimous Macedonian King, the bold and valiant Alexander, dedicated, presented, and humbly offered to the most holy father Pope Honorius II, the glory and support of the Church, and to our illustrious and generous father and mother—by us, Allessandro Alberico Cunio, cavalier, and Isabella Cunio, twin brother and sister—first reduced, imagined, and attempted to be executed in relief, with a small knife, on blocks of wood, and made even and polished by this dear sister, and continued and finished by us together, at Ravenna, from eight pictures of our invention, painted six times larger than here represented, engraved and explained by verses, and thus marked upon the paper, to perpetuate the number of them, and to enable us to present them to our relatives and friends, in testimony of gratitude, friendship and affection. All this was done and finished by us when only sixteen years of age."[1]

The book was, apparently, in its original binding of thin plates of wood, covered with leather, but without any gilding, ornamented only by crossed divisions marked with a heated iron. Papillon says that the engravings were cut in a crude, experimental manner, and that they appear to have been printed by rubbing the palm of the hand or a frotton many times over the paper. The tint of the ink was a pale, faded blue, mixed as water color. The field of the engravings was badly routed out; projections that soiled the paper appeared in several places, obscuring words, which had subsequently been written on the margin. Neither the engravings, nor the memoir bound with them, furnish us with dates; but there can be no doubt as to the period in which the engravings were ostensibly made, for Pope Honorius occupied the papal chair only between April 2, 1285, and April 3, 1287.

There is nothing improbable in the statement that prints like these could have been made in 1285. There may be a substratum of truth under the exaggerations raised by family pride and a love for the marvelous; but the memoir of the lives of the two Cunios, and the details furnished by Papillon about the appearance of the engravings, are altogether unsatisfactory.[1] Whatever opinion may be formed of the credibility

[1] Papillon, *Traité historique et pratique de la gravure en bois*, vol. I, p. 89. His description is very prolix and full of irrelevant matter. I have made use of the translation of Ottley, but have abridged it.

of the story of the two Cunios,[1] it must be admitted that their prints had no known influence in the development of engraving on wood. They were not imitated. The interval between the years 1285 and 1440 is almost an absolute blank in the annals of Italian engraving: it furnishes us neither trace nor tradition of engravings on wood. The oldest authentic Italian engravings on wood are in *The Meditations of John of Turrecremata*, a book printed at Rome in 1467; but these engravings cannot be claimed as illustrations of the development of the Italian practice of the art, for they were designed and cut by or for Ulric Hahn, a German printer.

This silence of the early chroniclers should not be construed as evidence that there was no engraving on wood; it is evidence only of the trivial nature of the work done. To specify the work is to justify the neglect. It consisted, so far as we know, only of stamps for the use of notaries, autographs for those who did not write, trade-marks for merchants' packages, outlined initials for inexpert scribes, and engraved blocks for manufacturers of textile fabrics. This paltry work seems specially inappropriate for the initiation of a great art destined to make a revolution in literature.

Engraving on wood was not considered as a great art by the earlier engravers. As it appeared to them, it was but a makeshift, a mechanical method of evading the labor of difficult drawing or of abridging its drudgery. To the chroniclers of this period, engraving was entirely unworthy of notice. No one could see that it had any marked merit. So far from deserving praise, the art of engraving and printing letters was

[1] This version of the origin of block-printing in Europe has been accepted by many authors, who find in it, or profess to find in it, the evidence that printing was derived from China and was first used in Italy. The wisest judgment passed upon its merits is that of Lanzi, who merely recites the legend, and concludes that "it is safest to say nothing about it." But Humphreys (*History of the Art of Printing*, second issue, page 209) submits the substance of a letter from a Russian book-collector, who asserts that, in 1861, he had seen, in the possession of a Mr. Herdegen of Nuremberg, seven prints which agreed precisely with those described by Papillon. I find no other description of these prints.

regarded as a confessed acknowledgment of inability to draw, more deserving of censure than of praise. There were in the thirteenth century workmen, now unknown, who produced exquisite workmanship in the carving of wood and stone, in the chasing of gold and silver, and in the copying of manuscripts. If these men were thought unworthy of notice, the rude engravers on wood would be entirely forgotten. The paltriness of the printed matter, and the perishable nature of the substances on which the printing was done, will account for the disappearance of most of the early prints. Nobody cared to preserve a bit of printed cotton cloth as evidence of the method of printing then in fashion. Nobody could foresee that it would be of any interest.

The trivial nature of the work cannot be considered as an evidence of the incompetency of the engravers to do work of merit. They left us no printing of permanent value, because they knew of no proper substance to print upon. The only materials available were parchment, papyrus and stiff cotton paper, all of which were unsuitable. Printing can be done to advantage only on paper, but paper was sparingly used in the fourteenth century. When paper came, printing followed.

VIII

The Introduction of Paper in Europe.

Paper Invented in China in the First Century...Paper-Making in Japan, with Illustration...Description of Process...An Illustration of Oriental Book-Making...The European Process like the Oriental...Paper known in Europe in the Fifth Century...Not used for Writing...Made of Cotton...Earliest Notice of Linen Paper...Differences of Opinion concerning its Introduction. Different Methods of Preparing Pulp...Early European Paper-Mills...Illustration of Paper-Mill by Jost Amman...Mills in Spain, France, Sicily and Italy...Possible Antiquity of the European Process...Paper not used by Copyists...Its Inferiority...Vellum Preferred...Palimpsests...Government Interference with Manufacturers of Paper...Changes of Fashion in Paper...Paper came in Proper Time.

It is peculiarly characteristic of all the pretended discoveries of the middle ages, that when the historians mention them for the first time, they treat them as things in general use. Neither gunpowder, nor the compass, nor the Arabic numerals, nor paper, are anywhere spoken of as discoveries, and yet they must have wrought a total change in war, in navigation, in science and in education. *Sismondi.*

ACCORDING to Chinese chronology, paper was invented in China at the close of the first century, or one hundred and forty-five years[1] after the Chinese invention of printing. All the printing that had been done before the invention of paper was on sheets or leaves of cotton or silk. This version of the antiquity of the Chinese invention is in some degree corroborated by a Japanese chronicle, which says that paper was exported from the Corea to Japan between the years 280 and 610 A. D. In time, the Japanese paper was made so superior to the Chinese, that there was no further need for importation. This superiority has been maintained to this day. In some branches of paper-making, the Japanese are

[1] Du Halde, as quoted by Ottley in his *Inquiry into the Origin of Engraving*, p. 9. There is another version placing the date at 170 B. C.

without rivals in either the eastern or western world. Two hundred and sixty-three kinds of paper are now made in Yeddo. Some of them may have their origin in reasons of habit, caprice or fashion, but most of them are made for specific uses. Papers are manufactured not only for writing and printing, but for hats, umbrellas, lanterns, clothing, dolls' dresses, twine, candle-wick, and an endless variety of useful or ceremonious purposes. An anonymous author has wisely remarked: "When a people contrive to make saucepans that are used over charcoal fires, fine pocket-handkerchiefs, and sailors' water-proof overcoats out of paper, they may be considered as having pretty thoroughly mastered the subject."

The illustration on the opposite page is the reduced facsimile of the engraving of a Japanese artist who has attempted to show how paper was made in his country in the eighteenth century. The grim old man who may be seen at the upper part of the illustration, with a leg in one page, and with head and body in another, is beating paper stock to a pulp.[1] His only tool is a forked club, with which he pounds on the stone, and macerates the leaves and inner bark of various trees that have been previously saturated in an adjoining tub that is supposed to contain a solution of caustic alkali. How the stock could be reduced to the requisite smoothness for paper pulp by this rough manipulation is a problem that no American paper-maker will undertake to solve. We only know that it is done and well done. The long tank in the centre of the left-hand page contains the pulp dissolved in water. Two men are taking out the pulp upon paper-moulds, or sieves of bamboo splints which have been wire-drawn and boiled in oil. The water taken up with the pulp is drained through the holes in the sieve, leaving upon the woven splints a thin and flabby web of paper pulp. The web is then couched on

[1] The artist was not restricted by the scant space that allowed him to show only the leg of the pulp-beater on the first page. He does this, and then, with an amusing unconsciousness of its impropriety, proceeds to draw the head and body on the following page, which, in the Japanese book from which this was taken, is the other side of the leaf.

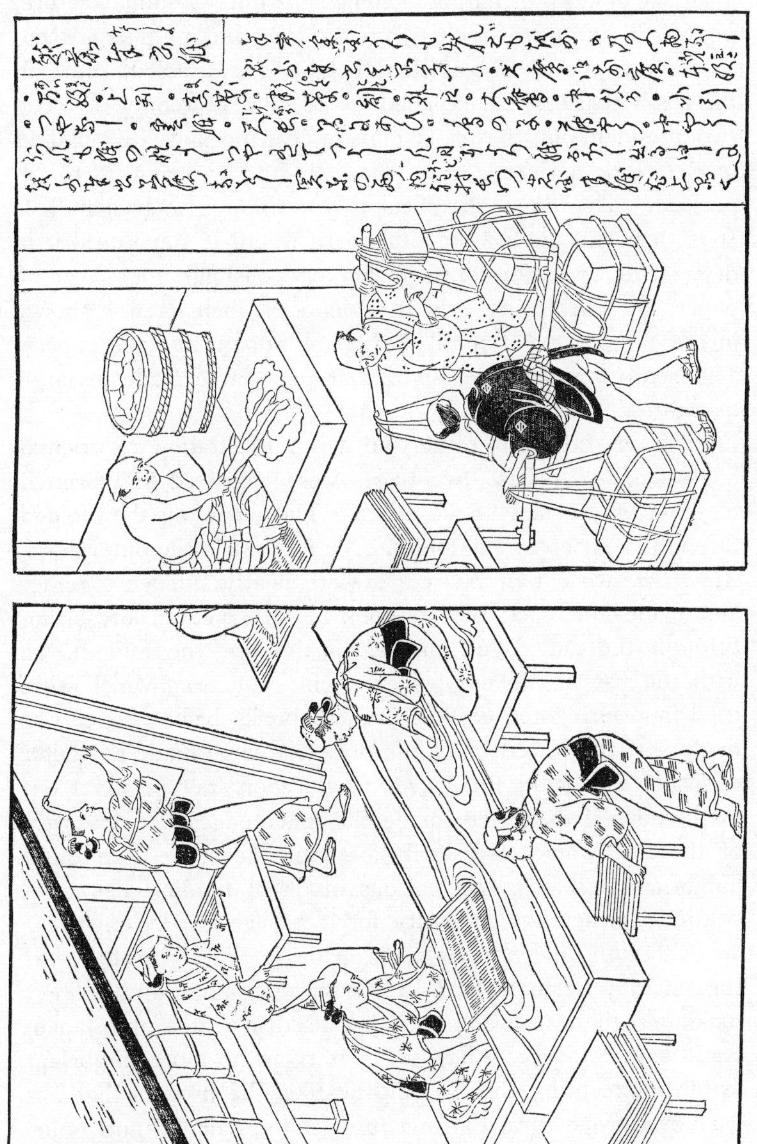

The Japanese Method of Making Paper.
[From Breitkopf.]

a surface of cloth or felt, or of some substitute of similar nature, on which, in turn, another layer of felt and pulp is placed. When the pile is of sufficient height it is pressed, until all the water that can be expelled by pressure is removed. The two attendants on the paper-makers near the tank are engaged in the work of interleaving the web and carrying it to be pressed. This done, the sheet is firm enough to be handled. It is then laid upon a smooth board where it stays until it is dry. The operation of surfacing or polishing the sheet of paper, by burnishing it with a smooth shell, is not shown in the engraving. But this finish was not given to all papers. The neatly corded bales show that paper was made in large quantities.

This engraving is of service as an illustration of oriental book-making. These two pages were engraved and printed together on one side of the paper. The sheet was then folded through the centre: the folded edge was made the outer edge, while the two cut or raw edges were neatly stitched together and made the back of the book. This method of sewing through the cut edges, instead of through the fold, began with the use of the cut leaves of silk or cotton, which were used in printing the earliest Chinese books before paper was made. If the cut edges of silk or cotton were made the outer edges of the book, the leaves would soon fray or ravel out in threads; if they were made the inner edges, the integrity of the leaf would necessarily be more secure. Like other habits and fashions, this curious mode of binding has been continued when the necessity for it has ceased to exist.

Although this engraving was made in the eighteenth century, it may be accepted as a correct representation of paper-making as it has always been practised in China and Japan. Rude as this process may seem, it is, in its more important features, excepting that of pulp-beating, the process that was used in Europe until the invention of the cylinder and Fourdrinier paper-making machines. Nor is this process entirely out of fashion. There are paper-makers yet living who have taken pulp out of the vats with hand moulds and deckle, and have couched it on felts, substantially by the same method that was in use in Asia fifteen hundred years ago.

Oriental paper-makers do not use rags nor raw cotton for making their pulp. They select different kinds of bamboo, and the bark and leaves of various trees, which they combine in unequal proportions, so as to produce for different kinds of paper the different qualities of strength, smoothness and flexibility. These materials are saturated in lime water, and are sometimes boiled to free them from useless matter. Barks are sometimes triturated with pestles in a mortar. While the greatest care is taken to prevent the cutting of the fibres in too short lengths, every expedient is made use of to split up the fibres in the finest threads. The result of this care is the production of papers of wonderful strength and flexibility.

It is admitted by all historians that the early European practice of paper-making was derived from Asia. How the knowledge of the art was transmitted to us from China, Persia or India, and where and when paper was first made in Europe are questions of controversy. The difficulty we encounter in an inquiry concerning its derivation is aggravated by the discovery that two kinds of paper—one, said to be made of cotton, and another, said to be made of linen or rags—were used in Europe at a very early period—a period in which we find no traces of the existence of a European paper-mill. Proteaux says that a thick card or card-like paper came in use during the fifth century,[1] when the manufacture of papyrus was declining. But its first use was not as a substitute for papyrus or parchment. It was called *charta damascena*, the card of Damascus; *charta gossypina*, or the cotton card; *charta bombycina*, or the silk-like card; *serica*, or the silky fabric. It was usually mentioned as a card; for it was so thick, and so unlike papyrus, that it was regarded as a different thing, and

[1] Proteaux, *Practical Guide for the Manufacture of Paper*, Paine's translation, p. 17. He does not name his authority for fixing the date in the fifth century, but it is not at all improbable that a card-like paper was then made for some other purpose than that of writing.

was defined by a different name. This cotton card or cotton paper was thick, coarse, woolly, yellow and somewhat fragile. It was so inferior to papyrus, parchment or linen paper as a writing surface, and was so generally neglected by professional copyists, that all the earlier chroniclers of paper-making have passed it by as unworthy of notice.

The linen paper, so called, came in use at a much later period, but there is great disagreement among authorities as to the date. Meerman, the author of a learned book on the origin of printing, offered a reward for the earliest manuscript on linen paper, which, he decided, could not have been used in Europe before 1270. Montfaucon, a learned antiquary, says that he could find no book nor leaf of linen paper of earlier date, but he thinks that it was known and used in Europe to a limited extent before 1270. Gibbon, citing the authority of Arabian historians, says that a linen paper was made in Samarcand in the eighth century, and leaves his reader to form the inference that not long after, paper found its way to Europe. Casiri, a Spanish author, who made a catalogue of the Arabian manuscripts in the Escurial, says that in this collection are many old manuscripts of the twelfth century on linen paper, including one of the year 1100. But we are not told that this paper was made in Spain; it may have been brought from the East. Tiraboschi, an Italian historian, says that linen paper is the invention of an Italian, Pace de Fabiano of Treviso, who flourished about the middle of the fourteenth century. But Peter Mauritius, abbot of a French monastery at Cluny, in a treatise written by him in 1120 against the Jews, says, "The books we read every day are made of the skins of sheep, goats and calves [parchment], of oriental plants [papyrus], or of the scrapings of old rags, or of any other compacted refuse material."[1] It would be a hopeless task to attempt to gather from these discordant

[1] The phrase *ex rasuris veterum pannorum*, here translated as the scrapings of old rags, has been construed by many authors as linen paper, in opposition to the "compacted refuse material," which is supposed to be cotton, or, at least, a mixture of cotton and cordage.

statements a satisfactory explanation of the origin or of the introduction of paper in Europe.

The modern paper-maker, who produces paper pulp from mixtures in variable proportions of all kinds of textile rubbish, will doubt the ability of any antiquary to distinguish linen from cotton paper, especially when Tiraboschi admits that cotton paper was made in Italy during the fourteenth century so closely resembling linen paper that only a paper-maker could perceive the difference. The microscope that enables the educated investigator to detect the characteristic features of every kind of vegetable fibre is really the only safe test[1] for determining the constituents of paper; but it does not appear that this instrument was ever used by the authors who have undertaken to discriminate between linen and cotton paper. The explanation of these contradictory statements must be sought in another quarter.

The peculiarities of the so-called linen and cotton papers are due more to their distinct methods of manufacture than to the material used. The earliest notice of the manufacture of paper in Europe clearly specifies the practice of two unlike methods. We are told that, in the year 1085, a paper-mill at Toledo, which had been operated by the Moors, passed into the hands of Christians, probably Spaniards, who made great improvements in the manufacture. The Moors made paper pulp by grinding the raw cotton, a process which hastened the work, but it shortened and weakened the fibres, making a paper that was tender and woolly. The Spaniards stamped the cotton and rags into a pulp, by pestles or stamps driven by water power, a method which preserved the long fibres that gave the fabric its strength. This paper, now known as linen paper, was then known as parchment cloth. The cotton paper of the antiquarians is, apparently, the paper that had its fibres cut by grinding; the linen paper was the paper made from pulp that had been beaten.

[1] See *The American Encyclopedia of Printing*, p. 329, for engravings of microscopic enlargements of some of the fibres used for paper.

The first European paper-mills seem to have been established by the Moors or Saracens who had direct intercourse with the East. Paper was made at Xativa, Valencia, and at other towns of Spain, by Moors and Spaniards, and the paper made at Xativa was much commended for its whiteness. We find mention, also, of a family of paper-makers in the island of Sicily in the year 1102. For many years the Moors were not only the largest manufacturers, but the largest consumers. In various cities of Spain, seventy libraries were opened for the instruction of the public, during a period when all the rest of Europe, without books, without learning and without cultivation, was plunged in the most disgraceful ignorance.[1]

Paper-Mill of the Sixteenth Century.
[From Jost Amman.]

In this illustration, which was first published by Jost Amman in his *Book of Trades*, we see something of the mechanism always used for preparing the pulp for paper. Large water-wheels, partially seen through the window, set in motion a wooden cylinder evenly spiked with projections. As the cylinder revolved, these projections tilted up, and then dropped heavy stampers of hard wood that beat against the torn and well-soaked rags lying within the tank. The stamping was continued until the macerated rags were of the consistency of cream. The stuff thus made was then transferred to tubs, at one of which a

[1] Sismondi, *Literature of the South of Europe*, chap. 2.

paper-maker is at work. The dipping out of the pulp with hand mould and deckle, the couching of the web on interleaving felts, and its transfer to be pressed by the brisk little boy, are the same processes in all points as those that have been described in the Japanese engraving. The processes of sorting and washing the rags, and of bleaching the half-made stuff are not shown in the cut, but they were not neglected. The screw press behind the paper-moulder is the only innovation of importance.

The development of paper-making in Europe cannot be traced with any degree of certainty. There are Italian authors who assert that linen paper was made in Lombardy and Tuscany as early as the year 1300, and that the Italian knowledge of the art was derived not from Spain or Sicily, but through the Greeks at Constantinople, who had been taught how to make paper by the Saracens. The earliest authentic mention of an Italian paper-mill is that concerning the mill of Fabiano, which had been in operation for some years before 1340, and which produced at that time nothing but the cotton card-paper. There is no record of paper-mills in the Netherlands during the fourteenth century. Paper was made at Troyes, France, in the year 1340. In the British Islands there was no paper-mill before that of John Tate, who is supposed to have established it in the year 1498. In Germany, a paper-mill was established at Nuremberg by Ulman Stromer about the year 1390.[1] But the different paper-marks in the home-made paper of German manuscripts of this period are indications that there were paper-mills in many German towns.

[1] The jealousy with which trades were then guarded is illustrated by the policy of Stromer. He obliged all his workmen to take an oath that they would not reveal the process, nor practise it on their own account. He had two rollers and eighteen stampers, and was about to put in another roller, when he was opposed by his Italian workmen, who probably thought that this extension of the works would give him a monopoly, and would deprive them of all opportunity of obtaining work from any rival manufacturer. The mutineers were brought before the magistrates and sent to prison. They afterward submitted and returned to work, but were allowed to renounce their oath of obligation.

The gradual development of paper-making in Europe is but imperfectly presented through these fragmentary facts. Paper may have been made for many years before it found chroniclers who thought the manufacture worthy of notice. The Spanish paper-mills of Toledo which were at work in the year 1085, and an ancient family of paper-makers which was honored with marked favor by the king of Sicily in the year 1102, are carelessly mentioned by contemporary writers as if paper-making was an old and established business. It does not appear that paper was a novelty at a much earlier period. The bulls of the popes of the eighth and ninth centuries were written on cotton card or cotton paper, but no writer called attention to this card, or described it as a new material. It has been supposed that this paper was made in Asia, but it could have been made in Europe. A paper-like fabric, made from the barks of trees, was used for writing by the Longobards in the seventh century, and a coarse imitation of the Egyptian papyrus, in the form of a strong brown paper, had been made by the Romans as early as the third century. The art of compacting in a web the macerated fibres of plants seems to have been known and practised to some extent in Southern Europe long before the establishment of Moorish paper-mills.

The Moors brought to Spain and Sicily not an entirely new invention, but an improved method of making paper, and what was more important, a culture and civilization that kept this method in constant exercise. It was chiefly for the lack of ability and lack of disposition to put paper to proper use that the earlier European knowledge of paper-making was so barren of results. The art of book-making as it was then practised was made subservient to the spirit of luxury more than to the desire for knowledge. Vellum was regarded by the copyists as the only substance fit for writing on, even when it was so scarce that it could be used only for the most expensive books. The card-like cotton paper once made by the Saracens was certainly known in Europe for many years before its utility was recognized. Hallam says that the use of this cotton paper was by no means general or frequent, except in Spain or Italy, and perhaps in the South of France, until the end of the fourteenth century. Nor was it much used in Italy for books.[1]

Paper came before its time and had to wait for recognition. It was sorely needed. The Egyptian manufacture of papyrus, which was in a state of decay in the seventh century, ceased entirely in the ninth or tenth. Not many books were written during this period, but there was then, and for at least three centuries afterward, an unsatisfied demand for something to write upon. Parchment was so scarce that reckless copyists frequently resorted to the desperate expedient of effacing the writing on old and lightly esteemed manuscripts. It was not a difficult task. The writing ink then used was usually made of lamp-black, gum, and vinegar; it had but a feeble encaustic property, and it did not bite in or penetrate the parchment. The work of effacing this ink was accomplished by moistening the parchment with a weak alkaline solution and by rubbing it with pumice-stone. This treatment did not entirely obliterate the writing, but made it so indistinct that the parchment could be written over the second time. Manuscripts so treated are now known as palimpsests. All the large European public libraries have copies of the palimpsests which are melancholy illustrations of the literary tastes of many writers or book-makers during the middle ages. More convincingly than by argument, they show the utility of paper. Manuscripts of the *Gospels*, of the *Iliad*, and of works of the highest merit, often of great beauty and accuracy, are dimly seen underneath stupid sermons, and theological writings of a nature so paltry

[1] Paper, whenever or wherever invented, was very sparingly used, and especially in manuscript books, among the French, Germans or English, or linen paper even among the Italians, until near the close of the fourteenth century. Upon the study of the sciences it could as yet have had very little effect. The vast importance of the invention was just beginning to be discovered. It is to be added that the earliest linen paper was of very good manufacture, strong and handsome, though perhaps too much like card for general convenience. *Literature of Europe in the Middle Ages*, chap. 1, sec. 65.

that no man living cares to read them. In some instances the first writing has been so thoroughly scrubbed out that its meaning is irretrievably lost.

Much as paper was needed, it was not at all popular with copyists. Their prejudice was not altogether unreasonable, for it was thick, coarse, knotty, and in every way unfitted for the display of ornamental penmanship or illumination. The cheaper quality, then known as cotton paper, was especially objectionable. It seems to have been so badly made as to need governmental interference. Frederick II of Germany, in the year 1221, foreseeing evils that might arise from bad paper, made a decree by which he made invalid all public documents that should be put on cotton paper, and ordered them within two years to be transcribed upon parchment. Peter II, of Spain, in the year 1338, publicly commanded the paper-makers of Valencia and Xativa to make their paper of a better quality and equal to that of an earlier period.

The better quality of paper, now known as linen paper, had the merits of strength, flexibility and durability in a high degree, but it was set aside by the copyists because the fabric was too thick and the surface was too rough. The art of calendering or polishing papers until they were of a smooth, glossy surface, which was then practised by the Persians, was unknown to, or at least unpractised by, the early European makers. The changes of fashion in the selection of writing papers are worthy of passing notice. The rough hand-made papers so heartily despised by the copyists of the thirteenth century are now preferred by neat penmen and draughtsmen. The imitations of medieval paper, thick, harsh, and dingy, and showing the marks of the wires upon which the fabric was couched, are preferred by men of letters for books and correspondence, while highly polished modern plate papers, with surfaces much more glossy than any preparation of vellum, are now rejected by them as finical and effeminate.

There is a popular notion that the so-called inventions of paper and xylographic printing were gladly welcomed by men of letters, and that the new fabric and the new art were immediately pressed into service. The facts about to be presented in succeeding chapters will lead to a different conclusion. We shall see that the makers of playing cards and of image prints were the men who first made extended use of printing, and that self-taught and unprofessional copyists were the men who gave encouragement to the manufacture of paper. The more liberal use of paper at the beginning of the fifteenth century by this newly created class of readers and book-buyers marks the period of transition and of mental and mechanical development for which the crude arts of paper-making and of block-printing had been waiting for centuries. We shall also see that if paper had been ever so cheap and common during the middle ages, it would have worked no changes in education or literature; it could not have been used by the people, for they were too illiterate; it would not have been used by the professional copyists, for they preferred vellum and despised the substitute.

IX

The Book-Makers of the Middle Ages.

Education controlled by the Church...All Books in Latin...Ecclesiastics the only Scholars and Book-Makers...Copyists in Constantinople...In Ireland...Charlemagne's Educational Policy. Copyists of France and their Work...The Scriptoriums of Monasteries...Errors of Copyists. Illuminators of Books...Bookbinders...Profuse Ornamentation of Books...Neglect of Books and Copying by Monks...Copyists and Book-Makers appear among the Laity...Regulations of the University of Paris about Copyists...Character of Medieval Books...Universal Appreciation of Pictures...General Use of Abbreviations...Paper Used only for Inferior Books...Rise of the Romance Literature...Its Luxurious Books...Book-Collecting a Princely Pastime...High Prices paid for Books of Merit...Fondness for Expensive Books retarded the Development of Printing.

With that of the boke losende were the claspis:
The margent was illumynid all with golded railles
And byse, enpicturid with gressoppes and waspis,
With butterflyis and freshe pecocke taylis,
Enflorid with flowris and slymy snaylis;
Envyvid picturis well towchid and quikly;
It wolde haue made a man hole that had be ryght sekely,
To beholde how it was garnyschyd and bounde,
Encouerde ouer with gold of tisseu fyne;
The claspis and bullyons were worth a thousande pounde;
With balassis and charbuncles the borders did shyne;
With aurum mosaicum every other lyne
Was wrytin.

Skelton.

FROM the sixth to the thirteenth century, the ecclesiastics of the Roman Catholic church held all the keys of scholastic knowledge. They wrote the books, kept the libraries, and taught the schools. During this period there was no literature worthy of the name that was not in the dead language Latin, and but little of any kind that did not treat of theology. A liberal education was of no value to any one who did not propose to be a monk or priest. Science, as we now understand the word, and classical literature, were sadly neglected. Scholastic theology and metaphysical philosophy were the studies which took precedence of all others. The knowledge derived through these narrow channels may have been imperfect, but it was a power. The church kept it to and for itself; hedging it in with difficulty and mystery, and making it inaccessible to poor people. The study of Latin would have been neglected, and its literature forgotten, if this dead language had not been the language of the Scriptures, of the canons and liturgies of the church, and of the writings of the fathers. Ecclesiastics were required, by virtue of their position, to study Latin, but there were many in high station, even as late as the fourteenth century, who were barely able to read,[1] and many more who could not write.

The manufacture by professional copyists of the books of devotion required for the services of the church, which had died of neglect in Rome, and which had been driven out of Constantinople by the hostility of the iconoclastic emperors, re-appeared in Ireland, with unprecedented elegance of workmanship. It does not appear that the diligence of the monks at Iona was of any permanent benefit to Ireland, but it was of great value to the corrupted religion and waning civilization of Western Europe. Irish missionaries founded schools and monasteries in England, and taught their Anglo-Saxon converts to ornament books after a fashion now known and described as the Saxon style. Books of great beauty, admira-

[1] Lewis Beaumont, an illiterate French nobleman, made bishop of Durham in 1330, was so inexpert at reading, that he could not read the bulls written for his people at his consecration. The word *metropoliticæ* occurred: the bishop paused, tried in vain to repeat it, and at last said, "Let us suppose that read." Then he came to the word *ænigmate*, before which he stopped in a fine wrath, and said, "By St. Lewis, he was no gentleman who wrote this stuff." . . . . At an entertainment given at Rome, during the same century, by the bishop of Murray, the papal legate from Scotland, the bishop so blundered in his Latin when he was saying grace, that his holiness and the cardinals could not refrain from laughing. The disconcerted bishop testily concluded in Scotch-English, by wishing "all the false carles to the devil," to which the company, who did not understand the dialect, unwittingly responded, Amen.

bly[1] written by unknown Irish copyists, are still preserved in Germany, France and Switzerland, to which countries Irish missionaries were sent from Iona between the sixth and ninth centuries. These missionaries revived the taste for letters.

Flaccus Alcuin, an Englishman and a graduate of Anglo-Saxon schools, the teacher and adviser of Charlemagne, was authorized by the great emperor to institute a policy which would multiply books and disseminate knowledge. It was ordered that every abbot, bishop and count should keep in permanent employment a qualified copyist who must write correctly, using Roman letters only, and that every monastic institution should maintain a room known as the *scriptorium*, fitted up with desks and furnished with all the implements for writing. The work of copying manuscripts and increasing libraries was made a life-long business. Alcuin earnestly entreated the monks to zealousness in the discharge of this duty. "It is," he writes, "a most meritorious work, more beneficial to the health than working in the fields, which profits only a man's body, whilst the labor of the copyist profits his soul." On another occasion, Alcuin exhorted the monks who could not write neatly to learn to bind books.

[1] At a period when the fine arts may be said to have been almost extinct in Italy and in other parts of the Continent, namely, from the fifth to the end of the eighth century, a style of art had been established and cultivated in Ireland absolutely distinct from that of all other parts of the civilized world. In the sixth and seventh centuries the art of ornamenting manuscripts of the sacred scriptures, and more especially of the gospels, had attained a perfection in Ireland almost marvelous. Westwood, *Palæographia Sacra Pictoria*, Book of Kells, page 1. Westwood further says, that in delicacy of handling, and minute but faultless execution, the whole range of palæography offers nothing that can be compared to these early Irish manuscripts, and those that were produced by their pupils in England. Wyatt, in a curt description of the famous Book of Kells, says that he tried to make a copy of some of its ornaments, but broke down in despair. "In one space of about a quarter of an inch superficial, he counted, with a magnifying glass, no less than one hundred and fifty-eight interlacements of a very slender ribbon pattern, formed of white lines, edged by black ones, upon a black ground." In this book, which he studied for hours, he never detected a false line or an irregular interlacement. Giraldus Cambrensis, a learned Welsh ecclesiastic of the twelfth century, who had carefully examined some of the Irish manuscripts at Kildare, says that the writer of this Book of Kells made the drawings from designs furnished by angels through the intercession of St. Bridget. Timms and Wyatt, *Art of Illumination*, p. 14.

The copyists of the middle ages may be properly divided in two classes: the class that considered copying an irksome duty and that did its work mechanically and badly; the class that treated book-making as a purely artistic occupation, and gave the most time and care to ornamentation. The book-makers who made search for authentic copies, comparing the

The Scriptorium.
[From Lacroix.]

different texts of books and correcting their errors, did not appear until after the invention of printing. The mechanical drudges, who were always most numerous, not only repeated the errors of their faulty copies, but added to them. Errors became so frequent that some of the more careful and conscientious copyists thought it necessary to repeat at the end of every book the solemn adjuration of Irenæus:

I adjure thee who shall transcribe this book, by our Lord Jesus Christ, and by his glorious coming to judge the quick and dead, that thou compare what thou transcribest, and correct it carefully according to the copy from which thou transcribest, and that thou also annex a copy of this adjuration to what thou hast written.

The illustration annexed, the fac-simile of a few lines from a Latin Bible written in the ninth century, is a fair example of the carelessness of many mechanical copyists. The words *In illo tempore* are not to be found in correct copies of the Vulgate;[1] the very awkward writing, the running together of words, the unnecessary contractions, and the misuse of capital letters, are flagrant blemishes that call for no comment.

INILLO TEPR.
ERat homo expharisei nichodem'
nomine princeps iudeorum.
Hic uenit ad ihm nocte et dixit ei

The Penmanship of a Copyist of the Ninth Century.
[From Lacroix.]

The letters of this book are of the Roman form, as had been commanded by Charlemagne; but this form of writing gradually went out of use, not only in France, but even in Italy and Spain. The unskillful writers who could not properly produce the plain lines and true curves of Roman letters, tried to hide the ungainliness of their awkwardly constructed characters by repeated touches of the pen, which made them bristle with angles. In the golden age of pointed architecture and superfluous ornamentation, this fault became a fashion. The pointed letters became known as ecclesiastic letters, and then there seemed to be a special propriety in putting finials and crockets on the letters of books of piety. It is to the failing skill and bad taste of inexpert copyists more than to their desire to construct an improved form of writing, that

[1] The text as it now appears in authorized copies of the Vulgate is: *Erat autem homo ex Pharisæis, Nicodemus nomine, princeps Judæorum. Hic venit ad Jesum nocte, et dixit ei.* John I, 3.

we may trace the origin of the Black or Gothic letter,[1] which, under a great many names and modifications, was employed in all books until supplanted by the Roman types of Jenson.

The copyists and calligraphers were stimulated to do their best by the religious zeal of wealthy laymen who frequently gave to religious houses large sums of money for the copying and ornamentation of books. It was taught that the gift of an illuminated book, or of the means to make it, was an act of piety which would be held in perpetual remembrance. For the medieval books of luxury thus made to order, the finest vellum was selected. The size most in fashion was that now known as demy folio, of which the leaf is about ten inches wide and fifteen inches long, but smaller sizes were often made. The space to be occupied by the written text was mapped out with faint lines, so that the writer could keep his letters on a line, at even distance from each other and within the prescribed margin. Each letter was carefully drawn, and filled in or painted with repeated touches of the pen. With good taste, black ink was most frequently selected for the text; red ink was used only for the more prominent words, and the catch-letters, then known as the rubricated letters. Sometimes texts were written in blue, green, purple, gold or silver inks, but it was soon discovered that texts in bright color were not so readable as texts in black.

When the copyist had finished his sheet, he passed it to the designer, who sketched the border, pictures and initials. The sheet was then given to the illuminator, who painted it.

[1] Petrarch's detestation of pointed letters and their admirers is amusing. After complaining of the difficulty he met in getting a fair copy of his writings, he commends the workmanship of a copyist to whom he applied, a penman who wrote Roman letters with great neatness.

His writing is not labored and tortured. It is suitable for our age, and, indeed, for all ages. Young people, always giddy, admirers of frivolity, despisers of useful things, have adopted the fashion of writing in bristling and undecipherable letters, of which accomplishment they are very proud. To me, these medleys and jumbles of angled letters, riding one on another, make nothing but a mess of confusion which the writer himself must read with difficulty. Whoever buys work of this character, buys not a book, but an unreadable farrago of letters.

The ornamentation of a medieval book of the first class is beyond description by words or by wood-cuts. Every inch of space was used. Its broad margins were filled with quaint ornaments, sometimes of high merit, admirably painted in vivid colors. Grotesque initials, which, with their flourishes, often spanned the full height of the page, or broad bands of floriated tracery that occupied its entire width, were the only indications of the changes of chapter or of subject. In printers' phrase, the composition was "close-up and solid" to the extreme degree of compactness. The uncommonly free use of red ink for the smaller initials was not altogether a matter of taste; if the page had been written entirely in black ink, it would have been unreadable through its blackness. This nicety in writing consumed much time, but the medieval copyist was seldom governed by considerations of time or expense. It was of little consequence whether the book he transcribed would be finished in one or in ten years. It was required only that he should keep at his work steadily and do his best. His skill is more to be commended than his taste. Many of his initials and borders were outrageously inappropriate for the text for which they were designed. The gravest truths were hedged in with the most childish conceits. Angels, butterflies, gob-

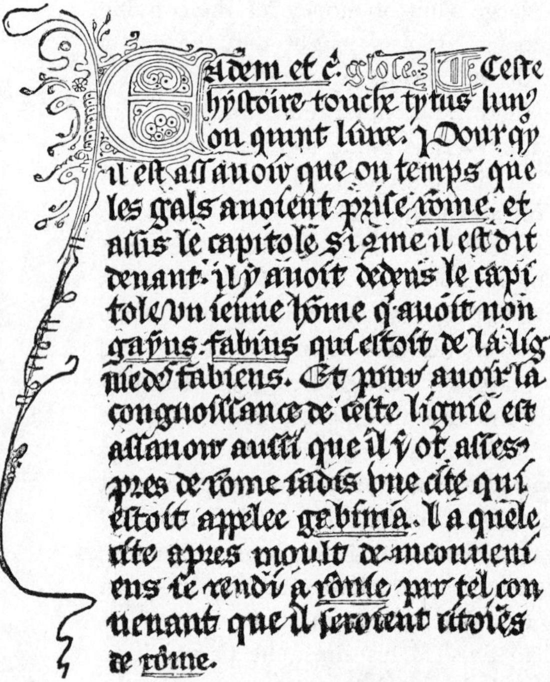
Eadem et c. glose. Ceste
hystoire touche tytus livi'
ou quint livre. Pour qy
il est assavoir que ou temps que
les gals avoient prise rome. et
assis le capitole si comme il est dit
devant. il y avoit dedens le capi
tole un ieune homme q avoit non
gayus. fabius qui estoit de la lig
nee des fabiens. Et pour avoir la
congnoissance de ceste lignie est
assavoir aussi que il y ot asses
pres de rome iadis une cite qui
estoit appelee gebinia. La quele
cite apres moult de inconveni
ens se rendi a rome par tel con
venant que il seroient citoiens
de rome.

A French Manuscript of the Fifteenth Century.
[From Lacroix.]

lins, clowns, birds, snails and monkeys, sometimes in artistic, but much oftener in grotesque, and sometimes in highly offensive positions, are to be found in the illuminated borders of copies of the gospels and the writings of the fathers.

The book was bound by the forwarder, who sewed the leaves and put them in a cover of leather or velvet; by the finisher, who ornamented the cover with gilding and enamel. The annexed illustration of bookbinding, published by Amman in his *Book of Trades*, puts before us many of the implements still in use. The forwarder, with his customary apron of leather, is in the foreground, making use of a plow-knife for trimming the edges of a book. The lying-press which rests obliquely against the block before him contains a book that has received the operation of backing-up from a queer-shaped hammer lying upon the floor. The workman at the end of the room is sewing together the sections of a book, for sewing was properly regarded as a man's work, and a scientific operation altogether beyond the capacity of the raw seamstress. The work of the finisher is not represented, but the brushes, the burnishers, the sprinklers and the wheel-shaped gilding tools hanging against the wall leave us in no doubt as to their use. There is an air of antiquity about everything connected with this bookbindery which suggests the thought that its tools

Medieval Bookbinding.
[From Jost Amman.]

and usages are much older than those of printing. Chevillier says that seventeen professional bookbinders found regular employment in making up books for the University of Paris, as early as 1272. Wherever books were produced in quantities, bookbinding was set apart as a business distinct from that of copying.

The poor students who copied books for their own use were also obliged to bind them, which they did in a simple but efficient manner, by sewing together the folded sheets, attaching them to narrow parchment bands, the ends of which were made to pass through a cover of stout parchment, at the joint near the back. The ends of the bands were then pasted down under the stiffening sheet of the cover, and the book was pressed. Sometimes the cover was made flexible by the omission of the stiffening sheet; sometimes the edges of the leaves were protected by flexible and overhanging flaps which were made to project over the covers; or by the insertion in the covers of stout leather strings with which the two covers were tied together. Ornamentation was entirely neglected, for a book of this character was made for use and not for show. These methods of binding were mostly applied to small books intended for the pocket: the workmanship was rough, but the binding was strong and serviceable.

The Medieval Illuminator.
[From Jost Amman.]

Books of larger size, made for the lecturn, were bound up in boards—not an amalgamation of hard-pressed oakum, tar, and paper-pulp, but veritable boards of planed wood, which were never less than one-quarter inch, and sometimes were two inches in thickness.[1] The sheets encased in these boards were gathered in sections usually of five double leaves. The sections were sewed on rounded raw-hide bands protected from cutting or cracking by a braided casing of thread. A well-bound medieval book is a model of careful sewing: the thread, repeatedly passed in and out of the sections and around the bands, sometimes diagonally from one corner of the book to the other, is caught up and locked in a worked head at the top and bottom of the back. The bands, often fan-tailed at their ends, were pasted and sometimes riveted in the boards. The joints were protected against cracking by broad linings of parchment.

For a book that might receive rough usage, and that did not require a high ornamental finish, hog-skin was selected as the strongest and most suitable covering for the boards. The covers and the back were decorated by marking them with fanciful patterns, lightly burnt in the leather by heated rolls or stamps, from patterns and by processes substantially the same as those used in manufacturing modern account-books. For a book intended to receive an ornamentation of gilded work, calf and goat-skin leathers were preferred. The gilding was done with care, elaborately, artistically, with an excess of minute decoration that is really bewildering, when one considers the sparsity and simplicity of the tools in use. To protect the gilding on the sides, the boards were often paneled or sunk in the centre, and the corners, and sometimes the entire outer edges of the cover, were shielded with thick projecting plates of brass or copper. A large boss of

[1] These boards were sometimes paneled from the inside of the cover. Scaliger tells us that his grandmother had a printed psalter, the cover of which was two fingers thick, containing in an interior panel a silver crucifix. Hansard says that he had seen an old book which contained in a similar recess a human toe, obviously a sacred relic of value.

brass in the centre, with smaller bosses or buttons upon the corners, was also used to protect the gilding from abrasion. On the cheaper books, bound in hog-skin, iron corners and a closely set studding of round-headed iron nails were used for the same purpose. To prevent the covers from warping outward, two clasps of brass were attached to the covers.

A Sumptuously Bound Book.[1]
[From Chambers.]

The book thus bound was too weighty to be held in the hand; it was so full of angles and knobs that it could not be placed upon a flat table without danger of scratching it. For the safety of the book and the convenience of the reader, it was necessary that the book should be laid on an inclined desk or a revolving lecturn, provided with a ledge for holding it up and with holdfasts for keeping down the leaves. The lecturn was really required for the protection of the reader. Petrarch, when reading an unwieldy volume of the *Epistles of Cicero*, which he held in his hands, and in which he was

[1] This is one of the finest existing specimens of antique bookbinding in the National Library at Paris. It is a work of the eleventh century, and encases a book of prayers in a mass of gold, jewels and enamels. The central object is sunk like a framed picture, and represents the Crucifixion, the Virgin and St. John on each side of the cross, and above it the veiled busts of Apollo and Diana; thus exhibiting the influence of the older Byzantine school, which is, indeed, visible throughout the entire design. This subject is executed on a thin sheet of gold, beaten up from behind into high relief, and chased upon its surface. A rich frame of jeweled ornament surrounds this object, portions of the decoration being further enriched with colored enamels; the angles are filled in with enameled emblems of the evangelists; the ground of the whole design enriched by threads and foliations of delicate gold wire. Chambers, *Book of Days.*

profoundly interested, repeatedly let the book slip and fall, and so bruised his left leg that he feared, for some time, that he would have to submit to its amputation.

When the book was not in use, it was laid sidewise on the shelf with the flat side fully exposed, showing to best advantage the beauty of the binding. Its metal-studded sides prevented it from being stood upright on the shelf. The book made for common use was frequently covered with oak boards banded with iron. When exposed in church, it was secured to a post or pillar with a chain.

The ornamented cover of the sumptuous book was even more resplendent than its illuminated text. Gilders, jewelers, silversmiths, engravers, and painters took up the work which the binder had left, and lavished upon it all the resources of their arts. A copy of the Evangelists presented by Charlemagne to a church in France, was covered with plates of gold and silver, and studded with gems. To another church the pious sister of Charlemagne gave a book glittering with precious stones, and with appropriate engraving upon a great agate in the centre of the cover. We read of another book of devotion covered with plates of selected ivory, upon which was sculptured, in high relief, with questionable propriety, an illustration of the Feast of Bacchus. The Cluny Museum at Paris contains two book-covers of enameled brass, one of which has on the cover a very elaborate engraving of the Adoration of the Wise Men. Books like these called for the display of a higher degree of

A Medieval Book with Covers of Oak.
[From Chambers.]

The mortise in the cover to the left was for the insertion of the hand when the book was held up for reading.

skill than could be found in monasteries. The mechanics who were called in to perfect the work of the copyists soon became familiar with all the details of book-making. Little by little they encroached on the province of the copyist, and in time became competent to do all his work.

During the twelfth century the ecclesiastical monopoly of book-making began to give way. Literary work had grown irksome. The church had secured a position of supremacy in temporal as well as spiritual matters; it had grown rich, and showed disregard for the spiritual and educational means by which its successes had been made. It began to enjoy its prosperity. The neglect of books by many of the priests of the thirteenth century was authorized by the example and precepts of Francis d'Assisi, who suffered none of his followers to have Bible, breviary or psalter. This new form of asceticism culminated in the establishment of the order of the Mendicant Friars, which, in its earlier days, was wonderfully popular. Founded for the purpose of supplying the spiritual administrations which had been sadly neglected by the beneficed clergy, who were not only ignorant but corrupt,[1] the new order ultimately

Book-Cover in Ivory, Byzantine Style.
[From Berjeau.]

[1] Wickliffe says that, in 1380, there were in England many "unable curates that kunnen not the ten commandments, ne read their sauter, ne understand a verse of it." The author of the *Plowman's Tale* accuses the clergy of faults worse than that of ignorance.

became even more neglectful of duty, more ignorant and more immoral. The leaders of the friars were men of piety, and some of them, disregarding the precept of the zealous founder of the order, were students and collectors of books; but the inferior clergy, with few exceptions, were extremely ignorant. They not only exerted a mischievous influence upon the people, but they showed to priests of other orders that the knowledge to be had from books was not really necessary. The class of monks who had devoted their lives to the copying, binding and ornamenting of books, imitated as far as they could the example set by the pleasure-loving, ignorant friars, and sought opportunities for relaxation.[1] The care of libraries was neglected for pleasures of a grosser nature. The duties of copyists and librarians passed, gradually and almost imperceptibly, into the hands of the laity.

The business of selling books, which had been given up during the decline of the Roman empire, re-appeared in the latter part of the twelfth century in the neighborhood of the new Italian universities of Padua and Bologna. To have the privilege of selling books to the students, the booksellers were

[1] Boccaccio, one of the enthusiasts of the fourteenth century in the labor of collecting the forgotten manuscripts of classical authors, has told the following characteristic story about the neglect of libraries and the abuse of books by the constituted conservators of literature. When traveling in Apulia, Boccaccio was induced to visit the convent of Mount Cassino and its then celebrated library. He respectfully addressed a monk who seemed the most approachable, begging that he would open to him the library. But the monk, pointing to a high staircase, said, in a harsh voice, "Go up; the library is open." Ascending the staircase with gladness, Boccaccio came to a hall, to which there was neither door nor bar to protect the treasures of the library. What was his astonishment when he saw that the windows were obstructed with plants which had germinated in the crevices, and that all the books and all the shelves were thickly covered with dust. With still greater astonishment, he took up book after book, and discovered that in a large number of classical manuscripts entire sections had been torn out. Other books had their broad, white margins cut away to the edges of the text. Full of grief, and with eyes filled with tears, at this sad spectacle of the destruction of the works of wise and famous men, he descended the staircase. Meeting a monk in a cloister, he asked why the books were so mutilated. The monk answered, "This is the work of some of the monks: to earn a few sous, they tear out the leaves and make little psalters, which they sell to the children. With the white margins they make mass-books, which they sell to the women." Benvenuto da Immola, as quoted by Didot, *Essai sur la typographie*, p. 567.

obliged to submit to a stringent discipline. The restrictive legislation of the University of Paris, for four centuries the greatest school of theology and the most renowned of the European universities, may be offered as a suitable illustration of the spirit shown to booksellers by all the schools of the middle ages. Through its clerical teachers, the church claimed the right to control the making, buying and selling of books. It extended its authority over parchment-makers, bookbinders, and every other class of mechanics that contributed in any way to their manufacture. The rules made by this university reveal many curious facts concerning book-making, and teach us, as a recent imperialist author has truly said, that the censorship of books is older than printing.

We command that the stationers,[1] vulgarly called booksellers, shall each year, or every other year, as may be required by the university, take oath to behave themselves honestly and faithfully in all matters concerning the buying, keeping or selling of books. In the year 1342, they were required, touching the price of books, to tell the truth, pure and simple, and without deceit or lying.

No bookseller could buy a book for the purpose of sale, until it had been exposed for five days in the Hall of the University, and its purchase had been declined by all the teachers and scholars.

The prices of books sold by the booksellers were fixed by four master booksellers appointed by the university. Any attempt to get a higher price entailed a penalty. No one could buy or sell books, or lend money on them, without a special permit from the university.

The profit of the bookseller upon the sale of a book was fixed at four deniers when sold to a teacher or scholar, and six deniers when sold to the public.

No *pots-de-vin*, or drink-money, nor gratuities of any kind, were to be exacted by the bookseller in addition to the fixed price.

Books should be made correct to copy, and be sold as correct in good faith. The bookseller should be required to make an oath as to their entire accuracy. Whoever sold incorrect books would be obliged to make the corrections, and would be otherwise punished.

[1] The word stationer which has been adopted in the English language has lost its first meaning in the French. It is here used to define a trader who sold books and all kinds of writing materials in a station, shop or store, in contradistinction to a class of peddlers or clerks who had no store or place of business, but who acted as couriers or agents between the buyer and maker.

No bookseller should refuse to lend a book to the student who wished to make a new copy from it, and who offered security and complied with the terms fixed by the university.[1]

Seal of the Masters and Scholars of the University of Paris.
[From Lacroix.]

Before any newly written book could be offered for sale, it must be submitted to the rector of the university, who had the power to suppress it,[2] or correct it, and who, if it was approved, fixed its price.

[1] The prices allowed to stationers in 1303 for the use of their copies seem pitiably small. A treatise on the *Gospel of Matthew*, 37 pages, was priced at 1 sol; *Gospel of Mark*, 20 pages, at 17 deniers; *St. Thomas on Metaphysics*, 53 pages, at 3 sols; a treatise on *Canon Law*, 120 pages, at 7 sols; *St. Thomas on the Soul*, 19 pages, at 13 deniers.

[2] If the book was objectionable, it was burned and the author was imprisoned. According to the Roman law, the condemnation of death attached not only to the author and buyer of a proscribed book, but to him who chanced to find it and did not burn it. In 1328, Pope John XXII condemned two authors who had written a book in eight chapters, full of grievous heresies—for they had undertaken to prove that the Emperor Louis of Bavaria had the right to discipline, install or depose the pope at his own pleasure, and that all the property of the church was held by it through the sufferance of the Emperor. Lacroix, *Histoire de l'imprimerie*, p. 26.

It does not surprise us to learn that the stationers did not thrive. Under the hard pressure of taxation and censorship, the imposition of arbitrary prices and compulsory loans, they found it very difficult to earn a living. They were obliged to add another business to that of book-publishing. A few became notaries; some sold furs, while their wives in the same shop sold "fripperies and like haberdashery"; others became the dressers of parchments and binders of books. Against these innovations the regents of the university made unavailing protest, severely censuring the base booksellers who "did not uphold the dignity of their profession, but who mixed it up with vile trades." But the necessities of the half-starved booksellers compelled the university to overlook the offense.

The best and largest books of the stationers were always of a theological nature. In a list given by Chevillier of the books sold in the fourteenth century by the booksellers to the university, are found in the foremost place, books on the *Canon Law*, the *Homilies of St. Gregory*, the *Book of Sacraments*, the *Confessions of St. Augustine*, the *Homilies of St. Augustine*, the *Compendium of Thomas Aquinas*,[1] and *St. Thomas on Metaphysics*, on *Physics*, on *Heaven and Earth*, on the *Soul.* Copies of the Gospels or the Scriptures, or even of the works of classical authors, were not in high request. The most popular books were elementary works on grammar and philosophy, for the use of students, and devotional works like creeds, catechisms, and prayers, which were largely bought by the more pious part of the people that were able to read.

The copyists made books for the more ignorant priests, books containing a synopsis of Christian faith and doctrine, or descriptions of important events recorded in the Scriptures. As an additional refreshment of the memory, and to make them more enticing to the buyer, these books were profusely illustrated with pen-and-ink drawings. The *Bible of the Poor*, and the *Mirror of Man's Redemption*, afterward popular as

[1] Erasmus, caustically, but truthfully, said of this huge book, "No man can carry it about with him, nor even get it in his head."

printed books, are favorable specimens of a class of illustrated manuscripts in common use among the inferior clergy as far back as the tenth and eleventh centuries. They were sold to the unlearned of the laity and to friars who could not read, but who could understand the allegories taught through the pictures. An increasing fondness for ornamentation and for pictorial illustration may be noticed among both learned and unlearned. Manuscripts of every description were adorned with pictures.[1] Abstruse theological writings and treatises on geometry and philosophy were often decked out with floriated borders and gaudily painted illustrations which would now be considered as suitable only for children. It would seem that it was through the pictorial attractions of a book, more than through its text, that men were led to admire literature.

The copyists made books of small size which were sold to students for trifling sums. Psalters, with leaves no larger than the palm of the hand, were sold for a sol. Elementary school-books, like the *Logic of Boethius*, were sometimes copied in a minute style of penmanship, and were still further contracted with abbreviations until the writing had the appearance of microscopic stenography. The minute penmanship may be regarded as evidence of the great scarcity of parchment, and the abbreviations as indications of the weariness of the writer.

The arbitrary order of the university, which compelled the booksellers to lend their books to scholars, shows that it was customary for a student or a poor man of letters to copy the books he needed. The little books sold for a sol were manifestly made for readers who could not even buy the vellum

[1] The National Library at Paris possesses two manuscript Bibles, of which one volume contains 5,122 pictures. Each picture is explained by two lines, one in Latin and one in French; each line is decorated by an initial and a finial in gold and bright colors. If the cost of each picture with its lines be estimated at sixteen francs (Didot's valuation), the value of this book would be 82,000 francs, exclusive of the cost of parchment, binding and copying. By the same estimate, the value of the second volume would be 50,000 francs. Didot pertinently asks the question: Where can we find, in the printed work of our day, an equal prodigality in illustration? *Essai sur la typographie*, p. 715.

required for a book of the usual size. It was necessary that books sold at this price should be of the cheapest materials, and that the text should be abbreviated by contractions[1] so that it would occupy but little space. The despised fabric of paper, and the remnants of vellum rejected by professional copyists after the skin had been cut up for leaves of folio or of quarto size, were cheerfully accepted by readers who valued a book more for its contents than for its appearance.

The scarcity of vellum in one century, and its abundance in another, are indicated by the size of written papers during the same periods. Before the sixth century, legal documents were usually written upon one side only; in the tenth century the practice of writing upon both sides of the vellum became common. During the thirteenth century, valuable documents were often written upon strips two inches wide and but three and a half inches long. At the end of the fourteenth century these strips went out of fashion. The more general use of paper had diminished the demand for vellum and increased the supply. In the fifteenth century, legal documents on rolls of sewed vellum twenty feet in length were not uncommon. All the valuable books of the fourteenth century were written on vellum. In the library of the Louvre the manuscripts on

[1] Abbreviations which deformed written language to such an extent that it is almost undecipherable to modern readers, were once esteemed a positive merit. The habit of making them was continued after printing was invented. In 1475, a printer of Lubec said, in commendation of one of his own books, that he had made free use of abbreviations, to get the whole work in one volume instead of two—a procedure, he thought, that deserved special praise, for he said that the contractions made the book more readable. The modern reader will be of a different opinion. The *Logic of Ockham*, in folio, printed at Paris in 1488, by Clos-Bruneau, contains, among other abbreviations, this bewildering passage:

(The text as printed.)

Sic hic e fal sm qd ad simplr a e pdu-cibile a Deo g a et silr hic a n g a n e pducibile a Do.

(With words in full.)

Sicut hic est fallacia secundum quid ad simpliciter. A est producibile a Deo. Ergo A est. Et similiter hic. A non est. Ergo A non est producibile a Deo.

In 1498, John Petit, of Paris, published a dictionary which professed to be *A Guide to the Reading of Abbreviations*. It was not published too soon, for the practice of making contractions had increased to such an extent that books with abbreviations were legible only to experts.

paper, compared to those on vellum, were as one to twenty-eight; in the library of the Dukes of Burgundy, one-fifth of the books were of paper. The increase in the proportion of paper books is a fair indication of the increasing popularity of paper; but it is obvious that vellum was even then considered as the more suitable substance for a book of value.

The esteem with which books were regarded by priests and scholars during the fourteenth century was shared by men of wealth, who coveted books, not so much for their contents as for their pictures, and as evidences of wealth and culture. A remarkable impulse had been given to literature and to the making of books by the troubadours of Southern France. Their songs of love and devotion to women, their encomiums of chivalry, and stories of battle and adventure, which were of their own age, fresh and full of life, and untainted by the influence of withered classical models, had most unbounded popularity in every grade of society. Uncultivated people, who would have yawned over the reading of *Homer* or the *Odes of Horace*, would listen with a keen delight to the songs of a Provençal minstrel, or to the reading of romances about Charlemagne and his Paladins, about Arthur and Merlin, and the Knights of the Round Table. To men who had regarded books only as dull treatises about theology, these romances were revelations of an unsuspected attractiveness in literature. How much these romances increased the respect for books, and led to the making of new copies, and to a more general knowledge of reading and writing, cannot be exactly stated; but their influence on the people was vastly greater than that of the books of the schools. During the fourteenth and fifteenth centuries, bocks about love and chivalry constituted the greater part of the secular literature of Europe. The most popular books of Caxton, the first English printer, and of the early printers of Paris, were of this character. To the ladies of France, the books of love and song were especially attractive. It was largely through their admiration that the workmanship of a new order of book-makers came in fashion.

To please their dainty tastes, copies were made with refinements of calligraphy never before attempted; the unwieldy sizes of folio and quarto were supplanted by small and handy duodecimos, and bindings of a more delicate character were introduced.

The nature of the new literature, and the effeminate taste of the newly made class of readers, seemed to call for changes in the old methods of making books. It was necessary that the massiveness and barbaric splendor of the monastic books should be supplanted by workmanship combining elegance, lightness and delicacy. It was necessary that the illustrations made for the lady's missal, or for a book of romance, should be designed, not by some grim old monk whose imagination had been cramped by his solitary life, and whose narrowness and severity were visible in all his workmanship, but by a courtier, an artist, and man of fashion, who knew the world, who knew how to please it, and how to paint it. To this class of men, the forerunners of courtly artists like Durer, Holbein and Rubens, the manufacture of the new books was intrusted. The new artists in book-making organized a nicer division of labor, and supervised and directed the work at every stage of its progress. A copyist selected for his skill wrote the text in prescribed places on the sheets, and, by the uniformity of his penmanship, gave character and connection to the work; one designer sketched the borders, and another outlined the initials; an illuminator filled in the outlines with gold-leaf and bright colors. Then came the artist, or miniaturist, who drew the illustrations and painted the fine pictures which gave the book its great charm. The artists were called miniaturists because their illustrations were miniature pictures, as artistically designed, and always more carefully painted than larger paintings made for the adornment of churches, halls and picture galleries. Avoiding the hard outlines and glaring pigments of the illuminator, the miniaturist painted in low tints, and with the nicest attention to harmony of color. The beauty of the work, which has been but little affected by time, is recognized to this day. The sheets which had been so artistically painted were as elegantly bound. They were covered with silk, velvet, satin, or bright-colored leather, embroidered with gold and pearls, studded with buttons of gold, banded on the corners with shields, and secured with clasps of precious metals engraved and enameled in the very finest style of decorative art. Admirable as the books are, they do not give us a high opinion of the intelligence of the artists, nor of the culture of their owners, for they are full of anachronisms and absurdities in the pictures and in the text.

This taste for elegant books, which began in the thirteenth century, became a princely amusement. In 1373, Charles V of France was the owner of more than nine hundred[1] books, most of which were written on fine vellum, superbly bound, and adorned with precious stones and clasps of silver or gold. His brothers fostered the same taste. Philip the Bold, Duke of Burgundy, gathered around him artists, authors, copyists, and bookbinders, and established a great library. His son, John the Fearless, largely increased it, but the most costly additions were made by Philip the Good, who, at the middle of the fifteenth century, enjoyed the distinction of possessing the most magnificent books in Western Europe. Books of equal beauty were also made in Italy, but there was no part of Europe where calligraphers, miniaturists and ornamental bookbinders found a higher appreciation of their skill than in Burgundy and the Netherlands. Nor did this taste for fine

[1] From a catalogue still extant, it appears that this library was composed chiefly of romances, legends, histories, and treatises on astrology, geometry and chiromancy. It was then valued at 2,223 French livres, rather more than the same number of pounds sterling. At this time, the price of a cow was about eight shillings, and of a horse about twenty shillings.—It is difficult to ascertain the real value of the money of the middle ages. Coins were frequently clipped to light weight by knavish traders, and were oftener debased at the mint when the royal treasury was low. Sellers everywhere knew that the value of a coin was not in its stamp, but in its quantity of silver, and they altered prices to meet the altered value of coin. But even in its most debased form, the silver coin of the middle ages had a very high purchasing capacity.

books soon go out of fashion. The business of making fine manuscript books was not entirely destroyed by the invention of printing. Lacroix, a French antiquary,[1] has shown us that copyists, illuminators, designers and painters found employment in the embellishment of books even as late as the last quarter of the seventeenth century.

During the middle ages, books of merit were everywhere sold at enormous prices. Illustrated and illuminated volumes in elegant bindings seem specially exorbitant, when we consider the greater purchasing capacity of money. Daunou says, that in a computation of the value of a large library of the fourteenth century, the average price of each manuscript book should be fixed at about 450 francs. Didot says that, of three hundred books contained in the library at Ratisbon, during the year 1231, the average price of each book was 600 francs. What proportion should be allowed for binding and illumination is not stated, but it can be proved that copying could not have been the labor of greatest expense. In the fourteenth century the price of copying a Bible at Bologna, exclusive of the value of binding, parchment and illumination, was 80 Bolognese livres. In the fifteenth century, the price of copying was steadily declining, while the prices of illuminating and binding were increasing.

Books were expensive, not so much through the labor of the copyist, who did the simplest and cheapest part of the work, but through the extravagant ornamentation put on

[1] He has given an extract from an ecclesiastical account book in which are found the items of expense for the making, binding, and presentation of the manuscript book *Royal Chants* to Princess Louise of Savoy.

To Jacques Plastel, for sketching the designs for forty-eight pictures, 45 livres; to Jehan Pichou, illuminator, for coloring the designs, 80 livres; to workmen of Jehan Pichou, 50 sols, and for *vin du marché* (in colloquial English, *treating* or drink money) with illuminator Pichou, 24 sols; to Jean de Béguines, priest, for engraving the ballads, 12 livres; to Guy-le-Flamenc, for illuminating the large initial letters, 13 livres, 3 sols; for vellum, 3 livres, 12 sols; for the binding, expenses of presentation to Louise of Savoy, and the journey to Amboise, 68 livres, 8 sols. Sum total, 366 livres. Lacroix, *Histoire de l'imprimerie*, p. 47.

them by the illuminator and the binder. The true office of the book was perverted. It was regarded, not as a medium of instruction, but as a means for the display of wealth and artistic tastes. The reader was really taught to value it more for its dress than for its substance; the book-maker was most appreciated when he made books so expensive that they were out of the reach of ordinary buyers. To the modern book-buyer, the prices asked for books of size and merit during the middle ages seem excessive, and especially so when they are contrasted with the prices then paid for food or labor.[1]

At the end of the fourteenth century, books of instruction were larger, more ornamental, and, to the unschooled reader, more pedantic and more forbidding than ever. We do not find in them any valuable contributions to knowledge, nor do we discover in the writers or teachers of the day any disposition to make knowledge easy to be acquired. The love of great books during this period, frequently noticed as one of the evidences of a true revival of literature, is, when critically examined, evidence only of the artistic tastes of book-buyers and of the exclusiveness of scholars. So far from paving the way for the introduction of printing, this trifling with litera-

[1] Stow says that a Bible "fairly written" was sold in 1274, in England, for 50 marks, equal to about 33 pounds. At this time a laborer's wages were 1½d. per day, and a sheep could be had for a shilling. — Roger Bacon, who died in 1292, said that he had spent more than 2,000 pounds for books. At this time the annual income of an English curate was £3 6s. 8d. — In 1305, the priory of Bolton gave 30 shillings for *The Book of Sentences*, by Peter Lombard. Hallam says that the accounts of the priory show that the jolly monks bought but three books in forty years. He estimates the equivalent in modern money of this 30 shillings at near 40 pounds. — *The Mirror of History*, a work in four volumes, was sold at Paris in 1332, with great formalities, for 40 livres of Paris. — In 1357, *The Scholastic History* was sold to the Earl of Salisbury for 100 marks, or about 67 pounds. At this time the pay of the king's surgeon was fixed at £5 13s. 4d. per annum and a shilling a day besides. — Wickliffe's translation of the *New Testament* was sold in 1380 for 4 marks and 40 pence. — Pierre Plaont bequeathed, in 1415, to the regents of the University of Paris, a big quarto Bible, which he said was worth 15 pounds. Chevillier says that a printed Bible of the same size in the seventeenth century could be had for 6 francs.

ture was one of the most formidable impediments in its path. It made despicable even the thought of an attempt to produce books by the simpler method of printing, then in its first stage of practical development.

The princely patrons of literature, the learned doctors of the universities, the copyists and stationers, the illuminators and miniaturists, must have seen the playing cards and prints then sold in all large cities, and, to some extent, must have known the process by which they were made. But they looked on them with a pitying contempt for the coarse tastes which could be satisfied with such rude workmanship. The distance in degrees of merit between printed playing cards and finely illuminated manuscript books seemed infinite. If the cards conveyed a suggestion of the possibility of printed books, the suggestion was rejected. To the dainty tastes of book-makers printing was a barbarous trade; to the wealthy book-buyer, a printed book would have been the degradation of art and literature. One may look in vain among the book-makers and scholars of the fourteenth century for any sign that heralded the coming of printing. Makers and buyers of books seem to have been fully satisfied with things as they were—with the established methods of book-making, with the organization of society and the state of education. And the professed patrons of literature would have been forever satisfied with this state of affairs. Under their exclusive patronage, books would have been made more and more sumptuously, and put more and more out of the reach of the people.

X

The Preparations for Printing.

Imperfect Preparation of the People of Southern Europe...Repression of Education in England. Early Gropings after Knowledge by English People...The Horn-Book and Clog...Injurious Effects of the Use of Latin in Books...Beginnings of Common Schools...Their Usefulness in Germany and Flanders...Indications of Mental Activity in the Arts...Favorable Condition of Germany as Compared with other States...Profligacy of the Clergy...Growth of Heresy...Early Translations of the Bible...Appreciation of Pictures by the Illiterate...The Dance of Death. Neglect of the People by their Constituted Teachers...Growing use of Paper...Increase of Self-taught Copyists...Guilds of Book-Makers in the North of Europe...Printing as an Aid to Writing...Printing Delayed by Considerations of Expense...Could not be Introduced until there were a Multitude of Readers...Books of Pictures preceded Books of Letters.

No great fact, no social state, makes its appearance complete and at once; it is formed slowly, successively; it is the result of a multitude of different facts of different dates and origins, which modify and combine themselves in a thousand ways before constituting a whole, presenting itself in a clear and a systematic form, receiving a special name, and standing through a long life. *Guizot.*

TO THE careless observer of the growth of learning and the state of the mechanical arts at the beginning of the fifteenth century, Italy might be regarded as the nation best prepared to receive and maintain any new method of book-making. The neatly engraved initial letters in manuscript books, the designs printed in many colors on woven fabrics, and the extended manufacture of images and playing cards, prove that the Italians knew how to print from blocks, and that they had mechanical skill in abundance. In spite of her civil wars, Italy was rich and prosperous, and famous all over the world, not only for her universities and learned men, but for the cultured tastes of her people. It would appear that all the conditions for the coming of block-book printing had been filled, and that its introduction should have followed as a consequence. But the conditions were only partly met.

To be ultimately successful, it was requisite that printing should begin with the plainest work, and that it should be adapted to the demands of very plain people; but the tastes of Italians were refined, and they could not tolerate rudeness in any form. With all its skill, wealth and culture, there was in Italy no true middle class, and, consequently, no suitable basis for the upholding of an art like xylography. The spirit which Woltmann has specified as the basis of printing,—"the impulse to make each mental gain a common blessing,"—was entirely wanting. As the professional book-makers, who were of the people, did nothing for the advancement of their order, the development of Italian printing had to stop with printed cards, cloths and images. The skill of Italian engravers culminated, not, as it did in Germany, in popular block-books, but in the more artistic and exclusive branch of copper-plate printing. The efforts of Italian scholars to revive the study of classical authors, however useful they may have been to the people of other countries, ended in Italy with a widening of the gulf that separated the ignorant from the educated. For the benefits of printed books, Italy is indebted to the skill of German printers, whose early productions had been excluded from Venice at the petition of her querulous card-makers.

It may seem equally strange that block-book printing was not invented in Spain, where textile fabrics were printed, and where paper was more largely made and used than in any portion of Europe. We there find schools, libraries, and signs of great mental activity. In poetry, architecture, music and other fine arts, the people of Spain were as advanced as the French or Italians. But the love of books, and the culture that comes only from their study, were not firmly rooted in the life and habits of common people. The education and social elevation of the few had been secured at the expense of the many, and literature and the literary arts had been so refined that they were in decay. Nothing seems to have been done to pave the way for the introduction of xylographic printing by attempts to educate the people.

The intellectual development of France resembled that of Italy and Spain—it was a development of the literature of the church, and of effeminate tastes among the wealthy, but from these the people derived no benefit. France was then passing through the horrors of what French historians call the "Hundred Years' War" with England, during which her population decreased at an alarming rate, and many of her arts and industries were irreparably injured. The princes and nobles were waging against each other a war of treason and assassination; the peasantry, on whom feudal laws pressed more severely than they did on any other people, broke out in the insurrection of the *Jacquerie*. In 1407, the pope laid the kingdom under interdict, and the withdrawal of the ministrations of the church were added to the horrors of civil and servile war and the miseries of foreign invasion. It was not a time for cultivating the arts of peace. There is, therefore, no block-book of the fifteenth century in the French language, and there is no reason to believe that any block-book printer ever attempted to establish his business on French territory.

Of all the states of Western Europe, England seems to have been most unfitted for the reception of printing. There were a few ecclesiastics who saw the importance of books, and who tried to found libraries, but the greater part of the clergy were very ignorant. They would not learn, nor would they allow common people to be taught. It was unlawful, even as late as 1412, for laborers, farmers and mechanics to send their children to school. A great opportunity for popular education was presented in Wickliffe's translation of the Bible, which could have been made an effective means for diffusing the knowledge of letters among a religious people. But in 1415 it was enacted that they who read the Scriptures in the mother tongue should be hanged for treason, and burned for heresy.

In spite of all these impediments, there was a slow but positive diffusion of knowledge among English people. How the knowledge was communicated is not clear, for notices of common schools in England, and indeed on the Continent, are infrequent and unsatisfactory. We have, however, some curious relics of the substitutes for books used by the people. One of them is the *Horn-Book*,[1] by which the children were taught their letters and the Lord's Prayer. The engraving annexed represents a book that is of no earlier date than the reign of Charles I, but it is a trustworthy illustration of the construction, if not of the matter, of the horn-books in use in the fifteenth century. Another of these substitutes is the *Clog*, a rude contrivance for marking the order of coming days, which may be considered as the forerunner of the printed almanac.

An English Horn-Book.

[From Chambers.]

[1] The horn-book was the primer of our ancestors, established by common use. It consisted of a single leaf, containing on one side the alphabet, large and small, in black letter or in Roman, with, perhaps, a small regiment of monosyllables, and the words of the Lord's Prayer. This leaf was usually set in a frame of wood, with a slice of diaphanous horn in front — hence the name horn-book. Generally, there was a handle to hold it by, and this handle had usually a hole for a string, whereby the horn-book was slung to the girdle of the scholar. It was frequently noticed by early chroniclers. Chambers, *Book of Days*.

The standard of English education was low, even in the universities. An eminent Italian man of letters, in England in 1420, complains of the scarcity of good books, and is not at all respectful to English scholars.[1] The Universities of Oxford and Cambridge had been established rather more than three hundred years, but they taught bad Latin. There were few books of merit in the English language: Wickliffe's translation of the Bible, and the poems of Chaucer, Lydgate and Gower, are all that deserve any notice. There was, as yet, no universally spoken English language: French was the language of the English nobility and of English courts and books of law, as late as the year 1362; merchants and mercantile companies kept their books in French; boys at school were required to translate

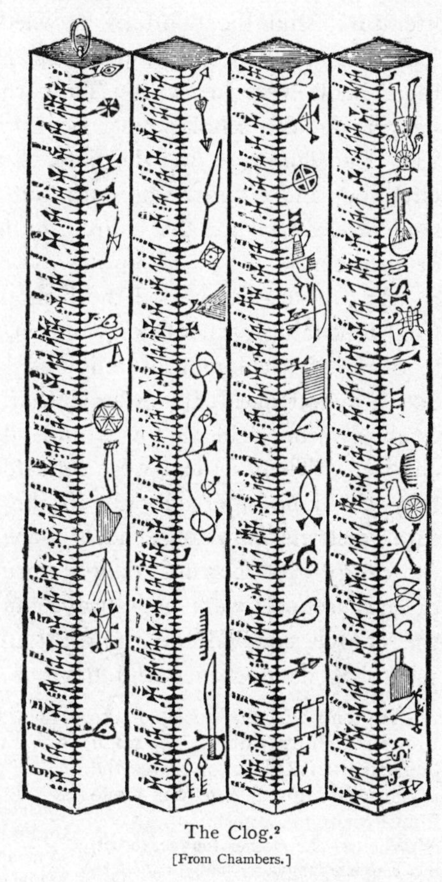

The Clog.[2]
[From Chambers.]

[1] Men given up to sensuality we may find in abundance, but very few lovers of learning, and those barbarous, skilled more in quibbles and sophisms than in literature. Poggio, as quoted by Hallam.

[2] It was a square stick of hard wood, and about eight inches long. The entire series of days constituting the year was represented by notches running along the angles of the square block, each side and angle thus presenting three months; the first day of a month was marked by a notch having a patulous stroke turned up from it, and each Sunday was distinguished by a notch somewhat broader than usual. The feasts were denoted by symbols resembling hieroglyphics. Chambers, *Book of Days*.

Latin into French.[1] The habitual employment of French as the language of the nobility, and of Latin as the language of literature, shut the doors of knowledge on those who spoke English only. In all countries the elementary text books of the schools were in Latin. To learn arithmetic, grammar or geography, the scholar must begin with the study of Latin. The dead language was the path to all knowledge: it was a circuitous and a wearisome path, but it was traveled by every student destined for the church, or for the profession of law or medicine.

At a very early period the bishops of the Catholic church tried to establish schools for children, but not so much for the teaching of secular as of religious knowledge. In the year 800 a synod at Mentz ordered that parochial priests should establish schools in all towns and villages to teach letters to children. These orders were repeated by other councils, but they could be enforced only in the larger cities. In many rural districts common schools were entirely unknown. As the clergy grew corrupt, they were neglected in cities.[2] The primary schools were not always taught by ecclesiastics, but the church claimed the right to supervise them, and made sure that its doctrines and dogmas should be fully taught.

[1] An entry in the books of the Brewers' Company during the reign of Henry V (1415–1430), states the reasons why this change was made from French to English.

Whereas our mother tongue, to wit, the English language, hath in modern days begun to be honorably enlarged and adorned, for that our most excellent King Henry V hath, in his letters missive, and in divers affairs, touching his own person, more willingly chosen to declare the secrets of his will; and, for the better understanding of the people, hath, with a diligent mind, procured the common idiom, setting aside others, to be commended by the exercise of writing; and there are many of our craft of brewers who have the knowledge of writing and reading in the same English idiom, but in others, to wit, the Latin and French, before these times used, they do not in any wise understand; for which causes, with many others, it being considered how that the greater part of the lords and trusty commons have begun to make their matters to be noted down in our mother tongue, so we also, in our own craft, following in some manner their steps, have decreed in future to commit to memory the needful things which concern us.

[2] In 1446, a petition was presented to the English parliament, to consider the great number of grammar schools that sometime were in divers parts of this realm, besides those that were in London, and how few there are in these days. Knight, *The Old Printer and Modern Press*.

These schools seem to have been most useful where they were not overshadowed by great institutions of learning. In the German countries that bordered on the Rhine, and more especially in the Netherlands, where there were no universities, and where the people had a large measure of personal liberty, we find many evidences of a steady progress in education,[1] and of improvement in social condition. The simple teachings of the schools were received by a plain but utilitarian people who put the knowledge to practical use. The newly developed mental activity did not run to waste, as it did in the universities, in unprofitable metaphysical speculations; it was at once applied to the varied requirements of art, trade and manufactures. When printing came, the common people were fully prepared for it, prepared not only to read books, but to make them. The invention was developed in proper order, and was preceded by improvements in mechanical arts.

As illustrations of this mental activity, it is not out of place to mention some of the many inventions of the men who had studied books only to aid them in studying things. We find gunpowder and fire-arms, glass windows and mirrors, clocks and watches, and numerous contrivances that add to the comforts of social life, some of which, like the tinning of iron, and the putting of chimneys to fireplaces, have seemed too paltry to deserve notice. Trivial as they may seem, when in contrast with the steam engine and railroad, the chimney and window were of the highest service as aids in bringing men from a qualified barbarism to civilization. It cannot be

[1] In the Netherlands we find the earliest development of the high school. The schools of the Brethren of the Life-in-Common, founded by Gerard Groot of Deventer, in 1385, which were forty-five in number in 1430, and double that number in 1460, were the first nurseries of literature in Germany. The fruits of this attention to education were freely gathered in the fifteenth and sixteenth centuries. The entire Bible was printed in the Flemish or Dutch language within the first thirty-six years of the sixteenth century in fifteen editions. . . . Thirty-four editions of the New Testament in that language alone appeared within the same period. . . . . There can be no sort of comparison between the number of these editions, and consequently the eagerness of the people of the Low Countries for biblical knowledge, considering the limited extent of their language, and anything that could be found in the Protestant States of the [German] Empire. Hallam, *Literature of Europe*, chap. VI, sec. 38.

proved that these contrivances were invented in Germany, but it is certain that they were there appreciated and used when they were entirely unknown in parts of Europe then supposed to be much more enlightened.[1]

The Germans and Flemings were regarded as a boorish people by the more polished Italians. In the artistic education that can be acquired only from intimate association with men of genius and works of art, the Northern people were deficient; but in the knowledge of useful arts, in originality of invention, in patience and thoroughness as manufacturers, they were superior. The Germans made linen, glass, carved wooden-ware, and useful articles of all kinds needed in home life. In the construction of fine mechanisms, like clocks and curious automatons, they had no rivals. The Flemings were celebrated as weavers, cutlers, goldsmiths, armorers, engravers of silver-ware, and as carvers of wood and stone. They were more than skillful mechanics.[2] Hubert and John Van Eyck, founders of the Flemish school of painting, and instructors of eminent Italian artists, may be regarded as representatives of the practical Flemish character, for they considered no branch of the arts of design as unworthy their attention; they painted on glass as well as on wood or canvas; they illuminated missals, and, as many bibliographers believe, made designs on wood for the engravers of block-books.

[1] Æneas Sylvius (subsequently Pope Pius II), writing near the middle of the fifteenth century, said that the kings of Scotland would rejoice to be as comfortably lodged as the second class of citizens of Nuremberg. Hallam says that Pope Pius also praised their well-furnished and splendid dwellings, their easy mode of living, the security of their rights and the just equality of their laws.

[2] Flanders, during the fifteenth century, was the richest and most densely populated part of Europe. It was famous for the extent of its foreign trade and the variety of its industry. It was not uncommon for one hundred and fifty ships in one day to enter the port of Bruges, in which city were mercantile agents from seventeen different nations. Flanders was full of industries, but its great business was the making of cloth. All the world, wrote an enthusiastic chronicler of the period, is clothed by Flanders. Ghent had fifteen thousand workmen employed on stuffs of wool; Ypres had four thousand makers of cloth; Courtray had six thousand drapers.

The steady progress made by the people of Flanders and Germany in arts and manufactures was largely due to their liberty. They were not altogether exempt from the bondage of feudalism: there was some discord in Germany, and never-ceasing strife between the nobles and middle class, but the German burgher maintained his independence and lived in comfort.[1] The need of peace and personal liberty as preparations for the introduction of printing may be more clearly perceived in a glance at the social condition of the people.

The discontent of common people at their treatment by constituted authorities was never greater than during the last twenty years of the fourteenth century. Southern Europe was afflicted by sanguinary wars, into which the rulers of the people dragged their unwilling peasantry.[2] Armed bands of

[1] As early as the twelfth century, the emperor Henry V undertook to curb the exactions of feudalism by the establishment of free cities, and by the grant of extraordinary privileges to mechanics and manufacturers. To the nobility and petty princes of Germany these privileges were a constant offense, and the occasion of many local strifes; but the burghers were industrious and public-spirited, and took care of their rights. To protect their trade from the rapacity of the princes on the Elbe and the coast, the cities of Germany, in the year 1249, established a mercantile organization, known as the Hanseatic League. In the fifteenth century, this league was constituted of traders from all parts of the Netherlands and Germany. It was so powerful that it monopolized the trade of Northern Europe: by threat of war it compelled Edward VI of England to grant extraordinary concessions; it made successful war against Sweden, Norway and Denmark. The Hanseatic League is a wonderful example of the sudden development of successful legislative and executive ability among men of little or no culture, who till then had been excluded from every position of honor in the state.

[2] Peasants could not claim exemption from arbitrary arrest or military servitude. They had no liberty to choose a residence, to learn a trade, to travel, to go to school, to marry, to keep property, to transact business, or to associate with others in any peaceable enterprise. Practically, they were but little better than slaves. Beaumanoir, a French jurist of the thirteenth century, defines the nature of their servitude in the plainest words. He says that:

> The third estate of man is that of such as are not free; and these are not all of one condition, for some are so subject to their lord, that he may take all they have, alive or dead, and imprison them whenever he pleases, being accountable to none but God; from others the lord can take nothing but the customary payments, though at their death all they have escheats to him.

discharged soldiers roamed about, robbing and murdering at will. Nobles secure in their castles sent out soldiers to make forays in adjacent districts, with no more pretext of law than is claimed by pirates. Outside of large cities there was no safety for life or property. To add to the general misery, famine desolated the most fruitful countries, and in some districts, the awful pestilence of the black death swept away half the population. Where the suffering was greatest, the people rebelled, but to no purpose. In France, the insurgents of the *Jacquerie*, in 1358, were massacred with savage ingenuity in cruelty;[1] in England, the Wat Tyler revolt of 1381 was put down with violence, and the people were remanded to the old villeinage.[2] In countries where there was no outbreak, a sullen resentment grew up against all authority, but more especially against that of the established church. The exactions and scandalous manners of the superior clergy afforded a sufficient provocation. There were two popes—one at Rome and one at Avignon; in many dioceses were rival bishops, holding authority under the rival popes. The heads of the church were at enmity with each other, and they ruled over God's heritage with the weapons and the spirit of temporal princes. The tribute of money which had been delayed or refused by recusant bishops, and the tribute of homage which had been denied by excommunicated kings or emperors, were paid in the misery and blood of the people. In the prolonged disputes between pope and king, and pope and anti-pope, the pious and loyal, who had been taught to honor those who were in authority, were unable to discern which of the two contestants was the true and which the false pope or bishop.

[1] The determination to keep the peasants enslaved was stronger than all enmities. During the insurrection of the *Jacquerie*, the English knights who accompanied King Edward III in his invasion of France made truce with the French nobles, and joined them in putting down this rebellion. Froissart, the chronicler of chivalry, admired this exhibition of magnanimity. For the sufferings of the peasants he has no sympathy.

[2] "Villeins you have been, villeins you are, and shall be,"—said King Richard to the miserable peasantry of Essex, after the killing of Wat Tyler,—"not as before, but in a bondage much more bitter."

From the teachings of each pretender the good turned away. The religious sentiment which had been shocked at the outrageous behavior of the anointed teachers forsook the old altars. It sought out new faiths and founded new sects.[1]

The teachers of the new sects were unwittingly preparing the people for the coming of printing by enforcing the duty of more careful reading and study of the Holy Scriptures. In the year 1380, Wickliffe completed a translation in English of the entire Bible. At the beginning of the thirteenth century, copies of a translation of the Scriptures in Provençal French, made by or under the direction of Peter Waldo, a wealthy merchant of Lyons, and the founder of the Waldenses, were circulated in Burgundy and upon the borders of the Rhine. There were many new translations, or at least of the gospels and psalms, in other European languages.[2] Men and women

[1] The ecclesiastical history of the thirteenth and fourteenth centuries, says Hallam, teems with sectaries and schismatics, various in their aberrations of opinion, but all concurring in detestation of the established church. The heresy which began during the twelfth century, or earlier, with the Manichees of Bulgaria, was made more and more formidable by the Albigenses of Languedoc, by the Waldenses of France and Germany, by the Vaudois of the Alps, by the Lollards of the Netherlands and England, and afterward by the disciples of John Huss of Bohemia, until the faith of the mass of the people was uprooted from its foundation. In Germany, enthusiastic but mystical priests like Eckhardt, Tauler and Suso, keeping themselves within the pale of the church, weakened its rigid discipline by preaching against the arrogant prerogatives of the clergy, and by commanding a higher worship of the heart and life.

[2] The British Museum contains a Bible in Flemish verse, known as the *Rym Bible*, written by Jacob von Maerlandt of Damne, near Bruges in Flanders. It is a manuscript of the fifteenth century, upon vellum, with ornamented capitals, and is one of many copies of a version of the Scriptures made in the year 1270.

Except the Waldensian translation in the Provençal language, this version is, consequently, the most ancient in existence, in the vernacular, and must have preceded by a century the versions of Raoul de Presles, of John Trevisa or the Hermit of Hampole. . . . . . The British Museum had another manuscript in prose, of parts of a Bible in Flemish, written in the fifteenth century. It is part of a translation made in the early part of the fourteenth century, and was the text used for the Bible printed in Delft in 1477. Sotheby, *Principia Typographica*, vol. III, p. 123.

The British Museum has, also, a manuscript in Flemish of five books of the Old Testament, made in the fourteenth century.

gathered together in secret places to hear them read.[1] The timid and irresolute, alienated from the church, and deterred from frequenting prohibited associations, set up altars of the most unpretentious character within their own houses. Too poor to buy books, and perhaps too ignorant to read them, they sought from the formschneiders and image-makers the emblems they needed as visible symbols of their faith. In this hungering after the instruction or consolation afforded by religious pictures, we see the origin of the block-books. A growing fondness for pictures is a marked peculiarity in the intellectual development of the age. It was not confined to the buyers of printed images: it was manifested in the paintings on the walls and windows of magnificent churches, in the pictorial playing cards then in the hands of all people, gentle and simple, and more than all in the fearful pictures of the *Dance of Death* upon the walls of convents, in the arcades of burying-grounds, and in market-places and town halls. In these hideous paintings, the saint saw the necessity of preparation for death; the sinner interpreted them as an assertion of the equality of all men and the final punishment of the

[1] It is a noteworthy fact that the first complaint of an unauthorized reading of the Bible came from the city where the Bible was first printed. Pope Innocent III, alarmed at the consequences of this innovation, and writing at the beginning of the thirteenth century, says he had been informed by the bishop of Mentz that:

No small multitude of laymen and women, having procured the translation of the Gospels, Epistles of St. Paul, the Psalter, Job and other books of Scripture to be made for them into French, meet in secret conventicles to hear them read and to preach to each other, and having been reprimanded for this by some of their parish priests, have withstood them, alleging reasons from the Scriptures why they should not be so forbidden. Some of them, too, deride the ignorance of their ministers, and maintain that their own books teach them more than they can learn from the pulpit, and that they can express it better. Although, Innocent proceeds, the desire of reading the Scriptures is rather praiseworthy than reprehensible, yet they are to be blamed for frequenting secret assemblies, for usurping the office of preaching, for deriding their own ministers, and for scorning the company of those who do not concur in their novelties. He presses the bishop and chapter to discover the author of this translation, which could not have been made without a knowledge of letters. He wished to know what were his intentions, and what degree of orthodoxy and respect for the holy see those who used it possessed. In another letter Innocent complains that some of the members of this association continued refractory, and refused to obey either the bishop or the pope. Hallam, *Middle Ages*.

The Abbot.

Death despoils the Abbot of his mitre and crozier, and drags him away. The Abbot resists, and is about to throw his breviary at his adversary.

The Mendicant Friar.

He is about to enter his convent with his money-box and wallet, when Death seizes him by the cowl, and compels him to leave the world.

The Preacher.

Death, with a stole about his neck, stands behind the Preacher, and holds a jaw-bone over his head, intimating that he is the more forcible teacher.

The Knight.

After escaping perils in numerous combats, the Knight ineffectually resists the onset of Death, and is vanquished by one thrust of the spear.

Holbein's Illustrations of the Dance of Death.

[From Douce.]

unjust. In the inexorable impartiality of the grinning and stalking skeleton who rudely dragged away the resisting noble and protesting priest, there was a ghastly irony which was keenly appreciated even by the illiterate.

The signs of awakening intelligence, as manifested in the general appreciation of pictures, images, playing cards and books, were entirely disregarded by the authorized teachers of the age, who could have used the method of xylographic printing by which images and playing cards were made, and could have led people from the contemplation of images and allegories of the *Dance of Death*,[1] to the study of books and letters. They had all the means within reach. There were engravers and printers in Venice in 1400; there is an obscure notice of image-cutters or engravers on wood in the records of the fraternity of St. Luke in Paris[2] for the year 1391. But

[1]At the beginning of the fifteenth century, paintings of the *Dance of Death* were in all the large cities of Europe. Woltmann has distinctly stated the causes which gave popularity to these horrible compositions.

The misery and unhappiness which at this period more than any other visited the nations of the West, increased more and more the ascetic views on the subject of death. The great aims and ideas of medieval life had passed away, and the ideas of the new period were now fast beginning to form themselves. . . . . Licentiousness prevailed in all lands; immoderate festivity and boundless excesses of sensuality gained more and more the upper hand. . . . . Upon this life of self-will and self-indulgence, of riot and revelry, the terrors of death burst all the more fearfully. In addition to the constant wars, the acts of violence and the shedding of blood which prevailed among men, we find the most various alarms in nature. Famine and desolating pestilences, and in the middle of the fourteenth century the Black Death, made their fearful and triumphal progress through Europe. To escape the dread and thought of this misery, men gave themselves up on the one side all the more passionately to the intoxication of the senses; but on the other they believed themselves struck by the vengeance of God, and sought for safety in contrition and repentance, which often led them into the most repulsive forms of ecstasy. But the most forcible sermons exhorting to repentance, the sermons that spoke to the people in the most intelligible form, were the figurative representations which proclaimed the almighty power of death. *Holbein and his Time* (Bunnèt's translation), p. 248.

[2] *Tailleres ymagiers*, the words of the record, may be construed as engravers on wood, or as carvers of wooden statuettes; but the *tailleres* were, probably, engravers. The fraternity of St. Luke consisted chiefly of men who made or contributed to the making of books: an engraver would properly belong to the guild. The words *tailleres ymagiers* suggest engraving quite as clearly as *formschneider* does in German.

neither the doctors of the universities nor the book-makers of Paris ever attempted to print books or pictures. Nor can it be shown that any one of the many persons laboring for the revival of literature at the beginning of the fifteenth century had anything to do with printing. The significance of this

Reduced Fac-simile of the Dance of Death, as shown in the Nuremberg Chronicle.
[Photographed from Mr. Bruce's Copy.]

fact should be fairly considered, for it is the proper explanation of the curious and childish literature of the block-books which followed the printed images.

Early printed work was the outgrowth, not of scholarship, but of comparative ignorance. The first block-printers were men outside the pale of literature, and not indebted to any school or scholar for the suggestion of printing. The first merchantable products of printing on paper were not books, but playing cards and images. The earliest purchasers of printing were men who could neither read nor write. The card-makers, who labored for the amusement of boyish tastes, were the ignorant nurses of an art which has preserved the learning of the world. They have had grand success. The once despised fabric of paper has displaced vellum; types do the work of reed and pen, and the work of perpetuating the literature of the world is done by mechanics.[1] Nor has this great revolution been restricted to mechanical processes in book-making. Medieval books are more than out of date: they are dead, beyond all revival. They are known to book-lovers chiefly by reputation. The writings of Anselm, Dun Scotus, Abelard, Peter Lombard, Albertus Magnus, Thomas Aquinas and Ockham, are read only through curiosity; they are as obsolete as the works of the old Greek philosophers.[2]

Although much had been done to prepare Germany and Flanders for the reception of printing, one thing was lacking. Printing waited for a wise appreciation of the utility of paper. For centuries paper had been regarded as a plebeian writing surface, unfitted for books, but good enough for shopkeepers, mechanics, and children who had or sought a smattering of education. It was necessary that the prejudices in favor of vellum should be uprooted, and that the practical superiority of paper should be recognized by men of higher authority than card-printers or poor scholars. This change in fashion was effectually made by the rich merchants of Flanders and Germany. The paper rejected of professional book-makers was not so strong nor so attractive as parchment, but it was flexible, durable, and much cheaper. There was no legislative intermeddling with its sale[3] as there had been with parchment.

[1] Laborde, a brilliant French writer on early printing, who traces the origin of printing to playing cards, acknowledges its very ignoble origin with evident mortification:—"What a mother for such a son!"

[2] The history of literature, like that of Empire, is full of revolutions; our public libraries are cemeteries of departed reputation; the dust accumulating upon these untouched volumes speaks as forcibly as the grass that waves over the ruins of Babylon. Hallam, *Middle Ages*.

[3] The University of Paris made no opposition to the free sale of paper. It was not subjected to taxes or duties in France, not even when oppressive taxes were levied on most manufactures. Didot, *Essai sur la typographie*, p. 730.

Everybody was free to buy and use it at his pleasure. The consequences of this contemptuous abandonment of paper to the people, who were supposed to be almost unfit to use it, were unexpected. Those who knew how to read and write found in paper a ready means of communicating their knowledge. The number of readers grew. With this increase of readers came also an increase of self-taught copyists and of unprofessional book-makers. In the commercial cities, where copyists were not subjected to the censorship of the universities, the practice of making books became as common as it had been exclusive. Book-making became a distinct trade, and shops were established for the sale of alphabets, primers, prayer books, creeds, and elementary text books for schools, all adapted, both in price and in subject, to the very humblest readers.[1] The names of some nooks and corners in London, Paternoster Row, Creed Lane, Amen Corner, Ave Maria Lane, show that these were the places in that city where manuscripts of a religious character were largely made and sold.

As the sale of these books and tracts increased, Northern copyists combined with each other for purposes of mutual protection, after the usage of all the tradesmen of the middle ages. We find a mention of the existence of the Company of Stationers of London in 1405. There were guilds of book-makers at Augsburg in 1418, at Nordlingen in 1428, at Ulm in 1441, at Antwerp in 1441, at Bruges in 1454. These are the years in which the guilds were first mentioned; but it is probable they were incorporated at earlier dates. The book-

[1] A school ordinance of Bautzen in Saxony, dated 1418, gives the names and prices of some of these books. For an *A B C* and *Pater Noster*, etc., 1 groschen; for a good *Donatus*, or child's grammar, 10 groschen; for a complete *Doctrinal*, 1 half-mark; for the *First Part*, 8 groschen. There has also been preserved the advertisement of one Dypold Lauber, a teacher and copyist of books at Hagenau in Germany, who lived during the middle of the fifteenth century, from which we may gather a clear notion of the books that were most salable among the people. His catalogue begins with the *Deeds of the Romans*, with illustrations. Then follow poetical works, romances of chivalry, biblical and legendary works, edifying books, religious books, books for the people, fortune-telling books, and other works of like character. Van der Linde, *Haarlem Legend of the Invention of Printing*, pp. 2, 3.

making fraternities of St. Luke, in Venice and in Paris, were constituted of copyists, calligraphers, illuminators and bookbinders; but the more practical Northern guilds admitted to membership printers and engravers, and every worker, however humble his work, who contributed to the making of a book. But this combination of copyists with engravers and printers did not at once lead to the printing of books. It did no more than pave the way for its introduction, by making people familiar with paper and printing. For a long time the workmanship of the rival arts was kept distinct; the copyist transcribed books, while the printers made images. But the time came when the copyist had to ask help from the printer.

The printing of books began, not as an independent art, but as an aid to the art of writing. A publisher[1] of London recently described and offered for sale a curious old book, partly printed and partly written, which illustrates the close alliance of labor once maintained between the copyist and the engraver. He describes the book as a folio of 17 leaves of vellum, on which are printed 69 engravings, twelve of them bearing legends, "representing scenes of Christian mythology, figures of patriarchs, saints, devils, and other dignitaries of the church, all colored and illuminated with oxidized gold, impressed in the midst of a manuscript text in German." The engravings of this book are small, about 3 inches long and 2¼ inches broad. They are enclosed by a double border of black lines, and are printed on the left side of the page. The designer of the illustrations was obviously an inexpert, not accustomed to drawing the letters of the inscriptions in reverse order on the block, for some of the letters are turned the wrong way. The engravings were printed before the descriptive text was written. The language of the text, old High German, contains obsolete words which were out of use before typography was invented. Quaritch attributes this

[1] Bernard Quaritch, *Catalogue of Block-Books*, 8vo. October, 1873, pp. 1373—1375. The title of the book, as he gives it, is *Ein Vorrede das Puch haist wochenlich Andach zu Seligkayt der weltlichen Menschen.*

book to unknown monks of Southern Germany, "about the year 1400." This copy of the *Weekly Meditations* is a favorable specimen of the combined workmanship of the copyist and the printer; but it is not the only one. Copies or fragments of manuscript books[1] with printed illustrations are in the British Museum, and in many European libraries.

These specimens of book-making during the period of its transition from writing to printing, give us some notions of the estimation in which the process of printing was held by the men who manufactured chap-books. It does not appear that they made use of printing because they thought it was a labor-saving process. They used it mainly, if not entirely, to supplement the deficient skill of the copyist. It was then as it is now—many could write, but few could draw. If the copyist who wrote the text had been competent to draw, the pictures would not have been engraved. Nor would these engravings have been made for one nor even for one dozen copies. We may properly suppose that enough copies were printed to justify the expense of engraving.

While it was expedient to engrave the pictures, it was inexpedient to engrave the text of a book. In many books, the letters constituted the largest part of the work, and to the engraver it was the more difficult part—the expense of engraving would more than offset all the advantages that might have been gained from printing. A full suite of blocks for the text would cost more than the writing of a hundred copies. To the stationer who could sell but few books, xylographic printing was not an economical process: the preliminary cost of engraving was too great. It would be an extravagant estimate to assume that the writer of the *Weekly Meditations* made one hundred copies of this book; but one

[1] They were common during the first quarter of the fifteenth century. Bernard, *De l'origine de l'imprimerie*, vol. 1, p. 102. Fournier, *De l'origine et des productions de l'imprimerie*, p. 176. Papillon, *Traité historique et pratique de la gravure sur bois*, vol. 1, p. 101. Guichard, *Notice sur le Speculum*, p. 118. They have been noticed also by Passavant. It is plain that copyists everywhere recognized the utility of engraving.

hundred copies would have been an edition much too small to justify the engraving of its text of seventeen pages. We must accept this as the reason why printing was so sparingly used by the early book-makers. They did not engrave blocks and print books, because there were not enough book-buyers to warrant the expense. This feature of printing—its entire dependence upon a very large number of book-buyers—may require a more extended explanation.

The small prices for which all popular modern books and newspapers are sold lead many into the error that printing is, necessarily and under all circumstances, a much cheaper method of making books than that of writing. As compared with writing, presswork, or the operation of impressing the types on the sheet, is much the quicker and cheaper process; but presswork is not the main branch of the art of printing. Before one impression can be taken, or one copy be made, types must be composed or blocks engraved at very great expense. The composition and stereotyping of the pages of an ordinary duodecimo book may be worth six hundred dollars. On an edition of ten copies the cost of such a book would be, for making plates only, sixty dollars per copy. If there were but one hundred copies, the expense of the plates would be six dollars per copy. Under these conditions few books would be published. But if an edition of one thousand copies should be printed, the cost of the plates would be only sixty cents a copy. In this instance, printing would be much cheaper than writing, but this reduced rate would not necessarily justify the expenses of printing. The risk of sale must be hazarded. No publisher would undertake at his own risk to print even one thousand copies,—much less a smaller number,—if he did not fully believe that the edition could be promptly sold. But the early book-maker did not have this confident belief in large and speedy sale. There were, comparatively, few book-buyers, and the publication of a book by the method of engraving and printing must have seemed very hazardous speculation.

It can be clearly seen that the cost of printing a book is in inverse ratio with the number printed. When the number is small, the cost per copy is great; when the number is great, the cost per copy is small. Printing is an economical process only for books of many copies. If there were not a very great number of book-readers and book-buyers, printing could not be practised to advantage.

In the fourteenth century this multitude of book-readers had not been created. One hundred copies would have been considered a great edition, and the engravers or printers who took such a hazard would have waited many years for purchasers. Their unwillingness to take an unwise risk has been often regarded as an evidence, not of their sagacity, but of their stupidity. There are writers who have taught that the project of a printed book was a grand conception, not to be imagined by any but a great inventor—an idea far above the capacity of any printer of playing cards or images; but the legends in the image prints teach us that the early engravers knew how to engrave the letters, and that they could have engraved entire books of letters if they had thought it expedient. The advantages or disadvantages of engraving books were considered by them as they would be by publishers of our own time, purely as an economical question. The early engravers decided that books of letters could be appreciated, and would be purchased, only by the educated, a class too small to reward the labor of the engraver. For the making of books, printing was not regarded as an economical process, and books were consequently made by the cheaper process of writing.

While it was unprofitable to engrave letters for books, it was profitable to engrave designs for printed fabrics, images and playing cards. On work of this character, the relations of cost and sale were completely reversed. The expenses for engraving one design, one image, or one suite of cards, was small; but the sale of the work printed from the blocks was generally very large. Fabrics that could be worn, cards that could amuse, and images that would serve as decorations or as aids to devotion, had attractions for all people, and especially for the poor and illiterate. Whoever printed merchandise of this nature could rightfully expect that it would be sold in such large quantities that the cost of engraving would be inappreciable.

The world was not ready at the beginning of the fifteenth century to apply its knowledge of printing with ink to the making of books. It was regarded as too expensive a process. It bided its time, waiting for more readers and book-buyers, for paper in greater supply and of better quality, for higher skill on the part of the engravers, printers and ink-makers. If there were no other evidences than those afforded by the partly printed and written books, it could be safely assumed that when the early engravers did begin to print books, they would be, not books of letters, but books of pictures.

XI

Block-Books of Images without Text.

General Appreciation of Pictures...Beginning of the Block-Books...Popularity during the Fifteenth Century...Neglected afterward...Childish in Character...The Bible of the Poor...Its Age as a Manuscript...Its Popularity. The First Edition...Its Designs and Engravings...Explanations of Fac-similes...Description of Printing...Not Printed by the Frotton...Anachronisms in Design. Dissimilarity of the Copies...Blocks destroyed in 1488...Price of Copies...Description of German Edition of 1470...The Apocalypse...Description of Illustrations...Probably of German Origin. The Canticles...Description of Fac-simile...Its Anachronisms...Its object...Quality of Engraving...The Story of the Blessed Virgin...Its Object...Description of Fac-simile...Its Absurdities. Exercise on the Lord's Prayer...Description of Fac-simile...Singular Perversion of the Prayer. The Book of Kings...Description and Fac-simile...The Grotesque Alphabet...A Mysterious Book...The Apostles' Creed...The Eight Rogueries.

I presume that nothing is in this life more useful to a man than to acknowledge his Creator, his condition, his own being. Scholars may learn this from the Scriptures, and the laymen shall be taught by the books of the laymen, that is by the pictures. Wherefore I have thought fit, with the help of God, to compile this book for laymen to the glory of God, and as an instruction for the unlearned, in order that it may be a lesson both to clerks and to laymen.

Preface to the Speculum Salutis.

THE sumptuary laws of the middle ages, which were made to restrain common people from imitating the dress and equipage of the nobility, were not extended to the making of books. The copyist or calligrapher was at liberty to decorate books according to his own fancy. There was no occasion for restrictive legislation. The admirable romances and books of prayer upon which the miniaturist had lavished his talents were beyond the skill of the vulgar copyist and beyond the means of the plebeian book-buyer. Only an artist could paint them; only a prince or patrician could buy them. But these books, although far removed from the multitude by price and rarity, were not above the capacity of the ordinary reader. The illiterate man who could find no attraction in a book of letters would readily acknowledge the charm of the pictures in a book like the *Bedford Missal.* In this universal appreciation of pictures, some of the early engravers of cards and images saw an opportunity. Men who would not buy books of letters would buy books of pictures. Books of the latter class were not only sure of sale, but they could be engraved on blocks at a comparatively small expense. They could be printed in quantities much more cheaply, and, above all, with more accuracy and uniformity than they could be drawn by hand. They could be painted or illuminated by stencil plates, and made acceptable to men of simple tastes. Here was the beginning of the block-books.

The term Block-Book is used to define the book printed entirely from engraved blocks, in contradistinction to the book printed from movable types. Bibliographers divide the block-books in two distinct classes: books of pictures without text, in which words descriptive of the picture are engraved at the foot of the page, or in cartouches proceeding from the mouths of the principal figures; and books of pictures with text, in which the explanations of the pictures are given in the form of a full page of text, which was commonly printed on the page opposite the picture.

It is admitted by all writers on typography that block-books of both classes were made before and after the invention of typography. That they were manufactured in large quantities by many printers, and in many cities or towns, during the fifteenth century, does not admit of doubt. It is claimed by one bibliographer that there are eight editions of the *Ars Moriendi;* by others, that there are six editions each of the *Bible of the Poor* and of the *Apocalypse*, and four of the *Mirror of Man's Redemption.* In some instances, the so-called later editions are reprintings, with slight alterations, of the same blocks that were used for the first edition; in other instances, the later editions were printed from blocks newly engraved. The number and variety of the editions are proof that there must have been a very large demand for the books; the alterations in the engravings are presumptive evidence of repairs to blocks badly worn by long use; the newly engraved blocks are evidently the replacement of a suite completely worn out; an edition different from the others in design may be accepted as the work of a rival or competing printer.

The few block-books known in the seventeenth century were regarded by bibliographers as prejudicial to the claims of contestants for the honor of the invention of typography. They were annoying facts which could neither be rejected nor accepted without hurt to favorite theories. There was a disposition on all sides to belittle them in number as well as in importance. The first writer who called attention to their value as relics could describe but nine block-books. Sotheby, writing about them in 1858, described in the *Principia Typographica* twenty-one block-books—not different editions of a few books, but twenty-one distinct works. Even with these additions, the list cannot be considered complete: it is possible that more will yet be found, but it is certain that many have been irretrievably lost.

The neglect of the block-books by early librarians seems almost justifiable when we consider their great inferiority to the typographic books that followed them. From a literary point of view, they were of no importance as works of instruction or authority. They were published during the fifteenth century, but they really belong to the twelfth and thirteenth centuries, during which period most of them were composed. The legends that explain their illustrations were written in Latin, but they are adapted to readers in a child-like state of development. It is not strange that they should have been put aside by the world when it had outgrown them. Childish as these books are, they are of high value to those who wish to note the growth of printing. They indicate the attainments of their authors and readers, and the artistic abilities of their designers and engravers. They show the quality of the paper, ink, and workmanship of the period. They prove that the art of printing from blocks was practised by many persons during the second and third quarters of the fifteenth century.

Legit' in cãtic' cãticoꝝ iiij°·ca°
q sponsus alloqt' sponsã et eã sumẽ
do dixit tota pulchra e amica mea
et macula no e in te · veni amica
mea veni coronaberis Sponsus vero
iste e xps qui assumẽdo eã sponsa
q̃ e aia sine macula oĩs pcci et
introducit eã i rqem etnã et coronat
corona imortalitatis
Legit' i apocal·xxi ca° q angel9
dei apphe dixit · iohãez ewangelistã
cũ eet i spu et uocs sibi oñdere
archana dei dixit ad eũ veni ondã
dab sponsa vxoriem agni Angel9
loqmb' ad oms in gnali vt re
maneãt ad auscultãdũ i spu agni
nũ inocẽte xpm aiaz innoceñ
te sonate
Dauid
ysaye · vj ·
Tanqŭ sponsus dũs pcedes de thalamo suo
· v ·
Tanqŭ sponsus decorauit me corona

Fac-simile of the Last Page of the Bible of the Poor.

[From Hansard.]

THE BIBLIA PAUPERUM, OR BIBLE OF THE POOR.

This is the most famous and the most creditable specimen of the early block-book.[1] The title, *Bible of the Poor*, seems to have been used at an early period to distinguish it from the Bible proper, a fair manuscript copy of which was sold in France, in the year 1460, for five hundred crowns of gold. The Bible proper, as then made, in two or more stout folio volumes of fine vellum, was the Bible of the rich; its epitome, in the shape of the book of forty pages of engravings, about to be described, was the Bible of the poor.

The author of the *Bible of the Poor* is unknown, but the designer of the illustrations was not the writer of the texts that explained the designs. There are frequent incongruities between the words and the pictures, which fully show that the author did not always understand the intent of the artist. It is probable that the illustrations were made first, and that, in the beginning, the *Bible of the Poor* was a book of pictures only.[2] Some German antiquarians say that the book, in its

[1] The engraver or the printer of the book published it, as all other books of this kind were published, without a printed title. It has been described by different authors under these titles: *Types and Antitypes of the Old and the New Testament; The Histories and the Prophecies of the Old Testament; The Typical Harmony of the Bible; Typical Illustrations of the Old Testament, and Antitypical Illustrations of the New*, or the *Story of Jesus Christ as told by Engravers*. Chatto calls it the *Bible for Poor Preachers*, and claims that it was written especially for their use. He objects to the title, *Bible of the Poor*, as leading to the erroneous opinion that the book was bought by the poor of the laity, who, he says, were unable to read in their own language, much less in Latin. This observation is true, yet Chatto's addition to the old title is not really needed. He overlooks the fact that the charm of the book was in its pictures, which could be appreciated by the poor of the laity as well as by poor preachers. In this sense, it was truly the *Bible of the Poor*.

[2] The British Museum has a French manuscript, entitled *Figures de la Bible*, in which the illustrations occupy nearly all the page, leaving room for little more than the text that describes the cuts. The same library has two copies in Latin verse of an abridgment of the Bible, in which the text occupies nearly all the page, while the illustrations are in miniature. These manuscripts of the fourteenth century are not *Bibles of the Poor*, but they show the fondness for books with biblical pictures.

original form, was designed and explained by a monk named Wernher, who was living in 1180, and was famous during his lifetime both as a painter and a poet. Other German authorities put the origin of the first manuscript as far back as the ninth century, attributing the work to Saint Ansgarius, first bishop of Hamburg. It seems to have been a popular manuscript, for copies written before the fifteenth century have been found in many old monasteries. These copies are not alike. Nearly every transcriber has made more or less alterations and innovations of his own; but the general plan of the book—the contrasting of apostles with prophets, and of the patriarchs of the Old Testament with the saints of the Christian Church—has been preserved in all the copies.

At least four distinct xylographic editions—two in Latin and two in German—of the *Bible of the Poor* have been discovered. Three of them were printed in Germany after the invention of typography.[1] The edition acknowledged as the first,[2] and supposed to have been printed before the invention of types, is in Latin, without date, place, or name of printer. Those who favor the theory of a German invention of printing say that it was printed in Germany between the years 1440 and 1460. Those who believe in the priority of Dutch printing say that it must be regarded as the work of some printer of Holland. This is the opinion of Berjeau, who republished the book in fac-simile. He says that the designs for the original editions must have been made in the Netherlands, probably by Van Eyck, between 1410 and 1420.

[1] 1. An edition in Latin, of fifty pages, and supposed to have been engraved and printed by Melchior Wohlgemuth of Nuremberg, between the years 1450 and 1460. Only one copy of this book is known. 2. An edition in German, of forty pages, by Friedrich Walther and Hans Hürning, at Nordlingen, 1470. 3. An edition in German, attributed to Sporer, at Erfurth, in 1475.

[2] Fifteen copies are known of the edition here specified as the first. Heineken, noticing little dissimilarities of design and engraving in many of these copies, says that they prove the existence of five distinct editions. For similar reasons, Sotheby says that there are six editions. The weight of authority favors the classification of these fifteen copies in one edition.

The illustration on the preceding page, which is the exact size of the original, gives a faithful representation of the last page of the first edition of this curious book.

Unlike most of the block-books, the *Bible of the Poor* was designed with architectural symmetry. An open frame-work divides each page in nine distinct panels or partitions, five of which are devoted to pictorial illustrations, and four to their explanation in words. The three large panels in the middle of the page illustrate historical subjects drawn from the Bible, of which the central panel is, in theological phrase, the *type*, and is taken from the New Testament. The pictures on either side are known as the *antitypes*, and are oftenest taken from the Old Testament. The texts that explain the pictures are placed in the corners of the page, or in scrolls near the figures.

To most readers the explanatory text is undecipherable. The obscurity is not only that of a dead language: a trained Latin scholar will always grope and often stumble in attempting to make a translation. All the letters are carelessly drawn and cut; the words are badly spaced, and are deformed with abbreviations. These faults appear more noticeable when the letters are contrasted with the designs. Whoever designed the figures on the wood drew with the bold and free hand of an artist who had proper confidence in his ability. Whoever engraved the figures cut the clean firm line that can be made only by an expert. But the cutting of the letters, although probably done by the engraver of the figures, is really barbarous. It is obvious that the designer, skillful as he was with figures, had no experience in drawing letters, and that the engraver was equally unsuccessful at a new kind of work.

The text and translation appended are the version of Dr. Horne, author of the *Introduction to the Study of Bibliography*, who has corrected the contractions of the original Latin. It is copied from the *Typographia* of Hansard.

Each page contains four busts—two at the top, and two lower down; together with three historical subjects. The two upper busts represent certain prophets, or other eminent persons, whose names are added beneath them. Of the three historical subjects, the *chief type*, or principal piece, is taken from the New Testament, and occupies the centre of the page, between the two *antitypes*, or subordinate subjects, which are allusive to it. The two busts, placed in the middle of the upper part of the page, represent David and Isaiah between two texts of the Bible, with brief explanations. The former of these, on the left of the Prophets, is from the Song of Solomon, Chapter IV, 7:

Legitur in Cantico Canticorum, quarto capite, quod sponsus alloquitur sponsam, et eam sumendo dixit: Tota pulchra es, amica mea, et macula non est in te. Veni, amica mea, veni, coronabere. Sponsus verus iste est Christus, qui in assumendo eam sponsam, quæ est anima sine macula omnis peccati, et introducit eam in requiem æternam; et coronat eum corona immortalitatis.

In the fourth chapter of the Song of Solomon it is read, That the bridegroom addresses the bride, and receiving her, says, Thou art all fair, my love, and in thee is no spot. Come, my love; come, thou shalt be crowned. The real bridegroom is Christ, who, in receiving the bride, which is the soul without spot of sin, also conducts her to eternal rest, and crowns her with the crown of immortality.

The second passage, on the right of David and Isaiah, is partly taken from the Book of Revelation, and runs thus:

Legitur in Apocalypsi xxi° capite, quod angelus Dei apprehendit Jhoannem Evangelistam cum esset in Spiritu, et volens sibi ostendere archana Dei, dixit ad eum, Veni, et ostendam tibi sponsam, uxorem agni. Angelus loquitur ad omnem generationem ut veniant ad auscultandum in sponsum, agnum innocentem Christum animas innocentes coronantem.

In the twenty-first chapter of the Revelation it is read, That the Angel of God took John the Evangelist when he was in the Spirit, and willing to show him the mysteries of God, said to him, Come, and I will show thee the bride, the wife of the Lamb. The Angel speaks to every generation, that they come and hearken to the bridegroom, the pure Lamb Christ, crowning innocent souls.

Under the bust of David, which is indicated by his name, is a scroll proceeding from his hand, inscribed:

Enim tamquam sponsus dominus procedens de thalamo suo.

Even as a bridegroom cometh out of his chamber. Ps. XIX, 5.

Beneath the corresponding compartment containing a bust of Isaiah, is the word *Ysaye*, and also the ordinal number LXI, referring to the sixty-first chapter of that prophet; and from the hand of the figure proceeds a label containing:

Tamquam sponsus decorabit me corona.

As a bridegroom, he hath adorned me with a crown. LXI, 10.

Toward the bottom of the plate are two other busts, similar to those at the top, and which represent the Prophets Ezekiel and

Hosea. From the figure that occupies the left-hand compartment extends a scroll, at one end of which is the word *Œzeciel*, with a number referring to the twenty-fourth chapter; and in the other part are the words:

Corona tua capite ligata fiet, et calciamenta in pedibus.	Thy tire shall be bound upon thine head, and thy shoes upon thy feet. XXIV, 17.

The corresponding scroll, attached to the other figure, contains, at one end, *Ozee*, with a reference to the second chapter; and in the other part are the words:

Sponsabo te mihi in sempiternum.	I will betroth thee unto me forever. II, 19.

In the central compartment, between the upper and lower busts, is depicted the Type, or principal subject. It represents the reward of righteousness in heaven; the designer having introduced the Redeemer as bestowing the Crown of Life upon one of the elect Spirits. The antitype, on the left, is the Daughter of Zion crowned by her spouse, with the following leonine verse underneath:

Laus anime vere, Sponsum bene sensit habere.	O soul divine! it rightly knew, To have the spouse was glory true.

The other antitype, on the right, represents an Angel addressing St. John, having beneath it this verse:

Sponsus amat sponsam, Christus nimis et speciosam.	And Christ, the bridegroom, far above Conception, the fair bride doth love.

And in the bottom space is this verse:

Tunc gaudent anime sibi quando bonum datur omne.	Then souls rejoice with great delight, When given is the diadem bright.

The first edition of the book contains forty engravings on wood, printed on one side only of the leaf. The prints face each other; two pages of illustrations are always followed by two pages of blank paper. The book was put together in sections of two leaves, a method of making a book contrary to prevailing usage. Manuscript books of that period were usually made up in sections of four double leaves, which were nested together in one section. This deviation from established usage was, apparently, caused through the error of the engraver, who cut, on the same block, the two pages which faced each other. It was, consequently, impossible to nest the leaves, or make them up in thick sections. Cracks in the wood block, which have made open seams or white gaps in the print, and which extend in straight lines over both pages, show conclusively that two pages were engraved on one block.

The book is without folios or paging figures to guide the reader, and also without signatures to guide the binder. The proper order of the pages was made manifest by engraving on each page a letter of the alphabet. Pages 1 to 20 are marked in alphabetical order from *a* to *v;* pages 21 to 40 have the same letters, but with a dot before and after each, .*a*. to .*v*.

The paper of the fifteen known copies of this edition of the book is of variable quality. Of itself, this variability is not sufficient indication that the paper was made by different makers, and printed at different times, but the different designs of the paper-marks lead directly to such a conclusion. Some copies have but one kind of paper-mark; others have two and three kinds; taking all copies together, there are at least fourteen distinct paper-marks. If each decided variation of the same design could be considered the mark of a different maker, the number could be doubled.

That the substance used for these engravings was wood, is clearly indicated by the occasional feathering or flatting out of border-lines, which, when crushed, show the fibres of wood in the impression. It seems that the engravings were cut on flat plates or blocks, that had been sawed or split on a line parallel with the fibres.

The ink is of a dull or rusty-brown color; on some pages light, and on others of darker tint, rarely ever of uniform tint on the same page. It has the appearance of a paste or a thick water color. This unevenness in color was produced by some imperfect method of inking the block—possibly by a hard-faced brush which shed color irregularly.

The shining appearance of the backs of the prints, in all places where the raised lines of the wood-cut have indented the paper, has been considered as sufficient evidence that the impressions were taken, not by a press, but by means of a frotton, or by friction, or by rubbing in some form or other. One writer of rare simplicity has hazarded the opinion that the back of the paper, or the frotton, may have been soaped to facilitate the work. But these methods of printing books are imaginary and entirely impracticable. The shining appearance on the back of the paper does not prove that the prints were made by friction. The gloss could have been produced by any press which gave a hard impression against a harder surface. It could have been produced by rubbing or smoothing down with a burnisher the indentations of the lines on the back of the paper, as is sometimes done by pressmen of this day when they take too hard an impression. Some copies of the book show the results of hard impression. Two of the four copies of the *Bible of the Poor* in the possession of the British Museum present lines deeply sunk in the paper, as if they had been printed from a press. Jackson, a practical engraver on wood, who had large experience in proving wood-cuts, has unwillingly accepted the unauthorized tradition of presswork by friction, but he has candidly stated its difficulties.

"Considering the thickness of the paper on which the block-books are printed—if I may apply this term to them—and the thin-bodied ink which has been used, I am at a loss to conceive how the early wood engravers have contrived to take off their impressions so correctly; for in all the block-books which I have seen, where friction has evidently been the means employed to obtain the impression, I have noticed only two subjects in which the lines appear double in consequence of the shifting of the paper. From the want of body in the ink, which appears in the *Apocalypse* to have been little more than water color, it is not likely that the paper could be used in a damp state, otherwise the ink would run or spread; and even if this did not exist, the paper in a damp state could not have borne the excessive rubbing which it appears to have received in order to obtain the impression. Even with such printer's ink as is used in the present day—which, being tenacious, renders the paper in taking an impression by means of friction, much less liable to slip or shift—it would be difficult to obtain clear impressions on thick paper from blocks the size of those which form each page of the *Apocalypse*, or the *History of the Virgin*. . . . A block containing only two pages [of the *History of the Virgin*, a block of smaller size than that used for the *Bible of the*

Poor] would be about seventeen inches by ten, allowing for inner margins; and to obtain clear impressions from it by means of friction, on dry thick paper, and with mere water color ink, would be a task of such difficulty that I cannot conceive how it could be performed. No traces of points, by which the paper might be kept steady on the block, are perceptible; and I unhesitatingly assert, that no wood engraver of the present day could, by means of friction, take clear impressions from such a block on equally thick paper, and using mere distemper, instead of printer's ink. As the impressions in the *History of the Virgin* have unquestionably been taken by means of friction, it is evident to me that if the blocks were of the size that Mr. Ottley supposes, the old wood engravers, who did not use a press, must have resorted to some contrivance to keep the paper steady with which we are unacquainted."[1]

This last hypothesis of an imaginary contrivance that kept the paper steady, is as untenable as the proposition that blocks were unquestionably printed by friction. The feat which is impossible now was impossible then. There is nothing in the appearance of the presswork of the block-books really inconsistent with the theory, that the books were printed under a rude press which was deficient in many attachments that are needed by the printer. The peculiar appearance of the presswork of this and of other block-books will be most satisfactorily explained by the hypothesis that they were printed on a press. The hypothesis of printing by friction is a conjecture for which there is no good authority. It seems to have been invented for a purpose. If the early chroniclers of printing had not been so anxious to magnify the merits of the early typographers, and to belittle the printers of block-books, we should have heard nothing of printing by friction.

The designs of the first edition have more merit than those of the earlier manuscript copies—more than those of subsequent editions printed by imitators. Neither the rudeness of the engravings, nor the flagrant anachronisms in architecture and in the costumes of the figures, are gross enough to conceal the ability of the designer, whose skill in grouping figures is manifest on almost every page.

[1] Jackson and Chatto, *Treatise on Wood Engraving*, pp. 78–80.

The illustrations have merit, but they are in the realistic and commonplace style of the designers of Germany and of Flanders during the fifteenth century. The want of ideality is painful. The designer certainly had no thought of irreverence, but many of the designs are really ludicrous. Some of the anachronisms are: Gideon arrayed in plate armor, with medieval helmet and visor and Turkish scimitar; David and Solomon in rakish, wide-brimmed hats bearing high conical crowns; the translation of Elijah in a four-wheeled vehicle resembling the modern farmer's hay-wagon. Slouched hats, puffed doublets, tight-legged breeches and pointed shoes are seen in the apparel of the Israelites who are not represented as priests or soldiers. Some houses have Italian towers and some have Moorish minarets, but in none of the pictures is there an exhibition of pointed Gothic architecture. The old Dutch stair-like gable is often delineated, and so is the round arch and latticed window of the Flemish house of the fourteenth century. With all its absurdities, this edition of the *Bible of the Poor* commanded the respectful attention of great artists like Albert Durer and Lucas von Leyden, who did not scruple to appropriate many of its designs.

One of the most puzzling peculiarities of the first edition of the *Bible of the Poor* is the dissimilarity of the copies. In some copies the dissimilarity is in the details of the framework; in others, it is in the foliage of trees, but it is, for the most part, confined to a few immaterial points. These differences seem to warrant the opinion stated by Sotheby that there were six distinct editions, each printed from a separate set of blocks; but this opinion cannot be reasonably defended. In all important features the copies are alike. The pages of the so-called different editions have the marks, even in little blemishes, of impressions from the same block—a uniformity which could not have been produced if each block had been re-engraved for each new edition. Why the various copies of the book should be alike in important, and unlike in minor features, cannot be explained. It has been suggested that the dissimilarities are the evidences of accident and repair; that when the block was injured, it was plugged, as is frequently done with wood-cuts in our own day, and the newly inserted plug was re-engraved with a new design. The explanation is not plausible. The differences generally appear in the same relative position on every page, and there are too many of them to be attributed to accident; they seem to have been made for some unknown purpose. Irregularities of like nature have been noticed in copies of the typographic books of the fifteenth century which are known to be of the same edition.

We do not certainly know when and where these blocks were engraved, but we do know when they were destroyed. Two books, published by Peter Van Os of Zwoll, in Holland, in 1488 and 1489, contain seventy-seven engravings on wood which were certainly cut from the blocks that had been used to print the original edition of the *Bible of the Poor.* To get the little cuts he needed to illustrate texts of movable type, Van Os must have partly destroyed the original blocks. In this act of destruction, we have a fact and a date which give a clue to the origin of the book. Copies of the first edition in folio form must have been printed before 1488. At this date, and perhaps for some time before, the blocks in folio form had no mercantile value; there was no longer any demand for the book in the neighborhood in which it had been made. That the country in which this first edition was printed and sold was Holland, seems probable when we find that the blocks were used for the last time, and in a mutilated form, in a town of Holland. This opinion is strengthened by the facts that the *Bible of the Poor* in folio form was then, and afterward, a salable book in Germany and in other countries, but it was not subsequently reprinted in the Netherlands in any form. The Dutch and Flemish architectural features in the designs, and the legends which attribute the work to Dutch engravers and printers, are of themselves unsatisfactory evidences of the origin of the book; but they cannot be entirely overlooked They lead to the conclusion that the book was printed in Holland, but they do not fix the date of printing, which may have been as early as the year 1425, or as late as 1450.[1]

The illustration on the following page is a fac-simile, but reduced in size, of the first page of the edition published in the year 1470, at Nordlingen, by Walther and Hurning. The panel in the centre of this fac-simile represents the Annunciation; on the left is the Temptation of Eve; on the right is Gideon with the Fleece. The busts at the top are those of Isaiah and David; at the foot, Hezekiah and Jeremiah. This edition, like the one previously noticed, was printed in rusty brown ink upon one side of the paper. The adherence of the printers to a rough method of printing seems strange when we consider that typographic books, printed with black ink and on both sides of the paper, were then known and sold in every part of civilized Europe. Walther and Hurning were, probably, printers of cards and images who tried to compete with typography.[2] Incompetent to practise the new art, and unable to make fine books, they made a German translation of the *Bible of the Poor*, and tried to sell it to German people. The Nordlingen edition is an obvious imitation of the Latin edition previously described, but it is a very feeble imitation. The designer was incompetent to his task, and the engraver was clumsy. The workmanship of this book is one of many

[1] The *Bible of the Poor* has always been considered as one of the most valuable of block-books, but copies have been sold at widely varying prices, as may be seen in the annexed statement, compiled from Sotheby's *Principia Typographica:*

Willet copy, 1813........245 guineas.
Inglis copy, 1826........ 36*l.* 15*s.*
Willet copy, 1833........ 36*l.* 15*s.*
Lucca copy, 1848...... .. 89*l.* 5*s.*
Stevens copy, 1849....... 11*l.* 12*s.*
Sykes copy, 1824........ 18*l.* 17*s.* 6*d.*
Rendorp copy, 1825...... 17*l.* 8*s.* 6*d.*
Devonshire copy, 1815...210*l.*

[2] Three typographic editions of the *Bible of the Poor* have been printed:—1. An edition by Albert Pfister, at Bamberg, in 1461. In this edition, the engravings are small and coarsely cut. 2. An edition by Anthoine Vérard, in Paris, about 1500. This edition is a close imitation, beautifully printed, of the first xylographic edition, with explanations in French on the back of the engraved pages and on supplementary leaves. 3. An edition of very different arrangement, having 118 small wood-cuts, printed by Giovanni Andrea Vavassore detto Vadagnino of Venice, between 1515 and 1520. Berjeau, *Biblia Pauperum*, p. 17.

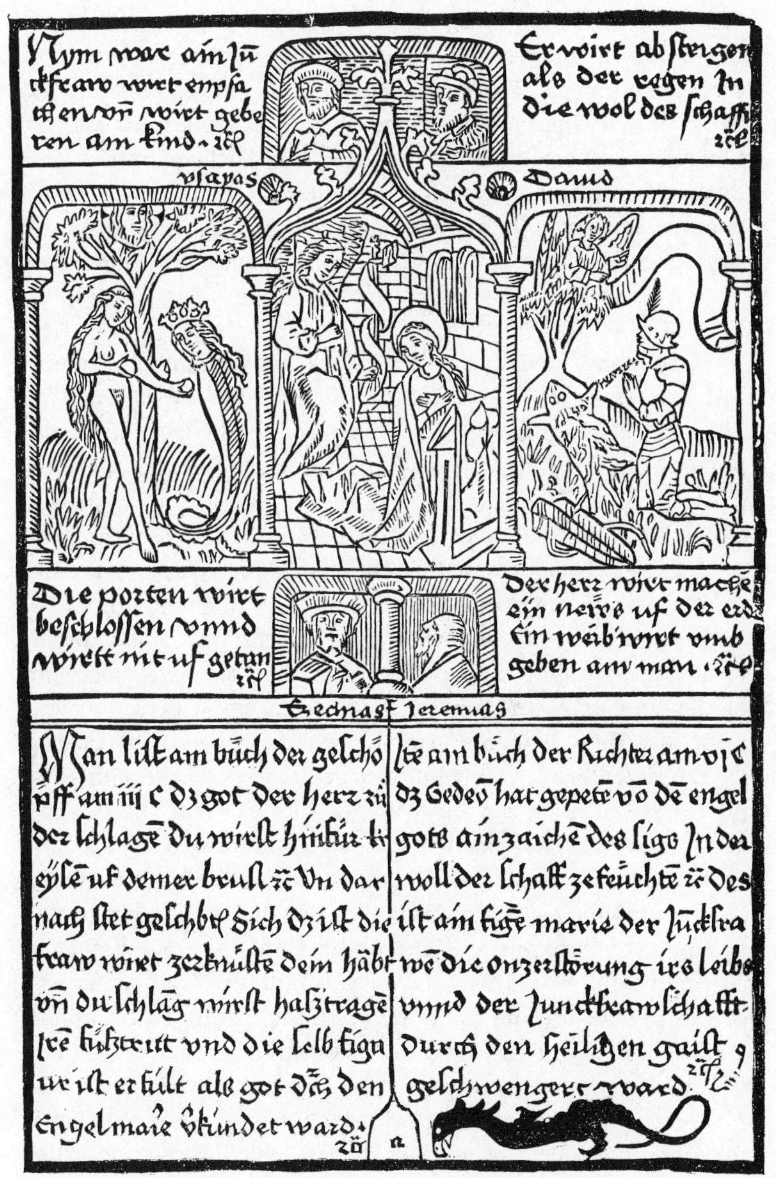

First Page of the Bible of the Poor as made by Walther and Hurning of Nordlingen, 1470.
The size of this print, in the original, is 7 by 10⅛ American inches.
[From Heineken.]

evidences which might be offered to prove that coarseness of engraving in undated block-books is by no means proof of their greater age. The facts point the other way. The block-books which contain engravings of high merit are, as a rule, the oldest; those made in the third or fourth quarter of the fifteenth century show decided decline in skill. Mean as this book is, it does not fully show the degradation that printing subsequently suffered from the hands of unskillful engravers.

THE APOCALYPSE OF ST. JOHN.

This is the name of an early block-book almost as famous as the *Bible of the Poor*, and of which there are at least six distinct xylographic editions. Some of them have fifty, and others have forty-eight leaves, printed upon one side only of the leaf. The dissimilarities in the designs and the engraving of these editions are decided and unmistakable: they are, no doubt, impressions from different suites of blocks, and each edition may be regarded as the work of a different printer.

As a literary production, the *Apocalypse* has small merit. It is not, as might be supposed, the text or an abridgment of the *Book of Revelation*. It is, in fact, only a book of pictures, and these pictures in many points border very closely on the ridiculous. One cannot shut his eyes to the ludicrous points, but neither can he overlook the fact that the designs of the book are not the work of an ignorant artist. Rudely as they have been cut, and badly as they were printed, there is strong character in the faces, and much artistic skill in the grouping of the figures. The designs are vigorous, but they are unlike the works of Van Eyck, or of the German artists of the period. There is nothing in the costumes or architecture which can be rated as decidedly German or Dutch. Chatto says the designs were probably intended to represent Mahomet as the Antichrist of the *Book of Revelation*, and that they may have been made by an exiled Byzantine artist who had been driven out of Constantinople after the taking of that city by the Turks in 1453. But this conjecture is not approved by careful bibliographers. It is generally supposed that the designs are of an earlier period. Maittaire, who says that it is the oldest[1] of all block-books, calls attention to the singular simplicity of the engraving, which is in almost plain outline. In this particular the *Apocalypse* is much inferior to the *Bible of the Poor*, for we see no attempt to give appearance of roundness to the limbs by curved shading lines, nor are there proper marks to indicate the shadows and folds in a dress. But the ruder workmanship of the engraver is more clearly shown in the letters. It may be that they were badly drawn upon the block, but it is plain that the engraver has frequently broken connecting lines. Bad presswork and bad ink have materially aggravated the fault; as printed, the lines of the engraver appear thicker than they were cut.

Each page has two illustrations with explanatory legends. Some of these illustrations represent the visions of St. John, but the designer has drawn them with the same disregard of time and place which may be noticed in the wood-cuts of the *Bible of the Poor.* The architecture is that of Germany in the fourteenth century; the men wear breeches and coats, conical, flat-topped and broad-brimmed hats; the soldiers are in chain or in plate armor, with the helmets and battle-axes of the middle ages. Nor do the improprieties stop here: many of the illustrations represent events in the life of the apostle which the artist did not find in the *New Testament.*

The illustration on page 213, which is a reduced copy of the first page in one edition of the *Apocalypse*, seems to have been derived from the fabulous life of St. John, supposed to have been written by Abdias, bishop of Babylon. Drusiana, a

[1] The great prices paid for copies of the book seem to show that this is a very general belief. Sotheby has wisely put some of them on record in his *Principia Typographica.*

Gaignat copy .... 300 francs.
La Vallière copy.. .... 800 "
Crevenna copy........... 510 florins.
Wilks copy, 1847 .... 74*l.*
Brienne-Laire copy......... 600 francs.
Lang copy, 1828 .... 45*l.*
Verdussen copy............ 240 florins.
Corser copy, 1873 (Quaritch), 550*l.*
Inglis copy................ 47*l.* 5*s.*
British Museum copy, 1845.. 160*l.*
Quaritch's, 1873..... ..... 200*l.*
Stowe copy, 1849........... 91*l.*

married lady of Ephesus, and one of the many converts of St. John, is an important personage in this fabulous life and in the illustration annexed. In the upper picture, St. John is represented as preaching to a magnate, whose robe or mantle is held by two attendants. Drusiana stands behind them. This picture is described in the legend:

Conversi ab idolis per predicacionem beati Johannis Drusiana et cetera.	Through the preaching of St. John, I have turned from idols Drusiana and others.

In the lower picture, St. John is represented as baptizing Drusiana in the Christian temple of Ephesus. Drusiana is judiciously abbreviated to suit the size of the baptismal font. Six armed men are before the barred door, endeavoring, by violence, to gain entrance, or to witness the ceremony. The picture is explained by the words:

Sts Johannes baptisans Drusiana.	St. John baptizing Drusiana.
Cultores ydolorum explorantes facta ejus.	The worshipers of idols watching his [St. John's] proceedings.

The edition of the *Apocalypse* named by Heineken as the first was planned by a practical book-maker, and was made up in sections of eight double leaves. The first and last pages of each section were probably engraved together on one block. They were certainly printed together by the following plan:

1—16	3—14	5—12	7—10
2—15	4—13	6—11	8— 9

Page 1 was engraved on the right, and page 16 on the left end of the block. Page 2 was on the left, and 15 on the right. This alternation was maintained on all sheets of the section.[1] The printed sheets, 1, 3, 5 and 7 were folded with the printed work on the inside; while sheets 2, 4, 6 and 8 were folded with the printed work on the outside. When the sheets were properly collected, two printed pages faced each other, and were followed by two pages of blanks. This method of making

[1] A section consists of two or more sheets folded together, so that one leaf will be within another, as sheets of folded letter paper are nested. If five quarter quires of letter paper were sewed together, and bound, the book so bound, in binders' phrase, would have five sections.

Fac-simile of the First Page of the Apocalypse.
Engraving in the original print is 7⅞ by 10⅓ American inches.
[From Heineken.]

up the book must have given the printer and the binder a great deal of trouble, but it was an efficient method, and the only one that should have been employed.

In most editions of the book, the ink is of the same rusty brown color that has been observed in the *Bible of the Poor*. In some copies it is almost gray; in others, nearly black. The first edition has engravings of the greatest merit, but it is badly printed. The paper-mark is a bunch of grapes, similar in design to that of a print in the collection of M. Weigel, entitled *The Adoration of the Three Kings*, which, it is claimed, was printed about the year 1425. But paper-marks are misleading evidences. We do not certainly know the date nor the country in which any edition of the book was printed. German bibliographers say that it was printed in Southern Germany; Dutch bibliographers say that it was printed in the Netherlands, probably by Coster of Haarlem; but all evidences that have been adduced to establish a certain date for the earlier editions of the book, or to prove that they were done at any time or by any printer, are unsatisfactory. Some copies of the book are interleaved with manuscript explanations, which are sometimes in the Dutch, and sometimes in the German language. The greater part of the copies have been found in Germany, and it is the opinion of the most eminent bibliographers that the first edition of the book, and most of the editions, were printed in Germany.

The catalogue of the library of Dr. Kloss contains the following note under the specification of a ragged copy of the *Apocalypse*: "At the end of this volume is a short note, written by Pope Martin V, who occupied the papal chair from 1417 to 1431." This indirect attestation to the age of the book has never been considered as trustworthy.

Another copy of the book, known as the Spencer copy, is bound up with a copy of the *Bible of the Poor*, and has on the binding an inscription to this effect: "Bound in the year of our Lord 1467 by me, John Reichenbach, in Gyllingen." The inscription is undoubtedly authentic.

Dibdin[1] alludes to an English clergyman who said that he was once the owner of one copy each of the *Apocalypse*, the *Bible of the Poor*, and the *Ars Moriendi*, all bound in one volume, on the cover of which was stamped an inscription certifying that "this volume was bound for the curate of the church in 142–." The last figure the clergyman had forgotten, but he was sure that the book was in its original binding, and that it must have been bound, and consequently printed, before 1430. The testimony is unsatisfactory.

THE CANTICLES.

This is a block-book[2] of sixteen pages, of small folio size. It is one of the few block-books which may be unhesitatingly pronounced as of Netherlandish origin. In general appearance it closely resembles the books previously noticed. The impressions are in brown ink, and on one side of the sheet; there are two illustrations on each page, and the two printed pages face each other; the explanations of the designs are in Latin, and are engraved in scrolls that surround the figures. According to some bibliographers, there are three editions of the book; according to others, the trifling variations which have been seized upon to justify the existence of a second and a third edition are only alterations or repairs that have been sustained by the original block. One edition contains at the head of the first page an engraved line, in the low Dutch or Flemish language, which may be translated thus: "This is the Prefiguration of Mary, the Mother of God, which, in Latin, is called *The Canticles*." Explanatory titles in block-books, and even in the earlier typographic books, are unusual. For this reason the genuineness of the inscription has been challenged, but it has been generally accepted as a true part of the original block.

[1] *Bibliotheca Spenceriana*, vol. 1, p. 4, as quoted by Ottley, p. 99.

[2] This book is sometimes described as *The History of the Virgin Mary, or The Prefiguration of the Virgin Mary from the Song of Songs.*

The illustration opposite is the fac-simile, reduced in size, of the first page of the *Canticles*. The design is imperfectly explained by the legends in the engraving.

Osculetur me osculo oris sui; quia meliora sunt ubera tua vino.	Let him kiss me with the kisses of his mouth, for thy love is better than wine.
Veni in hortum meum, soror mea sponsa messui myrrham meum cum aromatibus meis.	I am come into my garden, my sister, my spouse: I have gathered my myrrh with my spice.
Caput tuum ut Carmelus; collum tuum sicut turris eburnea.	Thine head is like Carmel; thy neck is like a tower of ivory.
Nigra sum, sed formosa, filiæ Jerusalem, sicut tabernacula cedar, sicut pelles Solomonis.	I am black but comely, O ye daughters of Jerusalem; As the tents of Kedar, as the curtains of Solomon.

The agriculturists of the upper illustration are in monastic habits: some are cutting and threshing grain; one is pounding the grain in a mortar and another is grinding it in a hand mill. In the open little house before the monk with a pestle, is a desk with two books. In this combination of agricultural work with the emblem or suggestion of study, Harzen sees an illustration of the daily work of the Brethren of the Life-in-Common, to whom he attributes the engraving and printing of this book. The brethren of this order were eminent as students and copyists of books, and had some distinction in the last quarter of the fifteenth century as printers, but their connection with this book cannot be established. [1]

The words at the top of one of the cuts are not the only Dutch feature in the book: the style of design is that of the Netherlandish school of art. The blocks have been drawn and engraved with much more care than those of the *Apocalypse*, or the *Bible of the Poor*. There is more of grace in the attitudes and draperies of the female figures of the *Canticles*, and less of that gross and unimaginative treatment of sacred personages which borders both on the ludicrous and the profane. But

[1] It is probable that the cowled farmers represent the lay brothers, then very numerous in nearly every thrifty monastery. The farmers, butchers, bakers, carpenters and useful mechanics were often permitted to wear the dress and share some of the privileges of the monks, on condition that they should do the servile work, and accept as a full reward the rich blessings of monastic prayers and masses.

Fac-simile of the First Page of the Canticles.

Engraving in the original print is 7¼ by 10½ American inches.

[From Heineken.]

the designer of the book presents the oriental love story to his readers with Dutch accessories. The bride of the Song of Solomon wanders about the streets of a city supposed to be Jerusalem, but the dwellings have high-peaked roofs, Dutch gables, and overhanging upper stories; she is assaulted by an armed and helmeted cavalier who carries on his shield the heraldic black eagle of some unknown German potentate; the pope, two cardinals and a bishop, with drawn swords in their hands and shields on their arms, look with great composure over Gothic battlements on the assault below. Writers who are skilled in heraldry say that there is a peculiar significance in the presentation of the devices and the arms on shields which are found in many places in the book. Some German authors see in these devices the arms of the German Empire, of Wittemburg and of minor German principalities. Those who believe that the book was printed in the Netherlands, see in the shields the arms of Burgundy, of Alsace, and of Flemish towns and cities. From these trivial evidences, the conclusion has been drawn by one class of partisans that the designer must have been a German, and, by another class, that he must have been a Hollander.[1]

[1] These devices give us no certain clue to the engraver or printer of the book, but they are of value in assisting us to ascertain the purpose for which the book was made. There are no old manuscript copies of the book, but there are many evidences that it was designed and produced for the first time in the fifteenth century. It would seem that this pictorial version of the *Canticles* was designed, not so much to illustrate the prefiguration of the Virgin Mary, as the termination of a great schism which had divided the Catholic church between the years 1378 and 1449. Christendom had been scandalized by the rule of two, and, for a short period, of three rival popes. It was believed that this schism in the church would have been closed by the action of the Council of Constance, which terminated in 1418; but this result was not accomplished until 1449, when Nicholas V became the only pope. The designer of the pictures has treated the return of Christendom to the rule of one pope as the reconciliation of Christ with the church. To give special significance to the subject, he has introduced the armorial shields of the magnates at the councils. It may be that the engravings were made in 1420, but it could be maintained with plausibility that they were made after the dissolution of the Council of Basle in 1448.

The engraved letters of this book are much more legible than those of the *Apocalypse* or the *Bible of the Poor*. The Dutch final *t* is frequently introduced. The paper-marks most frequently observed are the unicorn, the bull's head, and the letter P; but no information of value can be derived from the paper-marks, and but little from the designs and engravings.

Although we do not know whether the *Canticles* was printed in the second or third quarter of the fifteenth century, it may be admitted that it was printed in the Netherlands. We see the last trace of the blocks in the hands of the same printer who destroyed the engravings of the *Bible of the Poor*. A book, bearing the imprint of Peter Van Os, of Zwoll, 1494, has for its frontispiece the upper half of the first plate.

THE STORY OF THE BLESSED VIRGIN.

This is the bibliographic title[1] of a block-book which may be offered as a proper specimen of the popular religious literature of the fifteenth century. Sotheby mentions four distinct editions of the work. The one that has been most frequently described (whether first or last, is not known) consists of sixteen leaves, with four illustrations on each leaf, and a brief explanatory text in Latin. The designs have no artistic merit; the engraving is coarse, and evidently the work of a novice; the letters are legible, but they betray great inexperience in the use of the graver, and they do not, in any feature, resemble those of the block-books previously described. Some of them have mannerisms like those of Gutenberg's Bible. It is possible that the letters of one edition of the book are those of movable types, or that they were engraved on wood from a transfer taken from an impression of movable types. In all editions the letters have German peculiarities, but there is no edition which has the appearance of a first experiment in

[1] The full title of the book is, as given by Heineken, *The Story of the Blessed Virgin Mary, collected from the Evangelists and the Fathers, and Illustrated by Engravings*. Dibdin calls it, *The Defense of the Immaculate Conception of the Blessed Virgin Mary*.

printing. It is probable that all the editions were printed in Germany, and after the invention of typography.

The edition from which the annexed illustration was taken was roughly printed on one side of the paper, but in a very black ink. In other editions, which were printed from entirely different blocks, differing both in the size of the block and in the positions of the figures, the ink is of the customary rusty brown. The copy in black is supposed to have been printed on a press, and at a later date.

The object of the book is to show the reasonableness of the story of the Incarnation, and to defend the dogma of the Immaculate Conception. The bad taste of the author is more signally shown in the text than in the pictures. Arguments in support of the dogma are wrested from sacred history and heathen mythology, and the writings of the fathers of the church. The book is a curious compend of piety and unconscious irreverence, of high scholarship and gross stupidity, as will be more clearly shown by the following translation of the legends that explain the pictures on the opposite page.

Temple of Venus, with a man gazing at a lamp. If the light at the temple of Venus cannot be extinguished, why should not the Virgin generate without the seed of Venus? *Augustine de Civitate Dei*, XXI, 7.

Two Human Figures and a Statue. If a human being can be changed into stone, why, by divine power, should not the Virgin generate? *Albertus de Minoralium*, I, *in fine*.

A man gazing at water that reflects the moon. If Seleucus in Persia finds [reflected] light from the moon, why should not the Virgin, pregnant by a beautiful star, generate? *Augustine de Civitate Dei*, XX, 6.

Two men sawing a stone on which appear two human heads. If man can be painted on stone by the power of heaven, why should not the Virgin generate by the assistance of the Holy Spirit? *Albertus de Minoralium*, II, I.

The book begins with representations of St. Ambrose, St. Jerome, St. Gregory and St. Augustine. St. Ambrose, who is duly quoted from his *Hexameron*, book II, chapter 41, assigns reasons for the Immaculate Conception, by illogical reference to a bird without a mate. St. Augustine, who is represented as seated at a table, reading from his work, *De Mirabilibus*, book III, chapter 12, asserts the Immaculate Conception because many animals are produced without mating. St. Jerome and

Si lumen' phani veneris nullus ex
tinguere valet. quare absq3 veneris
semine virgo non generaret. augus
tinus. xxi. de ciuitate dei. capi. vij.

Seleucus in perside lucem lune si ha
bet. cur feta almo sidere vgo non ge
neraret. augustin'. xx. de, ciuitate dei.
capitulo sexto.

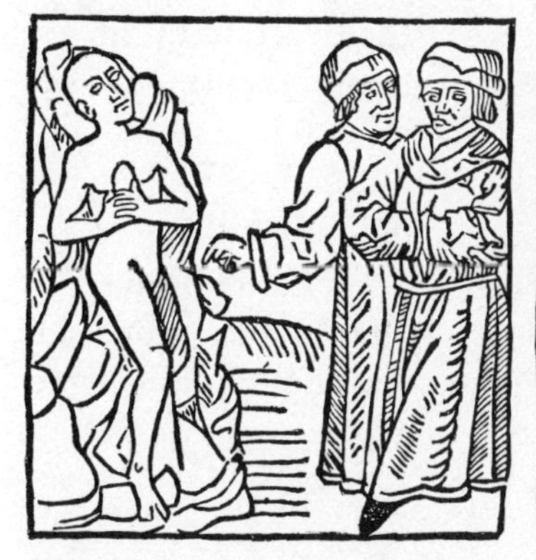

Si homo vi nature in saxū verti va
let. cur vi diuine cure virgo non ge
neraret. albertus primo minorali
um in fine.

Homo si in lapide vi celi pingi valet.
cur almi spūs opere vgo non genera
ret. albertus. ij. minoralium tractatu
ij. capitulo primo.

Fac-simile of a page of the Story of the Blessed Virgin.
Engraving in the original print is 7⅜ by 10½ American inches.

[From Heineken,]

St. Gregory expound the same doctrine. Fifty-four illustrations follow, each explained by a proposition that enunciates with great formality some of the marvels of natural science. We are told of bees without fathers, of birds impregnated by the bill, of geese born from trees, of asbestos that burns forever, of pearls made fruitful by the dew, of the phœnix restored by fire, and of many other absurdities. The authorities cited seem to have been selected with a truly catholic spirit: we find among them Valerius Maximus, Peter Comestor, Terence, Boethius, Job, Livy, and Isidore.

One edition of this work contains an imprint in sprawling and almost unreadable characters, which bibliographers interpret as the letters F. W. 1470. The letters F. W. were no doubt the initials of Frederich Walther of Nordlingen.

The quality of the science taught in this *History of the Blessed Virgin* enables us to form a just idea of the real value of the scholastic philosophy then regarded as the perfection of wisdom. The silly speculations set forth in the book were the husks upon which a devout people were fed.

AN EXERCISE ON THE LORD'S PRAYER.

This is the translated title of a thin block-book of ten leaves, which was intended to explain the Lord's Prayer by illustration. The blocks are printed in brown ink on one side of the paper. The *Exercise* is in the popular form of dialogue.

In the illustration No. 1, the monk *Frater* begs the angel *Oratio* to teach him the Lord's Prayer. And these are the lessons that are taught:

2. *Our Father who art in Heaven.* Christ, the Monk, and the Angel kneel.

3. *Hallowed be thy name.* The Monk, the Angel, Christ, and the Church represented by a female figure, are kneeling. On the right the Virgin and Holy Child.

4. *Thy kingdom come.* A representation of Purgatory: in the upper part, the wicked surrounded by flames; in the lower part, Jews and Pagans in the fiery lake.

5. *Thy will be done.* The Almighty in the clouds, and before him the Angel and the Monk kneeling. On the right, a good Christian and an Angel. In the centre, two bad men who are rejecting the Eucharist. In the foreground, the Jews and Pagans throw down the cup and are pouring out its contents.

Scroll in No. 5. Frater and Oratio kneeling before God. Fiat voluntas tua sicut in cœlo et in terra. Let Thy will be done in Heaven as on earth ... *The Angel to the right.* Qui stat videat ne cadat. Let him who may stand take heed lest he fall... *The Good Christian.*

Gratia Dei sum id quod sum. Thanks to God that I am what I am... *The Jews.* **Quis est Jesus filius fabri?** Who is Jesus but the son of the carpenter? *The Pagans.* **Quis noster dominus est?** Who is our Lord?.... *The Bad Christians.* **Ducamus in bonis dies nostros.** We guide ourselves to salvation.

6. *Give us this day our daily bread.* In the centre, three loaves of bread on a table, around which is Charity, robed as a queen, with three other figures. On one side the Monk and Angel kneeling; on the other, a Knight in armor.

7. *Forgive us our trespasses.* Christ standing on the altar, the blood pouring from his side in a basin, from which several persons fill their cups.

8. *Lead us not into temptation.* The disobedient, proud, gluttonous and avaricious surround a table. Death carries away the foremost.

9. *Deliver us from evil.* A representation of Hell. The disobedient man in the power of the Devil. The damned making supplication to the Almighty.

10. *Amen.* A view of Paradise, with the happiness of the blessed.

Fac-simile of the Fifth Illustration of the Exercise on the Lord's Prayer.
Engraving in the original print is 7⅛ by 7½ American inches.
[From Holtrop.]

Santander says that the book bears all the marks of the highest antiquity. Holtrop says that there is one copy of this work in which the Latin text is translated, and explained by engraved lines in Flemish at the bottom of each cut. Guichard describes a series of engravings on wood, consisting of eight designs like those just described, with a manuscript text in Flemish. It is, without doubt, a Flemish book. Of the many extraordinary commentaries which have been made on the *Lord's Prayer*, this, surely, is the most singular perversion. The prayer which begins with a recognition of the brotherhood of mankind, which tells us to believe in the all-embracing love of the Father, which teaches lessons of dependence, forgiveness and protection, is made the text for a denunciation of Jews and Pagans, and for the teaching of doctrinal notions about the Eucharist.

THE BOOK OF KINGS.

In this book, two separate illustrations, with their explanatory text, are printed together on each page. The *Book of Kings* might, therefore, be classified among the block-books without separate pages of text, but it really has a text of unusual length for a book of this class. In other features, it resembles the block-books previously described; its twenty pages are printed on one side of the leaf; the illustrations face each other, and are in the customary brown ink. The designs are rudely drawn, and are as full of anachronisms in architecture as the illustrations of the *Bible of the Poor*, but the architecture most frequently shown is in the pointed Gothic style. The engraving is coarse; every object is cut in bold and heavy outline; tints and shading lines are timidly used, and always in a crude manner. It was obviously intended that the illustrations should be developed by painting or by stenciling. The letters are drawn and engraved with more care than the pictures, but they are irregular in size and form. One of the peculiarities of the lettering is the final cross given to the small letter *t*, a peculiarity which is frequently

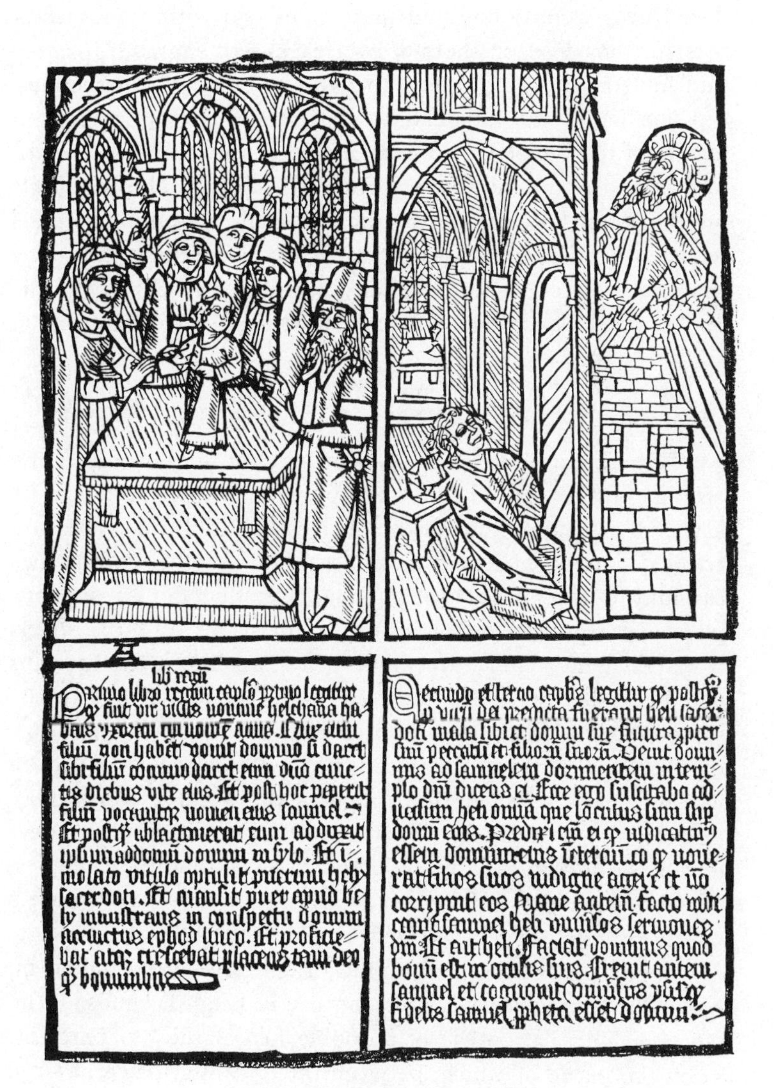

Libri regum

Primo libro regum capitulo primo legitur q fuit vir unus nomine helchana habens uxorem cui nomen anna. Que cum filium non haberet vovit domino si daret sibi filium commodo daret eum dno cunctis diebus vite eius. Et post hoc peperit filium vocavitqz nomen eius samuel. Et postqz ablactaverat eum adduxit ipsum in domum domini in sylo. Et immolato vitulo optulit puerum heli sacerdoti. Et mansit puer apud heli ministrans in conspectu domini accinctus ephod lineo. Et proficiebat atqz crescebat placens tam deo qz hominibus

Secundo et tercio capitulis legitur q postqz verba dei predicta fuerant heli sacerdoti mala sibi et domui sue futura pro eo quod peccatum filiorum suorum. Venit dominus ad samuelem dormientem in templo dni dicens ei. Ecce ego suscitabo adversum heli omnia que locutus sum super domum eius. Predixi enim ei q iudicaturus essem domum eius in eternum eo q noverat filios suos indigne agere et non corripuit eos. Mane autem facto indicavit samuel heli universos sermones dni. Et ait heli. Faciat dominus quod bonum est in oculis suis. Crevit autem samuel et cognovit universus ysrael q fidelis samuel propheta esset domini.

An Illustration from the Book of Kings.
Original is 7 by 8¾ inches.

[From Sotheby.]

noticed in some of the typographic work of Dutch printers. The leaves were not nested in sections one within another as was customary: each sheet of two leaves was engraved, printed and folded separately, so as to make a book of ten sections.

The book was intended to illustrate the more important events of the life of David as recorded in the books of *Samuel*, and in the *First* and *Second Books of Kings*. The fac-simile on the preceding page illustrates Hannah presenting Samuel to the priests in the house of the Lord, and Samuel called by the Lord out of sleep. Sotheby classifies it with the block-books of Holland, but Falkenstein attributes it to Germany.

THE GROTESQUE ALPHABET.

This is a curious block-book of twenty-four pages, of the original edition of which not one perfect copy is known. The leaves of the copy now on the shelves of the British Museum are 3¾ inches wide and 6 inches high. Sotheby, who has carefully examined its construction, says that the twenty-four pages were printed in sections of eight pages on three sheets of paper, with a thin watery ink of a sepia tint. The margins and blanks have been written on with an ink of nearly the same color as that of the printed cuts.

Another copy of this work has been found at Basle, in which, on the letter A (not found in the London copy), may be seen the date 1464. Another copy, in a library at Dresden, has the same date. Renouvier says that these copies, by German engravers, and of inferior execution, are transfers of the original, which was engraved in the Netherlands.

The history of the book in the British Museum is unknown, but it has many evidences of long use in English hands. The cover or binding consists of a double fold of thick parchment, upon the inside of which, between the folds, is written in large English characters, "Edwardus Lowes." On one side of the last leaf is the rough draft of a letter in the English language. The writing, which is found in scraps all over the book, is of the period of Henry VIII. Upon a sword-blade in the cut of the letter L is written in small characters the word London. In another place in the same cut are letters which are read by some as *Westmistre*—by others as *Bethemsted.* It is full of English writing, but it has not been proved that the cuts are the work of an English engraver. Chatto says of them:

——They were neither designed nor engraved by the artists who designed and engraved the cuts in the *Apocalypse*, the *History of the Virgin* and the *Poor Preachers' Bible.* . . . With respect to drawing, engraving and expression, the cuts of the *Alphabet* are decidedly superior to those of every block-book, and generally to all wood engravings executed before the year 1500, with the exception of such as are by Albert Durer, and those contained in the *Hypnerotomachia*, printed by Aldus at Venice in 1499. . . . I perceive nothing in them to induce me to suppose that they were the work of a Dutch artist; and I am as little inclined to ascribe them to a German. The style of the drawing is not unlike what we see in illuminated French manuscripts of the middle of the fifteenth century; and as the only two engraved words which occur in the volume are in French, I am rather inclined to suppose that the artist who made the designs was a native of France. The costume of the female to whom the words are addressed appears to be French; and the action of the lover kneeling seems almost characteristic of the nation. No Dutchman

Letter K of Grotesque Alphabet.
Original is 3½ by 4⅝ inches.
[From Holtrop.]

certainly ever addressed his mistress with such an air. He holds what appears to be a ring as gracefully as a modern Frenchman holds a snuff-box, and upon the scroll before him are engraved a heart, and the words which he may be supposed to utter: *Mon ame*—My soul.[1]

The real object of this book is not apparent. The figures were not engraved for the purpose of teaching the alphabet, for the designs are quaint, elaborate, and above the comprehension of young children. When the book was first made, the letters had a significance which seems to have been forgotten.

A Page from the Apostles' Creed.
Original is 5⅜ by 8⅛ inches.
[From Dibdin.]

THE APOSTLES' CREED.

This is the title given to a lost block-book, of which only seven leaves remain. The annexed illustration is a reduced fac-simile of the page that tells the story of the Resurrection. The four angels about the circle are sounding the last trump, and the dead are coming forth from their graves. The figures in the lower corners are those of Zacharias and Judas. In this book, and in nearly all the block-books, the subjects most frequently presented are those that illustrate the marvelous and terrible. The designs have merit, but the letters are badly engraved. The pictures are explained by a few lines in German. The

[1] The reading should be, *Mon cœur avez,*—you have my heart,—the word heart being represented not by letters, but by a drawing.

copy of the book described by Dibdin has on the fly-leaf the written memorandum V. W. 1471, but it is not probable that this writing has any reference to the date of printing.

THE EIGHT ROGUERIES.

This is a small block-book of eight leaves. Weigel places it among the earliest specimens of engraving on wood. The language in which the pictures are explained is High German. The pictures illustrate the Go-between, the Liar, the Cheat, the Counterfeit Goldsmith, the Cheating Merchant, the Church Robber, the Cheating Rope-maker, the Blacksmith that sells iron for steel. The designs are rude, but they are full of spirit and character, and the cutting of the figures has been done with ability and intelligence. The paper was printed on one side only and in dull brown ink. This book was found in the neglected library of an old South German monastery, in the heart of the neighborhood in which we find the earliest notices of printers and painters of images. As it is the only block-book of a decidedly non-religious character, it may be ascribed to some maker of playing cards, who practised the art of engraving before it was placed under the control of the Church.

A Page from the Eight Rogueries.
Original is 4 by 5⅜ inches.

[From Falkenstein.]

XII

Block-Books of Images with Text.

The Antichrist, with Fac-simile...How to Remember the Evangelists, with Fac-simile...How to Die Becomingly, with Fac-simile...Other Editions of this Work...Chiromancy of Doctor Hartleib, with Fac-simile...German Planetarium and Calendar, with Fac-simile...Wonders of Rome, with Fac-simile...Pomerium Spirituale, with Fac-simile...Temptations of the Devil, with Fac-simile. Life of St. Meinrat, with Fac-simile...Dance of Death, with Fac-simile...Mechanical Peculiarities of the Block-Books...All of Religious Character...Made for Priests, but seen by the People. Not Adapted to the Needs of the People...The Period of the Block-Books...Made in Germany and the Netherlands...Dates and Printers of the Books Unknown...Probably Made in the First Quarter of the Fifteenth Century...An Established Business before the Invention of Typography.

This, that is written in this little book, ought the priests to learn and teach to their parishes: and it is also necessary for simple priests that understand not the Scriptures, and it is made for simple people.... by cause that for to hear examples stirreth and moveth the people that ben simple more to devotion than great authority of science. *Caxton's Preface to the Doctrinal of Sapyence.*

DER ENDKRIST, OR THE ANTICHRIST. This book seems to have been written to warn men against the snares of heresy. Two distinct editions are known; each was printed from a different suite of blocks and by a different printer. The copy about to be described has thirty-eight leaves, twenty-six of which are devoted to the life of Antichrist, and eleven to a separate treatise known as the *Fifteen Signs*, which was bound up with the *Antichrist*, and of which it seems to be the proper sequel. The book is printed on one side of the leaf, in brown ink, and the illustrations face each other. The text begins with the words "Here beginneth of Antichrist, taken and drawn out of many books, how and of whom he shall be born." After a half-page wood-cut, which represents with needless grossness the birth of Antichrist, follow other engravings illustrating the more notable events of his life.[1] The fac-simile on the following page gives a correct notion of the lawlessness of the designs[2] of the book. It is obvious that they were not made by the artist who drew the illustrations for the *Bible of the Poor* or for the *Canticles*. The text which explains the wood-cuts is in the German language, but it is in a very careless form of German writing.

[1] The following synopsis of the work is condensed from the translation of the text of the book, as given by Sotheby in his *Principia Typographica*, vol. II, pp. 38–45:

Antichrist is born in Babylon. He yields himself to lust of women at Bethsaida. He is circumcised, and announces himself as the Messiah. He is instructed in magic and all sorts of evil. Elias and Enoch come down from Heaven and preach against him. Antichrist deceives the world by superior eloquence; he performs miracles; his apostles preach to the kings of Lybia and Ethiopia, and "the queen of the Amazons, and the Red Jews." All the kings of the world are converted to Antichrist; he condemns unbelievers to strange tortures; he kills Elias and Enoch. He repeats the history of the resurrection; he bids the whole world witness his ascent to Heaven from the Mount of Olives. The Almighty then gives the order—"Michael, strike him dead; I will no longer bear with the unjust." Antichrist is carried to Hell, where he is received by the Devil and his allies. Antichrist being dead, princes and people become Christians, and there is only one faith. But the people fear the Day of Judgment. These are some of the signs of the great and terrible day: The sea shall rise forty ells above the mountains; it shall then sink away and vanish. The sea shall burn. Trees and plants shall sweat blood. There will be earthquakes. Buildings and trees shall fall down in hopeless ruin. Stones shall fly up in the air. Wild beasts grow tame with fright, and run to men for help. The dead arise. Stars fall from Heaven. Heaven and earth are burnt up and chaos comes again. At this point the imagination of the designer was exhausted: he had done his best. The page following, which should have been filled with an illustration, is judiciously left blank. The last engraving is that of the resurrection of the blessed.

[2] The central figure in the lower illustration, the meek and priestly personage who, surrounded by gamboling devils, and with a monkey perched upon his back, walks with measured pace and uplifted eyes, is the Antichrist. This is the introduction to the explanatory text:

Antichrist is instructed by adepts, who teach him to make gold, the art of magic, and all sorts of evil. And this takes place at the city named Corosaym. And this stands also written in the *Compendium Theologiæ*. And our Lord curses the said city in his gospel, and says thus: "Woe to thee, Corosaym!"

Here, we see Antichrist goes from Capernaum to Jerusalem, and he there announces himself as holy. And hereof is also written in the book *Compendium Theologiæ*. And our Lord, in the gospel, also curses this city, and speaks thus concerning it: "Woe to thee, Capernaum!"

Der Enndkrist hat bey im maister · Die in lernen gold machen · Und ander zaubrey vnd pös list · Und das beschicht in der Stat genant Corosaym Und das stet auch geschriben in Compendio Theologie · Und vnser herr flücht derselben stat auch in dem Ewangelio, Do er spricht, Wee dir Corosaym

Hie gät der Enndkrist von Capharnaym · gen Iherusalem · Und heit sich da auf geben er sei hailig · Und dauon stat auch geschriben in dem püch Compendio Theologie · Und vnser herr flücht der selben stat auch in dem Ewangelio, Und spricht also · Wee dir Capharnaym

Fac-simile, reduced, of a Page of the Antichrist.

[From Heineken.]

The thirty-eight leaves of one edition are made up in one section. This bungling method of making up a book is sufficient evidence that the printer or engraver who placed these pages together had no education in practical book-making. But the bad method shown in the plan does not prove that the book is of great age. The copy under notice contains, in the German language, the imprint of *Junghannis, priffmaler*, or painter of cards, Nuremberg, 1472. Whether this Junghannis was the designer, printer or engraver is not known.

HOW TO REMEMBER THE EVANGELISTS.

This block-book[1] was, no doubt, intended for men, but a modern observer would say that it had been made for children. The time-honored method, still used for the child's alphabet, A was an apple, is the method of the *Ars Memorandi*. Compared with the block-books previously noticed, it is a book of high merit. It is a thin folio of thirty pages, fifteen of which contain a text of very large, clumsily drawn and compactly arranged letters within a rule-bordered frame; the remaining fifteen pages have full-page illustrations. The edition from which the annexed illustration was copied is in brown ink.

The designs are more eccentric than those of any known block-book, but the designer has shown no artistic ability in the grouping of his figures. The four Evangelists are symbolized—St. John by an eagle, St. Matthew by an angel, St. Luke by a bull, St. Mark by a lion—but they are presented to us in uncouth attitudes, and are surrounded or overlaid by some of the familiar objects frequently mentioned in the Gospels. These objects are numbered with Arabic figures referring to explanations in the text. The dove, for it must be so considered, although it looks like an owl, perched on the head of the symbolized St. John, may be accepted as the emblem of the Deity. The two heads beside the eagle are to be understood as those of Moses and of Christ. The musical instruments, a lute and three bells, on the breast of the eagle, indicate the contents

[1] The Latin title is *Ars Memorandi, notabilis per figuras evangelistarum.*

Fac-simile of a Page of the Ars Memorandi.
Engraving in the original print is 6¾ by 9¼ American inches.
[From Heineken.]

of the second chapter, the marriage at Cana. The fish recalls the pool of Bethesda. The numeral 3 points to the conversation with Nicodemus; the water-bucket and the crown refer to the woman of Samaria at the well; the five loaves and the two small fishes to the feeding of the multitude. The cross in the circle is the consecrated wafer of the Roman Catholic Church. The letters in the pages of text are unusually large; they are clearly cut, but are so compactly arranged that they frequently interfere with each other. The descriptive text is in Latin, but of very objectionable grammar and orthography. The knowledge it conveys of the Gospel is imperfect to the last degree, as may be more clearly seen in the following literal translation of the text provided for this illustration.

The Gospel of St. John has twenty-one chapters. *First Chapter.* In the beginning was the Word, from the eternity of the Word and the Trinity. *Second Chapter.* Nuptials were made in Cana of Galilee, and how Christ overturned the tables of all the money-changers. *Third Chapter.* But there was a man among the Pharisees named Nicodemus. *Fourth Chapter.* How Jesus asked the Samaritan woman to give him to drink near the well of Jacob, and about the law. *Fifth Chapter.* About the miracle in the fish pool, when Jesus told the lame man, Take up thy bed and walk. *Sixth Chapter.* About the feeding with five loaves and two fishes, and about the Eucharist.

The *Ars Memorandi* is considered by Schelhorn as one of the oldest of block-books, "if not the first, among the first." Von Aretin says that "it is worthy of observation that this book, one of the earliest of its kind, should be devoted to the improvement of the memory, when it was to be rendered of little consequence by the art of printing."

HOW TO DIE BECOMINGLY.[1]

At least ten distinct xylographic editions of this popular block-book have been identified, seven of which are in Latin and three in German. The text of the book is substantially the same in all editions, but the designs are dissimilar, and the engraving and printing are of unequal merit. Some copies are in black and others in brown ink; some are printed on

[1] The bibliographic title is *Ars Moriendi*, or, literally, The Art of Dying, but the work is more clearly described by the paraphrase *How to Die Becomingly*. It is also known as *The Temptations of Demons*.

one side and others on both sides of the paper. The origin of the book is not known, but it was a popular work long after types had been invented; before the year 1500, it had been printed either from types or from blocks, in Nuremberg, Paris, Rome, Florence, Verona, Lyons, Utrecht, Delft and Zwoll.

The edition about to be described, which Heineken names as the fourth, is a folio of twenty-four leaves. It is printed in brown ink, on one side, with printed pages facing each other. Eleven pages have illustrations, and thirteen pages are given to the text. The book is made up in workmanlike manner, in four sections of six leaves. The illustrations are crowded; the figures are grouped inartistically; the engraving is coarse.

The object of the book is to present the temptations that beset the dying. The first illustration represents the dying man as tempted by devils concerning his faith. The next illustration shows the good angels who enable him to remain steadfast. In like manner he is tempted by devils to despair, to impatience (in which the moribund is vigorously kicking an attendant), to vainglory, and to avarice; but through help of the angels, he triumphs over all his adversaries. The ninth illustration, which is reproduced on the following page, shows the dying man as resisting the last assaults of three emissaries of the devil. The vigorous action of these hideous goblins is in marked contrast with the composure of the relatives, who stand at a respectful distance. The horse and hostler show that the man on the death-bed was rich. The moral of the design is the vanity of riches. One of the devils, the one at the head of the bed, maliciously suggests, *Provideas amicis*—you should provide for your friends. Another devil, pointing to the house, calls out with grim irony—*Intende thesauro*—pay attention to your treasures. This illustration is followed by another in which a ministering angel exhorts the dying man to discard the devil's advice, and not leave his property to his relatives, but to give it to the church. In the last illustration, the spirit of the dying man exhales from his mouth in the shape of a manikin, which is received by the angels. The

Fac-simile of a Page of the Ars Moriendi.
Engraving in the original print is 6½ by 8¾ American inches.
[From Heineken.]

baffled devils make some frightful contortions and then depart. It is not a pleasant book. But the hideousness of the devils in the illustrations is not so revolting as the craftiness of the author who devised these ghastly scarecrows. The ostensible purpose of the book was the preparation of men for another world; its real object was the aggrandizement of the church, and for this purpose the writer of the book recommended the sacrifice of the desire to provide for one's family. It does not increase our respect for the piety or intelligence of the people to learn that this book was popular for more than a century.

The xylographic editions of this work which contain the names of the printers are in the German language. One of them has these words, *Hans Sporer*, 1473; another has the imprint of *J. W. Presbrm*, of Nuremberg; another is dated Leipsic, 1496. One of the typographic editions, dated 1473, is attributed to John Gensberg, of Rome; another, dated 1478, bears the imprint of Ratdolt, of Venice. An edition with a typographic text was printed in 1488 by Peter Van Os, of Zwoll, the same printer who last owned the blocks of the *Bible of the Poor*. In this edition the words in the scrolls are in the Flemish language, and the text is in Latin. The use of Flemish in the engraved blocks seems to warrant the belief that there must have been an earlier edition, entirely xylographic, but no such edition has been discovered.

THE CHIROMANCY OF DOCTOR HARTLIEB.

This is a folio of fifty-two pages, badly printed, in dark gray ink, on both sides of the paper. The designs are puerile and the engraving is coarse. The text of the book is in the German language. Some copies of the book contain at the foot of one page and outside of the border the name

iorg schapff zu augspurg

Other copies of the book have, in the same position, the name **irog scapff zu augspurg.** The spelling is different, and the shapes of the letters are different. No satisfactory explanation can be offered for these differences in books that are supposed to be printed from the same blocks. It may be that the name, inserted in a very exposed place, broke down under impression, and was carelessly re-engraved. This variation is a specimen of some of the perplexing changes to be found not only in block-books but even in early typographic books. The name is usually read as George Schapff, of Augsburg, who is supposed to have been the engraver and printer of the book in 1448. The workmanship is not to his credit: Chatto says "more wretched cuts were never chiseled out by a printer's apprentice as a head-piece to a half-penny ballad."

The matter is worthy of the manner. The book professes to teach the science of palmistry, or the telling of fortunes by wrinkles in the palm of the hand. The first page contains the title, in large letters, over a piece of ornamental border and lattice-work. The page that follows contains this dedication:

> "The hereinafter written Book of the Hand was made German by Doctor Hartlieb, through the Prayer and Bidding of the serene high-born Princess Dame Anna, *née* Brunswick, and Wife of the virtuous, blessed Prince, Duke Albert, Duke of Bavaria and Count of Voburg. This has come to pass on the Friday after the Conception of Mary, the most glorious Virgin. 1448."

The language is not clear: the date here given may be that of the translation, or of the engraving, or of the printing. The rudeness of design and engraving might lead an ordinary observer to the conclusion that the book was printed at an earlier date than 1448; but the insertion of a separate title-page, the printing of the pages on both sides of the paper, and the method of gathering the book in sections of eight leaves, teach us that the book should have been printed at a later date, when these improvements were in general use.

Doctor Hartlieb apprises his readers that he foretells the destiny of man by his right, and that of woman by her left hand. For this purpose he furnishes, on as many pages, forty-four large illustrations of the human hand, each covered with

Fac-simile of a part of a Page of the Chiromancy of Doctor Hartlieb.

[From Heineken.]

mystical characters, that are almost illegible by reason of bad printing. The illustration annexed, which is the first in the book, is intended to represent events that happen to people who have certain marks upon the palms of their hands. At one end of the picture are hanging and murder; at the other end, a kind deity is showering gold on the head of a bewildered peasant.

The childish book is an illustration of the intelligence of the ordinary reader of the period. It may be that the restrictive phrase, ordinary reader, is not warranted, for Doctor John Hartlieb was probably an honored graduate from a medieval university, and the Princess Anna, no doubt, was more carefully educated than the ladies of her court. Chiromancy was considered a science. Adrien Sicler dedicated a book on this subject to Camille de Neuf-Ville, Archbishop of Lyons and Primate of France. Books on chiromancy were printed at Lyons in 1492, at Strasburg in 1534, and at Bologna in 1504. The church tolerated the books of palmistry which did not interfere with the doctrine of moral responsibility, and which did not teach astrology or magic arts.

GERMAN PLANETARIUM AND CALENDAR.

These are two distinct works, which were often printed and bound together. The *Planetarium*, which is in German, describes, through a text in rhyme and by engraved illustrations, the influence of the planets on the destinies of mankind. The *Calendar*, which is in Latin, occupies but four pages, and contains at the end of the month of February the inscription, *Magister Johannes Gamundia.*[1] On another page is found the

[1] John of Gamundia was a mathematician and professor of astronomy. At his death, in the year 1442, he was chancellor of the University of Vienna. The calendars made by him were highly esteemed, and were engraved and printed for many years after his death. In his researches after old prints, the late R. Z. Becker, of Gotha, discovered one of the original blocks of a placard or poster edition of the *Calendar of John of Gamundia.* He describes it as about 10¾ inches wide, 15¼ inches long and 1½ inches thick. The block was engraved on both sides.

date 1468. There is a copy of the German *Planetarium* in the British Museum which contains only twelve printed pages. Berjeau describes it as a small quarto, and says, that although it is printed on both sides of the paper, it presents the appearance of impression by the frotton. The fac-simile illustration that is given underneath represents the influences of the planet Mercury. The artist before the easel is painting a Madonna; his servant is mixing colors with a muller; in the middle of

An Illustration from the Calendar of John of Gamundia.
[From Berjeau.]

the print is an organ-maker; to the right is a copyist; at his back are two gourmands; in the foreground is a sculptor at work on a statue; to the left is a goldsmith before his anvil. The descriptions of these works that have been given by the early German bibliographers are not clear. They represent the book as consisting of twenty-six pages printed on one side of the sheet, with the blank pages pasted together. The size of the page, the color of the ink, and the method used in gathering the sheets are not stated. It seems that there were at least two editions of each work, one in German and one in Latin, and that portions of the different editions were sometimes bound up in one book. Von der Hagen says that the first page of the copy examined by him contained an imperfect impression of one of the pages of the *Antichrist.*

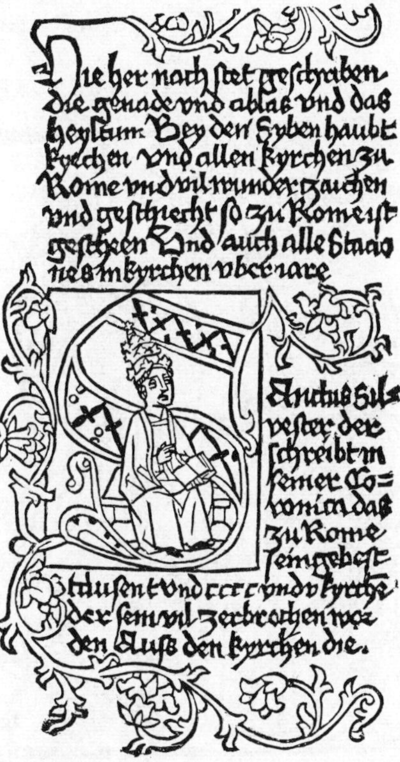

A Page from the Wonders of Rome, Original is 3¼ by 5⅝ inches.

[From Sotheby.]

THE WONDERS OF ROME.

This small quarto of one hundred and eighty-four engraved pages is an example of patience in obscure letter-cutting that is more characteristic of China than of Europe. The text is in German, and is fairly printed in black ink on both sides of the paper. The book is enlivened by a few illustrations which have small merit as designs. The *Wonders of Rome* is an ecclesiastic's description of the more important shrines of the holy city, with their consecrated relics. The first page of the book contains an engraving of the handkerchief of Saint Veronica, which, according to the legend, was placed on the face of Christ to wipe away the blood that dripped from the crown of thorns, and received therefrom the impress of his features. Under this design the papal arms and the triple crown, the crossed keys, and the letters S. P. Q. R. The arms of the pope are those of Pope Sixtus IV, who occupied the papal chair from 1471 to 1484, within which period it is supposed that the book was engraved and published for German readers.

POMERIUM SPIRITUALE, OR SPIRITUAL NURSERY.

An Illustration from the Pomerium Spirituale.
Original is 4⅞ by 5 inches.
[From Holtrop.]

The rightful place of this work is among the manuscripts that are partly written and partly printed, for its pictures were engraved and its text was written. The book contains twenty-six leaves of small folio, made up in one section. At the beginning of each of its twelve written chapters is the impression of an engraving on wood. The date 1440 is found in two of the engravings. The only known copy of this book is held by the Royal Library of Brussels. It is a curious circumstance that this copy, possibly in its original binding, which contains a printed date earlier than that of any other block-book, should also contain two printed leaves of the *Bible of the Poor.* Holtrop says that the book was composed by Henry Bogaert, canon of a monastery near Brussels, who was born in 1382 and died in 1469. He was the author of many small religious books, of which the *Exercise on the Lord's Prayer* is one. The illustrations of this book and of the *Pomerium Spirituale* were probably made at the same time and by the same engraver.

THE TEMPTATIONS OF THE DEVIL.

This is not a book, but a print on a single sheet eleven inches wide and sixteen inches high. It differs from the image prints in the pettiness of its cuts and the abundance of its text, for which reason it may properly be described among the

A Fragment of the Temptations of the Devil.
Original is 10 inches wide.
[From Koning.]

block-books with text. The nature of the work is clearly set forth in the preface, *The Temptations of the Devil, as he tempteth men to the Seven Mortal Sins.* The Devil, who, with a claw-hook in his hand, stands in the corner to the left, has beneath him the list of these seven sins. The tempted man is the monk near the centre of the print, who supplicates the aid of the angel, who hastens to his rescue. Below the angel are appropriate quotations from the Scriptures, which show that this print is but a medieval paraphrase of the story of Christ tempted by the Devil, as related by St. Matthew. It was engraved and printed in the form of a placard, that it might be fastened against a wall for the contemplation of the devout. The illustration shows only a portion of the upper part of this curious print, of which the British Museum has the only known copy. It is supposed to have been printed in the Netherlands.

THE LIFE OF ST. MEINRAT.

This book, which has an introduction of two pages in German, and forty-eight pages of illustrations, with brief descriptions below the pictures, tells the story of two bad men who murdered St. Meinrat, and who were immediately thereafter pursued by two crows. The illustration here presented represents the murderers on their way to execution, accompanied by the unrelenting crows. On the pages that follow are engravings of the murderers suffering under torture; it is shown how they were dragged at the heels of horses, and were broken and burnt on the wheel. The moral

A Page from the Life of St. Meinrat.
Original is 3⅛ by 5⅞ inches.
[From Dibdin.]

of this story is unmistakable: it is an awful crime to kill an ecclesiastic. The publication of so large a book to enforce so plain a truism is an intimation that some of the laity needed forcible illustrations of the danger of abusing the clergy.

THE DANCE OF DEATH.

Of this block-book of twenty-seven large pages, only two copies are known; one of them, which is in the Heidelberg library, is entirely xylographic, with a text in German; the other copy, in a Munich library, has also a text in German, but it is in manuscript. For each edition a different suite of blocks was used. Nothing is known about the printer of either book, nor about the date of its execution. The designs are really meritorious, and the engraving is obviously the work of a man who had experience in his art, but the merit of the work has been overshadowed by the superior designs of Holbein and the more masterly engravings of Lutzelberger. The characters or personages in this block-book are the same as those in the famous painting once at Basle.

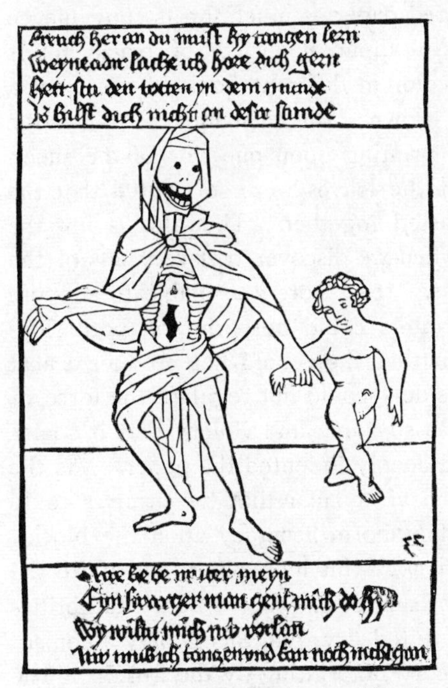

A Page from the Heidelberg Dance of Death. Original is 5½ by 8¼ inches.
[From Dibdin.]

These descriptions of the more famous block-books may be sufficient to show their paltriness from a literary point of view, and their rudeness as specimens of printing, but the books described are not enough in number to give us a correct notion of the activity of the early block-printers. It is probable that many books have been lost and forgotten; but we have, however, enough to warrant the belief that block-printing was an industry of some repute even as early as 1430.

One mechanical peculiarity of the block-books deserves a specific notice: all the block-books were printed on paper. The printers soon discovered that vellum was an intractable material, and they preferred paper as much for its convenience as for its cheapness. An apparent dislike of black ink is equally noticeable; the color in different books varies from a blackish gray to a dingy brown. But their most characteristic feature is the method of printing upon one side of the sheet. One chronicler says that the leaves were so printed that the blank sides might be pasted together. That this is not the true reason is apparent when we discover that very few of the books have pasted leaves. It is more reasonable to suppose that the earlier block-printers could not print on both sides of the paper. It is plain that they could not produce a neat impression even on one side—could not regulate the force of the impression, which was so harsh and violent that it sometimes spread the ink, and deeply indented the paper. As the margins are uneven, we have to infer that the printers could not place the sheets with uniform accuracy upon the blocks. Consequently, they could not print in register, and place the second page truly on the back of the first. Some authorities say that the paper was printed dry, but this is only a conjecture, made to suit the theory of printing by the frotton. The paper must have been dampened, for it was very thick, and as strong and as coarse as modern manila wrapping; it could not have been legibly printed until it had been softened.

With few exceptions, the block-books are of a religious character; but the religion taught is dogmatic and doctrinal more than devotional. We may safely assume that they were written by ecclesiastics in high station for the instruction of the ignorant monks, mendicant friars, and "unable curates."

Illiterate priests, to whom the descriptions or the legends of the pictures had been read, must have understood their historical and spiritual meaning, and must have found the pictures an aid to the memory, and suggestive of topics for preaching. Although made for priests, they were not beyond the reach of the people. As far back as the twelfth century, an English abbot sternly forbade, under penalty of excommunication, the lending of any books, "neither the large books with pictures, nor the small books without pictures." But the mandate was disregarded. Sooner or later, the books found their way to the hands of laymen, whose ignorance of Latin did not prevent them from admiring the pictures; and this admiration must have inspired many a reader with the desire to learn the strange language and to own the coveted book.

The *Life of St. Meinrat* is the only book which seems to have been written especially for the people. There are two, the *Antichrist* and the *Exercise on the Lord's Prayer*, which were, apparently, written to furnish suggestions to preachers against heresy. There was need for books of this character. The church was fermenting with dissent; a very large portion of the people had abandoned the old faith, and there was a general complaint among all priests that the churches were neglected. To recover this lost allegiance, and as an antidote to infidelity and heresy,[1] the church gave its assent to the circulation of image prints and block-books among the laity.

The poverty of the spiritual diet prepared for men who hungered for instruction and who leaned to heresy cannot be passed by without notice. It is strange that, in an age of

[1] Chatto says that the practice of distributing pictures or prints of a religious character at monasteries and shrines to those who visit them is not yet extinct in Europe.

In Belgium it is still continued, and, I believe, also in France, Germany and Italy. The figures, however, are not generally impressions from wood blocks, but are, for the most part, wholly executed by means of stencils. One of the latter class, representing the shrine of *Notre Dame de Hal*, colored in the most wretched taste with brick-dust red and shining green, is now lying before me. It was given to a gentleman who visited Halle, near Brussels, in 1829. It is nearly of the same size as many of the old devotional wood-cuts of Germany, being about four inches high by two and three-quarters wide. *Treatise on Wood Engraving*, pp. 57, 58.

growing disbelief, nothing was written for the people which can now be considered as of importance. We look in vain over the earlier block-books for a copy, in any language that the common people could read, of a book containing appropriate selections from the Scriptures. The *Lord's Prayer* was published but once, published in Latin, and strangely perverted from its true purpose. The *Ten Commandments*, in block-book form, were printed in German, but not before the last quarter of the sixteenth century. We find no selections from the *Psalms* or *Evangelists*. The stories of the *Bible*, always with a Latin text, were obviously prepared, not to teach lessons of piety to the people, but to instruct the priests in the mysteries of dogmatic theology. All are orthodox: there is no block-book that has the slightest taint of heresy.

It does not appear that any of these block-books were made by monks. The block-printers of a later period were laymen, and men of no note, and it seems probable that the earlier books, without names, places or dates, were also made by laymen, by the printers of cards and images. It is possible that they were made at the instance, and perhaps under the direction, of the ecclesiastics. But we find no evidences that they were printed in monasteries; the lazy habits and coarse tastes of the monks, and their general avoidance of every form of mechanical labor as beneath their sacred calling, make this conjecture inadmissible.[1]

The literary merit of the block-books was small, and their shabby mechanical execution made them contemptible. To readers accustomed to handle great books of tinted vellum, admirably written in letters that are yet as sharp and legible as modern types, these miserable little pamphlets on dingy paper, and with muddy letters, scarcely deserved the name of books. By the educated readers of the fifteenth century they

[1] The Brotherhood of the Life-in-Common may, perhaps, be regarded as an exception. Madden in his *Lettres d'un bibliographe* has shown that this fraternity were much interested in the production of books, and that they had a printing office in a monastery at Cologne; but he has not yet made it appear that they did the manual labor.

were rated as literary rubbish. Professors in the universities looked on them with the same contemptuous spirit which men of letters afterward manifested toward early newspapers. The attempts of early printers to furnish these poor substitutes for books to common people, so far from receiving any encouragement from scholars, met with their disdainful neglect. There were, indeed, a few praiseworthy exceptions, but the scholarship of the middle ages took sides with rank, in upholding all the conventional distinctions of society. They wished illiterate people to understand that books were the right of the educated only.[1]

The period in which block-books were printed cannot be fixed within exact limits. They did not go out of fashion when types were invented: the illustrated block-book *Opera Nova Contemplativa*, the Italian adaptation of the *Bible of the Poor*, was printed in Venice about 1512; but block-books of inferior merit were made after this date. Berjeau describes one, the *Innocentia Victrix*, probably engraved in China at the order of the Jesuits, which was printed in 1671. But these books are really the last specimens of a dying art; in the sixteenth century, they were practically obsolete. The period of their greatest popularity may be fixed between the years

[1] Southey says that, at the beginning of the sixteenth century, many educated men complained that the reputation of learning, its privileges and rewards, were lowered when it was thrown open to all men. It was seriously proposed in Italy to prohibit the publication of any book costing less than three soldi.

The amusing insolence manifested by authors, scholars and readers toward the early development of literature in any new field, or by a new method, is a subject that could be amply illustrated. The city of New-York furnishes a comparatively recent example in the field of journalism. The daily newspapers of 1835, which were then sold for six cents each, refused to recognize the rightful existence of the new daily then sold for one cent. So strong a prejudice was created against "the penny paper," that many timid men were afraid to be seen with the despised sheet in their hands: the six-penny papers were respectable, and the penny paper was vulgar. The same contemptuousness was manifested when duodecimos supplanted the folios and quartos—when books bound in cloth took the place of books bound in leather. The despised forms of printing have had their revenge. The rod of Aaron has swallowed its rivals.

1440 and 1475. As we approach the latter date, we find block-books containing the names and places of the printers. We see that they were made at Ulm, Nuremberg, and Augsburg,—the towns which have the earliest records of manufacturers of playing cards,—in the district in which old image prints like the *St. Christopher* have been oftenest discovered. It is probable that block-books were printed in Southern Germany at or near the time when the *St. Christopher* was printed, but we have no positive proof that any block-book was printed in 1423. The German book with earliest printed date is the *Chiromancy*, but its date of 1448 is not certainly the date of printing.

The evidences in favor of an early practice of block-book printing in the Netherlands are, in some features, even more incomplete. No early Dutch or Flemish block-book reveals the name of its printer. There are not many notices in old Flemish town-books concerning card-makers, or printers or painters of images. Yet there was, without doubt, an early practice of block-printing in the Netherlands. The Dutch traditions about early printing are more circumstantial than those of Germany; the *Brussels Print* dated 1418 is older by five years than the print of *St. Christopher;* the date of 1440 as printed in the wood-cuts of the *Exercise on the Lord's Prayer* is eight years earlier than the date of the *Chiromancy.*

The books themselves do not tell us, neither directly nor indirectly, whether they were first printed in Flanders or in Germany. They have been critically examined by many able men, but the unbiased reader will not fail to note that most inquirers have found only what they wanted to find. To the German critic, all the early block-books are German; to the Dutch critic, they are surely Dutch. To recite the arguments advanced by partisans, or even to state the facts wrested to the support of the arguments, would provide a tedious task for the reader. Nor would the fullest presentation of the facts lead to certain knowledge. The language oftenest found in the block-books is Latin, the language of the Church and of scholars in all countries during the middle ages, and it gives us no clue to the place where they were printed. The paper-marks have been carefully scrutinized, in the hope that they would reveal the manufacture of the paper at some date or in some place, but reasonings made from paper-marks are now regarded as uncertain and of no practical value. We learn nothing through the study of the shapes or fashion of the engraved letters, for German-like characters have been found in block-books known to be Dutch, and peculiarities supposed to be Dutch have been found in German books. Nor can we glean anything of real value from a critical examination of the designs, which could have been copied from manuscripts, or drawn in one country and printed in another.

The only mechanical feature which leads to positive conclusions as to age is the manner in which they were printed. The books printed in black ink and on both sides of the paper were certainly printed after the invention of typography, and by typographic apparatus. The books in brown ink and on one side of the paper are of an earlier period. There is a peculiar rudeness about the books in brown ink which is not to be found in typographic work, a rudeness which we know began with the makers of cards or printers of images. If we consider, as we must, that the block-books are only collections of image prints, which were put in the form of books as soon as paper became cheap and popular, we may conclude with confidence that they could have been made, and probably were made, in the first quarter of the fifteenth century.

The great popularity of the block-books even after 1450, when types had been invented, proves that the business of making them was then firmly established, and that it was not checked by the superior advantages offered by types. It is obvious that the block-printers of 1450 had long practice in the older method, that they were firmly attached to it, and would not abandon it in favor of the new invention. Their preference for the older method of xylography is very plainly shown by the numerous editions of the *Donatus*.

XIII

The Donatus, or Boy's Latin Grammar.

A Very Old Book...A Favorite with the Early Xylographers...Frequently Printed...Scarcity of Fragments...Printed by Typographic Process...Printed before and after Invention of Typography...Testimony of the Cologne Chronicle...Of Accursius...Of Scaliger...Of Sweinheim and Pannartz...Fac-simile of a German Donatus...Of a Dutch Donatus...The Arrangement of Words in the Donatus...Obscurity of the Letters...Fac-simile of a Dutch Horarium...Xylographic Editions are Imitations of Typographic Editions...Irregularities of Engraved Letters...The Donatus a Relic of the Past...Shows the Retrogressive Tendencies of the Teachers of the Period...The Pettiness of all Block-Books...An Evidence of the Limitations of Xylography.

Although the art of printing, as has been said, was discovered at Mentz, in the manner as it is now generally used, yet the first prefiguration was found in Holland, in the Donatuses which were printed there before that time. And from these Donatuses the beginning of the art was taken. *Cologne Chronicle of* 1499.

THE only block-book without pictures of which we have any knowledge is the *Donatus*,[1] or *Boy's Latin Grammar.* It received its name from its author, Ælius Donatus, a Roman grammarian of the fourth century, and one of the instructors of St. Jerome. The block-book is but an abridgment of the old grammar: as it was usually printed in the form of a thin quarto, it could, with propriety, be classified among primers rather than with books. When printed in the largest letters, it occupied but thirty-four pages; when letters of small size were used, it was compressed within nine pages. As the most popular of small works, and one constantly needed in every

[1] The full title of the book is *Donatus de octibus partibus orationis*, or Donatus on the Eight Parts of Speech. It is sometimes designated as *Donatus pro puerilis*, or the Donatus for Little Boys.

preparatory school, it met the conditions then required by the early publisher: it could be engraved at little cost, and the printed copies could be sold in very large quantities. How many xylographic editions of the book were printed has never been ascertained, but we are led to believe that the number was large when we learn that more than fifty editions were printed from types before the year 1500.

Fragments of the xylographic *Donatus* are scarce, and they are, for the most part, in a shabby condition. Many of them are the remnants of badly printed leaves which were rejected as spoiled by the printer. If it had not been for the frugal habits of the binders, who used them as stiffeners in the covers of books, we should have few specimens of this book. These waste leaves were put to this use because they were printed on parchment and had more strength than paper. And here we have to notice a remarkable difference between the block-books of images and the xylographic *Donatus*.

All the block-books are printed on paper, and the greater part are printed on one side of the sheet in brown ink. All copies of the xylographic *Donatus* are printed on parchment, on both sides of the leaf, and in black ink. Parchment was, no doubt, selected to adapt the book to the hard usage it would receive from careless school-boys, but the method of printing in black ink and on both sides is the typographic method, which was not in use, so far as we can learn, before the middle of the fifteenth century. We have to conclude that all copies of the *Donatus* printed in this manner were printed after the invention of types. The most trustworthy authorities say that there is no known fragment of an engraved *Donatus* that can be attributed to the first half of the fifteenth century.

In the manufacture of this grammar, the block-book printers competed successfully with type-printers for many years. But typography improved while xylography declined; at the end of the fifteenth century, the copies made from type were decidedly superior. The engraved copies of the book were gradually cast aside as rubbish, for they contained no pictures, and had no features to justify their preservation. We cannot wonder that copies of the engraved *Donatus* are scarce, but we must not infer from their present scarcity that they were not common before the year 1450. It is probable that more copies were printed of this than of any pictorial block-book; although we find no copies, we have trustworthy evidences that the *Donatus* was printed before types were made.

That the *Donatus* was engraved and printed before the invention of typography is distinctly stated in the book now known as the *Cologne Chronicle*, which was published in that city by John Koelhoff, in the year 1499. The name of the author is unknown, but he writes with the confidence of a clear-minded thinker and a candid chronicler. He says that the following statement was communicated to him, by word of mouth, "by Master Ulric Zell, of Hanau, now a printer in Cologne, through whom the art was brought to Cologne."

> Although the art [of printing], as has been said, was discovered at Mentz, in the manner as it is now generally used, yet the first prefiguration was found in Holland, in the *Donatuses* which were printed there before that time. From these *Donatuses* the beginning of the said art was taken, and it was invented in a manner much more masterly and subtle than this, and became more and more ingenious.[1]

Mariangelus Accursius, a learned Italian of the fifteenth century, made a similar acknowledgment of the indebtedness of the men whom he regarded as the inventors of typography to the unknown printers of the *Donatus* in Holland. He says:

> John Fust, a citizen of Mentz, and the maternal grandfather of John Schœffer, was the first who devised the art of printing with types from brass, which he subsequently invented in lead. Peter Schœffer, his son, added many improvements to the art. The *Donatus* and *Confessionalia* were printed first of all, in the year 1450. But the suggestion [of typography] was certainly made by the *Donatuses* that had been printed before in Holland, from wooden blocks.

This extract first appeared in an *Appendix to the Library of the Vatican*, which was written by Angelo Rocca, and pub-

[1] This extract is from the chapter entitled, "When, where, and by whom was found out the unspeakably useful art of printing books?" It contains statements of value, which will be quoted at greater length on an advanced page.

lished at Rome in 1591. Rocca says that this statement is in the handwriting of Mariangelus Accursius, who affixed his name to it. On this page it is not necessary to point out the many errors of Accursius about the origin of the invention at Mentz; it is enough to show that he believed that the *Donatus* was printed in Holland before types were made in Germany. It is not known, however, whether he acquired this information from the *Cologne Chronicle* or from another source.

Joseph Justus Scaliger, an eminent scholar of the sixteenth century, says that printing was invented in Holland, and that the first block-book with text was a breviary or manual of devotion. It seems that this book was like the *Horarium*, of which a fac-simile will be shown on an advanced page.

> Printing was invented at Dordrecht, by engraving on blocks, and the letters were run together as in writing. My grandmother had a psalter printed after this fashion with a cover two fingers thick. Inside of this cover was a little recess in which was placed a little crucifix of silver. The first book that was printed was a breviary or manual, and one would have thought that it had been written by hand. It belonged to the grandmother of Julius Cæsar Scaliger. A little dog destroyed it, much to his vexation, for the letters were conjoined, and had been printed from a block of wood, upon which the letters were so engraved that they could be used for this book and for no other. Afterward was invented a method of using the letters separately.

This record is of interest for its specification of Dordrecht in Holland as the birthplace of block-books, but it does not give any date, nor the name of the first printer. As it has not been corroborated by the testimony of any other chronicler, it is now regarded by the historians of typography as imperfect evidence—incorrect, probably, in its assertion of the priority of the breviary, but trustworthy so far as it shows that this learned antiquarian had some really valuable evidences concerning a very early practice of block-printing in Holland.

Sweinheym and Pannartz, the German printers, who introduced typography in Rome, and published more books than they could sell, in the year 1472 petitioned Pope Sixtus IV for relief. In the catalogue accompanying their petition they describe this *Donatus* as the "Donatus for Boys, from which we have taken the beginning of printing." Their language is not clear, for it may be interpreted as the first book printed by Sweinheym and Pannartz, or as the first book made by the art of printing.

The National Library at Paris has two very old xylographic blocks[1] of this book, which some bibliographers suppose were made about the middle of the fifteenth century.

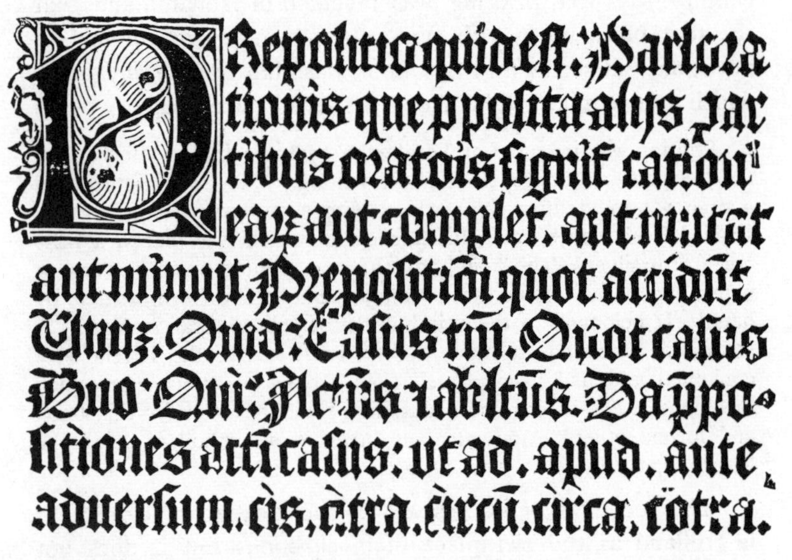

Prepositio quid est. Pars oracionis que preposita alijs partibus oratois significacion earum aut complet. aut mutat aut minuit. Prepositioni quot accidunt. Unum. Quid. Casus tantum. Quot casus. Duo. Qui. Actus et ablatus. Da preposiciones acti casus: ut ad. apud. ante. adversum. cis. citra. circum. circa. contra.

Fac-simile of part of a Block of the Donatus in the National Library at Paris.

[From Lacroix.]

The letters on these blocks were more carefully drawn and sharply engraved than the letters of any known block-book. The wood is worm-eaten, but the letters are neat and clear, and do not show any evidences of wear from impression.

One of these blocks has been attributed to John Gutenberg, for its letters resemble those of the *Mazarin Bible.* It

[1] There can be no doubt whatever about the genuineness of these blocks. They were bought in Germany, about two hundred years ago, by Foucault, the minister of Louis XIV of France.

has been conjectured that this block may have been one of Gutenberg's earlier experiments in printing. Apart from the similarity of the characters, there is no warrant for this conjecture. This similarity is entirely insufficient as evidence; it is not even proof of age. The block was probably engraved during the last quarter of the fifteenth century.

Koning, author of a treatise on early printing in Holland, has given in his book the fac-simile, which is here copied, of a fragment of a leaf from a xylographic *Donatus*. It was taken from the cover of a book printed by Gerard Leeu, of Antwerp, in 1490. Koning says that the fashion of the letters in this book is like that of letters in the manuscripts of Holland during the fifteenth century, and that they closely resemble the engraved letters of one edition of the *Ars Moriendi*. Holtrop gives a fac-simile of the entire page of a xylographic *Donatus* with similar letters, which he claims as a piece of early Dutch printing.

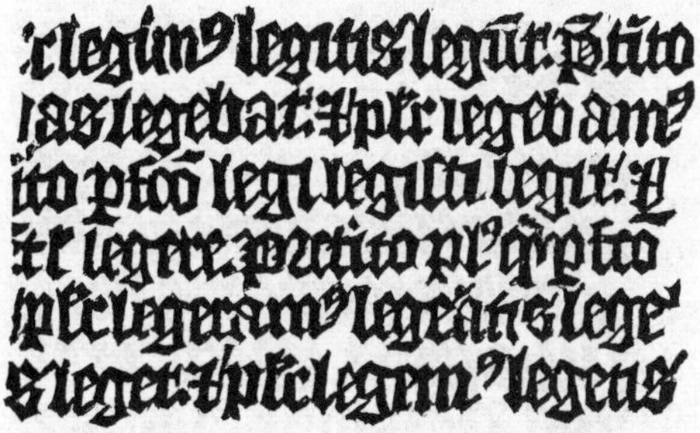
r legim9 legitis legũt. Ptito
las legebat. ⁊ plr legebam9
ito pfcō legi legisti legit.
r legere. preterito pl'qȝpfco
pfcr legeram9 legeratis legere
s leget. ⁊ pfcr legem9 legetis

Fac-simile of the Fragment of an early Donatus.
[From Koning.]

The arrangement of words in Koning's fac-simile of this fragment cannot be passed by without notice. The words are more readable than those of many block-books, but I have reset a small portion in modern type, that they might be more clearly contrasted with the modern method of composition. The words that do not appear in the mutilated fragment given by Koning are restored from the perfect copy of Holtrop.

THE OLD METHOD.

Lego legis legit. & plr legim' legitis legu't. Ptito ipfco legeba' legebas legebat. & plr legebam' legebatis legeba't.

THE MODERN METHOD.

Present Tense.		Imperfect Tense.	
Singular.	*Plural.*	*Singular.*	*Plural.*
Lego,	Legimus,	Legebam,	Legebamus
Legis,	Legitis,	Legebas,	Legebatis,
Legit,	Legunt.	Legebat,	Legebant.

This fac-simile gives an imperfect notion of the abbreviations, the blackness and obscurity of a page of the *Donatus*, but it is a fair specimen of the forbidding appearance of all the printed work of the fifteenth century. The illustration of the modern method of arranging the same letters shows the superior perspicuity of modern types and of modern typographic method. Not every reader of this age has a just idea of the extent of his obligation to what may be called the minor improvements of typography. It may be safely said that many men owe much of their scholastic knowledge to the systematic arrangement and the inviting appearance of modern types and books. The school-boy who glances over this fac-simile will quickly see the depth of the quagmire from which he has been delivered by the invention of types.

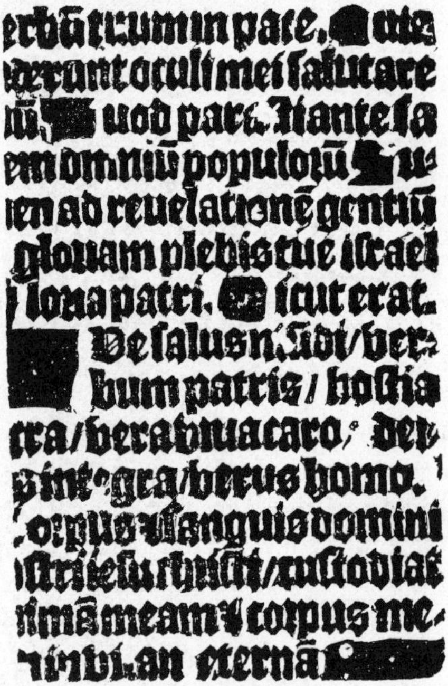

Fac-simile of an early Dutch Horarium.
[From Koning.]

To support his theory that this fragment of the *Donatus* is but a part of one of the many copies of the book which were printed in Holland before the invention of typography, Koning submits the fac-simile of a page from an old *Horarium*, or manual of devotion, which was copied by him from the original block. He says that this block once belonged to Adrien Rooman, a Haarlem printer of the seventeenth century, who had received it from one of the descendants of Coster. That Coster engraved or printed this block is highly improbable, but it is, without doubt, a very old piece of engraving. It can be fairly attributed to the fifteenth century, but no good evidence has been adduced to show that it was made before the invention of types. The block is practically worn out: the letters have been so flattened by impression that many of them are illegible.

It must here be noticed that the letters of this *Horarium* do not interlock, as they do in many of the block-books. A ruled line drawn between the printed lines will show only a few and unimportant interferences of letters. This evenness in lining, which is properly regarded as one of the peculiarities of typography, seems out of place in an early block-book. But it is not confined to the *Horarium.* There are copies of the xylographic *Donatus* that closely resemble typographic editions of the same period. They agree, line with line, page with page, and almost letter for letter, with the typographic model. That these xylographic copies were made from the engraved transfers of some typographic model is proved not only by the uniformity and parallelism of the letters, but by the square outline to the right of every page. These peculiarities are never produced in the workmanship of men who draw letters on a block.

It is not strange that the block-book printers should have imitated the work and the mannerisms of the typographers. It was easier to transfer the letters than to draw them; easier to cut the letters for a book of twenty or thirty pages than to cut the punches, make the moulds, and cast and compose the types. The blocks having been engraved, the block-printer had the superior advantage. His blocks, like modern stereotype plates, were always ready for use. He could print a large or small edition at pleasure. And what was of much more importance, he could print more legibly from his smooth plates of wood than the amateur typographer could from his uneven surface of lead.

The significance of the fact that letters were engraved by block-printers after typographic models will be more plainly seen when we examine the editions of the *Speculum Salutis,* a book which has been claimed by Dutch historians as the first production of the newly invented art of typography.

The irregular manner in which all the early xylographers drew and engraved letters on the block is fairly shown in this fac-simile of the imprint of Conrad Dinckmut, of Ulm, who affixed it to a *Donatus* printed by him in 1480. It will be seen that parallel lines ruled between the printed lines would interfere with almost every ascending or descending letter.

Octo partium orationis·
donatus·per Cunradum·
dinckmut Vlmensis Oppidi·
Civem impressus finit feliciter·

Reduced Fac-simile of the Imprint of Conrad Dinckmut.

[From De la Borde.]

The *Donatus* clearly shows the retrogressive tendencies of the teachers of that age. It was originally written for scholars who spoke in Latin, and who, when the book was first placed in their hands, knew the meaning of almost every word. In the fifteenth century Latin was a dead language, but the book that had been written a thousand years before received no modification adapting it to the capacities of the German or Dutch boys, to whom Latin was as strange as Chinese.[1] The

[1] Van der Linde says that the *Donatus* and *Abecedarium*, a religious primer hereafter to be noticed, are used in all the religious schools of Italy to this day.

I look with melancholy respect at an *Abecedarium*, a little octavo of four leaves, *Il Sillabario*, printed in our time in 1862, at Asti. Beneath the heading, Jesus Maria, the Alphabet follows, and after that the *Pater noster*, *Ave*, and *Credo*. Beside the *Sillabario*, I have a little grammar entitled *Donato ad uso delle scuolle secondarie. Nuova editione accresciuta e riformata.* Pinerola, &c., 1865. . . . The esteem in which these Catholic school-books, those foul springs from which, for instance, Erasmus drew the first elements of Latin, were held, was so great that the first efforts of the humanists to improve them were regarded as heresy, and heaven and earth were moved against such dangerous destroyers. . . . Donatuses were printed in every place where schools were established, and where the art of printing was introduced. *The Haarlem Legend*, p. 3.

rules and the explanations, as well as the text, were in Latin. The boy who began to study the book was compelled to translate the words and rules before he knew the simplest elements of the language. The difficulty of the task will be understood if we imagine an American boy beginning the study of German, not with a German grammar in which the explanations are in English, but with the grammar that is now used in the schools of Germany. We find no trace of any other school-book in the form of a block-book. There was no other book of equal popularity. To the scholar of the middle ages there was no science that could be compared with Latin; there was no knowledge like that of the words of the dead language. Words were held of more value than facts. The teachers of the fifteenth century clung to this obsolete book, and compelled their pupils to go through the same barren course of study that had been used in the fifth century. In this fixed purpose we see something more than the force of habit: there was a general unwillingness to make the acquisition of knowledge in any way attractive.

The limitations of xylography are plainly set forth in this review of the more famous block-books. During the first half of the fifteenth century, labor was cheap, skill in engraving was not rare, paper was in abundant supply, the art of block-printing was known all over civilized Europe, and there was a growing demand for printed work, but this rude art of block-printing was limited to the production of pictures. It was never applied to the production of books of size or merit. The *Wonders of Rome*, with its text of one hundred and sixty-eight pages, is its most ambitious attempt; but large as this work may seem when it is put in contrast with other block-books, it is really insignificant when compared with the works of the first typographers.

XIV

The Speculum Salutis, or the Mirror of Salvation.

Its Popularity as a Manuscript Book...Made for Mendicant Friars...Description of the Text...Fac-similes of Wood-cuts on First and Last Pages...Its Curious Theology...Four Editions of the Book...Their Peculiarities...Twenty Engraved Pages in one Edition...Strange Blemishes. Opinions of Bibliographers concerning the Date and Printer...Text of the Book Printed from Types...Fac-simile of the Types...Different Bodies of Types in Different Editions...Engraved Pages were Transferred from Types...Book Printed in Four Kinds of Ink...By Two Methods of Impression...Types and Cuts could not be Printed together...Opinions about the Quality of the Presswork...Strange Faults of Presswork...All Editions were Printed in Holland...Wood-cuts used for the last time by Veldener in 1483...Not Probable that Veldener Printed the Earlier Editions...Veldener did not use the Types...The Speculum is the Work of an Unknown Printer.

Everything about the book is uncertain. It may be that the book was printed from engraved blocks. There are persons who say that it was engraved; there is a librarian who says that it was written by hand..... I submitted the book to a type-founder, to an engraver, and to a printer, who decided that the book was printed with movable metal types that had been cast in a mould. *André Chevillier.*

THE *Speculum Salutis*[1] was popular as a manuscript for at least two centuries before the invention of typography. Heineken describes a copy in the imperial library of Vienna, which he attributes to the twelfth century. He says, such was the popularity of the work with the Benedictines that almost every monastery possessed a copy of it. Of the four manuscript copies owned by the British Museum, one is supposed to have been written in the thirteenth century, another copy is in the Flemish writing of the fifteenth century. The printed

[1] Sometimes described under the title of *Speculum Humanæ Salvationis.*

book contains forty-five chapters of barbarous Latin rhymes, the literary merit of which is clearly enough set before us in Chatto's faithful translation of four lines of the preface:

> Predictum prohemium huius libri de contentis compilaui
> Et propter pauperes predicatores hoc apponere curaui
> Qui si forte nequierunt totum libri sibi comparare
> Possunt ex ipso prohemio si sciunt historias predicare.

> This preface of contents, stating what this book's about,
> For the sake of all poor preachers I have fairly written out.
> If the purchase of the book entire should be above their reach,
> This preface yet may serve them, if they know but how to preach.[1]

In many features, the *Speculum* resembles the *Bible of the Poor.* As the designs are in the same style, and as the engravings show the same mannerisms, it has been supposed that both books were made by the same printer; but this conjecture is opposed by many facts and probabilities.

The illustration at the beginning of this chapter is a fac-simile of the upper part of the first pictorial page. In the compartment to the right may be seen the Fall of Lucifer. The rebellious angels having been transformed into devils, and by swords and spears thrust over the battlements of Heaven, are falling into the jaws of Hell, which is here represented, in the conventional style of medieval designers, as the mouth of a hideous monster filled with forks of flame. In the next compartment is the Creation of Eve in the garden of Eden. Here we see that the designer has modified the biblical narrative to suit his own notions: Eve is not formed from the rib of Adam, but is emerging from his side. At the bottom of this picture is this legend in abbreviated Latin, God created man after his own image and likeness.

[1] Jackson and Chatto, *Treatise on Wood Engraving*, p. 83.

The book was written for the instruction of the traveling mendicant friars who had, since the thirteenth century, gradually monopolized preaching and the pastoral work of the settled clergy. Provided with nothing but a little Church Latin, and therefore too ignorant to derive their discourses from original sources, they felt the want of homiletic and catechetical assistance as an aid to their understanding and memory. Picture books, with a brief explanatory text, were the best means of supplying this want. Hence originated representations of the mystic relation between the Old and the New Testament, of which the *Biblia Pauperum* is the first fruit. Van der Linde, *Haarlem Legend*, p. 3.

Fac-simile of the Upper Part of the First Pictorial Page of the Speculum Salutis.

[From Heineken.]

An illustration on the last page of the book represents the Parable of the Ten Virgins, to which is added the legend, The Kingdom of Heaven is likened unto Ten Virgins. The five foolish virgins are sadly descending into the mouth of the monster that represents Hell. Another illustration represents the prophet Daniel interpreting the writing on the wall.

Hessel's free translation of a large portion of the preface is really needed to show the theological teachings of the book.

This is the preface of the *Spieghel onser behoudenisse,* which will teach many people righteousness, and to shine as the stars in eternal eternities. It is for this reason that I have thought of compiling, as an instruction for many, this book, from which those who read it will give and receive instruction. I presume that nothing is in this life more useful to a man than to acknowledge his Creator, his condition, his own being. Scholars may learn this from the Scriptures, and the layman shall be taught by the books of the laymen, that is by the pictures. Wherefore I have thought fit, with the help of God, to compile this book for laymen to the glory of God, and as an instruction for the unlearned, in order that it may be a lesson both to clerks and to laymen. It will be sufficient to explain the matter briefly. I mean first to show the fall of Lucifer and the angels. Then the fall of our first parents and their posterity. Thereupon, how God delivered us by his assuming flesh, and with what figures he whilom prefigured this assuming. It is to be observed that many histories are given in this work, which could not be explained from word to word, for a teacher does not want to explain more of the histories than he thinks necessary for their meaning. And in order that this may be seen better and clearer, I give this parable. . . . . There was an abbey, in which stood a large oak, which, on account of the narrowness and smallness of the town, they were compelled to cut down. When it was cut down, the workmen came together, and each of them chose whatever he thought would suit his trade. The smith cut off the undermost block, which he thought suitable for a forge; the shoemaker took the bark for making leather; the swineherd, the acorns for feeding pigs; the carpenter, the straight wood for a roof; the shipwright, the crooked wood; the miller digs the roots up, as they are fit, on account of their solidity, for the mill; the baker uses the thin twigs for his oven; the sexton of the church, the leaves for decorating the church at festivals; the butler, the branches for barrels and mugs; the cook, the chips for the kitchen. . . . . Just now, as here every one chose his liking from the hewn tree, so they do with Holy Writ. The same method has been followed regarding the histories which will be explained. Every teacher collects from them what he thinks proper and useful. I shall follow the same way with regard to this work, leaving out altogether some part of the histories, that it may not offend those who will hear and read it. Let us also observe that Holy Writ is like soft wax, which assumes the shape of all forms impressed upon it. Does, for instance, the stamp contain a lion? the soft wax will contain the same; and if it bears an ear, the soft wax will bear the same figure. So one thing signifies, sometimes the Devil, and sometimes Christ. However, we ought not to be astonished at this manner of the Scriptures, for divers significations may be ascribed to the divers performances of a thing or a person. When David, the king, committed both adultery and man-

Fac-simile of the Upper Part of the Last Page of the Speculum Salutis.

[From Heineken.]

slaughter, he represented not Christ but the Devil. And when he loved his enemies, and did them good, he bore within him the figure of Christ and not of the Devil. . . . . This is why I have noticed these remarkable things here, for I thought it useful to those who study the Holy Scriptures, that they should not judge me, if they happened to find such things in this book, for the manner of translation and exposition is so. O good Jesus, give me works and a Christian devotion which may please thee. * * * * * *

Equally curious is the explanation of the marriage of the mother of God with Joseph. It appears from this, that it was not thought superfluous to justify a fact somewhat strange in regard to the doctrine of the supernatural incarnation of the second person of the Godhead. The author of the *Speculum* assigns eight reasons for this marriage. The first was, that Mary should not be suspected of unchastity; the second, that she might want the help of a man during her travels as well as elsewhere; the third, that the Devil might not become aware of the incarnation of Christ; the fourth, that Mary could have a witness of her purity; the fifth, that God wished that his mother should be married; the sixth, to prove the sanctity of marriage; the seventh, to prove that marriage is no impediment to blessing; the last, that married people should not despair of their salvation. Catholicism had already brought the world to the possibility of that despair. Van der Linde, *Haarlem Legend of the Invention of Printing*, p. 4.

The *Speculum* was printed at different times and places during the fifteenth century,[1] but the copies of greatest value are those which belong to four correlated editions—two in Latin, and two in Dutch—all without date, name, or place of printer. In these four editions the illustrations are obviously impressions from the same blocks; but each edition exhibits some new peculiarity in the shape or disposition of the letters. Those who favor the theory of an invention of typography in Holland maintain that these letters are the impressions of the first movable types, and that the curious workmanship of the book marks the development of printing at the great turning-point in its progress when it was passing from xylography to typography. As important conclusions have been drawn from the peculiarities of each edition, it is necessary that they should be described with precision. The order in which the four editions were actually printed is not certainly known. Six eminent bibliographers have arranged them in as many different orders. The order assigned to them here

[1] There is an edition, with a text in Latin and in German, which was printed at Augsburg in 1471; there are many editions in German only, some without dates, and others with dates of 1476, 1492, and 1500; a Flemish edition by Veldener in 1483; and various editions in French.

is purely conjectural, but it is based on the supposition that that should be the first edition in which the wood-cuts show the sharpest lines, and that the last in which the types and wood-cuts show the strongest marks of wear.

The *First Edition* is in Latin. Each copy of the book is made up of sixty-three leaves of small folio printed upon one side of the paper, but with printed pages facing each other, after the style of the block-books. The space occupied by the printed page is about 7¾ inches wide, and 10¼ inches high. The preface, in rhyme, is composed in broad measure, and occupies five pages. The fifty-eight pages of text that follow are also in rhyme; but they are made up with two columns to the page. At the top of each page is an engraving on wood, containing, on one block, two distinct designs, separated from each other by the pillar of an architectural frame-work. At the bottom of each design, and engraved upon the same block, is a line in Latin, which explains the design, and which serves as the text for the verses underneath. The letters of the preface and the text are impressions from Pointed Gothic types of the Flemish style. Every line of verse begins with a capital letter. The only mark of punctuation is the period, but it is rarely used. The book is without title, paging-figures, signatures, or catch-words. The wood-cuts are in brown, and the types in black ink. The brown ink is a water color which can be partially effaced by rubbing with a moist sponge; the black ink is an oil color, for it has stained the paper with the pale greenish tinge of badly prepared oil. As the back of every printed wood-cut is smooth and shining, while the back of every type-printed page is rough and deeply indented, it is obvious that the types of the text were not only printed with a different ink, but by a separate impression, and, perhaps, by a process different from that employed in printing the pictures. The two pages that appear on the same sheet were printed together, as may be inferred from their irregularities; if one page is out of register, or out of square, its mated page is out of register to the same degree. The engravings were printed before the types, as is clearly proved by the discovery that on some pages the types slightly overlap the cuts.[1]

The *Second Edition* is in Latin, and is like the first, with this odd exception: twenty pages of the text are printed from engraved blocks of wood. These xylographic pages are distributed in irregular order, as if by accident, as will be shown by the italic figures, which represent these pages, in the following table. It should be noticed that the xylographic pages,

First Section of Six Leaves.	Second Section of Fourteen Leaves.	Third Section of Fourteen Leaves.	Fourth Section of Fourteen Leaves.	Fifth Section of Sixteen Leaves.
– 5	. *6 – 19*.	20 – 33	34 – 47	48 – 63
1 – 4	. *7 – 18*.	. *21 – 32*.	35 – 46	49 – 62
2 – 3	8 – 17	. *22 – 31*.	36 – 45	50 – 61
	. *9 – 16*.	23 – 30	37 – 44	. *51 – 60*.
	. *10 – 15*.	24 – 29	38 – 43	52 – 59
	. *11 – 24*.	25 – 28	39 – 42	53 – 58
	. *12 – 13*.	. *26 – 27*.	40 – 41	54 – 57
				55 – 56

as well as the typographic pages, are always found in couples. The types are those of the first edition, but there are varia-

[1] There are two copies of the book which exhibit the blemish of a leaf made up of two distinct pieces of paper, each piece printed by a different impression, but so pasted together as to constitute one perfect page. We do not certainly know the cause that made this patchwork necessary, but it would seem that a gross blunder had been made in the printing-office; perhaps a transposition of lines by the compositor, or illegible presswork by the pressman. It was necessary that the sheet containing the error should be canceled and replaced. But the frugal printer refused to destroy the entire page for an error confined to but half a page. He tore off the lower half of the leaf, and replaced it by attaching a piece of white paper to the bottom of the upper half, which contained the engraving in brown ink. On this pasted piece of white paper, he took a corrected or perfect impression from the types. In this copy, the impression, which deeply indented the paper in the double thickness where it was pasted, proves that the types were printed after the engravings. There is another copy in which the illustration on the upper half of the sheet was canceled, and replaced by the same method.

tions in the composition and spelling of words, which prove that they must have been recomposed for this edition.

The *Third Edition* is in Dutch prose. The types are like those of the previous editions, with the exception of pages 49 and 60, which are printed in types of a smaller body. The face of the smaller types has all the peculiarities of the types of the earlier editions, and is apparently the work of the same letter-cutter. In the few known copies of this edition there are differences in typographic arrangement which show that types were altered between the first and the last impression.

The *Fourth Edition* is also in Dutch prose. All known copies of this edition are so badly printed that they have the appearance of spoiled or discarded sheets. Many authors have supposed that this must have been the first edition, and, perhaps, the first experiment with types; but a closer examination proves that the bad printing is owing, not so much to ignorance and to inexperience as to worn types and careless presswork—that this edition is really the last. The copy that is preserved by the city of Haarlem shows, in the handwriting of the sixteenth century, this inscription in Dutch: "The *Speculum Salutis*, the earliest production of Lourens Coster, the inventor of typography, who printed at Haarlem about the year 1440." Between the second and the third leaf has been inserted a portrait of Lourens Coster, "engraved by Vandervelde after Van Campen," with the words, in Latin, "Lourens Coster, of Haarlem, first inventor of the typographic art about the year 1440." Underneath this inscription is a Latin verse by Scriverius, in which he extols Coster as indisputably the inventor of typography. As the writing, the portrait, and the inscription were added a long time after the book had been printed, these additions cannot, consequently, be accepted as evidences of any real value.

Junius, the historian of Holland, writing in 1568, was the first to call attention to the *Speculum*. He noticed but one edition: it is not probable that he knew of the others. He said it was made by Coster from types of wood, in Haarlem, before the year 1440. Scriverius, a Dutch author, writing in 1628, said that it was printed by Coster from founded or cast types in or about 1428. Heineken, a German bibliographer, intimates that the blocks of the *Speculum* were engraved, and that the two Latin editions were printed in Germany after the invention of typography; but he concedes, rather grudgingly, that the Dutch editions were printed in Holland. Santander says that the book was printed in the Netherlands, but not before the year 1480.

The disagreements of bibliographers concerning this book have not been restricted to controversies about its date and printer. Some have said that there were no types in any of the editions, and that the letters, like the pictures, were cut on solid blocks of wood. This error is almost pardonable. The superficial observer of our own time will say that the characters of this book are not types, but badly engraved letters. They seem to lack the most distinguishing feature of types. The letters are not at all alike, as may be seen in the accompanying fac-simile. The variations in the shapes of the letters are so frequent that a modern printer would at once decide that the dissimilar letters could not have been cast in the same matrix. This is a curious defect, but it can be shown that the letters are types, and founded types. "The existence of a positive fact," says Chatto, "can never be affected by any arguments which are grounded on the difficulty of accounting for it." It is plain, however, that the types of the book were carelessly made by an inexpert type-maker, and perhaps by a clumsy method now out of use. Instead of making all the types of one character from one punch or original, the printer of this book made them from two, four, or six punches or originals. At this point it is not necessary to consider why so many punches were made. It is enough to say that there is real uniformity in the midst of all this diversity—that each letter is a duplicate, more or less faithful according to the wear it has received, of its own original. Careful tracings on transparent paper have been repeatedly made of a selected letter for the purpose of testing its agreement or disagreement with letters of the same kind on other pages, and the comparison establishes the fact that the letters are founded types.[1]

The errors of the *Speculum* are those of types. They show the inversion of letters in positions which preclude the possibility that they could have been formed upon engraved blocks. The occasional occurrence of a *c* for an *e*, of an *n* for a *u*, of an *ſ* for an *f*, and the "turning upside down" of other letters, are examples of errors which can be made only by compositors.

The unequal perspicuity of the letters in the *Speculum* is that of unequally worn types. Of two adjoining letters, one will be distinct, black, and deeply indented in the paper; the other will be of dull color, and of indistinct outlines. The distinct letter is a new and high type, which has received the full force of impression; the indistinct letter is an old and worn type which has been touched but feebly by impression. If all the letters had been engraved on one plate, they would have been of equal height, and should have been equally legible, or nearly so, under impression.

The four editions of the *Speculum* are, of themselves, presumptive evidence that each edition was printed from types. It is improbable that the printer would re-engrave blocks for a second edition when those of the first were in existence. If the first edition had been printed from types, and the types had been distributed, as is customary, the printer was obliged to reset them in order to make the second edition.

These four editions were certainly the work of the same printing office, and, without doubt, of the same printer, for

[1] Ottley, selecting one letter for examination from a great number of letters of the same kind, found that it was always the same where-ever it occurred, not only in the first, but in the second edition. Koning and Enchedé, pursuing a badly cast or defective letter, found that the peculiar blemishes of this letter re-appeared in other letters on many pages. This precision of form is the peculiarity of typography: it proves that the letters of unvarying uniformity could not have been made by any engraver on wood, but must have been produced by a mould.

the engravings are the same, and the types, ink, paper, and workmanship have similar defects and peculiarities. The first edition shows pages of types only; the next edition has types and blocks, but the types are like those of the first; then comes a third edition in the same types, but with two pages of types differing somewhat as to body and face; lastly an edition entirely in the old types, in a worn condition. Each edition has more or less connection with the others.[1]

English.

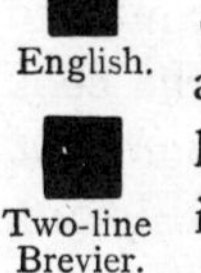
Two-line Brevier.

The body or dimension of the types used in the *Speculum* approximates the size known to all British and American printers as English; but it is rather larger than any of the modern standards. It is really intermediate between the body English and the little-used body of Two-line brevier or Columbian.[2]

The appearance of twenty engraved pages in the second edition of the *Speculum* cannot be explained with satisfaction. Bernard thinks that these pages are the relics of an earlier edition engraved, or at least attempted, on wood, which, for some unknown reason, were temporarily substituted for types.

[1] The Latin and Dutch editions of the *Speculum* maintain such a remarkable conformity with each other in the engravings, in the types, in the quality of the paper, in the presswork, and in every typographic feature, that it is evident that the four editions were published in the same country and by the same printer. As all bibliographers, whatever theory they may have concerning the origin of printing, attribute, without hesitation, the Dutch edition of the *Speculum* to Holland, the Latin editions should also be attributed to Holland. Guichard, *Notice sur le Speculum*, pp. 118 and 119. This is the opinion of all bibliographers except Heineken.

[2] The fac-simile given by Holtrop in his *Monuments typographiques* presents the following measurements, in American inches: In the Latin edition, described in this book as the first, 25 lines measure 5½ inches. In the Dutch edition, here described as the third, 27 lines measure 5½ inches. In the Dutch edition, here described as the fourth, 26 lines measure 5½ inches. As we find no indication of the use of leads or thin blanks to increase the distance between lines, it would seem that the types of the three editions were cast in different moulds. Sotheby's fac-similes, which seem to have been made with equal care, do not exactly agree with those taken from Holtrop's book. There are, no doubt, differences of size, not only in the fac-similes, but in the original copies of the book. Allowance must be also made for the unequal shrinkage on different leaves of the very thick paper, which may have been unequally dampened, and unequally extended before printing.

No trace of this imaginary edition has been discovered. It has been claimed that the engraver of these xylographic blocks was the probable inventor of typography. It is supposed that he matured the ideas he had cherished about movable types when he was engraving and printing the first edition of the book; that when he became fully convinced of their feasibility, he stopped the engraving of the blocks, and finished the work with types which were made for the purpose. This hypothesis is not reasonable. If the printer of the book suddenly abandoned blocks for types, the change would be abruptly marked in his work. The twenty pages at the beginning of the book would be xylographic, and all following would be typographic. But it will be perceived that the twenty pages are scattered, without any order, throughout the book. Instead of being the relics of an earlier edition, it is demonstrable that these xylographic blocks were cut from transfers obtained from a typographic edition. A traced drawing upon transparent paper, taken with accuracy from the first edition of the *Speculum*, and carefully laid over a corresponding xylographic page in the second edition, will show an agreement in the length of lines, in the abbreviation of words, and in the copying of little errors or blemishes, which could have been produced only by means of transferred drawing.[1] With this fact before us, the supposition of the priority of an engraved edition of the book is untenable. Dutch authors say that these xylographic blocks corroborate a Hollandish legend, in which it is stated that the materials of the printer of the *Speculum* were stolen. They suppose that the first typographer was obliged to engrave

[1] When a new engraving on wood, in imitation of an old one, is desired, the modern engraver does not redraw, but transfers the subject, substantially by the following process: The back of the print to be copied is moistened with a solution of alkali, or of benzine, which, soaking through the paper, forms a new combination with the oil in the ink. The black of the ink is thereby liberated, so that it can be completely removed by firm pressure. The print so treated is then laid, face downward, on the block, and the free black is transferred to the block by the pressure of a burnisher, or of a press. The black re-appears on the block, but in a properly reversed position, ready for the tool of the engraver.

Quo ꝯseqʒ vni⁹ nulle ꝛ duo fugarēt decē milia
Nisi qa de⁹ voluit ideo factū ē ita
Et quo vnis ꝯgregacio vna solū xp̄m cepisset
Nisi de⁹ ip̄m ī ptāte eoꝝ tradidisset
Hec aūt illusio q̄ xp̄o ī coronacione est illata
Olī fuit ī apemē ꝯcubinā regis p̄figurata
Apemē corōnā regalē de capite eius accepit
Et capiti suo in p̄ncia regis ipius iposuit
Jn synagō xp̄m corona .i. hōre debito spoliauit
Et ip̄m corona spinea ī· suā ꝯtumeliā coronauit
Apemē regi alaphas palmis dedit ī maxillā
Qd libēt rex sustinēs nō īdignabat̄ ꝯtra illā
ita rex celi sustinuit a iudeis alapas ꝛ colaphas
Et tn̄ nō ostēdit īdignacionē aliq̄ ꝯtra eos
Rex ille ꝯcubinā suā apemē in tm̄ amauit
q̄ oīa ab ip̄a sibi ꝑ ludo illata pacīēt portauit
Xp̄s synagoga multo pl⁹ amare ꝯprobatur
A qua tā magna cū tanta paciēa paciebatur
Talē paciēciā xp̄i olī rex dauid p̄figurauit
q̄ ab ōiq̄ semei tanta mala tā paciēt tollerauit
Semei piecit sup dauid lapides ligna ꝛ lutū
Sic synagoga iecit ī xp̄m palmas spinas ꝛ sputū
Semei dauid virū sāgūē ꝛ virū beleal vocauit
Synagoga xp̄m seductorē malefcū appellauit
Tercij regū ij° caplo

Fac-simile of part of a Page of the Speculum Salutis.

these twenty blocks to complete his imperfect edition. This hypothesis does not accord with other facts: the appearance of three successive editions of the book, each with a text of types, proves that the practice of typography was continued.

The provision of black ink for the types and brown ink for the cuts seems unnecessary, but Van der Linde's explanation of this peculiarity is plausible. He says that the oily black ink used on the types may have been rejected for the cuts because its greasy surface interfered with the brush of the colorist. It does not appear that the inquiry has ever been made, whether the brown ink of block-books was always brown. It is probable that this brown ink was once black. The variability of the color, so frequently remarked in all block-books, is the certain indication of a faded black writing ink. It was the fluidity of this writing ink that prevented its use on the types of the *Speculum;* the fluid collected in globules on the metal, spreading under impression, and blotting the paper. Oily ink was required for a surface of metal.

The unequal indentation of the letters indicates that the types were not of a uniform height. Nor is it probable that the engravings at the head of every page were always truly flat and of precisely the same height as the types. They were pieces of flat boards, which must have warped with every change from heat to cold, or from dampness to dryness.[1] In these irregularities we find the probable reason for the employment of two distinct methods of impression. Two impressions were needed as much as two kinds of ink.

[1] The neglect of engraving on wood by the early typographers has frequently been noticed as a strange fact. It was, no doubt, induced by the difficulties encountered in trying to print wood-cuts with types. The blocks would warp and crack in spite of all precautions. The evil was but partially checked by diminishing the size of the blocks. To evade the annoyance produced by warped blocks, some printers engraved large illustrations on separate pieces of wood, which were roughly fitted to each other, but not conjoined. Other printers printed the wood-cuts of their books by a separate impression. As these illustrations were printed in the same black ink which was used for the text, the double impression is rarely ever noticed, not even by the practical printer.

The types required strong, and the wood-cuts weak impression. If the impression had been graduated to suit the wood-cuts, the print of the types would not have been visible; if enough impression had been given to face the types, the wood-cuts, if in the same form, would have been crushed.

The quality of the presswork of the *Speculum* has been strangely misrepresented. Sotheby, who tries to establish the priority of Dutch printing, says that the ink in one edition is brilliant; that its types have great beauty and sharpness; that its presswork is equal in clearness to that of Gutenberg's Bible. In this high praise no other author joins: most critics say it is but a shabby piece of presswork. The Dutch authors, who wish to show the imperfections of typography in its infancy, call especial attention to the illegibility of the fourth edition in Dutch, which they claim as the first, and for that reason they rate it as an unusually clumsy piece of printing. Van der Linde says that the presswork of the *Speculum* does not differ materially from that of many books printed in the Netherlands during the last quarter of the fifteenth century.[1]

The wood-cuts were printed by the unknown process then made use of by all block-printers; the types were printed on a press which was fitted with at least one of the appliances of a well-made printing press; but the two editions in Latin, which are in verse, with lines of irregular length, show typographical blemishes of an extraordinary nature. In the blank spaces at the ends of the short lines are found impressions of letters never intended to be seen or read—of letters that do

[1] The Dutch folio of Jan de Mandeville, placed by Holtrop about 1470, as a work of printing, is so bad that the earliest editions of the *Speculum* are masterpieces by the side of it. The work of an unknown Schiedam printer of the latter part of the fifteenth century is equally bad. The Brussels incunabula of the Brotherhood of the Life-in-Common are bad; those of Arnold ter Hoorne at Cologne (1471–83) are sometimes barbarous. Heineken mentions a book printed in Augsburg in 1557, and says: "If the name of the engraver on wood and the date had not been found, one might think that this was the oldest book in the world." In the series of the different Dutch incunabula of this kind, the *Speculum* presents itself very favorably; it is not badly, but well printed; it is not a first experiment, but the fruit of practice. Dr. Van der Linde, *Haarlem Legend of the Invention of Printing*, p. 37.

not belong to the text—of letters not printed with ink, but embossed or jammed in the paper. On some pages entire words are found. These words and letters, which are always found within the square of the printed page, and in line with the types printed in black, are, undeniably, embossings of types from the same font. The printer who critically examines these embossed letters will be convinced that the types making them were used as bearers at the ends of the short lines, to shield adjacent types from hard impression: he will also know that they were printed on a press provided with a frisket.[1]

The period in which the early editions of the *Speculum* were printed will be the subject of the next chapter, but it may here be told when the wood-cuts were destroyed. In the year 1483, one John Veldener, then a printer at Culembourg, printed two editions of the *Speculum*, in the Dutch language, and in small quarto form. One edition contained 116 and another 128 illustrations, printed from the wood-cuts that had been previously used in the four notable editions. To make these broad wood-cuts, which had been designed for pages in folio, serve for pages in quarto, Veldener cut away the architectural frame-work surrounding each illustration, and then sawed each block in two pieces. Mutilated in this fashion, it was impossible afterward for any printer to use these blocks in the production of an edition in folio like any of those that have been previously described. Veldener's editions were not made by the method used by the printer of the earlier editions: the types and the wood-cuts were printed together,

[1] The frisket of the modern hand-press is a light frame-work of iron, which is covered like a kite, with a sheet of paper pasted to the edges. Just before the act of impression, this frisket is placed between the form of inked types and the sheet of paper prepared to receive the impression. The office of the frisket is to prevent the sheet from being blackened by anything but the face of the types. For this purpose, every part of the page to be printed is neatly cut out of the paper mask pasted on the frisket. Every part of the sheet that should remain unprinted is masked or covered by the uncut paper of the frisket. When the impression is taken, the sheet receives only the impression from the type, and is unsoiled by the ink that accumulates about the types and their fixtures.

in black ink and upon both sides of the leaf. The blocks were badly worn before they were mutilated: the finer lines of the engraving are flattened out, and retain too much ink, producing an effect of blackness and muddiness not shown in the impressions of the earlier editions. The fault is certainly in the cuts, and not in the presswork, for Veldener was an able printer. The wood-cuts printed by him in other books, at Louvain and at Utrecht, show neater presswork, although they are of feeble design and meanly engraved.

Although Veldener made use of the wood-cuts, he did not use any of the types of the *Speculum.* His book types are well known: as they are of different bodies and faces, they may be regarded as conclusive evidence that Veldener was not the printer of the early editions. It is probable that he bought from the printer of the first editions, or from his successors, the wood-cuts only. We may suppose that the types were worn out, and that the punches and matrices were also worn out or obsolete, for we find no traces of them in the books of any later printer. We have, therefore, to attribute all the books in which these types are found to a printer who preceded Veldener. We do not know the name of this printer, nor can we fix the date when he began to print, but it is evident that he was one of the earliest if not the first typographic printer in the Netherlands.

XV

The Works and Workmanship of an Unknown Printer.

The Speculum not the Work of an Experimenter...Improbable that this was his only Typographic Book...Twelve Books, Eight Faces of Types and Forty-two Editions attributed to him or his Successors...Hessel's Classification of these Types...Fac-simile of the Types of the Speculum. Fac-simile of the Fables of Lorenzo Valla...Fac-simile of the Peculiarities of Criminal Law. Fac-simile of the Epitaphs of Pope Pius II...The Donatus...Fac-simile of the Abecedarium. The Eight Faces of Types were made by the same Printer...An Indication that he Wore out Types rapidly...That he Sold many Books...Trivial Character of the Books...His Types not Made of Wood...Illustrations of Types of Wood...Their Impracticability Demonstrated...Books not made from Cut Types...Cause of the Dissimilar Appearance of the Types...Were Founded. The Press of the Unknown Printer...Its Defects...Indications of the Use of a Frisket.

If any shall suggest, that some of the Enquiries here insisted upon (as particularly those about the Letters of the Alphabet) do seem too minute and trivial for any prudent man to bestow his serious thoughts and time about, such persons may know that the discovery of the true nature and cause of any the most minute thing doth promote real knowledge, and therefore cannot be unfit for any Man's endeavours. *Bishop Wilkins*, 1668.

IF the printer of the *Speculum* was the rightful inventor of typography, his workmanship, as shown in the different editions of the book, clearly proves that he had passed the shoals of experiment, and was on the broad sea of successful practice. We can see, even without the help of the legends or chronicles, that he cut punches, made moulds and founded types of different faces and bodies; that he compounded ink in a proper manner, and printed his types upon a press constructed for the needs of his work; that he was successful both as a publisher and a printer. He practised printing not for amusement, nor in the way of scientific experiment, but as a business. Rude as his workmanship may appear, it fairly included all departments of the art: it was not experimental, but practical typography.

With these facts before us, it would seem proper to pass at once to the examination of the statements that have been made about the supposed printer of the book. But an examination at this point would be premature, for we have not, as yet, all the facts that are required. The four editions of the *Speculum* do not furnish enough evidence. It is not reasonable to suppose that two or three distinct fonts of type were made for no other purpose than the printing of four editions of this book. It is probable that the printer printed other books. But the early chronicles of Dutch printing tell us very little about these books. They are not only meagre in their recital of the more important facts connected with the invention, but are notoriously incorrect in their description of the minor details. They are unsafe guides. The books themselves, which reveal, to some extent, the process by which they were printed, are now regarded as of higher authority. We can accept the chronicles only so far as they corroborate the internal evidences of the books. It is proper that the books should be examined first.

The number of these books is greater than has been supposed, even by those who have favored the Dutch version of the invention of typography. Forty-three editions of twelve different works, printed from eight faces of types, are now attributed to the unknown printer of the *Speculum* or to his successors. In eleven works, the types resemble those of the *Speculum*, but the books are different as to character. They are in the form of small quarto or octavo, and are entirely destitute of illustrations. They are without name or place of printer, and, with one exception, are without date; they have no literary and no historical value; they differ but little, in a mechanical point of view, from numerous undated works of similar nature that have been assigned by bibliographers to the latter part of the fifteenth century. The places where these books or their fragments were found, and some of their peculiarities of workmanship, furnish evidences of value in an inquiry concerning their printer.

These books have been carefully classified according to their types, by J. H. Hessels, the translator in English of Van der Linde's *Haarlem Legend,* from which work the classification following has been copied. The types have been specified by numbers, and have been arranged according to the order in which they are described by Holtrop in his *Monuments typographiques.* It is not pretended that the order of these numbers indicates the order in which the types were made; numbers have been assigned to them only for convenience in reference and for the purpose of accurate classification.

TYPE I. In this character[1] the four notable editions of the *Speculum* were printed. In the same character were found the relics of six editions of the *Donatus.* The single leaf by which one edition of this book was identified, was pasted in a volume which once belonged to Sion Convent, at Cologne, and which contained several treatises printed by Ulric Zell, of Cologne. One of these treatises is dated 1467. Another leaf, now in the city hall of the city of Haarlem, was found in the original binding of an account book for the year 1474, which book was kept in the cathedral of that city. The account books of this church for the years 1476, 1485 and 1514, contain cuttings of leaves from the same edition. The first entry in the record of 1474 is to this effect: "*Item.* I have paid six Rhine florins to Cornelis the binder, for the binding of books."[2] Fragments of other little books printed in the types of the *Speculum* have been found:

An abridgment of the Liturgy, then known as the *Little Book of the Mass,*[3] a small quarto, with pages of twelve lines.

[1] For a fac-simile (from Holtrop) of this face of type see page 277.

[2] A fuller notice of Cornelis the binder will be given in the chapter on the Legend of Coster, in which his relations to early printing will be described. Attention may be called to the significance of the fact that no fragments of any book in the types of the *Speculum* have been found in the covers or binding of any manuscript book of earlier date than 1467.

[3] This work was in use as late as the reign of Charles V. It was enjoined by him that a printer should furnish without alteration "the little book commencing with the alphabet, the little book which directs how to bless the table (grace at meals), and the little book which directs how to answer at the holy mass." Van der Linde, *Haarlem Legend,* p. 2.

A Dutch version of the *Seven Penitential Psalms,* in the form of a very small quarto, containing but eleven lines to the page, printed on vellum, on one side only of the leaf. The only known copy of this work was found in Brussels.

Fragments on vellum of three editions of the *Doctrinal of Alexander Gallus,* a Latin grammar in rhyme, noticed by Van der Linde as the shabby compilation, by a priest of Brittany who lived in the thirteenth century, of the old Latin grammar of Priscianus. One of these fragments was found within the lining of a book printed at Deventer in 1495.

Four leaves of the *Couplets of Cato,* a small quarto which was then very popular in the schools.

TYPE II. The Dutch edition of the *Speculum,* which is described in this book as the third, contains, on pages 49 and 60, types which resemble those of other editions, and which

Jonas ghinc vtē walvisch na iij daghē
hernach. Des sonnēdaghes des middernachtes
die helle ghebrokē ofte verdoruē is hi wel si
nē lichaem ghegaē Cristus heeft sijn verrise
nis bi ionam ghefiguereert diē hi drie daghē
te ghilt inde buuc des walvischs Jonas was
inde scepe dat mid dē storm wart geworpē datt
dē dood dreichde alle dē genē die daer in warē
Doe seyde den scipper darumen hem inder zee

Type II. Fac-simile of the Small Types in the Third Edition of the Speculum.
[From Holtrop.]

seem to be the workmanship of the same letter-cutter. As these types are of a smaller face and body, they must have been founded in another mould. No fragments of any book in this smaller type have been found.

TYPE III. The types of this face are newer, but they resemble those of Type II; some capitals are identical, but others have differences which establish it as a distinct face. As it is of a larger body, it must have been founded in a different mould. A book which contains the *Fables of Lorenzo Valla* and the *Witty Speeches of Great Men*, two little works of some popularity in the fifteenth century, is the only known specimen of this type. The paper of this book, which is like that of the *Speculum*, contains many of the strange blemishes, previously described, of useless letters embossed in the white

Facecie morales laurentij vallensis
al's esopus grecus per dictum lauren
tiū translatus incipiunt feliciter
Prologus epl'aris
Laurentius vallensis insigni
viro arnoldo fonolleda salutē
Promiseram nuper me tibi cū
coturnices quas ipse venatus essem mis
surū · Eas capere ut homo venandi
insuetus cū nō possem · ad venatōnē

Type III. Fac-simile of the Types of the Fables of Lorenzo Valla.

[From Koning.]

lines and near the margins. As the written preface of the author is dated May, 1438, it is apparent that the book must have been printed subsequently to this date.

TYPE IV. Of this face, the fragments of four copies, and presumably of four distinct editions, of the *Donatus* have been found. This type, which does not closely resemble the faces previously described, was founded on a body a little larger than Paragon. The largest book in this type is a treatise on the Roman Law, apparently an abridgment of the fifth book of the *Pandects of Justinian.* It is described in the preface as *The Peculiarities of Criminal Law, by Lewis of Rome.* This treatise, which consists of forty-four pages, is printed in the form of small folio, twenty-six lines to the page. It was the largest book and contains the largest type of the unknown printer.

TYPE V. The forty-fifth page and all subsequent pages of the book previously described are devoted to a *Treatise and Epitaphs by Pope Pius II*, and a *Eulogy on Lorenzo Valla.* In these names we find sure indications of the probable age of the book: Cardinal Piccolomini or Æneas Sylvius was made Pope Pius II in the year 1458; Lorenzo Valla died in 1457. The book must have been written and printed after these dates. The workmanship of this part of the book is of superior character: the types were fairly founded on a body about the size of Great-primer; they were decently printed in good black ink and on both sides of the paper, but the remarkable defect of embossed letters which has been noticed as one of the blemishes of the *Speculum* is also noticeable in this book.

Type IV. Fac-simile of the Types of the Peculiarities of Criminal Law.
[From Koning.]

This Type V seems to have been more frequently used than any other type in the list, but it was always on petty books or pamphlets. One book printed in it has only twenty-four pages, but it is made up of four distinct tracts: *William of Saliceto on the Health of the Body; Torquemada on the Health of the Soul; A Treatise on Love, etc., by Pope Pius II; The Iliad of Homer*, or more definitely, a commendation of the *Iliad.* Two editions of this book have been discovered. A fragment of one edition was found in the binding of a work printed by Jan Andrieszoon, of Haarlem, in the year

1486. Another book in the same type, which consists of ten leaves, contains an abridgment or an epitome of the *Iliad*, with a preface by Pius II in praise of Homer. Of this book two editions were printed. Six editions of the *Donatus*, four editions of the *Doctrinal of Alexander Gallus*, and one edition of the *Couplets of Cato* were also printed in this type.

Epitaphiũ publij virgilij maronis·
Pastor arator eques·pavi colui superavi
Capras rus hostes·fronde ligone manu
Ex capris pastis·rure lato·est hoste subacto
Nec lac nec segetes·pascuaq3 nulla tuli
Epitaphium Marci tullij ciceronis·
Largus est exundans leto dedit ingenij fons
Ingenio magnus est·cervix cesa·nec unquã
Sanguine causidici maduerũt rostra pusilli

Type V. Fac-simile of the Types of the Epitaphs of Pope Pius II.
[From Koning.]

TYPE VI. An edition of the *Donatus*, twenty-seven lines to the page, is the only known book in this type, which was founded on Great-primer body.

TYPE VII. Four leaves of a *Donatus* on vellum, taken from the binding of a book printed in Strasburg in the year 1493, and belonging to a convent in North Brabant, are all that is known of this type, which closely resembles the character described as Type V.

TYPE VIII.[1] Impressions from this face of type have been found in the fragments of only two books. Two broad bands of parchment printed upon one side only with the text of a

[1] Hessels does not describe this as Type VIII, but as the *Type of the Enschedé Abecedarium.* He thought it "advisable to separate these two little works [the *Donatus* and the *Abecedarium*, which are printed in this face], to a certain extent, from the others" but he admits that the types of these books bear the family likeness and cannot be omitted.

Donatus, which were discovered in the cover linings of a manual of devotion, printed at Delft in 1484, are the only known relics of one of these books. The types are barbarous, of singularly ungraceful cut, of uneven height and out of line, evidently founded by a man who had no skill in type-founding. They are printed in pale ink which is readily removed by the application of water. The presswork is as slovenly as the type-founding, but the composition was done with some care and intelligence. The lines of type are nearly even as to length, and the words, when broken, are properly divided in syllables. It is evident that the compositor knew how to space and divide words, but the font of type that he used was not provided with hyphens or marks of punctuation. The fashion of the letter is in the Dutch style as may be seen in the final *t* with the perpendicular bar.

The other fragment in this type is a little pamphlet of eight pages, printed on parchment and upon one side only. It is described by some as a *Horarium*, or a little book of prayers; by others as an *Abecedarium*, or a child's primer. It contains the Alphabet (all the small letters but not the capitals), the Lord's Prayer, the Ave Maria, the Apostles' Creed, and two prayers. The Alphabet has the *k*, a letter that was not used in the Latin language; it has no *w*, this letter being formed by the union of the two characters *v*. Holtrop says that the types seem to have been made for the Dutch language.

The "turning upside down" of four letters on the second page of this little work proves that the letters are impressions from movable types.

Line 2. *Paue* should be Pane.
Line 3. *Cotidiaun* should be Cotidianu.
Line 5. *uobis* should be nobis.
Line 6. *uostra* should be nostra.

This little tract was discovered in 1751 by the celebrated type-founder Enschedé, of Haarlem, in a manuscript breviary of the fifteenth century, among the books of the descendants of John Van Zuren, a printer of Haarlem in 1561.

If barbarous type-founding and shabby printing could be accepted as conclusive evidence of the superior antiquity of the book in which these faults occur, the *Abecedarium* should be the oldest piece of printed matter. One cannot imagine a printed book with more slovenly workmanship. Its types present all the irregularities of the *Donatus* previously described. The pages have but nine lines of types to each page, yet they are very crooked. This crookedness was partially produced by an unskillful fastening, or locking-up of the types, but it is plain that the types were of irregular size as to body, and that the letters were badly adjusted upon the bodies. Some types are high and others low to paper, and there are types that are legible at one end of the face and not at the other. The presswork is wretched: we see the evidences of too weak and badly distributed ink and of uneven impression. The text shows many faults of composition in the division of syllables.

First Page.
The Enschedé Abecedarium.
[From Holtrop.]

To the observer who is not an expert in typography, the workmanship of the book seems that of a man who had no experience in any department of printing: the faults do not appear to be those of a badly taught printer, but those of an experimenter.

For this reason the *Abecedarium* has been claimed by the Dutch historians of typography as the first production of the inventor of the art. They say that it was printed before any edition of the *Speculum*, and probably in the first quarter of the fifteenth century. A closer

Second Page.
The Enschedé Abecedarium.
[From Holtrop.]

examination of the book does not lead to this conclusion: the printer of the book was, no doubt, a careless workman, but he had been taught the trade. The fragments of the tract are in four pieces, but they were printed in one form of eight pages, and by one impression. This artificial arrangement of the pages, in the arbitrary position which allows them to be folded together in regular order, reveals an expertness in little technicalities on the part of this early printer which is somewhat unexpected. The method of printing sheets imposed in forms of eight pages was not in fashion before it was adopted by Aldus Manutius, of Venice, in his edition of Virgil dated 1501. It is not an invention of the first, but of the last quarter of the fifteenth century, to which period this book belongs.[1]

The types of the book were not set up by an experimenter or ignoramus. The comparatively even outline to the right of every page shows that the compositor tried to space out his lines and to give every page an appearance of uniform squareness. As full and even-spaced lines are not to be found in any edition of the *Speculum*, nor in any of the first books of the early printers, we may conclude that the *Abecedarium* was printed at a later date, when this improvement had been adopted by all printers.

It has been maintained that the book must be very old, because it is printed on one side only, after the fashion of the block-printers. This is an improper inference, for each fragment has the appearance of a spoiled impression which was rejected before the sheet had been perfected by printing on the other side. The unfilled space for the initial letter shows that the work on the sheet was never completed.

[1] Berjeau, who accepts this *Abecedarium* as one of the first products of the invention, says that impositions of eight pages seem more complex than they really are — that the printer had but to fold a sheet, to mark the pages and then unfold the sheet, to see the method at a glance. This reasoning is specious, but it is inconclusive. It was the argument of the courtiers with Columbus after he had stood the egg on its end. Anybody can do it. Simple as the process may seem, the imposition of eight pages of type in one form was not done by any of the early printers, and we have to infer that they did not know how to do it.

The eight faces of types show their relation to each other, not only by common features, but by the occasional appearance of two faces in one book. That they were never used by any printer of Germany, nor by any known printer of the Netherlands, is acknowledged even by those who dispute their age. That they were founded and used in the Netherlands, and probably in Holland, may rightfully be inferred from the language of two editions of the same book, from the Dutch fashion of the letters in all the books, and from the fact that all existing copies or fragments of works in these types have been discovered in the Netherlands. That they were the work of one printer, or of the successors of that printer, is highly probable. But this admission involves difficulties. These eight faces of types were founded on as many different bodies: four of these faces are on bodies nearly the size of English; two of them are on bodies about the size of Great-primer. The modern printer is at a loss to imagine why his unknown predecessor should have cut so many punches and made so many fonts of types with faces closely resembling each other, yet so unlike that they could not be used together. His perplexity is increased when he discovers, after careful measurement, that each face on English body and each face on Great-primer body was cast in a new or different mould. It would seem that the unknown printer of the *Speculum* not only incurred the needless expense of cutting new punches and making new moulds for every new font of types, but that he intentionally introduced in his printing office bodies so nearly alike that they could not, in the shape of single types, be distinguished apart.

The questions at once arise, Why were so many faces and bodies of types that could be readily mistaken for each other, and were so liable to be mixed together, allowed in one office? Why were so many punches cut for such trivial differences of face, and so many moulds made for such slight differences of body? These questions can be answered only by conjectures fairly derived from the remarkable workmanship of the books.

The harsh indentation of the types in the paper shows very clearly that the types were roughly used, and that they wore out rapidly. We can see, also, that the method of making types was as imperfect as the method of obtaining impression. It is possible that the matrices and moulds wore out as fast as the types, but they could not have been renewed if they had not been made by a much quicker and cheaper method than that of modern type-founders. It is not at all probable that these different types were in use together. We may suppose that as soon as a font of types was worn out, it was replaced by another font, which may have been cast from new matrices and a new adjustment of mould. A new font made in imitation of the old one, but made without scientific method, and without regard to exact accuracy, would show the difference in face and body which seems so strange to the modern printer.

These eight fonts of type seem all the more unnecessary when we consider the trivial nature of the unknown printer's works.[1] The *Speculum* is the only book of respectable size; the others are so diminutive that they could be classified as pamphlets. They were cheaply made, adapted, apparently, to the wants of school-boys, and were probably sold for small sums. It is evident that the books met with ready sale. We find four editions of the *Speculum* in two faces of type and in two languages; nineteen editions of the *Donatus* in six faces of type; six editions of the *Doctrinal* in two faces; and twelve editions of other books.

From the character of the books, one might judge that they had been printed for the use of some school, and at the suggestion, or under the direction, of the authorities of the church. The *Abecedarium* was a primer for small children. The books most frequently published, the *Donatus* and the *Doctrinal*, were those most needed by very young scholars.

[1] Caxton, who printed thousands of pages in folio, made use of but eight fonts. Blades, *Life and Typography of Caxton*, vol. II, p. xxvii. Gutenberg, who practised printing for thirty years, did his work with not more than six fonts of type. Schœffer, who was a printer and publisher for forty-three years, made use of but six fonts.

The *Couplets of Cato*, the curt treatise on the *Roman Law*, and the *Praise of the Iliad*, are, in size and subject, the books that would be suitable for a boy's school in the middle ages. The *Treatises* of Saliceto and Torquemada, the *Witty Sayings of Great Men* and the *Eulogy* of Pope Pius II, may also be included in the list of books that were intended to be used in schools for the teaching of morals. The character of these works is more juvenile than that of any other typographic printer of that century. Whoever compares them with the ponderous theological works that were printed by Mentel, Gutenberg and Schœffer, and by numerous printers in Germany, and subsequently in the Netherlands, will at once see that this unknown printer made books for boys where other printers made books for men.

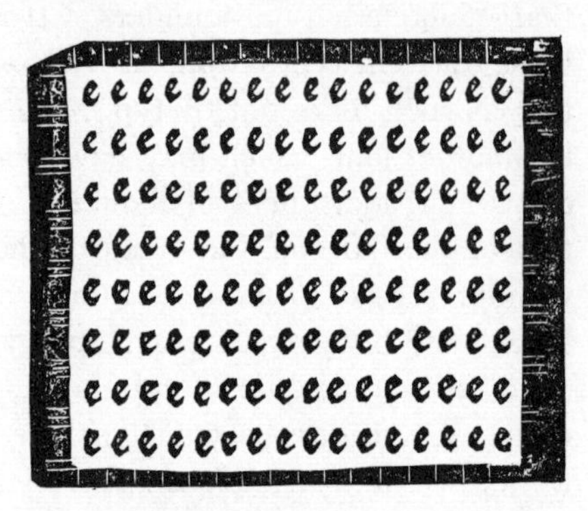

1. Experimental Letters Drawn on Wood.

[From De la Borde.]

Probably he could secure no other buyers. His workmanship was so rude that it could not be sold to an intelligent or critical reader. His process was suitable only for the cheapest work and the simplest tastes.

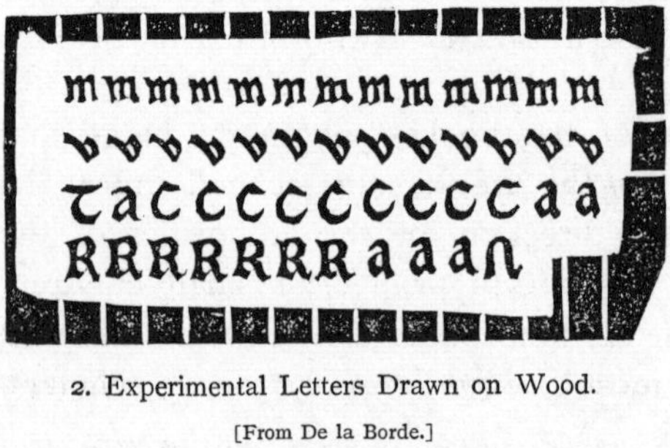

2. Experimental Letters Drawn on Wood.

[From De la Borde.]

It is unnecessary to prove that the types of these books, like the types of the *Speculum*, were founded in a mould. They show the same features, and must have been made by the same process. It is, however, necessary to show that neither these types, nor any types made in the infancy of the art, could have been cut on wood or metal. There is a tradition, which has found its way in many popular treatises on typography, and even in encyclopædias, that the first types were cut or sawed out of wood. We are told that separate letters, drawn at graduated distances, were engraved on blocks of wood, and that a saw cutting through the intervening spaces separated the fixed letters and made movable types. According to Meerman, the uncouthness of the types of the *Abcedarium* is fully explained by the acceptance of this tradition. It is necessary, at the outset, to show the impracticability of these imaginary types of wood. This can be done in no better way than by presenting the illustrations of Leon De la Borde, one of the most eminent defenders of the theory. In these engravings, we see how the letters were drawn on the blocks, how lines were marked out to guide the saw that cut them apart, and how the dissected letters were recombined in new positions.

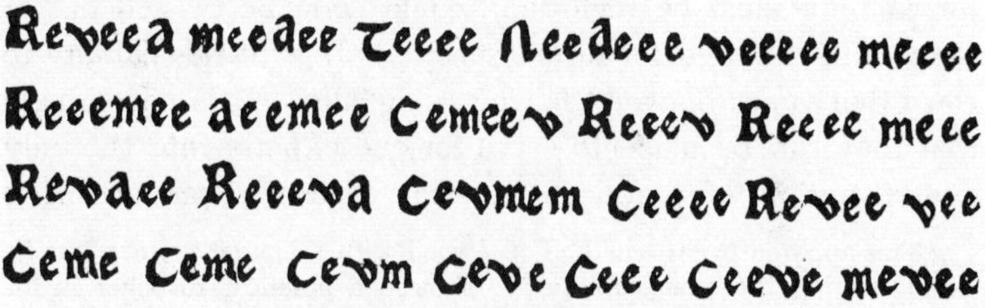

3. Types made from the Experimental Letters.[1]

[From De la Borde.]

But this illustration really proves the reverse of what was intended: it proves that types may be cut out of wood, but that they cannot be used after they have been cut. In this third illustration, the lines of type are separated by leads,[2] but the types stand more unevenly in line than the letters of any xylographic book. It is obvious to every printer that they could not have been printed at all, if they had not been

[1] Leon De la Borde, *Debut de l'imprimerie à Strasbourg*, pp. 70, 72.

[2] Leads are very thin pieces of metal which are inserted between the lines of types to increase the distance between the lines, and to give the printed page a more open and inviting appearance.

leaded. As an imitation, the illustration is of no value, for it illustrates a method of arranging types which was never practised by the unknown printer, whose types were always composed without leads. This pretended demonstration must be put aside as a complete failure.[1]

Those who have written in defense of types of wood have failed to see that the cutting of the faces is the least difficult part of the work. The real difficulty is in the cutting of the bodies—in making bodies so accurate that they can be interchanged with facility, in all kinds of combinations, without showing distortion in the line of the face. In small types made of wood this accuracy is not possible. Even if it were possible to cut them, it would be impossible to use them. No care could keep them from warping. Types must be wet with ink, and they must be cleansed with lye or water; they must be exposed to changes from heat to cold, from dampness to dryness. Under these influences, the little skewers of wood, for so they must be regarded, would soon be twisted out of shape, and unfitted for future service. It is in this liability to warp that types of wood fail most signally. It is not enough that they can be made to serve for one experiment; the only demonstration of practicability that a printer can accept is

[1] This apparently easy method of demonstrating the practicability of types of wood has been attempted by many writers. Wetter, the author of a valuable history of printing, published in his book a page printed from types of wood, which he offered as conclusive evidence that types of wood could have been made and were made by the early printers. But his types of wood are larger than those of the *Speculum*, and they are also provided with leads to keep them in line. Notwithstanding these precautions, they are more out of line than the types of the *Speculum*. Meerman, in his *Origines Typographicæ*, printed a few words from types of wood with a similar result; but he showed a practical disbelief in his own theory, by engraving all the facsimiles of the alleged types of wood upon plates of copper. The substitution of copper for wood was, virtually, an acknowledgment of the impracticability of wood types. Schinkel, a Dutch printer, was more successful than either Meerman or Wetter in obtaining a good impression from small types of wood, but he subsequently admitted that his success was but a trick, and that it did not prove that they could be used in the ordinary practice of printing. Léon De la Borde afterward conceded that types of wood would be impracticable.

that of repeated distribution and recomposition, a feat which has never been done. That types of wood were tried by the inventor of typography is probable; that single leaves were printed, experimentally, is possible; but the statement that any printer used them repeatedly in the printing of books, cannot be admitted. No book was ever printed in Europe with small types of wood. It is time, says Van der Linde, that criticism made a bonfire of these imaginary types.[1]

The hypothesis of types of wood has been given up reluctantly. It was considered that the singular variety of letters, so noticeable in all the books of the unknown printer, and so contrary to the usage of the modern type-founder, could have been produced only by engraving the types. A demonstration of the impracticability of bodies of wood seemed to

[1] The impracticability of types of wood is cleverly stated by Enschedé:

"I have exercised printing for about fifty years, and I have cut letters and figures for my father's and my own printing office in wood of palm, pear, and medlar trees; I have now been a type-founder for upwards of thirty years; but to do such things as those learned gentlemen [Junius and Meerman] pretend that Laurens Coster and his heirs have done, neither I nor Papillon [the most clever wood-engraver of France] are able to understand, nor the artists Albrecht Durer, De Gray, and Iz. Van der Vinne either; but such learned men who dream about wooden movable letters make Laurens Janzoon Coster use witchcraft, for the hands of men are not able to do it. To print a book with capitals of the size of a thumb, as on placards, *House and Ground*, which are cut in wood, and which I have cut myself by hundreds, would be ridiculous; to do it with wooden letters of the size of a pin's head is impossible. I have made experiments with a few of a somewhat larger size. I made a wooden slip of Text Corpus [a body about the size of Long-primer], and drew the letters on the wood or slip; thereupon I cut the letters. I had left a space of about the size of a saw between each letter on purpose, and I had no want of fine and good tools; the only question now was to saw the letters mathematically square off the slip. I used a very fine little saw, made of a very thin spring of English steel, so cleverly made that I doubt whether our Laurens Janszoon had a saw half as good; I did all I could to saw the letters straight and parallel, but it was impossible; there was not a single letter which could stand the test of being mathematically square. What now to do? It was impossible to polish or file them. I tried it, but it could not be done by our type-founder's whetstones, as it would have injured the letters. In short, I saw no chance, and I feel sure that no engraver is able to cut separate letters in wood, in such a manner that they retain their quadrature, for that is the most important part of the work of type-casting. If, however, I wished to give my trouble and time to it, I should be able to execute the three words, *Spiegel onzer Behoudinis*, better than the Rotterdam artist has done in the Latin works of M. Meerman; but it is impossible, ridiculous, and merely chimerical, to print books in this manner." Van der Linde, *Haarlem Legend*, pp. 72, 73.

destroy with it the only reasonable explanation of the greatest peculiarity of these types. To place this imaginary method of making types on unassailable ground, Meerman offered a modification of the theory. He supposed that the first printers of Germany founded little cubes of metal, with truly squared bodies, upon one end of which the faces were subsequently engraved. The misconstruction of the language of a chronicler of the sixteenth century—who, in trying to explain the process of making types, carelessly placed the cutting of the punch after the founding of the type—seemed a full warrant for this conjecture. It is, however, but a conjecture: there is no credible authority for the statement that the printers first cast the bodies and then cut the faces. Cut types, if made at all, were made only in the way of preliminary experiment. The method is as impracticable as it is absurd. "He must have been an imbecile," says Bernard, "who could not see that the process of founding in a mould which made the body would also make the face."

The allusions to letter-cutting that are so frequent in all the earlier notices of type-making can be readily explained. The cutting is not that of types used for printing, but of the punches by which the printing types were made. The types of the early printers were made by two classes of workmen: he who poured the melted metal was the founder; he who made the model letters was the cutter. Performing the more artistic and the more difficult part of the work, the punch-cutter was properly regarded as the maker of the types.

The variety of faces in the types of the unknown printer can be explained in a much more satisfactory manner than by attributing them to the accidental slips or deviation of the graving tool. The letters of the manuscript books of that century were not uniform; it was not necessary that printed letters should be uniform. The fashion of the day did not require it. On the contrary, it did seem desirable that the letters should be printed with the variety of shapes to which readers were accustomed. Whether this variety of shape in type was the result of design, of accident, or of necessity need not now be considered; in this place it is enough to say that all the early printers made many varieties of the letters which they most frequently used.[1] It should, however, be noticed that this apparent taste for variety of form was confined to the small or lower-case letters. Two forms of a capital letter are rarely found in the same book, but the same form of capital is occasionally used with two faces of lower-case types that are decidedly different.

The dissimilarity of the small types has been made greater by faults of type-founding and of presswork. In all copies of the *Speculum* the careful observer will see the impressions of types with imperfect faces. There are many half-formed letters, with little peculiarities of appearance which can be satisfactorily explained only by the conjecture that the types in leaving the mould, carried with them the impress of defects in the matrices. We can see that the types were unequal in height, and that the over-high types have been flattened out under impression. This flattening-out of the soft metal has produced a strange appearance of compactness, making letters that were really separate seem connected. The ink, which

[1] This taste for variety in the shape of letters was more clearly exhibited in Greek and German than in Roman types. The Greek types of the sixteenth century are so full of ligatures and variants, that they are undecipherable to the scholar who has been taught the language only in modern text books. So far from trying to make letters readable, the literati of that period tried to make them obscure: they were evidently determined not to make the acquisition of the language easy for their successors. When Francis I of France established the royal printing office, he engaged a skillful Greek penman to design additional varieties of contractions. Two centuries afterward, Pierre Fournier, the younger, a typefounder of Paris, commended the Greek types of his own manufacture as much less complicated than any Greek types then in use. But I count 776 characters in the font. More than 300 of Fournier's contractions, once esteemed as admirable graces, have been rejected by modern typefounders. Blades, who has made a careful analysis of the characters used by Caxton, shows that in the face described by him as 1 there are at least 167 distinct characters. But 24 of these are capitals and 81 are double letters. In faces 2 and 2* there are 380 characters, exclusive of figures, spaces and marks of punctuation.

was sometimes thin and gray and sometimes thick and strong black, was applied by an imperfect method which has filled the counters of some letters until they are almost illegible, while it has not fairly covered the faces of other letters. The singular irregularities of a collection of types, apparently new on one page and worn-out on another, which have provoked the astonishment of many critics, are chargeable, not to the condition of the types, but to faulty methods of inking and impression. Few persons have a proper notion of the changes that can be given to the appearance of the best modern types by substituting wet for dry paper, hard for light impression, and thin for thick ink.[1]

How the types of these and of other early books were founded cannot be learned from the vague descriptions of the early chroniclers of typography. We have to conjecture the process from the workmanship of the books. The discrepancies in the bodies and the imperfections of the faces indicate that the process was rude and unscientific, and that the mould was not of metal. It is possible that the maker of these types followed the example of other founders in metals, and made types in moulds of sand.[2] There are some peculiarities in his types which almost confirm this conjecture. The difficulty encountered in fitting matrices to these moulds, or in adjusting the mould of the face of the letter in proper position on the body, a difficulty that calls for no explanation, may be the reason why the types are so often out of line, crookedly set on body and of irregular height to paper. The feebleness of the sand mould, its liability to damage, and the necessity for its frequent renewal are, possibly, the reasons why we find in the

[1] Blades, in his *Life and Typography of William Caxton*, has given a practical illustration of these changes in Plate IX B, which also illustrates the feasibility of types of pure lead, for a notice of which see next page.

[2] The most approved process in the modern art of stereotyping is that in which the mould is made of calcined gypsum or plaster. The same material is used by type-founders in the manufacture of the largest types of metal. The cheapness of sand, and the ease with which it can be worked, make it the most serviceable of materials for all founders who wish to produce cheap castings.

impressions of the unknown printer types of so many bodies, and with such singular defects.[1] The rounded edges, spotted stems and deficient lines of many of the letters seem the faults of types unskillfully founded in moulds of sand, from metal insufficiently hot, poured in without the force that is needed to make it penetrate all the finer lines of the matrix.[2]

Koning, the author of a prize essay on the invention of typography by Coster, expresses his belief in the theory that the types of the *Speculum* were made from punches of wood and were founded in matrices of lead. His belief in the use of these rude implements is based on the well known fact that matrices of lead were frequently used by the earlier German and Dutch printers. Enschedé of Haarlem had in his type-foundry matrices of lead, which he claimed were used by Peter Schœffer in the fifteenth century. Firmin-Didot, the eminent

[1] To satisfy his own doubts as to the feasibility of casting small types in moulds of sand, Bernard, of Paris, gave to a brass-founder the types of a few Roman capital letters as the models from which he requested founded duplicates. He charged the founder not to dress nor finish the face of the founded letters, nor to give them more than ordinary care. The founded letters so made were printed by Bernard in his history as practical illustrations of the feasibility of sand moulds. They lack the finish of types made by the professional type-founder; they look like badly worn types, but they are legible. The brass-founder assured Bernard that a workman could make one thousand similar types in one working day. Bernard then gave to this founder separate types of a word in Gothic letters and requested him to furnish duplicates of these types founded on one body. The duplicates returned showed the very defects of the types of the *Speculum;* the thick lines were spotted, and the letters were out of line. Bernard's impression shows that the movable types which made the word were jostled or trivially disturbed at the instant of moulding. A disturbance of this nature would explain the irregularity of line and the rounding of the edges. The spotted and ragged edges of the founded word were probably caused by the roughness of the moulding sand, or by the sticking fast to the mould of bits of metal. It is a proper inference that in both cases the defects were the imperfections of the same process. The experiment of Bernard fully proved the feasibility of making small types in sand moulds.

[2] In the sand mould, the hot metal is poured in; in the metal mould, whether worked by hand or machine, the hot metal is forced or cast in. The phrase "casting type," which implies a sudden throw or violent jerk, has entirely supplanted the older phrase of "founding type."

type-founder of Paris, says that punches of wood and matrices of lead were used in his type-foundry for the casting of large ornamental types even as late as the beginning of the present century. His description is as curious as it is instructive.

> ...I have often made use of this process,...which is to sink in lead, a character cut on wood, at the instant when, melted by heat, the lead is about to harden. Matrices of lead made by this process are subsequently justified for height and for lining, like other matrices, Then, by the ordinary process of stereotyping, one may take from this matrix, a duplicate in metal, which, after having been dressed, is replaced in the matrix in lead, and fitted up to a mould. The melted metal poured in this mould, not only makes the body of the type, but at the same time solders itself to the stereotype [nested in the matrix] which makes the face of the type. By this process one may take from a matrix in lead, a type as perfect as that which is obtained in the ordinary manner. But these matrices in lead will only make a limited number of stereotypes....By taking the precaution to cool occasionally a matrix in lead, one can obtain from sixty to eighty types, without being obliged to re-enter the old matrix with the punch of wood, or to make a new matrix from the same punch. For vowels, and for the letters that are more frequently used, it is necessary to increase the number of matrices. But whenever the punch re-enters the matrix, the form of the punch undergoes some alteration from the effects of the pressure and the heat. It often happens that the punch is burned during the little time that it is buried in the hot metal. It then becomes necessary to re-engrave the punch. These are the reasons why differences in shape are to be found in the letters that are most frequently used.[1]

Whether the types of the unknown printer were founded entirely in sand, or in matrices of lead, cannot be positively determined from the appearance of the letters, for it seems that either method of founding would produce types showing similar defects. It is probable that the punches were cut on wood, and sunk in hot metal as described by Didot, and that the types of the *Speculum* were not only cast in lead matrices, but that the matrices were sometimes conjoined, and that two or more letters were cast together on one body. There is a closeness of fitting in some of the words which cannot be

[1] Didot, *Essai sur la typographie*, p. 607.

explained with entire satisfaction by the hypothesis that this closeness is the result of flattening out under pressure. One is strengthened in this belief when he discovers that it was not an uncommon practice in the type-foundries of the fifteenth century to join the matrices. Six of the matrices owned by Enschedé, and by him attributed to Schœffer, were made to be combined. These leaden matrices were pierced through their sides with a gimlet-hole, in which an iron wire was inserted to bind them together, and keep them securely on the mould. The method was faulty, for it could not keep the matrices in proper position; it could not produce types uniform as to height and true as to line.[1]

The thick faces and flattened lines of the types in many of the unknown printer's books show that his types were of very soft metal, probably of pure lead. To satisfy his doubts on this subject, Enschedé cast in some of his antique moulds types composed almost entirely of lead. The experiment succeeded: he was convinced that practical types of lead could be founded in matrices of lead.[2] Blades carried this experiment to a more successful conclusion, for he put the types to practical use. He had cast for him a collection of types in

[1] The process seems impracticable, but whoever carefully studies the British and American patent reports, will find specifications of inventions in typography that are much more absurd. There can be no doubt of their use. Koning cites one M. Fleischman, who had not only seen conjoined matrices in the type-foundry of C. Hardwich, of Nuremberg, but had experimentally cast types from them in an old mould that appears to have been made for this express purpose. Speckelinus, Paul Pater, Meerman, Schoepflin, Spiegel, and other early chroniclers, have specifically mentioned types pierced with a hole, and bound together with wire. These so-called types were either punches or matrices. Koning, *l'Origine, etc., de l'imprimerie*, p. 12.

[2] Benjamin Franklin, in his autobiography, has given a curious description of his attempt to supply his defective printing office with types cast in matrices of lead:

"Our printing house often wanted sorts, and there was no letter-foundry in America; I had seen types cast at James's in London, but without much attention to the matter; however, *I contrived a mould*, and made use of the letters we had as puncheons, *struck the matrices in lead*, and thus supplied in a pretty tolerable way all deficiencies. I also engraved several things on occasion; made the ink; I was warehouseman, and, in short, quite a factotum."

"unmixed lead," with which he printed five hundred impressions on rough and dry paper. He says that the types showed no appreciable wear; but this is not surprising, for we have evidences that they were printed by an expert pressman on an iron press provided with every appliance requisite for a nice adjustment of the impression.

It is not at all probable that the press of the unknown printer had these handy appliances. All the printing presses made before the nineteenth century had wooden frames, with beds of slate or stone, and platens or pressing surfaces of wood. Impression was given by the direct action of a screw, the force applied being regulated only by the discretion of the pressman. Knight, in his essay on Caxton, says the press of that printer was a modification of the cheese-press, provided with an attachment that permitted the form of types to be moved in and out of the press. German authors say that the first printing press was a modification of the wine-press. Bernard says it was, probably, an improved form of coining or stamping press. But these are only conjectures. We can find no engraving nor any verbal description of the form of the printing press in use during the fifteenth century. The general neglect by all artists and writers of this important auxiliary to printing is an indication that no importance was attached either to the mechanism of the press or to the principle of impression. It seems to have been generally understood that, whatever merit there might have been in the invention of printing, no noteworthy inventive skill had been shown in the construction of the press. It was not only a rude but an old contrivance.

We have many evidences that the press of the unknown printer was of the rudest construction. Some pages have the marks of strong pressure in one corner and of weak impression in another—manifestly the result of the printer's inability to regulate or control the force he exerted. The margins of the *Speculum* are of unequal width; the type-work is rarely ever parallel with the engraving at the head or at a proper distance from it. On some pages, the types overlap or bite on the wood-cuts; on other pages they are too near or too far from them. One of the reasons why the *Speculum* was printed on one side only was the deficiency in this press of any contrivance for determining the proper position of the sheet before the impression was taken. The pressman could not print one page truly and squarely on the back of another page. Koning says that the printer did not have the least idea of the means to be used for accomplishing this result.[1] This defect of the press can be seen in the pages of the small books without illustrations: they were printed on both sides, but the modern printer would condemn the work as seriously out of register.

The most remarkable peculiarity in the presswork of the *Speculum* is the embossed letters at the ends of the short lines.[2] They are most noticeable in the two Latin editions, which contain lines of unequal length. To the modern printer the purpose to be accomplished by the use of the old and worn types that produced these embossed letters is apparent at a glance. They served as bearers or guards to shield newer and better types in exposed positions from an impression which

[1] *Dissertation sur l'origine, l'invention, etc., de l'imprimerie*, p. 18.

[2] It has been shown that book types must be on square bodies. As a necessary consequence every form of types must be squared. If the lines of types in any page are not of uniform length in the metal, and the page is not truly squared, the form cannot be handled nor printed. But although the lines are of uniform length in the metal, they do not always appear so in print. The last line of a paragraph is frequently short; lines of poetry are always of an irregular length. To make the form square, and yet produce this desired irregularity at the end of every short line, the compositor inserts metal blanks, technically known as quadrats. As these blanks are about one-third shorter than the letters, they are not touched by the inking roller; they receive no ink and take no impression, and are consequently invisible to the reader. Quadrats are now regarded as an indispensable part of every font of types, but the appearance of the *Speculum* shows that the printer of the book had to do his work without them. That he knew the utility of quadrats is apparent, for he used low types as spaces between words. His imperfect press compelled him to reject quadrats at the end of short lines, and to fill the blanks with bearers.

could not be regulated. This exposed position was at the ends of the long lines; the types that projected beyond their fellows received the hardest impression, and the printer knew no better method of shielding them than by the insertion of worn types at the ends of the shorter lines above and below.[1]

This expedient was insufficient. On the margins of many copies of the *Speculum* can be detected (for the grain of wood is unmistakable) the marks of impressions against wood. It seems that the pages of types were fastened in a mortised block of wood of the same height as the types. This block of wood not only served as a chase to hold the types, but as a bearer to shield the types from uneven impression. It steadied the descent of the platen, and diffused the impression equally over the entire surface. These bearers shielded the types from undue impression, but they made a new difficulty, for they were of the same height as the types. The inking of a form so constructed must have blackened with equal impartiality the types of the text, the worn types used as bearers, and the wooden chase. To lay a sheet of white paper over such a form would smear and blacken it at the ends of short lines and in the margins where no color was required. It became necessary to put a mask over these bearers, so that the ink on the bearers would not be transferred to the paper.

This mask was substantially the same contrivance which modern printers call the frisket. It shielded the white sheet from contact with ink where ink was not required, but could not shield it from impression. It really strengthened and deepened the impression, producing the embossed letters in the short lines and the marks of wood in the margins. On

[1] To protect types in places similarly exposed, stereotypers insert at the extreme ends of short lines types of flat face expressly designed for this object, which are usually known as guards. When the plates have been made perfect in other points, the guards are no longer needed, and are cut away. When books were printed on hand presses during the first half of this century, pressmen sometimes pasted on or tacked on thin strips of wood around the forms of types to shield the ends of lines from injury. It is a strange surprise to encounter this modern method of protecting types from injury in one of the earliest books.

some pages the slipping or displacement of this paper mask caused the false letters to be printed in black; on one other page the mask slipped so trivially that one-half of the false types was printed in black, while the other half was embossed in white; on another page the mask slipped over the text type, and obscured the end of the line. These were exceptional errors; the general execution of this part of the work shows that the printer was a man of some intelligence, and that with imperfect materials he performed a very difficult task.

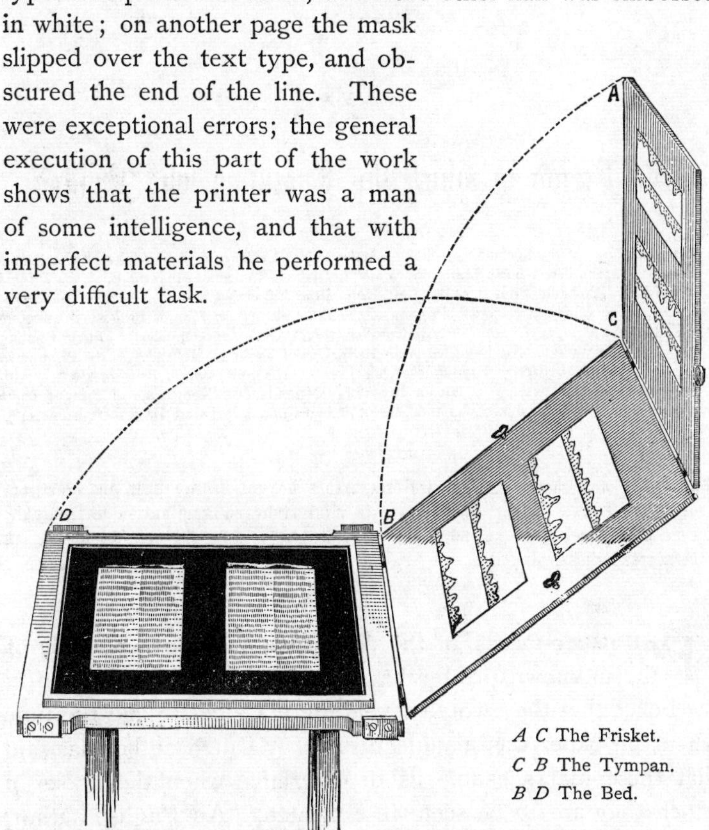

A C The Frisket.
C B The Tympan.
B D The Bed.

The Frisket, Tympan and Bed of a European Hand Printing Press.

The operation of presswork begins with inking the form on the bed of the press, which, in this illustration, is supposed to contain a form not unlike that of the *Speculum*, nested in a chase type-high. The sheet is laid on the tympan against guides that keep it in place. The frisket, containing the paper masks cut out to sink the irregularities of the form, is folded down in the line A B, partially covering the paper on the tympan. The tympan is then folded over on the line C D, which operation brings the paper down on the face of the form, ready to receive the impression. These are the appliances of a modern press. The frisket of the unknown printer was of much simpler construction, probably nothing more than a mask of paper laid on the form of types by hand.

XVI

The Period in which the Speculum was Printed.

The Paper-Marks of the Speculum, with Fac-similes...Not Evidence of Age...The Earliest Dated Annotation...Earliest Known Manuscript copy in Dutch...Indications that the Book was Printed at Utrecht...Probably Printed in the Last Half of the Fifteenth Century...Review of the Evidences...The Cambray Record...Printers of the Fraternity of St. John at Bruges...Testimony of Zell in the Cologne Chronicle...All Unsatisfactory...Discordant Opinions...Dutch Printing probably Xylographic...No Evidence of an Early Use of Types in Holland...Early Printing in Haarlem...Jacob Bellaert...Fac-simile of his Types...His Successors...Brito of Bruges, with Fac-simile of his Types...Was not an Inventor...Netherlandish Knowledge of Printing came from Cologne...Map of the Netherlands...Not probable that Types were Used there before 1463.

The utility and charm of historical researches do not depend upon the exactness of their results. Inasmuch as error is misfortune, so examination is profitable, even that which does no more than declare as evident the opinion which had been regarded as plausible.

Daunou.

THE paper-marks[1] of the *Speculum* and of other works of the unknown printer have been repeatedly examined in the belief that they would reveal the place where and the time when the paper was manufactured. A Dutch author has said that these marks enable us to determine when the books in which they are to be seen were printed. An English author,

[1] A paper-mark is an opaque design on the web of the paper, placed there to enable the buyer to identify a particular manufacture. It is made by bending the wires on which the moist pulp is couched in some peculiar shape which leaves its impression on the paper when it is perfected. Certain sizes of paper are even now known by the names of marks that are no longer used. Foolscap once bore the mark of a fool's head with cap and bells; Post once had the mark of a post-boy's horn. Paper-marks are now made chiefly for the finer qualities of writing papers. The illustrations of old paper-marks, on the following pages, were taken from Koning, and are about one-eighth of the original size.

who devoted the larger part of a folio volume to a review of the paper-marks of the block-books, undertook to prove from them that the *Speculum* must have been printed before 1440.

All known copies of the *Speculum* contain a variety of dissimilar paper-marks. Among them are the hand, the dolphin, the lily, the unicorn, bulls' heads, the letter P, the letter Y, the letters M A, the spurred wheel, and the papal keys. Many of these marks are found in the paper of the *Canticles* and the *Bible of the Poor.* It is evident that papers bearing so great a variety of paper-marks were not made at one mill, and probably not in the same district. They were not made in Holland, at least not during the first half of the fifteenth century, for there were then no paper-mills in that country. The early records of the treasury of the city of Haarlem, which are written on papers containing paper-marks like those of the *Speculum,* show that the paper was bought at Antwerp. Koning thinks that the *Speculum,* and the block-books which are printed on the same paper, must have been printed between 1420 and 1440; that the paper of the books was made in Brabant; and that many of the paper-marks are the initials or arms of the house of Burgundy. According to Koning, the letter P stands for Philip the Good, Duke of Burgundy, who reigned from 1419 to 1467; the letter Y stands for Ysabella of Portugal, who married Philip in 1430; M A stand for Margaret, who was countess of Holland before that state was ceded to Philip in 1433. These are very confident assumptions; they require a careful examination.

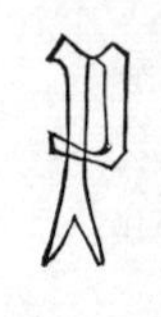

A closer investigation has elicited these facts: the letter P has been found in the accounts of the Count of Holland at the Hague for the year 1387; paper bearing the same P was used by many printers of the Netherlands, by one printer in Paris, and by several printers in Germany in the last quarter of the fifteenth century. It is found in paper made before and after the reign of Philip, and in cities over which Philip never ruled. Paper containing the letter Y was used in 1395, before Ysabella was born; it was in use for many years after she was dead; paper with the letters M A joined to the arms of Bavaria must have been made before her daughter Jacqueline was married, or, in other words, before 1422, an earlier date than can be claimed for any typographic book. The rude paper-mark of the bull's head was in frequent use between the years 1370 and 1523 in the Netherlands and in Germany; it is found in the great Bible of Gutenberg. It is, therefore, of no value in an inquiry concerning the date of any book in which it has been found.

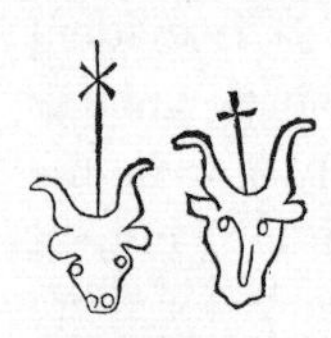

The paper-mark of the lily was used even in the fourteenth century; in the fifteenth it was as common as the bull's head. It is found in books that were printed in Cologne and in Paris, in Utrecht, Gouda, Delft, Louvain and Deventer. Paper marked with the unicorn was frequently used by the later Netherlandish printers. It did not go out of use until 1620. It is found in so many shapes that it is impossible to determine by it the date, or the printer, of any book on which it was used.

When we find that these marks were used in manuscripts before the fifteenth century, and in printed books at the end of the fifteenth century, we have to conclude that they are almost worthless as evidence[1] in an inquiry concerning the printer of the *Speculum.* Instead of proving that the *Speculum* must have been printed between 1420 and 1440, they really show, so far as paper is connected with the question, that the various editions of the book could have been printed in the third, and perhaps in the fourth, quarter of the century.

[1] Water-marks have much less weight in bibliography than some writers have attributed to them. In very few instances can a prime limit be fixed for their use; and, as the marks might be repeated, and the paper itself kept for any length of time, and imported to any place, they cannot be used as evidence either of the date when, or place where, they passed through the press. Blades, *William Caxton*, vol. II, p. XVIII. — The results of the examination of the paper-marks are, for the present, mostly negative. Van der Linde, *Haarlem Legend*, p. 86.

We have a clearer indication of the period of the unknown printer in the fragments of his work that have been discovered in the cover linings of manuscript and printed books bound in the latter part of the fifteenth century. It is obvious that the fragments are older than the bindings, but it is not probable that they are much older, for no fragment has been found in any book made before the year 1467. The larger portion came from bindings made after 1470.

A copy of *William of Saliceto on the Health of the Body* contains a written memorandum or annotation to this effect: "This book was bought by Lord Conrad, abbot of this place, XXXIIII [?], who died in the year 1474." Conrad du Moulin was abbot between the years 1471 and 1474 only. Another inscription in the same book states that it once belonged to the Convent of St. James at Lille.[1] These inscriptions have been cited to show that the unknown printer preceded every other typographic printer in the Netherlands; but the precedence claimed is unimportant, for we know that Ketelaer and De Leempt printed books at Utrecht in 1473.

In a public library at Haarlem is a manuscript copy of a version of the *Speculum* in the Dutch language—an admirably illustrated book of 290 leaves of vellum—which contains these inscriptions: "This book was finished in the year of our Lord 1464, on the 16th day of July. . . . An Ave Maria to God for the writer. . . . . This book belongs to Cayman Janszoen of Zierikzee, living with the Carthusians near Utrecht."[2] Van der Linde says that the text of the two editions in Dutch described on a previous page, is really an abridgment of the text of this Utrecht manuscript of 1464.

This fact established, the claim that the Dutch editions of the book were printed before this date becomes untenable. Nor is there positive evidence that the book was printed anywhere out of Utrecht. Utrecht was the residence of David, a prince of Burgundy and a notable patron of literature; it was also the residence of the bishop of the diocese; it had a

[1] Hessels, *Haarlem Legend*, p. xvii. [2] *Haarlem Legend*, p. 35.

gymnasium (as the high school of the time was then designated) of some reputation; it was a favorable location for an early printer; it was in Utrecht that the mutilated blocks of the *Speculum* were printed by John Veldener in 1483.

The book containing the *Eulogy* on Pope Pius II, which must have been printed after the year 1459, and the *Abecedarium,* with its evenly spaced lines and its arrangement in octavo, are specimens of the typography, not of the second, but of the third, quarter of the fifteenth century. The Latin editions of the *Speculum* were, no doubt, printed before the Dutch editions; but when we consider the activity of nearly all the early printers, and their frequent publication of popular books, it is hazardous to concede to the Latin editions a priority of more than five years. But Dutch bibliographers claim that the earlier editions of the book were printed at least thirty-three, perhaps fifty, years before the arrival of German printers in the Netherlands. To support this claim, they refer to passages or annotations in old manuscript books, which seem to show that printed books were common in the Netherlands during the middle of the century. These passages and annotations demand critical examination.

There is an entry in an old diary which, on its first reading, produces the impression that printed books were sold in Bruges as ordinary merchandise in the first half of the fifteenth century. This entry was made by one Jean le Robert, abbot of St. Aubert in Cambray, then a city of Burgundy.

Item. For a doctrinal *getté en molle,* which I sent to Bruges for in the month of January, 1445, from Marquart, the first copyist at Valenciennes, for Jacquart, twenty sous, currency of Tours. Little Alexander had a similar copy for which the church paid.

Item. Procured at Arras a doctrinal for the instruction of the Lord Gerard, which had been bought at Valenciennes, and which was *jettez en molle,* and which cost twenty-four groots. He [Lord Gerard] returned to me this doctrinal on All Saints' Day, in the year '51, saying that he set no value on it, and that it was altogether faulty. He had bought another copy in paper for ten patards.[1]

[1] Bernard, *De l'origine et des débuts de l'imprimerie,* vol. I, pp. 97 and 98.

The importance of this document depends entirely upon the construction of these words, *getté en molle.* Bernard says that they have always been regarded in France as the equivalent of printing, or of printed letters.[1] The literal meaning of the words is, *cast in mould.* So construed, no words could more clearly define founded types. This construction of the phrase would prove the existence of a typographic printer in Bruges at least as early as 1445. The dry, matter-of-fact way in which the words were used would show that books of this description were not novelties; that they were sold in Arras and in Bruges; that book-buyers were critical about their workmanship, and knew how they were made.

This construction of the phrase has been keenly disputed. Van der Linde says that the books were printed, but not from types—from blocks that had been *getté en molle,* or put into form, or put into readable shape, by the art of engraving. He cites authorities showing that the word *molle* or *mould* had been applied to forms of manuscript.[2]

Dr. Van Meurs proposes a new construction—that *getté en molle* has nothing to do either with types or blocks. "Who does not perceive, while reading the Cambray document, that in 1451, the term *getté en molle* is used in contradistinction to *in paper?* Do not these terms make us rather think of books in loose sheets as opposed to sheets that are bound? What can *molle* mean but form? What is a book *getté en molle* but a book brought together in a form, or in a binding, in oppo-

[1] Bernard, *De l'origine et des débuts de l'imprimerie,* vol. I. p. 98.

[2] The phrase could be applied to the forms of the letters in the books, without regard to the quality or any peculiarity of the printing or the binding. Two forms of writing were then in use: one, a black angular, and somewhat condensed form of Gothic character, which is defined in Fournier's *Manuel typographique* as *lettres de forme,* or letters of precision; the other, a round, light-faced, more careless and more popular form of letters, named by him as *lettres de somme.* To this day, carefully written but disconnected letters, whether upright or inclined, are colloquially known as *print* letters. The doctrinal which was put in form may have been written in *lettres de forme.* The phrase *gette en molle* could have been fairly applied to these precise letters, in contradistinction to the more careless shapes of the *lettres de somme.*

sition to another book in paper, or in a paper cover?" This conjecture is reasonable. No one knows of an early edition of this book from engraved blocks. As the seller of one copy was a copyist we may conclude that both copies were written.

Equally unsatisfactory to an unprejudiced reader is the misconstruction of the word printer in the list of the different arts or trades embraced by the Confraternity of St. John the Baptist, at Bruges. It has been inferred that the printers here noticed were printers of types, and that typographic printing was done in 1454, when the following list was written:[1]

Librariers en boeckverkopers, or booksellers.
Vinghettemakers, or painters in miniature.
Scrivers en boucscrivers, or scriveners and copyists of books.
Scoolemeesters, or schoolmasters.
Prentervercoopers, or image sellers.
Verlichters, or illuminators.
Prenters, or printers.
Boucbinders, or bookbinders.
Riemmakers, or curriers who prepare skins for parchment-makers.
Perkementmakers en fransynmakers, or makers of parchment.
Guispelsniders, or makers of decorations for bound books.
Scoolevrowen, or schoolmistresses.
Lettersnyders, or engravers of letters.
Scilders, or painters.
Drochscherrers, or shearers of cloth.
Beeldemakers, or makers of images.[2]

We have here a careful and, probably, a complete specification of all trades contributing to the manufacture of books, but there is no mention of type-makers nor of typographers.

[1] Leon de Bubure, in a paper published in the *Bulletins de l'académie royale de Belgique*, 2d series, vol. VIII, No. 11, shows that printing was practised at Antwerp as early as 1417. He submits an extract from the records of the city in which it appears that one Jan the printer publicly acknowledged, August 5th, 1417, that he was indebted to William Tserneels, manufacturer of parchment, in the sum of 2 pounds 12 shillings 4 pence, for which he bound himself and his chattels. It seems that this Jan the printer received a very liberal credit, for there are other acknowledgments of obligations for larger amounts, all incurred in 1417. After this date his name does not again appear on the record.

[2] Van der Meersch, *Imprimeurs Belges et Neèrlandais*, vol. I, p. 92.

In 1442 there was an organized society of book-makers in the city of Antwerp, known as the Fraternity of Saint Luke. Like the association of Bruges, it comprised every trade that contributed to the making of books. The trade of printer is in their list, as it is in that of the Confraternity of Saint John of Bruges; but in this list there is no mention of the makers or printers of types. The printers of the fraternities were, no doubt, the printers of playing cards, images and block-books.[1]

The earliest notice of book-printing in the Netherlands is that of the *Cologne Chronicle* of 1499, which is to this effect:

This highly valuable art was discovered first of all in Germany, at Mentz on the Rhine. And it is a great honor to the German nation that such ingenious men are found among them. And it took place about the year of our Lord 1440, and from this time until the year 1450, the art, and what is connected with it, was being investigated. And in the year of our Lord 1450 it was a golden year [jubilee], and they began to print, and the first book they printed was the Bible in Latin; it was printed in a large letter, resembling the letter with which at present missals are printed. Although the art [as has been said] was discovered at Mentz, in the manner as it is now generally used, yet the first prefiguration [*die erste vurbyldung*] was found in Holland [the Netherlands], in the *Donatuses*, which were printed there before that time. And from these *Donatuses* the beginning of the said art was taken, and it was invented in a manner much more masterly and subtile than this, and became more and more ingenious. One named Omnibonus, wrote in a preface to the book called Quinctilianus, and in some other books too, that a Walloon from France, named Nicol. Jenson, discovered first of all this masterly art; but that is untrue, for

[1] Some of the evidences that have been adduced to prove the priority of typographic printing in the Netherlands are really ludicrous. In 1777, Desroches, a member of the Academy of Brussels, published a pamphlet, in which he undertook to prove that the art of printing books was practised in Flanders in the beginning of the fourteenth century. His authority was an old rhymed chronicle of Brabant, written by Nicholas, clerk of the city of Antwerp. In that part of the chronicle which narrated events before 1313, it is stated of one Ludwig, that "He was one of the first who discovered the method of Stamping which is in use to this day." Desroches construed the word *Stampien* as printing. But the context shows that this Ludwig was a fiddler, and that he had invented nothing more than a method of beating time by stamping with the foot. In other examples which might be adduced, it is plain that the word translated as printing does not mean printing with ink. This word has been made to serve in notices of embossing, stamping, stenciling and moulding.

there are those still alive who testify that books were printed at Venice before Nicol. Jenson came there and began to cut and make letters. But the first inventor of printing was a citizen of Mentz, born at Strasburg, and named Junker Johan Gutenberg. From Mentz the art was introduced first of all into Cologne, then into Strasburg, and afterward into Venice. The origin and progress of the art was told me verbally by the honorable master Ulrich Zell, of Hanau, still printer at Cologne, anno 1499, and by whom the said art came to Cologne.[1]

Ulrich Zell is a candid and a competent witness, yet he narrates not what he had seen, but what he had heard. He was but a mere child, possibly unborn, when Gutenberg began to experiment with types at Strasburg about the year 1436, or sixty-three years before this chronicle was printed.

Zell's statement is the earliest acknowledgment of the priority of book-printing in Holland, but it is an incomplete and unsatisfactory acknowledgment. He names Gutenberg, but he does not name the printer of the *Donatus*. He specifies the period between 1440 and 1450 as the time, and Mentz as the place, and the great *Latin Bible* as the first product, of the German invention; but he does not specify the year nor the city in which the *Donatus* was first printed. The only specifications are—in Holland,[2] before Gutenberg, and by an inferior method. It is apparent that Zell did not have exact knowledge of the details of early Dutch printing, and that he could not describe its origin nor its peculiarities with accuracy.

We cannot supplement Zell's imperfect description of early Dutch printing with knowledge or with inferences that might

[1] Hessel's translation, as given in *The Haarlem Legend* of Van der Linde, p. 8.

[2] Van der Linde takes exception to this part of the chronicle. He says that Zell's knowledge of geography was confused, and that he wrote Holland where he should have written the Netherlands. His reasons for suggesting this correction are, that the manufacture of block-books and the prints of images, and the cultivation of literature and of literary arts, during the first half of the fifteenth century, were in their most flourishing condition in the cities of Bruges, Antwerp, Brussels and Louvain, all of the Southern Netherlands, while they were comparatively neglected in Haarlem, Leyden, Delft and Utrecht, of the Northern Netherlands. At that period Holland had not taken its place as the foremost state of Europe, in its championship of liberty and civilization.

be derived from a critical examination of the Dutch *Donatuses.* These books, described by him as the prefiguration of typography, have been destroyed. There is no known copy of the *Donatus,* neither typographic nor xylographic, which can be attributed to a period before that of Gutenberg's first experiments in Strasburg. The early typographic copies have the full-spaced lines, which were not in use before 1460 in any book; the xylographic copies are about as old, and, for the most part, are imitations of the typographic editions. Guided by these facts we have to conclude that it is not probable that the *Donatuses* of Zell were printed from types.

The frequent repetition of the statement that *the* art was invented in Germany shows there was no confusion in the mind of the writer concerning the relative importance of the German and the Dutch method of printing. He clearly perceived, although he obscurely described, two distinct methods of book-printing: the first, the method used for printing the *Donatus,* which method was imperfect and but a prefiguration; the second, the method that was more masterly and subtile, the method that now is used. The second method was, without doubt, the making of accurate types in metal moulds, and the printing of great books. It was not the second invention, but the invention, inasmuch as it was the only invention that had a practical value. The *Donatus* was printed, but it was not printed by *the art.* It was *the art as it is now used,* the only practical art of making types and books, of which Gutenberg was the first inventor.

According to German historians, the first method was xylography. They say that it was the sight of some lost or now unknown copy of an engraved *Donatus,* which gave to Gutenberg the suggestion of the more subtile invention of movable types; that this *Donatus* was not taken as a model for imitation—it served only as the suggestion of an entirely new method. Dutch historians say that it is unreasonable to assume that this *Donatus* was engraved on wood. There is force in the argument that it is not probable that Ulrich Zell, the printer, who furnished the writer of the chronicle with his facts, and who, as a German, was proud that typography was a German invention, would have ascribed the first rude practice of printing to Holland, if this practice had been nothing but xylography. It cannot be supposed that Gutenberg was so ignorant of the productions of German formschneiders that he believed xylographic printing was done only in Holland. They say that the suggestive *Donatus* which was made in Holland should have been a typographic book, printed as the *Speculum* was printed, from types founded by an inferior method—a method that was never imitated.

It will be seen that the statement of the Cologne chronicler is so ambiguous that it can be wrested to the benefit of either side of the question. It can be used to support the hypothesis that there were two inventions of typography—one Dutch, one German—one of little and the other of great merit—both alike in theory, but unlike in process and in result. But it is not worth while to consider the probability of a very early invention of typography in Holland until we can find the evidences which will compensate for the deficiencies of Zell.

This evidence is wanting. The statement attributed to Ulrich Zell is the only acknowledgment made by any writer, Dutch or German, during the fifteenth century. In view of the pretensions subsequently made, the silence of the earliest Dutch writers and printers seems unaccountable. Many of the printers were learned and patriotic men, proud of their art and of their country, but in none of their books do we find any claim for Holland as the birthplace of typography. Nor was this claim made by any of the great men of Holland. Erasmus, the scholar, the guest and corrector of the press for John Froben, the friend and correspondent of Thierry Martens, first scholarly printer in the Netherlands, should have known something of the introduction of typography in his native country; but the only mention that he made of the origin of the art was to attribute its invention to Germany. Before the year 1480, three chronicles of the events of the century had been printed in Holland, but in none of them is any notice made of early printing in Holland. The printers of Holland who followed their business in other cities never claimed Haarlem as the birthplace of typography. Before the year 1500, there were Dutch printers who put on record, in imprints attached to their books,[1] their belief in the statement that printing had been invented in Germany. It does not appear that there was then any knowledge of the legend of Haarlem.

At this point it may be proper to record what is exactly known about the old printing offices of this town. The first Haarlem book with a printed date is of the year 1483. It is a little religious book that contains thirty-two wood-cuts and a peculiar face of type that had been used the year before by one Gerard Leeu of Gouda. The printer's name is not given, but a colophon at the end of the book distinctly says that it was printed at "haerlem in hollant." From the same press, by the same printer, and with the same types, seven other books were printed before the year 1486. In one of these books, dated 1484, is printed the name of the printer, Jacob Bellaert of Zierikzee. There is no evidence that he had been taught typography in Haarlem, nor that he succeeded to any old printing office in that town. Bellaert was from Zierikzee; his types and his wood-cuts had been procured from Gerard Leeu of Gouda. The types are of a condensed form, superior to those of the *Speculum*, fairly lined, obviously cast in moulds

¶ Hier eyndet dat boeck welck ghe-
hieten is bartholomeus vanden pro-
prieteyten der dinghen inden iaer ons
heren M.CCCC.eñ lxxxv.optē heyli
ghen kersauent. Ende is gheprint en
de oeck mede voleyndt te haerlem in
hollant ter eren godes ende om lerin
ghe der menschen van mi Meester JA
COP BELLAERT gheborē van ze-
rixzee.

Fac-simile of the types of Jacob Bellaert.
[From Holtrop.]

[1] Van der Linde, *Haarlem Legend*, p. 66.

of metal, entirely unlike those of the unknown printer. The engravings have many peculiarities of design and cut which are not to be found in any known block-book.

Jan Andrieszoon was the second printer of Haarlem. In 1485 he opened a printing office with a stock of old and worn types, printed seven books, four with and three without a date. There is no evidence whatever that connects him or his works with the unknown printer. The competition of two rival printers in a small town produced the usual result. As no book can be found with the imprint of either printer after 1486, we have to infer that the printers closed their offices and abandoned typography.

The imprint of Haarlem does not again appear on any book before 1507. The name of the third printer is supposed to be Hasback, who, in 1506, had an office in Amsterdam, which he removed to Haarlem. His enterprise was unsuccessful, for no book of a later date can be attributed to him.

There is neither record nor tradition of any typographic printer in Haarlem between the years 1507 and 1561. The account books of the treasury of the town contain entries which show that its typographic work was done at Leyden. Coornhert and Van Zuren, "sworn book-printers at Haarlem," were also unsuccessful, for we have no evidences of their work after the year 1562.

In 1581, Anthonis Ketel was in possession of a printing office in Haarlem, but typography cannot be considered as securely established in that town before 1587, in which year one Gillis Rooman began to print. He continued to work as printer until 1611, when he was succeeded by Adrien Rooman.

There is nothing in this list of unsuccessful printers which assures us that typography had been invented or cherished in Haarlem. Nor is there even any recorded evidence of an early printing of block-books. There was, at an early date, in Haarlem a guild composed of painters, goldsmiths, sculptors, and of other artisans; but we can find no engraver on wood, no *prenter* or *figuersnyder* among the members. "The harvest of history," writes Dr. Van der Linde, concerning Haarlem, "on the field of typography may be scanty; on the field of xylography it does not yield anything."

This recital of the names and the fortunes of the earlier printers of Haarlem is not altogether irrelevant; it furnishes a proper introduction to the legend of Haarlem. The first printer in Haarlem, Jacob Bellaert, whose art must have been a wonder to simple people, closed his office after two or three years of unsuccessful labor, and probably went to some other place. The printers who followed him at long intervals were equally unsuccessful. Van der Linde thinks that it is around the first printing office of Haarlem that the vague traditions have clustered.

In none of the notices of early Netherlandish printing do we find any mention of Coster of Haarlem, or any description of printing by types. There is extant, however, an allusion, which cannot be passed by unnoticed, to the printed work of one Brito of Bruges, who, about 1481, printed a little book entitled *The Book of Doctrine for the Instruction of Christians.* The first page of this book says that it is a copy of two great tablets in the Church of Our Lady of Terouanne; the last page has this inscription in six lines of faulty Latin rhyme:

Aspice presentis scripture gracia que sit
Confer opus opere. spectetur codice codex
Respice q̄ munde. q̄ terse. q̄qȝ decore
Imprimit hec ciuis Brugēsis Brito Johānes
Inueniēs artem nullo monstrāte mirādam
Instrumēta quoqȝ non minus laude stupēda

Fac-simile of the Types of John Brito.[1]

[From Holtrop.]

[1] Behold what favor is due to the writing! Compare work with work and examine copy with copy [i. e. notice the uniformity of the letters]. Consider how clearly, how neatly, how handsomely, John Brito, a citizen of Bruges, prints these works, having discovered a very wonderful art, nobody having instructed him, and the very astonishing implements also, not less praiseworthy.

Brito was a member of the Fraternity of Saint John the Baptist, between the years 1454 and 1494, but he was not industrious as a printer, for Campbell can attribute but four books to him. Van Praet[1] says that he was engaged by the bishop of the church to paint or to affix this *Book of Doctrine* on the great tablets, which he did by the wonderful art of stenciling, with the very astonishing instruments of perforated letters, nobody having instructed him. Proud of his work, he attached this inscription. When he printed the composition in the form of a book he repeated the inscription. It is not possible that Brito intended to convey the notion that he had invented typography. So far from inventing types, Brito did not even make the types that he used in this book. They are the types of Veldener of Utrecht.[2]

From the early records we can glean nothing which will demonstrate that typography was practised in any part of the Netherlands before 1472. The workmanship of all known Netherlandish printers after this date is of every degree of merit and of demerit, but in all their books it shows the impressions of types founded in moulds of hard metal, and properly printed on a press, on both sides of the paper, and in black ink. As it is a style of workmanship entirely unlike that of the unknown printer, it is a proper inference that typography came into the Netherlands, as it did into all other countries, through the pupils and by the method of Gutenberg.

The table annexed will show how late was the beginning of typography in the Netherlands. It also shows that printing "by the art that is now used," was introduced almost simultaneously in three different towns of the Netherlands. In the year 1473, John of Westphalia was first printer at Alost;

[1] Van Praet says that the word *imprimit*, or printed, was frequently used by the scribes and copyists of that period as the equivalent of *scripsit*, or wrote. It was also used to describe painting by stencils. *Notice sur Colard Mansion*, p. 11.

[2] The same face of types was used by Machlinia of London. It would seem that Veldener was not only working as a printer, but that, even at this date, he was doing business, to some extent, as a manufacturer of types for the trade.

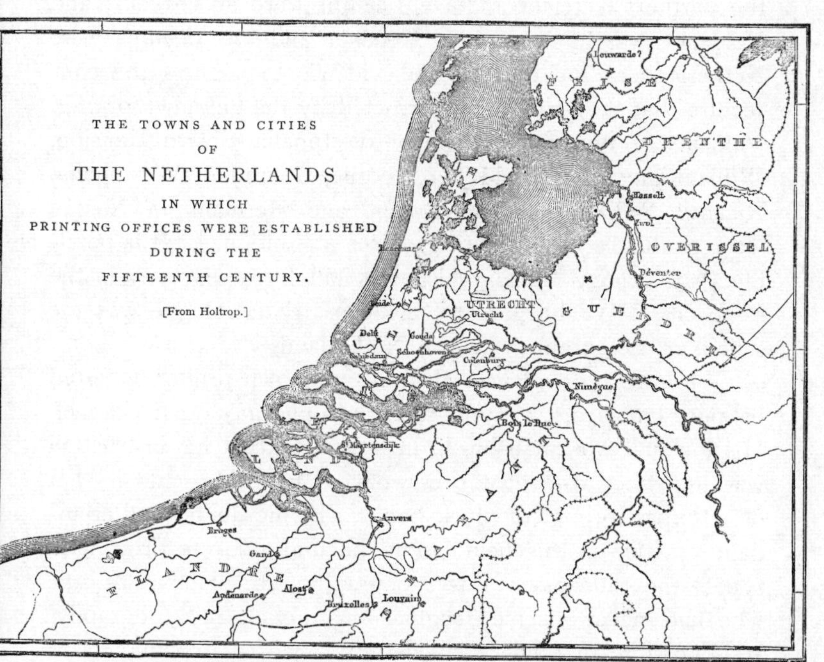

Utrecht . . . Nicholas Ketelaer, Gerard de Leempt, 1473–1474.
William Hees . . . . . . 1475.
John Veldener . . . . . . 1478–1481.

Alost . . . . . John of Westphalia . 1473–1474.
Thierry Martens . . . 1474–1490.

Louvain . . John Veldener . . . . . 1473–1477.
John of Westphalia . 1474–1496.
Conrad Braem . . . . . 1475–1481.
Conrad of Westphalia . . . . 1476.
Hermann of Nassau, Rud. Loeffs, 1483.
Egidius van der Heerstraten . . . . 1485–1488.
Louis de Ravescot . . 1488.
Thierry Martens . . . . 1498–1500.

Brussels . . Brotherhood of the Life-in-Common, 1476–1487.

Gouda . . . Gerard Leeu . . . . 1477–1484.
Godfrey de Os . . . . . . 1486.
Godfrey de Ghemen.
Unnamed Printer . . . 1486.

Bruges . . . . Colard Mansion . . . 1475–1484.
John Brito . . . . . .

Deventer . . Richard Paffroed . . 1477–1500.
Jacques de Breda . . 1485–1500.

Delft . . . . . . Jacob Jacobzoon . . . 1477–1479.
J. Van der Meer . . . 1480–1487.
Unnamed Printer . . 1488–1494.

St. Maartensdyk . . Werrecoren . 1478.

Nimeguen . Gerard Leempt . . . . 1479.

Zwoll . . . . . Unknown Printer . . 1479.
Peter von Os . . . . . . 1480–1500.

Audenarde . Arn. l'Empereur . . . 1480–1482.

Hasselt . . . Pereg. Bermentlo . . 1480–1481.

Antwerp . . . Matt. Van der Goes, 1482–1491.
Gerard Leeu . . . . . . 1484–1493.
Thierry Martens . . . 1493–1497.

Leyden . . . . Henry Henry . . . . . . 1483–1484.

Gand . . . . . Arnold l'Empereur . 1483–1489.

Culenburg . John Veldener . . . . . 1483–1484.

Bois-le-Duc . Gerard Leempt . . . 1484–1487.

Schoonhoven . . Brotherhood . . . 1495–1500.

Schiedam . . Unnamed Printer . . 1498–1500.

Haarlem . . . Jacob Bellaert . . . . . 1483–1486.

the partners Ketelaer and De Leempt were at Utrecht; and Veldener was at Louvain. Ketelaer and De Leempt were Netherlanders, but there is no evidence to confirm the conjecture that they had been instructed by the unknown printer. Veldener of Wurtzburg, John of Westphalia, Colard Mansion, William Caxton, Arnold Ter Hoorne, Conrad of Westphalia, Richard Paffroed, Conrad Braem, and Hermann of Nassau were graduates from printing offices at Cologne.[1] It is possible that Thierry Martens also was taught typography in the same city. We have many evidences that Cologne was the school of typography for the Netherlands.

We have no evidences that the unknown printer acquired his poor knowledge of typography through any other channel. His unequal workmanship is an indication that his instruction was imperfect; the neat presswork of his wood-cuts is that of an expert printer of block-books, who, no doubt, had abundant practice in this field before he undertook to print with types; the rudeness of his typographic work is that of one who had never received regular instruction in typography. It is possible that he received only a verbal explanation of the processes of the art,[2] and that he tried, unaided, to graft the new into the old method. His workmanship seems to be that of an imitator, a curious mixture of skill and of ignorance, but its inferiority to the workmanship of other printers of his time is not proof of its greater age or of his originality; it proves only his imperfect instruction or greater incapacity. So far from showing the first steps in an immature invention, his books truly show the degradation of a perfect method. They show the ignorance of a badly taught typographic printer, and

[1] The date usually assigned for the introduction of printing in Cologne is 1466, but some authors suppose, and Hessels and Madden say it is probable, that Ulric Zell began to print there as early as 1462.

[2] We have in this country two remarkable illustrations of attempts to make types by men who had no experience in type-founding. Benjamin Franklin's experiment is mentioned in the note on page 303. In 1794, Wing and White of Hartford, men entirely ignorant of type-founding, undertook to make type, never having seen a type-mould.

the prejudices of an old block-printer who had adopted the newer method with reluctance. We have seen that Walther's edition of the *Bible of the Poor* is every way inferior to the first edition, and have drawn from it the conclusion that there was a wonderful degradation of the art of engraving on wood. When we establish a comparison between the great *Bible* of Gutenberg and the *Speculum* of the unknown printer we have similar premises, and have to form the similar conclusion, that the arts do not always improve with age, and that the pupil or the imitator is often inferior to the master.

The evidences in favor of the priority of the unknown printer are very slight. It may be conceded that he was the first printer of the Netherlands, but it has not been proved, nor is it probable, that he printed with types earlier than the year 1463. Still more improbable is the assumption that he was an independent inventor of printing. We have to judge of the merits of this pretended invention as we do of every other—by its fruits. It had no fruit. The facts that this unknown printer made no mark on his age—that he left no work worthy of his alleged invention—that neither he nor his printed work was noticed by any of the chroniclers of his day—that he had no pupils, no successors, no imitators—should be sufficient to prove that he was not an inventor but an imitator.

By many authors the question of his possible priority has been decided, not from an examination of known and proved facts, but from the assertions of prejudiced and untrustworthy witnesses. The frequent presentation of the statement of the *Cologne Chronicle*, and of the legends that find their support in it, has not been without effect. There is a general belief in the tradition that types were first made in Haarlem by Coster, and that the German method was the outgrowth of the Dutch method. This proposition has been repeated so frequently and so confidently that it becomes necessary to give a critical examination to the legend of printing in Haarlem.

XVII

The Legend of Lourens Janszoon Coster.

Coornhert's Notice of Printing in Haarlem...Notice by Van Zuren...By Guicciardini...The Statement of Junius...Fac-simile of Scriverius's Portrait of Coster...Sketch of Junius's Life and Works. Examination of his Statement...Vagueness of the Date...Junius's Story is Incredible...Wood Types could not be Used...Metal Types made too soon...This story an Imitation of a Spurious German Story...Fust was not the Thief...Absurdity of the Accusation...Evidence of Cornelis. Our knowledge of Cornelis from other Sources...Cornelis not an Eye-Witness...Talesius not a Satisfactory Witness...Disappearance of the Art more Wonderful than its Invention...Legend Cherished for Patriotic Reasons...Its Growth and its Exaggerations.

He who is satisfied, as regards a fact like that of the invention of typography, with the simple assertion of people who talk of things which are said to have happened more than a century before their time, is destitute of scientific morality: he is ignorant of the passion of truth; in short, he belongs to the plebeians. We have not only the right to reject the fable fabricated by Junius,...but as honest men we are bound to do it. *Van der Linde.*

IN the year 1561, Jan Van Zuren and Dierick Coornhert, with other partners, set up a printing office in Haarlem. Van Zuren was a native and burgomaster of the town of Amsterdam; Coornhert, who was a notary and an engraver, is said to have been the instructor of the famous engraver Goltzius. Their first book was an edition of *Cicero de Officiis*, to which they prefixed the following quaint dedication:

To the burgomaster, sheriffs and councilors of the town of Haarlem, D. V. Coornhert wishes as his honorable and commanding masters, salvation to soul and body.

"I was often told, in good faith, honorable, wise, and prudent gentlemen, that the useful art of printing books was invented first of all here at Haarlem, although in a very crude way, as it is easier to improve on an invention than to invent; which art having been brought to Mentz by an unfaithful servant, was very much improved there, whereby this town, on account of its first having spread it, gained such a reputation for the invention of this art, that our fellow-citizens find very little credence when they ascribe this honor to the true inventor, as it is believed by many here on incontestable information, and is undoubtedly known to the elder citizens. Nor am I ignorant that this fame of Mentz has taken so deeply root in the opinion of all, by the heedless carelessness of our forefathers, that no proof, however apparent, however clear, however blameless it may be, would be capable of removing this inveterate impression from the hearts of the people. But—for truth is no less truth when known only to a few, and because I implicitly believe what I have said before, on account of the trustworthy evidence of very old, dignified, and grey heads, who often told me not only the family of the inventor, but also his name and surname, and explained the first crude way of printing, and pointed with their finger the house of the first printer out to me—I could not help mentioning this in few words, not as an envier of another's glory, but as a lover of truth, and to the promotion of the honor of this town; which proper and just ambition seems to have also been the cause for the re-establishment and recommencement of this printing office (as a shoot from the root of an old tree). For it often happened, when the citizens talked to each other about this case, that they complained that others enjoyed this glory unjustly, and (as they said) without anybody contradicting them, because no one exercised printing in this town."[1]

The claim of Haarlem to the invention of printing is confidently stated, but Coornhert has neglected to give the name or describe the process of the inventor, to fix the date of the invention, or to specify any of its products. He and his venerable informants, the "honorable, wise and prudent gentlemen," knew all these matters, but Coornhert prudently kept silence. It is worthy of notice that Coornhert admits that, in 1561, "the fame of Mentz" had taken so deep a root in the minds of many people that no proof could remove it.

A full notice of the details of early printing might have been considered out of place in the preface to a classic text book, but it would have been pertinent in a "*Dialogue on the First Invention of the Typographic Art*," which was the title of a book said to have been written by Jan Van Zuren. Of

[1] Hessel's translation as given in the *Haarlem Legend*, p. 50.

this dialogue nothing is known but the introduction. Whether the author grew weary of his task, and abandoned it before completion, or whether the manuscript was destroyed, as is alleged, during the siege of Haarlem in 1573, cannot now be ascertained. All we know of this manuscript is through Peter Scriverius, who, diligently gleaning every scrap of history that favors the Haarlem invention, has preserved the preface. It is too long and rambling for a literal translation; this is the substance, which Van Zuren approached with great delicacy:

> He does not wish to deprive Mentz of its rightful honors, but he will see that the honors of Haarlem are not altogether lost. The town of Mentz, so justly lauded, first introduced this art, received from us, in public life. The first crude foundations of this excellent art were laid in our town of Haarlem. Here the art of printing was born. No doubt it was here carefully cultivated and improved; here it remained during many years, until at last it accompanied a foreigner and made, at last, its public appearance at Mentz.

Here again is a noticeable absence of names, dates, books, evidences and authorities.[1] From beginning to end there is nothing in this statement but naked assertion.

One fact of real value may be gleaned from the preface of Van Zuren and the dedication of Coornhert. There was even then in Haarlem a strong prejudice against Mentz; there was a wavering belief among some of the townsfolk that printing had been invented in Haarlem, and that the pretension of

[1] The comments of a modern critic on the strange omissions of this positive statement are to the point:

"This forgetfulness of Coornhert has always seemed to me one of the most striking peculiarities of the Haarlem legend. How can it be! Here is a man, very learned, very patriotic, who appreciates the importance of the discovery, who contends with zeal to establish for his country the honor of being the cradle of the greatest of modern inventions. He knows the name, the family name and the family of the inventor, and he does not divulge them to his fellow-citizens! This surpasses belief. And what shall we say of the burgomaster Van Zuren? He writes a special treatise to retrieve the glory of the invention to the honor of the city of which he is a magistrate, but it never occurs to him that he should honor the memory of the inventor — I will not say by a monument of some kind, for that might be demanding altogether too much — but at least by a mention, by some souvenir, by giving his name to some street, or still less, by a simple record in a book. It is not possible to find another example of a forgetfulness so incredible." C. Ruelens, *Bibliophile Belge*, vol. III, 1868.

Mentz was unfounded. Whether this prejudice had been fostered by the obscure language of Zell, or whether it took its rise in the conceit of the simple people of the town, who may have thought that Ballaert, the first printer at Haarlem, was also the first printer in the world, cannot now be ascertained. There was a prejudice, and Van Zuren and Coornhert thought that it would be to their interest as printers to propitiate it.

The publication of these mysterious allusions to an early printer in Haarlem strengthened the belief of Hollanders in the legend. It was imposed as veritable history on intelligent foreigners who were unable to disprove it. Luigi Guicciardini, a Florentine nobleman, for many years resident of Antwerp, and who there wrote and published, in 1567, a *Description of the Low Countries*, was the first author of distinction who gave a world-wide publicity to the legend. In his book he says:

According to the common tradition of the inhabitants and the assertion of other natives of Holland, as well as the testimony of certain authors and records, it appears that the art of printing and stamping letters and characters on paper in the manner now used, was first invented in this place [Haarlem]. But the author of the invention happening to die before the art was brought to perfection and had acquired repute, his servant, they say, went to reside at Mentz, where, giving proofs of his knowledge in that science, he was joyfully received, and where, having applied himself to the business with unremitting diligence, it became at length generally known, and was brought to entire perfection, in consequence of which the fame afterward spread abroad and became general that the art and science of printing originated in that city. What is really the truth I am not able, nor will I take upon me to decide, it sufficing me to have said these few words that I might not be guilty of injustice toward this town and this country.[1]

The story is told as it had been heard, without comment, and without hearty belief. It will be noticed that no really important fact has been added to supplement the previous story. We are still in the dark as to the name of the printer, the date of the invention, and the titles of his books. The authors mentioned by Guicciardini were probably Coornhert

[1] Ottley's translation as quoted in Johnson's *Typographia*, vol. I, p. 12.

and Van Zuren; the inhabitants who gave him information were probably the same men who had previously given it to these printers. Guicciardini's story differs from theirs in one point only. His description of the translation of typography from Haarlem to Mentz does not impute dishonesty to the workman who carried it thither. The insinuated accusation of theft was not repeated by the scrupulous Italian.

Guicciardini's book, which was of marked merit, was published in an age of credulity. It was translated and reprinted in many languages. This legend of an unnamed inventor at Haarlem was taken up by other writers. It was published as valid history by George Braunius of Cologne, in his geography, dated 1570–88; by Michael Eytzinger of Cologne, in a book on the Netherlands, dated 1584; by Matthew Quade of Cologne, in a compend of history and geography dated 1600; by Noel Conti of Venice, in a universal history, dated 1572. These authors have been frequently quoted as men who had examined and confirmed the legend; but it is obvious that they copied the statements of Guicciardini without investigation. Their approval of the legend must be considered as an exhibition of credulity rather than of knowledge.

The specification of the name of the alleged proto-typographer of Haarlem was made for the first time in a book now known as *Batavia*, which was published in 1588, and of which Hadrianus Junius or Adrien de Jonghe was the author. The story of the invention, as here related, is far from complete, but it is positive and definite: it gives the time, the place, the book and the man. It can be fairly presented only in an unabridged translation of the author's words:

About one hundred and twenty-eight years ago, there dwelt in a house of some magnificence (as may be verified by inspection, for it stands intact to this day) in Haarlem, near to the market, and opposite the royal palace, Laurentius Joannes, surnamed Æditus or Custos, by reason of this lucrative and honorable office, which by hereditary right appertained to the distinguished family of this name. To this man should revert the wrested honor of the invention of the typographic art, which has been wrongfully enjoyed by others. A just judgment should give to him before all others, the laurel which he has deserved as the most successful contestant.

When strolling in the woods near the city, as citizens who enjoyed ease were accustomed to do after dinner and on holidays, it happened that he undertook as an experiment to fashion the bark of a beech tree in the form of letters. The letters so made he impressed the reverse way, consecutively, upon a leaf of paper, in little lines of one kind and another, and the kindness of his nature induced him to give them, as a keepsake, to the grandchildren of his son-in-law [Thomas Pieterzoon]. He had succeeded so happily in this that he aspired to greater things, as became a man of cultivated and enlarged capacities. By the aid of his son-in-law, Thomas Pieterzoon, to whom were left four children, most of whom attained the dignity of burgomaster (I say this that all the world may know that this art was invented in a reputable and honorable family, and not among plebeians), he invented, first of all, an ink thicker and more viscid than that of the scribes, for he found that the common ink spread or blotted. Thereupon he made, by the addition of letters, explanations for pictures engraved on wood.

Of this kind of printing I myself have seen some stamped block-books, the first essays of the art, printed on one side only, with the printed pages facing each other, and not upon both sides of the leaf. Among them was a book in the vernacular, written by an unknown author, bearing the title of *Spieghel onzer behoudenis* [the edition in Dutch of the *Speculum Salutis*]. This book was among the *a b c s* of the art—for an art is never perfected at its inception—and the blank sides of the leaf were united by paste, to hide the uncouthness of the unprinted pages. He subsequently changed the beech-wood letters for those of lead, and these again for letters of tin, because tin was a less flexible material, harder, and more durable. To this day may be seen in the very house itself, looking over on the market-place as I have said (inhabited afterward by his great-grandchild, Gerrit Thomaszoon, who departed this life but a few years since, and whom I mention only to honor), some very old wine flagons, which were made from the melting down of the remnants of these very types.

The new invention met with favor from the public, as it deserved, and the new merchandise, never before seen, attracted purchasers from every direction, and produced abundant profit. As the admiration of the art increased, the work increased. He added assistants to his band of workmen; and here may be found the cause of his troubles. Among these workmen was a certain John. Whether or not, as suspicion alleges, he was Faust[1]—inauspicious name for one who was

[1] An attempted play or pun on the Latin *faustus*, happy. But the German printer's name was not Faust, but Fust. This pun was the origin of the error.

equally unfortunate and unfaithful to his master—or whether he was another of the same name, I shall not trouble myself to ascertain—for I am unwilling to disturb the *shades* of the dead, inasmuch as *they*[1] must have suffered from the reproaches of conscience as long as *they* lived. *This* man, although bound by oath to [preserving the secrets of] the typographic art, when he knew himself to be perfectly skilled in the operations of type-setting, in the knowledge of type-founding, and in every other detail appertaining to the work, seized the first favorable opportunity—and he could not have found a time more favorable, for it was on the night of the anniversary of the nativity of Christ, when all, without distinction, are accustomed to assist at divine service—and flew into the closet of the types, and packed up the instruments used in making them that belonged to his master, and which had been made with his own hands, and immediately after slunk away from the house with the thief. He went first to Amsterdam, thence to Cologne, and finally regained Mentz, as it were to an altar of safety so it is said, and as if beyond all possibility of a recapture, where, having opened his office, he reaped an abundant reward from the fruits of his theft. That is to say, within the space of a year, or about 1442, it is well known that he published by the aid of the same types which Laurentius had used in Haarlem, the *Doctrinal* of Alexander Gallus, the most popular grammar then in use, and also the *Treatises* of Peter of Spain, which were his first publications.

These are the facts. Nearly all of them are from old men worthy of belief, who, each in turn, have accepted and transmitted them, as they would pass a lighted torch from hand to hand. I knew these facts long time ago, and have positive knowledge from other sources which have attested and confirmed them. I remember that Nicholas Gallius, the preceptor of my boyhood, a man of tenacious memory, and venerable with gray hairs, narrated these circumstances to me. He, when a boy, had more than once heard Cornelis, an old book-binder and an under workman in the same printing office, when not an octogenarian and bowed down with years, recite all these details as he had received them from his master, embracing the inception of the enterprise, the growth and cultivation of the rude art, and other transactions connected therewith. But as often as he made mention of the theft, he involuntarily would burst into tears at the recollection of the infamy of the sequel; and then the anger of the old man

[1] In Junius's description of the thief, there is a strange confusion of singular and plural. Beginning with the specification of one John as the thief, the story ends with an intimation that there were two thieves. This substitution of *they* for *he* is not a typographical error, nor is it a slip of the pen. It seems to have been intended to sustain the insinuation of the complicity of Fust in this theft.

The true Effigies of Laurenz Ians Koster Delineated from his Monumentall Stone Statue, Erected at Harlem.
MEMORIÆ SACRUM.
LAURENTIO COSTERO, HARLEMENSI, ALTERI CADMO, ET ARTIS TYPOGRAPHICÆ CIRCA AN. DOM. M.CCCC.XXX INVENTORI PRIMO,
BENE DE LITERIS AC TOTO ORBE MERENTI, HANC Q.L.C.Q.
STATUAM, QUIA ÆREA AUT MARMOREA DEFUIT, PRO MONUMENTO POSUIT CIVIS GRATISSIMUS
PETRUS SCRIVERIUS
1635.
A

[From Moxon.]

would flash up, as he thought of the glory of the invention that had been stolen with the other theft; and he wished, if his life had been spared, that he might have been able to set forth the thief in irons, ready to be pronounced a subject for the executioner; and then again he was wont to consign his sacrilegious head to the direst punishment, and to curse and execrate the nights which he had passed upon the same bed for many months with that villain. These details do not disagree with the words of Quirinius Talesius, burgomaster; for I acknowledge that a long time ago I received nearly the same story from him as was received from the mouth of the bookbinder.[1]

The story of Junius is the real foundation of the modern legend of Haarlem. All that had been written before is of little value; all that has been written since is but in explanation of its obscurer features. Before any criticism is given

[1] The full title of the book from which this translation was made is *Hadriani Ivnii Hornani, Medici Batavia. In qua præter gentis & insulæ antiquitatem, originem, decora, mores, aliaque, ad eam historiam pertinantia, declaratur quæ fuerit vetus Batavia. Ex. offic. Plantiniana*, 1588, 4to. Hadrianus Junius was born at Hoorn, in the year 1511. His education, as a boy, was received at a grammar school in Haarlem; as a young man at the university of Louvain. In 1537, with one Martin Costerus, he made a tour in foreign countries. In 1540 he obtained from the university of Bologna the degree of doctor of medicine. Two years afterward he was living in Paris. In 1543 he went to England, and for six years succeeding, he was employed as physician to the duke of Norfolk. Soon after the death of the duke, he published in London a Greek lexicon, which enhanced his reputation as a scholar, but did not mend his fortunes. In 1559 he returned to Haarlem, where he married a lady of wealth. Three years after his marriage he accepted the appointment of tutor to the crown prince of Denmark, but finding that the position or the climate was disagreeable, he resigned the office. In 1563 he was appointed town physician, and rector of the Latin grammar school at Haarlem, which appointments he held until 1569. About this period he wrote *Nomenclator*, a lexicon in eight languages, and *Batavia*, a description of Holland. At various times he was formally invited to enter the service of the kings of Hungary, Poland and Denmark. William of Orange sent from Delft for his services as a physician: at a meeting of the deputies from the States, he nominated Junius as the historian of Holland. In 1574 he was made town physician at Middleburg, with a liberal salary and a free living. When Haarlem was captured in 1573 by the Spaniards, the library of Junius was plundered, and many of his manuscripts were destroyed. He took this calamity greatly to heart, and died at Arnemuiden in 1575. Justus Lipsius said he was the most learned Netherlander after Erasmus.

to this important document, the capability and credibility of the learned author of *Batavia* should be considered.

The learning of Junius cannot be questioned; but Junius must be judged not by his dead reputation, but by his living performance. *Batavia,* although written in unexceptionable classical Latin, is not a valuable, nor even a mediocre book. The author was not above the pedantry and the bad taste of his age. His book is full of classical allusions, lugged in, not to illustrate the subject, but to display the author's omnivorous reading;[1] his style is rhetorical, and his arrangement of facts is bewildering. These faults would be overlooked, if we could be sure of his so-called facts; but one cannot read many pages of *Batavia* without being convinced of the credulity of the author, and of the thorough untrustworthiness of many of his

[1] The publication of *Batavia,* the work upon which the fame of Junius rests, seems to have been suggested to William of Orange by Junius himself, who expected to receive from the States a salary for his services as historian. In 1565, the question of salary, first named at 200 pounds of 40 groots, was put to vote. The prudence of the Dutch character is shown in the deliberations of the deputies. Haarlem, Delft, Leyden, and Gouda assented; Dordrecht and Amsterdam requested time for its consideration. Dordrecht afterward consented, but on condition that the money should be paid out of the taxes; that Junius should publish a volume every year; and that he should publish nothing without the approval of the States. In the meantime other States receded from their action, saying that the publication was ill-timed during a period of general distress. After some influences had been used, the States gave a grudging and qualified assent. In 1570, Junius petitioned for the payment of 200 guilders, as he had then finished the first book of the history. The petition was not favorably received, and its consideration was postponed for one year, at which time it was finally decided by the deputies to pay Junius 300 guilders, to prohibit him from publishing the first volume of the book with a dedication to the States, and to release him from all obligation to continue the work. This disparaging treatment of the author prevented the publication of the book with the completeness and at the time Junius had proposed. After his death the manuscripts of *Batavia* were collected and transcribed by his son Peter, who, with Peter Douza, undertook the publication. The book was published during 1588, from the office of Christopher Plantin, at Antwerp. The selection of a printer in a neighboring city shows that there was then no competent printer at Haarlem. It is another evidence of the indifference of the people of Haarlem toward typography.

descriptions. His defenders must confess that the book would have been of higher authority, if he had been more chary of rhetoric and more exact in description.[1]

The fixing of the period in which the inventor lived seems to have been made with a studied carelessness and intended obscurity. If we deduct the 128 years from the year 1568, the year in which the manuscript of *Batavia* was completed, we have the date 1440. In this year Coster lived. When he was born, when he died, and how long he had been occupied with the practice of printing, is not related. If we infer that Junius intended that this year 1440 should be considered as the year of Coster's death, the inference is purely conjectural. He does not say so. It may be supposed, but it is not said, that Coster printed with types before 1440. Whatever may have been the intention of Junius, the year 1440 was at first accepted by the authorities of Haarlem as the true date of the

[1] He relates not as a legend, but as veritable history, that the virgin Soter, who possessed but three pennies, gave them for the building of a church in Dordrecht. Other three pennies were miraculously and regularly found in her purse, and were as regularly bestowed, until the church was built. He repeats, with simplicity, the story of the eleven thousand virgins of Cologne, who came from England to the now unknown port of Verona in Holland. He says that a certain stone in a church in Leyden was once a loaf of bread, and that the transubstantiation was made by a curse. He formally records the delivery by one Margaret, countess of Hennenberg, of 365 babies—a miracle, writes Van der Linde, "that makes you think of an upset pot of shrimps." Junius adds that this would be a miracle beyond belief, if it had not been attested by the authority of public monuments. . . . but he accepts the common belief. These examples of the credulousness of the author of *Batavia* warn us not to accept his criticisms on other traditions. Junius begins his description of printing at Haarlem with a solemn declaration of his intention to tell the truth. The declaration of candor is not needed: what the reader of *Batavia* does need is, not the protestation of the intention of the author to tell the truth, but some convincing evidence of his ability to distinguish the true from the false. His preface is long, pedantic, and in every way irrelevant, as may be inferred from a glance at the following classical names which he has sprinkled in the first paragraph: Carneades, the Daughter of Time, Democritus, Phœnicians and Egyptians, Cadmus, Athenians, Greeks and Thebans, Cecrops, Philostratus, Linus, Tacitus, Palamedes, Hyginus, Carmenta, Evander, Crassus, Scævola and Plutarch!

invention of typography.[1] It was thought that the fixing of the invention within this year would sufficiently establish the priority of Coster, for the year 1442 was the date then assigned to the rival invention in Germany. The authority of Junius for the year 1440 was, no doubt, a pedigree of the Coster family, of which he makes no mention.

There are troublesome entanglements connected with this date of 1440. Subsequent defenders of the legend, who tried to supply the deficiencies and correct the errors of Junius, made discoveries which compelled them to acknowledge that Lourens Janszoon (supposed by them to be Lourens Janszoon Coster) died in the year 1439. If he died in 1439, and if we believe that the invention was made in 1440, then he did his typographic work in the year after his death.[2] The absurdity of this date was clearly perceived when it was afterward discovered that Gutenberg had been engaged as early as 1436 in experiments with printing. To preserve the appearance of probability, the date of the invention was removed to 1423, so as to allow Coster time for experiment and for the perfection of his invention.

The name of the inventor is as uncertain as the date of the invention. Junius names him Laurentius Johannes, surnamed Æditaus, or Custos. In the pedigree, the name was

[1] In the year 1630, Adrien Rooman, of Haarlem, published a print which contained the engraved representation of a printing office, to which he put the words—"Invented at Haarlem about 1430;"—but "The magistrates and citizens of Haarlem, in everlasting remembrance of the event and the man," erected a monument in front of the Coster house, with an inscription on it, which fixed the date at 1440.

[2] Lambinet caustically observes that the romance of Junius obeys the dramatic law of unity, in time, place, and hero: the typographic art is invented complete in one day. The vague language of Junius has been used as a proper warrant for a very liberal construction of the date. When Van Lennep objected, in 1823, to the chimerical year of the invention, 1423, fixed upon by a Haarlem committee, the synod enjoined him: "If he will again carefully read the account of Junius, and not forsake, out of his prejudice, all common sense, he will plainly see himself, and be obliged to acknowledge, that Junius said not a single word about the time of the invention." Van der Linde, *The Haarlem Legend*, p. 68.

written Lourens Janssoens Coster. Surnames were not then in common use; the son was identified through a name which described him in words as the son of his father. Lourens Janssoen Coster is literally, Lourens, son of John, the keeper, or the sexton.[1] He is most widely known in typographical literature by the name of Coster.

By the record, it appears that Coster was both a printer and a publisher. He cut blocks and made types, he mixed printing inks, he printed books, he employed many workmen, he had an honorable reputation as a printer, he reaped abundant profit from the sale of his merchandise. These statements are inconsistent with the eulogy which represents him as an idle man who experimented with types for amusement.[2]

That Coster knew nothing whatever about printing when he took his walk in the wood may be properly inferred from a careful reading of the story. His experiments with bark seem to have surprised and amused him as much as they did his

[1] There has been much dispute concerning the functions of this keeper. Junius says that this Lourens Janszoon was the keeper of a church; that this keepership was an honorary office which belonged to Coster's family by hereditary right. The duties of the office seem to have been those of a church trustee. Some writers say that this custos was nothing more than a sexton, but it is of no moment whether custos means sexton or trustee. The care with which Junius introduces evidences of the respectability of Coster's house and the dignity of his family implies his fear that there might be, on the part of a heedless reader, some doubt concerning the social position of a custos. Nothing is said of the ancestors of Coster. Probably, there was reason for this omission. Coster's distinction in Haarlem was not that of patrician blood. His wealth was not, so far as we can learn, derived from any inheritance, nor could it have been acquired through the emoluments of a custos, which was an honorary but not a lucrative office. He had been engaged in some occupation which Junius considered derogatory to his dignity. Of this occupation we shall hear more hereafter.

[2] The assurances of his wealth, leisure and respectability seem to have been provoked by the published statements, with which Junius was familiar, that Gutenberg, the rival German inventor, was of noble birth. It is not the only instance in which the Dutch legend is the echo of the German history. The first coincidence is that Coster, like Fust, was indebted to his son-in-law for valuable assistance in perfecting typography. And both sons-in-law were named Peter.

grandchildren. There is nothing unreasonable in this part of the legend, but faith fails us when Junius says that Coster printed his book with types of wood.[1] The statement must be put aside as entirely unworthy of belief, for it has been shown that types of wood are impracticable, and that the types of every known edition of the *Speculum* were made of founded metal.

No part of Junius's statement is more incredible than his description of the ease with which Coster solved the problem of typography. Coster knew nothing of printing; but having carved a few letters on bark, and having cherished the idea that books could be printed from single types, he undertook to make—not types, but wood-cuts. Eager to realize his idea of typography, he began work with a formidable task of engraving. Here is an absurdity. To design, engrave, and print the illustrations of the *Speculum* was a task almost as great as that of making the types. If the engravings were not in the possession of Coster before he made this experiment (and Junius does not authorize this hypothesis), it is not possible that he could have added to his task by attempting so many large wood-cuts. What follows is equally incredible. He passed from the work of cutting letters and pictures to that of making types without hesitation or experimentation;

[1] If Junius had not said that Coster changed the characters of wood for letters of lead and of tin, and that the false workman was expert in composing letters and in founding types, there might be some doubt whether these characters of wood were made disconnected or conjoined. His language is obscure, for he has used the words form and character as the equivalent of type, where these words could be applied with equal propriety to a letter engraved on a block. This obscurity was not caused by the poverty of the Latin language, for he afterward described types with clearness. There was obviously some confusion in the mind of Junius. It is not certain that he clearly understood the broad difference between typography and xylography; it is certain that he intended to convey the idea that Coster was the inventor of printing in its broadest sense—the inventor of printing from blocks as well as from movable types. The absurdity of this broad claim must be obvious to all who have read about early image prints and playing cards and the printed fabrics of Italy and Sicily.

he struck out the correct method of making the types at the outset. His only mistake with types was in the selection of materials; wood was laid aside for lead, and tin supplanted lead; his greatest difficulty was encountered in the manufacture of the ink. If this story is true, then typography was invented through inspiration, for its origin was unlike that of all great mechanical inventions.

Junius describes this pretended invention of typography, not as he knew it was done, but as he thought it should have been done. Ignorant of the necessity for that strict accuracy of body, which is the vital principle of typography, and which can be secured only by the most ingenious mechanism, he thought, as thousands have thought, that the merit of the invention consisted in the conception of the idea. The construction of the mechanism he has skipped over as a little matter of mechanical detail entirely unworthy of notice. He tells us nothing about it. He shows the extent of his reading and the weakness of his judgment, by treading in the footsteps of German authors who attempted to describe the German invention of typography, not from positive knowledge, but through the exercise of a lively imagination. He makes Coster follow the road which they say was taken by Gutenberg: first, the types of wood; then, engraved letters on blocks of wood; next, types of lead; lastly, types of tin.[1]

The artful insinuation that John Fust was the false workman is discreditable. Junius does not unequivocally say that Fust was the thief, but his language authorizes the calumny. That John Fust of Mentz could not have stolen the implements of Coster will be positively established by records of

[1] The wine-flagons of Thomaszoon may have had some features which carried conviction to the observer of the seventeenth century, but the modern reader of the story will fail to see that they should have been made of worn-out types. But the tin wine-flagons and the noticeable house on the market-place are not to be despised. Useless as proofs of the credibility of the legend of Junius, they illustrate to some extent the pedigree of the Coster family, a pedigree with which Junius was well acquainted, but for which he could find no place in his legend. These wine-flagons were the pewter pots of a tavern about a century old.

the highest authority. The Dutch historians of typography who defend the story of Junius, say that Junius did not know the name of the real thief, but that the name of Fust is properly inserted, because Fust was honored as the inventor of typography in Mentz; that there was, probably, a complicity between Fust and the false workman, and that Fust was, for that reason, properly mentioned as the real offender.[1]

The determination of Junius to fasten this theft on Fust is shown in his statement that the thief regained or returned to Mentz, as to "the altar of safety." At that time Paris, Rome and Venice had more schools and scholars, more book-readers and buyers than Mentz, and offered greater inducements for the founding of a printing office. These were the cities to which printers from Mentz subsequently went, and to which a thievish printer from Haarlem should have gone. But Junius finds it necessary to send him to Mentz to explain the introduction of typography in Germany.

The charge of theft is not corroborated by the discoveries of bibliographers. The two books which Junius says were printed in Mentz in 1442, with the types of Coster, cannot be traced to Mentz. Fragments of a copy of the *Doctrinal* of Alexander Gallus, the work of some unknown printer, have been found, not in Mentz, but in the Netherlands. The types

[1] There were many Johns among the early printers of Mentz: John Fust, John Gutenberg, John Petersheim, John Meydenbach. When it was thought proper to acquit Fust of this accusation, John Gutenberg was selected as the man; but the discovery of records which proved that Gutenberg was making experiments in typography at Strasburg during the year 1436, compelled the withdrawal also of this accusation. Meerman, with a skill in casuistry equal to the occasion, then undertook to prove that there were two Gutenbergs—brothers, but with different surnames—Johan Gensfleisch, the elder, and Johan Gutenberg, the younger; and that it was the elder brother who betrayed Coster and revealed the secret to John Gutenberg. It was a weak artifice. German historians have fully proved that Gutenberg's brother Frielo had nothing to do with typography; that John Gensfleisch, the elder, was an uncle, not a brother,—old, rich and blind—of all men, most incapable of any attempt at the purloining or practising of an intricate art like printing. There is no evidence to inculpate Petersheim or Meydenbach.

of this book resemble those of the *Speculum*, but they are sufficiently unlike to establish the fact that they could not have been cast from the matrices used for the *Speculum*. This edition of the *Doctrinal* could not have been printed at Mentz.

The zealous indignation of Cornelis does not compensate us for his mysterious concealment of the name of the thief.[1] His evidence is extremely unsatisfactory. Cornelis, who was in the employ of Coster when the theft was made, who knew the process, who bound the printed work, who was an old resident of Haarlem, who had business relations with every printer that succeeded Coster, of all men, should have been the one most

[1] The story of theft is not only improbable, but it is unsupported by external evidence. Jacobus Koning, a diligent searcher in the archives of Haarlem, discovered that, on and after Christmas day, 1440, the constabulary of Haarlem were often sent to Amsterdam upon important business. The inference attempted is that the constables were in search of the workman who stole Coster's implements. The records do not say that they were sent for a thief. Their business was of another nature. There had been a great mortality in Haarlem, and the officers of the town had left it while the pestilence was raging. The journeys of the constables were made to the temporary residences of the magistrates who, from a more healthy city, sent directions for the government of the town. Koning knew this fact but suppressed it.

The accusation of unfair practice, is frequently made by men who have been defeated in a fair contest. Whenever such an accusation is accompanied, as it was in this instance, with dramatic details, it effects a lodgment in the popular belief, from which it is not easily removed. Junius was not the first, nor the last, to use this discreditable but effective method of making-up a case. There is an old French record which narrates how Nicholas Jenson was sent from Paris to Mentz in the year 1458 to get a knowledge of the German invention. Jenson did acquire this knowledge, and became an eminent printer. His detractors say that he stole the secret; his eulogists say that he learned nothing, that he was the real inventor.—The story of Richard Atkyns about the English theft is too full of absurdities for criticism.—Sometime between 1520 and 1570, Daniel Specklin wrote a chronicle of Strasburg, in which he relates that printing was invented at that city in the year 1440, by John Mentel; that Mentel's unfaithful servant, one John Gensfleisch, stole the secret, not the punches, and took it to Mentz.—There is a popular legend in Italy that Pamphilo Castaldi invented printing types at Feltre in the year 1450; that John Fust, who happened to be in the town, abstracted the knowledge of the invention, carried it to Mentz, and arrogated all the honors of the rightful inventor.

competent to describe the work of Coster. But the information that he has furnished through Junius is ridiculously trivial, scanty as to facts and dates, inconsistent, and, in some points, entirely untrue.

Before we accept all that Junius has said about Cornelis, it will be well to learn what we can about him from other sources. The first entry in an account book of the cathedral of Haarlem for the year 1474 is to this effect: "Item. . . . I have paid to Cornelis, the binder,[1] six Rhine florins for binding books." Similar items, describing Cornelis as a bookbinder, are found in similar account books between the years 1485 and 1515. Payments were also recorded to Cornelis for coloring the initial letters of the "bulls of the indulgences." After the year 1515 his name appears no longer as a bookbinder; in 1517 another binder did the work of the church. Seiz mentions an old book, printed by Jacob Bellaert of Haarlem in 1485, on the last leaf of which was written: "Bought at Haarlem in the Cruysstraet, of Cornelis the bookbinder, in May, 1492." The register for the year 1522 contains this entry: "Cornelis the bookbinder was buried in the church. For the making of his grave, twenty pence." There can be no doubt that there was a bookbinder Cornelis at Haarlem, and that the Cornelis of Junius is the Cornelis of the church record. The dates in these records will enable us to test the accuracy of one portion of the chronology of the legend.

Junius said that Cornelis told his story before he was an octogenarian. Eighty years might properly be considered as the limit of his life, which, according to the record, ended in 1522. If, to ascertain the date of the birth of Cornelis, we deduct eighty years from 1522, the result would show that he must have been born in 1442. But this was at least one year, perhaps two years, after the alleged theft. If Cornelis lived to the age of ninety years, the allowance of ten years more would not reconcile the discrepancy. Cornelis would have

[1] It was on the inner cover or the fragment of a typographical binding of this account book that *Donatus* was found. See page 259.

been a child of eight years of age; but the story of Junius requires, not a child, nor even a boy, but a man, an under-workman, the associate and room-mate of the false workman. To call it by the mildest name, here is a grievous blunder. The blunder is not in the record of the church, in which the chronology is consistent, for it represents Cornelis as beginning to work for the church when he was about thirty-two years of age. It would be a waste of time to show that the chronology of Junius is impossible: it is enough to say that the first link in the attempted chain is broken, and that Cornelis could not have been an eye-witness of the facts.[1]

It is a suspicious circumstance that the testimony of Cornelis should be recorded for the first time nearly half a century after his death. Hasback, Andrieszoon and Bellaert, the early printers of Haarlem, should have heard from Cornelis this story about Coster and his invention. The people of Haarlem, we are told, were proud of Coster, and envious of the honors conceded to Gutenberg. Why the printers and the people of Haarlem allowed the important testimony of Cornelis to remain unpublished for so long a time is a question that cannot be answered.

At this late day, it is impossible to discover the kernel of truth that may be concealed in the heart of so great a husk of fiction. It may be that Cornelis, who seems to have been a simple-minded man, and who appears as a binder in the church record about nine years before Bellaert opened his printing office, imagined that this first printing office in Haarlem was the first printing office on the globe. There may have been a theft of types and of secrets from the office of Jacob Bellaert at or about 1485. Cornelis blundered about dates, and his inaccuracies have been exaggerated by the gossip of the next generation. These are possible conjectures.

[1]Lambinet had reason to speak of the aged witnesses, Cornelis, Gallius and Talesius, as "walking and talking centuries." Van der Linde characteristically describes the story of Junius as "a story in which all the authorities hear the principal facts in their infancy, but only to communicate them to each other in their second childhood."

But we must remember that this story of Cornelis is not told by himself, but by Junius.

One of the authorities referred to by Junius is Talesius, burgomaster of Haarlem when Junius was writing *Batavia.* In referring to him, Junius is careful in his choice of words. "My account does not disagree with that of Talesius. . . . I recollect that I have heard from him nearly the same story." This is a timid assertion—one that Talesius could have modified in some of its features. Talesius himself has not spoken. Talesius was, in his youth, the secretary, and, in mature age, the intimate friend of Erasmus, to whom he must have spoken about the legend, but he did not make Erasmus believe it.[1]

The mysterious disappearance of the practice of the art from Haarlem is even more wonderful than its introduction. The tools may have been stolen, but the knowledge of the art must have remained. Coster may have died immediately after the theft, but his son-in-law Thomas Pieterzoon, and the workmen, who knew all about the details of typography, were living, and able to go on with the work.[2] The making of books may have been temporarily suspended, but the curious

[1] Erasmus says: "All those who apply themselves to the sciences are under no small obligations toward the excellent town of Mentz, on account of the excellent and almost divine invention of printing books with tin letters, which, as they assure us, was born there."

[2] To satisfy these doubts, and to bridge the chasm between Coster of 1440 and Bellaert of 1483, Meerman undertook to show that Coster's three grandsons, Peter, Andrew and Thomas, continued the practice of typography and printed many small works. Dr. De Vries maintained that "there was after Coster's death, until about 1470, an uninterrupted, carefully concealed practice of printing. . . . That there existed in Holland for many years a seminary of the practicers of the art is confirmed by many and strong evidences." But De Vries offers conjectures for evidences. History is silent about the printing office that was conducted by the sons of Coster. This office and these printers were really created by Meerman to fill a disagreeable gap in the story of Junius—a gap not seen by any of his numerous commentators from Scriverius to Seiz. There is no book that bears their names; there is no record that mentions them as printers; there is not even a tradition that they had anything to do with printing. If their names had not appeared upon the pedigree of Gerrit Thomaszoon, we should know nothing of them. The typographical successors of Coster are as fictitious as their progenitor.

public who clamored for them should have persuaded Coster's successors to fill their wants. The new art of printing which found so many admirers should not have been completely forgotten fifty years afterward. There is nothing in the story of Junius to satisfy these doubts. If we accept his account of the invention, we must rest contented with the belief that typography in Haarlem died as suddenly as it was born, leaving behind as its only relics one edition of the *Speculum* and the old wine-flagons of Thomaszoon. The same strange fatality followed the alleged thief John who fled to Mentz and printed two books in 1442. Immediately after, his types, his peculiar process and his printed books disappear forever.

The improbable features of this legend were not seen in the uncritical age in which *Batavia* was written. Patriotic Dutchmen did not wish to see them. Holland, at the close of the sixteenth century, was flushed with pride at her successful resistance to the power of Spain. Grateful to the men who had made her famous, she exaggerated the services of all her eminent sons. Coster was not forgotten. The name of Junius gave authority to the Haarlem legend, and the story of Coster was read and believed throughout the Netherlands. There were dramatic features connected with it which pleased the imagination and fastened themselves to the memory. To people who had no opportunity to examine the evidences, the legend of Haarlem soon became an article of national faith, to disbelieve which was to be disloyal and unpatriotic. But this enthusiasm would have subsided if it had not been nourished. If subsequent writers had added nothing to this legend of Junius, it would not be necessary to write more about it. Long ago it would have been put aside as untrue. But the legend has grown: it has been almost hidden under the additions that have been made to it. The snow-ball has become a snow-heap. It is necessary to expose the falsity of the additions as well as of the legend, and to show how recklessly this chapter of the history of typography has been written.

XVIII

The Growth of the Legend.

Perversion by Bertius... Romance of Scriverius... Date of Invention removed to 1428... Illustration of First Statue to Coster... Date of 1420 given by Boxhorn... Rooman's Date of 1430... History and Chronology of Seiz... Doubts of Hollanders... Discrepancies in the Dates on Medals... Meerman and his Unsatisfactory System... Fac-similes of Medals... Koning and his Prize Essay... Dr. De Vries's Theory... Radical Disagreements of the Authors... All Versions Enlargements of the Legend as given by Junius... An Article of Patriotic Faith in Holland... Monuments to Coster. Illustration of Last Statue.

Who is there that has not opinions planted in him by education time out of mind, which by that means came to be as the municipal laws of the country, which must not be questioned, but are to be looked on with reverence... when these opinions are but the traditional grave talk of those who receive them from hand to hand without ever examining them? *Locke.*

At the end of the sixteenth century, the legend had two strong supports—the authority of an eminent scholar, and the patriotic pride of the Hollanders, who accepted it as truthful history. It did not, however, pass the ordeal of criticism unharmed: the weaker points of the legend were exposed by many German authors, and the weight of their objections compelled Dutch writers to attempt new explanations. Bertius,[1] writing in 1600, and evidently perplexed by the carelessness with which Junius had noticed Coster's first experiments, says, but without producing any proof, that "Coster invented the art of printing with engraved blocks or xylography . . . . the three-fold villain John Faust stole the invention." Here we see the unavoidable result of Junius's

[1] Wolf, *Monumenta Typographica*, vol. I, pp. 193 and 621.

malignant innuendo: Bertius does not hesitate, as Junius did, to name Fust as the false workman who stole Coster's tools.

Peter Scriverius thought it necessary, in 1628, to enlarge and embellish the story of Junius. He wrote a new version of the invention, which appeared with a curious poem called the *Laurecrans*.[1] This, says Scriverius, was the manner of it: In the year 1428, Laurens Coster, then a sheriff of Haarlem, strolled in the Haarlem wood. He took up the branch of an oak-tree, cut a few letters in relief on the wood, and after a while wrapped them up in paper. He then fell asleep, but while he slept, rain descended and soaked the paper. Awakened by a clap of thunder, he took up the sheet, and, to his astonishment, discovered that the rain had transferred to it the impress of the letters. Here was the suggestion of xylography, which he at once followed to a successful conclusion. He printed a great many block-books and a *Donatus*, but finding to his surprise that letters cut upon a solid block could not be used for other work, he thereupon invented typography. John Gutenberg, who had been employed as a workman, stole the tools and the secret. Disheartened with this misfortune, Coster abandoned printing and died. He proceeds:

It is my opinion that the art was first invented ten or twelve years before the year of our Lord 1440 (in which the most trustworthy authors agree), in Holland, at Haarlem. Junius has told its beginning and progress before us. And although he discovered some particulars about the invention, yet he has (I may be allowed to say it without disturbing his ashes) his errors, and may not be pronounced free from inadvertence. To-day (A. D. 1628) is just two centuries since the excel-

[1] *Laurecrans voor Laurens Coster von Haarlem, eerste Vinder von de Boeckdruckery, etc.* Haarlem, 1628. Reprinted in Dutch, with description in Latin, in Wolf's *Monumenta Typographica*, vol. 1, pp. 209-451. The poetry of Scriverius is as whimsical as his prose. Here is his charge of theft against John Gutenberg:

Ah, rascal! ah, are you there? is it you Hans Gutenberger?
Why does this name become you? Yes, two-fold rascal, and worse!
Notorious by theft, oh shameless man!
This word is still too mild for your villainy.
Because you concealed Laurens' good and carried it away,
And stole it falsely: so hear we now speak
Of Goedenbergher's praise; however they disguise it,
By the Goeden-berg they betray the Guyten-(rogue)berg.

lent and valuable art of printing made its appearance (A. D. 1428). Not in the manner that is used now, with letters cast of lead and tin. No, it did not go on like that; but a book was cut, leaf for leaf, on wooden blocks . . . . We must not think that every letter was cut separately on wood, and that these letters were collected and put together to a line, and in a certain number of lines. . . . . Our acute Laurens first cut the letters, twisted and close to each other, in the manner of writing on wood or tin; but afterward, when he was so successful, he changed his method of working, and, having invented the matrices, cast his letters. (!)

I will not say further how the noble art of engraving and printing of engravings is connected with the invention of printing, which arose afterward. But just as the dexterous Jan Fuyst imitated the appropriate art of printing, so the excellent and talented printers and designers, who also handled the artistic chisel and knife, contrived to multiply and publish their engravings, cut after the printing of the Haarlem figures. And all have been instructed by, and got their first experience from, our clever and talented Laurens Koster.[1]

Scriverius has given dates and new details, but he has not thrown any clear light on the subject. He has not made the story of Junius more credible, but he has exposed himself as a romancer and a fabricator. In trying to mend the legend, he has destroyed it. If the story of Scriverius is true, then that of Junius is false, for they contradict each other. The statements of Junius were based on the pedigree and the gossip of the old men of Haarlem; the statements of Scriverius were based on nothing, for he had no authorities which the most lenient critic could accept.

Scriverius said that Lourens Janszoen or Laurens Koster was the inventor of xylography as well as of types. After an examination of the *Speculum*, he had wit enough to see what Junius did not, that the printer of the book must have had practice with blocks, and that printing on blocks necessarily preceded printing with types. His description of the growth of the new art is not at all satisfactory. The careless manner in which he skips over the invention of matrices and the making of the moulds is that of a man who knows nothing

[1]Condensed from Hessels' translation in *Haarlem Legend*, p. 113–14.

about type-founding, neither from instruction nor observation. Encouraged by the praise which Scriverius had received for his performance, Marcus Zuerius Boxhorn undertook to place the date of the invention eight years earlier. In his *Dissertation on the Invention of Typography*, printed by Vogel at Leyden in the year 1640,[1] Boxhorn says that the invention was made in 1420. Here we encounter a curious fact. The story of Junius had been published less than fifty years, yet the writers disagreed concerning the date of the invention. Believers in the legend had been taught by one teacher that typography was invented in 1440—by another, in 1428—by another, in 1420. And it is a noticeable circumstance that the authors farthest removed from the date of the invention were the most positive in their statements. The later writers, who knew the least, give us the earlier dates.

Adrien Rooman, a printer of Haarlem, and apparently a conservative and conciliatory man, thought that these differences could be most satisfactorily adjusted by fixing the date midway between the extremes. He was not in the possession of any newly discovered facts, and had no authority for the arbitrary selection, but this incompetency did not prevent him from publishing a portrait of Coster, with an inscription which made the year 1430 the date of the invention.

To the thinking men of Haarlem the assumptions of Boxhorn were as unsatisfactory as those of Junius and Scriverius. There was an air of improbability, or at least of uncertainty, about the statements of all the authorities, which filled their minds with doubts as to the truth of the legend. The statue to Coster, which was soon after put up in the Doctors' Garden, had no date of invention on the pedestal. To remove these doubts, Seiz[2] undertook, in 1742, to furnish "a true and rational account of the invention" by Coster. The truth and reason of this new description of the invention of Coster are most strikingly illustrated in its chronology.

[1] Wolf, *Monumenta Typographica*, vol. 1, pp. 813-868.

[2] Seiz, *Annus Tertius Sæculoris Inventæ Artis, etc.* Haarlem, 1742.

The Statue of Coster in the Doctors' Garden.

[From Seiz.]

1428 . . Laurens Coster engraved a few letters upon the bark of a tree.
1429 . . He gave one year to experimental engraving on wood.
1431 . . He printed the *Temptations of Demons* or *Ars Moriendi.*
1432 . . Printed the *Bible of the Poor.*
1435 . . He began to engrave and print an edition of the *Donatus.*
1436 . . He cut separate letters or single types out of lead.
1437 . . After prolonged experiment, he abandoned this method.
1438 . . He invented a method of casting types of lead.
1439 . . He began to print an edition of the *Donatus*, and the Dutch edition of the *Speculum.* In this year Gutenberg took service with Coster, and began to print for him, by which he earned the title of the Book-printer of Haarlem. (!)
1440 . . Gutenberg absconded with some knowledge of the invention. He was able to cut, but not to cast types. (!)
1441 . . He established a printing office in Mentz.
1442 . . Gutenberg printed an *A b c* book, the *Doctrinal* of Alexander Gallus and the *Treatise* of Peter of Spain. By this time Coster had repaired the damages of the theft.
1443 . . Coster printed the second edition of the *Speculum* in Dutch.
1444 . . Coster printed a Latin edition of the *Speculum.*
1446 . . Gutenberg also induced Gensfleisch, called afterward Faust, (!) and Meydenbach to join him in printing a *Latin Bible.*
1457 . . Coster's art was well known, and excited the envy of the Archbishop of Canterbury and of King Henry VI of England.
1457 . . The Archbishop persuaded the king to get a knowledge of the art from Gutenberg, the first book printer of Haarlem. (!)
1459 . . Turnour and Caxton, who were sent on this mission, bribed Frederick Corsellis, a workman of Coster, to run away from Haarlem in disguise. To prevent his escape, Corsellis was taken to Oxford, in which town he began to print in 1468.
1467 . . Coster died, about the same time that Gutenberg and Faust died. (!) His printing office ceased to exist.[1]

Seiz has not told us where he obtained this curious information, but we shall make no mistake if we attribute it to an imagination disordered by national pride. His chronology is so absurd that serious criticism would be a waste of time.

Notwithstanding the strong efforts of Seiz to remove the impression created by the contradictory accounts of his predecessors, the citizens of Haarlem seemed to be involved in

[1] Condensed from Hessels' translation in *Haarlem Legend*, p. 123.

greater doubts than ever about the chronology of the invention. For, in 1740, upon the occasion of the third jubilee of Coster's invention, two silver medals were struck, with legends curiously unlike. We here see that the name of the inventor is printed in different forms; one medal bears the date 1440, and the other contains the date 1428. These irregularities prepare us for what is to follow.

Medals in Honor of Coster.

[From Seiz.]

In 1757, Gerard Meerman, subsequently a distinguished champion of the Haarlem legend, wrote "that the pretentious assertion of the invention of printing by Laurens Coster begins to lose credit more and more. The particulars that have been related by Seiz are mere suppositions, and the chronology of Coster's invention and enterprise is a romantic fiction."

But, in the year 1760, Daniel Schoepflin, an eminent scholar of Strasburg, wrote a valuable contribution to the history of typography, under the title of *Vindiciæ Typographicæ*. Meerman was provoked to emulation. He had not believed in the legend, but he thought that he could construct a theory of the invention, which would, to some extent, concede the claims of the rival cities of Haarlem, Strasburg and Mentz. In this illogical manner, by the construction of a theory before he was in possession of the facts, he began to write the *Origines Typographicæ.* The entire book was published in 1765, with a portrait of Lourens Coster by the eminent Dutch engraver Houbraken, and a portrait of Meerman himself by Daullé. In the matter of scholarship, Meerman was thoroughly qualified for his task. He wrote in a clear style and with admirable method. But he knew nothing of the mechanics of printing nor of type-founding, and, unfortunately, he was too conceited to accept correction or instruction even from the hands of experts like Enschedé, Fournier and others. In trying to make facts suit theories, he went so far as to order the engraver of a fac-simile to stretch the vellum of a *Donatus* so that the types used upon this *Donatus* should appear to be the same as the types of the *Speculum.*

Medals in Honor of Coster.

[From Seiz.]

These are the conclusions submitted by Meerman as the result of his study of, and reflection on, the legend of Haarlem:

Typography was invented by Louwerijs Janszoen, also known as Laurens Coster, who, at various times between 1422 and 1434, filled the office of sheriff, treasurer and sacristan. He was of noble blood, but a bastard of one of the

Brederodes. He died sometime between 1434 and 1440. He invented typography about 1428 or 1430, using only movable types of wood. All that Junius has written about an invention of lead and tin types by Coster is incorrect. He thinks it useless to consider the engraving of letters upon solid wood-blocks, for this is not typography, and is not printing as we now understand it. Laurens was robbed on Christmas night, 1440, by Johan Gensfleisch the elder, who carried the art to Mentz. The son-in-law and heirs of Coster continued his business for some time after his death, but with little appreciation, as they were overshadowed by the superior invention of Gutenberg and Schœffer. Coster printed but one edition of the *Speculum* from types of wood. His successors printed the other Dutch edition and the two Latin editions from engraved metal types. The contributions of different inventors toward the perfect invention are acknowledged in this manner: Laurens Coster was the first to demonstrate the feasibility of typography by his use of wood types; John Gensfleisch was the first to make cut or engraved metal types; Peter Schœffer was the inventor of cast or founded metal types; John Gutenberg and John Fust were printers who invented nothing.

Meerman had fair warning from the type-founder and printer John Enschedé that his theories of wood types[1] and of cut metal types were preposterous. He did not heed the warning. He wrote, not for printers, but for bibliographers who believed in the practicability of wood types, and he did not mistake his readers. The bibliographers, who knew little or nothing of the theory or practice of type-making, were not competent to criticise the mechanical part of his theory. He hoped to disarm the prejudices of German authors by his frank acknowledgment of the contributions of Schœffer and Gensfleisch as co-inventors. The novelty of his theory, the

[1] John Enschedé then said that "Jansen Koster used no wooden movable letters, as later, and still living scholars [Meerman] assert—scholars who know nothing of the mechanism of type-founding—and who, therefore, gently swerve from the path of simple truth." Meerman's reason for rating this Dutch edition of the *Speculum* as first of all was the inferior appearance of the types and the printing, which inferiority, he maintained, had been produced by wood types and want of experience in presswork. Fournier told him truly that the types of his alleged first edition were metal types; that the printing of the book was inferior because the types were worn out; that his first edition had all the signs of a last edition—but Meerman refused this explanation.

judicial equity with which he decreed to Coster, Gensfleisch and Schœffer what he said was their share in the honors of the invention, the temperate tone and calm philosophic spirit in which the book was written, the breadth of scholarship displayed in exact quotations from a great number of authors, won admirers in all countries. The theory of Meerman about a contributive invention need not be examined here: it has been entirely refuted by many French and German authors; it was abandoned even by Hollanders[1] at the beginning of the present century. The authority of the book is at an end.

The conviction that all previously written defences of the legend were untenable, caused a scientific society of Holland to offer a prize for the best treatise on the invention. Jacobus Koning was the successful competitor. In 1816, he published, under the sanction of the society, the essay that had won the prize, under the title of "*The Origin, Invention and Development of Printing.*" It was an inquiry of more than ordinary merit—the first book on the subject which showed evidences of original research. Koning tried to supplement the many deficiencies of Junius with extracts from the records of the old church and town of Haarlem, which he had studied with diligence. He brought to light a great deal of information about one Laurens Janszoon, whom he confounded, as Meerman had done, with Lourens Janszoon Coster. This is the substance of his discoveries and of his conclusions therefrom:

Koning describes the inventor as Laurens Janszoon Koster, and not as Lourens Janszoon. He says that Koster was born about 1370; that there are no records of his early life, and that his name does not appear on any of the registers of Haarlem, municipal or ecclesiastical, until he became a man of middle age. After this period of his life, notices are frequent. He was the sacristan of a church from 1421 to 1433. He was, at different times, alderman and presiding alderman, treasurer of the town, lender of money to the city, officer in the citizens' guard, member of the grand council, and deputy to a

[1] Dr. De Vries, the most eminent defender of the legend in this century, said: "The work of the learned but not very judicious Meerman had done more injury to the cause of Haarlem than the writings of all other antagonists."

convocation of the States—clearly a man of wealth and distinction. There was a great pestilence in Haarlem in the latter part of the year 1439, and Koning says it seems probable that Koster was one of its many victims. Koster's only child was a daughter named Lucette, who married Thomas, the son of Pieter Pieterzoon—the Peter mentioned by Junius. Pieterzoon had three children, but with them the family name was lost. This Laurens Janszoon Koster invented xylography and typography. He experimented with types of wood, but did not use them for practical work. His types were founded in matrices of lead, and in moulds of metal; he invented printing ink, and printed his books with inking balls on a press. His materials were rude, but the process was substantially the same as that of modern printers. He printed the first edition of the *Speculum* in 1430, and sixteen other books before his death. His business as a printer was continued for some years, but in a feeble manner, by his grandsons. The thief of Koster's process was Frielo Gensfleisch.

In the town records Koster is not noticed as a printer, but Koning described his method of printing, his punches, moulds, matrices, presses, inking balls, ink, types, and printing office furniture, with as much boldness as if he had been eyewitness to the entire process. Nor was this his only error. It has since been proved that he willfully suppressed many important facts in the records which are of great importance in an examination of the life and services of Coster. It is plain that he was more intent on pleasing the national pride than on revealing the truth.

The speculations of Koning were destroyed by the keen criticisms of the authors who followed him. Dr. Abraham De Vries[1] set aside impatiently nearly all the ingenious theories devised by former commentators. He repudiated the statement that Coster had been a sexton or sacristan, or that he invented engraving on wood. Warned by the failures of his predecessors, he advanced no new theory about the peculiarities of Coster's typographic process; he professed to be satisfied with the bald statement of Junius, and dogmatically maintained that Coster "was the inventor of typography, of the proper art of printing, the first who invented and practised

[1] *Eclaircissemens sur l'histoire de l'invention de l'imprimerie.* 1843.

the art of printing with movable and cast letters, and so gave the example to Mentz. . . . In the beginning, the art was secretly practised as a trade in manuscripts, not only during the lifetime of the inventor, but by his successors after his death." De Vries placed the invention about 1423.

It is not necessary to protract this review of the different versions of the legend, nor yet to point out the fatal disagreements and inaccuracies of these versions. It is plain that all the authors who have maintained the claims of Coster have taken their leading facts from Junius. It is equally plain that they have been dissatisfied with his statements and have tried to fill up the gaps in the evidence with conjectures. But they have not made the legend any more credible. The exact nature and date of the invention, the name of the inventor, his method of making types, the books he printed, the thief who stole his process, the fate of his printing office, the total disappearance of the knowledge of the new art—these and other features of the positive statement first made by Junius are enveloped in as complete a mystery as they were when *Batavia* was written.

With all its inconsistencies and improbabilities, the legend has been accepted as essentially truthful by many eminent bibliographers in France and England. Of late years it has encountered but feeble opposition from German writers. In many modern books on printing, Coster has been recognized either as the inventor or as one of the co-inventors of the art. There has been a general belief that, however absurd the legend might be in some minor matters of detail, it had a nucleus of truth. Coster's place in typographical history, at the middle of the present century, seemed almost as firmly fixed as that of Gutenberg.

In Holland, this legend of the invention of printing by Coster was an article of national faith which only the bold man dared to deny. It has produced results which could never have been foreseen by the vain old man Gerrit Thomaszoon, in whose conceit the fable originated. Haarlem is dotted with monuments to the memory of Coster. Certain days in June and July are observed as festivals in commemoration of the invention. In the Hout, or Haarlem Wood, where Coster is said to have received his first suggestion of types, an imposing cenotaph has been placed. Carved on this stone are the arms of the sheriff Laurens Janszoon, and the year 1423, which is offered as the date of this suggestion. An acknowledgment of Coster as the inventor of typography may be seen in the ancient cathedral of Haarlem, on a black marble tablet, which was put in place during the month of June, 1824, by King William I. In almost every well appointed public office or private house of Haarlem is some pictorial recognition of Coster as the inventor of printing.

The Statue on the New Monument to Coster.

[From Noordziek.]

In the year 1851, an association of patriotic Hollanders placed in front of the rebuilt Coster house a memorial stone with this inscription: "The house of Coster: the birthplace of typography." The date of this birth is judiciously omitted. The tablet of the old Coster house contained an inscription in honor of "Laurens Coster, sheriff, of Haarlem, inventor of typography about the year 1430." The vitality of the legend has also been preserved by the issue of a great many medals, prints and papers, and by the repeated assertion of the civic authorities that Coster was the original and unquestionable inventor of typography.

XIX

The Downfall of the Legend.

The Vague Inscription on the Last Monument...Relics in the Costerian Museum...Fac-simile of Janszoon's Autograph...The Coster Pedigree...Made by Gerrit Thomaszoon...Legend began with the Pedigree...Pedigree has been Falsified, and is of No Authority...Search by Van der Linde for Records concerning Coster...Archives of the Town and Church of Haarlem represent Coster as a Tallow-Chandler and Innkeeper...Coster living at Haarlem in 1483...The Record of the Chair-Book...No Evidence that Coster was a Printer...Lourens Coster has been Confounded with Laurens Janszoon...Illustration of the House of Coster...Other Fac-similes of Portraits of Coster...Their Curious Dissimilarity...Absurdity of the Legend.

We see in a square at Haarlem the monument of the fictitious personage Laurens Coster. It presents a sad figure. Behind this statue, sneering in mockery, is another colossal monument, which dominates and belittles it—a statue visible to us, but to Hollanders invisible—the statue of Ridicule. *Helbig.*

IN the year 1856, on the sixteenth day of July, the day accepted as the anniversary of the invention, a statue of Coster was put up in Haarlem. The tablets of the pedestal bear inscriptions which are thus translated by Hessels:

LOURENS JANSZOON COSTER.

HOMAGE OF THE
NETHERLAND NATION.
MDCCCLVI.

INVENTOR OF
THE ART OF PRINTING
WITH
MOVABLE LETTERS
CAST OF METAL.

The date of the invention and the profession or position of the inventor are omitted. We cannot ascertain from the monument whether Coster was a sheriff or a sexton, whether he invented printing in 1423 or 1440. It may be inferred that there had been disagreements among the eminent men who erected this work of patriotism, and that they could not heartily accept the date of any version of the legend. On this great occasion the Costerian Museum[1] of Haarlem was enriched with a pedigree of the Thomaszoon family, an old document frequently referred to by some defenders of the legend as an incontestable evidence of its truth. The pedigree was, without doubt, a genuine relic. Its dingy vellum surface, written over in many handwritings, was surrounded by an embroidered border blackened with age. Its history could be traced through three centuries. Gerrit Thomaszoon, the aged descendant of Coster mentioned by Junius with such marked respect, was the person by or for whom this pedigree was made in or about the year 1550.[2] This Gerrit Thomaszoon had kept an inn in the house once occupied by Coster, and it is supposed that the pedigree was one of the decorations of a wall in his house. There is a special significance in this date of 1550.

Autograph of Laurens Janszoon.
[From Koning.]

This pedigree, which describes Coster as the inventor of printing, was written at least one hundred years after the discovery of the invention and the death of the inventor. It was written when Cornelis, the only eye-witness known to

[1] This Museum then contained, among other relics, copies of the *Apocalypse*, the *Ars Moriendi*, the *Canticles*, the *Donatus*, the *Speculum*, the *Temptations of Demons*, and other printed works that have here been noticed in the chapter on The Works and Workmanship of an Unknown Printer, most of which were claimed as the work of Coster's office. The wood block of the *Horarium* (see page 260), some official documents, some autographs of the sheriff Louwerijs Janszoon, a picture said to be a likeness of Coster, several engravings of Coster (curiously dissimilar, and one of which is an undeniable forgery), are also contained in this Museum. Van der Linde denounced the Museum as a municipal show-booth. *The Haarlem Legend*, p. 164.

[2] Gerrit Thomaszoon died about 1563 or 1564. In the year 1611, the pedigree belonged to Adrien Rooman, the town printer at Haarlem. At his death it fell into the hands of Dr. John Vlasveld. For nearly two centuries it was unknown to the public. In 1809, it was sold at auction, Jacobus Koning paying for it, and for an old wood-cut, supposed to be the work of Coster, four hundred guilders.

history, had been dead nearly thirty years. It is, however, and too much stress cannot be laid on this fact, the oldest document in which mention is made of Coster as a printer. There are valid reasons for the belief that Coster's merit as an inventor had never been recognized in any way before the record was made on this pedigree. When we consider the order of the dates, it is obvious that it was from this much suspected document that Coornhert derived the information he published in 1561. "The old, dignified and grey heads" described by Van Zuren in 1561, "the aged and respectable citizens" of Guicciardini (1566) and Junius (1568), were Gerrit Thomaszoon and his friends, among whom we may properly include Gallius and Talesius. And it may be added that the more circumstantial story of Junius was first published when Gallius and Talesius were dead, and when there was no man living who could controvert or modify any part of his story.

There can be no doubt that the legend began with this pedigree. It is not at all probable that the vain old man Gerrit Thomaszoon, who was proud of the ancestor in whose house he lived, kept his friends in ignorance of it. It was not unknown to Junius. There is a similarity of uncertainty between an ambiguous date (1440 or 1446) on this pedigree and the mysterious circumlocution of Junius in his use of the words "about one hundred and twenty-eight years ago," or 1440, which is enough to show that Junius had not only seen the pedigree, but that he took it as an authority for this date. Whether Scriverius saw it cannot be confidently maintained; he does not mention it. Gerard Meerman knew of its existence, but he did not reprint it. He made use of it, however, in the construction of a new genealogy of the Coster family, in which he added and altered items in the most unwarrantable manner. Koning studied it with diligence: he frequently alluded to it as a document of the highest importance, but he did not reprint it, nor even describe it in general terms.

The withholding of this pedigree from public examination, and the evasion of its description by the authors who had examined it, are suspicious circumstances. We see that men who wrote hundreds of pages of speculations to support the claims of Coster—men who translated and reprinted many columns of irrelevant chaff for the sake of one little kernel of grain—willfully suppressed what they maintained was a most convincing evidence of the truth of the legend. It was not suppressed because it was too long: the entire pedigree can be printed in two pages.

The reasons for withholding the pedigree were apparent when it was put in the Museum. The reading of the words in the first row at once produced the impression that its importance had been vastly overrated; that its information was of little value; that it was almost worthless as evidence of the priority of Dutch typography. Dr. Van der Linde, who made a critical examination of the writing soon after it was placed in the Museum, revealed the astonishing fact that the most important entry had been falsified. This entry, which contains the only portion of any interest in an inquiry concerning the invention of printing by Coster, consists of the following lines:

"Sijn tweede wijff was Lourens Janssoens Costers dochter die deerste print in die werlt brocht Anno 1446."	"His [Thomas Pieterzoon's] second wife was Lourens Janssoen's Coster's daughter who brought the first print in the world in the year 1446."

The date first written was 1446, but in this column, and in others, objectionable entries have been effaced and falsifications have been attempted. The figure 6 has been partially rubbed out; it has been replaced by a 0, so that the careless reader will construe the date as 1440. There can be no hesitation whatever on this point; the figures first written surely were 1446. "We see here a fable arise before our very eyes. A Haarlem citizen has a pedigree made for him, probably to put it up in his inn. . . . . . But the frame wants lustre, and so the pedigree is linked by the probably totally fictitious Lucye, the second wife, to a Haarlemer—to a Haarlemer who (the awkwardness and naïveté of the expression may not surprise us at all in such a product of family vanity) brought the first print in the world."[1]

We may waive all criticism of the faulty grammar of the pedigree and proceed to more important matters. It may be conceded that the pedigree was written by an ignorant man who intended to say that it was Coster, and not his daughter, who brought the first print in the world. By the word print Thomaszoon may have meant a playing card, the engraved figure of a saint, a block-book, or a book made from movable types. If he meant any product of xylographic printing, the statement is totally false, and deserves no consideration. If he meant typography, his failure to express that meaning is unfortunate. But his intention is really of but little importance. A bald statement on a pedigree, written by an ignorant and conceited man, about one hundred years after the great event he professed to record, of the details of which he obviously knew nothing, cannot be used to overthrow established facts in the history of typography.

It is unsatisfactory in other points. The alteration of the date, and the unexplained erasures have destroyed whatever validity the document may have had. It may be put aside; as an authority it is worthless. Its obscure notice of the invention of printing is but a frail foundation for the colossal superstructure which Junius erected. It is plain that Junius must have been conscious of its weakness as a basis for the legend; he had doubts of its accuracy, and dared not refer to it. He preferred the oral testimony of the dead Cornelis.

The discovery of this falsification induced Dr. Van der Linde to make, "with a zeal and patience worthy of a better cause and of a better reward," a laborious investigation in the archives of the town and church of Haarlem for authentic

[1] Van der Linde, *The Haarlem Legend of the Invention of Printing*, p. 42. In the singular words "who brought the first print in the world" we may find the cause of that mysterious indefiniteness of description which may be observed in all the authorities. It is more than an indication that the story of Junius is based on the pedigree and on information derived from Thomaszoon and his friends.

information concerning Coster. He had cause to think that history had been falsified by other historians of the legend. Through the study of the archives, Van der Linde ascertained that there lived in Haarlem, in the fifteenth century, a citizen whose name was Lourens Janszoon Coster, the son of one Jan Coster who died in 1436. The results of the search were as curious as they were unexpected, as will be fully understood after an examination of this translation of the originals:

1441 .. On the evening of the 13th, settled with lou koster for 15 pounds and 12 pounds of oil, each pound an ancient butdrager, and 34 pence for soap and tallow candles, together 22 guilders 3 pence.

1441 .. Louwerijs Janssoen, for 72 pounds of candles, which have been burnt by the guards in the town hall during the year—for each pound an ancient butdrager.

1441 .. Louwerijs Jans, aforesaid, for the candles burnt in the tower in honor of Our Lady, during this year, as was agreed with him.

1442 .. Lourijs Coster, paid for having repaired the lantern of Our Lady in the tower.

1442 .. Lourijs Coster, for 40 pounds of tallow candles which the guards in the town hall burnt; cost each pound an ancient butdrager.

1442 .. Paid to lou coster 8 guilders for oil and soap.

1442 .. To lou coster for soap, candles and other things, 15 pence.

1447 .. On the 14th day of March, paid to Louwerijs Coster for 5 pounds of candles burnt in the tower in honor of Our Lady.

There can be no mistake about the business of this man. The Lourens Janszoon Coster described on the old pedigree as the famous man who brought the first print in the world, and in *Batavia* as a wealthy citizen, a man of leisure and of enlarged mind, and the inventor of engraving on wood and typography, was certainly an obscure tallow-chandler, who sold oil and candles.[1] The anti-climax is sufficiently absurd, but worse remains. The archives give us more than a clue to the origin of Coster's wine-flagons. It seems that, some time

[1] There is, of course, no reason why a chandler could not have invented typography, but we have no evidence that this chandler invented anything. Our knowledge of the tastes of the man, as shown in his selection of a new business, is enough to prove that he was not at all like the later chandler, Benjamin Franklin, with a leaning to types and letters.

after 1447, this Lourens Janszoon Coster gave up the business of chandler in favor of his sister Ghertruit Jan Costersdochter, and that he chose for his new occupation the duties of a tavern-keeper. Van der Linde found this fact clearly stated in the treasury accounts of the town of Haarlem.

1451 .. Lou coster[1] paid, for two menghelen of wine which were sent to the burgomaster a year ago.
1454 .. A dinner was offered to the count of Oostervant on the 8th day of October, 1453, at lou coster's; indebted to him for it XVII guilders.
1468 .. Louris Coster and other citizens are summoned to the Hague.
1474 .. Louris Janszoon Coster pays war taxes.
1475 .. Louris Janszoon Coster pays a fine for "buyten drincken" (to drink beyond the premises).
1483 .. Received of Louris Janszoon Coster for ferry toll for his goods when he left the town, 8 rex guilders.

We here see that the name of Louris Janszoon Coster was recorded in the town-book for the last time under the date of 1483, when he paid ferry toll for his goods, and was allowed to leave the town. It is not known where he went or where he died, but it is plain that the story of his death in 1439, as related by Meerman and Koning, must be untrue.

There might have been a doubt as to the identity of the chandler with the innkeeper, if Van der Linde had not investigated in another direction, and made gleanings from the books of an old association, whose records are as trustworthy as those of the archives of the town and the church. This association, which still exists, under the name of the *Holy Christmas Corporation*, is thus described by Van der Linde:

It is one of those fraternities which had the lofty aim of eating and drinking. This corporation is already very old, for it celebrated its third jubilee in 1606. Its fifty-four brethren and sisters preserved each a chair for their meetings. According to these statutes, these chairs, if they were not disposed of by a last will, were inherited by

[1] The variable orthography of the name of Coster, which is here copied literally from the records, is a sufficient explanation of the irregularities in the spelling of his name which are to be found in all the authorities. I have adopted the orthography as I find it in the book of Van der Linde.

the eldest and nearest blood relation in the branch from which they came.... The corporation remaining in existence, the right of property in the chairs continued, by uninterrupted transmission, until our time.

In the register of the names of the occupants of the chairs are found the following entries under the heading of chair 29:

1421 .. Jan Coster, by....
1436 .. Lourijs Coster, by inheritance.
1484 .. Frans Thomas Thomasz, by ....[1]
1497 .. Gerret Thomas Pieterz, by inheritance from his father.
1564 .. Cornelis Gerritz, by inheritance from his father.
1589 .. Anna Gerritsdr., by purchase from her cousin.

The names of the successive owners of chair 29 are continued in the book, but they are of no interest in this inquiry.

The archives of the church and town of Haarlem contain the names of other Costers, but there is no other Coster who will answer the description of Junius and Thomaszoon. The Lourens Janszoon Coster of the pedigree, the Louwerijs Janssoen (so called only after the year 1441) or Lourijs Coster of the archives, and the Lourijs Coster of the chair-book are, without doubt, the different names of the same man. This is the man who, according to Thomaszoon and Junius, brought the first print in the world. But he appears as a printer only in the pedigree. The archives and the chair-book do not so describe him; they tell us nothing of his invention, nor of the alleged stealing of his types, nor of his death in 1439. The town-book says that he was living in 1483. In none of these documents does he appear as sheriff, sexton, or treasurer.

It is obvious that the legend of Coster the printer rests entirely upon the pedigree and its amplifications by Junius.

[1] The exact nature of the relationship between Laurens Janszoon Coster and Gerrit Thomaszoon is not clearly defined, but the archives of the town and the vellum pedigree corroborate each other in establishing the existence — of Lourens Janszoon Coster (son of Jan Coster), tallow chandler and innkeeper, who left Haarlem in 1483 — of Thomas Pieterszoon (probably the son-in-law of Coster), sheriff, who died in 1492 — of Gerrit Thomaszoon (according to the pedigree, a great-great-grandson of Lourens Janszoon Coster), a sheriff and an innkeeper. He was, also, a sacristan or church-warden.

But the pedigree is of no authority. Its information is not confirmed by the records; its falsifications and its suspected history compel every candid reader to reject its evidence altogether. We have to accept in preference the testimony of the archives, and have to admit that there is no credible evidence that Coster printed anything at any time. The Lourens Janszoon Coster of typographical history is as fictitious a personage as the Cadmus of Greek mythology. He is really more fictitious, for he is the representative of two men.

The revelations of Dr. Van der Linde show that Lourens Janszoon Coster has been confounded with Laurens Janszoon or Louwerijs Janszoon,[1] who was a man of some distinction, a wine merchant, innkeeper, councilor, sheriff, treasurer and governor of the hospital. He is the man of civic offices, of wealth and high social position, who has been described by Koning. He is the man whom Meerman represented as an

[1]For this unwarrantable confusion of the names and deeds of the two men Junius and Scriverius are responsible. Junius, who wrote in Latin, caught at the word Coster, which he found in the pedigree, as a subject for the display of his critical ability. He explains and expounds it: "Lourens Janszoon, surnamed Coster, by reason of the office which belonged to the family by hereditary right." There was no need for this absurd expansion of the meaning of the word *custos*. This attribution of an honorable office to an insignificant man was purposely made to give him a dignified position. Gerrit Thomaszoon, who knew that Coster was a man of no note, gave him only the distinction of the first printer. This was not enough for Junius, who thought that he would be deficient in patriotism if he did not make Coster as reputable as his rival Gutenberg, who was represented as of noble blood. The word Coster was his opportunity, and he made the most of it. It is not probable that Junius studied the archives of Haarlem for the purpose of getting exact information about Coster, but it is possible that he had read or heard of Lourens Janszoon, the wealthy man, and that he confounded him with Coster, the chandler. Whether he made this confusion with intent or in ignorance cannot now be ascertained, but we can see that the wealth and respectability of Janszoon were attributed to Coster. Scriverius perpetuated the blunder. He found a document signed by Louwerijs Janszoon, as sheriff, in 1431. Without further research, he leaped to the conclusion that this man who died in 1439, who had nothing in common with Coster but similarity of name and similarity of occupation as innkeeper, was the very Lourens Janszoon Coster who, according to Junius, invented types and practised printing in 1440.

unrecognized member of the noble family of Brederodes. But he is, certainly, not the man described on the pedigree as the Coster who brought the first print in the world. He is not the man described by Junius who lived "about one hundred and twenty-eight years ago," or in 1440, for the records of the church of St. Bavo prove that Laurens Janszoon died and was buried in 1439. It is not at all probable that Thomaszoon or Junius made any mistake in the name, and that it was this Louwerijs Janszoon who brought the first print in the world. There is no more evidence in favor of Janszoon as an inventor of printing than there is in favor of Coster. The most careful searching of the records fails to bring to light any evidence that he was engaged in the practice of printing.

That Lourens Coster kept a tavern may also be inferred from the fact that the house he lived in was always known as a tavern. The engraving of this house on the following page shows how the edifice appeared in 1740. Junius said that it was a house of some pretension in 1568, and that it stood on the market-place near the royal palace; but Van Zuren had previously noticed it as a house falling to decay. In 1628, Scriverius said that the house had been "changed and was divided among three masters:" the part supposed to be the Coster residence was called *The Golden Bunch of Grapes*, and it was even then used as a tavern. When John Bagford first saw the house, in 1706, it was a cheese shop. In 1761, Moses Van Hulkenroy, a printer, lived in part of it, and the other part was occupied as an inn, then known as *The Golden Fleece*. In 1813, the centre building was used as a public house. It fell into ruins on the 13th of May, 1818, but it has since been rebuilt, and a tablet inserted in memory of Coster. It is probable that this house was an inn when Junius wrote *Batavia*, and that he refrained from mentioning this circumstance lest it might degrade Coster. But we now know that Coster, and Pieter Thomaszoon, his son-in-law, who succeeded him in business, and that Gerrit Thomaszoon, the author of the pedigree, were all innkeepers. The wine-flagons, to which

The House of Coster.

[From Seiz.]

Junius points so triumphantly, were a proper portion of the furnishings of an inn. To the modern reader, who has been informed that a part of this house has always been a drinking tavern for the refreshment of the men of Haarlem, these pewter mugs, or flagons, as Junius names them, are not, as he would have us believe, indisputable evidence that their first owner must have been a printer.

The falsity of the legend is abundantly established by the dissimilarity of the many engraved likenesses, which from time to time have been presented as portraits of Coster. The earliest representation of the alleged inventor was published by Scriverius,[1] not quite two centuries after Coster is said to have died. The only attest to the accuracy of the portrait is Scriverius himself, and it need not be said that he is not a trustworthy witness. There have been many variations of this well-known engraving. Van der Linde suggests that this engraving by Scriverius may be a portrait of Gerrit Thomaszoon, appropriated for the exigency. There is a peculiarity in the engraving which plainly proves that the portrait could not have been painted during the lifetime of Coster. The "true effigies of Laurenz" carries in his right hand a matrix of the letter A of the Roman form, but letters of Roman form were not used at Haarlem in 1440. Books attributed to Coster have letters in the Gothic style.

Laurens Janszoon Coster.
[From Maittaire.]

[1]Moxon's copy of this engraving is shown on page 333 of this book.

In 1630, a new portrait of Coster was published by Adrien Rooman, with Latin and Dutch verses attached. Boxhorn mentioned this engraving in such a manner that strangers were led to believe it was a statue that had been erected to Coster.

A Spurious Portrait by Van den Berg.
[From Koning.]

A Portrait attributed to Van Oudewater.
[From Koning.]

Jacob Van Campen was induced to make another painting of the grim features in a more truly artistic style. His idealized head of Coster was engraved by Cornelis Koning, whose reproduction of the painter's fancy has ever since been accepted as an authentic portrait.[1] The round cap, the furred

[1] Van der Linde tells a curious story about Hollandish credulity:

The most amusing imitation was that of an amateur artist of the last century, C. Van den Berg, who wished to play the collector J. Marcus a trick. He engraved a small wood-cut after the portrait of Van Campen, with the name *Laur' Jassoe*, in old-fashioned style, underneath. With a little soot and dirt, he gave the copies an antique appearance, and made Marcus happy for a few weeks. The poet Langendijk, the type-founder Enschedé, and other amateurs, each got a copy. Van den Berg was too honest to mean anything more than fun; he told afterward to Marcus himself the value of that antique wood-cut. Although every investigator could and ought to have known these things, yet Jacobus Koning was bold enough, in the second nomenclature of his collection of rare books and manuscripts, to describe a copy of this portrait as "*printed by*, or at the time of, Lourens Janszoon Koster." . . . . . . The Haarlem painter L. Van der Vinne, in his youth, painted, in the beginning of the former century, a study, after a drawing of Van Campen. But lo! in 1762, this picture is offered for sale by Van Damme at Amsterdam (the same who produced the false inscriptions respecting the imaginary Corsellis of Oxford), provided at the back with a very old inscription, *Lours Jans to Harlem* MCCCCXXXIII, and the monogram A O, which was explained to mean Albert Van Oudewater. Excellent discovery! Here was a genuine contemporaneous portrait by a painter of the fifteenth century! A trifle, however, was wanted to make the joy perfect. Albert Van Oudewater, who had painted the celebrated inventor of printing in 1433, was born in 1444! This history is full of despairing irony from beginning to end. Just as the sheriff Lourens Janszoon invents the art of printing *after his death;* just as Cornelis works at *Donatuses before his birth;* just as the chandler Lourens Janszoon Koster entirely forgets his invention *during his lifetime;* so the painter Albert Van Oudewater becomes a zealous Costerian *long before he was born.*" Van der Linde, *The Haarlem Legend*, p. 145.

robe, and the matrix in the extended hand, are the features of the Scriverius portrait; but the head is that of another man. The stony face which Scriverius presented as the image of Coster was somewhat softened by the pencil of Van Campen, but after he had exhausted upon it all the resources of his art, it still remained a grim and unsatisfactory head, a head without any expression of genius or even of culture—the head of a hard innkeeper, but not of an inventor. It was a biting satire upon the story of Junius, all the more offensive because the portrait had as strong claim to authenticity as the legend.

The Laurens Janszoon of Meerman.
[From Meerman.]

Meerman refused to accept this head as a faithful portrait. He produced a new likeness of the inventor, and claimed for it a superior truthfulness. In the same year, 1765, Van Osten de Bruyn published an engraving of the same head, with this explanation: "Laurens Janszoon, sheriff, of the town of Haarlem, inventor of the noble art of printing . . . after an old picture bought from William Cornelis zoon Croon, the last descendant of Laurens Janszoon, who died, unmarried, at Haarlem in 1724." We find no vouchers for the authenticity of this portrait. Croon was the man by or for whom the vellum pedigree was continued. He was equally interested with the originator of the pedigree, Gerrit Thomaszoon, in upholding the legend. Whether Croon was ignorant of the fact that Laurens Janszoon, the sheriff, was not Lourens Janszoon Coster, is not so clear; but it is clear that the portrait submitted by Croon does not resemble the portrait furnished by Scriverius. Gockinga asserts that the engraving made by Meerman (after Croon's portrait) is like the engraved head of Sir Thomas More of England. Van der Linde says that the Coster of Meerman closely resembles the engraved portrait of a once celebrated inquisitor, one Ruard Tapper of Enkhuizen.[1] The Coster of Scriverius and the Coster of Meerman are certainly different men.

Everywhere but in Holland[2] and Belgium, Dr. Van der Linde's exposure of the spuriousness of the legend has been accepted as the end of all debate. Coster must hereafter be regarded as one of the heroes of fiction and not of history. With the downfall of Coster, fall also all the speculations concerning an early invention of printing[3] in the Netherlands by an unknown or unnamed printer.

[1] The striking dissimilarity between the calm philosophic face of the Coster of Meerman and the sour look and misanthropic features of the Coster of Scriverius is neatly explained by Dr. Abr. De Vries:

> The portrait given by Scriverius was painted from a sketch or study made after Coster's death, and was, necessarily, gloomy and cadaverous; but no portrait, however beautiful, unless it was a true and genuine likeness, could satisfy the truth-loving Scriverius. The truth was to be well founded if he endorsed it. The cadaverous hue and the marks of death in Van Campen's picture are strong evidences for the genuineness and faithfulness both of the original representation and of Van Campen's copy!

[2] In Holland, Dr. Van der Linde's book has been denounced as impolitic and unpatriotic, but it has not, as yet, met with a suitable answer. The indignation manifested toward the author has been so violent that he, a native Hollander, has found it expedient to remove to Germany.

[3] The only positive evidence which seems to give a color of probability to the assertion that typography was first practised in the Netherlands is the fact that an unknown printer had printed there some little books before the arrival of Ketelaer and De Leempt, in 1473. Whoever this printer may have been, it still remains to be proved that he did any typographic work before 1463.

XX

John Gutenberg at Strasburg.

Gutenberg's Place as an Inventor... His Birth at Mentz... Subsequent Residence in Strasburg. Early Suits at Law... His Probable Marriage... Is Sued by Claus Dritzehen... The Judge's Statement... Testimony of the Witnesses... Gutenberg the Chief of an Association... Engaged in a Secret Art... Notices of a Press and of a Mysterious Tool of Four Pieces... Notices of Forms that were Melted, and of Printing... Decision of the Judge... Gutenberg's Reputation for Knowledge of Curious Arts... Polishing Stones... Making Mirrors... The Secret Art was Printing with Founded Types... Secret was not in the Press... Illustration of Old Screw Press... Testimony of the Earlier Authors... Tool of Four Pieces was a Type-Mould... Fac-simile of Garamond's Mould... Fac-simile of an Early Donatus... Gutenberg's Financial Embarrassments and Failure.

But whoever were the inventers of this Art, or, (as some Authors will have it,) Science, nay, Science of Sciences (say they), certain it is, that in all its Branches it can be deemed little less than a Science... For my part, I weighed it well in my thoughts, and I find... that a Typographer ought to be a man of Science. By a Typographer, I do not mean a Printer... I mean such a one, who by his own Judgment from solid reasoning with himself, can either perform, or direct others to perform, from the beginning to the end, all the Handy-works and all the Physical Operations relating to Typographie. Such a Scientifick man was doubtless he who was the first Inventer of Typographie. *Joseph Moxon*, 1683.

MOXON did not overrate the rank of typography among the arts. It is a science, and, like all sciences, is the fruit of the knowledge which comes only by study. Like all sciences, it came in the fullness of time, when the world had been prepared for it, but it came only to him who had qualified himself for its handiworks from beginning to end. In the description of the work of John Gutenberg about to be related, imperfect as it must be by reason of our ignorance of his thoughts and plans, we shall clearly see that the invention of typography was not, as Junius would have us believe, the result of a happy thought or of a flash of inspiration. It was not born in a day. To use the sound language of an old chronicler, it was thought out and wrought out.

The work of Gutenberg will require a treatment different from that given to the work of Coster. It is not necessary to introduce the subject by a description of his books, by proof of his existence from writings made a century after his death, and, by a train of fine speculative reasoning, to show that he should have been the printer of the books ascribed to him by conjecture. Our knowledge of Gutenberg is incomplete, but it is positive as far as it goes. He did not put his name on any book, but he certainly printed many books; it does not appear that he ever boasted that he was the inventor of typography, but this honor was conceded to him by many printers soon after his death. His antagonists in courts of law, as well as the friends who put up tablets to his memory, have told us, as plainly as could be desired, that he was a master of many curious arts, and that he had made a broad and unmistakable mark on his time.

There is no record of the birth of Gutenberg,[1] but it is the belief of his German biographers that he was born at Mentz about 1398 or 1399. His parents were, Frielo Gensfleisch and Else Gutenberg. Their two[2] children were, John Gutenberg,[3] named after his mother, and Frielo Gensfleisch. Frielo junior was always called Gensfleisch, but John, whose relation to the Gensfleisch family must have been well known, was sometimes described as John Gensfleisch, junior. A legal document of

[1] There is no known authentic autograph of Gutenberg. In his day the name was written by other persons, Guttemburg, Gudenburch, Goodenberger, Guthembergius, Gudenbergh, Kuttenberg, and in many other ways. The form of spelling used in this book is the one that is preferred by the German bibliographers. Gensfleisch, in German, is goose-flesh; Gutenberg is good hill.

[2] Bodmann, a librarian at Mentz, said that he had discovered two old documents which set forth that Gutenberg had a brother, Conrad, and two sisters, Hebele and Bertha. Helbig says that these documents, as reprinted by Fischer, are spurious.

[3] It seems that Else Gutenberg was the last surviving member of her family. According to a German custom prevailing at that time, a son was, under certain circumstances, permitted to take the name of his mother when it was feared that her family name might become extinct.

the city of Strasburg names him John, called Gensfleisch, alias Gutenberg, of Mentz.[1]

The infancy and youth of Gutenberg were passed amid scenes of strife. In Mentz, as in many other cities of Germany, the burghers made persistent encroachments on the privileges of the noblemen, and met with as persistent resistance. The municipal disorder which followed their frequent collisions was seriously aggravated by the disputes of the rival archbishops who held office under rival popes. The burghers, as the larger body, claimed the larger share of the city offices, and the right to take the lead on occasions of ceremony and in the administration of affairs. In the year 1420, the burghers of Mentz made preparation for the entertainment of the Emperor, on the occasion of his visit to the city. Circumvented by the action of the noblemen, who greeted the Emperor first, the burghers retaliated by the destruction of the houses and goods of the more obnoxious nobles. In their rage, they demanded of them humiliating guarantees, and put them under restrictions so galling, that Frielo Gensfleisch and many others preferred to go in exile.[2]

[1] The name of the brother of Frielo Gensfleisch, senior, was John Gensfleisch, senior. He is the man improperly described by Meerman as the elder brother of John Gutenberg. The identity of his baptismal name with that of the inventor of printing has been the occasion of many mistakes. The uncle has been confounded with the nephew. The family was wealthy: it had, in or near Mentz, three houses or estates, known as Zum Gudenberg, Zum Jungen and Zum Gensfleisch. The members of the family were sometimes called Sulgeloch or Sorgenloch, from a property on which they resided outside of Mentz.

[2] This is the version of chroniclers in the interest of the nobles. The childish dispute about precedence seems an insufficient cause for the quarrel. It was, probably, the occasion, but not the cause. It was the spark which set on fire the stifled resentment of the burghers against a long course of neglect and of misgovernment. The Gensfleisch families seem to have been always prominent in the civil disturbances of Mentz. Gutenberg's great-great grandfather took sides with one of the rival archbishops, and, in 1332, aided him in burning some convents, for which he was put under ban by the Emperor Louis. In the same year, he and other noblemen made themselves so offensive to the burghers that they were obliged to flee for their lives.

It is not known where the Gensfleisch family took refuge. It is supposed that Strasburg was the city selected, for this is the city in which we find the earliest notice of Gutenberg.

In 1430, the Elector Conrad III granted a full amnesty to many of the exiled citizens of Mentz, and summoned them to return. Johan Gutenberg was specifically named in the proclamation, but he continued to dwell abroad. During this year, his mother Else, then a widow, negotiated, through her son, for her pension of fourteen guilders which had been allowed to her by the magistrates of Mentz. In 1432, he visited Mentz, probably on business relating to this pension. These are the only known records of his early manhood.

Nothing is known about his education. Some writers have represented him as an engraver on wood or a printer of cards or of block-books at an early age. It is possible that he may have received instruction in the arts of block-printing and engraving, and that he may have traveled far and wide in quest of greater knowledge,[1] as was and is customary with German artisans; but we have no evidence on this point. It must be confessed that the first thirty years of his life are virtually blank.

The most important actions of his after life would have been obscured quite as thoroughly, if it had not been his fate to appear many times, either as complainant or defendant, before the courts of his country. It is from the records of these courts that we glean the story of his life. He first appears as complainant in a suit at law which shows his high

[1] Charles Winaricky, a learned Bohemian, wrote a dissertation on the birthplace of Gutenberg — *Jean Guttenberg, né en* 1412 *a Kuttenberg en Bohème*, 12mo. Brussels, 1847 — in which he tried to prove: that Gutenberg was born in the year 1412, in the town of Kuttenberg in Bohemia, from which town he derived his name; that he was a graduate of the university of Prague; that he acquired his knowledge of metallurgy from the metal workers of that old mining town; and that his proficiency in many curious arts was the result of his Bohemian education. Winaricky's book abounds with curious information, but his reasoning is largely based on conjecture. It cannot be used to discredit the positive dates and facts of many German records.

spirit and audacity. The magistrates of Mentz had neglected or refused to pay to Gutenberg the sum of money which he claimed as his due. Gutenberg, waiting for his opportunity, caused to be arrested the clerk or recorder of the city of Mentz, who happened to be in Strasburg. This sudden arrest seems to have been a great annoyance to the magistrates of Strasburg, who feared that it would endanger the friendly relations of the two cities. At their request he consented to relax his hold on the unfortunate clerk.[1] This is the first plain proof we have of his residence in Strasburg in 1434.

In the same year he formally authorized his mother to act for him in the adjustment of some business between him and his brother Frielo. This authorization, which is recorded in the city books of Mentz and of Frankfort, would imply that he was, or intended to be, absent.

In 1436 he appeared as defendant before the tribunal of Strasburg. Anne, called Zur Isernen Thur (Anne of the Iron Gate), sued Gutenberg for a breach of promise of marriage. The judgment of the court is not given. Most writers on the subject believe that the suit was withdrawn, and that the case was closed by marriage. After this suit, the name of Ennel Gutenberg, who, according to Schoepflin, is none other than this Anne, appears on the tax-roll of the city of Strasburg. It does not appear that Anne had any noticeable influence

[1] This is the form of complaint: "I, Johan Gensfleisch, the younger, also called Gutenberg, declare by this letter, that the worshipful sage burgomaster and the council of the town of Mentz owe me every year a certain interest, according to the contents of letters which contain, among other things, that, if they do not pay me, I am at liberty to seize and imprison them. As I have now to claim much rent in arrears from the said town, which they were hitherto not able to pay me, I caused M. Nicolaus, secretary of Mentz, to be seized, whereupon he promised me and swore to give me 310 valid Rguilders, to be paid at Oppenheim, before the following Whitsuntide. I acknowledge, by this letter, that the burgomaster and council of Strasburg have induced me to relieve of my own free will, in honor and love of them, the said M. Nicolaus from his imprisonment, and from the payment of the 310 guilders. Given on Sunday (12th of March), 1434."

The ease with which Gutenberg relinquishes his monetary claim, and which at once shows him to be a better knight than financier, exhibits a trait of character which explains much in his later fate. Van der Linde, *Haarlem Legend*, p. 13.

over his subsequent life; she did not follow him to Mentz; it is not certain that she was living in 1444.

In the year 1439, John Gutenberg again comes before the court, and again as defendant. The testimony brought out on this trial reveals Gutenberg to us as an experimenter and inventor. The official record[1] is long, and full of matter that seems irrelevant, but it presents a curious picture of the time, which deserves study. This is the judge's statement of the case, as delivered by him on the 12th day of December, 1439:

WE,[2] Cune Nope, master and counselor at Strasburg, hereby make known to all who shall see this writing, or shall hear the reading thereof, that George Dritzehen, our fellow-citizen, has appeared before us in proper person, and with a full power of attorney for his brother Claus Dritzehen, and has cited John Gensfleisch, of Mentz, called Gutenberg, our fellow-resident, and has deposed that the late Andrew Dritzehen, his brother, had inherited from his deceased father valuable effects, which he had used as security, and from which he had realized a considerable sum of money; that he had entered into copartnership with John Gutenberg and others, and [with them] had formed a company or association, and that he had paid over his money to Gutenberg [the chief] of this association; and that for a certain period of time they had carried on and practised together their business, from which *they had reaped a good profit;* but that, in consequence of the speculations of the association, Andrew Dritzehen had made himself personally liable, in one way and another, for the *lead* and other materials which he had purchased, and which were necessary in this art, or trade, and which he [George] would also have been responsible

[1] For more than three hundred years this important document, with other records of the courts of Strasburg, rested unknown and undisturbed in the old tower *Pfennigthurm*, in which place it was discovered by Wenkler, the keeper of the records. He communicated this fact to Schoepflin, who, perceiving its value, made it the great feature of the *Vindiciæ Typographicæ*. The record is imperfect, for it does not contain all the testimony of all the witnesses. Whether this deficiency is due to the neglect of the recorder, or to the decay or mutilation of the record, has not been fully explained. Schoepflin, who says it is written in an almost obsolete German dialect hard to be understood, reprinted it in full, accompanied with a translation in Latin, which has been censured as inaccurate. Dr. Dibdin, and a few carping bibliographers, who looked with disfavor on all newly discovered documents which obliged them to revise their own theories, have tried to throw discredit on this record, but its authenticity is now recognized as beyond controversy. The records were placed in the Library of Strasburg for safety, but they were destroyed by the Prussians during the siege of that city in 1870.

[2] Conventionally used for I.

for and would have paid; but inasmuch as in this interval Andrew had died, he [George] and his brother Claus had requested with importunity of John Gutenberg that he should receive them in the association in the place of their late brother, or else, that he should account to them for the money that he [Andrew] had put in the association; but that he [Gutenberg] was unwilling to comply with their request, alleging, as an excuse, that Andrew Dritzehen had not, as yet, paid his proper quota into the association. Now he, George Dritzehen, believed that he was abundantly able to prove that this agreement was just as he had represented: he had pleaded that Gutenberg should take him and his brother Claus in the association, in place of their late brother, for they were his lawful heirs, or that Gutenberg should return the money which their late brother had invested, or that he should at least give the reason why he would not accede to their demand.

In answer, John Gutenberg had replied that the complaint of George Dritzehen seemed to him very unjust, inasmuch as he could sufficiently establish, through many notes and writings (the nature of which George and his brother Claus could have learned after the death of Andrew Dritzehen), under what rules the association was formed. In truth, Andrew Dritzehen came to him many years ago, and *had asked him to communicate and to teach to the said Andrew many secrets:* it was for this reason, and to comply with his request, that *he had taught him how to polish stones*, *from which art Andrew Dritzehen had derived a good profit.* Afterward, after a long interval of time, he [Gutenberg] had made agreement with Hans Riffe, mayor of Litchtenau, to *work up a secret* for the fair at Aix-la-Chapelle, and they were associated together after this fashion: Gutenberg was to have two shares of the business, and Hans Riffe one share. This agreement came to the knowledge of Andrew Dritzehen, who begged Gutenberg to communicate and teach him this secret also, for which Andrew Dritzehen promised to be his debtor, on Gutenberg's own terms. In the meantime, the elder *Anthony Heilmann had made the same request* in favor of his brother Andrew Heilmann; whereupon he [Gutenberg] had considered these two applications, and he had promised, at their solicitation, to make known to them the secret, and also to give and grant to them the half of the profits, in this wise: that they two should have one share, Hans Riffe one share and he [Gutenberg] one share; but that, as a consideration, the two should give to him [Gutenberg] 160 guilders for the trouble that he would have in teaching them, and *for the communication of the secret*, and that they should, afterward, each give him 80 guilders additional. At the time when they were determining their agreement it was understood that the fair would be held that same year, but when they were all ready, and prepared to work out the secret [*i. e.* to manufacture the merchandise intended for the fair] the fair was postponed to the following year. Thereupon, they [Anthony and Andrew] *had made request that Gutenberg would hide nothing from them which he knew or would discover of secrets and inventions*, and they at once proposed to him to name his terms; and it was then agreed that they should add to the sum first named 250 guilders, making in all 410 guilders; and that they should at once pay 100 guilders in cash—of which sum, at that time, Andrew Heilmann paid 50, and Andrew Dritzehen paid 40—so that Andrew Dritzehen remained a debtor to the amount of 10 guilders. It was also understood that the two partners should pay the 75 guilders due and unpaid, at three different dates which were stipulated; but before the expiration of these dates Andrew Dritzehen had died, still in debt to Gutenberg. At the time when the agreement was made, it had been decided that the accomplishment of their secret [the duration of copartnership] should occupy five entire years: in the event of the death of any one of the four partners, during this five years, *all the implements pertaining to the secret*, and all the merchandise that had been manufactured, should be vested in the remaining partners, and that the heirs of the partner who had died should receive, at the end of five years, 100 guilders. Consequently, and because the contract, which is expressed in these very terms, and which contract was found at the house of Andrew Dritzehen, fully set forth all these stipulations, and those that preceded it, as he John Gutenberg hopes to prove by good witnesses, he demands that George Dritzehen and his brother Claus should deduct the 85 guilders which were still due to him from their late brother, from the 100 guilders, and then he would consent to return to them the 15 guilders, although he was still fairly entitled, according to the terms of the contract, to several years, before this money should be payable. As to the declaration made by George Dritzehen that the late Andrew Dritzehen, his brother, had taken much money by the pledge of his goods and of his inheritance from his father, he did not think it worth consideration, for he [Gutenberg] had not received from the goods or inheritance anything more than he had before first stated, except a half-omen of wine, a basket of pears, and a half-fuder of wine, which Andrew Dritzehen and Andrew Heilmann had given to him; that, moreover, the two men had consumed the equivalent of this and more besides at his house, for which they had never been asked to pay anything. Moreover, when he, George Dritzehen, demanded to be admitted in the partnership as an heir, he knew very well that this claim was no better founded than any other;

and that Andrew Dritzehen had never been security for him, neither for lead, nor for any other matter, except on one occasion before Fritz von Seckingen; but he had, after his death, satisfied this obligation; and it is for the purpose of establishing the truth of these assertions that he demands that the depositions should be heard.

The depositions contain the most curious portions of the pleadings, for it will be noticed that Gutenberg and Dritzehen have not described the secret. Gutenberg did not wish to divulge it, and Dritzehen probably hoped to discover it in the evidence, which begins mysteriously and dramatically.

Barbel von Zabern, the mercer, testified that on a certain night she had talked with Andrew Dritzehen about various matters, and that she had said to him: "But will you not stop work, so that you can get some sleep?" He replied to her, "It is necessary that I first finish this work." Then the witness said, "But, God help me, what a great sum of money you are spending! That has, at least, cost you 10 guilders." He answered, "You are a goose; you think this cost but 10 guilders. Look here! if you had the money which this has cost over and above 300 guilders, you would have enough for all your life; this has cost me at least 500 guilders. It is but a trifle to what I will have to expend. It is for this that I have mortgaged my goods and my inheritance." "But," continued the witness, "if this does not succeed, what will you do then?" He answered, "It is not possible that we can fail; before another year is over, we shall have recovered our capital, and shall be prosperous: that is, providing God does not intend to afflict us."

This dialogue puts two of the partners in a clear light: the domination of Gutenberg and the faith of Dritzehen are perfect. Unmoved by the cold distrust of shrewd Madame Zabern, Dritzehen persists in his work, trusting confidently in the genius of Gutenberg and the success of the process. "It is not possible that we can fail." In the testimony of the next witness we find the first clue to the secret.

Dame Ennel Dritzehen, the wife of Hans Schultheiss, dealer in wood, testified that Lorentz Beildeck [personal servant to Gutenberg] came on a certain day to her house, where Claus Dritzehen, her cousin, happened to be, and said to the latter, "Dear Claus Dritzehen, the late Andrew Dritzehen had *four pieces lying in a press*, and Gutenberg begs that you will take them away *from the press*, and that you will *separate them*, so that no one can see what it [the tool or implement made of four pieces] is, for he does not wish that anyone should see *it*." This witness also testified that when she was with Andrew Dritzehen, her cousin, she had assisted him night and day when he was on this work. She also said that she knew very well that Andrew Dritzehen, her cousin, had, during this period, mortgaged his capital; but as to how much of it he had devoted to this work, she knew nothing.

The nature or the purpose of this tool of four pieces lying in the press is not explained by any of the witnesses. It seems that Gutenberg feared that it would, when fitted together, be readily understood, and would reveal the secret. His inquietude about it is also set forth by Hans Schultheiss.

Hans Schultheiss testified that Lorentz Beildick came one day to his house with Claus Dritzehen, where this witness had conducted him. It was at or about the time of the death of Andrew Dritzehen; Lorentz Beildick said, "Your late brother, Andrew Dritzehen, has *four pieces lying down in* [or underneath] *a press*, and Gutenberg begs that you will take them out and separate them, so that no one will be able to see what *it* is." Claus Dritzehen searched for the pieces, but could not find them. This witness heard, a long time ago, from Andrew Dritzehen that the work had cost him more than 300 guilders.

It is obvious that these four pieces were not a part of the press. Properly put together, they constituted one tool. Another witness repeats the story, describing this tool as *it*.

Conrad Sahspach testified that Andrew Heilmann came to him one day when he was in the market square and said: "Dear Conrad, Andrew Dritzehen is dead, and as you are the man who made the press, and know all about the matter, go there, and *take the pieces out of the press, and separate them*, so that nobody can know what *it* is." But when this witness went to look after the press (it was on St. Stephen's day last) the thing [it] had disappeared. This witness said that Andrew Dritzehen had once borrowed money from him, which he used for the work. He knew that he had mortgaged his property.

It does not appear that there was any secret about the construction of the press. Sahspach, who was not one of the partners, was authorized, not to disjoint the press, but to remove and disconnect the form of four pieces in the press, which seems to have been the key to the secret.

The poverty and the subsequent despondency of Andrew Dritzehen are described by Hans Sidenneger, who testified that Andrew had mortgaged all his property. His honesty is acknowledged by Werner Smalriem, who testified that he had lent him money and had been repaid. His anxiety about his debts, and his death, which seems to have been the result of overwork, are briefly related by Mydehart Stocker.

Mydehart Stocker deposed that the late Andrew Dritzehen fell sick on St. John's Day, or about Christmas time. When he fell sick, he was laid upon a bed in the room of this witness. And this witness went to him and said, "Andrew, how are you?" And he answered, "I believe that I am on my death-bed.

If I am about to die, I wish that I had never been connected with the association." Witness said, "Why so?" He responded, "Because I know very well that my brothers will never agree with Gutenberg." Witness said, "Is not your partnership governed by a written agreement? Are there not evidences of the nature of your obligations?" Andrew said, "Yes. Everything has been done properly by writing." Witness then asked how the association had been formed. Dritzehen then told him how Andrew Heilmann, Hans Riffe, Gutenberg and himself, had formed a partnership, to which Andrew Heilmann and himself had brought 80 guilders, at least, so far as he recollected. When the partnership had been made, Andrew Heilmann and himself went one day to the house of Gutenberg at Saint Arbogastus. When there, *they discovered that Gutenberg had concealed many secrets which he had not obligated himself to teach to them.* This did not please them. Thereupon they dissolved the old partnership, and formed a new one. [Here follows a repetition, substantially, of the statement made by Gutenberg, concerning the indebtedness of each partner.]

The insolvency of Andrew Dritzehen is set forth in the testimony of the priest who attended him before his death.

Herr Peter Eckhart, curate of St. Martin, said [as a priest, he was not sworn], that the late Andrew Dritzehen sent for him during Christmas week that he might have his confession. When he came to his home, he found him ready to confess. He [the priest] asked him if there was debt due by him to any person, or if any person owed him, or if he had given or done anything which it was necessary that he should reveal. Then Andrew Dritzehen told him that he was in partnership with many persons, with Andrew Heilmann and others, and that he had incurred an obligation in an enterprise to the amount of 200 or 300 guilders, and that, at that time, he was not worth a stiver.

Gutenberg's need of money, and Dritzehen's liability for money lent to the association, are proved by another witness.

Thomas Steinbach deposed that Hesse, the broker, once came to him, asking him if he knew where he could place some money, with little risk of loss. Witness had recommended him to John Gutenberg, Andrew Dritzehen and Anthony Heilmann, who needed money. Witness took up for them 14 lutzelbergers, but he really lost 12½ guilders by the transaction. Fritz von Seckingen was their surety, and his name was inscribed [as endorser] on the books of the house of commerce [probably some kind of banking-house].

The most explicit evidence concerning this form of four pieces is given by Lorentz Beildick, the servant of Gutenberg.

Lorentz Beildick testified that John Gutenberg, on a certain day, sent him to the house of Claus Dritzehen, after the death of Andrew, his brother, with this message—that he should not show to any person the press in his care. Witness did so. Gutenberg had instructed him minutely, and told him that Claus should go to the press and should *turn two buttons, so that the pieces would be detached one from the other;* that these pieces should be afterward placed in the press or on the press; that when this had been done, *no one could comprehend its purpose.* Gutenberg also requested Claus Dritzehen, if he should leave his house, that he should at once repair to his house [John Gutenberg's], who had some things to tell to him in person. This witness remembers perfectly that John Gutenberg was not indebted to the late Andrew, but that, on the contrary, Andrew was indebted to John Gutenberg. Witness also testified that he had never been present at any of their meetings since Christmas last. Witness had often seen Andrew Dritzehen dining at the house of John Gutenberg, but he had never seen him give to Gutenberg as much as a stiver.

The bold manner in which Beildick denied the payment of money by Andrew Dritzehen, seems to have greatly exasperated George Dritzehen, who threatened him with a prosecution for false evidence, or perjury. There was a scene in the court. George Dritzehen cried out, sarcastically, "Witness, tell the truth, even if it takes us both to the gallows." Beildick complained to the judge of this intimidation, but it does not appear that the affair had further consequences.

Reimboldt, of Ehenheim, testified that he was at the house of Andrew before Christmas, and asked him *what he intended to do with the nice things with which he was busy*. Andrew told him that *they had already cost him more than 500 guilders*, but that he hoped, when the work was perfected, to make a great deal of money, with which he would pay witness, and would also receive a proper reward for his labor. Witness lent him 8 guilders, for he was then very needy. Witness's wife had also lent money to Andrew. Andrew once came to her with a ring, which he valued at 30 guilders, and which he had pawned to the Jews at Ehenheim for 5 guilders. Witness further said that he knew very well that Dritzehen had prepared two large barrels of sweet wine, of which he gave one-half omen to Gutenberg, and one-half omen to Mydehart. He had also given Gutenberg some pears. On a certain occasion Andrew had requested witness to buy for him two half-barrels of wine, and Dritzehen and Heilmann, jointly, had given one of these half-barrels to Gutenberg.

That the work on which Dritzehen was engaged was of a novel nature may be inferred from the fact that his visitors could not give names to his tools or his workmanship. They speak of *it*, *that thing*, *the nice things*, *the form of four pieces*, etc. Madame Zabern is surprised at the cost of that thing; Reimboldt wonders what he intends to do with these nice things. It is obvious that this mysterious work is not that of polishing stones or gems, nor the making of mirrors, for it cannot be supposed that these witnesses, and one of them a woman, would be ignorant of the purpose of a mirror, or would grossly underrate the value of gems, or polished stones. But there is one witness who testifies that Dritzehen said his enterprise was that of making mirrors.

Hans Niger von Bischoviszheim testified that Andrew Dritzehen came to him and told him that he was in great need of money, for he was deep in an enterprise which taxed his resources to the utmost. Witness asked him what he was doing. Dritzehen then informed him that *he was making mirrors*. When witness threshed his grain, he took it to market at Molsheim and Ehenheim, and sold it, and gave Dritzehen the money. This witness also corroborated the testimony of Reimboldt as to the giving of wine to John Gutenberg. He took the wine in his own cart to Gutenberg, who was then at Saint Arbogastus.

It may be inferred from this testimony that Dritzehen was still deriving some profit from the old work of making mirrors.

Fritz von Seckingen testified that Gutenberg had borrowed money of him, and that Anthony Heilmann was on his bond. Andrew Dritzehen, who should have done so, evaded this obligation, and never signed the bond at all. Gutenberg paid up the entire sum at the time of the last fair during Mid-Lent.

Gutenberg's partner gives some curious details about the partnership, and intimates that the *forms* were of metal.

Anthony Heilmann testified that, when he learned that Gutenberg wished to take Andrew Dritzehen as a third [partner] in the company formed for the sale of mirrors at the fair of Aix-la-Chapelle, he *begged him with importunity to take also his brother Andrew*, if he wished to do a great favor to him, Anthony. But Gutenberg told him that he feared that the friends of Andrew would pretend that this business [or secret] was that of sorcery, an imputation he wished to avoid. Heilmann persisted in his request, and finally obtained a document, which he was obliged to show to the two future partners, and about which they found it necessary to have a consultation. Gutenberg took the document to them, and they decided that they would comply with its terms, and in this way the affair [of partnership] was settled. In the midst of these negotiations, Andrew Dritzehen begged this witness [Anthony Heilmann] to lend him some money, and he then said that he would willingly oblige him, if he would give good security. And he lent Dritzehen 90 pounds, which Dritzehen took to Gutenberg, at Saint Arbogastus. .... The witness asked him, "What do you wish to do with so much money? You do not need more than 80 guilders." Dritzehen replied that he had need for more money; that it was but two or three days before the [vigil of] Annunciation (March 25), on which day he was bound to give 80 guilders to Gutenberg. [Here follows an elaborate explanation of the financial standing and the rights of each partner.] After that, Gutenberg said to this witness that it was necessary that he should draw his attention to an essential point [in the agreement], which was, that all the partners were on a footing of equality, and that there should be a mutual understanding that each should conceal nothing from the others; and that this arrangement would be for the common benefit. The witness was content with this proposition, and communicated it with praises to the other two. Some time after this, Gutenberg repeated his words, and the witness responded with the same protestations as before, and said that he intended to be worthy of the trust. After this, Gutenberg drew up an agreement as the expression of this proposition, and said to this witness: "Consult well among yourselves, and see that you are agreed on this matter." They did so consult, and they discussed for a long time on this point, and even sought the advice of Gutenberg, who, on one occasion, said: "*There are here now many things ready for use, and there are many more in progress; the goods you acquire are almost equal to your investment in money. In addition to all this, you get the knowledge of the secret art.*" So they soon came to an agreement, and it was decided that the heirs of the deceased partner should have for that partner's investment, for the *forms*, and for all the materials, 100 guilders; but they should have it only after the five years. Gutenberg said that this provision would be of great advantage to them, for, if he chanced to die, he would abandon to them everything to which he was entitled, as his share of the property; and yet they would be obliged to give to his heirs only the 100 guilders, as they proposed to do with each other. It was also decided that in case of the death of any one of the partners, the others should not in any wise be obliged to teach, to show, or to reveal the secret to his heirs. It was a provision as favorable to one as to another. . . . This witness also testified that Gutenberg, a little while before Christmas, sent his servant to the two Andrews, to fetch *all the forms.* These forms *were melted* before his eyes, which he regretted on account of *several forms.* When Andrew Dritzehen died, there were people who would have willingly examined the *press.* He told Gutenberg to send and prevent it from being examined. Gutenberg, in effect, did send his servant to put *it* in disorder, and to tell the witness that, when he had the time, he wished to talk with him.

The testimony of the last witness is the shortest, and it is remarkable as the only testimony which defines the work.

Hans Dünne, the goldsmith, testified to this effect: within the past two or three years he had received from John Gutenberg about 100 guilders, which sum had been paid to him exclusively *for work connected with printing.*

The testimony of eighteen other witnesses was taken,[1] but, according to Schoepflin, Dünne's is the last testimony on the official record. The judge gave the following decision:

WE, master and counselor, after having heard the complaint and answer of the parties, the depositions and the testimony . . . and after having examined the contract and the agreement. . . Considering that there is a contract which fully establishes the manner in which these arrangements were projected and carried out:· We do command that Hans Riffe, Andrew Heilmann and Hans Gutenberg shall make an oath before God that the matters that have transpired are warranted by the contract that has been cited; and that this contract had but one supplementary agreement, under seal, which would have been

[1] The eighteen witnesses were Master Hirtz, Jacob Imerle, Midhart Honöwe, Heinrich Bisinger, Wilhelm von Schutter, the wife of Lorentz Beildick, M. Jerge Saltzmütter, Stösser Nese von Ehenheim, Martin Verwer, Henrich Seidenneger, M. Gosse Sturm, of Saint Arbogastus, Hans Ross, the goldsmith, and his wife, Andrew Heilmann, Claus Heilmann, Heinrich Olse, Hans Riffe and Johan Dritzehen. Their testimony is not on the record. It is unfortunate that we have lost the testimony of M. Gosse Sturm, of Saint Arbogastus, and Ross, the goldsmith. It is probable that these men, who had intimate relations with Gutenberg, could have described this secret art with greater clearness.

agreed to by Andrew Dritzehen if now living; and that Hans Gutenberg shall also take oath that the 85 guilders have not been paid to him by Andrew Dritzehen; and from this time this amount of 85 guilders shall be deducted from the sum of 100 guilders, about which there has been controversy; and he [Gutenberg] shall pay to George and Claus Dritzehen 15 guilders; and, in this manner, the 100 guilders will be paid in conformity to the contract that has been cited.

The oath, according to this form, has been taken before us by Hans Riffe, Andrew Heilmann and Hans Gutenberg, with this qualification on the part of Hans Riffe, that he was not present at the first meeting [of the partners]; but that, as soon as he did meet with them, he had approved of their action or agreement.

The taking of this oath, and the payment of the fifteen guilders by John Gutenberg, terminated the suit in his favor.

The record is enough to give us a clear idea of the character and position, if not of the process, of John Gutenberg. At this time, December, 1439, and for some time previous, Gutenberg was neither in poverty nor in obscurity. He had already acquired a local reputation for scientific knowledge. He did not seek for partners or pupils; they came to him. Among the number we find Hans Riffe, the mayor of Lichtenau, whose confidence in Gutenberg, after three years of partnership, is implied in his testimony. Anthony Heilmann, the lender of money, seems to have been equally satisfied with his brother partner. The action of the judge, in accepting Gutenberg's oath as conclusive, proves that he was a man of established character. The deference paid to him by all the witnesses shows that he was not merely a mechanic or an inventor, but a man of activity and energy, a born leader, with a presence and a power of persuasion that enabled him to secure ready assistance in the execution of his plans. His reputation had been made by success. George Dritzehen said that his brother had received a good profit from his connection with Gutenberg. The eagerness and the faith of Andrew, the pertinacity with which his brothers pressed their claim to be admitted as partners, the solicitation of Heilmann on behalf of his brother, are indications that the men were sanguine as to the success of Gutenberg's new invention. The expected profit was attractive, but it was not the only advantage.

In that century it was not an easy matter to learn an art or a trade of value: no one could enter the ranks of mechanics even as a pupil, without the payment of a premium in money; no one could practise any trade unless he had served a long period of apprenticeship. These exactions hopelessly shut out many who wished to learn; but men who had complied with all the conditions were often unwilling to teach, or to allow others to practise. Many trades were monopolies. In some cases they were protected by legislative enactments, like that accorded to the Venetian makers of playing cards. So far as it could be done, every detail of mechanics was kept secret, as may be inferred from the old phrase "art and mystery," still retained in indentures of apprenticeship in all countries. One of the consequences of this exclusiveness was that many mechanical arts were invested with unusual dignity.[1] The sharply defined line which, in our day, separates art from trade and mechanics did not then exist.

The testimony shows that Gutenberg had a knowledge of three distinct arts. The one earliest practised, from which Dritzehen derived a good profit, was the polishing of stones or gems. The second, was that of making mirrors. Gutenberg was not the inventor of this art, but he was one of the

[1] After the development of the towns, all members of the nobility did not seek their occupation exclusively in deeds of knighthood. Industry, art, and the refinement of town life gradually superseded the warlike spirit of the nobility, to whom the town offered distinguished dignities and situations, while enterprises of commerce and industry gave them distinction and riches. The privilege of coining money, especially, was often farmed out to an association of ancient families. At Mentz this association consisted of twelve families (Münzer-Hausgenossen), among whom was also the family of Gensfleisch. They possessed, moreover, the privileges of the valuation of coin, of the assize of weights and measures, or offices for the exchange of money and of the sale of gold and silver staves to the mint. Such employment brought them chiefly in connection with the goldsmiths, whose work consisted, at that time, of one of the most considerable trades, which comprised mechanics and chemistry, nay, the whole dominion of plastic and graphic art, in its application to metals, whether separate or in conjunction with diamonds and other precious materials. They were mostly patricians who established powder-mills, paper-mills and similar new manufactories. Van der Linde, *Haarlem Legend*, p. 17.

first to practise it.[1] The early German mirrors were small, but they had broad frames, and were richly gilt and adorned with carved or moulded work in high relief. Ottley thinks that the press was used for pressing mouldings for the frames of mirrors, and that the lead was used for the metallic face.

The third art is imperfectly described. If Dünne's testimony had been lost, it would not appear that this art was printing, for there is no mention of books, paper, ink, types, or wood-cuts. The lead, the press, and the goldsmith's work on things relating to printing, could be regarded as materials required in the art of mirror-making. But "the thing," and "the nice things," which provoked exclamations of surprise at their great cost, could not have been looking-glasses.

Dünne said, very plainly, that this art was printing; but Dünne's testimony could be set aside, and Gutenberg's connection with typography at the period of this trial could be inferred from other evidence. The thoroughness of the workmanship in the books printed by Gutenberg after 1450 is a thoroughness which could have been acquired only by practice. Before he began this practice he must have devoted much time to experiment and to the making of the tools he needed. No inventor, no printer can believe that the skill

[1] Glass mirrors, almost unknown in the fourteenth century, were regarded as novelties in the fifteenth. It seems that they were first made in Germany. Winaricky lays great stress on the fact that the Bohemians were the earliest and the most skillful workers in glass, and that they also excelled as lapidaries and metallurgists. He says, but without proof, that the art of polishing stones and making mirrors was acquired by Gutenberg in Bohemia. The learned Beckmann says that

"Early German mirrors were made by pouring melted lead or tin over a glass plate while yet hot as it came from the furnace. In and around Nuremberg, convex mirrors were made by blowing with the pipe in the glass bubble while it was still hot a metallic mixture with a little salts of tartar. When the bubble had been covered and cooled, it was cut in small round mirrors. These small convex mirrors were called *ochsenaugen*, or ox-eyes. They were set in a round board, and had a very broad border or margin. One of them in my possession is two and a half inches in diameter. . . . This art is an old German invention, for it is described by Porta and Ganzoni, who both lived in the beginning of the sixteenth century, and who both expressly say that the art was then common in Germany. Curious foreigners often attempted to learn it, and imagined that Germans kept it a secret."

he subsequently showed as a printer could have been attained by the labor of a few months or years. If it is also considered that Gutenberg was poor, and that he collected the money he needed with great delay and difficulty, the doubt may assume the form of denial. It is a marvel that he was so well prepared at the end of the ten years which Zell says were given up to investigation.

It would be gratifying to know the form in which the idea of typography first presented itself to Gutenberg; but there is in this case, no story like that of Franklin and the kite, or of Newton and the apple. Zell, in the *Cologne Chronicle*, says that the first prefiguration of Gutenberg's method was found in the *Donatuses* published in Holland before 1440. That the xylographic *Donatus*, the only block-book without cuts, was the forerunner of all typographic books, may not be denied. That some stray copy of a now lost edition of the book may have suggested to Gutenberg the superior utility of typography is possible, but the suggestion was that of the feasibility of a grander result by an entirely different process. For, although typography took its beginnings in an earlier practice of xylography, it was not the outgrowth[1] of that practice. It took up the art of printing at a point

[1] The most common prejudice is the supposition, *à priori*, legitimated strictly scientifically by nothing, that printing with movable types was only an improvement on that with wooden blocks on which the letters were cut; that it was a development of it, an extension, a fortunate application, the highest step of the ladder, consisting of playing cards, images of saints, pictures with super, sub and other scriptions, texts without pictures. In short, xylography, in a technical, logical and reformatorical sense, would be the mother of typography. But it is such only in the sense of an external impulse, of an external push to meditating on quite *another* means than wood or metal engraving, or *another* mode of obtaining books. Zell finds that push in the block-Donatuses, but the inspiration of genius, the first invention of a quite independent art, of a totally new principle, which has nothing in common with wood and metal engraving, he ascribes . . . to Gutenberg. In Gutenberg's mind, the grand idea arose that all words, all writing, all language, all human thoughts, could be expressed by a small number, a score of different letters, arranged according to the requirements; that, with a large quantity of those different letters, united as one whole, a whole page of text could be printed at once, and, repeating this process continually, large manuscripts could be swiftly multiplied. . . . This thought, this idea, begot the invention of typography. . . . Every other explanation is at once unhistorical and unpsychological. *Haarlem Legend*, p. 11.

where xylography had failed, and developed it by new ideas and new methods. Typography was an invention pure and simple. In the theory and practice of block-printing, there was nothing that could have been improved until it reached the discovery of the only proper method of making types.

It may have been from his experience in the melting and pouring of lead, in the engraving of designs for the frames of his mirrors, in the use of a press for the moulding of the designs for these frames, that Gutenberg derived his first practical ideas of the true method of making types. Whatever the external impulse which led Gutenberg to printing, it was so strong that it compelled him to abandon the practice of all other arts. After this trial we hear no more of him as a maker of mirrors, or a polisher of gems.

The record of the trial before Cune Nope is not the only evidence we have that Gutenberg's unknown art was that of typography. Wimpheling, one of the most learned men of his age, and nearly contemporary with Gutenberg, gives the following testimony concerning early printing in Strasburg:[1]

> In the year of our Lord 1440, under the reign of Frederic III, Emperor of the Romans, John Gutenberg, of Strasburg, discovered a new method of writing, which is a great good, and almost a divine benefit to the world. He was the first in the city of Strasburg who invented that art of impressing which the Latin peoples call printing. He afterward went to Mentz, and happily perfected his invention.

In another book, in which Wimpheling pays compliment to the intelligence of the people of Strasburg, he writes:

> Your city is acknowledged to excel most other cities by its origination of the art of printing, which was afterward perfected in Mentz.

The *Chronicle of Cologne*[2] is as explicit as to date, but not as to place. It specifies 1440 as the date of the discovery of printing "in the manner that is now generally used."

[1] Wolf, *Monumenta Typographica*, vol. I, p. 586.

[2] See page 315 of this book. The chronicler is in error in specifying Mentz as the place where the art was discovered, but the specification of the period between 1440 and 1450 as that in which "the art was being investigated" by John Gutenberg is sustained by other testimonies.

The evidence of the witnesses on the trial agrees with the testimony afforded by the chronicles: it is plain that Gutenberg had not perfected his invention in 1439. From his lonely room in the ruined monastery of Saint Arbogastus, to which he retreated for the sake of secrecy, Gutenberg gave work to Dünne, the goldsmith, to Saspach, the joiner, and to Dritzehen, his old workman. It would seem that they were not producing work for sale, but were making tools which required a great deal of labor. Dritzehen worked night and day, Madame Schultheiss helping him. At the death of Dritzehen, the work expended on the art had cost a great deal of money, but it was still incomplete. The testimony shows that it had been intended that the salable work to be produced by the partnership should be exposed for sale at the great fair of Aix-la-Chapelle in the summer of 1439. The postponement of this fair[1] to the year 1440 was a grave disappointment. If the object of the partnership was the making of popular books of devotion, we can understand the reasonableness of the hopes of great profit when the books should be laid before the pious pilgrims. The sudden death of Andrew Dritzehen was the occasion of more delay. Gutenberg, fearing that the public, or George Dritzehen, would get possession of the secret, melted the forms and suspended the work. Then followed a litigation which lasted nearly one year, during which period it seems no work was done.

There are many conflicting opinions about the character of the printing so obscurely mentioned in the testimony of the witnesses. Schoepflin says it was block-printing. In the four pieces lying in the press, he sees four pages of engraved

[1] The pilgrimage to ancient Aix-la-Chapelle took place every seventh year, and, commencing on the 10th of July, lasted fourteen days, during which time the ordinary service in the church did not take place, but a free market was held. The concourse of people was uncommonly great on that occasion, so that, for instance in the year 1496, 142,000 pilgrims were counted in the town, and 80,000 guilders in the offering boxes on one day. Aix-la-Chapelle possessed relics of the first rank, as the swaddling-clothes of Christ, his body-cloth at the Crucifixion, the dress worn by Mary at his birth, and the cloth on which St. John the Baptist was beheaded. Van der Linde, *Haarlem Legend*, p. 18.

blocks; in the two buttons, which Dr. Van der Linde says are improperly translated by him as two screws, he finds a screw chase that held the four pages together. This conjecture is in every way improbable. All the processes of block-printing should have been as well known at that time in Strasburg as they were in Venice, Augsburg and Nuremberg. Something more novel than this form of printing would have been required to secure the coöperation of shrewd men like Riffe and Heilmann. The enthusiasm of Dritzehen, and the eagerness of all parties to learn the new art, and to have a share in its profits, cannot be satisfactorily explained by the conjecture that this art was simple block-printing.[1]

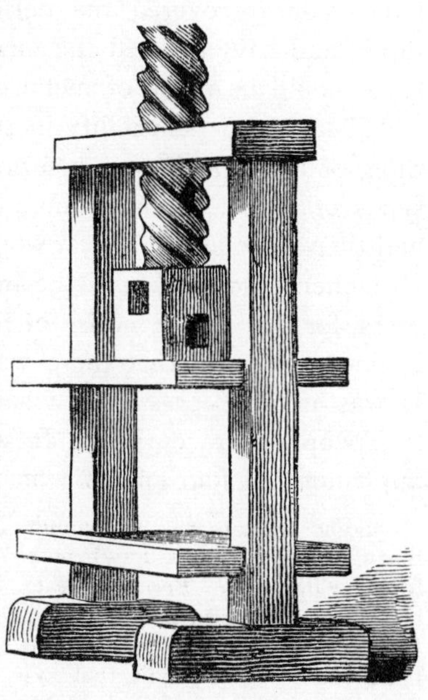

A Medieval Press.

[From Duverger.]

[1] There is no evidence that Gutenberg had been taught xylography, or any of the many branches of book-making. He was not, for that reason, incompetent to invent an entirely new branch. The history of great inventions shows that many inventors never received a thorough technical instruction in the arts or trades which they undertook to reconstruct. Jacquard, inventor of the automatic loom, was, in his boyhood, a bookbinder and a type-founder. Arkwright, inventor of the spinning jenny, was a barber until he was thirty years of age. Stephenson, inventor of the locomotive, tended a steam boiler, but had not served time as a machinist nor as a carriage-builder. Fulton, inventor of the steamboat, was not a sailor, machinist nor ship-builder. Morse, inventor of the electric telegraph, was an artist, not a mechanician, nor even a man of science. Koning, inventor of the cylinder printing machine, was not a printer. The greatest inventions have been made by men not within, but without, the arts they improved. It would seem that a thorough technical education in any art or trade cramps the inventive faculties, disqualifying the expert from making any attempt at radical changes, permitting him to attempt improvement in the details only.

Gutenberg may have begun his experiments in typography by the use of engraved types or punches of wood;[1] but he must have soon discovered the defects and limitations of xylography and have reached the unalterable conclusion that useful types could be made of metal only.

There is no plausibility in the theory of Fischer, that the thing of four pieces was a form of four pages or columns of types of wood. Nor is there any evidence that Gutenberg had then done any practical work. The practice of printing in Dritzehen's house cannot be inferred from the presence of a press, for there is no notice of paper, printed sheets or books. It does not seem that there was a mystery about the press. It was not the press, but what was in it, concerning which the people were curious. It was the imperfectly described implement of four pieces which gave the partners anxiety.

[1] Some authors will not admit that Gutenberg derived any benefit from xylography. Bernard treats block-printing as an art so paltry, that he refused to describe the block-books, or to admit that xylography had any noticeable influence, direct or indirect, on the invention of types. Van der Linde says that history knows nothing of Gutenberg as a xylographer—that there is no documentary evidence that he ever cut or printed a block. These disclaimers—obviously provoked by the absurd statements of other authors that Gutenberg invented xylography, that he printed with types of wood, that typography is the natural outgrowth of xylography—cannot be accepted without qualification. The fact remains that Gutenberg, his associates and pupils, were benefited by the highest technical skill of that time in all the processes of engraving in relief, in the compounding of inks, in the construction and use of presses, and in the manipulation of paper. Compared with the invention of the type-mould, these may seem trivial matters, but the success of Gutenberg's new ideas about printing depended upon his attention to every process that promised aid. It is not probable that the man who hired joiners and goldsmiths could have neglected to avail himself of whatever skill the block-printers possessed. The experience in printing acquired by the block-printers was far from contemptible, but the educating influences they had exerted over the book-buying public were of great importance. It was Gutenberg's discernment of the fact that the block-printers had created a demand for printed work which could never be satisfied by the method of xylography, which gave him the impulse to seek for a more scientific method. Block-printing, although in no sense the mother of typography, was its forerunner, and for that reason alone demands respectful consideration.

Nor was the tool of four pieces the only object of value. Gutenberg assured the partners that the things had cost him nearly as much as he asked of them for their shares in the enterprise, but more were to be made. In the event of the death of a partner, his heirs were to be paid their claim on the *forms* and tools. When Dritzehen died, Gutenberg sent for *all the forms*, which were melted before his eyes,[1] which act he subsequently regretted on account of the *forms*. It was a rash act, but Gutenberg's fears were aroused, and he preferred to destroy the tools rather than allow George Dritzehen to get a knowledge of his secret.

In the practice of printing, the word form means a collection of composed types, arranged in readable order, secured together as one piece, in an iron band or chase, and prepared to receive impression.[2] In all printing offices it has this meaning. That the forms so frequently mentioned in this record of the trial were of metal is clearly implied in the statement

[1] This passage has been translated by Ottley: Gutenberg sent "to fetch all the forms that they might be loosened, and that he might see it [done], and that the joinings of some of the four pieces might be renewed." This translation makes the action of Gutenberg unintelligible. Bernard's translation is: "Gutenberg sent to get the forms, so that he could be sure that they had been separated; these forms had given him a great deal of solicitude." This is obviously a very free and evasive translation. Wetter, who interprets the passage as descriptive of block-printing, says that "the words are too obscure for us to infer anything definite from them. We are in no case to understand by the word *formen* separate letters, but whole blocks." This is an unwarrantable assumption, and in contradiction to the statement that the forms were melted. Van der Linde says that "the words are plain. Translators have stopped at the words *zurlossen* and *ruwete*. *Zurlossen*, or *zerlassen*, means melting, and *ruwete* is dialect for *reuete*, repented."

[2] The commonest meaning of the word form, in most European languages, is a shape or figure prepared by carving; but it has also been applied, colloquially, to the mould made from this carved shape, and also to the article made from the mould. A type-founder's punch is the form of a letter; the mould in which the type is cast is the form or former of the letter; the types prepared for printing are also known as the form. On a future page it will be shown that the word *formen* as used in the trial, was also used at a later date to describe the most important tools in Gutenberg's printing office at Eltvill.

that Gutenberg melted them. These forms, or formens, were, without doubt, implements connected with typography; but whether they were types, or matrices, or moulds, or a collection of types, is not so clear. If they were types, it will seem strange that they were not accurately described as letters of metal by some of the witnesses who saw them. If we regard them as matrices, they may have been "the nice things" alluded to by Reimbolt, the use of which he did not understand.[1] It is possible that Dritzehen was making matrices and fitting them to the mould. If the *forms* were matrices, they and the punches could have cost five hundred guilders.

If the "nice things" were matrices, there must have been a type-mould, and it was this mould which was the key to the invention. The mould was the only implement connected with typography which would at once lay open to an intelligent observer the secret of making types. Of all his tools, this was the one that had received the greatest amount of care and labor, and it should have been the one that Gutenberg would be anxious to conceal. It may be supposed that the thing of four pieces that was opened by two buttons was the mould.[2] Why it should have been kept in or under the press cannot be explained. But if Dritzehen was fitting up matrices, it was proper that he should have the mould at hand. The conjecture that the thing of four pieces was a type-mould, is not free from difficulties, but it seems the only one that makes intelligible the action of the witnesses.

[1] Here we may recall the surprise of Madame Zabern at the cost of the work. She would not have hazarded the low estimate of ten guilders, if Dritzehen had been surrounded by many types or printed sheets. The only tools appertaining to typography, which have a value out of all proportion to their apparent cost, are the punches, matrices and moulds. The modern inexpert would underrate the value of a similar collection as grossly as did Madame Zabern.

[2] It could not have been four pages of metal types, for types disconnected and put in disorder, in or under the press, would have betrayed the secret almost as plainly as if they had been in order. Nor could it have been any attachment to a press like the frisket or tympan. It is impossible to name any jointed or buttoned tool of four pieces, connected with composition or presswork, which would suggest to an inexpert the secret of typography.

The gravest difficulty in the way of this conjecture is, that the type-mould of modern type-founders has, including the matrix, but three detachable pieces. As this mould is substantially of the same form as that known to have been used by Claude Garamond, the eminent type-founder of Paris, in 1540, it has been supposed, and properly, that this mould of three pieces must have been used before Garamond, by all

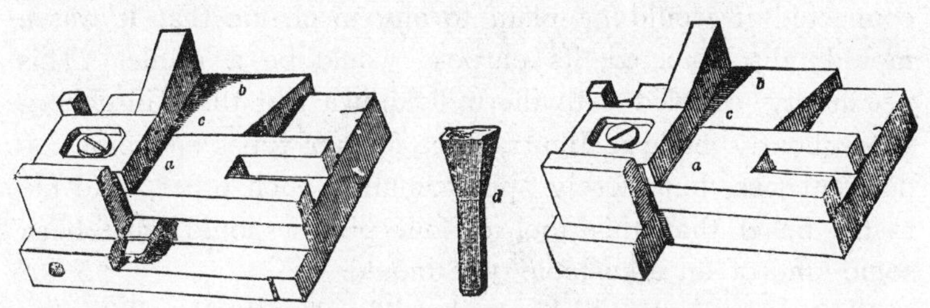

Fac-simile of the Type-mould of Claude Garamond.

a. The place where the body of the type was cast. *b. c.* The mouth-piece in which the fluid metal was poured. *d.* The type as cast, with the metal formed in the mouth-piece adhering to it.

[From Duverger.]

the early printers. But it was not the only form of mould. At the beginning of this century every type-founder found it expedient to use at times, a type-mould somewhat different in its construction—a mould which, with the matrix, consisted of four detachable pieces. The merit of this mould was its adaptability, within limits, to any size of body. Its disadvantages were its difficulty of nice adjustment and its liability to inaccuracy—faults which have obliged all American type-founders of this day to discontinue its use entirely. It is, without doubt, a very old form of mould, but it was never a popular one, having been used chiefly for casting bodies of irregular size.[1] Mr. Bruce has showed me one of these early moulds—a mould long out of use, preserved only as one of the earlier relics of his old type-foundry. Its construction is

[1] Bernard gives this form of type-mould a passing notice. He says:

M. de Berny showed me one of these primitive mechanisms in his own foundry. This mould, which is still [1853] in use, is constructed with two kinds of knees [or squares] enabling the type-maker to adjust it in various ways so as to cast any body desired. *De l'origine*, etc. vol. I, p. 44, note.

too complex for description by words, or even by engraving; but it may be sufficient to say that, with the matrix, it consisted of four pieces, and was so constructed as to allow of an enlargement and nice adjustment in either direction of the space provided for casting the body of the type. The pieces were held together by stiff springs, but buttons could have been used for the same purpose. When these pieces were connected it would be plain to any mechanic that it was a mould; disconnected, its purpose would be a riddle. This peculiarity, coupled with the well known fact that Gutenberg subsequently made at Mentz, three fonts of types on bodies of different size, but closely approximating each other, lead me to the belief that this tool of four pieces should have been some kind of an adjustable type-mould.

The only book which can be offered with plausibility as the work of Gutenberg in Strasburg is a *Donatus*, of which four leaves are now preserved in the National Library at Paris. This *Donatus* is a small quarto, containing twenty-seven lines to the page. The similarity of the types of this book, both in face and body, to those of the *Bible of 42 lines*, suggests the thought that both books were the work of the same printer; but the cut of the letters, the founding of the types and the printing of the book are vastly inferior.

It is possible that Gutenberg may have printed some books at Strasburg, but we do not know anything about them. There were many difficulties connected with the proper development of typography, and he may have labored over them many years without any satisfactory result.[1] His earlier experience could not have been materially different from that of other inventors: he may have been kept for years on the threshold of success, vainly trying to remove some obstruction which blocked up his way. If we suppose that Gutenberg

[1] The inability to produce any book printed by Gutenberg at Strasburg was the occasion of the following pithy answer: Koch had asserted before the Institute, that Strasburg was the cradle of printing. Schaab interrupted him, "Yes, but it is a cradle without a baby."

began, as a novice would probably begin, by founding types of soft lead in moulds of sand, the printer will understand why he would condemn the types made by this method. If he afterward made a mould of hard metal, and founded types in matrices of brass, we can understand that, in the beginning, he had abundant reason to reject his first types for inaccuracies of body and irregularities of height and lining. To him as to all true inventors, there could be no patching up of defects in plan or in construction. It was necessary to throw away all the defective work and to begin anew. Experiments like these consume a great deal of time and quite as much of money. The testimony shows that the money contributed by some of the partners in the association had been collected with difficulty. We may suppose that when this had been spent to no purpose, they were unable or unwilling to contribute any more.

Fac-simile of the Types of a Donatus attributed to Gutenberg at Strasburg.
[From Bernard.]

It may be that the failure of the Strasburg associates was due solely to the audacity of Gutenberg, whose plans were always beyond his pecuniary ability. Even then he may have purposed the printing of the great *Bible of 36 lines* in three volumes, which he afterward completed in an admirable manner. In trying to accomplish much, he may have failed to do anything of value. Whatever the reason, it is certain that his partners abandoned Gutenberg and his invention. We read no more of Riffe and Heilmann in connection with typography.

There is evidence that Gutenberg was financially embarrassed after the trial. On the second day of January, 1441, Gutenberg and the knight Luthold von Ramstein gave security for the annual payment of five pounds to the Chapter of St. Thomas at Strasburg, in consideration of the present sum of one hundred pounds paid by the chapter to Gutenberg. On the fifteenth day of December, 1442, John Gutenberg and Martin Brether sold to the same corporation for the present sum of eighty pounds, an annual income of four pounds, from the revenues of the town of Mentz. Gutenberg had inherited this income from his uncle, Johan Lehheimer, secular judge of that city. The tax-book of the city shows that he was in arrear for taxes between the years 1436 and 1440. In the tax-book for 1443, it is plainly recorded that Gutenberg's tax was paid by the Ennel Gutenbergen who is supposed to have been his wife. Gutenberg had reason to be disheartened. He had spent all his money; had alienated his partners; had apparently wasted a great deal of time in fruitless experiments; had damaged his reputation as a man of business, and seemed further from success than when he revealed his plans to his partners.

It is the common belief that Gutenberg went direct from Strasburg to Mentz. Winaricky, on the contrary, says that he forsook Strasburg for the University of Prague, at which institution he took the degree of bachelor of arts in 1445, and in which city he resided, until it was besieged, and he was obliged to leave, in 1448. There is no trustworthy authority for either statement. The period in his life between 1442 and 1448 is blank, but it is not probable that he was idle.

XXI

Gutenberg and his Earlier Work at Mentz.

Gutenberg appears in Mentz as a Borrower of Money...Was then Ready to Begin as a Printer. Donatus of 1451...Letters of Indulgence of 1454 and 1455...Made from Founded Types...Circumstances attending their sale...Fac-simile of Holbein's Satire...Fac-simile of the Letter dated 1454, with a Translation...Almanac of 1455...Gutenberg's two Bibles...Dates of Publication Uncertain...Bible of 36 lines, with Fac-simile...Evidences of its probable Priority...Apparently an Unsuccessful Book...John Fust, with Portrait...Fust's Contract with Gutenberg in 1450. Probable Beginning of the Bible of 42 lines...Description of Book, with Fac-simile...Colophon of the Illuminator...Must have been Printed before 1456...Fust brings Suit against Gutenberg. Official Record of the Trial...Gutenberg's Inability to pay his debt...Suit was a Surprise...Portrait of Gutenberg...Fust deposes Gutenberg and installs Schœffer at the head of the Office.

There is material in this event for an affecting drama: a genial inventor, indefatigably occupied in realizing an idea, an usurious and crafty money-lender, abusing the financial carelessness of a genius, to get him more and more into his power; a clever servant courting the daughter of the usurer, and conspiring with him against the great master; the inventor robbed of all the fruit of his exertions during many years, at the moment that it was ripe to be gathered. *Van der Linde.*

GUTENBERG'S last act upon record in Strasburg was the selling out of the last remnant of his inheritance. The first evidence we have of his return to Mentz is an entry, on the sixth day of October, 1448, in a record of legal contracts, in which he appears as a borrower of money. It seems that Gutenberg had persuaded his kinsman, Arnold Gelthus, to borrow from Rynhard Brömser and John Rodenstein, the sum of 150 guilders, for the use of which Gutenberg promised to pay the yearly interest of 8½ guilders. Gutenberg had no securities to offer; Gelthus had to pledge the rents of some houses for this purpose. How this money was to be used is not stated, but it may be presumed that Gutenberg needed it for the development of his grand invention. His plans, whatever they were, met with the approbation of his uncle John Gensfleisch, by whose permission he occupied the leased house[1] *Zum Jungen*, which he used not only for a dwelling, but as a printing office.

At this time Gutenberg was, no doubt, nearly perfect in his knowledge of the correct theory of type-founding, and had also acquired fair practice as a printer. Helbig thinks that he had ready the types of the *Bible of 36 lines*. Madden says that he was then, or very soon after, engaged in printing a small edition of this book. There is evidence that these types were in use at least as early as 1451. Two leaves of an early typographic edition of the *Donatus*, 27 lines to the page, printed on vellum from the types of the *Bible of 36 lines*, have been discovered near Mentz, in the original binding of an old account book of 1451.[2] In one word the letter i is reversed, a positive proof that it was printed from types, and not from blocks. The ink is still very black, but Fischer says that it will not resist water.[3] As this fragment shows the large types of the *Bible of 36 lines* in their most primitive form, it authorizes the belief that it should have been printed by Gutenberg soon after his return to Mentz.

During the interval between 1440 and 1451, about which history records so little, Gutenberg may have printed many trifles. He could not have been always unsuccessful: he could not have borrowed money for more than ten years, without

[1] Schaab says that there is on record in Mentz a document which proves that John Gensfleisch leased this house in October, 1443. Reasoning from the two disconnected facts, that this house was used by Gutenberg for a printing office, and that it had been leased by Gensfleisch in 1443, careless readers have assumed that John Gensfleisch was the first printer in Mentz, and that he was either the true inventor of printing, or the unfaithful workman who stole the invention of Coster or of Mentel. It is not necessary to repeat what has been written concerning the impossibility of a theft from the fictitious Coster, nor about the absurdity of representing the uncle as a printer.

[2] Fischer, *Essai sur les monuments typographiques*, p. 70.

[3] Bernard refuses this statement. He says that the fragments of other editions of the *Donatus* in this type, supposed to be of the same period, which he inspected in the British Museum, show ink that is permanent.

a demonstration of his ability to print and to sell printed work. It is probable that he had to postpone his grand plans, and that his necessities compelled him to begin the practice of his new art with the printing of trivial work. There is evidence that the branch of typography which is now known as job printing is as old as, if not older than, book printing. This evidence is furnished in the *Letters of Indulgence*, which have distinction as the first works with type-printed dates.

Three distinct editions of the *Letters of Indulgence* are known. The copies are dated 1454 or 1455, but are more clearly defined by the number of the lines in each edition, as *Letters* of *30*, or *31*, or *32 lines*. Each *Letter* is printed from movable types, in black ink, upon one side of a stout piece of parchment, about nine inches high and thirteen inches wide. The form of words is substantially the same in all editions, and all copies present the same general typographical features, as if they were the work of the same printing office. In all copies, the presswork is good; they seem to have been printed by a properly constructed press on damp vellum with ink mixed in oil. The types

Fac-simile of the Types of the Donatus of 1451.
[From Fischer.]

of the three editions have a general resemblance,[1] yet they differ seriously as to face and body. They were certainly cast from different matrices and adjustments of the mould,[2] and were composed by different compositors. In the edition of *30 lines*, the types of the text are on a body smaller than English, and those of the large lines are on Paragon body; in the edition of *31 lines* the types of the text are on English body, and those of the large lines approximate Double-pica body.

Pica Body.

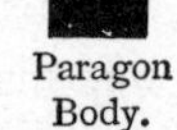

Paragon Body.

English Body.

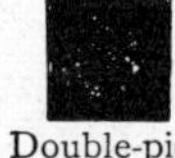

Double-pica Body.

The types on Double-pica body are those of the *Donatus* of 1451 and the *Bible of 36 lines;* the types on Paragon body are those of the *Bible of 42 lines.* The appearance of these types in the *Bibles* is presumptive evidence that the printer of the *Bibles* was the printer of the *Letters.* The small types are unique; they were never used, so far as we know, for any other work. The large initials may have been engraved on wood, but the text and the display lines were founded

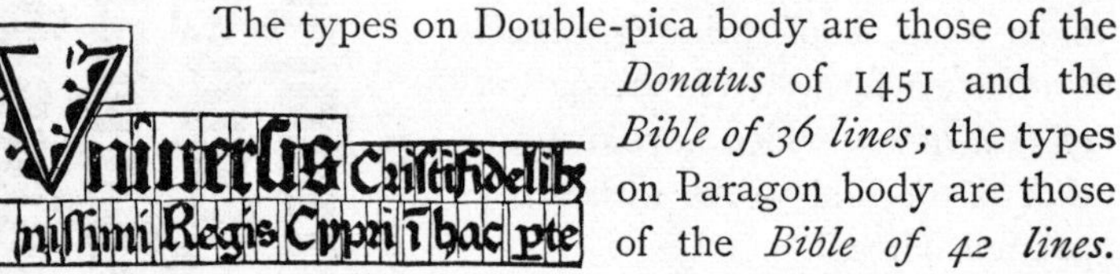

[From De la Borde.]

[1] The text letters are of the form known to librarians as *lettres de somme*, or letters of account, which may be understood as the carelessly made letters then used in books of account. The letters of the large lines are of the form known as *lettres de forme*, or letters of precision, the angular and carefully made letters of fine books. The *lettres de somme* will be defined in this book under the name of Round Gothic; the *lettres de forme*, under the name of Pointed Gothic.

[2] Deceived by the close fitting-up of the matrices, earlier writers said that the letters were xylographic. The comments of Dr. Van der Linde on this error are pertinent: .... It was thought necessary to find the wooden letters of the imagination, and hence bibliography presents the dismal spectacle that almost all monuments of the excellent invention, that fruit of a vigorous mind, of a simple, but ample and grand idea, have been declared by would-be connoisseurs one by one to be xylographic. This caused the double trouble of first making out, with much verbosity and an air of perspicuity, incontrovertibly typographical masterpieces to be wood, and then afterward putting aside this pedantry and returning to the simple truth. The origin of typography presents nowhere anything narrow-minded, worthless, or trifling, for it belongs to the *grand* facts of history, but trifling minds have soiled it with their own littleness. *Haarlem Legend*, p. 77.

types. The illustration on the previous page shows that although the matrices were fitted with closeness, each type was founded on a square body.

The circumstances connected with the publication of the *Letters* require more than a passing notice, for they present the first specific indication of a demand for printing. These circumstances give us a glimmer of the corruption of some of the men who sold the indulgences—a corruption which, in the next century, brought down upon the sellers and the system the scorn of Holbein and the wrath of Luther.

Fac-simile of Holbein's Satire on the Sale of Indulgences.

[From Woltmann.]

The canon at the right absolves the kneeling young man, but points significantly to the huge money-chest into which the widow puts her mite. Three Dominicans, seated at the table, are preparing and selling indulgences: one of them, holding back the letter, greedily counts the money as it is paid down; another pauses in his writing, to repulse the penitent but penniless cripple; another is leering at the woman whose letter he delays. The pope, enthroned in the nave, and surrounded by cardinals, is giving a commission for the sale of the letters.

On the twelfth day of April, 1451, a plenary indulgence of three years was accorded by Pope Nicholas V to all who, from May 1, 1452, to May 1, 1455, should properly contribute with money to the aid of the alarmed king of Cyprus, then threatened by the Turks. Paul Zappe, an ambassador of the king of Cyprus, selected John de Castro as chief commissioner for the sale of the indulgences in Germany. Theodoric, archbishop of Mentz, gave him full permission to sell them, but held the commissioner accountable for the moneys collected. The precaution was justified. When the dreaded news of the capture of Constantinople (May 29, 1453) was received, John de Castro, thinking that Cyprus had also been taken, squandered the money he had collected. De Castro was arrested, convicted and sent to prison, but the scandal that had been created by the embezzlement greatly injured the sale of the indulgences. As the permission to sell indulgences expired by limitation on May 1, 1455, Zappe, the chief commissioner, made renewed and more vigorous efforts to promote the sale. It was found that, in the limited time allowed for sale, the customary process of copying was entirely too slow. There was, also, the liability that a hurried copyist would produce inexact copies; that an unscrupulous copyist or seller would issue spurious copies. These seem to have been the reasons that led Zappe to have the documents printed, which was accordingly done, with blank spaces for the insertion of the name of the buyer and the signature of the seller.

The typography of this *Letter of 31 lines* is much better than that of the *Donatus*, but it has many blemishes. The text is deformed with abbreviations; the lines are not evenly spaced out; the capital letters of the text are rudely drawn and carelessly cut. The white space below the sixteenth line, and the space and the crookedness in the three lines at the foot, are evidences that the types were not securely fastened in the chase. These faults provoke notice, but it must be admitted that the types were fairly fitted and stand in decent line. They were obviously cast in moulds of metal; it would be impracticable to make types so small in moulds of sand.

Eighteen copies of these *Letters of Indulgence* are known, all bearing the printed date of 1454 or of 1455. The places where they were sold having been written on the document by the seller, we discover that they must have been sold over a large territory, for one was issued at Copenhagen, another at Nuremberg, and another at Cologne. The large number of copies preserved is evidence that many copies must have

Vniuersis Cristifidelibus presentes litteras inspecturis Paulinus Chappe Consiliarius Ambasiator et procurator generalis Serenissimi Regis Cypri in hac parte Salutem in domino Cum Sanctissimus in christo pater et dominus noster dominus Nicolaus diuina prouidentia papa quintus. Afflictioni Regni Cypri misericorditer compatiens. contra perfidissimos crucis christi hostes. Theucros et Saracenos gratis concessit omnibus christifidelibus vbilibet constitutis ipsos per aspersionem sanguinis domini nostri ihesu christi pie exhortando qui infra trienium a prima die Maii anni domini Mccccliii incipiendum pro defensione catholice fidei et Regni predicti de facultatibus suis magis vel minus prout ipsorum videbitur conscientiis. procuratoribus vel nunciis Substitutis pie erogauerint vt Confessores ydonei seculares vel Regulares per ipsos eligendi confessionibus eorum auditis. pro commissis etiam Sedi Apostolice reseruatis excessibus criminibus atque delictis quantumcumque grauibus pro vna vice tantum debitam absolutionem impendere et penitentiam salutarem iniungere Necnon si id humiliter petierint ipsos a quibuscumque excommunicationum suspensionum et Interdicti Aliisque sententiis censuris et penis ecclesiasticis a Jure vel ab homine promulgatis quibus forsan innodati existunt absoluere. Iniuncta pro modo culpe penitentia salutari vel aliis que de Jure fuerint iniungenda Ac eis vere penitentibus et confessis. vel si forsan propter amissionem loquele confiteri non poterint signa contritionis ostendendo plenissimam omnium peccatorum suorum de quibus ore confessi et corde contriti fuerint Indulgentiam ac plenariam remissionem semel in vita et semel in mortis articulo ipsis auctoritate apostolica concedere valeant. Satisfactione per eos facta si superuixerint aut per eorum heredes si tunc transierint Sic tamen. quod post indultum concessum per vnum annum singulis sextis feriis vel quadam alia die ieiunent. legitimo impedimento ecclesie precepto Regulari obseruantia. penitentia iniuncta voto uel alias non obstantibus. Et ipsis impeditis in dicto anno uel eius parte Anno sequenti uel alias quam primum poterint ieiunabunt. Et si in aliquo annorum vel eorum parte dictum ieiunium commode adimplere nequiuerint Confessor ad id electus in alia commutare poterit caritatis opera que ipsi facere etiam teneantur Dummodo tamen ex confidentia remissionis huiusmodi quod absit peccare non presumant Alioquin dicta concessio quo ad plenariam remissionem in mortis articulo et remissio quo ad peccata ex confidentia vt premittitur commissa nullius sint roboris uel momenti Et quia deuotus Judocus Ott von Apspach ——— iuxta dictum indultum de facultatibus suis pie erogauit merito huiusmodi indulgentiis gaudere debet In veritatis testimonium Sigillum ad hoc ordinatum presentibus litteris testimonialibus est appensum Datum Maguntie sub Anno domini Mccccliiii die vero vltima Mensis Decembris

Forma plenissime absolutionis et remissionis in vita

Misereatur tui etc. Dominus noster ihesus christus per suam sanctissimam et piissimam misericordiam te absoluat Et auctoritate ipsius beatorumque petri et pauli apostolorum eius ac auctoritate apostolica michi commissa et tibi concessa Ego te absoluo ab omnibus peccatis tuis contritis confessis et oblitis Etiam ab omnibus casibus excessibus criminibus atque delictis quantumcumque grauibus Sedi apostolice reseruatis Necnon a quibuscumque excommunicationum suspensionum et interdicti aliisque sententiis censuris et penis ecclesiasticis a Jure vel ab homine promulgatis si quas incurristi dando tibi plenissimam omnium peccatorum tuorum indulgentiam et remissionem Inquantum claues sancte matris ecclesie in hac parte se extendunt. In nomine patris et filii et spiritus sancti Amen.

Forma plenarie remissionis in mortis articulo

Misereatur tui etc. Dominus noster ut supra Ego te absoluo ab omnibus peccatis tuis contritis confessis et oblitis restituendo te vnitati fidelium et sacramentis ecclesie Remittendo tibi penas purgatorii quas propter culpas et offensas incurristi dando tibi plenariam omnium peccatorum tuorum remissionem. Inquantum claues sancte matris ecclesie in hac parte se extendunt. In nomine patris et filii et spiritus sancti Amen.

Jo. abbas monasterii sancti burckardi
ad promissa deputatus

Reduced Fac-simile of a Letter of Indulgence, dated 1454.

[From De la Borde.]

Translation.

all the faithful followers of Christ who may read this letter, Paul pe, counselor, ambassador, and administrator-general of his ious majesty, the king of Cyprus, sends greeting: hereas the Most Holy Father in Christ, our Lord, Nicholas V, by e grace, pope, mercifully compassionating the afflictions of the dom of Cyprus from those most treacherous enemies of the Cross hrist, the Turks and Saracens, in an earnest exhortation, by the kling of the blood of our Lord Jesus Christ, freely granted to all faithful followers of Christ, wheresoever established, who, within e years from the first day of May, in the year of our Lord 1452, d piously contribute, according to their ability, more or less, as it d seem good to their own consciences, to the procurators, or their ties, for the defense of the Catholic religion and the aforemend kingdom,—that confessors, secular and regular, chosen by thems, having heard their confessions for excesses, crimes, and faults, ever great, even for those hitherto reserved exclusively for the tolic see to remit, should be licensed to pronounce due absolution them, and enjoin salutary penance; and, also, that they might lve those persons, if they should humbly beseech it, who, perchance t be suffering excommunication, suspension, and other sentences, ures, and ecclesiastical punishments, instituted by canon law, or ulgated by man,—salutary penance being required, or other satison which might be enjoined by canon law, varying according to the e of the offence; and, also, that they might be empowered by olic authority to grant to those who were truly penitent, and cond their guilt, or if perchance, on account of the loss of speech, they not confess, those who gave outward demonstrations of contrition fullest indulgence of all their sins, and a full remission, as well g life as in the hour of death—reparation being made by them y should survive, or by their heirs if they should then die: And enance required after the granting of the indulgence is this—that should fast throughout a whole year on every Friday, or some other of the week, the lawful hindrances to performance being prescribed e regular usage of the Church, a vow or any other thing not standn the way of it; and as for those prevented from so doing in the d year, or any part of it, they should fast in the following year, any year they can; and if they should not be able conveniently to fulfill the required fast in any of the years, or any part of them, the confessor, for that purpose shall be at liberty to commute it for other acts of charity, which they should be equally bound to do: And all this, so that they presume not, which God forbid, to sin from the assurance of remission of this kind, for otherwise, that which is called concession, whereby they are admitted to full remission in the hour of death, and remission, which, as it is promised, leads them to sin with assurance, would be of no weight and validity: And whereas the devout *Judocus Ott von Apspach*, in order to obtain the promised indulgence, according to his ability hath piously contributed to the above-named laudable purpose, he is entitled to enjoy the benefit of indulgence, of this nature. In witness of the truth of the above concession, the seal ordained for this purpose is affixed. Given at *Mentz* in the year of our Lord 1454, on the *last day of December*.

THE FULLEST FORM OF ABSOLUTION AND REMISSION DURING LIFE: May our Lord Jesus Christ bestow on thee His most holy and gracious mercy; may he absolve thee, both by his own authority and that of the blessed Peter and Paul, His apostles; and by the authority apostolic committed unto me, and conceded on thy behalf, I absolve thee from all thy sins repented for with contrition, confessed and forgotten, as also from all carnal sins, excesses, crimes and delinquencies ever so grievous, and whose cognizance is reserved to the Holy See, as well as from any ecclesiastical judgment, censure, and punishment, promulgated either by law or by man, if thou hast incurred any,—giving thee plenary indulgence and remission of all thy sins, inasmuch as in this matter the keys of the Holy Mother Church do avail. In the name of the Father, and the Son, and the Holy Ghost. Amen.

THE PLENARY FORM OF REMISSION AT THE POINT OF DEATH: May our Lord [as above]. I absolve thee from all thy sins, with contrition repented for, confessed and forgotten, restoring thee to the unity of the faithful, and the partaking of the sacraments of the Church, releasing thee from the torments of purgatory, which thou hast incurred, by giving thee plenary remission of all thy sins, inasmuch as in this matter the keys of the Mother Church do avail. In the name of the Father, and the Son, and the Holy Ghost. Amen.

Joseph, abbot of the Monastery of Saint Burckard,
Duly qualified to make this engagement.

been printed. It is probable that Gutenberg was required to compose and print the form at three different times; but we do not know why he found it necessary to make a new face of text type for the second and third editions,[1] for it is very plain that the types of the first edition were not worn out.

The Appeal of Christianity against the Turks, sometimes called the *Almanac of 1455*, is another small work attributed to Gutenberg. It is a little quarto of six printed leaves, in German verse, in the large type of the *Bible of 36 lines*. As it contains a calendar for the year 1455, it is supposed that it was printed at the close of 1454. Its typographical appearance is curious: the type was large, the page was narrow, and the compositor run the lines together as in prose, marking the beginning of every verse with a capital, and its ending by a fanciful arrangement ·:· of four full points. It is the first typographic work in German, and the first work in that language which can be attributed to Gutenberg. But one copy of this book is known.

Gutenberg's fame as a great printer is more justly based on his two editions in folio of the *Holy Bible* in Latin. The breadth of his mind, and his faith in the comprehensiveness of his invention, are more fully set forth by his selection of a book of so formidable a nature. There was an admirable propriety in his determination that his new art should be fairly introduced to the reading world by the book known

[1] It is possible that other books, now lost and forgotten, may have been printed in the small types, but Helbig thinks that the types were made expressly for the *Letters of Indulgence*, as bank-notes are now made, with the intention that the copies of each edition should be exactly alike in appearance, and that they should be difficult of imitation. Bernard dissents from the belief that the *Letters of Indulgence* were printed by Gutenberg. He attributes them to some printer of unknown name in Mentz, supposed by him to have been either the false workman described by Junius, or some graduate or seceding malcontent of Gutenberg's printing office. But we have no evidence of a typographical printer before Gutenberg. Jäck has endeavored to prove that two *Letters* were printed by Pfister of Bamberg. De la Borde thinks one of the faces of type used in the *Letters* was cut by Schœffer in a friendly competition with Gutenberg. These conjectures cannot be made plausible.

throughout Christendom as *The Book.* These two editions of the *Bible* are most clearly defined by the specification of the number of lines to the page in the columns of each book: one is the *Bible of 42 lines*,[1] in types of Paragon body, usually bound in two volumes; the other is the *Bible of 36 lines*,[2] in types of Double-pica body, usually bound in three volumes.

It is not certainly known which was printed first. Each edition was published without printed date, and, like all other works by Gutenberg, without name or place of printer. They were not accurately described by any contemporary author. In the sixteenth century they were obsolete, and the tradition that they had been printed by Gutenberg was entirely lost. When a copy of the *Bible of 42 lines* was discovered in the library of Cardinal Mazarin, and was identified as the work of John Gutenberg, it was not known that there was another edition. The *Bible of 42 lines* was consequently regarded as the first—as the book described by Zell, which, he says, was printed in 1450. This belief was strengthened by the subsequent discovery, in another copy of this edition, of the certificate of an illuminator that, in the year 1456, he had finished his task of illumination in the book. More than twenty copies of this edition (seven of which are on vellum) have been found, and they have generally been sold and bought as copies of the first edition.

The *Bible of 36 lines* was definitely described for the first time by the bibliographer Schwartz, who, in 1728, discovered a copy in the library of a monastery near Mentz. In the old manuscript catalogue of this library was a note, stating that this book had been given to the monastery by John Guten-

[1] It is sometimes described as the *Mazarin Bible*, and sometimes as *Gutenberg's First Bible*.

[2] This is known as the *Bamberg Bible*, because nearly all the known copies of this edition were found in the neighborhood of the town of Bamberg; as *Pfister's Bible*, because it has been attributed, incorrectly, to Albert Pfister, a printer of Bamberg; as the *Schelhorn Bible*, because it was fully described by the bibliographer of that name; as *Gutenberg's Second Bible*, because it is the belief of many authors that it should have been printed by Gutenberg about 1459, after his rupture with John Fust.

berg and his associates. Schwartz said that this must have been the first edition. A still more exact description of this edition was published by Schelhorn in 1760, under the title of *The Oldest Edition of the Latin Bible.* He said that this must have been the edition described by Zell.

The *Bible of 36 lines* is a large demy folio of 1764 pages, made up, for the most part, in sections of ten leaves, and usually bound in three volumes. Each page has two columns of 36 lines each. In some sections, a leaf torn out, possibly on account of some error, has been replaced by the insertion of a single leaf or a half sheet. The workmanship of the first section is inferior: the indentation of paper by too hard pressure is very strongly marked; the pages are sadly out of register; on one page the margins and white space between the columns show the marks of a wooden chase and bearers, which were used to equalize impression and prevent undue wear of types. This section has the appearance of experimental or unpractised workmanship. It is apparent, almost at a glance, that the printer did not use a proper chase and bearers, nor a frisket, nor points for making register.[1] All other sections were printed with the proper appliances, with uncommon neatness of presswork, in black ink, with exact register, and with a nicely graduated impression, which shows the sharp edges of the types with clearness.

The types of this book closely resemble, in face and body, many letters being identically the same, the types of the display line in the *Letter of Indulgence of 31 lines*, and of the *Donatus of 1451.* In some features they resemble the types of the *Bible of 42 lines.* It is possible that the types of each edition were designed and made by the same letter cutter, and that they were made for and used by the same printer. This opinion is strengthened after an inspection of the mannerisms of the composition, which are those of the *Bible of 42 lines.* The colon, period, and hyphen are the only marks of punctuation. The lines of text are not always full: the hyphen

[1] Bernard, *De l'origine et des debuts de l'imprimerie,* vol. II, p. 30.

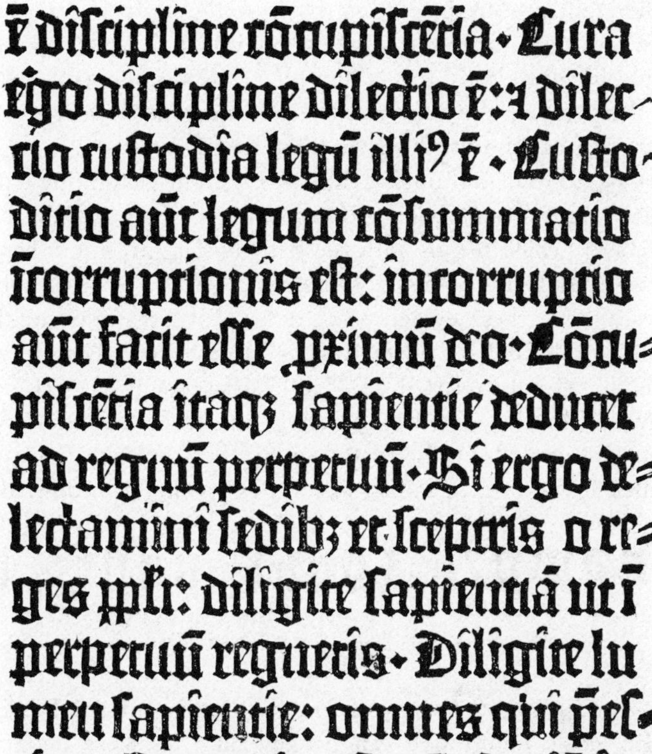

ē discipline cōcupiscētia. Cura
ergo discipline dilectio ē: ⁊ dilectio custodia legū illi⁹ ē. Custo-
ditio aūt legum cōsummatio
icorruptionis est: incorruptio
aūt facit esse ꝑximū deo. Cōcupiscētia itaq; sapientie deducet
ad regnū perpetuū. Si ergo de-
lectamini sedib; et sceptris o re-
ges ppli: diligite sapientiā ut ī
perpetuū regnetis. Diligite lumen sapientie: omnes qui p̄es-
tis pplis. Quid est aūt sapiētia
et quēadmodū facta sit referā
⁊ non abscondam a vobis sa-
cramenta dei: sed ab inicio na-
tivitatis īvestigabo: et ponā ī
lucem scientiā illius. ⁊ non p̄te-
ribo veritatē: neq; cum īvidia

Fac-simile of the Types of the Bible of 36 Lines, with the Rubricator's Marks on the Capitals. Verses 17 to 22 of the Sixth Chapter of the Book of Wisdom.

[Photographed from a Fragment of the Original in the Collection of Mr. David Wolfe Bruce.]

is frequently seen projecting beyond the letters. A blank space was left for every large initial which, it was expected, would be inserted by the calligrapher. Red ink was not used by the printer; the rubricated letters were dabbed over with a stroke from the brush of the illuminator.

One copy of the book contains a written annotation dated 1461. An account book of the Abbey of Saint Michael of Bamberg, which begins with the date March 21, 1460, has in its original binding some of the waste leaves of this Bible. These, the earliest evidences of date, prove that this edition could not have been printed later than 1459. That it was done in 1450, as asserted by Madden, has not been decisively proved, but the evidence favoring this conclusion deserves consideration. Ulric Zell's testimony that the first *Bible* was printed in 1450 from missal-like types,[1] points with directness

et rum con pp per us s contractions pro

Some of the Abbreviations of the Bible of 36 lines.

[From Duverger.]

to the *Bible of 36 lines*, for there is no other printed Bible to which Zell's description can be applied. Its close imitation of the large and generous style in which the choicer manuscripts of that period are written marks the period of transition between the old and the new style of book-making. The prodigality in the use of paper seems the work of a man who had not counted the cost, or who thought that he was obliged to disregard the expense. As not more than half a dozen copies are known, it is probable that the number printed was small. Nearly all the copies and leaves of this edition were found in the neighborhood of Bamberg. This curious circumstance may be explained by the supposition that the entire edition, probably small, had been printed at the order of, or

[1] In the year of our Lord 1450, they began to print, and the first book they printed was the *Bible* in Latin: it was printed in a large letter, resembling the letter with which, at present, missals are printed. *Cologne Chronicle* of 1499.

had been mortgaged to, one of the many ecclesiastical bodies of that town. There is evidence that Gutenberg frequently borrowed money from wealthy monasteries. The imperfect workmanship of the first section is, apparently, the work of a printer in the beginning of his practice, when he had not discovered all the tools and implements which he afterward used with so much success.[1]

The *Bible of 36 lines* should have been in press a long time, for it cannot be supposed that Gutenberg had the means to do this work with regularity. His office was destitute of composing sticks and rules, iron chases, galleys, and imposing stones. Deprived of these and other labor-saving tools, without the expertness acquired by practice, frequently delayed by the corrections of the reader, the failures of the type-founder and the errors of pressmen, it is not probable that the compositor perfected more than one page a day. He may have done less. Even if, as Madden supposes, two or more compositors were engaged on this, as they were upon other early work, the *Bible of 36 lines* should have been in press about three years.[2]

The newness of the types seems to favor the opinion that this must be the earlier edition. The same types, or types cast from the same matrices, were frequently used in little books printed between the years 1451 and 1462, but they always appear with worn and blunted faces, as if they had

[1] In the first essays of printing, great difficulties were encountered. For when they [the first printers] were printing the Bible, they were obliged to expend more than four thousand florins before they had printed three sections. Trithemius, as reprinted by Wolf, *Monumenta Typographica*, vol. II, p. 654.

[2] These evidences, which seem to favor the theory of the priority of the *Bible of 36 lines*, combine many features of probability, but they are not free from objections. Too little is known about the book to warrant a positive statement as to its age. In nearly all the popular treatises on printing, the *Bible of 42 lines* is specified as the first book of Gutenberg, but it is the belief of many of the most learned bibliographers, from Zapf to Didot and Madden, that the *Bible of 36 lines* is the older edition. The theory that it must have been printed by Gutenberg between 1457 and 1459, and the proposition that it may have been printed by Albert Pfister of Bamberg at or soon after that time, will be examined on an advanced page.

been rounded under the long-continued pressure of a press, or had been founded in old and clogged matrices.

Gutenberg deceived himself as much as he did his Strasburg partners, in his over-sanguine estimate of the profits of printing and the difficulties connected with its practice. His printed work did not meet with the rapid sale he had anticipated, or the cost of doing the work was very much in excess of the price he received. The great success which Andrew Dritzehen hoped to have within one year, or in 1440, had not been attained in 1450. During this year Gutenberg comes before us again as the borrower of money. If he had been only an ordinary dreamer about great inventions, he would have abandoned an enterprise so hedged in with mechanical and financial difficulties. But he was an inventor in the full sense of the word, an inventor of means as well as of ends, as resolute in bending indifferent men as he was in fashioning obdurate metal. After spending, ineffectually, all the money he had acquired from his industry, from his partners, from his inheritance, from his friends,—still unable to forego his great project,—he went, as a last resort, to one of the professional money-lenders of Mentz. "Heaven or hell," says Lacroix, "sent him the partner John Fust."[1]

The character and services of John Fust have been put

[1] His name is often improperly written as Faust. In all the books subsequently printed by Fust and his partner, Schœffer, the name appears as Fust. It was so written and printed by all his contemporaries, and is so seen, wherever it occurs, in the record of the famous trial he instituted. It is so spelt in the church record of his burial. During his lifetime, and for at least thirty years after his death, the name is always given as Fust. The notorious reputation subsequently made by Dr. John Faust, who was born in Wurtemberg in 1480 (several years after the death of Fust), who studied magic in Cracow, and, by his learning and wickedness, horrified wise men like Luther and Melancthon; whose life, deeds and death are involved in a mystery that dramatists have turned to such good account, has been transferred by carelessness to John Fust, the printer. The confusion has been perpetuated by a legend. The fable, not yet weeded out of treatises on printing, that Fust was arrested in Paris for selling bibles, supposed to have been manufactured at the instigation of the devil, has served to foster the error.

before us in strange lights. By some of the earlier writers he was most untruly represented as the inventor of typography, as the instructor, as well as the partner, of Gutenberg. By another class of authors he has been regarded as the patron and benefactor of Gutenberg, a man of public spirit, who had the wit to see the great value of Gutenberg's new art, and the courage to unite his fortunes with those of the needy inventor. This latter view has been popular: to this day, Fust is thoroughly identified with all the honors of the invention. The unreasonableness of this pretension has sent other writers to the opposite extreme. During the present century, Fust has been frequently painted as a greedy and crafty speculator, who took a mean advantage of the needs of Gutenberg, and basely robbed him of the fruits of his invention.[1]

John Fust.
[From Maittaire.]

It is possible that Gutenberg knew John Fust, the money-lender, through business relations with Fust's brother, James, the goldsmith; for we have seen that, during his experiments in Strasburg, Gutenberg had work done by two goldsmiths. What projects Gutenberg unfolded to John Fust, and what allurements he set forth, are not known; but the wary money-lender would not have hazarded a guilder on Gutenberg's invention, if he had not been convinced of its value and of Gutenberg's ability. John Fust knew that there was some risk in the enterprise, for it is probable that he had heard of

[1] Those who favor this view of Fust's character, find a peculiar significance in the radical meaning of his name, Fust—in German, fist, the symbol of all that is hard, close, grasping, and aggressive.

the losses of Dritzehen, Riffe and Heilmann. In making an alliance with the inventor, Fust neglected none of the precautions of a money-lender. He really added to them, insisting on terms through which he expected to receive all the advantages of a partnership without its liabilities.[1]

The terms were hard. But Gutenberg had the firmest faith in the success of his invention: in his view it was not only to be successful, but so enormously profitable that he could well afford to pay all the exactions of the money-lender. The object of the partnership is not explicitly stated, but it was, without doubt, the business of printing and publishing text books, and, more especially, the production of a grand edition of the *Bible*, the price of a fair manuscript copy of which, at that time, was five hundred guilders. The expense that would be made in printing a large edition of this work seemed trivial in comparison with the sum which Gutenberg dreamed would be readily paid for the new books. But the expected profit was not the only allurement. Gutenberg was, no doubt, completely dominated by the idea that necessity was laid on him—that he must demonstrate the utility and grandeur of his invention,—and this must be done whether the demonstration beggared or enriched him. After sixteen years of labor, almost if not entirely fruitless, he snatched at the partnership with Fust as the only means by which he could realize the great purpose of his life. The overruling power of the money-lender was shown in the begin-

[1] These were the terms of the contract, made in August, 1450:

The partnership between Gutenberg and Fust should be for five years, in which time the work projected by Gutenberg should be completed.—For the purposes of this partnership, not specified, Fust should advance to Gutenberg 800 guilders, at 6 per cent. interest. The tools and materials made by Gutenberg for the uses of the partnership should remain mortgaged to Fust, as security for this loan of 800 guilders, until the whole sum should be paid.—When the aforesaid tools and materials should be made, Fust should, every year, furnish Gutenberg with 300 guilders to provide for the payment of the paper, vellum, ink, wages and the other materials that would be required for the execution of the work.—For these advances Fust should have one-half of the profits made from the sale of the products of the partnership.—Fust should be exempted from the performance of any work or service connected with the partnership, and should not be held responsible for any of its debts.

ing of the partnership. Gutenberg had ready the types of the *Bible of 36 lines*, and had, perhaps, printed a few copies of the work—too few to supply the demand. Another edition could have been printed without delay, but it was decided that this new edition should be in a smaller type and in two volumes. It was intended that the cost of the new edition should be about one-third less than that of the *Bible of 36 lines*. Gutenberg was, consequently, obliged to cut a new face and found a new font of types, which, by the terms of the agreement, were to be mortgaged to Fust.

Fust did not assist Gutenberg as he should have done. Instead of paying the 800 guilders at once, as was implied in the agreement, he allowed two years to pass before this amount was fully paid. The equipment of the printing office with new types was sadly delayed. At the end of the two years, when Gutenberg was ready to print, he needed for the next year's expenses, and for the paper and vellum for the entire edition, more than the 300 guilders allowed to him by the agreement of 1450. Fust, perceiving the need of Gutenberg, saw also his opportunity for a stroke in finance, which would assist him in the designs which he seems to have entertained from the beginning. He proposed a modification of the contract—to commute the annual payment of 300 guilders for the three successive years by the immediate payment of 800 guilders. As an offset to the loss Gutenberg would sustain by this departure from the contract, Fust proposed to remit his claim to interest on the 800 guilders that had been paid. Gutenberg, eager for the money, and credulous, assented to these modifications.

The delays and difficulties which Gutenberg encountered in the printing of this edition were great, but no part of the work was done hastily or unadvisedly. He may not have received practical education as a book-maker, but he had the rare good sense to accept instruction from those who had. The *Bible of 42 lines* was obviously planned by an adept in all the book-making skill of his time. It was laid out in 66 sections, for the most part of 10 leaves each. To facilitate the division of the book in parts (so that it could be bound, if necessary for the convenience of the reader, in ten thin volumes), some of the sections have but 4, some 11, and some 12 leaves. The book proper, without the summary of contents, consists of 1282 printed pages, 2 columns to the page, and, for the most part, with 42 lines to the column.[1]

A wide margin was allowed for the ornamental borders, without which no book of that time was complete, and large spaces were also left in the text for the great initial letters. It was expected that the purchaser of the book would have the margins and spaces covered with the fanciful designs and bright colors of the illuminator. In some copies, this work of illumination was admirably done; in others it was badly done or entirely neglected. The rubrics were roughly made by dabbing a brush filled with red ink over a letter printed in black. On the pages of 40 lines, the summaries of chapters were printed in red ink; on other pages the summaries were written, sometimes in red and sometimes in black ink.

[1] There are two kinds of copies, with differences which seem to justify the opinion that they belong to two distinct editions. In one kind, all the copies have 42 lines to the column, and all the summaries of chapters are written and not printed. In the other kind, the first eight pages of the first section have 40 lines to the column; the ninth page has 41 lines; the tenth and all other pages (except two 40-line pages in the book of *Maccabees*) have 42 lines; and the pages of 40 and 41 lines have their five summaries printed in red ink. The same face of type is used in both kinds of copies, but the pages of 40 and 41 lines occupy the same space as the pages of 42 lines, beginning and ending, for the most part, with the same words. Bernard says that the 40-line pages were reset by Peter Schœffer after Fust had acquired the unsold copies of the *Bible*, with intent to lead the purchaser of the book to form the belief that it was an entirely new edition. Other writers suggest that a portion of the first section may have been spoiled, and replaced by a subsequent reprinting. But the differences are not confined to the first section. In many other sections there are differences in the spelling and abbreviation of words which clearly prove that the two kinds of copies were printed from separately composed and distinct forms. The double composition of every page for the same edition seems a ridiculous waste of labor, but the proofs of this double labor are unmistakable.

It would seem that it was Gutenberg's original intention to print all the summaries in red ink, and that he was obliged, for some unknown reason, to have them written in.

The general effect of the typography is that of excessive blackness,—an effect which seems to have been made of set purpose, for the designer of the types made but sparing use of hair lines. It may be that the avoidance of hair lines was caused by difficulties of type-founding. The type-founding was properly done: the types have solid faces and stand in line. The letters are not only black but condensed, and are so closely connected that they seem to have been spread by pressure. Double letters and abbreviations were freely used. Judged by modern standards, the types are ungraceful; the text letters are too dense and black, and the capitals are of rude form, obscure, and too small for the text. The presswork is unequal: on some vellum copies, the types are clearly and sharply printed; on other copies, they show muddily from excess of ink. On the paper copies, the ink is usually of a full black, but there are pages on paper and on vellum, in which, for lack of ink and impression,[1] the color is of a grimy gray-black. Van der Linde and others say that the ink will not resist water, but the ink on the fragments of vellum belonging to Mr. Bruce stood a severe test by water, without any weakening of color. The register on the paper copies is very good; on the vellum copies it is offensively irregular, a plain proof that the vellum had been dampened, and had shrunk or twisted before the second side was printed.

It has been said that this *Bible of 42 lines* was printed with intent to cheat purchasers, so that it might be sold as a manuscript. There is a legend that Fust did attempt the cheat at Paris, but there is no good authority for the libel, which scarcely deserves examination. There were, no doubt, during the fifteenth century, many who could not perceive

[1] Bernard says that over-colored and under-colored pages are by no means rare. He attributes this unequal blackness to imperfections in the inking implements. *De l'origine de l'imprimerie*, vol. I, p. 182.

the dissimilarities between manuscript and printed books, but these men were not book-buyers. To the intelligent book-buyer, the features of dissimilarity were conspicuous.[1] It is not at all probable that Gutenberg entertained any thought of deception: he imitated his manuscript copy only because it was in an approved style of book-making.

Although the types of this *Bible* are obsolete, there is something pleasing in their boldness and solidity to a reader who is wearied with the small trim letters, light lines and apparently paler ink of modern books. The effect of rugged strength is relieved by the flowing lines, vivid colors and complex ornamentation of the odd borders and initials which have been added by designer and illuminator. How much of the pleasure derived from an inspection of the work is due to the skill of the printer, and how much to the art of the illuminator, has not always been judicially weighed by those who represent the book as a specimen of perfect printing. It cannot be denied that the most attractive features of the book are those made, not by printing, but by illumination, but it is plain that the designs and ornamentation are not of a character appropriate to the text. They would not be allowed in any modern edition of the book.

The workmanship of the printer in his own proper field is wonderful when we regard the circumstances under which it was done, but it would not satisfy the requirements of a modern publisher or book-buyer. It is of its own time, with the faults of that time, in manner and matter. The promise of legibility, which seems warranted by the bold and black types, is delusive. The ordinary Latin scholar cannot read the book, nor refer to any passage in it, with satisfaction. It is without title and paging figures. The blank spaces which indicate changes of subject, and give relief to the eye, were seized by the illuminator. Verse follows verse, and chapter follows chapter, and one line chases another with a grudg-

[1] See the fac-similes of Sotheby and Humphreys. The written summaries of this Bible, as they present them, are unlike the printed text.

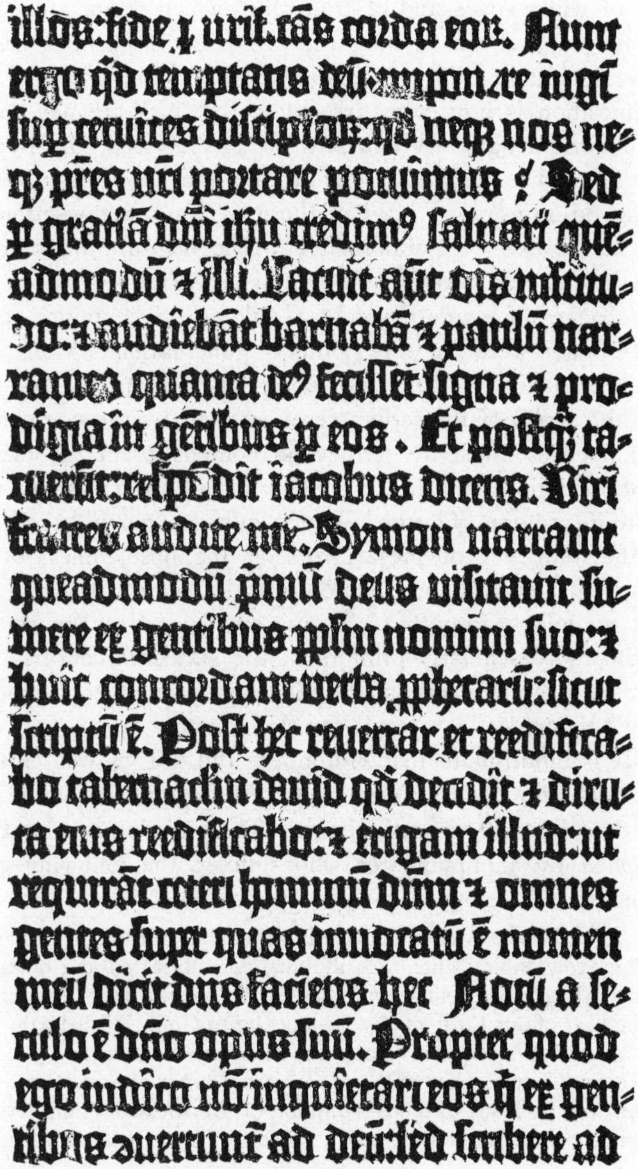

illos: fide purificās corda eorū. Nunc
ergo qd temptatis deū imponere iugū
sup ceruices discipulorū: qd neq; nos ne-
q; patres nři portare potuimus? Sed
p gratiā dñi ihu credim⁹ saluari quēadmodū ꝛ illi. Tacuit aūt oīs multitu-
do: ꝛ audiebāt barnabā ꝛ paulū nar-
rantes quanta de⁹ fecisset signa ꝛ pro-
digia in gētibus p eos. Et postq; ta-
cuerūt: respōdit iacobus dicens. Viri
fratres audite me. Symon narrauit
queadmodū primū deus visitauit su-
mere ex gentibus ppl'm nomini suo: ꝛ
huic concordant verba ꝓphetarū: sicut
scriptū ē. Post hec reuertar et reedificabo tabernaculū dauid qd decidit: ꝛ diru-
ta eius reedificabo: ꝛ erigam illud: ut
requirāt ceteri hominū dñm ꝛ omnes
gentes sup quas inuocatū ē nomen
meū dicit dñs faciens hec. Notū a se-
culo ē dño opus suū. Propter quod
ego iudico nō inquietari eos q ex gentibus ꝯuertunt ad deū: sed scribere ad

Fac-simile of the Types of the Bible of 42 Lines, with the Rubricator's Marks on the Capitals. Verses 10 to 20 of the Fifteenth Chapter of the Acts of the Apostles.

[Photographed from a Fragment of the Original in the Collection of Mr. David Wolfe Bruce.]

ing of white space and of true relief which is not atoned for by the dabs of red in the rubrics, nor by the profuse wealth of ornamentation in the centre column and margins. The composition is noticeably irregular: the lines are not always of uniform length. When a word was divided, the hyphen was allowed to project and give to the right side of the column a ragged appearance. When there were too many letters for the line, words were abbreviated. The measure was narrow, and it was only through the liberal use of abbreviations that the spacing of words could be regulated. The period, colon and hyphen were the only points of punctuation.

The manuscript taken for copy was not strictly accurate, and the errors of the scribe were repeated by the compositor. The liberties taken by scribe and compositor in the making of abbreviations, and in the spelling out of abbreviations, were a prolific source of error. It was quite as much on account of the frequency of these errors, as the obsoleteness of the types, that this famous edition was so soon laid aside and was so quickly forgotten. It was supplanted by the editions of the more scholarly printers of the sixteenth century, who collated a great many manuscript and printed copies before they prepared a new copy for the printer.

It is unfortunate that Gutenberg did not, as was customary with the book-makers of that time, put his name and the date of printing on the book. The omission was partially supplied by an illuminator who suffixed the following colophons or subscriptions to his copy of the book:

First Volume. Here endeth the First Part of the Old Testament of the Holy Bible, which was illuminated, rubricated and bound by Henry Albech, or Cremer, on Saint Bartholomew's Day (August 24), in the year of our Lord 1456. Thanks be to God. Hallelujah.

Second Volume. This Book was illuminated, bound and perfected by Henry Cremer, vicar of the Collegiate Church of Saint Stephen in Mentz, on the Feast of the Assumption of the Blessed Virgin (August 15), in the year of our Lord 1456. Thanks be to God. Hallelujah.

As the second volume was illuminated nine days before the first volume, it may be supposed that, on this copy, the work of illumination was started on the sheets, as soon as they had been printed and before they were bound. It is possible that the last sheet was printed in 1456, but it is a more general belief that the work was completed in 1455.

There is no tradition about the number printed. At the close of the century, three hundred copies were regarded by printers of Italy as a proper number for an edition in folio. It is not probable that Gutenberg printed so large a number. Unbound copies were sold at different times and places, not long after publication, for various sums ranging from twelve guilders to sixty crowns.[1] It does not appear that the books provoked any enthusiasm: no chronicler of that time thought it worth while to give them even a passing mention. We have to suppose that they attracted no more attention than the books of a copyist. It appears, also, that the *Bible of 42 lines*, from a mercantile point of view, was a very unsuccessful enterprise. This is the evidence.

On the sixth day of November, 1455, Fust brought a suit for the recovery of the money advanced to Gutenberg. As Gutenberg was unable to pay the demand, we may suppose that the *Bible* had not been completed, or, had not met with a ready sale. The suit of John Fust has been the occasion of discordant criticism. Dibdin fully justifies his action, and intimates that Gutenberg was really a trickster, who would have defrauded Fust if he had not resorted to summary proceedings. The defenders of Fust, who are few, have to admit that he here appears as a keen man of business, destitute of sentiment, and of ungenerous disposition. Sympathizers with Gutenberg denounce Fust as a cunning schemer, who had made the terms of the partnership rigorous with the secret determination to get possession of the invention through Gutenberg's inability to keep his contract.

This is the record of the proceedings before the court:

[1] At the sale of the Perkins library near London, June 6, 1873, a copy of the *Bible of 42 lines*, on vellum, was sold for £3,400, and a copy on paper for £2,690—more than the first printers got for all the copies.

INSTRUMENT of a certain day, when Fust produced an account and confirmed it by an oath. In the name of God. Amen. Be it known to all who shall see this public document or hear it read, that, in the year of our Lord 1455, on Thursday, the 6th of November, between eleven and twelve at noon, at Mentz, in the large dining-hall *(refectorium)* of the convent of bare-footed friars, appeared before me, notary, and the witnesses to be mentioned hereafter, the honorable and prudent man Jacob Fust, citizen of Mentz, and has, in behalf of Johan Fust his brother, also present, shewn, said and exposed, that to the said Johan Fust on the one side and Johan Gutenberg on the other, should be administered the oath, according to judgment passed on both the parties, and for which this day and this hour had been fixed and the hall of the convent assigned. In order that the friars of the said convent, who were still assembled in the hall, should not be disturbed, the said Jacob Fust did ask through his messenger, whether Johan Gutenberg, or any one for him, were present in the convent, in order to finish the matter. At this message came into the said refectorium the reverend Heinrich Gunther, pastor of St. Christopher's at Mentz, Heinrich Keffer, and Bertolf von Hanau, a servant of Johan Gutenberg, and when they had been asked by Johan Fust whether they had been authorized by Johan Gutenberg, they answered that they had been sent by Junker Johan Gutenberg to hear and see what should happen in this case. Thereupon Johan Fust begged leave to conform to the stipulations of the verdict, after he had waited for Johan Gutenberg till twelve o'clock, and was still waiting for him. He reads the sentence passed on the first article of his claim, from word to word, with its pretension and response, which runs as follows: First, that he, according to the written agreement, should lend Johan Gutenberg about 800 florins in gold, *with which he was to finish the work, and whether it would cost more or less was no matter to Fust;* and that Johan Gutenberg was to pay six per cent. interest for this money. He had indeed lent him these 800 guilders on a bond, but Gutenberg was not satisfied, but complained that he had not yet received the 800 guilders. For that reason, Fust, being desirous of doing him some service, lent him 800 guilders more than he was bound by his contract to do, for which 800 guilders Fust had to pay forty guilders as interest. And, although Gutenberg had bound himself by contract to pay six per cent. interest on the first 800 guilders, yet he had not done so for a single year, but Fust had to pay this interest himself to the amount of 250 guilders. For, at present, Gutenberg having never paid interest, and Fust having been obliged to borrow this interest from Christians and Jews, for which he had paid about thirty-six florins, his payments, together with the capital, amount to about 2,020 guilders, of which he demands reimbursement. Thereupon, Johan Gutenberg answered that Johan Fust had agreed to lend him 800 guilders, *with which money he was to arrange and make his tools*, and that these *tools* should remain as security for Fust. But Fust had moreover agreed to give him every year 300 guilders for *expenses*, and to advance also *wages*, *house-rent*, VELLUM, PAPER, INK, etc. If, afterward, they did not agree, Gutenberg should then pay the 800 guilders back, and the tools should be free from mortgage; it should be understood, that with the 800 guilders he had to make the *machine*, which was to be a pledge. He hopes not [that any one shall pretend] that he was obliged to spend these 800 guilders *on the work of the books* [*i. e.*, on vellum, paper, etc.] And, although it is said in the contract that Gutenberg was to pay six per cent. interest, Fust had told him that he had no intention of accepting this interest from him. Moreover, he had not received the 800 guilders in full and at once according to agreement, as Fust had pretended in the first article of his claim; and as for the second 800 guilders, he is ready to give an account of them, but declines to give him interest or usury for them, and hopes that he is not bound by law to pay them. We pass, therefore, sentence according to pretension and response: When Johan Gutenberg has submitted an account of all receipts and disbursements spent *on the work to their common profit* [*i. e.*, printing], this work shall be added to the 800 guilders; if he has spent more than the 800 guilders, which did not belong to their common profit, he should pay it back; if Fust is able to prove, on oath or by witnesses, that he has borrowed the money on interest, and did not lend it out of his own resources, then Gutenberg is bound by contract to pay it.

Now, after this sentence had been read in presence of the aforesaid witnesses, Johan Fust has, with raised fingers, in the hands of me, public notary, taken the oath by all the saints, that everything was comprised according to truth and sentence, in an act which he placed in my hands. He confirmed it on oath, as truly as God and the saints may help him; and the contents of this document were as follows:

I, Johan Fust, have borrowed 1,550 guilders, which have been received by Johan Gutenberg, and spent on our common work, for which I have paid an annual interest, and still owe a part of it. Therefore, I count for every hundred guilders which I have borrowed in this way, six guilders per annum; and for the money spent on our common work, I demand the interest according to judgment passed.

The said Johan Fust demands from me, public notary, one or more public acts of this matter, as many and as often as he should want them; and all these matters recorded here, happened in the year, indiction, day, hour, papacy, month, and town aforesaid, in the presence of the honest men, Peter Grauss, Johan Kist, Johan Knoff, Johan Yseneck, Jacob Fust, citizens of Mentz; Peter Gernsheim and Johan Bone, clerks of the city and diocese of Mentz, asked and summoned as witnesses. And I, Ulrich Helmasperger, clerk of the diocese of Bamberg, by imperial authority, public clerk of the Holy See at Mentz, sworn notary, have been present at all the aforesaid transactions and articles with the witnesses mentioned. Therefore, being requested to do so, I have signed with my hand, and sealed with my common seal, this public act, written by another, as testimony and true record of all the aforesaid matters.[1]

ULRICUS HELMASPERGER, *Notary.*

The suit brought by Fust was, apparently, a surprise, for it cannot be supposed that Gutenberg would have been so completely unprepared to meet his obligation if he had not been led to believe that Fust would postpone the collection of his claim. The enforcement of this claim before the book was published, or at least before money had been derived from its sale—taken in connection with the facts that the delay in the publication of the book, and Gutenberg's inability to pay his debt, were largely due to the delay of Fust in furnishing the money as he had promised—seems to warrant the charge that Fust meditated the despoilment of Gutenberg at the formation of the partnership. Gutenberg's defense before the court was very feeble: it is that of a man who knew he had no hope of success. He did not appear in person, but trusted his case to his workmen. Fust was more adroit; he was voluble and positive, and his relative, Jacob Fust, was one of the judges. But the fates were against Gutenberg: the hard terms of the contract he had signed compelled an adverse decision.

That Fust did Gutenberg a grievous wrong is very plain; that Gutenberg had managed the business of the partnership with economy and intelligence is not so clear. At no period of his life did the great inventor show any talent for financial administration. He was certainly deficient in many qualities that should be possessed by a man of business, and Fust may have thought that he was fully justified in placing his money

[1] Hessels' translation, as printed in the *Haarlem Legend*, pp. 24 and 25.

John Gutenberg...From an Old Print in the National Library at Paris.
[From Lacroix.]

interests in the hands of a more careful manager. This, a copy of the oldest engraving known of Gutenberg, presents him to us as a man of decided character, not to be cajoled or managed by a partner in business. The thin curving lip and pointed nose, the strongly marked lines on the forehead, the bold eyes and arrogant bearing of the head reveal to us a man of genius and of force, a man born to rule, impatient of restraint, and of inflexible resolution. We have but to look at the portrait of Fust to see that he, also, was accustomed to having his own way, and that he and Gutenberg were not at all adapted to each other as partners.

But Fust would not have broken with Gutenberg if he had not been prepared to put a competent successor in his place. In Peter Schœffer, a young man twenty-six years old, who had been employed in the printing office, Fust discerned an intelligent workman who gave promise of ability as a manager. Schœffer, who then hoped to win the hand of Fust's daughter Christina, was, no doubt, more complaisant than the irascible Gutenberg. As he was afterward married to her, it may be thought that she approved his suit in its beginning, and that her influence with her father was used to its utmost in favor of the removal of Gutenberg and the advancement of Schœffer. It was fully understood by the three conspirators that Gutenberg could make no proper defense; it was determined that he should be expelled from his place in the partnership and that Schœffer should succeed him in the management of the printing office. When every thing had been arranged, Gutenberg was summoned to appear before the court.

The plot was successful in all points. Fust won the suit almost without a struggle: under the forms of law, he took possession of all the materials made by Gutenberg for the common profit, and removed them to his own house. With the types, presses and books went also many of the skilled workmen, and Peter Schœffer was at their head. From an equitable point of view, Fust was amply recompensed. He got the printing office that he coveted, and, with it, the right to use the newly discovered art of Gutenberg. It appears that he was content. There is no evidence that he afterward made any attempt to collect the claim which was, legally, unsatisfied even after the surrender of Gutenberg's printing materials and the printed books.

XXII

The Later Work of Gutenberg.

Establishes a New Printing Office...Calendar of 1457...Not probable that the Bible of 36 lines was printed at this time...Gutenberg Embarrassed by Debts...Letter of Indulgence of 1461, with Fac-simile...Catholicon of 1460, with Fac-simile and Colophon...Indifference of Gutenberg to Fame. Pamphlets attributed to Gutenberg...Celebration of the Mass, with Fac-simile...Mirror of the Clergy, with Fac-simile...The War between the Rival Archbishops...The Siege and Sack of Mentz...Gutenberg's Office removed to Eltvill...Gutenberg made a Gentleman of Adolph's Court...End of Gutenberg's Labors...His Death in 1468...Disposition of his Types...His Services not fully Appreciated...True Nature of his Invention...His Merit acknowledged by Writers of his Time...Tablets of Gelthus and Wittig...Permanency of Gutenberg's Invention.

Why should we talk about monuments of bronze or marble to commemorate the services of Gutenberg? His is a monument which, more frail than any other, will survive them all: it is the Book. *Madden.*

GUTENBERG had been legally deprived of his printing office and of the exclusive right to his great invention, but he was not left friendless and utterly impoverished. Nor was his spirit broken by this great calamity. The reflection that Fust was owner of the materials made for printing the *Bible of 42 lines*, and was about to enjoy all the emoluments of the new art, aroused Gutenberg to rivalry. He was nearly sixty years of age, but he was vigorous in mind, if not in body, and evidently retained all his old power of persuasion. When he determined to found a new printing office, he found helpers: Conrad Humery, a physician, and also clerk of the town of Mentz, provided him with the means, and some of his old workmen came over to join his fortunes.

Gutenberg had some materials toward the equipment of a new office. Fust's mortgage covered only the materials made with Fust's money for the common profit; it did not cover the large types on Double-pica body, which were used upon the *Bible of 36 lines*, and other materials which might have been made in Strasburg. As these types were subsequently used in several little books which may be attributed to Gutenberg, we may conclude that he retained the punches and matrices in his own possession.

We have indirect evidence that the new printing office of Gutenberg was in operation at the close of the year 1456. With the types of Double-pica body he printed on one side of the paper, obviously made to be pasted on a wall, a broadside, now known as the *Calendar of 1457*. Of this curious document, only the half of a copy has been found—a fragment which contains the festivals and notable days for six months. It is fairly printed in black ink on coarse paper.

It is the belief of several historians that Gutenberg, hot with anger at the bad faith of Fust, in wresting from him the honor of printing the first *Bible*, immediately undertook in his new office to publish a rival edition of the same book, or the edition herein described as the *Bible of 36 lines*. The annotation in one copy of the book of the year 1459, which is supposed to be the date of publication, accords with the conjecture that the book begun in 1456 could have been finished in three years. But there is no evidence that it was begun in 1456, while there are many indications that it was done or should have been done in 1450. Gutenberg had earned fame as a printer[1] in 1458, but no writer of that time has said that he was then at work on the *Bible of 36 lines*.

[1] Philip de Lignamine, in a book entitled *A Continuation of the Chronicles of the Popes*, which he printed in Rome in 1474, writes concerning the year 1458: "Jacob Gutenberg of Strasburg, and another called Fust, very skillful in the art of printing with characters of metal on parchment, each printed three hundred leaves daily at Mentz." Jacob is an error of memory or of typography, and the mention of Strasburg as Gutenberg's birthplace is incorrect, but the statement that he printed in 1458 is, no doubt, true. It seems the testimony of a printer, whose knowledge of the facts had been derived either from personal observation, or from the reports of workmen once employed at Mentz.

We have evidence, also, that he was embarrassed by his debts. After the year 1457 he was unable to pay the four pounds annually to the chapter of St. Thomas at Strasburg, as he had agreed to do in 1442. The chapter summoned him to appear before a court at Rottweil in Suabia, in 1461, but to no purpose, for he was unable to satisfy this debt. His printing materials were owned by Conrad Humery, and not liable to seizure. It is by no means clearly established that he was, even then, carrying on business in his own name. Helbig thinks it was the fear of legal proceedings, if he had

Notum sit vniuersis pntes lras inspecturis Q quia
dioc pro repacone ecclie Nuhusen et ad op9 fabrice ipi9 intantu co
pro duodecim dieb9 disponi possit Idcoqz particeps Indulgenciaꝝ in
dnm nrm pium papa scdm cocessaꝝ esse debebit videlicet q elige po
mortis articulo 9fessorem ydoneum q eum ab omib9 Sentencijs e
inquas nondu incidisse declarat9 est Necno et ab omib9 crimib9 pct
casib9 ecia sedi aplice reseruatis absolue et plenaria remissione aucte
possit Sic tn q satisfaciat si alicui p eu satisfactio impendeda sit Et s
vl loco sexte ferie qn aliunde in illa ieiunare tenetur alio die in sep
pietatis iuxta dictamen sui confessoris maxie ad fabricam dicte ecc
faciat Et in obediecia sedis aplice ac pfati sctissimi dni nri pij pap
bulla dicti dni pape pij pleni9 contietur In cui9 testimoniu Sigillu
Reynhardu Epm ac Rudolphum decanu wormacien pro hac indu
a dicto dno pio sumo pontifice est data facultas pntibus est appe
Millesimoquadringentesimosexagesimoprimo

Fac-simile of the Types of the Letter of Indulgence of 1461.

[From Bernard.]

made himself very conspicuous, that prevented him from putting his name on his books. This omission has made it difficult to specify the books and pamphlets which are supposed to have been printed by him about this time.

One of these works is *The Letter of Indulgence of 1461*, an indulgence granted by Pope Pius II to all who should contribute to the restoration of a church at Neuhausen. It is printed in a new face of type, which should have been made before 1460. The types of this indulgence resemble those of the *Letters of Indulgence* of *30 lines* and of *31 lines*, but they were cast from different matrices and in a different mould. They seem to be the production of an incompetent punch-cutter; the letters were rudely cut, the matrices were not properly fitted up, and the types do not line. The press-work, upon new types, is good.

In the same face of type, but upon a body a little larger, Gutenberg printed the *Catholicon*[1] *of 1460*, a great folio of 748 pages of double columns, with 66 lines to each column. In some copies of the *Catholicon,* the summary of contents is printed in red ink, and ornamented with an engraving which fills one side of the first page. The composition is as rude as that of the *Bibles;* the right side of each column is always ragged from careless spacing. The colophon annexed states that the book was printed at Mentz in 1460, but it does not give the name[2] of the printer. The silence of Gutenberg concerning his services is remarkable, all the more so, when this silence is contrasted with the silly chatterings of several printers during the last quarter of the fifteenth century,—of whom Peter Schœffer may be considered as the first, and Trechsel of Lyons the last,—each insisting that he, whatever others might have done before him, was the true perfecter of printing. There is no other instance in modern history, excepting possibly that of Shakespere, of a man who did so much and who said so little about it. This colophon is the only passage in this book, and, indeed, in any of his works, which can be attributed to Gutenberg:

[1] This *Catholicon* was written, or edited, as the title informs us, by John of Genoa, of the fraternity of preachers, or mendicant friars. It contains an elaborate Latin grammar and an etymological dictionary in five divisions. It was a text book of authority in the higher schools.

[2] Van Praet says that Gutenberg, as a noble, dared not advertise his connection with a mechanical art. This is absurd, for Gutenberg's connection with printing in Mentz had been known for at least ten years, and printing was not then regarded as a business derogatory to the standing of a noble. Wetter says that Gutenberg was humiliated by the superior workmanship of Fust and Schœffer. But the work of these printers was not of such unquestionable superiority. Helbig's conjecture seems most plausible, but Gutenberg may have been so intent on the personal satisfaction he derived from the realization of his ideas, that he was comparatively indifferent to the gratification derived from notoriety.

By the assistance of the most High, at whose will the tongues of children become eloquent, and who often reveals to babes what He hides from the wise, this renowned book, the *Catholicon*, was printed and perfected in the year of Incarnation 1460, in the beloved city of Mentz (which belongs to the illustrious German nation, and which God has consented to prefer and to raise with such an exalted light of the mind and of free grace, above the other nations of the earth), not by means of pen, or pencil, or stencil plate, but by the admirable proportion, harmony and connection of the punches and matrices.[1] Wherefore to thee, Divine Father, Son and Holy Ghost, triune and only God, let praise and honor be given, and let those who never forget to praise [the Virgin] Mary, join also through this book in the universal anthem of the Church. God be praised.

Leuus . a . um . an leua exponitur.
Lex legis . dr a lego . gis . legi qz legitur . Et est
lex ius scriptū asciscens honestū . ꝓhibens cont'
riū . ul' lex ē scriptū populo ꝓmulgatū magistra
tu querente et populo respondente . Solebat enī
magister ciuitatis cum aliquā legem uellet institu
ere ascendere pulpitū in media concōne et querē
a populo si uellet illud ratū esse . et accepta rūsio
ne a populo deinceps ꝓ lege habebat' . fm hug .
¶ Et scias q lego . gis . cor' le in pnti s in pterito
prod . Vnde lex legis tenet naturam huius pteri
ti legi . cum primam prod . Xv . Non decet illa legi
q sunt contraria legi . De lege nali uide in consciā
Lexis inte ptatur pausacō uel sermo . et in bar
barolexis s hug . Pap uero dicit . Lexis grece lati
ne locucō . i . quelibet silla ul' uox que scribi deb3

Fac-simile of the Types of the Catholicon of 1460.

[From Bernard.]

[1] In Germany, the punch or the model letter is known as the *patrice*, a word obviously derived from the root of the Latin *patronarum* of the text. The reversed duplicates of punches, here translated as matrices, are noticed in the text as *formarum*, a variation of the word form, which we find so often in the record of the Strasburg trial. "The admirable proportion, harmony and connection of the punches and matrices," should be understood, not as a commendation of the beauty of the printed letters, but as a specification by the inventor of what he conceived was the great feature of typography, the making of types of different faces and thickness on bodies of absolute uniformity, so that they could be combined with ease. It should be noticed that the invention or the use of isolated letters or types is not boasted of; it was the method of making the types which the inventor regarded as the most admirable feature of his invention.

The dignified and reverential language of this colophon, so unlike the vainglorious imprints of Fust and Schœffer and the commonplace subscriptions of Pfister, is almost enough of itself to show that the printer of the *Catholicon* was John Gutenberg. That he should attribute the invention to the assistance and favor of the Almighty, might be expected from a man thoroughly imbued with religious sentiment, but why Gutenberg should, in this and in all other books, neglect to mention himself as the man through whom the invention was accomplished is an irregularity which cannot be explained. This neglect is strange, for Fust and Schœffer had boasted, in an imprint to the *Psalter of 1457*, of their skill as printers.

Five little pamphlets with texts in a new face of Round Gothic on English body, and with chapter headings in types resembling the text types of the *Bible of 42 lines*, have been attributed to Gutenberg. They are: *A Treatise on the Celebration of the Mass*,[1] a book of 30 leaves; *A Calendar*, or *An Almanac* for 1460, in Latin, a quarto of 6 leaves; *The Mirror of the Clergy*, by Hermann of Saldis, "happily perfected and printed at Mentz," a quarto of 16 leaves; *A Treatise on the Necessity of Councils*, etc., a quarto of 24 leaves; *A Dialogue between Cato, Hugo and Oliver about Ecclesiastical Liberty*,

[1] This work is attributed to Gutenberg, chiefly on the authority of this inscription, which was found in a copy in the possession of the Carthusian Friars at Mentz:

> The Carthusian Friars near Mentz, through the liberality of John Gutenberg, own this book, which was made by his wonderful art, and by the skill of John Nummeister, clerk. In the year of our Lord 1463, on the 13th calend of July [June 19].

Helbig doubts the genuineness of this annotation, and intimates that it may be the work of Bodmann, a librarian at Mentz, who has been suspected of attempts to foist spurious documents on those who were eager to know more of the life and labors of Gutenberg. In his treatise on the *Typographic Monuments of Gutenberg*, Fischer, on the authority of Bodmann, printed the copy of a verbose document which set forth that John Gutenberg and Frielo Gensfleisch assented to the action of their sister Hebele in conveying to the Convent of Saint Clare, of which she was then a nun, her share in the paternal inheritance. It also recites that John Gutenberg will give to the convent a copy of every book to be printed by him. This document, which is dated 1459, is not accepted as genuine by discreet bibliographers.

a quarto of 20 leaves.[1] It is possible, but not certain, that Gutenberg printed these books. *A Treatise on Reason and Conscience*,[2] by Matthew of Cracow, a small quarto of 22 leaves, and *A Summary of the Articles of Faith*, by Thomas Aquinas, a quarto of 12 leaves, printed in the types of the *Catholicon*, may be confidently accepted as the work of Gutenberg. But one copy or fragment of some of these works is known. Gutenberg may have printed many other works which have been destroyed and forgotten.[3]

De dominica infra octauam a-
scensionis domini.
Dominica pxima post die ascensiois dni
officiu dnicale Exaudi ptotu cu suffragijs
duob Alla. Seqntia. et pfacoe de festo ascen
sionis necno Glia in excelsis Credo et item mis-
sa dnicaliter dicetur.

Fac-simile of the Types of the Treatise on the Celebration of the Mass.
[From Fischer.]

The existing copies or fragments of pamphlets and books printed before 1462 are enough to prove that printing met

[1] Bernard says that some of these works were probably printed by an unknown printer at Mentz (not the printer of the *Indulgence of 31 lines*); but this conjecture of two printing offices, about which history and tradition are silent, which never produced any work of value, cannot be accepted.

[2] A copy of this book in the National Library at Paris has an annotation which sets forth that "Henry Kepfer of Mentz put this book in pledge for twelve days, and has not reclaimed it. . . ." Henry Kepfer was one of Gutenberg's workmen who appeared for him on the trial.

[3] Fischer says that a library at Mentz once contained several pamphlets printed by Gutenberg in the large types of the *Bible of 36 lines*. He gives fac-similes of the illuminated initials in one of these pamphlets, which closely resemble those of the *Psalter of 1457*. This similarity is more than an indication that the letters of this *Psalter* were made by Gutenberg.

with a qualified degree of appreciation. Gutenberg and Fust must have given employment to many presses and workmen: there was a demand for printed work of all kinds from almanacs to dictionaries, and the printers had reason to believe that they would be amply rewarded for their labor. Their hopes were destroyed by the sack of Mentz in 1462.

Similiter dicendū est si facta est aliqua ad
dicō erronea: sicut fuit addicō arrij vel si sine
addicōe impertinēte baptizās nullomō credat
fieri posse baptismū. Sbi pbabiliter dubitat
de obmissis an sint de substātia. an de addicōe
an impediūt baptismū an nō. ad formā cōdi-
cōnalē recurratur. que sup̄ posita est in prima
specie de materia scz de emendādis circa mate
riam. Si tn̄ obmissa sunt illa que nō sunt de
substātia. ut ego. et amē. vel sine omi malitia
facta est diminucō vel addicō. vel corrup cō cir

Fac-simile of the Types of The Mirror of the Clergy.

[From Bernard.]

The city of Mentz then held the first place in the league of the free cities of the Rhine, but her prosperity[1] was declining. Unceasing civil strifes had driven away the more feeble part of her population. In 1461, it was the wreck of its earlier greatness: it had but 50,000 inhabitants and was burdened with debt. Diether, Count of Isenburg, was then archbishop and elector of the city, by the consent of the majority of the inhabitants; but the rival archbishop, Adolph II, Count of Nassau, supported by Pope Pius II, claimed the archbishopric, and made war upon Diether. The consequences of the war, which nearly ruined the city, are forcibly stated by Schaab.

[1] In the tenth and eleventh centuries, Mentz, then the capital of Germany, contained a population of about 100,000 inhabitants. It was the most powerful city of the empire, the great city where the emperors were crowned. In the fourteenth century, it was so strong that it could send out of its walls 10,000 armed citizens to destroy the strongholds of the noble robbers who had ravaged its commerce.

This enmity between two archbishops was the cause of one of the most terrible days to the town of Mentz. It was the 28th of October, 1462, the day on which Christianity celebrated the anniversary of the apostles Simon and Judas. Mentz had remained faithful to the archbishop Diether. Adolph therefore tried to conquer it by stratagem and treason. Traitors were gained over in the town, who entailed upon a half thousand of their fellow-citizens death, and endless misery on many more. By the treachery of some wicked persons the town was assaulted during the night between the 27th and 28th of October, 1462, by the followers of Adolph; its noblest citizens were murdered, the most of them robbed of their possessions, and driven from the town. All kinds of mischief were committed toward those who remained behind. Neither age, rank, nor sex was exempted. The booty was sold publicly in the cattle-market, and the money divided between the soldiers.[1] Of the expelled citizens only a few gradually returned in secret to their relations. But the town, so populous before, remained empty, and all industry was destroyed. The elector Adolph II found it necessary, on the Saturday after St. Thomas's day of the same year, to issue a proclamation whereby he promised to all who wished to trade or to exercise a profession in Mentz, protection for their persons and possessions, to induce a few to return. A town, a short time before flourishing with commerce and industry, had been robbed in a few days of its privileges and utterly destroyed.[2]

In the general sack of the city, the house of Fust was burned, and his printing materials were destroyed. During the three years that followed no books of value were printed in Mentz. We do not know how Gutenberg was affected: we find no authoritative statement that his printing office was destroyed; it is not even certain that his office was then in the city of Mentz. In the year 1466, the printing office which contained his types was in active operation at Eltvill, a village not far from the city. As this was the place where Gutenberg's mother was born, and where she had an estate, it is probable that Gutenberg found some advantage in making it his residence, soon after his separation from Fust. Eltvill was also

[1] Helbig says that all the larger houses that had not been destroyed by fire were confiscated. The booty was divided in three parts: Adolph took the first and the best part, the nobles of his army claimed the second; the soldiers, "a band of mercenary savages," took the remainder. *Notes et dissertations*, p. 52.

[2] Hessels' translation.

the place which Adolph II had selected for his residence before he made his attack on Diether. It may be presumed that Eltvill was the place where Adolph first knew of Gutenberg and his works.

In 1465, Adolph II made Gutenberg one of the gentlemen of his court for "agreeable and voluntary service rendered to us and our bishopric." The nature of the service is not defined. Gutenberg was certainly not a soldier. His German biographers do not believe that, as diplomatist or politician, he had favored the cause of the destroyer of the liberties of his native city. Helbig thinks the words used are purely conventional, and that this distinction was conferred on Gutenberg because he was connected with the old nobility of the city. It is a more common and a more reasonable belief that Adolph recognized, to some extent, the utility of Gutenberg's invention, and took this method to honor the inventor.

We, Adolph, elected and confirmed archbishop of Mentz, acknowledge that we have considered the agreeable and voluntary service which our dear and faithful Johan Gutenberg has rendered to us and our bishopric, and have appointed and accepted him as our servant and courtier. Nor shall we remove him from our service as long as he lives; and in order that he may enjoy it the more, we will clothe him every year, when we clothe our ordinary suite *(unsern gemeinen hoffgesind)*, always like our noblemen, and give him our court dress; also every year twenty mout of corn and two voer of wine for the use of his house, free of duty, as long as he lives, but on condition that he shall not sell it or give it away. Which has been promised us in good faith by Johan Gutenberg. Eltvill, Thursday after St. Antony, 1465.[1]

[1] Schaab says that an aristocratic appointment at the court procured this nobleman a comfortable life. Voluntarily he followed the princely court, where he had a free table and fodder for his horses. Even for his dress he received cloth in the court colors, and generally wore a kind of mantle, called Tabard. It was in accordance with the premorals of that time to carouse at court. They went there with empty cups and returned with full ones. The princes tried not before the sixteenth century to put a check to this excess by special orders. The elector Johan Schweikard von Kronenberg ordered, even in the year 1605, to leave the *grossen Saumagen*—this was the name of the cups then used—for the future at home.... However comfortable and German-like all this may look, miserable were these court-wages, this dress, these alms presented to the inventor of typography. But no, it is perfectly in harmony with the general course of earthly things. Van der Linde, *Haarlem Legend*, p. 29.

The man who had invented an art which promised to renew the literature of the world, who had printed two great *Bibles*, a *Latin Dictionary*, and many minor works relating to religion, had surely rendered service to the first ecclesiastical dignitary of Germany.

Here Gutenberg's work ends. If not disqualified by the infirmities of age from the management of his printing office, his position as courtier must have compelled his attendance at the court of the archbishop. Possibly, the rules of the court required Gutenberg to withdraw from business. Whatever the reason, we see that the printing office at Eltvill passed into the hands of his relatives by marriage, the brothers Henry and Nicholas Bechtermüntz. It does not appear that these men had been formally instructed as printers in Mentz. As they acquired no rights of proprietorship in this office, as they were men of middle age, rich, of noble birth and of high civic position, it may be supposed that they took charge of the office to oblige Gutenberg and the archbishop, and, perhaps, from a pure love of the new art.

In the year 1467, this printing office at Eltvill produced a book now known as the *Vocabularium ex quo*, called so because these first words of the work serve to distinguish it from other vocabularies. It is an abbreviation of the *Catholicon*, and for that reason is described in the colophon as an *opusculum*, or a little work; but it is a heavy quarto of 330 pages. It is printed with the types of the *Catholicon*, and shows the same peculiarities of composition. The colophon says that "this little book was made, not by reed, nor pen, nor stencil plate, but by a certain new and subtile invention . . . by Henry Bechtermüntz, of blessed memory.[1] . . . Nicholas Bechtermüntz, and Wygand Spyess of Orthenburg."[2]

Gutenberg could not have abandoned his printing office with much regret. He had abundantly demonstrated the

[1] Henry Bechtermüntz had died before the book was finished.

[2] The *Vocabularium ex quo* was reprinted by Nicholas Bechtermüntz, in the same types and in the same form, in the years 1469, 1472, and 1477. Only one copy is known of the first edition of the book.

utility of his invention and his own ability as a printer by the publication of two great books and many pamphlets. His art had been adopted in five German cities: it was then making its entry in Rome; it was eagerly sought for by the king of France. A future of unbounded popularity and usefulness was before it. The young men to whom Gutenberg had taught the practice of printing had so improved that they were his equals and superiors, and the old man of quite seventy years could not cope with these competitors. His ambition for pre-eminence in his own art, or for the wealth that should have been derived from its practice, if he ever had such aspirations, had to be given up. It was time that he should quit the stage.

Gutenberg did not long enjoy the leisure or the honors of a courtier. In February, 1468, he was dead. Nothing is known of the cause or the circumstances of his death, nor is there any mention of a surviving family. We have to conclude that John Gutenberg, the inventor of the greatest of modern arts, died, weighed down by debts, and unattended by wife or child. The disposition of his printing office is stated in the following document:[1]

I, THE undersigned, Conrad Humery, doctor, acknowledge by this writing, that his eminence the prince, my gracious and dear lord Adolphus, archbishop of Mentz, has generously delivered to me certain formen [matrices or moulds], characters [types], instruments, utensils, and other implements connected with printing, which John Gutenberg left after his death, which materials belonged and still belong to me:[2] but, for the honor and the satisfaction of his eminence I am bound, and I pledge myself, by this document, never to put them to use but in the city of Mentz, and further, to sell them, at a fair price, to a citizen of Mentz in preference to any other. In testimony whereof, I have put my seal to these presents, which have been made in the year of our Lord 1468, on the Friday after Saint Matthew's day [26th of February].

[1] From the preface to a curious and little-known poem entitled *Encomion Chalcographiæ*, by Arnold Bergellanus, as reprinted by Wolf in his *Monumenta Typographica*, vol. I, p. 5.

[2] It appears from this, that Humery, who owned the printing office, had neglected to properly record or establish his title. It was through the grace of the archbishop, who understood the matter, that he was spared the trouble of re-establishing his right by legal process.

In this strange document we again find the word *formen*, and the *formen* are specified first, as if they were the most valuable tools. As types are specifically described, it is plain that these *formen* must have been matrices or moulds.

Humery kept his word. The types and tools of Gutenberg remained with Nicholas Bechtermüntz until his death. They were then transferred to the custody or the possession of the Brothers of the Life-in-Common, who had a printing office at Marienthal, near Eltvill, as early as 1468. That this place was regarded as a part of Mentz may be inferred from the imprint they put on their first book, which is to this effect: Dated in our city of Mentz on the last day of August, 1468. Eltvill was the chosen residence of the archbishop, and under his jurisdiction, and might properly be considered as a dependency or a part of the city of Mentz.

For some unknown reason these Brothers of the Life-in-Common made no use of the types of Gutenberg. In the year 1508, they were sold to Frederic Hauman of Nuremberg, who established a printing office in Mentz, and who used these types in many of his books.[1] The house that had been occupied by Hauman as a printing office was subsequently used for the same purpose by Albinus, a printer of

[1] One day when I was reading this interesting passage [of Bodmann, concerning the types of Gutenberg], the idea presented itself to me that it would be well to examine with care a certain volume printed by Frederic Hauman, which was in a neglected corner of my library. I took it up, not thinking that I should make any discovery. I knew that the last productions of the presses of Nicholas Bechtermüntz were printed with other types than those of Gutenberg, and that, among the known impressions of the Brothers of the Life-in-Common at Marienthal, none were executed with these characters. But judge of my astonishment, of my joy, perhaps, when I recognized in this neglected book not only the types of the *Catholicon* of 1460, the only ones appertaining to Gutenberg that could have been employed in the books that proceeded from the presses of Eltvill, but also the types that had been used in the *Letters of Indulgence* of 1454 and 1455, in the *Appeal against the Turks* of 1455, the *Calendar of 1457* described by Fischer, the *Bible of 36 lines*, and all the characters of Albert Pfister—or, to be brief,—when I recognized the most ancient types of John Gutenberg. Helbig, *Une découverte pour l'histoire de l'imprimerie*, p. 4.

Helbig gives a list of seven books, of little value, printed by Hauman, in these types of Gutenberg. He expresses his astonishment that they had not before been identified, but he offers no explanation of the singular fact that these types were not used by any printer between 1469 and 1506.

the seventeenth century. The types of Gutenberg were in this house at the end of the sixteenth century, for Serarius, in his *History of Mentz*, says that he had seen them there.[1]

Humery's promise that, in the sale of the printing materials then contemplated, he would give preference to a citizen of Mentz, was obviously made at the request of the archbishop. It follows that the types of the dead printer were then regarded as relics of value of which the city should be proud. This request, which would not have been made without occasion, seems to confirm the conjecture that Gutenberg had previously sold the types, or at least the matrices, of the *Bible of 36 lines* to Albert Pfister, of the monastic town of Bamberg. It is not probable that the deed of gift would have been clogged with this stipulation, if there had been no sale.

This request of the archbishop is the only evidence we have that Gutenberg's work was appreciated, but the appreciation came when he was dead. No contemporary writer noticed the *Bible of 42 lines*, and no one during his lifetime suitably honored Gutenberg as a great inventor. The archbishop, who knew the merit of the man, and pitied his misfortunes, had not a word to say in the document that made him a courtier of his services as an inventor or printer.

This indifference or want of perception seems inexcusable, but it was not altogether without cause. The readers of that time were somewhat familiar with printed impressions in the form of block-books, and the *Bible of 42 lines* may have seemed to them but a block-book of larger size and of higher order. Knowing that engraving, ink, paper, and impression upon surfaces in relief, were used in both processes, the ordinary book-buyer could have inferred that type-printing was the natural outgrowth of the older and well-known art of block-printing. According to this view, Gutenberg invented little or nothing; he did but little more than combine some old and well-known processes; he distinguished himself more by the great size of his books than by the novelty or merit

[1] Helbig, *Une découverte pour l'histoire de l'imprimerie*, p. 4, note.

of his process. It is but proper to expose this sophistry, for it is perpetuated to this day in several books on typography.

This grave error did not originate with the first printers, who knew the full difference between type and block-printing. They knew that Gutenberg was indebted to the earlier block-printers for a great deal of his knowledge, but they knew as well that his system of printing was a great and an original invention, for they clearly understood, what the ordinary book-reader did not, the value of its characteristic feature. And here it may be repeated, for the error is common and it is necessary to be emphatic, that the merit of Gutenberg as an inventor is not based upon his supposed discovery of the advantages of movable types, but upon the system by which he made the movable types. All the printers of that period recognized the fact that Gutenberg's method of making the types, or the type-mould, with its connections, was the proper basis or starting-point of the invention. Schœffer, who first printed a notice of the new art, speaks of it as the "masterly invention of printing and also of type-making," implying that the art of printing was inseparably connected with that of type-making. John Gutenberg, in the *Catholicon*, has not a word to say about isolated types, nor about a combination of types: the admiration which he invokes for the masterly invention should, in his view of the matter, be bestowed on its system of making the types, or on the "admirable proportion, connection and harmony of the punches and matrices."

Gutenberg made no effort to secure for himself his rightful honors as the inventor of printing, but his friends who knew the nature and value of his services were not neglectful. We have abundant evidence that Gutenberg was the man, and Mentz the place, where printing was invented.

Trithemius, from information furnished by Peter Schœffer, said, in a book written before 1490, "About this time (1450), the admirable and then unheard-of art of composing and printing books, by means of types, was conceived and invented at Mentz, by a citizen of Mentz, named John Gutenberg."

Matthias Palmer, in 1474, said that John Gutenberg, a knight of Mentz, had invented the art of printing books.

Ulric Zell's testimony, given in 1499, is equally explicit.[1]

Polydore Virgil, in his treatise on *Inventions*, says, in the first edition, that printing was invented by one Peter [probably Peter Schœffer], but in the second edition of 1517, he corrected the error, and attributed the invention to Gutenberg.

Wimpheling, in 1499, wrote and published at Heidelberg some verses praising Gutenberg, in which he said, "Blessed Gensfleisch! through you Germany is famous everywhere. Assisted by Omniscience, you John, first of all, printed with letters in metal. Religion, the wisdom of Greece, and the language of the Latins, are forever indebted to you." Two professors at Heidelberg, at an earlier date (1494), had written panegyrics on Gutenberg as the inventor of typography, in which he is honored above all the great men of antiquity.[2]

Two friends of Gutenberg who, no doubt, knew all about his invention, put up tablets to his memory, in which his merit as an inventor is distinctly acknowledged. The inscriptions on these tablets have not received the attention which they merit. The tablet first placed was put up not long after his death by his relative, Adam Gelthus, near his tomb in the church of St. Francis. This is a translation of the inscription:

> To John Genszfleisch, inventor of the art of printing, and deserver of the highest honors from every nation and tongue, Adam Gelthus places this tablet, in perpetual commemoration of his name. His remains peacefully repose in the church of St. Francis of Mentz.[3]

[1] See pages 315 and 316 of this book.

[2] Many authors who do not mention Gutenberg speak of Mentz as the city in which printing was first practised. Van Laar, at Cologne, in 1478; Caxton, at Westminster, in 1482; the archbishop Berthold of Mentz in 1486; Meydenbach of Mentz in 1494—these are a few of the many writers who have certified to this fact. A cloud of witnesses, says Van der Linde, join in the song of Celtes: "You wind yourself, already, O broad-waved Rhine! to the town of Mentz, which first of all printed with metal letters." Van der Linde, *Haarlem Legend*, p. 32.

[3] In the year 1742, the Jesuits, who then had control of the church of Saint Francis, tore it down in order to rebuild another edifice upon the same ground. The tablet and the tomb of Gutenberg were destroyed. The inscription on this tablet was published for the first time in a book printed by Peter Friedburg at Mentz in the year 1499. Helbig, *Notes et dissertations*, p. 10.

Gelthus properly describes Gutenberg's invention as *the* art of printing. In a practical view, there was no other.

Equally instructive is the pithy inscription on the second tablet, which was put up by Ivo Wittig,[1] in the court of the house of the Gensfleisch family, where Gutenberg is supposed to have died,[2] and which was then used as a law school.

> To John Gutenberg, of Mentz, who, first of all, invented printing letters in brass [matrices and moulds], and by this art has deserved honor from the whole world, Ivo Wittig places this stone in commemoration, 1508.[3]

Ivo Wittig, who had probably known Gutenberg, and who clearly understood his process, is not content with a paraphrase of the Gelthus inscription. In plain words, he specifies the key of the invention: Gutenberg, first of all, made types in brass moulds and matrices. In other words, it was only through the invention of the type-mould and matrices in brass that printing became a great art. This inscription shows that

[1] Ivo Wittig was an ecclesiastic of eminence, chancellor and grand rector of the University of Mentz, to which he gave his large library of books and manuscripts. When the Swedes approached Mentz, this precious library was removed. Unfortunately, it was put on a boat of the Rhine which was wrecked, and his rare collection of books was lost. Helbig says it is an irreparable loss, for Wittig was deeply interested in printing, and his collection, no doubt, contained materials of the highest importance concerning its history.

[2] This is an error. This house is not connected with the history of printing in any other way than in being the residence of Gutenberg when a child. When the Gensfleisch family were sent or went in exile, their houses were confiscated. It is not probable that Gutenberg died in the house bearing his name.

[3] The Jesuit Serarius says that he saw this tablet one hundred years after it was erected. Between 1632 and 1636, when the Swedes were in Mentz, this house was sacked, but the tablet was spared. In 1741, it was taken down and placed in the wall in the court of a house belonging to the University. But this monument, which escaped the barbarity of the Swedish soldiers, was destroyed by the conscripts of the French republic, who were lodged in this house between the years 1793 and 1797. Helbig says it is probable that these ruffians suspected John Gutenberg of aristocratic tendencies. They did not know that the old citizen of Mentz was, unwittingly, the leader of all democrats, revolutionists and reformers, the man above all others, who, by his invention, had paved the way for the French revolution.

Wittig, then professor of history in the University, and probably the most learned man in Mentz, regarded John Gutenberg as the true inventor of printing.

Considered from a mechanical point of view, the merit of Gutenberg's invention may be inferred from its permanency. His type-mould was not merely the first; it is the only practical mechanism for making types. For more than four hundred years this mould has been under critical examination, and many attempts have been made to supplant it. Contrivances have been invented for casting fifty or more types at one operation; for swaging types, like nails, out of cold metal; for stamping types from cylindrical steel dies upon the ends of thin copper rods—but experience has shown that these and like inventions in the department of type-making machinery are impracticable. There is no better method than Gutenberg's. Modern type-casting machines have moulds attached to them which are more exact and more carefully finished, and which have many little attachments of which Gutenberg never dreamed, but in principle and in all the more important features, the modern moulds may be regarded as the moulds of Gutenberg.

Gutenberg's merit as an original inventor, although never properly recognized during his life, was never denied. But this merit was disallowed and set aside after his death by the sons and friends of Peter Schœffer. They said that printing was only half invented by Gutenberg, and that the complete invention is really due to Gutenberg's assistant and successor. As this claim has been repeated by many authors, it is necessary, for the vindication of Gutenberg, to review the work and workmanship of Peter Schœffer and John Fust.

XXIII

The Work of Peter Schœffer and John Fust.

Schœffer a Copyist at Paris in 1449... Fac-simile of his Writing... Enters the Service of Gutenberg. Psalter of 1457, with Fac-simile of Types and Initials in Colors... Accurate Register of Initial made by Painting the Cut... Evidences of Painting... Fac-simile of Colophon in Colors... Different Theories concerning the Method of Printing... Schœffer's First Claim as an Inventor. Psalter probably Planned by Gutenberg... Fac-similes of the Types of the Rationale Durandi and of the Bible of 1462... Trade-Mark of Fust and Schœffer... Fac-simile of the Types of the Constitutions... Jenson's Mission to Mentz... Printing not a Secret... Death of Fust... Partnership of Schœffer and Conrad Fust... Fac-simile of Types of 1468... Schœffer becomes a Judge... Schœffer's Claim to the Invention of Matrices... Statements of John Schœffer and of Trithemius... Their Improbability... Statement of Jo. Frid. Faustus... Its Untrustworthiness.

The man who enters the service of Gutenberg and Fust at Mentz after 1450, when the invention was completed, and has yet the courage to declare in 1468, that he, Petrus, entered first of all the sanctuary of the art, is, notwithstanding all his technical ability as a typographer, a bragger, against whose information we ought to be on our guard. *Van der Linde.*

PETER SCHŒFFER was born at Gernszheim, a little village situated on the Rhine, near Mentz, about the year 1430. Before he was twenty years of age, he was copying books at Paris, as is clearly enough shown in the colophon of an old manuscript book, which says that "this book was completed by me, Peter, of Gernszheym, or of Mentz, during the year 1449, in the most glorious University of Paris." This isolated fact is the only authority for the assertion that Schœffer was a calligrapher, engaged by Gutenberg to design the letters and ornaments of the *Bible of 42 lines.* He may have been qualified for this service, but the thin letters and angular ornaments of his colophon are not like the thick types and flowing lines of Gutenberg's Bible. Like all poor students of his time, Schœffer was a copyist, but we have no evidence that he was a calligrapher or an illuminator. As a student of the University of Paris, he was qualified to read and correct the proofs of a Bible in Latin, and this may have been the duty for which he was engaged. If so, he was not really needed in the printing office until the types were founded, or until 1453; but whether he came then or before, it is obvious that he entered the printing office as a boy from school, and that all he knew of printing was taught him by Gutenberg. He proved an apt scholar. Fust's confidence in his ability is enough to show that he had added skill to his knowledge, and that, when Gutenberg departed, he was competent to supervise and manage all the departments of the printing office.

Reduced Fac-simile of a Colophon written by Schœffer.

[From Madden.]

Bernard thinks that Schœffer's first work in his new place was to change the appearance of the *Bible of 42 lines*[1] by the cancellation of eight pages of 42 lines, and the substitution of pages of 40 lines, with summaries printed in red ink. The extraordinary licence then enjoyed by copyists allowed the compositor to abbreviate the words of a manuscript copy

[1] Bernard's conjectures as to the reason for this change are plausible. He says: The sales of the *Bible* had not been so great as Fust had expected. Envious copyists had probably fostered a prejudice against the printed Bible as purely mechanical copying, and for that reason, or on account of its known errors, inferior to the ordinary manuscript. Fust hoped to remove these objections, and to attract purchasers by giving the unsold copies the appearance of a new edition. Madden does not accept this hypothesis. He thinks that the two kinds of copies were composed at the same time by different compositors, who, setting their types from dictation, not seeing the manuscript copy, made their abbreviations without uniformity, and, as a necessary consequence, produced pages of unequal length. This explanation is quite as reasonable.

of 42 lines, until they were crowded into the space of 40 lines. The page was made of full length by leading out, or by widening the lines with bands of stout parchment.

The first book published by Fust, after his separation from Gutenberg, was the *Psalter*[1] *of 1457*, a folio of 175 leaves, which is almost as famous as the *Bible of 42 lines*. Only seven fair copies of the edition of 1457 are known, and all of them are on vellum. The leaves of this book are nearly square, smaller in size than those of the *Bible of 42 lines*, but, like that book, they are made up, for the most part, in sections of ten nested leaves. The size of the printed page is irregular, but most pages are about 8 inches wide and 12 inches high. The Psalms are printed in types of Double-paragon body, and the introductory or connecting text in types of Double-great-primer body.[2] As the cut or fashion of these types is like that of the Bibles of Gutenberg, it is possible that they were designed by the same hand. The leaf was not broad enough for the large-sized types, but a very large portion of it was given up to the initial letters and their pendants, which are of unusual dimensions. The space allotted to the print is small: but a few lines of the large types could be put on a page, and on many pages it was necessary to use small types. The fault of uneven or ragged outline on the right side of the page, which has been noticed in the *Bible of 42 lines*, is repeated more strikingly in the *Psalter*. Here and there spaces were made for plain chant notes of music, parts of which appear in printing ink, while other parts seem to have been retraced with a pen.

It is obviously an imitation not only of the copyist's but of the illuminator's work upon a fine manuscript. It was intended that the book should show the full capacity of the newly discovered art. Letters and lines in red ink are to

[1] It could, with more propriety, be called a ritual. The psalms are followed by prayers, collects, litanies, the service for the dead, hymns, etc. But it is always described as a psalter.

[2] The rubricated capital letters on the larger body, which are very large and square, might be regarded as another incomplete font, for which small letters had not been provided.

be found on every page, and there are many very large and profusely ornamented initials in red and blue inks. To the young reader who is accustomed to the severe and colorless style of modern printing, the boldness and blackness of the stately text types of this *Psalter*, the brightness of its rubrics, and the graceful forms of its two-colored initials, are really bewildering. They lead him to the belief that the workmanship of the book is of the highest order. This has been the opinion of many eminent authors;[1] the *Psalter of 1457* has been called the perfection of printing.

The initial letter B, the largest in the book, which is at the beginning of the first Psalm, *Beatus vir*, has been often reproduced, and commended as an example of skillful engraving, brilliant color and faultless register. The design is beautiful, and admirably fitted for relief printing, but it is not in the Gothic or German style: the palm-leaf fillet-work is oriental, and was probably copied from some Spanish manuscript, the illuminator of which had been taught in the Moorish schools. In a few copies, the letter is red and the ornament is blue; in other copies, the colors are reversed. In all copies the thin white line which separates the red from the blue is always of uniform thickness: there is no overlapping or meeting of the adjacent colors. The register is without fault in all the copies. The quality of the ink has been greatly praised: we are told

[1] Savage said, before he had critically examined the ink of the book:

It is a curious fact that, under Fust and Gutenberg, the process [of printing in colors] should be carried nearly to perfection; for some of the works they printed, both in the quality of the ink and in the workmanship, are so excellent that it would require all the skill of our best printers, even at the present day, to surpass them in all respects: and I do not hesitate to say, that, in a few years after, the printers were actually superior to us in the use of red ink, both as to color and as to the inserting of a great number of single capital letters in their proper places in a sheet, with a degree of accuracy and sharpness of impression that I have never seen equaled in modern workmanship. *Decorative Printing*, London, 1822, pp. 6 and 7.

After a closer inspection, Savage discovered that the red was painted.

Papillon declared that the red ink was of the most perfect beauty. Chatto said that this earliest known production [of the press of Fust and Schœffer] remains to the present day unimpaired as a specimen of skill in ornamental printing. The art of printing was perfected by Fust and Schœffer. Jackson and Chatto, *Wood Engraving*, p. 168.

Adorem9 dñm qui fecit nos, Ps' venite aiã Servite.
Beatus vir qui
non abijt in Euouae.
consilio impiorũ et in
via pctõr nõ stetit: & in
cathedra pestilẽcie nõ se=
dit. Sed ĩ lege dñi vo
lũtas ei9: et in lege eius meditabit die ac
nocte. Et erit tanq̃ lignũ qđ plãtatũ iste

Fac-simile of Part of the First Page of the Psalter of 1457.

[From Humphreys.]

that the black of the text is very deep and glossy, that the red has a vividness of color, and the blue a delicacy of tint, not to be found in the productions of any modern printer. It has been asserted that this *Psalter* is more neatly printed than any modern book; that Schœffer, with rudely made types, a rough press of wood, and with small experience in, or scientific knowledge of, ink-making, succeeded in producing presswork that has never been excelled on modern presses. These bold assertions require careful examination.

The few experts in printing who have examined copies of this book have been so cowed by the rulings of eminent bibliographers that they have not, apparently, dared to trust their own observation. Savage was the first to refuse the dictum of authorities and tell us what he saw with his own eyes. He distinctly says that the blackness of some notes of music was made by retracing with a pen[1] the faded lines of a paler printed color. Bernard[2] and Humphreys[3] plainly say that in the fine copy of the *Mentz Psalter* at the British Museum, some lines of text have been written in by hand. Humphreys thinks that this filling in of lines may have been done when the book was published. We have here trusty evidence that the printing of the *Psalter* was imperfect: that in some places the ink was too weak,[4] and that the deeper

[1] He says the ink was dull yellow: On some of the leaves where music is given there is an appearance as if the oil in the ink had penetrated through the vellum and tinged the opposite side of the leaf with a dingy yellow. This had been supposed to be the case, but I find that the original tune had been printed with a dull yellow ink, and that subsequently a different one had been written in over the first, with black ink to match the color of the text; and so exactly is this effect produced that, if it were not for the remains of the printing of the original tune, it might pass unsuspected of being any other than the production of the press. *Practical Hints on Decorative Printing*, pp. 49 and 51.

[2] *De l'origine*, etc., vol. I. p. 225.

[3] *History of Printing*, p. 85.

[4] Some writers say that the earliest printing inks were gum-water colors, which could be washed off the vellum with a wet sponge. But the ink of the *Psalter* was a true printing ink, a smoke-black mixed with oil. The modern pressman, who has ineffectually tried to make ordinary printing ink stick to parchment imperfectly cleansed of oily matter, will at once attribute this failure of the printer of the *Psalter* to the oiliness of the vellum and the weakness of his printing ink.

Pn̄s spalmorꝝ codex · venustate capitaliū decorat⁹
Rubricationibusq̄ sufficienter distinctus,
Adinuētione artificiosa imprimendi ac caracterizandi ·
absq̄ calami ulla exaratione sic effigiatus, Et ad euse=
biam dei industrie est ꝯsummatus, Per Johēm fust
Ciuē magūtinū · Et Petrū Schoffer de Gernszheim,
Anno dn̄i Millesimo · cccc · lvij · In vigilia Assūpcōis,

Fac-simile, slightly reduced, of the Colophon of the Psalter of 1457.

[From Falkenstein.]

color was produced by painting the letters with a pen. The brilliancy of the black ink has consequently been unwisely praised, for it is a triumph not of printing, but of painting.

The same observation may be applied to the colored ink of the great initials. Savage denies the statement of Papillon that the red ink is of the most perfect beauty: he says that "it is a very heavy brick-dust color." Heineken says it is a dull red. A closer examination of the book revealed the fact to Savage that the initials also had been retraced or painted.

> I could not avoid expressing my astonishment at seeing in some pages two distinct red inks: one, the dull color before spoken of, and the other, a red which, in printing, might fairly be called of the most perfect beauty; and I had nearly left it with the belief that there were two inks, red and blue, used in the printing of the book, which, for brilliancy of color, would set at defiance all the efforts of the present day to equal them. Some accidental circumstance caused me to view the book in a different light, when I discovered that the beautiful red was not printed but written in, so exactly like the type that it could only be ascertained by the want of indentation in the paper, which is invariably produced by pressure in the process of printing. By the same means, I also ascertained that the fine delicate blue was painted. Thus the colors produced by printing in the capital letters are reduced to two, namely, dull blue and dull red.[1]

It is not difficult to explain this curious circumstance. The red and blue printing inks first used by Schœffer were so dull and faded that he would not suffer them to be compared with the brighter colors of fair manuscripts. He was compelled to brighten the colors by painting. Although sold as a printed book, the *Psalter* was the joint work of the printer and the illuminator, and the features which the modern bibliographer most admires are those made by the illuminator.

The process employed by the printer of the *Psalter* for securing an exact register of the colors was just as irregular. It is an error to assume that the two-colored initials were printed as similar work is now printed, by two impressions. Bernard says that the red and the blue blocks of the initials,

[1] *Practical Hints on Decorative Printing*, p. 50.

each engraved on a separate piece of wood, were made to fit each other, so that the red block should fit accurately in the mortised blue block. In the process of printing, each block was separately inked, but the red block was dropped in the mortise of the blue block before impression was taken.[1] After these painstaking preparations, exact register was inevitable.

Blades does not accept this explanation. He thinks that the engraving for the red and the blue ink was done on one block, which was not printed with ink, but was embossed in the paper as a guide to the colorist. He says that his examination of the two-colored initial letters of a Bible made by Sweynheim and Pannartz in 1467 proves that they were not printed, but embossed, in the white paper; that the paper mask on the frisket was left uncut over the engraving, so as to shield the white paper from the ink, and to deepen the indentation of the engraved lines; and that the illuminator made use of this indentation, as he would of a pencil drawing, to guide his pen or brush when laying on the colors. He further says[2] that a similar operation was carelessly done in parts of the *Psalter of 1457;* that some of the spiral lines, finials and ornaments were left uncolored, but that the process was plainly exposed by the indentation of the engraved lines.

It is not necessary to accept Blades' opinion that the coloring was done entirely with pen or brush: the few uncolored lines in the initials of the *Mentz Psalter* may be regarded as blemishes occasioned by an accidental overlapping of the mask on the frisket. Savage's statement that the blocks were printed with ink is too positive to be disputed. Nor is it necessary to accept the hypothesis of Bernard that the blocks were engraved in two pieces and mortised, that they might be printed by one impression. We may rightfully suppose

[1] This method of printing in colors was patented by Solomon Henry of Great Britain in 1786, and in another form by Sir William Congreve in 1819, and by him applied to the printing of maps. *Abridgment of Specifications relating to Printing*, London, 1859. Improvements in machine presses have put out of use these methods of printing in colors.

[2] *Life and Typography of William Caxton*, vol. II, p. liii, note.

that Schœffer tried to imitate the work of the illuminator by the imitation of his method. To engrave the initial and the ornament around it on one block, to paint the letter in one color and the ornament in another, and to print both colors by one impression, seemed the surest way to do the work. That this was the intention of the designer of the letters is evident from the manner in which the colors are divided. Contrary to the usage of the illuminators, who were fond of interweaving colors, each color was kept apart in a mass, that it might be inked with greater facility. And this inking was probably done with a brush. Blue ink was painted on the letter, and red ink on the ornament, at a great sacrifice of time, but with neatness and without any interference of the colors.[1] It should not surprise us that exact register was secured, but it was more a feat of painting than of printing.[2]

Setting aside the colors, the workmanship of the *Psalter* is not neater than that of the *Bible of 42 lines*. The right side of every page is much more ragged[3] through bad spacing; typographical errors[4] are more frequent; the lines are often bowed or bent in the centre from careless locking up. The presswork is not good; the pages are dark and light from uneven inking, and the types have a grimy appearance, as if

[1] Blades shows fac-similes of the printed work of Colard Mansion, in which we see that his red and black were printed by the same impression. *Life and Typography of William Caxton*, vol. I, p. 43. Also, plates III and VIII.

[2] The modern printer who may regard this method of color-printing as puerile and wasteful of time, must be reminded that, slow as it may now seem, it was a quicker method than that of hand-drawing and painting. The difference between the old and the modern process of printing in colors will be fully stated, by saying that Schœffer printed, probably, but forty copies of this initial in one day, and that the modern pressman on a machine press would be required to produce, from two impressions, about twenty-five hundred copies in one day. Far from being a specimen of the skill of the early printers, this initial B is a flagrant example of their inexperience and the rudeness of their methods.

[3] See fac-simile, plate 15, *Humphrey's History of Printing*.

[4] See fac-simile on page 455 for the frequent transposition of the letters *t* and *c*. Also in first line of same fac-simile, *Presens spalmorum* for *Presens psalmorum*.

they had been inked with foul balls and printed on over-wet vellum. The colophon or imprint attached to this book says:

> This book of Psalms, decorated with antique initials, and sufficiently emphasized with rubricated letters, has been thus made by the masterly invention of printing and also of type-making, without the writing of a pen, and is consummated to the service of God, through the industry of Johan Fust, citizen of Mentz, and Peter Schœffer of Gernszheim, in the year of our Lord 1457, on the eve of the Assumption [August 14].

This imprint is ingeniously worded. Fust and Schœffer do not say, in plain words, that they were the inventors of printing; they invite attention to the red ink and the two-colored initials which were here used in printing, with fine effect. They speak of rubricated printing and of the invention of printing as if they were inseparable. They suppress the name of Gutenberg, and induce the reader to believe that Fust and Schœffer were not only the first to print with letters in red ink, but the first to discover and use the masterly invention. This insinuated pretense had the effect which was, no doubt, intended. By many readers of that century, Peter Schœffer was regarded as the man who planned and printed the *Psalter*, the man who made the types, not only of this book, but of the *Bible of 42 lines.* Made bold by the silence of Gutenberg, Schœffer allowed, if he did not positively authorize, the statement to be made by his friends, that he was the true inventor of printing; that he took up the art where Gutenberg left it incomplete, and perfected it.

Before this assertion can be examined, it will be proper to consider the date of 1457 in the imprint of the *Psalter.* If Schœffer planned and printed the book, he did all the work in the twenty-one months following Gutenberg's expulsion from the partnership. This is an unreasonable proposition, for the book should have been in press or in preparation as long as the *Bible of 42 lines.* It is quite probable that the *Psalter* was planned and left incomplete by Gutenberg. The types, which are like those of Gutenberg's *Bible,* are unlike any types subsequently made by Schœffer. The great initials in colors are of the same design as the initials of the *Donatuses* shown by Fischer, and by him attributed to Gutenberg. The careful manner in which they were engraved indicates experience as well as skill on the part of the engraver; but it is not possible that the engraver was Schœffer, or any workmen attached to his office, for Schœffer never after printed any engravings on wood of equal merit.[1] The sumptuous style of the *Psalter* is unlike that of any book afterward made by Schœffer; it is in a style which he did not originate, and could not sustain. He reprinted it in 1459, in 1490, and in 1502, but the later editions were not printed so well as the first.[2] The inferiority of the later workmanship is evidence that the master mind who planned the work was not at the head of the printing office.

On the sixth day of October, 1459, Fust published the *Rationale Durandi*, or the exposition, by Durandus, of the services of the church. It is a folio of 160 leaves, 2 columns to the page, in types on English body, 63 lines to the column. It has many rubricated letters and lines, and ends with a colophon, in red ink, worded like the *Psalter of 1457*, but with the addition of the words, "clerk of the diocese of Mentz," after the name of Peter Schœffer. The statement in the colophon, that it was made without the writing of a pen, is not entirely true. There are two kinds of copies: one has printed capitals like those of the *Psalter*, the other has illuminated initials. To provide suitable spaces for these written initials, which are of large size, the types were overrun and re-arranged.

If Schœffer had been an able calligrapher, he would have

[1] Fournier thinks that *all* the letters of the *Psalter* were cut on wood. *De l'origine, etc., de l'imprimerie,* p. 231. But Bernard says: "After a careful study of many copies, I declare that this book is certainly printed with types of founded metal, and founded, too, with admirable precision." *De l'origine et des débuts,* etc., vol. I, p. 224.

[2] The last edition of the book, printed by his son, John Schœffer, in 1516, shows the great initial B entirely in red ink. It proves that the letter previously printed in two colors was engraved on one block. It proves also that the original method of painting the letter in two colors had been found expensive and impracticable.

demonstrated his ability by the production of types of finer proportions than those of Gutenberg. If he was an expert type-founder, and the inventor of the type-mould, he should have proved his skill by casting types of neater finish. The first types made by him or by his order after his separation from Gutenberg are exhibited in the *Rationale Durandi*, but they do not warrant the opinion that he was a very skillful designer or an ingenious type-founder. The combination of Gothic and Roman which he there exhibited is evidently an imitation of the Round Gothic face used by Gutenberg in the *Letters of Indulgence* and the *Catholicon.* Schœffer's types present no features of superiority: they show mannerisms of engraving so like those of Gutenberg's types as to lead to the opinion that both were made by the same punch-cutter.

Secũdo loco. pascal' cere⁹ bñdicet'. Cir̃ qd sci-
endũ ē qꝫ ĩ pñcipio officij tot⁹ in eccl'a dꝫ ignis
extingui. ꝛ nou⁹ de lapide pcusso cũ calibe
vl' ex cristallo soli obiecta dꝫ elici ꝛ de sarmēto foueri
ignis vet⁹ veterē sig'ficat legē. cui⁹ figurē in mōte
xp̄i cōplete fuere. ꝛ ideo velut extincte cessaē debue-
rũt. Si de lapide id ē de xp̄o. qui ē lapis angularis. q̄
verbē crucis pcussus spm̄ scm̄ nobis effudit vel de
cristallo inter solem ꝛ lunā mediāte. id est xp̄o qui

Fac-simile of the Text Types of the Rationale Durandi.

[From Bernard.]

In the following year (1460), Schœffer and Fust finished a stout folio, which was printed in a Round Gothic face on the larger body of Great-primer. This book, the *Constitutions* (or Body of Divinity) *of Pope Clement V, with the Commentaries of Bishop John Andrew*, has been much admired by bibliographers for its composition. The fac-simile on a following page shows the text of the pope nested in the commentaries of the bishop—truly "a rivulet of text in a meadow of notes." In some pages the text occupies about one-third, in other pages about one-sixth, of the space assigned to the print.

The composition of pages so unevenly balanced must have taxed the ingenuity of the compositor, but he was materially aided by the licence permitting frequent use of abbreviations.

These types are cast in evener line than the types of the *Rationale*, but the face is not of neater cut. The presswork is not good. The colophon, which is like that of the *Psalter*, states that the red letters have been printed by the masterly invention of type-making; but the red letters are the ones interspersed in the text. The great initials were not printed;

Pñs hoc opusculuz finitū ac cōpletū. et ad
eusebiaz dei industrie in ciuitate Maguntij
per Johannē fust ciuē. et Petrū schoiffher de
gernshejm clericū diotes eiusdez est consū=
matū. Anno incarnacōis dñice. M.cccc.lxij.
In vigilia assumpcōis glo'se virginis marie.

Fac-simile of the Types of the Bible of 1462.
[From Bernard.]

the blank space left for them was filled up by the illuminator. This book was even more popular than the *Psalter;* it was reprinted four times, but always in the same form.

In 1462 Schœffer printed a new edition of the *Latin Bible*, in the Great-primer types of the *Constitutions*, in folio form, two columns to the page, and 48 lines to the column. It is the first Bible with printed date. According to modern taste, Schœffer's change from Pointed Gothic to Round Gothic was not happy, for the new face is inferior in design and execution. But the Round Gothic permitted the compression of the book within fewer pages, and was a more economical letter for the printer. The second volume has, in some copies, a colophon worded like that of the *Psalter of*

The Mark of Fust and Schœffer.

¶ Ad id. nõ sufficit q̃ citari nisi exp̃matũ id q̃d ad sniam audiẽ-
dam. ff. q̃ sen. sine ap. rescin. l. i. §. Itẽ cũ ex edcõ. fa. d̃ testi. cũ oli.
in fi. de do. et otu. eũ qui. li. vi. nã si h̃ in sũmarijs fortius in alijs
ut sepius dixi. ar. q̃ in alijs cauẽ in q̃b⁹ s̃uat̃ iudicio℞ figu-
¶ Nõ p̃ẽptorie ra sit nc̃ce p̃ẽptoriũ exp̃mi. ubi nõ fit trina cita
cio ad sniaꝫ audiẽdã. q̃d vid̃r tenere Jo. xxiiij. q. iij. de illicita. s.
de of. del. o sulwit. Inno. d̃ accu. ad peticõꝫ. guil. in spe. de cita. §.
viso de tpe. v̇. als aũt.
et in. v̇. quid si lata.

¶ In sc̃ptis. p̃ferat q̃d
est. j. et huius otrariũ
tenebat egi. in dec̃ no-
uit: etiã solũ ex vi illius
v̇bi de plano. et p̃ hoc
no. duo in quib⁹ ouenī-
unt iste et alie cause. s.
q̃ in hijs nc̃ce sit diffi-
nitiam in sc̃pto p̃ferri.
Itẽ q̃ iudex sic in alijs
ita in hijs hꝫ illam p̃se
ipsũ p̃ferre. et de utro-
q̃ satis no. de. sen. et re
iudi. c. fi. li. vi. ubi vide-
as nõluit q̃ scripturaꝫ
q̃ in sentẽtijs reqritur
p̃ placõnem iudicis in
hijs cauẽ p̃termitti. ne
p̃ id otingẽt occultari
veritatẽ p̃palatã. et in

¶ Sentẽtiam vero diffini-
tiuã citatis ad id licet non
p̃emptorie p̃tib⁹ in scriptis
et p̃ ut magis sibi placue-
rit. et stãs uel sedẽs p̃ferat
etiam si ei videbitur oclusi-
one nõ fcã p̃ ut ex peticõe
et p̃bati's. et alias actitatis
in causa fuerit faciendum.
¶ Que omia etiam in illis
casib⁹ in quib⁹ p̃ aliã ostõꝫ

indicio diffinitã. et p̃ oñs victorẽ ridiculose et frustra in tali p̃-
cessus iudicio laborasse. est ius in hijs cauẽ ad alias que req̃
¶ Stans. in hoc diuersiũ runt figurã iudicio℞ que ferri debẽt
a iudice sedente. de quo vide no. in p̃d. dec̃. fi. de re iudi. li. vi. in
glo. penl. Et vid̃r q̃busdã hoc induci etiã p̃ solum illud v̇bũ de
plano ut dixi in p̃n. huius p̃tis. et h̃ tenebat egi. in dec̃. nouit.
¶ Cõclusione. ista lr̃a vid̃r velle q̃ in alijs causis requirentib⁹
figurã iudicio℞ necessaria sit oclusio. Et de ocl̃one habetur. s.
de p̃cu. auditis. de causa pos. pastoralis. et in cõstitutione cle-

Fac-simile of a part of a Page of the Constitutions of Pope Clement V.

The paragraph marks were written in red ink.

[From Humphreys.]

1457, setting forth that "this little book was made by the masterly invention of printing and of type-making, without any writing of a pen;" in other copies, obviously of the same edition, this clause does not appear. This is but one of many variations in this book which can be satisfactorily explained only by Madden's theory of a double composition.

The war between Diether and Adolph for the possession of the electorate of Mentz was the occasion of some curious proclamations which were printed in the types of Schœffer.[1] Two editions, one in Latin, one in German, of a *Bull of Pope Pius II against the Turks*, dated October 22, 1463, have also been attributed to Schœffer.

The capture and sack of Mentz brought great misfortune to Fust and Schœffer. We are told that the house and materials of Fust were burned; but it is plain that he saved his punches and matrices, for we see that the old faces of type were used in all the later books of Fust and Schœffer. The printed proclamations of Adolph show that Fust soon refurnished his office, and began to print. With his fellow-citizens, he suffered from the paralysis to industry inflicted by the war. There was no encouragement for enterprise. There is no book bearing the imprint of Fust and Schœffer between the years 1462 and 1464. The unemployed workmen of Fust and

[1] The one first printed is dated April 6th, 1462: it is a manifesto, from Diether, notifying all people that he is the lawful ruler, and that Adolph is the usurper. This document, which is in German, contains 106 lines of Great-primer type, and is printed on a sheet of the size 12½ by 17¼ inches. But when Adolph captured Mentz, he issued counter proclamations. First of all was a proclamation dated August 8, 1461, from the Emperor Frederic III, announcing the deposal of Diether. It was printed on a half sheet, in German, and in the types of the *Bible of 1462*. The other proclamations were bulls or briefs in Latin, against Diether, from Pope Pius II, dated at Tivoli. All of them are in Round Gothic types on English body. The first bull warns the people to shun Diether as they would a pestilent beast; the second is the warrant for the installation of Adolph; the third orders the clergy to obey Adolph; the fourth orders the people to obey Adolph, and releases them from allegiance to Diether. The fifth bull relates to a different matter: it sets forth the unsuccessful mission of Cardinal Bessarion to the Turks. Bernard, *De l'origine*, etc., vol. I, p. 242.

Schœffer were obliged to leave the city. In leaving it, they carried with them the knowledge of the new art, which, in a few years, they established in all the larger cities of Europe.

The *Bible of 1462* found few purchasers in Mentz. The demand in the city had already been supplied with the *Bibles of 36 lines* and of *42 lines*, and buyers from abroad shunned a city subject to siege and to civil war. Leaving Schœffer to take care of the business of the printing office, Fust took the unsold *Bibles* to Paris, where he believed they would find a more generous appreciation. For it seems that, in 1458, the king of France had sent Nicholas Jenson to Mentz to get a knowledge of the practice of typography, the fame of which had then reached France, and it is supposed that Jenson gave to Fust the information that there was a demand for printing in Paris. This is the official record of the proposed mission.[1]

> On the third day of October, 1458, the king [Charles VII], having learned that Messire Guthemburg, chevalier, a resident of Mentz in Germany, a man dexterous in engraving and in types and punches, had perfected the invention of printing with types and punches, curious concerning this mystery, the king ordered the chiefs of the mint to nominate some persons of proper experience in engraving of a similar nature, so that he could secretly send them to the said place, to obtain information about the said form [type-mould] and invention, there to hear, to consider, and to learn the art. This mandate of the king was obeyed, and it was directed that Nicholas Jenson should make the journey, by means of which the knowledge of the art and its establishment should be achieved in this realm, and it should be his (Jenson's) duty to first give the art of printing to the said realm.[2]

[1] Bernard, *De l'origine*, vol. II, p. 273.

[2] We do not know whether Jenson acquired his knowledge of printing secretly or openly—in the office of Gutenberg or Schœffer, or elsewhere, but he succeeded in his undertaking. Nor is the date of his return to Paris known. Madden thinks that Jenson was taught the art not in Mentz, but in Cologne. During his absence, Charles VII died. On the 15th August, 1461, Louis XI, his son, was crowned at Rheims. A lover of books, and the founder of the great National Library, the king should have been deeply interested in the mission of Jenson, but he had formed a strong dislike to all the officers that had been appointed by his father, and began his reign by dismissing the court favorites. Jenson was treated as one of their number. All his efforts to get a suitable recompense for what he had done, and money to establish an office in Paris, were unavailing, and he was obliged to abandon Paris. He went to Venice, and made himself famous by his new design of Roman letter, and by the admirable presswork of his books.

The description of printing here given is singularly exact. It is not surprising that the existence of the new art was then known in Paris, for the colophon to the *Psalter of 1457* had announced the masterly invention; but it is strange that this document specified its characteristic features—the *formen*, or the matrices and type-mould, the types, punches and engraving. We see that the secret was revealed; that Frenchmen in 1458 had a correct idea of the vital principle of printing, and that all they required was a knowledge of its manipulations.

Eager to prevent the threatened rivalry of Jenson, Fust appeared in Paris, in 1462, with copies of the *Bible*,[1] while Jenson was ineffectually soliciting the new king to aid him. So far from being persecuted in Paris, Fust was received with high consideration, not only by the king, but by the leading men of the city. He was encouraged to establish in Paris a store for the sale of his books, and to repeat his visit.

In 1465, Schœffer printed the *Decretals of Boniface VIII*, a folio of 141 leaves, each page containing a text in large types, surrounded by notes in small types. Red letters and lines are introduced, but there are no engravings, and the presswork is in no point better than that of the *Bible of 1462*. The colophon exhibits an unscrupulous appropriation of the

[1] These *Bibles* have been the occasion of an incredible legend which was first told by one John Walchius. It would not deserve repetition here if it had not so often appeared in modern literature. He says that Fust offered one copy of this *Bible* to the king for sixty crowns, and another copy to the archbishop for fifty crowns. To tempt indifferent purchasers, he abated his price until it was but forty crowns, a price so small and so insufficient as to excite the greatest wonder. The purchasers of different copies, fearing trickery, compared their copies. Instead of discovering imperfection, they found an unvarying uniformity which was unaccountable. Meanwhile Fust was still offering for sale other copies, and all were exactly alike. As it was clearly impossible that any copyist could write so many books with this precision, it was obvious that Fust was in league with the Devil, and that the *Bibles* were their joint production. The logical process by which this conclusion was reached is not stated; but we are told that complaint was made, that Fust was arrested, and thrown in prison, from which he was not released until he had revealed the secret. The absurdity of the story is transparent. Bernard has shown that it rests on no valid authority.

words of the colophon of the *Catholicon of 1460*;[1] but, unlike the printer of that book, Fust and Schœffer here advertise themselves as the men most intimately connected with the great invention. We can plainly see their strong desire to be regarded as the first printers, but there is as yet no clear statement that Schœffer was the real inventor of printing.

In the same year was printed by Fust and Schœffer an edition of *The Offices of Cicero*, a small quarto of 88 leaves, in their smaller size of Round Gothic types. To make the book of proper thickness, and perhaps to improve the appearance of the types, which show signs of wear, Schœffer put thick leads, about one-tenth of an inch thick, between the lines. As it is the first book in which leads of perceptible thickness were used, this real improvement in printing may be attributed to Schœffer. This edition of *Cicero* is also distinguished as the first book in which Greek letters were printed; but these letters were not types—they were engraved on wood in a rude manner.[2] This edition of *Cicero* has the following colophon:

> This very celebrated work of Marcus Tullius, I, John Fust, a citizen of Mentz, have happily completed, through the hands of Peter, my son, not with writing ink, nor with pen, nor yet in brass,[3] but with a certain art exceedingly beautiful. Dated 1465.[4]

The *Cicero* was reprinted on February 4, 1466. Soon after its publication, Fust made another journey to Paris.[5] Before he could perfect his arrangements for the sale of his books, Paris was depopulated by the plague, and it is the common

[1] See page 435 of this book.

[2] In this year Conrad Sweinheym and Arnold Pannartz, who had established a printing office in the monastery of Subiaco, near Rome, printed an edition of *Lactantius*, in which Greek types were used.

[3] The phrase, *neque œrea*, must be understood as, not by engraving *in* brass or copper plates, or not by the process then employed by the copper-plate printers.

[4] The use of the words, Peter, my son, may be understood as the first acknowledgment by Fust of the marriage of his daughter to Schœffer.

[5] The Library of Geneva has a copy of this edition of *Cicero*, which contains, in his own handwriting, the acknowledgment of Louis de Lavernade, first president of Languedoc, that the book had been presented to him in Paris, by John Fust, in July, 1466.

belief that Fust was one of its victims. This is not certainly known, but he was dead on the thirtieth day of October, 1466, the date of the first mass instituted for him at the Church of Saint Victor at Paris, where his body was buried.[1]

After Fust's death, Peter Schœffer took his place at the head of the printing house. It seems, however, that he had a partner, one Conrad Fust, or Conrad Hanequis, who was, no doubt, the Henlif mentioned in the record of the Church of Saint Victor.[2] A book belonging to the Church of Saint Peter of Mentz contains the following record of their application for the manuscript of a book to which they wished to refer:

On Tuesday evening, January 14, 1468, the dean and the canons of the chapter being assembled in the court of Rhingrave, the discreet man, Conrad Fust, citizen of Mentz, respectfully requested of their reverences that they would be pleased to lend to him, and also to Peter, the husband of his daughter, a book from the library of our church, to be used as a copy, namely: the *Saint Thomas* [of Aquinas], entitled *Liber super quarto sententiarum*, and of which they wish to make many copies. The canons, considering that this request was just and pious, and that it would be productive of good, consented to the request, on condition, however, that he should replace this book, together with the *Decretals of Boniface*, and further, that he should give proper security to the canons. It was so done.[3]

[1] The record of this church says that the mass was instituted to John Fust, printer of books, "by Peter Scofer and Conrad Henlif," who gave to the church the *Epistles of Saint Jerome*, printed on parchment, and valued at 12 crowns of gold. In 1473, Schœffer established another mass for Fust and his wife Margaret, with the Dominicans at Mentz, for which he gave a copy of the *Epistles of Jerome* and of the *Constitutions of Pope Clement V*. As two books were here required, it shows that the price of books was rapidly depreciating.

[2] Bernard says that this Conrad was the son of John Fust, and that Christina Fust, who married Schœffer, was Conrad's daughter. The only evidence that this Christina was Conrad's daughter is the statement in the application, which is printed above. But this statement is not enough to overturn the contradictory statements of other writers of that day, who had better knowledge of the true relationship of all the parties. Wetter thinks that Conrad was another son-in-law to Fust. We know very little about him. It does not appear that he had any thing to do with printing before the death of Fust, nor did he exercise any known influence as a printer. His name is not to be found in any of Schœffer's books. It is not known when he died.

[3] This manuscript was returned, as had been agreed. It was probably used to collate the text of their edition of this book, a big folio of 548 double-columned pages in types on English body, which was completed by Schœffer and Conrad Fust, June 13th, 1469.

Soon after Gutenberg's death, Schœffer put forth this artful claim for recognition as one of the inventors of the new art:

Moses, in the plan of the tabernacle, and Solomon, in the plan of the temple, did nothing more than imagine a meritorious work. The merit of constructing the temple was greater than Solomon's thought. Hiram and Beselehel, greater than Solomon, improved on the plans of Solomon and Moses. He who is pleased to endow mighty men with knowledge has given us two distinguished masters in the art of engraving, both bearing the name of John, both living in the city of Mentz, and both illustrious as the first printers of books. In company with these masters, Peter hastened toward the same end.[1] The last to leave, he was the first to arrive; for he excelled in the science of engraving, through the grace of Him only who can give genius and inspiration. Hereafter every nation may procure proper types of its own characters, for he excels in the engraving of all kinds of types. It would be almost incredible were I to specify the great sums which he pays to the wise men who correct his editions. He has in his employ, the professor Francis, the grammarian, whose methodical science is admired all over the world. I, also, am attached to him, not by any greed of filthy lucre, but by my love for the general good, and for the honor of my country. Oh that they who set the types and they who read the proofs would free their texts from errors! The lovers of literature would certainly reward them with crowns of honor when with their books, they come to aid the students in thousands of schools.[2]

Portrait of Peter Schœffer.
[From Dahl.]

[1] This passage is an allusion to the running of the disciples to the sepulchre where Christ had been laid. "So they ran both together; and the other disciple did outrun Peter, and came first to the sepulchre . . . . yet went he not in. . . . . Then cometh Simon Peter following him, and went into the sepulchre." St. John, XX, 4, 6.

[2] *Institutes of Justinian, 1468.*

In this colophon, Schœffer claims superior skill as a letter-cutter. This pretension must be tested by his works. His first types, on English body, appeared in 1459, at least four years after Gutenberg's expulsion from the partnership; his next types, on Great-primer body, appeared in 1462; his last types, a very bold-faced Round Gothic on English body, were first shown in 1462, and this new face is but a font of small letters fitted to the capitals of the English of 1459.[1] These are the only types made by Schœffer. If we compare them with the types of Gutenberg, it will be perceived that they are fewer in number and of inferior design and execution. It is absurd for Schœffer to claim even equal merit with Gutenberg either as letter-cutter or type-founder. Schœffer's real merit is to be found in his eminence as a man of business. He was, no doubt, chosen as Gutenberg's successor, for his presumed ability as a manager and a sharp financier. This presumption was warrantable. His subsequent management of the printing office shows that he was a thorough man of business—a born trader. He has not shown that he was a mechanic or an inventor. Like John Fust, he practised printing, not because he loved it for its own sake, but because he loved its excitement and its promised rewards.

Sperioꝛib⁹ nup dieb⁹ peni
tioꝛa quedā grāmatice ru-
dimēta certo p oꝛdmē nu-
mero pōdere et mensura in
vnū cobercē ingēti laboē conatus sū
quo discētis et certioꝛ mens fieret ab

Fac-simile of the Types of the Latin Grammar of 1468.
A bold-faced Round Gothic on English Body.
[From Bernard.]

[1] It seems that this was done to avoid the expense of making a new mould, and to save the labor of cutting new capital letters—an evasion of duty not at all creditable to the alleged inventor of the type-mould. Gutenberg made four sizes of Pointed Gothic—the Paragon of the *Bible of 42 lines*, the Double-pica of the *Bible of 36 lines*, the Double-great-primer and Meridian of the *Psalter of 1457*—and three sizes of Round Gothic, the large English of the *Letter of Indulgence of 31 lines*, the small English of the *Letter of Indulgence of 30 lines*, and the Pica of the *Catholicon of 1460*. They were cast on seven distinct bodies. Schœffer's three faces of types, one of them imperfect, were cast on two bodies.

Schœffer established agencies for the sale of his books in Lubec[1] and Frankfort,[2] and probably in other cities. He sold not only his own books, but those of other printers.[3] We have many evidences that he was unwearied in the prosecution of his business, which seems to have been attended with much risk of loss.[4] His prosperity was at its highest point in 1476, in which year he printed four large books. After 1480, his interest in the printing office began to decline. Between 1490 and 1502, but six books were issued from his office. It is worthy of note that his last book was the fourth edition of the *Psalter*, the book with which he began his typographical career.

During his later years, Schœffer was made a judge. His official duties prevented him from giving close attention to his printing office; but printing was neglected by him because it had almost ceased to be profitable. He had competitors, not only in Rome, Paris and Venice, but in all the larger cities of Germany, and even in Mentz and Strasburg—competitors who were more skillful as printers and more shrewd as publishers. They had perceived that the art of printing would be of little advantage to them, and of little service to the world, if its practice was confined to the servile imitation of manuscript books, or if it expected to derive a generous support exclusively from the rich, or from men of taste and men of letters. The younger printers saw that it was necessary that books

[1] He consigned his books to one Hans Bitz of Lubec, who died, leaving the debt unpaid.

[2] To become a freeman of the city of Frankfort, Schœffer paid a tax of 10 pounds 4 shillings.

[3] There is in Paris a treatise by Dun Scotus, printed by Anthony Koburger of Nuremberg in 1474, which contains a bill of sale written by Peter Schœffer, which states that the book was sold to one John Henry for three crowns of gold.

[4] His agent in Paris was Hermann Stathoen, who died there in 1474, before he had been made a citizen. According to the French law, all his effects reverted to the crown. The books of Schœffer were seized by the king's commissioners, and were scattered and sold before his partner Conrad Fust, or Henlif, could make a reclamation. He appealed to the king, Louis XI, who ordered that Schœffer should be recompensed by the payment of 2,425 crowns. This was a large sum for that day: it was nearly four times as large as the sum fixed on in a valuation of all the books in the Louvre in 1459.

should be made more cheaply, and in more convenient forms. With this end in view, they introduced the cheaper size of octavo, which was much handier than the unwieldy folio or quarto. The rubricated letters and lines were supplanted by initials and borders engraved on wood and printed with the types in black ink. The fashion of surrounding a text with notes, and of making notes and text in measures of different width and length on every page, was abandoned: the text was put at the top and the notes at the bottom. Signatures, catch-words, paging-figures, blank spaces between chapters, and the division of matter in paragraphs, were introduced. But the greatest innovation was in the letters themselves. When Nicholas Jenson introduced Roman types, and proved the superior legibility of light and simple lines, the popularity of the sombre Gothic in Southern Europe came to an end. The new fashions were adopted by many printers in Germany, but they were not approved by Schœffer, who resisted them till his death. In his judgment, the only model for a printed book was the Gothic manuscript copy, and he copied it as closely as he could, with all its imperfections.[1]

This curt review of the works and workmanship of Peter Schœffer should be enough to show that his reputation as the father of letter-founders, and the inventor of matrices and the type-mould, is entirely undeserved. His types show that he had no skill as a letter-cutter or mechanic. It is not possible that a man who has shown such feeble evidences of mechanical ability could have been the first inventor of the matrices and the type-mould. While Gutenberg and Fust were living, Schœffer never made the claim that he was the inventor, or even a co-inventor, of printing. But when they were buried, he claimed that he was superior to both, and that he was really the first to enter the sanctuary of the art. In 1468, he

[1] His son, John Schœffer, who had some control over the printing office before his father's death, timidly and tardily introduced paging-figures, but they were not regularly used in his later works. We may suppose that the father disliked the innovation. The invention of leads is the only improvement that can be attributed to Schœffer.

falsely said that although Gutenberg was the first inventor, he was the man who perfected the art. It seems that he must have told his friends many things about his pretended services which he was unwilling to print. In 1503, John Schœffer said in his first book that he was a descendant of the inventor of the almost divine art of printing. In 1509, he says in another book that his grandfather was the first inventor of printing. In 1515,[1] he printed this extraordinary statement:

The printing of this chronicle was completed in the year of our Lord 1515, in the vigil of the Virgin Margaret, in the noble and famous city of Mentz, where the art of printing was first developed, by John Schœffer, descendant of the honest man, John Fust, citizen of Mentz, and inventor of the before-mentioned art. It was in the year 1450, in the 13th indiction, under the reign of the very illustrious Roman Emperor Frederic III, the very reverend father in Christ, Lord Theodoric, grand cup-bearer of Erpach, prince elector, occupying the archiepiscopal chair in Mentz, that this John Fust began to devise, and finally invented, solely through his own genius, the art of printing. Aided by divine favor, in the year 1452, he had so far improved and developed his art, that he was able to print; in which work, however, he was indebted for many improvements to the ingenuity of Peter Schœffer of Gernszheim, his workman and his adopted son, to whom, in acknowledgment of his many services and his skill, he gave the hand of his daughter, Christina Fust. These two men, John Fust and Peter Schœffer, carefully retained to their own advantage the secrets of the art; and for this purpose, they demanded from their workmen and servants an oath that they should not in any way divulge the process. Notwithstanding this precaution, in the year 1462 the knowledge of the art was carried by their workmen to distant countries, and printing thereby secured a wide development.

[1] Ten years before, John Schœffer had conceded full justice to Gutenberg, and had told the story with more truth. In the dedication of an edition of Livy, printed by him in 1505, John Schœffer uses this language: "Will your Majesty [addressing the Emperor Maximilian] deign to accept this book, printed in Mentz, the city in which the admirable art of typography was invented, in the year 1450, by the ingenious John Gutenberg, and was afterward perfected at the cost and by the work of John Fust and of Peter Schœffer . . ." This acknowledgment did not prevent the Emperor from making a subsequent official declaration, in the privilege or copyright for a grand edition of Livy, published by the same printer, and dated December 9, 1518, that the grandfather of John Schœffer had invented printing [*chalcographia*]. So much for the strength of audacious falsehood! Bernard, *De l'origine et des débuts*, vol. I, p. 309.

The thorough dishonesty of this statement is abundantly proved by its suppression of the name and services of Gutenberg. It is also evident that the writer could not, or dared not, point out the improvements which he alleges were made by Schœffer. This deficiency was soon supplied by a more credulous writer. About 1514, Trithemius,[1] one of the most learned men of that century, wrote the following description of the invention, which he says he had from Peter Schœffer himself:

It was at this period (1450) in Mentz, a city of Germany on the Rhine, and not in Italy, as some people have falsely asserted, that this admirable, and till then unheard-of, art of printing books by the aid of types was planned and invented by John Gutenberg, a citizen of Mentz. When he had spent all his property in his search after this art, and was almost overwhelmed with difficulties, unable to find relief from any quarter, and meditating the abandonment of his project, Gutenberg was enabled by the counsel and by the money of John Fust, also a citizen of Mentz, to finish the work which he had begun.

They first printed, with engravings of letters on blocks of wood, arranged in proper order in the manner of ordinary manuscripts, the vocabulary then called the *Catholicon;* but with the letters on these blocks they were not able to print anything else, for the letters were not movable, but fixed and unalterable upon the blocks, as has been stated. To this invention succeeded another much more ingenious. They discovered a method of founding the forms of all the letters of the Latin alphabet, which they called matrices, from which [matrices] they again founded types, either in tin or in brass, strong enough for any pressure, which [types?] before this had been cut by hand. In right earnest, I was told, nearly thirty years ago, by Peter Schœffer of Gernszheim, citizen of Mentz, the son-in-law of the first inventor, that this art of printing had encountered, in its first essays, great difficulties. For, when they were printing the *Bible*, they were obliged to expend more than 4,000 florins before they had printed three sections [sixty pages]. But the Peter Schœffer already mentioned, at that time a workman, but afterward son-in-law, as has been said, of the first inventor, John Fust, a man skillful and ingenious, devised a more easy method of founding types, and thus gave the art its present perfection. And the three men kept secret among themselves, for a while, this method of printing, up to the time when their workmen were deprived of the work, without which they were unable to practise their trade, by whom it was divulged, first in Strasburg, and afterward in other cities.

[1] *Annales Hirsaugienses*, vol. II, p. 421.

There are many inaccuracies in this statement. Gutenberg and Fust are represented as foolishly squandering money in vain efforts to invent xylography, a method of printing then in common use in many cities of Germany, Italy and Holland. The *Catholicon*, which is mentioned as one of the productions of block-printing, was printed from metal types in 1460. In the beginning, Gutenberg is acknowledged as the inventor of printing, yet, a few lines further, we are told that Fust was the first inventor. And it seems that Gutenberg could do nothing with his invention until helped by the advice, as well as the money, of John Fust. After the improved invention,[1] Gutenberg and Fust fell in hopeless difficulties, having spent four thousand florins before they had completed sixty pages of the *Bible*. From these difficulties they were extricated by Peter Schœffer, "son-in-law of the first inventor," who invented a more easy method of making types, and who gave the art its present perfection, and without whose aid the earlier inventions would have been of little value. The intention of the writer is plain: Gutenberg, Fust and Schœffer may be regarded as co-inventors, but Schœffer did the most effective service.

It is a curious fact that this paper, which has been so often quoted as evidence in favor of Schœffer's invention of matrices,

[1] The description of the more ingenious method of "founding the forms of all the letters of the Latin alphabet, which they called matrices, from which [matrices] they again founded types, either in tin or in brass," has been denounced by many writers on typography as the confused statement of a man who did not thoroughly understand what he related, and who has reversed the proper order of the process of type-making. A more careful reading will show that Trithemius attempted to describe the process of matrix-making, which is set forth in page 302 of this book. He says the types were made either of brass or of tin, for his memory failed him, and he could not recollect that it was the matrix which should have been of brass, and the type of tin. The characters "which before this had been cut by hand" may be regarded not as types, but as punches of soft metal. They would necessarily be damaged by pressure in the semi-fluid metal selected for making the matrices. The tools which Trithemius vainly tried to describe were the punch of steel and the mould and matrices of brass. That punches and matrices of wood or of soft metal unequal to hard pressure were used by the earlier printers is proved by the variable shapes of their types.

positively says that matrices had already been used by Fust and Gutenberg. Before Schœffer's name is mentioned, it is said that "they" [Fust and Gutenberg] discovered a method of making matrices. Trithemius says that Schœffer's contribution to the invention was "a more easy method of founding types, by which he gave the art its present perfection." He does not explain this easy method. We do not know whether his claimed improvement was in the mould or matrix, in its construction or in its manipulation; but it was not origination or invention, it was improvement only. The passage which seems to say that the first types were cut by hand does not require much comment. Trithemius may have misunderstood, and incorrectly reported, what he heard, or Schœffer may have misrepresented the facts. It is evident that Trithemius is in error; for cut types, cut either as to body or as to face, never were, never could have been used. The most trustworthy evidences tell us that the earliest types were cast in a mould.[1]

If the word *formen*, which is found in the record of the trial of Strasburg, be construed as the same word must be construed in the colophon to the *Catholicon of 1460*, in the acknowledgment of Dr. Humery in 1468, and in the order of the King of France in 1458, then we have the most complete evidence that the matrices and the accompanying type-mould were used by Gutenberg long before he knew Schœffer.

It was not necessary that Trithemius should have told us that he derived this curious information from Peter Schœffer. In these perversions of truth we may see the vanity of the man who had already boasted that he was the first to enter the sanctuary of the art. The unreasonableness of his claim

[1] The impressions of Gutenberg, which clearly show that his types were cast and not cut, should outweigh the statements of all the chroniclers; but it may be proper to recall attention to the fact that the types of the *Bible of 42 lines* were used by Schœffer in 1476, and that the types of the *Letters of Indulgence* and of the *Bible of 36 lines* were in use by Hauman at the end of the fifteenth century. If these types had been cut, they would have been soon worn out. The reappearance of these faces fifty years after they were first used shows that the types of Hauman must have been cast from the matrices of Gutenberg.

to the invention of matrices, or to the perfection of printing, may be inferred from the fact that, although he was a judge, a man of distinction, and a successful publisher for more than forty years, during the period when the value of printing was fully appreciated, he was never noticed in any way as a great benefactor. Neither the emperor nor elector gave him any distinction as the founder of a great art; no one put up a stone to his memory, honoring him as an inventor; no printer of that century regarded him as aught more than a thrifty publisher. His reputation has been created entirely by his own boasts and those of his family; and it is a most damaging circumstance that these boasts were not made until Gutenberg and Fust were dead, and that the statement written by Trithemius was not published until all the witnesses to the invention were dead, and there could be no contradiction.

There are many facts which show the falsity of Schœffer's claim. Setting aside the evidences in favor of the probable priority of the types of the *Bible of 36 lines*, the record of the lawsuit between Gutenberg and Fust virtually tells us that the types of the *Bible of 42 lines* had been made, perhaps in 1452, but not later than 1453. That these types were founded in matrices, were of neater cut, more exact as to body, and better founded than any afterward made by Schœffer, is apparent at a glance. They prove that the true method of type-making had already been found. If Schœffer invented the matrices from which these types were made, he should have perfected this invention in 1451. But Schœffer was a copyist at Paris in 1449, and it is not certain that he was with Gutenberg before 1453. Here we encounter an impossibility. It cannot be supposed that a young collegian, fresh from books, without experience in mechanics, could invent, off-hand, a complicated method of type-making, upon which Gutenberg had been working for many years.

There is still another version of this invention of matrices by Schœffer, the version of Jo. Frid. Faustus, which has been often paraded as conclusive testimony in Schœffer's favor.

John Fust, of Mentz, was the first to perceive the losses suffered by scholars through the scarcity of books. He labored diligently to invent some new method of multiplying them, so that they could be furnished to readers at reduced and reasonable prices. High Heaven, kindly favoring his sincere prayers and his most laudable intention, revealed to this excellent man the most approved form and mainstay of his invention. In the beginning, he cut the letters of the alphabet for children, on a block of wood, in high relief. With much loss of time and labor, he waited for the invention of a more suitable ink; for writing ink blotted and made the printed letters unintelligible. He experimented with soot from a candle, with which he was able to print, but the impression would not adhere to the paper. At last he invented an ink which was black, adhesive and permanent. Then he began to print on a press and to publish little books for children, which everybody bought, for the price was trivial, and buyers praised the printer. Fust was stimulated to attempt larger work, and he thereupon printed the *Donatus* in exactly the same manner. But the engraved pages of this book, cut out of the solid block, displayed many imperfect letters, and many copies were worthless. It then occurred to the inventor, at the right time, that he might print books with separate types, and that it was not at all necessary that the letters should always be cut on solid blocks. Whereupon he cut up the wood blocks, and saving all the types that had escaped injury, he made new combinations with them. This is the true origin of the composition of movable types. This new method of making types called for a great expenditure of time and labor; it delayed the work, hindered the development of the new art, and made many miserable difficulties for the inventor.

Fust had many workmen, who assisted him in making ink and types, and in other work. Among them was Peter Schœffer of Gernszheim, who, when he perceived the difficulties and delays of his master, was seized with an ardent desire to accomplish the success of the new art. Through the special inspiration of God, he discovered the secret by which types of the matrix, as they are called, could be cut, and types could be founded from them, which, for this purpose, could be composed in frequent combinations, and not be singly cut as they had been before. Schœffer secretly cut matrices of the alphabet, and showed types cast therefrom to his master, John Fust, who was so greatly pleased with them, and rejoiced so greatly, that he immediately promised to him his only daughter, and soon after he gave her to him in marriage. But even with this kind of type, great difficulty was experienced. The metal was soft and did not withstand pressure, until they invented an alloy which gave it proper strength.

As they had happily succeeded in this undertaking, Fust and Schœffer bound their workmen by oath to conceal the process with the greatest secrecy; but they showed to friends, whenever it pleased them, the first experimental types of wood, which they tied up with a string and preserved. My uncle, Doctor John Fust, testified that he had seen, with the manuscripts which were bequeathed by the inventor, these experimental types of wood, and that he had held in his hands the first part of his edition of the *Donatus*.[1]

The unknown author further says that John Gutenberg was one of the friends to whom Fust and Schœffer showed the wood types; that Gutenberg, professing to admire their ingenuity, took a great interest in their enterprise, and lent Fust and Schœffer money, thereby entangling them in an agreement, from which they could not extricate themselves until Gutenberg had acquired a right to use the invention, by which use he wrongfully enjoys the honor of first inventor. Here we may stop. It would be a waste of time to expose, one by one, the falsehoods of a statement so flatly contradicted by many unimpeachable evidences. It is very clear that the writer had no new facts to tell us about the invention. He has told us not how it was made, but how he wished it had been made that it might redound to the honor of the Fusts.

What later writers have said about the value of Schœffer's services need not be considered, for they also have produced no new facts: they have based their opinions entirely on the incorrect information of Faustus, Trithemius and Schœffer. We may pass, without further delay, to the examination of the claims made for other alleged inventors of printing.

[1] This version is found in *Wolf's Monumenta Typographica*, vol. I, pp. 466 and 469, under the heading of *The Statement of an Unknown Author*, and is attributed by Wolf to one Jo. Frid. Faustus of Aschaffenburg (who died in 1620), or to his son. Wolf admits (p. 452, note) that the identity of the author is not clearly established. It is probable that the statement was written by a descendant of John Fust, who was predisposed to magnify his services and those of his partner. Van der Linde calls the writer an arch liar. Bernard rejects the entire statement as unworthy of credit, or even of notice.

XXIV

Alleged Inventors of Printing.

Discovery of the Book of Four Stories, with Imprint of Albert Pfister...Its Types the same as those of the Bible of 36 lines...Pfister regarded as an Inventor of Printing...Description of Book of Four Stories...Its Colophon...Book of Fables...Colophon and Fac-simile...Other Books by Pfister...Pfister not a Type-founder...Probably an Engraver on Wood...Could not have Printed the Bible of 36 lines...Pfister probably got his Knowledge of Printing from Gutenberg...Paul of Prague's Notice of Printing at Bamberg...Sebastian Pfister...Pamphilo Castaldi...Absurdity of the Legend...John Mentel and his Epitaph...Gebwiler's Statement...Fac-simile of the Arms of the Typothetæ...Specklin's Statement...Plain Falsifications of History...Known Facts about Mentel and his partner Henry Eggestein.

It is, perhaps, possible to show of all inventions that somewhere somebody must have been very near to it. To assert of any invention whatever, that it could or should have been invented long ago, is nothing but chicane: we are to prove, incontrovertibly, that it was really invented, or else be silent. *Lessing.*

SCHELHORN'S opinion that the *Bible of 36 lines* was the Bible described by Zell—the book printed by Gutenberg in 1450—did not meet with the approval of those who had copies of the *Bible of 42 lines.* Men who had paid very large prices for the copies of an edition supposed to be the first, were loth to have it degraded to the inferior place of a second edition. The testimony of Zell was unceremoniously set aside; the written date of 1460 in one copy of the *Bible of 36 lines* was regarded as indicating the date of printing, and the book was declared the work of Gutenberg between 1455 and 1460. Another hypothesis was soon presented. In 1792, Steiner, a clergyman at Augsburg, announced the discovery of the *Book of Four Stories* with the imprint of Albert

Pfister, Bamberg, 1462. Soon after, Camus read before the National Institute at Paris, a critical description of the book, in which he proved the identity of its types with those of the *Bible of 36 lines*. Thereupon, incautious readers rushed to the hasty inference that, as Pfister had made use of the types of the *Bible of 36 lines*, the Bible must have been printed by Pfister. Critics of authority did not hesitate to say that Albert Pfister, a printer unknown for three centuries, and of whom there is no tradition, might have been an inventor of printing, the rival, and perhaps the predecessor and teacher, of John Gutenberg. As we know Pfister only through his books, it will be proper to examine their workmanship before this hypothesis can be considered. They are not numerous: sixteen books and pamphlets have been attributed to him, but his claim to eight has been disproved.[1]

The *Book of Four Stories*, a thin folio of 60 leaves—a version made for childish readers of the biblical descriptions of Joseph, Daniel, Esther and Judith—may be offered as the most characteristic specimen of Pfister's style. The types of this book are those of the *Bible of 36 lines*, but they are much worn. If they were not the identical characters, they were cast in the mould and matrices that had been used for the types of the *Bible*, for the types of both books agree in face and in body. The *Book of Four Stories* has fifty-five engravings on wood, six of which are repeated, each occupying the space of about eleven lines, or 2¾ inches, of the text. The engravings are coarse; they have no artistic merit, and are in every way inferior to those of the *Bible of the Poor* or the *Speculum Salutis;* they abound in puerile absurdities, and seem to be the work of a maker of cards or images. The text of the book is in German rhyme, but the lines follow each other, without break, as in a text of prose. A capital

[1] Five of the disputed works are the *Donatus of 1451*, the *Bible of 36 lines*, the *Letters of Indulgence of 1455*, the *Calendar of 1457* and the *Almanac of 1455*. The chief reason for attributing these works to Pfister is that they exhibit the types of the *Bible of 36 lines*.

letter indicates the beginning of each line of poetry, and a lozenge-shaped period denotes its ending. The presswork is decidedly inferior: the deeply indented paper shows that the printer could not regulate the pressure on the types; the muddiness of the letters comes from the use of a thin ink, and the faulty register from a shackly press. The colophon or subscription of this book, a translation of which is submitted, specifies the date, the place of printing and the printer:

Every man, in his heart, desires to be learned and well read. Without books and without teacher, this cannot be. If it were otherwise, all of us would know Latin. These reflections have engaged me for a long time. To good purpose have I sought out and gathered the four stories of Joseph, Daniel, Judith, and also of Esther. God granted protection to these four personages, as He always does to the good. This little book, which is intended to teach us how to amend our lives, was completed in Bamberg, in which city Albert Pfister printed it, in the year which is numbered one thousand four hundred and sixty-two,—which is the truth,—soon after the day of Saint Walpurgis, who is able to obtain for us grace abundant, peace, and everlasting life. May God give them to all of us. Amen.

The *Book of Fables*, a folio of 88 leaves, printed with the types of the *Bible of 36 lines*, is another work which fairly exhibits the style of Pfister. It contains eighty-five fables, each illustrated with a coarse engraving on wood, in which monkeys represent men. The text is in rhyme, but the lines follow each other without break. The colophon says:

At Bamberg this little book was finished, after the Nativity of Jesus Christ, as one counts, one thousand four hundred years and sixty and one,—such is the truth,—on the day of Saint Valentine. God save us from His sufferings.

Another book attributed to Pfister is known as *Belial*, or the *Consolation of the Sinner*. It is a folio of 95 leaves, which exhibits on the last leaf the words *Albrecht Pfister zu Bamberg*. Pfister also printed two editions of the *Bible of the Poor*, one in Latin and one in German, each containing eighteen engravings. His treatment of the old block-book is that of a mechanic and not of an artist: the designing, engraving and printing are of the lowest order. He also printed the *Complaint against Death*, and the *Judgment of*

Fac-simile of an Illustration in the Book of Fables by Albert Pfister.
[From Heineken.]

Man after Death. All were printed with the types of the *Bible of 36 lines*, and they were, apparently, his only types.

That Pfister was not a type-founder seems clearly enough established through the fact that he did all his typographic work with only one size and face of type. In all his books, the letters of the Latin alphabet appear old and worn, but the *w*, *k*, and *z*, characters of the German alphabet, are new and sharp. The types had evidently been used before for books in Latin, but not by Pfister, for the *Bible of the Poor* seems to have been the only book he printed in that language.

The *Book of Fables* bearing the date of 1461 seems the earliest of Pfister's books, but it was published without any explanation stating that it was made by a new art. It may therefore be presumed that he began to print with types before 1461. The profusion of wood-cuts in his books is an indication that he was an engraver on wood—probably a maker of playing cards, images, and block-books, who had profited by an early opportunity to perceive the advantages of types. As a seller and maker of chap-books, he would prefer the types because they explained his pictures more cheaply than the slower process of engraving letter by letter; but his persistent use of types which other printers would have condemned as worn out, shows that he did not make and could not renew them. It is not probable that a man who seems to have rated his wretched wood-cuts as the most meritorious feature of his books could have invented types. It is possible, however, that an image printer of low aims and slender ability could have perceived the economical advantages of types, and may have purchased a discarded font for the sole purpose of printing explanations to his engravings. And this seems the only conjecture that will explain Pfister's ownership of the types of the *Bible of 36 lines*.

The conjecture that Pfister printed the *Bible of 36 lines* will not bear a critical examination. It is not enough to show that our first positive knowledge of the types and the copies of this book begins with Pfister and Bamberg. It still remains to be proved that Pfister made the types and printed the copies. The proof is wanting and the probabilities are strongly adverse. The *Bible of 36 lines* is unlike any book of Pfister's in size, character, and workmanship. It is not possible that the man who began his career as a printer with an admirable edition of the Latin Bible in three volumes folio, could have ended it with the publication of shabby little books in German, intended for children. A declension like this is without a parallel in typographical history.

It has been supposed that Pfister got his types and his imperfect knowledge of typography from Gutenberg after the dissolution of the partnership between Fust and Gutenberg, but Pfister could have gotten them before. There is a blank in Gutenberg's history between the years 1442 and 1448, about which we know nothing. That he was then at work on his problem; that he must have communicated more or less of his secrets to the many unknown workmen and associates who succeeded Dritzehen, Saspach, Heilmann and Dünne; that he may have been induced to try his fortunes at Bamberg before he went to Mentz; that Albert Pfister may have been one of his workmen who followed him to Mentz and acquired some skill in the art,—these are conjectures that deserve consideration. But they are conjectures only: we have no exact knowledge concerning the introduction of typography in Bamberg. It is plain, however, that the appearance at Bamberg, in 1461,—a year before the sack of Mentz, the date usually fixed on as that of the dispersion of the printers, and the general divulgement of the secret,—of a book printed in the worn types of the *Bible of 36 lines*, and the subsequent discovery near this city of many copies of this book, which could not have been printed by Pfister, are indications that Gutenberg must have had business relations with Bamberg which are of importance in the history of printing.

The only documentary evidence which seems to favor the hypothesis that Pfister might have printed the *Bible of 36 lines* is the following curious notice of early printing, which was written about 1463, by Paul of Prague, for a contemplated but unfinished encyclopedia of arts and sciences:

The *libripagus*[1] is an artisan who skillfully engraves on plates of copper, iron, hard wood, or other substances, images, writing, or anything he fancies, and afterward quickly prints them on paper, or on a wall, or on a smooth board. He cuts whatever he pleases, and is a man who can apply his art to pictures. When I was at Bamberg, a man engraved the whole Bible upon plates, and in four weeks skillfully preserved this engraving of the whole Bible on thin parchment.

Pfister's name is not mentioned, but he was, probably, the *libripagus* here noticed. The story is not credible. The whole *Bible* was not printed in four weeks, neither at Bamberg nor elsewhere; nor was it ever engraved upon plates. The only book of Pfister's to which this statement could be applied, is his edition of the *Bible of the Poor.*

We do not know when Pfister died; his last dated work is of the year 1462. Sebastian Pfister, who is supposed to be Albert's son, was at the head of a printing office at Bamberg in the year 1470, and then printed a little book which seems to have been his first and last venture in printing.

Pamphilo Castaldi of Feltre, Italy, to whom a statue was erected in 1868, has also received the undeserved honor of an inventor of printing. This commemoration of the man by the people of a great nation seems to require in this book at least a statement of the legend on which his claims are based. This is the legend, abridged from a long panegyric on Castaldi's services by one of his countrymen:

Pamphilo Castaldi was born in Feltre, of noble parents, at the end of the fourteenth century. He was highly educated and intelligent. Although a poet and a lawyer of good reputation, his love for literature induced him to open a school for polite learning, which soon became famous, and attracted students from foreign countries. None of his pupils acquired greater fame than John Fust, who is called by the historians of Feltre, Fausto Comesburgo. This Faust resided with

[1]There is no English equivalent for *libripagus,* which means a workman who is an engraver, a printer, and a stenciler. Like other writers of his day, Paul of Prague had to coin a word to define printers, who for many years after were called *typographi, typothetæ, chalcographi, excusores* and *protocharagmatici.* Most writers called printers *impressores,* or impressors, from the process of impressing types. This word, which was finally accepted in all European languages, has served to foster the error that the vital principle of printing is impression.

Castaldi in Feltre as early as 1454. In the year 1442, Castaldi had seen a proof of Gutenberg's attempts at the invention of typography. Gutenberg at that time (1442) was supported by the money of Faust and the skill of Schœffer, his partners. After ten years of experiment, Gutenberg had done nothing more than print from blocks of wood and with metallic characters. He had not yet invented movable types, for the *Bible of 1456* should be classified with the block-books.

Castaldi, more ingenious or more fortunate, had already discovered movable types before the arrival of Faust in Feltre. It is well known that, a century before the publication of the *Mentz Psalter of 1457*, initial letters and capital letters formed of glass were manufactured at Murano, and used in Italy. These glass letters were, probably, the invention of Pietro de Natali, bishop of Equilo. Castaldi had noticed that these letters were of advantage to the scribes, who printed them in their manuscript books. He at once saw that it would be possible to print entire books, instead of occasional letters, with movable types. The facility with which this discovery had been made caused him to undervalue its importance. He gave the idea to Faust, who, returning to his partners in 1456, or a little before, enabled them to appropriate the invention of Castaldi. They greedily adopted this invention, and, in 1457, they produced the *Psalter*, the first book printed with movable characters of wood.[1]

The only portion of this absurd story which has any claim to respect is that about the early use in Italy by copyists of engraved or moulded initial letters. That they were, or could have been, made by the glass-blowers of Murano, and that Castaldi may have amused himself with experiments in stamping consecutive letters or lines, is possible. All else is pure fiction. It does not appear that Castaldi printed anything of value: we have no relics of his experiments in the form of a book, or even of a leaf, a line, or a letter. Nor did his dreams or teachings about the possible value of types ever incite any of his Italian pupils to make and use types.

To those who think that the merit of the invention of printing is in the conception of the idea of movable types, this legend about Castaldi is instructive. It reveals to us a man who is represented as having a very clear idea of the

[1] Ticozzi, Stefano, *Storia dei letterati e degli artisti del dipartimento della Piave*, Belluno, 1813. See, also, *L'imprimerie*, No. 58, October, 1868.

importance of types, who did nothing with his great discovery. His discovery, if it can be so called, was useless. He cannot be rated as an inventor of printing, for he printed nothing.

John Mentel, of Strasburg, who died in December, 1478, and was buried in the great cathedral of that city, has there a tablet to his memory, which contains the following inscription:

Here I rest: I, John Mentel, who, by the grace of God, was the first to invent, in Strasburg, the characters of typography, and to develop this art of printing, which should be perpetuated to the end of the world, to such a degree of perfection that a man can now write as much in a day as another could have done in a year. It is but just that thanks should be rendered to God, and without vanity, to me myself; but as this homage could not otherwise be rendered in a proper manner, God has ordained, as the reward for my invention, that the stones of this cathedral should serve for my mausoleum.[1]

The claim that Mentel was the inventor of typography was first made in 1520 by John Schott,[2] son of Martin Schott, who had married Mentel's daughter and inherited his business.

[1] Bernard, *De l'origine*, vol. II, p. 94. This vain and scandalous inscription was probably made by one of Mentel's descendants. It is not stated when this tablet was erected. Bernard supposes that it is a second tablet, which was put up in place of one made soon after his burial.

[2] It was probably provoked by the false assertion of John Schœffer, that Peter Schœffer, his father, and John Fust, his grandfather, were the proper inventors, to the exclusion of Gutenberg. Schott, knowing that Mentel's claims as an inventor were as valid as those of Fust or Schœffer, placed on his books, after 1520, an armorial shield containing a crowned lion, with this inscription: "Arms of the Schott family, granted by the Emperor Frederic III to John Mentel, the first inventor of typography, and to his heirs, in the year 1466." There are doubts concerning this patent of nobility. When it was demanded many years afterward, it could not be produced [*De l'origine*, vol. II, p. 69]. It may have been granted to Mentel, not as the first printer, but as the first printer in Strasburg. Schœpflin, who speaks of this document as if he had seen the original, denies that it gave to Mentel the title of inventor of printing [*Vindiciæ Typographicæ*, p. 98, note]. There was a tradition that the Emperor Frederic III had given to a corporation of master printers known as the Typothetæ, an heraldic shield, representing an eagle holding in one claw a composing-stick, and in the other claw a copy-guide, surmounted by a griffin distributing ink with two balls. But these are not the arms displayed by Schott, nor did Mentel, nor his successor Flach, make any display of them in their books.

In the year 1521, Jerome Gebwiler, misled by the assertions of Schott, undertook to controvert the pretensions of Fust and Schœffer as the first printers. He writes that printing was practised in Strasburg by John Mentel, who had obtained the new art of chalcography, or of making books with tin pens (types) about the year 1447; that Mentel, and Eggestein, his partner, made an agreement that they should keep secret the new art; that John Schott, whom he praises, showed him a manuscript book, without date, written by Mentel, in which were drawings of typographic instruments, and observations on the manufacture of printing ink. It was by similar methods that John Schott induced James Spiegel to declare, in a book printed in 1531, that John Mentel invented printing in Strasburg in the year 1444.[1] John Schott is also the authority for the following version of the invention which was found in an old manuscript chronicle attributed to Daniel Specklin.

The Arms of the Typothetæ.

[From Hansard.]

In the year 1440, the admirable art of printing was discovered in Strasburg by John Mentel. His son-in-law, Peter Schoiffer, and Martin Flach at once made use of the discovery; but a servant of Mentel, called John Gensfleisch, after stealing the secret, fled to Mentz, where he soon established the new art, through the help of Gutenberg, a very rich man. Mentel was so affected with grief by this perfidy that it caused his death. In honor of the art, he was buried in the monastery or cathedral church, and a representation of his press was cut on his tombstone. God swiftly punished the servant Gensfleisch, by striking him with blindness for the remnant of his life. I have seen the first press (of Mentel) and the types cut on wood, which were of syllables and words. They were pierced through the sides, that they could be conjoined by a wire and kept in line. It is to be regretted that these types, the first of the kind, should have been lost.[2]

[1] In another book Spiegel says 1442.

[2] Meerman, *Origines Typographicæ*, vol. II, p. 199. It is not clearly proved that Specklin, who was a magistrate of Strasburg at the close of the sixteenth century, is the author of this statement. Bernard says that this version contains about as many errors as words.

These impudent falsifications of history would have been soon forgotten if they had not been renewed in the seventeenth century, by one James Mentel, a physician of Paris, the supposed descendant of John Mentel, who published two little books on the history of printing, in which he enlarged and distorted the versions of Gebwiler, Spiegel and Specklin. To support his claim, he did not scruple to alter the text and pervert the meaning of the authors from whom he pretended to quote.[1] It was a useless work, for no impartial critic can accept the statements of Mentel or of his predecessors. For these statements, like those in behalf of Coster, Castaldi and Schœffer, were made, for the first time, long after the invention had been perfected, by men who had the desire and the temptation to misrepresent the facts. All of them are tainted with the same calumny—the accusation that Gutenberg stole his knowledge of the invention—and all of them are contradicted by public records of undoubted authority.

Neither Mentel's books nor the records of Strasburg give any warrant to the hypothesis that Mentel was an inventor of printing. His name appears for the first time on the tax list of the city of Strasburg, in the year 1447. He is called a *goltschriber*, and is enrolled with the goldsmiths. In another record of the city, for the same year, his name appears in a list of artists and painters, but he is not described as a printer. The earliest notice of him as a printer was made by Philip de Lignamine of Rome, who said, in 1474, that John Mentel of Strasburg, *since 1458*, had there a printing office, in which he printed three hundred sheets a day, "after the manner of Fust and Gutenberg." By this statement we may suppose that Mentel practised printing soon after the dissolution of the partnership between Fust and Gutenberg. It was, no doubt, from Mentz that he got a knowledge of typography, for it cannot be shown that he was taught the art by any of Gutenberg's early associates in Strasburg, nor is there any reason to believe that he was an independent inventor. We

[1] Lichtenberger, *Initia Typographica*, p. 56.

have no evidence that he experimented with types, or that he printed anything in Strasburg between 1439 and 1457. It is not even established that Mentel was the first practical printer in Strasburg, for there is evidence that he began to print there in partnership with one Henry Eggestein, who was a man of superior ability and of greater distinction, a master of arts and philosophy.[1]

Mentel did not affix his name to any of his books before 1473, but he had then printed many large theological works.[2] Schœpflin says that he soon made himself rich by his industry and his sagacity in the selection of salable books. He was a shrewd publisher, the first who issued a descriptive catalogue, and employed agents for the sale of his works.

[1] The first book printed at Strasburg with a date was a copy of the *Decretals of Gratianus*, a folio in two volumes, which bears this imprint: "By the venerable Henry Eggestein, master of liberal arts, and citizen of the renowned city of Strasburg, in the year 1471." This was not his first book, for in another book printed in the same year, he tells the reader that he has printed "innumerable volumes of law, philosophy and divinity." He printed two or three editions of the *Bible* in Latin, and one in German, and many other books in folio. The types of these books are unlike those used by Mentel. Eggestein was recorded in the tax list among the city officers, and was afterward bishop's chancellor in the court of Strasburg. The partnership between Mentel and Eggestein was of short duration. The date of Eggestein's death is not known: his name is not found in any books printed with his types after 1472.

[2] It is supposed that he printed the *Bible* in German and in Latin, *Questions of Conscience*, *A Concordance of the Bible*, *The Epistles of Saint Jerome*, *The City of God*, *The Specula of Vincent of Beauvais*. All these books are thick folios—many of them in types on English body. Some are in two, and the last named in eight, volumes. Other works have been attributed to him, but Madden says that some of them (books with a curious form of the letter R—which others say were the work of Zell) were printed at the Monastery of Weidenbach.

XXV

The Spread of Printing.

First Printers of Germany...Mentel at Strasburg...Zell at Cologne...Keffer and Koburger at Nuremberg...Fac-simile of a part of Koburger's Map...Zainer at Augsburg...Fac-simile of Zainer's Birth of Eve...John of Westphalia and Martens at Louvain...Mansion at Bruges. Gerard Leeu at Antwerp...First Printers of Italy...Sweinheym and Pannartz at Rome...De Spira at Venice...Jenson's Types...Venice famous for Printing...Cennini at Florence...The Ripoli Press...Zarot at Milan...Appearance of Publishers...First Printers of France...Gering, Crantz and Friburger at Paris...The Printers of Elegant Books...First Printers in Spain and Portugal...In England...Caxton at Westminster...Printing did not find a general Welcome. Made Popular by the Cheapness of Books...Injudicious Selection of Books for Publication. Demand for Books in the Vernacular...First Check on the Liberty of the Press.

About this time, the crafte of Enpryntyng was fyrste founde in magounce in Almayne, which crafte is multiplyed through the world in many places, and bookes ben had grete chepe and in grete nombre by cause of the same crafte.

Caxton, 1482.

IN CENTRAL AND NORTHERN EUROPE.

WHEN two rival printing offices had been established at Mentz it was no longer possible to keep secret the processes. Every printer who handled the types and every goldsmith who helped to make the tools must have felt a weakening of the obligation of secrecy. The sack of Mentz was a greater misfortune, for it dissolved all obligations and sent the printers to other cities to found new offices. Not one of these printers has told us when and how he began to print on his own account. All we know about the introduction of printing in many of the large cities has been gathered from the dates of books and the chance allusions of early chroniclers. It is from these imperfect evidences that the following tables of the spread of printing have been made up. They are based on the chronological arrangement of Santander's *Dictionary*, but the names and dates have been collated with those of Cotton's *Typographical Gazetteer*, and other works of authority, and some alterations have been made.

Place.	Printer.	Date.
Mentz	John Gutenberg	1450
Bamberg	Albert Pfister	
Strasburg	Mentel and Eggestein	1458
Cologne	Ulric Zell	1462
Augsburg	Gunther Zainer	1468
Nuremberg	Henry Keffer	1469
Munster in Argau	Helyas Helye	1470
Spire	Peter Drach	1471
Ulm	John Zainer	1473
Buda (Hungary)	Andrew Hess	1473
Mersburg	Lucas Brandis	1473
Laugingen		1473
Esslingen	Conrad Fyner	1473
Marienthal	Bros. of Life-in-Com	1474
Lubec	Lucas Brandis	1475
Burgdorf		1475
Blaubeuren	Conrad Mancz	1475
Pilsen		1475
Rostock	Bros. of Life-in-Com	1476
Geneva	Ad. Steynschauer	1478
Prague		1478
Eichstadt	M. and G. Reyser	1478
Wurtzburg	Dold, Ryser, *et al.*	1479
Leipsic	Marcus Brand	1481
Aurach	Conrad Fyner	1481
Erfurt	Wider de Hornbach	1482
Memmingen	Albert de Duderstadt	1482
Passau	Stahl, Mayer, *et al.*	1482
Reutlingen	John Ottmar	1482
Vienna	John Winterburg	1482
Magdeburg	Rauenstein *et al*	1483
Stockholm	John Snell	1483
Winterberg	John Alacraw	1484
Heidelberg	Fred. Misch	1485
Ratisbon	John Sensenschmidt	1485
Brinn	Stahl & Preinlein	1486
Munster	John Limburg	1486
Sleswick	Stephen Arndes	1486
Frisia		1488
Kuttenberg	Von Tischniowa	1489
Ingolstadt	John Kachelofen	1490
Hamburg	J. and T. Borchard	1491
Wadstein		1491
Czernigov	Tzernoevic	1492
Zinna		1492
Fribourg	Kilianus Piscator	1493
Luneburg	John Luce	1493
Copenhagen	Gothof. de Ghemen	1493
Oppenheim		1494
Freisingen	John Schæffler	1495
Offenburg		1496
Tubingen	John Ottmar	1498
Cracow	John Haller	1500
Munich	John Schobser	1500
Olmutz	De Baumgarten	1500
Pfortzheim	Thomas Anselmus	1500

This is but a brief list for the vast and populous country north of Italy and east of France and the Netherlands.[1] Not less remarkable is the fact that some cities now deservedly famous for their printing were among the last to acquire a knowledge of the art, and those that gave it feeble support.

The master printers at Mentz before 1500, not previously named, were: Erhardus Reuwich, whose first book was dated 1486; Frederic Misch, who began after 1490; Jacob Meydenbach (a witness at the trial of 1455), between 1491 and 1496; and Peter Friedburg, between 1494 and 1497. There may

[1] For a table of the chronological order in which printing was established in the Netherlands, see page 323 of this book.

have been others, whose names are lost, but the printers are few; they cannot be compared, either in number or in influence, with those of many smaller cities during the same period. Long before Schœffer died,[1] Mentz had ceased to be a great school and centre of printing.

STRASBURG. The statement of Lignamine, that Mentel printed at Strasburg after 1458, has been corroborated by the recent discovery in the Freiburg library of a Latin *Bible* in two volumes folio, which is known to have been printed by Mentel, and which contains the subscriptions of the illuminator and the written dates, in one volume of 1460, in the other of 1461.[2] As this book should have been in press at least two years, it may be regarded as evidence that printing was practised here as early as in Bamberg. Strasburg gave greater encouragement to printers than Mentz, for sixteen master printers were working there before 1500.

COLOGNE. The first printer at Cologne was Ulric Zell. He was an industrious printer for more than forty years, but he never printed a book in German, nor did he adopt any of the improvements of the printers of Italy. He adhered rigidly to the severe style of his master, Schœffer, printing all his books from three sizes of a rude face of Round Gothic types. He was not a skillful nor even a correct printer, but he was a shrewd publisher, and accumulated a large property. Madden supposes that he went to Cologne in 1462, and

[1] The high reputation of Schœffer's office was fairly sustained by his son John, who died in 1531. Peter Schœffer, junior, another son, was equally able, for he printed books in Hebrew, Latin, German and English. He found no proper encouragement at Mentz, and had to establish his office successively at Worms, Strasburg and Venice. His last known work, with date 1542, was printed at Venice, where it is supposed he died. Ives Schœffer, son of Peter, junior, who succeeded John Schœffer in the management of the office at Mentz, was an industrious publisher from 1531 to 1552, the supposed year of his death. Victor, the son of Ives, gave up the business, and the name of Schœffer disappeared from the roll of printers at Mentz. Helbig, *Notes et dissertations*, etc., p. 47–50.

[2] A description of this *Bible*, with other particulars of importance, was given by Dr. Dziatzko, the librarian at Freiburg, in a letter to Hessels, and by him printed in the introduction to the *Haarlem Legend*, p. XXII.

was engaged by the Brotherhood of the Life-in-Common at Weidenbach, near that city, to assist them with his new art of printing in their pious task of making books.[1] His name appears for the first time in a book dated 1466, which date may be accepted as indicative of the time when he left the monastery and began to print on his own account in the city.

At the close of the fifteenth century, twenty-two printing offices had been established at Cologne. Among them was that of Arnold Ter Hoorne, who, despite his occasional bad presswork, deserves special notice as one of the first printers who made use of Arabic figures.

NUREMBERG. Henry Keffer, who appeared as a witness for Gutenberg in the suit at law in 1455, is supposed to have established himself as a printer at Nuremberg about 1469. His name appears, for the first time, in the imprint of a book dated 1473, from which it seems that he was hired by John Sensenschmidt, a wealthy man of that city,[2] who aspired to be a publisher. In 1473, Anthony Koburger began to print at Nuremberg. In a few years he acquired great reputation as printer and publisher: he had twenty-four presses at Nuremberg and offices at Basle and at Lyons. Lichtenberger says that he printed twelve editions of the *Bible* in Latin and one in German. That he merited his honors is implied by the testimony of Jodocus Badius, his rival at Paris, who frankly said he was an honest merchant and the prince of printers. The success of Koburger did not materially interfere with the

[1] The Brotherhood were forbidden by the vows they had taken to ask for alms or accept gifts, and were required to live by the labor of their hands. They devoted themselves to the duties of teaching school and copying books. At Weidenbach they were remarkably successful. They built a church in 1490 with the money they had made from the sale of manuscript and printed books. Madden says that the monastery of Weidenbach was not only a publishing house, but a prominent school of typography, and that there are reasons for believing that it gave instruction to Caxton, Jenson, Mansion and other eminent printers.

[2] This John Sensenschmidt subsequently went to Bamberg, and in 1481 there published the *Bamberg Missal*, with a text in Pointed Gothic types of five-line pica body, probably the largest text types ever used in a book. It was admirably printed and rubricated.

prosperity of his rivals, for there were seventeen master type-printers and many block-printers at Nuremberg before 1500. Koburger's most curious book is the *Nuremberg Chronicle*

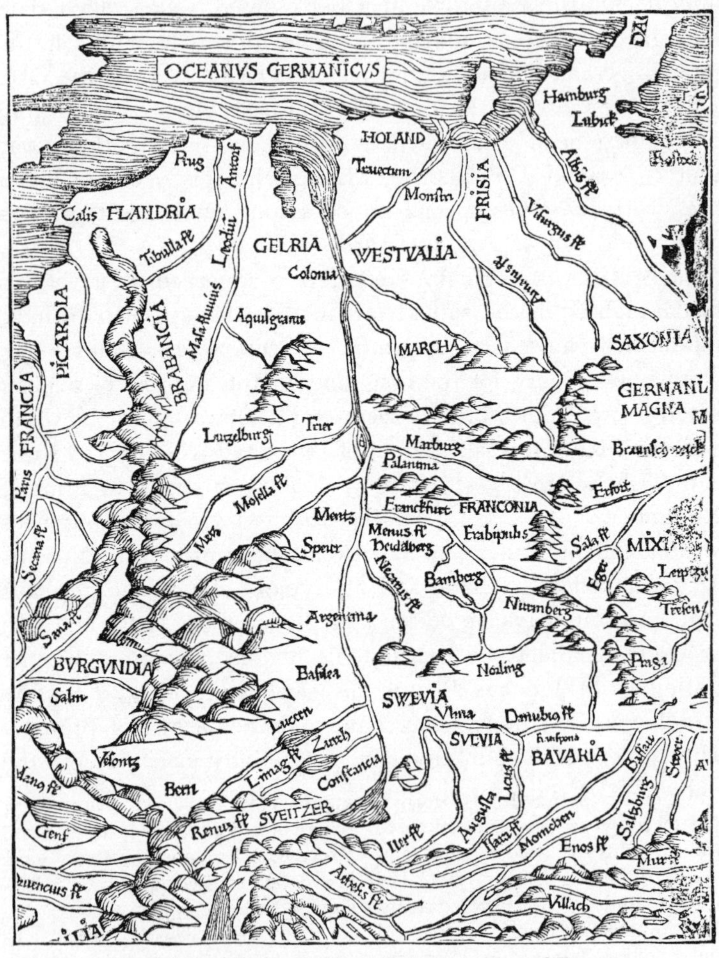

Fac-simile, reduced, of part of Koburger's Map of Europe.

[Photographed from Mr. Bruce's copy of the Nuremberg Chronicle.]

of 1493, a large and thick folio, edited or compiled by Hartmann Schedel, as a summary of the history, geography and wonders of the world. It contains more than two thousand impressions[1] of wood-cuts, "made by Wolgemuth and Pleydenwurff, mathematical men, and cunning as designers."

AUGSBURG. The practice of typography was brought to Augsburg in 1468 by Gunther Zainer of Reutlingen, who is

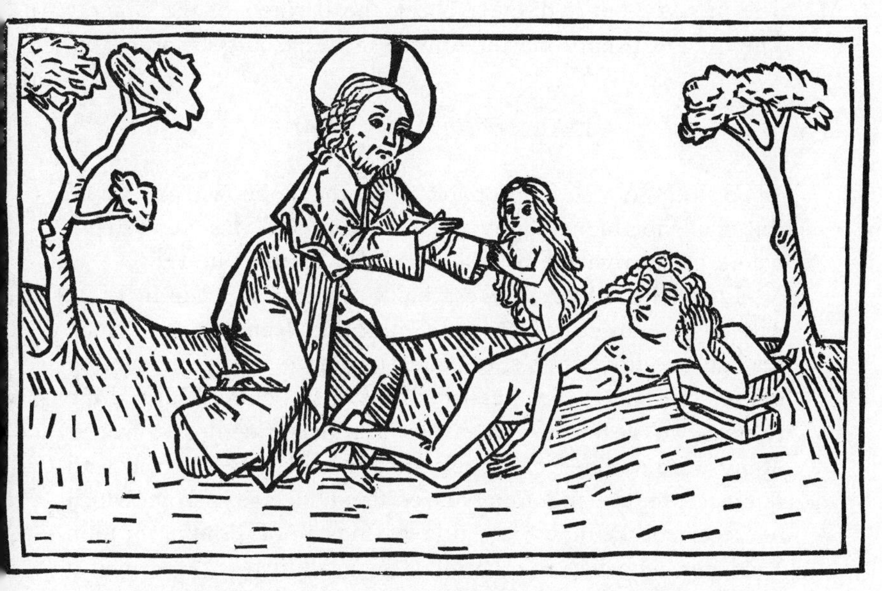

The Birth of Eve, from Zainer's Edition of the Speculum Salutis.

[From Heineken.]

supposed to have been taught at Strasburg. He was the first printer in Germany who printed a book in Roman characters.

[1] These two thousand impressions were taken from about three hundred cuts—for the cut that served for the portrait of Paris of Troy was used for Odofredus of Germany and the poet Dante of Italy. Wood-cuts professing to represent cities and battles in Greece and Syria were repeated for battles and cities in France and Germany, with an indifference to the anachronisms and a cool disregard of the incredulity of the reader that are amazing. The author had a keen relish for the marvelous—for men with one eye, with immense ears, with enormous legs, and like monstrosities. The *Dance of Death*, which is reproduced on page 185 of this book, is one of the most meritorious designs, but most of them are of small value. The fac-simile of Koburger's map on the opposite page should be contrasted with the map of Germany in any modern atlas. It is presented as an illustration of the medieval notion of geography, and as one of the first attempts at map-printing.

He and his rivals, Bamler, Schüssler and Sorg,[1] illustrated their books so freely with wood-cuts as to provoke the remonstrance of the fraternity of block-printers of Augsburg.[2] This opposition may have caused Zainer's retirement from business in 1475, but it did not check the business of the others.[3] There were twenty master printers at Augsburg before 1500.

IN THE NETHERLANDS.

UTRECHT. It is probable that the unknown printer of the four notable editions of the *Speculum* was at Utrecht before the arrival of Ketelaer and De Leempt in 1473.[4]

LOUVAIN. John of Westphalia came to Louvain in 1472, with some matrices of Round Gothic and Roman types which he had acquired in Venice, and began to fit up a printing office. In 1473, he published his first book. During the twenty-two years he was in business, he printed 120 works. Many were editions of the classics, and all were selected with reference to the requirements of the University, from which he received the honorary title of Master of Printing. John Veldener, who began to print at Louvain in 1473, received a similar title. He boasted that he was expert in all branches of the graphic arts, but his skill was that of a mechanic. As

[1] In 1477, Sorg printed the first illustrated edition of the whole Bible; in 1483, a description of the council of Constance, containing nearly one thousand engravings.

[2] Representing that the use of wood-cuts by typographers was an infringement on the vested rights of the guild, the block-printers induced the magistrates to pass a law commanding printers not to use wood-cuts. Not deriving the benefits they expected from this restriction, the block-printers proposed to concede to the typographers the right to use as many cuts as they pleased, providing they would agree to use only the wood-cuts made by regular engravers.

[3] In 1472, Melchior of Stanheim, abbot of the monastery of St. Ulric at Augsburg, established a printing office in his monastery, buying types and tools from other printers. He bought five presses of Schüssler for 73 florins, and had five other presses made for him by a joiner of Augsburg. The equipment of his office cost 702 florins, which was then regarded as a large sum.

[4] See chapter XV and pages 322–325 of this book for a fuller description of the works of this printer.

a publisher, he could not compete with John of Westphalia.[1] Thierry Martens, of Alost, was employed by John of Westphalia, probably as editor, soon after he arrived at Louvain. After receiving suitable instruction, Martens was allowed to print some little books at Alost in 1473. He began to print at Alost in his own name in 1487. Necessity or the love of change compelled him to move his printing office many times between Louvain and Antwerp. In 1529, he forsook printing and retired to Alost, where he died in 1534, at the age of eighty-eight years. In his business life of almost sixty years he printed, beside many other works, about 150 books in Greek, Hebrew and Latin. He had a critical knowledge of six languages, and his ability as an editor was acknowledged by many scholars who were his friends and correspondents. Erasmus wrote his epitaph, and the town of Alost has put up a statue to commemorate his worth.

BRUGES. The name of Colard Mansion, a calligrapher of high merit and afterward the first typographer at Bruges, is found in the records of a corporation of book-makers, between the years 1454 and 1473. As his name does not re-appear before 1482,[2] it is supposed that he abandoned the guild and learned printing. In 1476, he printed a little book in a new face of type in the French style. He was a skillful but not a prosperous printer, for he was obliged to eke out his scant income as a printer by occasional jobs of illumination. Soon after 1484, he left Bruges. It is not known where he went or when he died. John Brito, who succeeded Mansion, was for many years the only typographic printer at Bruges. This neglect of printing in a city renowned for the elegance of its manuscripts and the skill of its calligraphers shows that the professional book-makers regarded printing as an inartistic and mechanical method of making books.

[1] See notes on pages 281 and 322.

[2] Many bibliographers say that he went to Cologne in 1473. Madden regards him as a pupil of the monastery at Weidenbach. Blades thinks that he was self-taught, or taught by some unknown printer, and that, as early as 1472, he began his typographic work at Bruges, in which he was assisted by William Caxton.

GOUDA and ANTWERP. Gerard Leeu, the most industrious[1] printer of his time, began to print at Gouda in 1477, but he went to Antwerp in 1484, where he continued to print until his death in 1493. Imitating Verard of Paris, he gave his later years to the translation and printing of romances and popular books. In 1493, he began to print Caxton's *Chronicle of England*, in English and obviously for sale in England, but he died before the work was finished.[2]

IN ITALY.

This is the order in which printing was established in Italy:

Place.	Printer.	Date.	Place.	Printer.	Date.
Subiaco	Sweinheym & Pannartz	1465	Mondovi	Antonio Mathiae, *et al.*	1472
Rome	Sweinheym & Pannartz	1467	Jesi	Frederic Veronensis	1472
Venice	John de Spira	1469	Cremona	Paravisinus, *et al*	1472
Milan	Anthony Zarot	1470	Parma	Andrew Portiglia	1473
Foligno	John Nummeister	1470	Brescia	Thomas Ferrandus	1473
Trevi	John Reynard	1470	Messina	Henry Alding	1473
Verona	John of Verona	1470	Vicenza	John de Reno	1473
Treviso	Gerard de Lisa	1471	Como	De Orcho, *et al*	1474
Bologna	Balthazar Azzoguidi	1471	Turin	Fabri and John de Petro	1474
Ferrara	Andrew Belfort	1471	Genoa	Matthew Moravus, *et al.*	1474
Naples	Sixtus Riessinger	1471	Modena	John Vurster	1475
Pavia	Antonio de Carcano	1471	Trent	Hermann Schindeleyp	1476
Florence	Bernard Cennini	1471	Palermo	Andrew de Wormatia	1477
Fivizano	Jacobus and others	1472	Ascoli	William de Linis	1477
Padua	Balt. de Valdezochio	1472	Lucca	Bart. de Civitali	1477
Mantua	Pietro Adam de Michael	1472	Casal	William de Canepa	1481

Cotton, in his *Typographical Gazetteer*, specifies thirty-seven other places in Italy in which printing was done before 1500.

[1] He printed eight books in 1478; seven in 1479; nine in 1480; ten in 1482. In fifteen days he printed three books, one of 85, and another of 305 leaves. During the seventeen years he was in business he printed 150 books. His last book at Gouda was dated June 23, 1484; on the 18th of September, 1484, he published at Antwerp, a book of 400 pages. Fifteen days after, he completed another book. During the first six months of 1485, he published one volume each month. One of these books had 34, and another 76 engravings specially cut for the work.

[2] The colophon of this book is a queer piece of mysterious English: . . . Enprentyd in the duchye of Braband, in the town of Andewarpe, in the yere of our Lord M. CCCC. XCIIII. By maistir Gerard de Leew, a man of grete wysedom in all maner of kunyng: whych nowe is come from Lyfe unto the doth, which is grete harme for many of poure man. On whas sowle God almythy for hys hygh grace haue mercy. Amen. Van der Meersch. *Imprimeurs Belges et Néerlandais*, vol. I, p. 119.

SUBIACO and ROME. Conrad Sweinheym and Arnold Pannartz, two printers from Germany, set up a press in the monastery of Subiaco, near Rome, and there produced in 1465 the books first printed from types in Italy. To please the tastes of their Roman readers they made a new font of Roman types. It was not a successful effort, for the traces of Gothic mannerisms are noticeable in almost every letter. Not meeting with the encouragement they desired, the two printers removed to Rome in 1467. They began to print on a grand scale, making new fonts of Roman, Greek and Round Gothic types, enlisting the services of Bishop John Andrew as reader and corrector, and undertaking the publication of many large classical works. They did not prosper. In the year 1472, they petitioned the pope for relief, setting forth that they had printed 11,475 copies of twenty-eight works, a very large portion of which had not been sold, and that they were in great distress. In 1473, Sweinheym withdrew from the partnership, and began to engrave on copper maps for an edition of *Ptolemy's Geography*. He died before the book was published, in 1478. Pannartz died in 1476.

Ulrich Hahn, a printer of Bavaria, went to Rome in 1465, and began to print there in 1467. His first book was in Round Gothic types, but his Italian readers induced him to make for his second book a rude form of Roman types. He employed Campanus, an eminent scholar, as reader and corrector, and associated himself with Simon Nicholas de Lucca, who acted as editor and publisher of his books. At this time there were in Rome many printing offices, and the number increased, notwithstanding the complaints of Sweinheym and Pannartz, and also of Philip de Lignamine, that more books were printed than could be sold. Before the year 1500, there were or had been thirty-seven master printers at Rome.

VENICE. John de Spira, so called from Spire, the city in which he was born, was the first typographer at Venice. He began in 1469, by the publication of the *Letters of Cicero* in types of Roman form. Soon after, he published an edition in folio of the *Natural History of Pliny*, which is regarded as one of the finest specimens of the printing of the fifteenth century. Proud of his fine work, but fearing competition, De Spira solicited and obtained from the senate, September 18th, 1469, exclusive rights as a printer in Venice for five years. The privileges seem to have been forfeited by his death in 1470; but his printing office was managed with ability by his brother Vindelin, who succeeded to the business.

Nicholas Jenson, the "man skilled in engraving," who had been sent to Mentz in 1458, and who, according to Madden, had thoroughly qualified himself in the monastery of Weidenbach, seems to have been the first of several printers who hastened to Venice to profit by the forfeiture of De Spira's privilege. In 1471, he published his first book,[1] the *Decor Puellarum*, in neat light-faced Roman types on Great-primer body. His experience at the mint of Tours as an engraver gave him a decided advantage over all his rivals. Roman types had been made before by Sweinheym, De Spira and Hahn, but never before had punches been so scientifically engraved, nor types so truly aligned. It is not surprising that the efforts of his predecessors should pass for naught, and that Jenson has ever since been regarded as the introducer of Roman types. But Jenson discovered, as Hahn and De Spira had done, that, to secure buyers in Germany, it was necessary to print books in Gothic characters. With this object in view, he cut several fonts of Round Gothic, one on Bourgeois and one on Brevier body, the smallest sizes of types made in the fifteenth century.

As a printer, Jenson is entitled to high praise. None of his competitors showed so much taste and skill in the details of book-making. It is noticeable in every feature—in the tint and texture of his paper, in the glossy blackness of his ink, in the clearness and solidity of his impressions, in the

[1] The printed date of this book is M.CCCC.LXI. It is a curious circumstance that this exact printer should begin with an error which makes his first publication appear ten years earlier than it was.

uniformity of register and of color on every page. Jenson's merits were recognized by Pope Sixtus IV, who, in addition to other marks of favor, bestowed upon him the title of count palatine. He died in 1481: His printing office passed into the hands of an association of which Andrew Torresani of Asola was the manager. In time, Aldus Manutius, a partner in this association, married a daughter of Torresani, and got control of the office, the reputation of which he increased by his scholarship, by his numerous editions of the classics, and by his introduction of Italic types, but not by superior skill as a typographer. As a type-founder, printer and ink-maker, Jenson had no rival and left no proper successor.

At the close of the fifteenth century, Venice took the lead of all cities, not only in the number of its printing offices, but in the beauty of its types and printing. Printers in other countries knew that they would secure for their types the highest commendation by announcing them as the true Venetian characters. Santander specifies 201 master printers who had been in business at Venice before 1500. Bernard estimates the number of books then and there printed at two million volumes.

FLORENCE. Bernard Cennini, an eminent goldsmith of Florence, began to print with types at that city in the year 1471. He said that he and his sons Peter and Dominic made the tools and types and did all the work without instruction, but the exact manner in which Cennini describes the cutting of punches and the founding of types makes this statement doubtful. Cennini never earned any reputation as a typographer, for it does not appear that he printed any book after 1471. Santander names twenty-two master printers at Florence before 1500. The most noticeable of the number is Dominic de Pistoia, an ecclesiastic who founded a printing office in 1474, which is known in history as the Ripoli Press. Dominic was the abbot of a monastery, but he proved an active and intelligent publisher. He deserves notice chiefly for his care in keeping his accounts, which give us our most trustworthy information concerning the materials and usages of the early printers.[1]

MILAN. Anthony Zarot began to print at Milan in 1470 or 1471, having been hired by Philip de Lavagna, who seems to have been a capitalist and a publisher. In 1472, Zarot persuaded four citizens of Milan to unite with him in a new association for the printing and publishing of books. The articles of agreement are curious, and deserve preservation.[2] The association seems to have been remarkably prosperous, for in 1472 it had seven presses at work. In 1473, the pub-

[1] In 1479, Dominic made this contract for printing a book The publisher Boniface should furnish the paper, and should pay 10 livres for 200 copies of a book of 23 or 24 leaves of royal octavo or ordinary quarto. If he printed more than 200 copies, he should forfeit all claims for work done. In another contract, made in 1480, Dominic agreed to print 100 copies of a book of 100 or 120 pages for 4 florins in gold. The prices for printing seem insufficient, but the cost of labor was small. The compositors of the Ripoli Press were the sisters of a convent.

[2] The partnership should be for three years. Zarot bound himself to furnish all the types, Latin and Greek, Roman and Gothic, and to make all the ink. The four associates were to furnish the money. One of them, De Burgo, should advance 100 ducats as soon as they could keep four presses steadily at work. If any partner should obstruct the business, he should lose all his rights. Rent should be paid out of the general fund. Profits should be divided in three parts, of which Zarot should have one part, and the four associates, two parts. Zarot should pay the associates one third the actual cost of the presses and other implements, which should become his property at the termination of the partnership. Current expenses should be paid out of the general fund from the profits of sales. The priest Gabriel (a partner) should be the agent, treasurer and general manager. He should have one copy of every book printed. Books for publication should be selected at a general meeting of all partners. The corrector and the copyists should be paid in printed books. Every workman should be bound by oath to keep the secrets of the partners, and was forbid to give any book to any other master printer of the city. If any partner wished to print a book on his own account, and could not agree with his associates, he would be permitted to have it done elsewhere.— Peter and Nicholas de Burgo immediately asked for the use of three presses or more, for works on common and civil law and medicine, they providing and paying for the presses and for working them, and half the current expenses of the office. They also agreed to give one-fourth of the profits, to pay a bonus of 25 ducats, and one copy of each book, provided the society would not sell it under price.

lisher Philip de Lavagna and his new partner Montanus made an agreement with Christopher Valdarfer, another printer at Milan, for the exclusive use of two presses.[1]

There was no part of Europe in which so great an enthusiasm was shown for printing as in Italy.[2] The only open opposition which the new art encountered was made in 1472, by the copyists of Genoa, who complained that the typographers were greedy, and that they deprived the copyists of their livelihood by undertaking to print little books.

IN FRANCE.

Place.	Printer.	Date.	Place.	Printer.	Date.
Paris	Ulrich Gering, *et al.*	1469	Hagenau	Henry Grau	1489
Lyons	Buyer and Le Roy	1476	Dol	Peter Metlinger	1490
Angers	De Turre and Morelli	1477	Grenoble		1490
Chablis	Pierre le Rouge	1478	Orleans	Matthieu Vivian	1490
Poitiers	J. Boyer and G. Bouchet	1479	Dijon	Peter Metlinger	1491
Toulouse		1479	Angoulême		1491
Caen	Ferrandus and Quijone	1480	Cluny	Michael Wenssler	1493
Vienne	Pierre Schenck	1481	Nantes	Etienne Larcher	1493
Promentour	Loys Guerbin	1482	Limoges	John Berton	1495
Troyes	Guillaume le Rouge	1483	Provins	G. Tavernier	1496
Chambery	Antonius Neyret	1484	Tours	Matthieu Lateron	1496
Bréand-Loudéhac	R. Foucquet	1484	Avignon	Nicol Lepe	1497
Rennes	Pierre Belleesculée	1484	Treguier		1499
Abbeville	Dupré and Gerard	1486	Guienne		1500
Rouen	Guillaume le Talleur	1487	Perpignan	J. Rosembach	1500
Besançon		1487			

PARIS. About the close of the year 1469, Ulrich Gering, Michael Friburger and Martin Crantz began to print at Paris. To please the classic tastes of the doctors of the university who had invited them, their first book appeared in types of Roman form. They were not skillful printers, for Chevillier says that letters half formed and half printed are noticeable

[1] It will be seen that the business of publishing is almost as old as that of printing. Valdarfer agreed to set up the types of the books produced at the rate of 24 imperials (?) for every 20 pages. The wary publishers took the precaution to specify in the agreement that the blank pages should not be counted.

[2] The Senate of Lucca, by a vote of 38 to 9, voted to pay the priest Clement, a professional calligrapher and bookbinder (who had applied for the means to go to Venice and get a knowledge of the art), a subvention of two florins monthly, on condition that he should practise his art as a public officer, teaching all who wished to learn. Clement declined the offer.

in their earlier works, but they were industrious publishers. Like Jenson, they found it expedient to cut and cast types of the Round Gothic fashion, for the Roman character was most admired by scholars. In 1477, Crantz and Friburger abandoned printing, but Gering continued to print until his death in 1510. He willed a large property to the university.

In 1473, Peter Keyser and John Stol, after a three years' service with Gering, set up a rival printing office, the result of which was a reduction in the price of books.[1] This competition did not prevent other printers from founding offices in Paris, but it did compel some to improve the quality of their work, and to seek a new class of readers. Antoine Verard in 1480, and Phillipe Pigouchet in 1484, founded a new school of printing, when they undertook to make prayer-books and romances in imitation of the style of the miniaturists.[2] Thielmann Kerver, who commenced to print in 1497, was almost as famous as a printer of ornamental books. The growing taste for fine books did not prevent the publication of solid literature. In 1495, Jodocus Badius, a printer of great learning, who had been proof-reader for his father-in-law, Trechsel of Lyons, established an office at Paris, and began to print for men of education. In the following year came the famous Henry Stephens, first of a long line of printers eminent for their scholarship and diligence as editors and publishers of classical and critical text books. Before the year 1500, there were, or had been, sixty-nine master printers in Paris.

LYONS. Lyons must have offered unusual inducements to master printers, for there were forty printing offices in that city before the year 1500. The printers of Lyons were busy

[1] Gering reprinted the books of Keyser and Stol as soon as he could procure copies. Each house boasted of the superior accuracy and greater cheapness of its own publications.

[2] In this style the pages were surrounded by narrow pictorial borders in pieces of irregular length. These pieces were repeatedly used on different pages, but always in new combinations, so as to present some feature of novelty. The groundworks of the borders were generally stippled. The large illustrations in the text were in outline, obviously intended for coloring. Red letters were often printed on every page, but the larger initials were painted.

publishers, and their competitors in Italy complained with reason of their piratical editions. They made liberal use of engravings on wood and copper-plate illustrations. They were also the first printers to sell cheap books in showy bindings.

IN SPAIN AND PORTUGAL.

Place.	Printer.	Date.	Place.	Printer.	Date.
Barcelona	N. Spindeler	1473 or 1478	Murcia	Juan de Roca	1487
Valencia	Cordova and Palomar	1474	Tarragona	John Rosembach	1488
Saragossa	Matthew Flandrus	1475	Lerida		1488
Seville	A. Martinez, *et al*	1476	San Cucufute des Valles		1489
Segorbe		1479	Lisbon	R. Samuel Zorba	1489
Tolosa	Henry Mayer	1480	Pampeluna		1489
Burgos	De Basilea	1485	Zamora		1490
Salamanca		1485	Leiria	Abraham Dortas	1492
Soria	Eliezar ben Alanta	1485	Grenada	Meynard Ungut	1496
Xerica		1485	Madrid		1499
Toledo	John Vasquez	1486	Montserrat	John Luchner	1499

IN GREAT BRITAIN.

The first book printed in English, the *Recuyell of the Historyes of Troye*, a stout folio of 351 leaves, does not contain the date of printing, nor the name and place of the printer, but it appears from the introduction that it was translated from the French by William Caxton between the years 1469 and 1471. When and where it was printed is a vexed question.[1]

The monogram which was exhibited by Caxton in his later books—s W. 74. C. t—is interpreted by Madden as *William Caxton, 1474, Sancta Colonia.* It is an indication that a notable event in his life was represented by the year 1474 and the city of Cologne, and it seems to authorize the conjecture that at this time and place he published his first book. In 1475, Caxton printed, in the office of Mansion at

[1] Blades thinks that it was printed at Bruges by Colard Mansion and William Caxton, about 1472. Madden thinks it was printed at the monastery of Weidenbach by Mansion and Caxton, who went there about 1474 to learn practical typography. Other bibliographers say that it was printed by Zell at Cologne. The types of this *Recuyell* are thoroughly French, and are like the larger types used by Mansion. Bernard thinks that these types were made and first used at Cologne, by the order of the Duke of Burgundy for the French edition of the same work.

Bruges, *The Game and Playe of the Chesse.* In 1477, he was "in the abbey of Westminster, by London," and then and there published *The Dictes and Sayings of Philosophers.* He was then a very old man, but he did good service as a printer before his death in 1491. Blades estimates the entire product of his press at 18,000 pages, nearly all of which were of folio size. Compared with his great rivals on the Continent, Caxton cannot be accorded high rank as editor or publisher, but there was no printer of his time who labored more diligently.

In 1480, Lettou and Machlinia began to print at London. Wynken de Worde, Richard Pynson, Julian Notary and William Faques were also printers of that city before 1500.

In 1480, Theodoric Rood, of Cologne, printed at Oxford. In the same year, an unnamed printer, known to bibliographers as *The School-master of St. Albans,* was at Saint Albans.

The first printing press in Scotland was put up at Edinburgh in 1507; the first in Ireland at Dublin in 1551.

Printing was first practised in the New World in the city of Mexico, by Juan Cromberger, or his agent Pablos, between 1536 and 1540.[1] The second printing press in North America was put up by Stephen Daye at Cambridge, in 1638, and the first work printed on it, the *Freeman's Oath,* was dated 1639.

The German origin of printing is fairly shown by the names, unquestionably German, of nearly all the men who introduced printing in Southern Europe. The workmanship of these men leads to the same conclusion, for the expert will see in their books evidences of the use of the punch,

[1] Thomas, in his *History of Printing,* said that printing was done in Mexico before 1569. The subsequent discovery of Mexican books with earlier imprints has compelled a gradual putting back of the date to 1540, which is that of the earliest existing book. There is a tradition about a Mexican book said to be printed in 1536, but the book is not in existence, and the correctness of this date has not been proved. Harrisse quotes an author who says that printing was taken to Mexico in 1532, by the Viceroy Mendoza, and that Pablos was the first printer. But Mendoza did not go to Mexico until 1535. Pablos was the foreman of Cromberger, who had one office in Seville and one in Mexico.

Statue of Gutenberg at Strasburg.

[From St. Nicholas.]

mould, press, and frisket. Whether done well or ill, printing was done with the tools and by the methods of Gutenberg.

Printing did not meet with general welcome, but the neglect or opposition it encountered did not come largely from the copyists. The business of the copyist of cheap books was injured, but the only complaint that I have met came from the copyists of Genoa. The calligrapher was indifferent to the growth of the new art, for his skill was never in higher request nor more handsomely rewarded than at the close of the fifteenth century. So far from injuring the business of the calligrapher, printing really improved it, for it largely increased the production of books intended for illumination. The neglect of literary men to note the *Bible of 42 lines* and the *Catholicon* of Gutenberg, the delayed establishment of a printing office at Paris, the indifference shown to printing in the great book-making town of Bruges, and the insufficient patronage bestowed on the early printers at Rome, are evidences that there was, in the beginning, a prejudice against printed books much more powerful than that of the copyists. The bibliophiles of the time looked on printed books as the productions of an inartistic trade. The admiration which has been recently invoked for the *Bible of 42 lines* as a book of nearly perfect workmanship was not expressed by any early book-buyer. It does not appear that any book-lover of that period regarded this work, or the art by which it was made, as of high merit. The error seems pardonable, for the printed book was not as attractive as the manuscript, and no one foresaw the future of printing. Gutenberg may have had a clearer idea than any man living of its capabilities, but it is not probable that he foresaw the wheels within wheels which his types would put in motion, or heard the clash and roar of the innumerable presses for which there should be no night and scarcely a Sunday of rest, or dreamed that books, schools, libraries, newspapers and readers were yet to appear in a world then undiscovered, in numbers so great that they could not be counted.

The activity of the early printers is remarkable. The task of preserving the literature of the world was fairly done at a very early date. There were not many books that promised to be salable and profitable, and some of them were scarce, and copies were obtained with difficulty—but nearly every valuable book was found and printed. Naudé, the librarian of Cardinal Mazarin, said that, before the year 1474, all the good books, however bulky, had been printed two or three times, to say nothing of many worthless works which should have been burned. The same work was often printed in the same year, by four or five rival printers in as many different cities. The catalogue of Hain very minutely describes 16,290 editions, which, at the low estimate of 300 copies for each edition, represents a total production of 4,887,000 books.[1]

The attention of the literary world was first arrested, not by the possibilities of future usefulness in printing, but by the growing cheapness of books. The early printers offered their books at less than the market prices of manuscripts, but in a few years they were obliged to reduce the prices still lower. The market was soon glutted, and the prices fell rapidly and irretrievably. Chevillier says that, at the close of the century, the price of many books had been reduced by four-fifths. In the preface to a book printed at Rome in 1470, John Andrew, the bishop of Aleria, addressing Pope Pius II, says:

"It reflects no small glory on the reign of your holiness that a tolerably correct copy of such a work as formerly cost more than a hundred crowns may now be purchased for twenty; those that were worth twenty, for four at most. It is a great thing, holy father, to say, that in your time the most estimable authors are attainable at a price little exceeding that of blank parchment or paper."

[1] This is Hallam's enumeration of the books printed in large cities before 1500:

Florence	300	Nuremberg	382
Milan	629	Leipsic	351
Bologna	298	Basle	320
Rome	925	Strasburg	526
Venice	2835	Augsburg	256
London	130	Louvain	116
Paris	751	Mentz	134
Cologne	530	Deventer	161

If allowance be made for the books that are lost, these numbers are too small, but the list will give a correct idea of the comparative activity of the early printers at different places. During this period were published 291 editions of Cicero, 95 of Virgil, 57 of Horace, 91 of the Latin Bible and many hundreds of the decretals and digests of canon law.

The failure of many early printers to make their business profitable was largely caused by their injudicious selection for publication of bulky theological writings which cost a great deal of money to print, and were salable only to a small class. It was unwisely supposed that printing would receive its great support from the ecclesiastics. With this object in view, the first printers printed almost exclusively in Latin, and generally in the expensive shape of folio, the books which could be read only by the learned, and bought only by the wealthy.[1] The printers' hopes of profit were rarely ever realized. Only a few like Zell, Mentel and Schœffer became successful merchants of books on dogmatic theology. It was soon discovered that printing could not be supported by ecclesiastics. The printers who had been induced to set up presses in monasteries did not long remain there, nor did the printing and publishing offices which they left prosper for many years. Books of devotion were never in greater request, but books published by the church did not fully meet the popular want.

Nearly all the books printed by Gutenberg and Schœffer were in the Latin language. Whether they overlooked the fact that there was an actual need for books in German, or whether they were restrained in an attempt to print in German, cannot be decided. Other publishers saw the need, and disregarded the restraint, if there was any, to the great inquietude of ecclesiastics, who seem to have had forewarning of the mischief that would be made by types. On the fourth

[1]The Bishop of Angers in 1470 paid 40 crowns of gold for a copy of the *Bible of 1462*. The *Catholicon* of Gutenberg sold for 41 crowns of gold in 1465. A copy of Mansion's edition of the *Consolation of Philosophy* by Boethius, brought 40 crowns in 1481. A missal was sold in 1481 for 18 gold florins. Bernard notes a sale in which a printed copy brought a higher price than a manuscript. A copy on vellum of the *Summary of St. Thomas* by Schœffer, was sold at Paris for 15 crowns of gold. A manuscript of similar size was sold for 10 crowns. It is difficult to form just conclusions from these prices, for the bindings of the books have not been described. Hallam says that the florin was worth about four francs of present money, equivalent, perhaps, to twenty-four in commodities, and that the crown was worth rather more. Another estimate allows to the money of the fifteenth century eight times its present purchasing power.

day of January, 1486, Berthold, the archbishop of Mentz, issued a mandate in which he forbade all persons from printing, publishing, buying or selling books translated from the Greek or Latin, or any other language, before the written translation had been approved by a committee which should be appointed for the purpose from the faculty of the University of Mentz. The penalties were excommunication, confiscation of the books, and a fine of 100 florins of gold.[1]

In Italy the revival of classical literature opened a new field for the publisher, but the demand for Latin authors was limited. In this country, and in others, eagerness for books in the native language was manifested; for books that plain people could read; for books that represented the life and thoughts of the living and not of the dead. The world was getting ready for new teachers and for a new literature—for Luther and Bacon, for Galileo and Shakespeare.

[1] The mandate is too long for an unabridged translation, but the following extracts will fairly set forth the reasons for his action:

Although, by a certain divine art of printing, abundant and easy access is obtained to books in every science . . . yet we have perceived that certain men, led by the desire of vainglory or money, do abuse this art; and that which was given for the instruction of human life is perverted to purposes of mischief and calamity. For, to the dishonoring of religion, we have seen in the hands of the vulgar certain books of the divine offices and the writings of our religion translated from the Latin into the German tongue. . . . Some volumes on this subject, certain rash unlearned simpletons have dared to translate into the vulgar tongue, whose translation . . . many learned men have declared unintelligible, in consequence of the very great misapplication and abuse of words. . . . Let such translators, if they pay any regard to truth, say whether the German language be capable of expressing that which excellent writers in Greek and in Latin have most accurately and argumentatively written on the sublime speculations of the Christian religion and the knowledge of things. They must acknowledge that the poverty of our idiom renders it insufficient, . . . they must corrupt the sense of the truth in the sacred writings . . . which, from the greatness of the danger attendant upon it, we greatly dread; for who would leave it to ignorant and unlearned men and to the female sex, into whose hands copies of the Holy Scriptures may have fallen, to find out the true meaning of them ?

This was not the first restriction imposed on the liberty of the printers, for the University of Cologne in 1479 had assumed the right to control the printing of books by Quentell and Winters.

XXVI

The Tools and Usages of the Early Printers.

Punches made by Goldsmiths...Styles of Types imitated from Manuscripts...Popularity of the Gothic...Moulded Matrices...Types made without any System...From an Adjustable Mould. Appearance of Early Types...Large Fonts made...Importance of Mould...Rudeness of Early Composition...Method of Dictation...Faults of Compositors...Slowness of Improvement...Construction of the Hand-Press, with illustration...Inking Balls, with illustration...Slowness of Pressmen...Printing in Colors...Printing Ink...Ingredients used by the Ripoli Press...Moxon's Complaints about Ink...Neglect of Engraving on Wood...Peculiarities of Paper...The Degradation of Engraving...Proof-reading at Weidenbach...Faults of First Editions...Superiority of Printed as compared with Manuscript Books...Permanence of Gutenberg's Method.

All invention is progressive. . . . When a new machine is produced, we do not say, Why, it only consists of a number of wheels and cylinders, therefore, surely there is nothing new in it! All the parts may be old, and yet the combination be quite new. To analyse an invention into its several parts, would be equivalent to finding that a poem was only composed of the letters of the alphabet, or the words in a dictionary. *Dircks.*

THE first processes in the practice of typography—the cutting of punches and making of moulds—demanded a degree of skill in the handling of tools and of experience in the working of metal rarely found in any man who undertook to learn the art of printing. They were never regarded as proper branches of the printer's trade, but were, from the beginning, set aside as kinds of work which could be properly done by the goldsmith only. Jenson, Cennini, Sweinheym and Veldener seem to have been the only printers of the fifteenth century who had the preliminary education that would warrant them in attempting to cut punches with their own hands.

Not every goldsmith[1] could do this work with neatness, and for this reason, as well as for the sake of economy, many beginners bought their matrices from the printers who owned punches. In some cases the types were bought outright, but matrices which gave the means of renewing a worn-out font must have been preferred. That there was a trade in matrices before type-foundries for the trade were established is shown by the appearance of the same face of type in many offices. The Round Gothic types cut by Jenson were frequently used by printers in France and Germany. Certain faces of types used by Caxton and by Van der Goes, by Leeu and Bellaert, by Machlinia and Veldener, are identically the same, and must have been cast from matrices struck from the same punches.

The styles of the early types were not invented by printer or punch-cutter. The Pointed Gothic letters of Gutenberg's *Bibles* and of the *Psalter of 1457* are like those of the choice ecclesiastical manuscripts of that period. The Round Gothic letters of the *Catholicon* and of the *Letters of Indulgence* are of the form then used by German copyists in popular books. In Italy, the first types were cut in imitation of the popular form of Roman letters, or in the southern fashion of Round Gothic; in the Netherlands, they present the peculiarities of Flemish writing; in France and Burgundy, they were, for the most part, in the favorite French style of *Bâtarde ancienne*. In no instance did the printer invent a new style: he did

[1] Gutenberg's employment of the goldsmith Dünne at Strasburg, and the payment to him of a big sum for work connected with printing, can be most satisfactorily explained by the conjecture that Dünne was hired to cut punches and make a mould. I find no mention of punch-cutting or mould-making at Mentz, but there is, in the accounts of the Ripoli Press, an unequivocal notice of one John Peter of Mentz, who was selling matrices to the printers of Florence in 1476. It is evident that this John Peter had experience in this branch of typography. The Ripoli Press bought of him, in 1477, the matrices of a full font of Roman, for 10 florins in gold. John Peter was not the only punch-cutter. In 1478, the Ripoli Press paid the goldsmith Benvenuto 110 livres for the punches of three fonts—two of which were of Roman and one of Gothic face. In 1481, another goldsmith, Banco, made a sale to the manager of the Ripoli Press, of "100 little letters, 3 big letters, and 3 vignettes on copper."

no more than direct his punch-cutter to imitate, as closely as he could, the letters of a meritorious manuscript. In this matter, as well as in the arrangement of types, he followed the fashion set by an approved copyist or calligrapher. The peculiar characters[1] of different languages were produced as they were required, somewhat slowly and of unequal merit, by different printers. The limitations of typography were not fully perceived, and many unsuccessful attempts were made to produce types and sectional wood-cuts that could be used in the construction of maps, ornaments and pictures.[2]

The Gothic character was more popular than the Roman, but there were mechanical reasons why many printers preferred it. It was not so quickly cut, but its broad face, free from hair-lines, was more readily founded. It could be inked with facility and printed with more evenness of color, and it would not show wear as soon as the Roman. Early printers, who had no Roman, were loud in their praises of the Gothic.[3] It was preferred by Verard, Pigouchet, Kerver, and nearly all French and Flemish printers. It did not entirely go out of fashion in Southern Europe nor in France until the close

[1] Square notes of music, partly written, partly printed, are seen in the *Psalter of 1457*. Greek letters were made by Schœffer and Sweinheym, but the first book in Greek was printed by Paravisinus at Milan in 1476. Hebrew types were made at Soncino in 1488. At the close of the century, a German printer at Paris made an imitation of writing, but the letters were not connected, and the only penmanlike features were in the capitals. About 1500, Manutius had the engraver Francis of Bologna cut punches for Italic types, in imitation of the handwriting of Petrarch.

[2] Jacob Bellaert of Haarlem combined isolated engravings, cut for the purpose, in the belief that each combination would seem a new engraving. Kerver tried to give variety to his pages by varying combinations of detached pictorial borders. But it was quickly demonstrated that typography could deal successfully with letters only. The large ornamental initial letters of books were not cast, but cut, sometimes on wood, oftener on metal. Small and ornamented capital letters were cast by Mentel of Strasburg, and by Ratdolt of Venice in 1477.

[3] Colonna and Manthen at Venice said that their Gothic was a "sublime letter." John Herbort, in 1483, said his was "a most captivating letter, unquestionably excelling all others." Nicholas Prevost said his book was printed "in types the most beautiful and most becoming for polite literature." Chevalon said his Gothic was "the polite and fashionable letter."

of the sixteenth century. It might have been supplanted by Roman characters in Germany, if there had not been at this time a strong prejudice against Roman customs and fashions of all kinds. Attempts at change were frequently made, but they were always unsuccessful.

The steel bought for the type-foundry of the Ripoli Press was probably intended for punches. The use of this metal in other type-foundries may be inferred from the sharpness, when new, of many fonts of early types. That the moulds were of brass is indicated by the allusions of early writers and printers to types made in brass. The matrices were of copper, but it is not probable that they were struck in cold metal, for it required great force and still greater discretion to strike the punch truly, and the risk of breaking it had to be hazarded. For the matrices of the large types of Gutenberg's *Bibles* and the *Psalter of 1457*, copper softened by heat[1] should have been, and probably was, provided.

When the secrets of type-making had been divulged, the printers who found difficulties in making or buying matrices tried to evade its necessary conditions and cheapen its processes. The types of wood with holes for wire, described by Specklin and others, must have been punches of wood which had been made in the belief that it would be cheaper to cast words than to cast and compose single letters. The matrices of lead noticed by Enschedé were probably made by striking the punch of wood in half-melted metal, after the process described by Didot. The punch of wood, burned by contact with hot metal, was repaired, altered and renewed; the matrix of lead,[2] clogged by the adhesion of metal, became defaced, and was soon worn out. Every change in punch or matrix produced a corresponding change in the cast type.

[1] In France, the punches are struck in hot copper to prevent their breakage.

[2] I know by experience that the ordinary metal used for types can be cast in a matrix of lead to the number of 125 or 150 types before the matrix will be destroyed. After 50 or 60 castings, there will be an alteration in the mould; the finer lines will disappear and ruder lines be presented. This will account for the differences that the same letters present on every page. *Magazin Encyclop. de Millin*, 1806, vol. 1, p. 74, as quoted by Bernard, vol. 1, p. 299.

The types of the fifteenth century were made without system. The dimensions of each body and the peculiarities of each face were determined chiefly by the manuscript copy which had been selected as the model. No printer had any idea of the advantages to be derived from a series of regularly graduated sizes, nor of the beauty of a series of uniform faces, nor of the great evils they would impose on themselves and their successors by the use of irregular bodies.[1] A classification by scale of the types of any printer of this period will show that there are often wide gaps between the larger, and confusing proximities between the smaller, bodies.[2]

As the size of every body is determined by the mould in which it is cast, it would seem that there must have been a separate mould for every distinct body.[3] But this inference is encumbered with fatal objections. The type-mould of hard metal is, and always has been, a very expensive tool, and it cannot be supposed that any early printer made two or four moulds for one body when one mould would have served. It

[1] Gutenberg's larger bodies were irregularly graduated and of Pointed Gothic face; his smaller bodies were not separated at proper distances, and were of Round Gothic face. The unknown printer had four faces and four bodies of the size English. Caxton had two faces and two bodies each of the sizes Paragon, Great-primer and English. The types of many printers at Paris and Venice show irregularities of body which seem remarkable and inexplicable to the modern printer.

[2] The smallest sizes which I have met in any book of the fifteenth century are in the *Decretals of Gregory*, printed in black and red by Andrew Torresani at Venice in 1498, in which book the text is in Bourgeois and the surrounding notes are in Brevier. Nonpareil was first made by Garamond of Paris about the middle of the sixteenth century. Diamond was made by Jannon of Sedan about 1625. Nothing smaller was attempted until 1827, when Henry Didot, then 66 years old, cut a font on the French body of 2½ points—a body known to American printers as Brilliant, or Half-nonpareil—about twenty-five lines to the American inch.

[3] It has been suggested that these distinct bodies were founded in sand moulds; that a new pattern for the body was made every time a new font was cast; and that the irregularities in body are the results of unintended or undetected variations in the pattern. But this hypothesis cannot be accepted. The small bodies, the sharp edges, close fitting-up and even lining of the types, are peculiarities which could not have been produced by a sand mould, nor by a mould of any plastic material.

is much more probable that he tried to make one mould serve for two or more bodies. The inventor of the mould may have thought that it should be constructed with adjustments, so that it should cast different bodies as well as different widths of types. The practicability of a mould of this description is properly demonstrated by the old-fashioned adjustable mould for irregular bodies, or by the mould used for casting leads, which can be so enlarged or diminished that it will cast many bodies or thicknesses. If we suppose that this mould was used by Gutenberg for casting the two bodies of the *Letters of Indulgence*, and by the unknown printer of the Netherlands for his four bodies of English, and that it was, of necessity, newly set or adjusted each time a new font was cast, we shall at once have a precise explanation of irregularities which are unaccountable under any other hypothesis. Casting types without the system, standards and gauges which modern type-founders use, it is not surprising that the first printers made types with differences of body. It was the impracticability of casting in this primitive mould, at different times, types of uniform body, that compelled later type-founders to discard it, and to use instead a mould for each body.

The casting of the types, which was always done in the printing office, was then adjudged a proper part of a printer's trade. The earlier chroniclers said the first types were made of lead and tin. The Cost Book of the Ripoli Press specifies these metals, and obscurely mentions another which seems to have been one of the constituents of type-metal. If this conjecture can be accepted, types were probably made in the fifteenth century, as they are now, of lead, tin and antimony.[1] Not one of the millions of types founded during the fifteenth

[1] See page 66 of this book. Was this obscure metal antimony? The text books say that antimony was, for the first time, set apart as a distinct metal in 1490, by Basil Valentine, a monk of Erfurt. But Madden says that a book supposed to have been printed at Cologne, before the year 1473, plainly describes antimony as a metal frequently used and much abused by many monks of the thirteenth century in their pharmaceutical preparations. *Lettres d'un bibliographe*, 4th series, p. 115.

century has been preserved, nor is there in any old book an engraving or a description of a type. This neglected information has been unwittingly furnished by a careless pressman in the office of Conrad Winters, who printed at Cologne in 1476. This pressman, or his mate, when inking a slackly justified form, permitted the inking ball to pull out a thin-bodied type, which dropped sideways on the face of the form. The accident was not noticed; the tympan closed upon the form, and the bed was drawn under the platen. Down came the screw and platen, jamming the unfortunate type in the form, and embossing it strongly in the fibres of the thick wet paper, in a manner which reveals to us the shape of Winters' types more truthfully than it could have been done even by

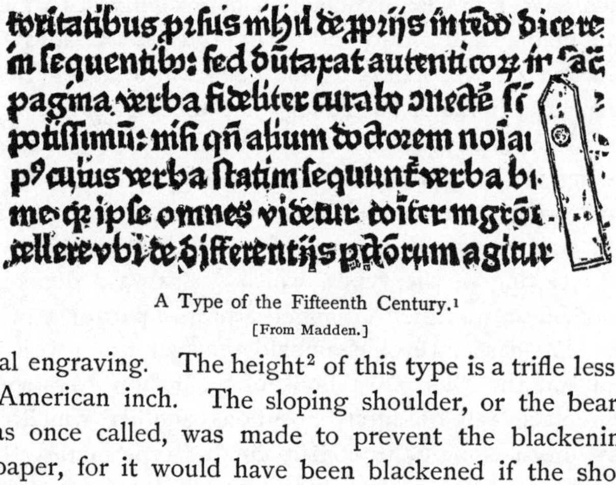

A Type of the Fifteenth Century.[1]

[From Madden.]

special engraving. The height[2] of this type is a trifle less than one American inch. The sloping shoulder, or the beard, as it was once called, was made to prevent the blackening of the paper, for it would have been blackened if the shoulder had been high and square.[3] The circular mark, about one-

[1] *Lettres d'un bibliographe*, 4th series, p. 231.

[2] It agrees exactly with the old French standard (of 1723) for height of type, which was 10½ geometric lines, or, by modern French measure, 24 millimetres. Fournier, *Manuel typographique*, vol. I, p. 125.

[3] The sloping shoulder, which was in general use in the first quarter of this century, was discarded to meet the requirements of the new art of stereotyping. It was found that these sloping shoulders made projections in the plaster mould, which imperiled the making of an accurate cast. The blackening of the sheet from square shoulders was prevented by altering the mould and placing the shoulder lower on the body.

tenth of an inch diameter, on the side of the type, was firmly depressed in the metal, but did not perforate it. As this type had no nick on the body, it is apparent that the circular mark was cast there to guide the compositor. When the type was put in the stick with the mark facing outward, the compositor knew, without looking at the face, that it was rightly placed. There is no groove at the foot. Duverger says that the early types had no jet or breaking-piece; that the superfluous metal was cut off, and the type made of proper height by sawing.[1] These details may seem trifling, but they are of importance: they show that, in the more important features, the types of the early printers closely resembled ours.

There is a disagreement among bibliographers about the quantity of types ordinarily cast for a font by the early printers. Some, judging from appearances which show that one page only was printed at an impression, say that they cast types for two or three pages only; others maintain that they must have had very large fonts. That the latter view is correct seems fully established after a survey of the books known to have been printed by Zell, Koburger, Leeu, and others. It would have been impossible to print these books in the short period in which we know they were done, if the printer had not been provided with abundance of types.[2] As the types were made in the printing office, by a quick method, from an alloy which could be used repeatedly for the same purpose, the supply was rarely limited by fear of expense.

The trades of compositor and pressman, and possibly that of type-caster, were kept about as distinct then as they are now. There were more compositors than pressmen, and the

[1] See page 399 of this book.

[2] Bernard believes that Gutenberg cast for the *Bible of 42 lines* at least 120,000 types, or enough for two sections, or forty pages. He supposes that twenty pages were perfected, and ready for press or under press, while the succeeding twenty pages were in the compositor's hands. This would be the method adopted by the modern printer, and it may have been the method of Gutenberg, but it is probable that the difficulties connected with the new art compelled him to print the book more slowly, and with imperfect system. But the printers who followed him certainly used quick methods.

compositors, says Madden, in the heroic age of printing, were not boys, but men of education and intelligence. The early printers who were taught the business that they might become masters had to pay a premium for their education.[1] In the brief time that they gave to the work, their education must have been more theoretical than practical. As the branch of composition required the largest number of workmen, and more intelligence, and less manual labor than any other, it was usually selected by the pupil for practice. Of type-casting and presswork he learned no more than was sufficient to enable him to direct the labors of his future workmen. The knowledge of the trade which the pupil coveted was the ability to practise it on his own account, and this knowledge was, in most instances, satisfactorily acquired when he got a theoretical knowledge of its secret processes.

The frequent specification of the *formen* in the earliest notices of printing shows that the mould, with its accompanying matrices, was regarded as the key to the knowledge and practice of the art. As the moulds were made by master mechanics, not bound to secrecy, and as the earlier compositors had some knowledge of the process of type-casting, it was not difficult for a journeyman to become a master printer. When he had bought a type-mould and matrices, he could go to any city and begin to print books. He could cast types and mix ink as he needed them; he could buy paper and the constituents of type-metal in any large town; properly instructed, any joiner could make the press.[2]

The annexed illustration, a fac-simile of one of Amman's engravings of a printing office, is from his book dated 1564.

[1] Caxton said that he had "practysed & learned at [his] grete charge and dispense to ordeyne this said booke in prynte."

[2] Many of the early master printers practised their trade for a few years in one place, and a few years in another, roving about from town to town with a seeming indifference to change which seems unaccountable to the modern printer, who knows how expensive it is to move a printing office. The roving habits of the masters will not seem so strange when it is known that the equipment of the early office was simple, and that the more expensive tools could be carried with little difficulty.

The case for the type is of one piece and is resting on a rude frame. All the boxes are represented as of the same size, but this is probably an error, for it is an error which is frequently made by designers of this day.[1] In this, and in many other early illustrations of type-setting, the compositors are seated on stools. In Italy and in Paris, women were employed as compositors. In the wood-cut used by Jodocus Badius[2] for a trade-mark, we see a hard-featured dame before a narrow case, composing types with judicial deliberation. She has in her left hand a narrow composing stick, made to hold but two or three lines of small types. The early stick was not like the neatly finished iron tool of our time, with steel composing rule and an adjustable screw and knee adapting it to any measure.

Presswork and Composition as done in 1564.

[From Jost Amman.]

It was a real stick of wood, a home-made strip of deal, with the side and end-piece tacked on. For every measure, a new stick or a retacking of the movable piece was required. The date of the introduction of the stick cannot be fixed, but it was used, without alteration for many years, by the printers of all countries. It is possible that some of the early printers

[1] The engravings of cases shown by Moxon have boxes of unequal size. No doubt, they were so made from the beginning, for a day's experience would teach any compositor that his case must have a larger box for the letter e than for the letter x.

[2] See page 528.

had no sticks. The peculiar workmanship of the unknown printer and of Albert Pfister shows that the types were taken direct from the case and wedged in the mortised blocks of wood which served for chases. Blades attributes the uneven spacing and irregular endings of lines in the early printed books of Caxton and of other printers, to their ignorance of the advantages of a composing rule, without which types could not be readily moved to and fro, and adjusted.[1]

In the following illustration, the compositor has the copy before her in the shape of a book, but Conrad Zeltner, a learned printer of the seventeenth century, said that this was not the early usage; that it was customary to employ a reader to read aloud to the compositors, who set the types from dictation, not seeing the copy. He also says that the reader could dictate from as many different pages or copies to three or four compositors working together.[2] When the compositors were educated, the method of dictation may have been practised with some success; when they were ignorant, it was sure to produce many errors. Zeltner said that he preferred the old method, but he admits that it had to be abandoned, on account of the increasing ignorance of the compositors.

[1] Bernard says that sticks of wood were used by Christopher Plantin, "king of printers." It is characteristic of the taste of his time, that Plantin had sticks of wood, although he boasted that some of his types were cast in [matrices of] silver.

[2] Madden, in his first collection of *Lettres d'un bibliographe*,—the most curious piece of analytical criticism that has appeared in typographical literature—has demonstrated that the method of dictation was practised in the office at Weidenbach. In this series of letters he critically examines three books, printed at this office with the same types, and at the same time, and points out the peculiar errors of three different compositors, who, not seeing the copy, were misled by their misapprehension of the dictated words. He claims that these books were the practice work of three amateur compositors who were then learning the trade. Each compositor had copies of his own workmanship printed as evidences of his skill, or as a memento of his errors. Novel as they may seem, I am inclined to accept the conclusions of Madden. Many copies of early printed books, known to be of the same edition, or done at the same time, show variations in the typographical arrangement which cannot be explained by any other hypothesis than that of a double composition by compositors working from dictation.

No feature of early printing is more unworkmanlike than that of composition. Imitating the style of the manuscript copy, the compositor huddled together words and paragraphs in solid columns of dismal blackness, and sent his forms to press without title, running-titles, chapter-heads and paging-figures. The space for the ornamental borders and letters of the illuminator seems extravagant when contrasted with the pinched spaces between lines and words. The printer trusted to the bright colors of the illuminator to give relief to the blackness of the types, not knowing that a purer relief and greater perspicuity would have been secured by a wider spacing of the words and lines. The obscurity produced by huddled and over-black types was increased by the neglect of simple orthographical rules. Proper names were printed with or without capitals, apparently to suit the whim of the compositor. The comma, colon and period, the only points of punctuation in general use, were employed capriciously and illogically. Crooked and unevenly spaced lines and errors of arrangement or making-up were common. Madden has pointed out several gross blunders, caused by the transposition of lines and pages and an erroneous calculation of the space that should be occupied by print. Words were mangled in division, and in the display of lines in capital letters, in a manner that seems inexcusable. But no usage of the early compositor is more annoying than his lawless use of abbreviations. Imitating the example of Procrustes, he made the words fit, chopping them off on any letter or in any position, indifferent to the wants of the reader or to the proprieties of language.[1] Whatever opinion may be entertained concerning

[1] The composition of Schœffer's edition of the *Decretals* has been injudiciously praised by Bernard. In the fac-simile on page 463, it will be noticed that the page is crooked, and that the justification and making-up are very faulty. In a copy of Torresani's edition of the *Decretals*, the frequent contractions make the work almost unreadable. This book has been highly commended for its even spacing; but it is a sufficient answer to say that any printer could space admirably, even in the narrowest measure, if allowed to mangle words to suit his convenience.

the deterioration of printing in other branches, it is, beyond all cavil, certain that in the art of arranging types so that the meaning of the author shall be made lucid, the modern compositor is much the more intelligent mechanic.

Improvements were made slowly. The method of spacing out lines so as to produce a regular outline at the right side of every page had been practised before, but it was not in general use even as late as 1478. Arabic figures, instead of Roman numerals, were first used by Ter Hoorne of Cologne, and by Helye of Munster in 1470. Signatures to guide the binder in putting together in order the different sheets of a book were first used in printed books by Zarot of Milan in 1470. As the alphabetical letters of these signatures often had to be doubled, and sometimes quadrupled in thick books, it became necessary to print a full list of the signatures at the end of every book as an additional guide to the binder. This list, *registrum chartarum*, seems to have been first used by Colonna at Venice in 1475. The clumsiness of doubled alphabetical letters should have led to the use of Arabic figures for signatures, and should have suggested paging, but these reforms were not adopted for many years afterward.[1] A table of errata, two pages folio, was exhibited by Gabriel Peter of Venice in 1478. The first full title, if a few lines in compact capital letters can be so called, was made by Ratdolt of Venice in 1477, but his example was not rapidly followed by rival printers. Running-titles and open chapter-headings are innovations of the next century. The printers of the fifteenth century who wished to free themselves from dependence on the illuminator filled up the white spaces about chapter-headings with bits of engraving on wood or metal.

[1] The statement made by Lacroix that one book was paged in 1469 does not prove that this was the usage. In some books printed at Venice during the last ten years of the fifteenth century, the leaves (not the pages) are numbered on every odd page. But this was not the common practice. In the *Statius* of Aldus, printed at Venice in 1502, and in the Italian translation of the *Commentaries of Julius Cæsar*, printed by Bernard Venetus of that city in 1517, neither leaves nor pages are numbered.

Galleys, or trays of wood to keep in place the composed types, were not known; the types were placed line after line, perhaps letter by letter, in the mortised block of wood which served for the chase. Nice justification was impossible. If two pages were put in one mortise, one of these pages would often be out of square—an irregularity which has led some bibliographers to think that each page was separately printed from a separate form. The locking-up or tightening of the types, which was roughly done, often made the types crooked, springing them off their feet and making the spaces work up.[1]

The neglect of the early printers to praise their presses is remarkable when contrasted with their frequent praises of the marvelous art of type-making. It is inferential evidence that the press was then regarded as an old contrivance, and not worthy of notice, but this conclusion cannot be unreservedly accepted. The principle of pressure was old, and for that reason, was undervalued by printers, but the mechanism of the press was new. That the printing press was an invention of merit will be perceived at a glance when it is compared with the screw press which is supposed to have served as the basis of construction.[2] That a proper method of doing presswork was devised in the infancy of the art may be inferred, not only from the permanency of the primitive form of press, all the important features of which are still preserved in the modern hand-press, but from the meritorious presswork of the first books. The *Bibles* of Gutenberg were certainly printed on a press which quickly gave and quickly released its pressure, and which had the attachments of a movable bed, tympan and frisket, and contrivances for neatly inking the types and for keeping the paper in position.

Jodocus Badius of Paris was the first printer who published engravings of the printing press. It cannot be asserted

[1] Some early chases held their types not with quoins, but by the pressure of screws. A German printer's hand-book, dated Leipsic, 1743, has diagrams of imposition in which the pages are fastened by screws perforating the chase. Quoins and bevels were not an early invention.

[2] See page 395 for illustration of primitive screw press.

that they are minutely accurate representations of the press then in use, but they will serve to show its general construction. Two features provoke hostile comment. Contrary to modern usage, the piles of white paper and printed paper are unhandily placed on the off-side of the press, and the stalwart pressman pulls home the bar with both arms. The platen

Presswork and Composition as done in 1520.

[From Blades' fac-simile of the print of Badius.]

Two upright beams, or cheeks, supporting a thick cross-piece, or cap, made the frame-work. The cap held in place the screw and spindle which gave the impression, and the descent of the spindle was steadied by the large square collar, or till, which was supported by the cheeks. The point of the spindle pressed against the impressing surface, or platen, which was held in place by iron rods connecting it with the collar. The bed of the press and the form of types are concealed by the tympan drawer, which, with tympan and frisket, have been folded down and run under the platen. See illustration on page 307, and explanation on page 280, for the uses of these parts. The bed was of stone, but every other large piece was of wood. Iron was used only for the spindle, the core of the bar-handle, for nuts and bolts, and the minor pieces for which no other material would serve.

seems altogether too small when contrasted with the great screw, the heavy frame, and the two-handed pull of the pressman. The smallness of this platen was not an error of the designer. Moxon, who has minutely described the press of his time, says that the platen of an ordinary press should be of the size 9 by 14 inches, and that the coffin, or trough in which the bed was placed, should be 28 inches long and 22 inches wide. In other words, the platen was purposely made so that it could impress less than half the surface of the bed; it could print only one-half of one side of the sheet.[1] Small as this platen may seem, it was large enough for the frame-work of wood. It gave great resistance under pull, and severely taxed the strength of the pressman. A platen of double size would have defied the pressman; it would have sprung under pressure and have broken the bed of stone.

The types were inked by balls, an appliance which is not more than fifty years out of fashion. These balls were made of untanned sheepskin, stuffed hard with wool, and mounted with handles. The gluey ink was evenly distributed by forcibly rocking their curved surfaces against each other. This done, the balls were then beaten upon the types in the form.

When we learn that the early presses were made almost entirely of wood, and put together by ordinary joiners, we may infer that many were unscientifically built,[2] and shackly.

[1] *Mechanick Exercises*, vol. 1, pp. 52, 69. To the printer who has seen only the press in which the platen covers the bed this may seem an absurd method, but it was a method in general use even as late as the beginning of this century. Men are yet living who have printed books by the method shown in the cut—pulling down the bar when one-half of the form was under the platen—releasing the pressure—running the other half of the bed under the platen—and finishing the presswork of the other half of the sheet by a second pull.

[2] There should have been a gradual improvement in the construction of the press, as there was in the making of the types, but there was no decided change for two centuries. Moxon, in 1683, commending the "new fashion" presses of Blaew, denounced the "old fashion presses as make-shift, slovenly contrivances practised in the minority of this art." Nor was Blaew's press perfect. To insure proper register, Jackson (who undertook, at Venice in 1745, to print wood-cuts in colors) was obliged to reconstruct the press of Blaew.

All the materials for presswork were imperfect. The types, cut to length by a saw, were of uneven height; the paper was usually of very rough surface and of irregular thickness; the platen of wood, rarely ever truly flat, must have given unequal pressure at different corners. It was necessary that some substance should be put between the platen and the white sheet which would compensate for these irregularities. This substance was a woolen blanket, in two or more thicknesses, which spread or diffused the impression. The wetting of the paper, which made it soft and pliable, materially aided the pressman, but his great reliance seems to have been on strong impression. All the old cuts of presses represent the pressman tugging at the bar with a force which seems out of all proportion to the size of the form.

Early Inking Balls.

[From a Playing Card of Sixteenth Century.]

The early press was rude, and the method of printing was unscientific, but in many offices the pressman was superior to his press and his method. By doing his work slowly and carefully he often did it admirably. It was always done slowly, with a waste of time which, if allowed in the modern practice of printing, would make books of excessive price. Some notion of this waste may be had after an examination of the letters of the *Psalter of 1457*, in which exact work was produced by painting, not by printing proper. That the performance of the press even on ordinary black work was slow, is indicated by the great number of presses used by the early printers, and is proved by the plain statement of Philip de Lignamine, who said that the printers of Mentz printed three hundred sheets a day. This seems a small performance.[1]

The accurate register of the first books was produced by placing the white sheet on four fixed points which perforated the four corners of the leaf when the first side was printed. In printing the back of the page, the half-printed sheet was hung on the same points, from the same point-holes, and was impressed in the same position. Blades notices the four point-holes in some of Caxton's books, and it is probable that the mysterious pin-holes in other books are the marks of points. It was soon discovered that register could be had with two points, which were placed in the centre of the sheet where the marks would be hidden by the binder.[2]

[1] It must also be remembered that on the early printing press two pressmen were required for the work—one to beat or to ink, and one to pull or to print. The ordinary task of the hand-pressman of New-York in 1840 was rated at 1500 impressions, but these impressions were made by one man (working an inking machine) and one pull on forms of large size. Considering the surface printed, the performance of one hand-pressman in 1840 was about eight times more than that of one pressman in 1458.

[2] Words and lines were sometimes printed in red in a text of black, with a nicety of register rarely equaled by any printer during the first years of this century. The early method of printing red with black, has been described by Moxon. The black form was first printed with quadrats in the places that should be occupied by the red words or lines. This done, the form remaining on press, the quadrats were taken out and the vacant space partially filled with "underlays" of reglet, about one-sixth inch thick. On these underlays the types to be printed in red were placed, which adjusting made them about one-sixth of an inch higher than the types of the black form. The bearers were then raised, the impression was readjusted, a new frisket was put on, and the pressman was ready to print red as he had printed the black. This method of printing red with black, a clumsy method at best, which can be practised only on small forms on the hand-press, has been out of fashion for many years.—The color work of the early printers has been overpraised. Superior, no doubt, to that of printers of the last century, who tried to do more work in less time, it cannot be compared with the color work of our time. The rubricated *Book of Common Prayer* printed by Welch, Bigelow & Co. of Cambridge, Massachusetts, the *Specimen Book* of Charles Derriey of Paris, the *French-English Dictionary* of George Bellows of Gloucester, England, may be offered as specimens of modern color presswork which show an exactness of register and a purity of color and of impression not to be found in any early book.

The printing ink of the fifteenth century, as we now see it, is of unequal merit. In the books of Jenson it appears as an intense, velvety, glossy black; in the *Bibles* of Gutenberg it is a strong, permanent black, without gloss; in the *Psalter of 1457* it appears in some places as a glossy black, and in others as a faded color which had to be retouched with the pen; in the works of the unknown printer it is a dingy and smearing black; in the books of some printers it is a paste color which can be rubbed off with a sponge; in nearly all, it is uneven, over-black on one page and gray on another.[1]

The general impression that early printing ink is blacker and brighter than modern ink is not always correct. Early ink seems blacker, because it is shown in greater quantity, for the early types were larger, of broader face, without hair lines, and could be over-colored without disadvantage.[2] The same ink applied to the small thin Roman types of our time,

[1] This unevenness does not prove the use of two distinct inks. In some instances, it was caused by the negligence of the pressman who applied an unequal quantity of ink upon different pages. In many instances, it was produced by the variable qualities or conditions of the paper or vellum. If the paper laid out for one form differed from that used for other forms in being too coarse or too dry, or over-wet, or if the vellum had been polished too much or too little, or had not been entirely freed from lime and grease, it would take up from the types, during each condition, a variable quantity of color, and produce prints of a different degree of blackness. These variations in color are most noticeable in books of vellum. In a prayer book printed by Kerver in 1507, the ink is black wherever the vellum is smooth, and gray where it is rough. In another edition of the same book on paper, printed by Kerver in 1522, the ink is not so black as it appears on the smooth vellum, but the color is more uniform. Equal carefulness seems to have been taken with each book, and the ink was, no doubt, substantially the same. Some of the early printers sorted their sheets *after* printing, separating the under-colored from the over-colored and binding each together.

[2] In trying to avoid the gloominess of early printing, modern printers have gone too far in the opposite direction. The fault of imperfect blackness which is justly censurable in many modern books is largely due to what Hansard calls the "razor-edged" hair lines and thin stems of modern types which give the printer no opportunity to show black color. Readers have been taught to prefer a feminine elegance in types, a weak and useless imitation of copper-plate effects, to the masculine boldness, solidity and readableness of the old-style letter of the last century.

would seem dull and gray. The microscopic examination of any early ink will show that the black is not fine and not thoroughly mixed with proper drying oil. But this imperfection is comparatively unimportant. It is a graver fault in some early inks that they are not firmly fixed to the paper.[1]

There is no trustworthy account of the invention of printing ink, but the types and the inks were undoubtedly invented together. One was the proper complement of the other. It may be supposed that Gutenberg acquired the knowledge of the newly found properties of boiled linseed oil[2] from German painters. It is certain that he used oil as the basis of his ink, and that it was also used by his pupils and successors. And it has been in use ever since, for there is no substitute.

INGREDIENTS OF PRINTING INK USED BY THE RIPOLI PRESS.

Ingredients.	*Tuscan Currency.*	*American Currency.*
Linseed Oil, bbl. . lir.	3 10 0	$3.17
Turpentine, lb. . .	4 0	.18
Pitch, Greek.	4 0	.18
Pitch, Black.	1 8	7½
Marcassite.	3 0	.13½
Vermilion	5 0	.22¾
Rosin	3 0	.13½
Varnish, hard. . . .	8 0	.36
Varnish, liquid. . .	12 0	.54
Nutgalls	4 0	.18
Vitriol	4 0	.18
Shellac	3 0	.13½

We have not been told how the ink was compounded. Our nearest approach to this knowledge is through the Cost Book of the Ripoli Press for 1481, which specifies and prices the materials. As no

[1] Mr. Ticheborne, a recent contributor to *Chambers' Journal*, says that the older printing inks are more easily saponified and washed off by alkalies than those of the last century. Some of the old inks he found so sensitive, that on introducing them to a weak solution of ammonia, the printed characters instantly floated off the surface of the pages. His explanation, that the oil had not been properly prepared by boiling, and was not changed into an insoluble varnish, and "resinfied," is, no doubt, correct. A practical ink-maker, in a series of papers to *L'imprimerie* (vol. I, p. 129), says that in many books of the fifteenth century, the adhesion of the color to the paper is very weak, and that the ink can be made pale or washed off with a moist sponge.

[2] Lanzi refers to an Italian manuscript of 1437 in which it is asserted that the new method of painting in oil, as practised by the Germans, must begin with the process of boiling linseed oil. *History of Painting in Italy.* Bohn's edition, 1852, vol. I, p. 86.

mention is made of smoke-black, we have to infer that pitch was burnt to make this black. Linseed oil, as the most bulky ingredient, very properly occupies the first place. The real value of nutgalls and vitriol is not so apparent: they were important ingredients in writing ink, and the Italian printer may have thought them indispensable in printing ink. Shellac and liquid varnish were used to give a glossy surface.

Printers soon discovered that printing was an art of too many details, and that the manufacture of printing ink was its most objectionable duty. There was risk of fire in the boiling of linseed oil; discomfort and dirt were connected with the manipulation of the ingredients; and in inexpert hands, waste and failure were of frequent occurrence. In all large cities, ink-making was set apart and practised as a distinct trade. As a necessary consequence, the quality deteriorated through the competition that followed. Moxon's criticism of ink made in England in 1683 could be applied without any injustice to much of the ink of the fifteenth century.[1]

[1] Our *Inck-makers* to save charges, mingle many times *Trane-Oyl* among theirs and a great deal of *Rosin;* which *Trane-Oyl* by its grossness Furs and Choaks up a *Form*, and by its fatness hinders the *Inck* from drying; so that when the Work comes to the *Binders*, it *Sets-off;* and besides is dull, smeary and unpleasant to the eye. And the *Rosin*, if too great a quantity be put in, and the *Form* be not very *Lean-Beaten*, makes the *Inck* turn yellow: And the same does the New *Linseed-Oyl*.——*Secondly*. They seldom *Boyl* or *Burn* it to that consistence the *Hollanders* do, because they not only save labour and Fewel, but have a greater weight of *Inck* out of the same quantity of *Oyl* when less *Burnt* away than when more *Burnt* away; which want of Burning makes the *Inck* also, though made of good old *Linseed-Oyl*, Fat and Smeary, and hinders its Drying; so that when it comes to the *Binders* it also *Sets-off*.—— *Thirdly*. They do not use that way of clearing their *Inck* the *Hollanders* do, or indeed any other way than meer Burning it, whereby the *Inck* remains more *Oyly* and *Greasie* than if it were well clarified.——*Fourthly*. They, to save the *Press-man* the labour of *Rubbing* the *Blacking* into *Varnish* on the *Inck-Block*, *Boyl* the *Blacking* in the *Varnish*, or at least put the *Blacking* in whilst the *Varnish* is yet *Boyling-hot*, which so *Burns* and *Rubifies* the *Blacking*, that it loses much of its brisk and vivid black complection. —— *Fifthly*. Because *Blacking* is dear, and adds little to the weight of the Inck, they stint themselves to a quantity which they exceed not; so that sometimes the *Inck* proves so unsufferable *Pale*, that the *Press-man* is forced to *Rub* in more *Blacking* upon the Block; yet this he is often so loth to do, that he will rather hazard the Content the Colour shall give, than take the pains to amend it: satisfying himself that he can lay the blame upon the *Inck-maker*. Moxon, *Mechanick Exercises*, vol. II, pp. 76, 77.

Gutenberg, Schœffer, Zell, Mentel and many early printers of France and Italy neglected engraving on wood.[1] It may be that this neglect originated in the difficulties of printing

Reduced Fac-simile of a large Wood-cut, said to be of the Fifteenth Century.

[From Jackson.]

types and wood-cuts together,[2] or in a despisal of the rude productions of the block-printers,[3] and in the intention of the

[1] No exception need be made for the initial letters of the *Psalter of 1457*. The thin curved lines of the ornamental portions of these letters could not have been cut on the flat boards then used by all engravers on wood. The absence of cracks and broken lines, after long service, in every print taken from these cuts is presumptive evidence that they were cut on metal. The ornamentation is unlike that of the professional engravers of block-books and at once suggests the thought that they were cut on brass or type-metal by the hand that cut the types of the text.

[2] That the early printers did encounter serious difficulties in the use of wood-cuts in type forms is proved by their selection of blocks of smaller size. Full-page cuts are rare in the books of Koburger, Leeu and Veldener. Von Os of Zwoll cut up the blocks of the *Bible of the Poor*. Blades says that Colard Mansion printed the types and wood-cuts that appeared on the same page by two impressions. Sad experience in the warping and cracking of blocks of wood in forms of types was, no doubt, the reason for this extra labor. This difficulty seems to have been avoided by Pigouchet, Kerver and the printers of ornamental books, whose cuts have all the mannerisms of engraving on metal.

[3] The disconnection between the arts of engraving on wood and typography is fairly indicated by the quarrel between the type-printers and block-printers of Augsburg.

typographers to make emphatic the superiority of their branch. Wood-cuts were freely used by typographers in the heart of Germany and in the Netherlands, the districts where we find the earliest notices of block-printing, but they are generally of a low order. Many of them are barbarous, as faulty in cutting as in drawing, and pleasing only to uncultivated tastes. It is probable that, about this time, many of the more skillful engravers and designers[1] abandoned the practice of xylography, attracted, no doubt, by the superior advantages offered by the newly invented art of copper-plate printing. The art of engraving on wood, although it afterward enlisted the services of artists like Durer and Holbein, could not compete with this formidable rival. It suffered a long eclipse, from which it did not emerge until the days of Bewick.

The quality of the paper in early books is as unequal as the printing. In the *Bible of 36 lines*, the paper is thick and strong, of coarse fibre, yellowish, apparently made from sun-bleached flax; in the books of Schœffer, and of the later German printers, the paper is thinner, but dingy and harsh; in the books of the Venetian printers, it is often very thin, usually of smooth surface and a creamy white tint that seems to have been unchanged by time. Different qualities are often noticeable in the same book. There were many paper-mills from which the printers drew their supplies, and every mill made different qualities. Blades says that it was the practice to sort the paper before printing, separating the rough from the smooth, and the thin from the thick, and to print and bind together sheets of similar quality. The sizes required by printers were small. The books first made were printed on sheets about 16 by 21 inches, one leaf of which was as large as could be printed by one pull of the press. The sizes 15 by 20, 14 by 18 and 12 by 15 inches were common, and

[1] Some engravers on wood who would not work with typographers undertook a new branch of printing—the making of prints, thirty or forty inches long, for the decoration of interior walls. Becker has published a collection of these large prints, taken from the original blocks, some of which he says were made before 1500. See cut on page 535.

in request for quartos and octavos. The largest size seems to have been royal, about 20 by 25 inches. The Cost Book of the Ripoli Press gives names and prices to nine distinct qualities or sizes of paper, but it does not define the weights and measurements. The smallest size and cheapest quality, possibly a pot foolscap, was put down at the price of 2 lire 8 soldi (about $2.18) per ream; the largest and best, probably royal, at 6 lire 8 soldi (about $5.80) per ream.[1]

The Fall of Lucifer, as shown in Zainer's Edition of the Speculum Salutis.
An Illustration of the Degradation of Engraving on Wood.
[From Heineken.]

The paper made for the *Bibles* of Gutenberg and for the earlier books was the ordinary writing paper of the period. Made from linen rags that had not been weakened by caustic alkalies or by steam-boiling and gas-bleaching processes, and strongly sized by the dipping of each sheet in a tub contain-

[1] If Florentine money had eight times the purchasing power of its American equivalent, these were high prices. They justify the observation of Keyser and Stol, printers at Paris in 1486, that the price of paper was out of all proportion to the price of printed books.

ing a thin solution of glue, it was strong and of hard surface. But the qualities which commended the paper to the copyist were objectionable to the printer. The hard surface caused harsh impression, and strong sizing made the damp sheets stick together. It was soon discovered that unsized paper, which, according to Madden, was about half the price of the sized, was easier to print. It would take a clearer impression, and more thoroughly imbibe the oily ink. These advantages could not be overlooked, and, consequently, hard-sized papers went out of fashion. By far the largest part of the books printed during the last quarter of the fifteenth century were of unsized or half-sized paper.

The early printer tried to gratify luxurious tastes by printing copies on vellum, but its inordinate price, and the great difficulties then encountered in printing, obliged him to give it up as an impracticable material. When book-lovers found that able printers like Kerver and Pigouchet printed paper more neatly and evenly in color, vellum[1] went out of fashion.

We do not know what system or method was observed in early proof-reading. Madden has pointed out many curious errors in three distinct copies of a book printed at Weidenbach about 1464, which seem to show that the compositor of each copy read the proof of his own work, and read it badly. Possibly this was the method of many of the amateur printers of that century, whose books, according to Schelhorn, bristle with horrid and squalid errors. It could not have been the method of Gutenberg, whose *Bibles*, although not free from faults, were obviously read with care. Nor was it the method of careful printers, for there is evidence that many of them

[1] Vellum was made out of the dressed skins of very young kids and lambs; parchment from the skins of sheep and goats. The vellum was very thin, flexible and highly polished; the parchment was thick and horn-like; but each substance was prepared by nearly the same process. The skin, when freed from hair, was put in a lime-pit, until it was deprived of its fat. It was then stretched on a frame, pared with a knife, rubbed with lime and pumice-stone, and repeatedly dried and wet, and rubbed and stretched, until the surface was made faultlessly smooth.

enlisted the services of eminent scholars as proof-readers or correctors of the press.[1] These correctors did a double duty; they corrected the errors of the compositors and those of the

A Print of 1475, probably the work of an amateur engraver.

[From Heineken.]

manuscript copy.[2] From the frequency and earnestness of the complaints then made concerning faulty manuscript texts,

[1] See page 469 for the testimony of Schoeffer's proof-reader.

[2] The copyists, underpaid by the stationers, did their work recklessly, abbreviating words so freely that it was often impossible to discover the meaning of the author. The faults of the calligrapher, who preferred beauty to accuracy, and of the young scholar, who rashly undertook to correct errors — tended to the same result. Fichet, a professor of the University of Paris, who seems to have been the first man of letters who esteemed printing, said, in a complimentary letter to Gering, Crantz and Friburger, that books were becoming barbarous through the faults of the copyists. Bouhier, a later president of the University, said that the books of the copyists were monstrous, and often unintelligible.

it seems that the copyists needed correction more than the compositors. But the correctors were not always equal to the task. Some of them were grossly incompetent, and still further corrupted the texts they undertook to improve.[1] Considering the difficulties the early printers encountered in getting correct copies and competent readers, it is surprising that their books are not more full of faults. The errors of early printed books have been frequently commented on, but the remarks of Prosper Marchand are, perhaps, the most emphatic:

> It is a prejudice altogether too common, a prejudice which dealers in old books have kept alive and profited from, to think that the editions of the fifteenth century are more accurate because they were printed from manuscript copies. Many of these editions were printed from faulty texts, picked up by chance, or selected without judgment by printers who were unable to see their faults, and were still further corrupted by the ignorance and rashness of their editors and correctors. I know that this is a kind of literary blasphemy, but it is warranted by respectable authority. . . . They are deceived who think that books are accurate in proportion to their age. For the most part, the older they are, the more inaccurate they are.[2]

[1] Marchand quotes at length an author who says that John Andrew, the corrector for Sweinheym and Pannartz, was a very presumptuous meddler with texts. When he met a word he did not understand, he printed it in Latin, or put in words at a venture, often making the text more unintelligible than ever. Another ecclesiastical reader, Bishop Nicholas Perotti, was quite as great an offender.

[2] Marchand, *Histoire de l'imprimerie*, vol. 1, pp. 97–103, and notes. In support of this assertion he cites the opinions of Schelhorn, Maittaire, Naudé, and other eminent bibliographers, and gives many specifications of the inaccuracies of the early printers from Fust and Schœffer to Froben. Not even Aldus Manutius escapes, for Marchand quotes at length the accusation of Erasmus that the *Homer*, *Cicero*, and *Plutarch* of Aldus were *depravatissima*. This criticism is hardly warranted by the errors of these editions, and is decidedly unjust in its reflection on a printer whose industry and carefulness as an editor have never been surpassed, and who, in his edition of *Plato* of 1513, offered a gold coin for every mistake that should be discovered. This damaging accusation would probably never have been made if Erasmus had not quarreled with Aldus, and had not thought it necessary to deny with much asperity that he had served as a corrector of the press in the Aldine office. As a corrector, Erasmus was not beyond reproach, as will be more clearly seen in his reading of the *Greek Testament*. Froben's lamentation over the two pages of errata in this book (published by him, but corrected by Erasmus) shows how much easier it is to discover errors after commission than it is to correct them in time. Stung by the taunts of critics, Erasmus said that if the Devil did not preside over typography, there must have been a diabolical malice on the part of the compositors.

Inaccurate as early printed books may have been, they were more correct than those of the copyists. The errors of a faulty first edition were soon discovered and the faulty editions were supplanted by the perfect. It is not the least of the many benefits of printing that it has effectually prevented the accidental or intentional debasement of texts.

The inferiority of the tools of the early printing office could be plainly exhibited by contrasting them with those of our time—the early hand-press with the modern cylinder printing machine—the entire collection of types made in the fifteenth century with the specimen book of any reputable modern type-founder. But the pride of the young printer in improvements that have been most largely made in this century should be modified by the reflection that there has been no change in the theory, and there have been but few changes in the elementary processes of printing. The punch, matrix and mould, the tympan, frisket and points, the use of damp paper and oily ink, of curved surfaces for applying the ink, and of blankets for diffusing the impression, are still in fashion. Printing is done quicker, cheaper, with more neatness and accuracy, with more regard for the convenience of the reader, with many new features of artistic merit, and in varieties and quantities so vast that there can be no comparison between early and modern productions—but it is the same kind of work it was in the beginning. It has not been made obsolete by lithography or photography, nor by any other invention of our time. The method invented by Gutenberg still keeps its place at the head of the graphic arts.

AUTHORITIES CONSULTED.

BECKMANN JOHN. A History of Inventions, Discoveries and Origins. Translated by William Johnston. 12mo. 2 vols. London, 1846.

BERJEAU J. PH. Biblia Pauperum. Reproduced in Fac-simile.......with an Historical and Bibliographical Introduction. Folio. London, 1859.

—— —— Le Bibliophile Illustré for 1861. Imperial 8vo. London, 1862.

—— —— Book-worm for 1866. Imperial 8vo. London, 1866.

BERNARD AUG. De l'origine et des débuts de l'imprimerie en Europe. 8vo. 2 vols. Paris, 1853.

BIBLIOPHILE BELGE BULLETIN DU. 8vo. Vols. I to IX. Brussels, 1845—1852.

BLADES WILLIAM. The Life and Typography of William Caxton, England's First Printer, etc. Royal 4to. 2 vols. London, 1861—1863.

BREITKOPF JOH. GOTTL. IMMAN. Versuch den Ursprung der Spielkarten, die Einführung des Leinenpapieres, und den Anfang der Holzschneidekunst in Europa. 4to. 2 vols. in one. Leipsic, 1784.

CAMPBELL M.-F.-A.-G. Annales de la typographie Néerlandaise au XVe siècle. 8vo. La Haye, 1874.

CAMUS. Notice d'un livre imprimé à Bamberg en 1462. 4to. Paris, an VII.

CRAPELET G.-A. Études pratiques et littéraires sur la typographie. 8vo. Paris, 1837.

DAUNOU ——. Analyse des opinions diverses sur l'origine de l'imprimerie. 8vo. Paris, an XI.

DE LA BORDE LÉON. Débuts de l'imprimerie à Strasbourg, ou recherches sur les travaux mystérieux de Gutenberg dans cette ville, et sur le procès qui lui fut intenté en 1439 à cette occasion. 8vo. Paris, 1840.

—— —— Débuts de l'imprimerie à Mayence et à Bamberg, ou description des lettres d'indulgence du pape Nicholas V pro regno Cypri, imprimées en 1454. Royal 4to. Paris, 1840.

DE VRIES A. Éclaircissemens sur l'histoire de l'invention de l'imprimerie. 8vo. La Haye, 1843.

DIDOT M. AMBROISE FIRMIN. Essai sur la typographie. 8vo. Paris, 1851.

DOUCE FRANCIS. Holbein's Dance of Death...with a Dissertation, etc. 12mo. London, 1872.

FALKENSTEIN KARL. Geschichte der Buchdruckerkunst in ihrer Entstehung und Ausbildung. 4to. Leipsic, 1840.

FISCHER GOTTHELF. Essai sur les monuments typographiques de Jean Gutenberg, mayençais, inventeur de l'imprimerie. 4to. Mayence, an X.

FOURNIER le jeune P. S. Manuel typographique. 16mo. 2 vols. Paris, 1764—1766.

GRESSWELL WILLIAM PARR. Annals of Parisian Typography, etc. 8vo. London, 1818.

HAIN L. Repertorium Bibliographicum, in quo Libri Omnes ab Arte Typographica Inventa usque ad Annum MD. typis expressi, etc. 8vo. 2 vols. Stuttgardt, 1826—1838.

HALLAM HENRY. Introduction to the Literature of Europe in the Fifteenth, Sixteenth and Seventeenth Centuries. 8vo. 2 vols. New-York, 1841.

—— —— View of the State of Europe during the Middle Ages. 8vo. 3 vols. Boston, 1853.

HANSARD T. C. Typographia: an Historical Sketch of the Origin and Progress of the Art of Printing, etc. 8vo. London, 1825.

HEINEKEN C. H. Idée générale d'une collection complette d'estampes, avec une dissertation sur l'origine de la gravure et sur les premiers livres d'images. 8vo. Leipsic and Vienna, 1771.

HELBIG HENRI. Une Découverte pour l'histoire de l'imprimerie. Pamphlet, 8vo. Brussels, 1855.

—— —— Notes et dissertations relatives à l'histoire de l'imprimerie. Pamphlet, 8vo. Brussels, without date. (From Vol. XVIII of the *Bibliophile Belge.*)

HOLTROP JOH. GUIL. Catalogus Librorum Sæculo XV° Impressorum, quotquot in Bibliotheca Regia Hagana asservantur. 8vo. Hagae-Comitum, 1856.

—— —— Monuments typographiques des Pays-Bas au quinzième siècle. Folio. La Haye, 1868.

HUMPHREYS H. NOEL. A History of the Art of Printing from its Invention, etc. Folio. Second Issue. London, 1868.

JACKSON JOHN and CHATTO W. A. A Treatise on Wood Engraving, etc. Second Edition. 8vo. London, 1861.

JACOB P. L. (Lacroix.) Curiosités de l'histoire des arts. 16mo. Paris, 1858.

JOHNSON J. Typographia, or the Printers' Instructor, including an Account of the Origin of Printing. 24mo. 2 vols. London, 1824.

KONING JACQUES. Dissertation sur l'origine, l'invention, et le perfectionnement de l'imprimerie. 8vo. Amsterdam, 1819.

LACROIX PAUL (Bibliophile Jacob), E. FOURNIER et F. SERÉ. Histoire de l'imprimerie et des arts et professions, etc. Imperial 8vo. Paris, 1852.

LA CAILLE JEAN DE. Histoire de l'imprimerie et de la librarie où l'on voit son origine et son progrés jusqu'en 1689. 4to. Paris, 1689.

LAMBINET P. Recherches historiques, littéraires et critiques sur l'origine de l'imprimerie. 8vo. Brussels, an VII.

LANZI ABATE LUIGI. The History of Painting in Italy, etc. Translated by Thomas Roscoe. 12mo. 3 vols. London, 1852.

MADDEN J.-P.-A. Lettres d'un bibliographe. Series I to IV. Royal 8vo. Versailles and Paris, 1868—1875.

MAITTAIRE M. Annales Typographici ab Artis Inventæ Origine ad annum MDCLXIV. 4to. 5 vols. Hagae-Comitum, 1719—1741.

MARCHAND PROSPER. Histoire de l'origine et des prémiers progrès de l'imprimerie. 4to. La Haye, 1740.

MEERMAN G. Origines Typographicæ. 4to. 2 vols. Hagae-Comitum, 1765.

MERLIN R. Origine des cartes à jouer, etc. 4to. Paris, without date.

MOXON JOSEPH. Mechanick Exercises: or the Doctrine of Handy-Works. Applied to the Art of Printing. Small 4to. London, 1683.

MUNSELL JOEL. A Chronology of Paper and Paper Making. 8vo. Albany, 1870.

NICHOLS ——. The Origin of Printing, etc. 8vo. London, 1774.

OTTLEY WILLIAM YOUNG. An Inquiry into the Origin and Early History of Engraving upon Copper and on Wood. 2 vols. 4to. London, 1816.

—— —— An Inquiry concerning the Invention of Printing, etc., with an Introduction by J. Ph. Berjeau. 4to. London, 1863.

PASSAVANT J. D. Le Peintre-Graveur. 8vo. 6 vols. Leipsic, 1860.

RINGWALT J. LUTHER. American Encyclopædia of Printing. Imperial 8vo. Philadelphia, 1871.

SANTANDER SERNA DE LA. Dictionnaire bibliographique choisi du quinzième siècle. 8vo. 3 vols. Brussels, 1805—1807.

SAVAGE WILLIAM. Practical Hints on Decorative Printing. 4to. London, 1822.

SCHOEPFLIN JO. DANIEL. Vindiciæ Typographicæ. 4to. Strasburg, 1760.

SEIZ J. C. Annus Tertius Sæcularis Inventæ Artis Typographicæ. 8vo. Haarlem, 1743.

SISMONDI J. C. L. SIMONDE DE. Historical View of the Literature of the South of Europe. 12mo. 2 vols. New-York, 1860.

SOTHEBY S. LEIGH. The Typography of the Fifteenth Century, etc., exemplified in a Collection of Fac-similes. Folio. London, 1845.

—— —— Principia Typographica. The Block-Books, or Xylographic Delineations, etc. Folio, 3 vols. London, 1858.

SKEEN WILLIAM. Early Typography. 8vo. Colombo, Ceylon, 1872.

THOMAS ISAIAH. History of Printing in America, etc. . . . with a concise view of the discovery of the art. 8vo. 2 vols. Worcester, 1810.

TIMPERLEY C. H. A Dictionary of Printers and Printing, etc. Royal 8vo. London, 1839.

TYMMS W. R. and WYATT, M. D. The Art of Illumination as Practised in Europe from the Earliest Times. Royal 8vo. London, without date.

VAN DER MEERSCH P. C. Recherches sur la vie et les travaux des imprimeurs Belges et Néerlandais, etc. Royal 8vo. Gand et Paris, 1856.

VAN DER LINDE. The Haarlem Legend of the Invention of Printing by Lourens Janszoon Coster Critically Examined. From the Dutch by J. A. Hessels, with an Introduction, etc. 8vo. London, 1871.

WEIGEL T. O. and ZESTERMAN. Die Anfänge der Druckerkunst in Bild und Schrift, etc. Imperial 4to. 2 vols. Leipsic, 1866.

WETTER J. Kritische Geschichte der Erfindung der Buchdruckerkunst durch Johann Gutenberg zu Mainz. 8vo. 1836.

WOLTMANN ALFRED. Holbein and His Time. Translated by F. E. Bunnètt, 8vo. London, 1872.

WOLF JO. CHRISTIAN. Monumenta Typographica, qvæ Artis hujus præstantissimæ Originem, Laudem et Abusum posteris produnt, etc. 16mo. 2 vols. Hamburg, 1740.

INDEX.

ADDITIONAL NOTES AND CORRECTIONS.

Page 24. In the second line of foot-note, change two-thirds to four-ninths.

27. The exact date of the complete invention of copper-plate printing is unfixed. Vasari says that Finiguerra's discovery was made in 1450, but that the Italian practice of making plate prints began about 1460. It is obvious that the alleged discovery in 1450 of the fact that the blacking placed in incised lines could be transferred to paper by pressure was not the complete invention of copper-plate printing. Much more had to be done. The earliest dated Italian print by this method is of the year 1465. The earliest authentic German print is dated 1446. There are others attributed to the years 1422, 1430, 1440, but they are not accepted as genuine by Passavant. See *Peintre-Graveur*, vol. I, pp. 192–197.

Senefelder's first suggestion of lithography was entertained in 1796, but his vague notions about printing from stone did not assume a practical shape before 1798. He did not receive, and perhaps was not entitled to, his patent before 1800.

64. On page 447, the date of the erection of this stone by Wittig is put down at 1508, which is the date given by Bernard and by many others. But Wetter, from whose book this statement was taken, knowing that Wittig was dead in 1507, altered the date to 1507. Helbig does not accept either date. He thinks that it should be 1504. *Notes et dissertations*, pp. 10, 11.

82. It is possible that engraving on wood was done in England in the first half of the fifteenth century. Ottley, in his *Inquiry concerning the Invention of Printing*, page 198, describes an English print of the crucifixion, with legend in English, which he says may be as old as the St. Christopher. This is the legend: "Seynt Gregor. with oyer [other] popes & bysshoppes yn seer, Haue graunted of pardon XXVI. mill yeer. To yeym yat befor yis fygur on yeir knees Devoutly say .V. pater noster .&.V. Auees." Weigel has given other fac-similes of early English engraving.

96. Chatto says that Gringonneur was paid 56 sols about 1393. Passavant says 50 sols. Lacroix says 1392, and estimates the value of 56 sols in modern money at 180 francs.

111. In foot-note, last line of small type, change chap. I to chap. II.

150. Change John I, 3, to John III, I.

150. Lacroix gives the date of 1292 for the employment of the seventeen book-binders at the University of Paris.

218. The date of the termination of the Great Schism is usually put at 1447, but it was not fully ended until Pope Felix V abdicated the papal chair in 1449, and ordered the church to submit to Nicholas V.

250. Passavant (vol. I, p. 50) says that there is in the library at Heidelberg a copy of a xylographic edition of the Lord's Prayer, a block-book of ten leaves, which may be attributed to the fifteenth century.

319. Holtrop says that Bellaert's name is first mentioned in 1485, as it appears in the fac-simile.

378. A document has been recently discovered at Strasburg which proves that Frielo Gensfleisch, the elder brother of John Gutenberg, was in Strasburg in 1429. This document is the signature of Frielo to a receipt for 26 florins due him on an annuity. See *Book-worm* for January, 1868.

397. It is not probable that this tool of four pieces was the press. Ottley, who thinks that Gutenberg's secret was not that of printing (*Inquiry concerning Invention*, p. 41), says, "there can be no doubt that presses of different kinds were known long before the invention of typography" (p. 37), and that "five of the witnesses, none of whom were partners, knew all about the press" (p. 40). It may also be added that the repetition by different witnesses of the order to separate the four pieces and put them in a disjointed form in the press, or on or under the press, is evidence that the four pieces did not constitute the press nor any part of it. Nor can it be supposed that Gutenberg had sent to his home a bulky press to have, as has been asserted, its "joinings renewed." This work should have been done by Sahspach, the joiner who built it. Although I believe that Gutenberg afterward invented the printing press, I think that the press here mentioned was nothing more than the screw press of the carpenter—the wooden vise or press of a workman who needed it when using a file. A printing press would not be needed until the types were made, which it appears were not even then ready. The fact that Gutenberg, Dritzehen, Dünne, and Sahspach worked apart is proof that the proposed printing office was not furnished—that the men were making tools, and the tools were probably moulds and matrices. I have accepted Van der Linde's translation of *zurlossen* as melting, for it is warranted by many evidences that the tool of four pieces and the *formen* were of metal. Ottley's translation, making *zurlossen* mean a loosening or unjointing, or breaking-up, with a view to renewal or reconstruction, could also be accepted.

405. Bernard questions the accuracy of the date of the *Donatus of 1451*, but it is the belief of Fischer and of many others that it was printed in 1451.

413. Compare the spacing in the *Bibles* of Gutenberg with that of the *Psalter of 1457*, as shown in pages 453 and 455. In Gutenberg's *Bibles*, there are some evidences of attempts to keep the lines even; in the *Psalter*, the nicety of full lines or of even spacing was disregarded.

451. Madden admits that Schœffer was a copyist at Paris, but doubts the inference that he was a student of the University. His doubt seems to be based on the faulty Latin of the colophon.

455. I am not entirely satisfied with the fac-simile of types on this page. It is a copy of the fac-simile made by Falkenstein, the only one accessible to me of the edition of 1457. It is, no doubt, a correct representation of form and of general appearance, but the outlines of the letters are suspiciously sharp. They do not accord in this feature with the types shown on page 453. In Falkenstein's fac-simile, the ornamental work about the letter P is a dull bluish purple, so made by printing deep blue over lines previously printed in dull red. I have not attempted to imitate this dull purple color (of which I find no notice save in the book of Papillon), for I believe that this use of purple was exceptional. It was probably caused by an imperfect cleansing of the red block, the after application of the blue and the mixing on the block of both colors, forming a dull purple.

465. Madden doubts the genuineness of the record of the proposed mission of Jenson to Mentz.

467. I have accepted the statement of Bernard that leads were first used in 1465 in the *Offices* of Cicero, but a re-examination of the fac-simile in Sotheby's *Typography* (No. 90) of the *Treatise on Reason and Conscience* convinces me that the types of this work were leaded. As Gutenberg abandoned printing in 1465, it is probable that the *Treatise* is really older than the *Offices*. If so, Gutenberg was the first to use leads.

498. Some bibliographers regard Martens as the predecessor of John of Westphalia, and as a graduate of one of the typographical schools at Cologne. Holtrop thinks that Martens was the pupil of John of Westphalia, his corrector and associate, but not his partner or predecessor.

506. La Caille and Santander say that Gering died in 1510; Van der Meersch says 1520.

529. The weakness of the early press is abundantly proved by the smallness of the forms and the absence of large and black wood-cuts in all books printed before 1800. The inability of the hand-press (even when made of iron, as it was in 1824) is set forth by Johnson in his *Typographia*, vol. II, p. 548. It is there stated that an engraver who had been at work for three years on a wood-cut 11½ by 15 inches, was dismayed by the discovery, after a fair trial, that his block was too large to be properly printed on any variety of English press then in common use. The Clymer press, just introduced, was then tested. By lengthening the bar, and getting two men to pull, a few fair impressions were obtained, but the block soon broke under pressure. This wood-cut was only about half the size of the two-page cuts which are now regularly and easily printed for the popular illustrated papers on machines at the rate of 1,000 an hour.

530. The most admirable feature of the best early printing is its simplicity. The types were uncouth, but they were made with single purpose, to be easily read, not to show the skill of the punch-cutter. This object would have been fully accomplished if the compositor had refrained from abbreviations and had spaced his words with intelligence. The pressman did his part of the work fairly, and honestly impressed the types on the paper with unexceptionable firmness and solidity. The readable method of doing presswork is, unfortunately, out of fashion. A perverted taste requires the modern printer to use thin types, dry glossy paper, as little ink and as weak an impression as is consistent with passable legibility. This general fondness for delicacy is not at all favorable to the production of readable books.